THE MICROLIGHT FLYING MANUAL

R.D. CAMPBELL AND J. JONES

Airlife
England

First published in Great Britain by Aviation Training Publications Ltd
1982

First published by Airlife Publishing Ltd 1990

Reprinted 1995

British Library Cataloguing in Publication Data
Campbell, R. D. (Ronald D.)
The microlight flying manual — 3rd ed
1. Microlight aeroplanes. Flying
I. Title II. Jones, J. (John)
629.1325217

ISBN 1 85310 189 3

Printed in Great Britain by Livesey Ltd.

Nothing in this Manual must be taken as superseding the Legislation, Rules, Regulations, Procedures and Information contained in the Air Navigation Order, the Air Navigation (General) Regulations, Rules of the Air and Air Traffic Control Regulations, the UK Air Pilot, NOTAMS, Aeronautical Information Circulars, or the Recommendations, Restrictions, Limitations and Operating Procedures published in Aircraft, Engines or Systems Manuals and Certificates or Airworthiness, or any Civil Air Publication or similar document published by the Civil Aviation Authority.

Airlife Publishing Ltd.
101 Longden Road, Shrewsbury, England.

ACKNOWLEDGEMENTS

The authors wish to express their grateful acknowledgements to the Civil Aviation Authority, British Microlight Aircraft Association, Nicklow Engineering Ltd., Castrol Ltd., Breen Aviation Ltd., and the National Air Traffic Services for permitting reproduction of certain material in this manual.

Acknowledgements are also made to those members of the Civil Aviation Authority, British Microlight Aircraft Association, Chargus Gliding Co., Dragon Aircraft Co., International Airtour Ltd., and Julian Doswell, Managing Director of Breen Aviation Ltd for their help and support in the production of this manual.

Contents

INTRODUCTION

The first practical aeroplane came into existence in 1903 when the Wright brothers achieved sustained and controlled flight in a heavier than air flying machine. Since then progress in technology has produced aircraft capable of carrying hundreds of passengers at breathtaking speeds across great distances, so producing transport facilities which are of tremendous benefit to mankind.

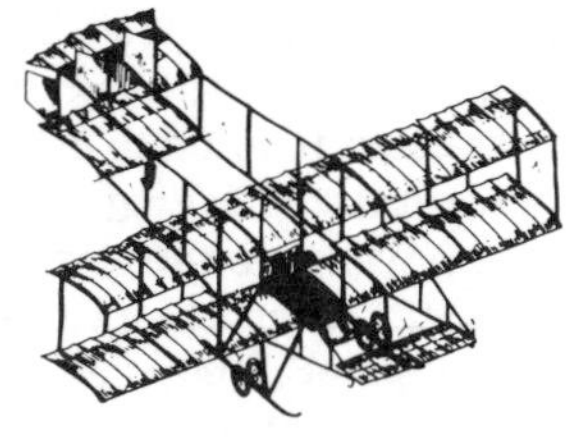

An Early Aeroplane

Hand in hand with this development have come vast increases in the number of small and medium sized aircraft ranging from two seat trainers to those carrying 4 or more passengers. Up until the time of the Wright brothers achievement, the only form of controlled (and not so controlled flight) was made by man carrying gliders which were essentially a framework of wing and fuselage. These gliders continued to be developed in parallel with powered aircraft and a whole new recreational and sporting movement was built around the use of these simple structures, which today, have become very sophisticated in their design.

A Glider

In the 1960's a new type of heavier than air vehicle emerged, the Hang Glider. This consists of a fabric wing beneath which the pilot sits in a framework of lightweight metal tubes. Control of the aircraft is achieved by the pilot moving his body, a method known as 'weight shift'. The advent of hang gliders and their relatively low cost brought flying within the reach of many people who could not afford the more conventional forms of flying as a pastime. To support this development a whole new industry has been born, but, since any form of gliding activity is limited by Newton's law of gravity it was not long before enthusiasts of the hang gliding sport began experimenting with fitting small engines to their hang gliders and from this the Microlight aeroplane has emerged.

A Hang Glider

In a sense the wheel has turned a full circle in that small single and two seat flying machines of maximum simplicity and minimum cost are now available to many more individuals who aspire to fly for pleasure. However, unlike the journey into the unknown taken by the Wright brothers in their first experiments, modern materials and production methods have made available safe reliable flying machines for those who have a wish to take up this activity.

A Microlight

Introduction

Those who accept the challenge of microlight flying will obtain considerable pleasure and sense of achievement from their efforts, but like the activities of mountain climbing, scuba diving, water skiing, etc, flying is a sport which demands not only skill but the exercise of personal responsibility. It is also one which requires consideration to other aviators and to the general public. For example, at the present time the engines fitted to microlight aircraft are often noisy which can cause annoyance to those who do not share our interests, and although progress in engine technology will undoubtedly lead to positive reductions in the noise levels of these engines it behoves all pilots engaged in microlight operations to ensure as best they can that their activities do not aggravate others to an extent which could encourage a flurry of regulatory restrictions.

Whilst the simplicity and economy of microlight aircraft are no doubt the greatest motivating factors which attract people to this sport, it must be appreciated that many things have to be learned before becoming a competent microlight pilot. With this in mind it would be pertinent to point out that one problem faced by all authors of training manuals is that of "taking the complex and making it as simple as possible". In attempting to do this the danger arises in oversimplifying and thus leaving the reader with a false impression that there is less to know than is actually the case. Whereas this may not cause great problems in some of the skills we learn in everyday life the environment of flight demands that you have a comprehensive understanding of the subject if you are to become a safe pilot. Bear in mind that the only creatures born with the intuitive and natural ability to fly are the birds, and if you wish to emulate these creatures and still be safe, you will need to apply yourself to learning through a sound understanding of the subject, coupled with adequate physical practice.

This manual has been specifically written to ensure that the reader has the opportunity to learn and understand the problems involved in flying a microlight aircraft, but in reviewing the following pages an aspiring pilot may be daunted by the amount of information it contains. Therefore it would be sensible at this stage to point out that you are not expected to learn the contents of this manual by heart, but just glancing through the pages will convince you of its value as a work of reference and it will be an important addition to your bookshelf.

In addition to this, it contains the necessary study material which you will need in order to pass the written examinations for a Private Pilot's Licence (aeroplanes Group "D"), as well as giving you an insight into some important aspects of microlight flying and the training you will have to undertake.

In conclusion it must be said that although this manual is specifically written to cover the ground subjects necessary to a basic understanding of the environment of flight, it cannot teach you how to fly. This part of your training can only be taught by your flying instructor. The manual should therefore be used to give you a grasp of the many items of knowledge which you will be required to learn in order to prepare yourself for your flying instruction and to assist you to develop into a safe competent pilot.

AN INTRODUCTION TO THE GROUND TRAINING SUBJECTS OF THE MICROLIGHT TRAINING COURSE

When a person first learns to fly, whether in a fixed wing aeroplane, microlight or other type of flying machine, his immediate concentration centres on how to control the aircraft and develop his physical reflexes to achieve judgement in handling the controls so that the aircraft does what he wants it to do.

However, in flying, judgement involves two specific areas, one which relates to the development of physical skills and the other which relates to the making of correct decisions. Lack of judgement in making decisions usually stems from a lack of appreciation or failure to properly comprehend the many items of knowledge which in themselves form the basis of understanding, and without which, the correct decision in handling a particular situation cannot be made without a large element of luck.

In order to operate any aircraft in safety, a pilot will need to develop the elements of skill and good judgement, the quality of these requirements will largely be based upon the acquisition and correct application of knowledge.

Pilots operate in an unforgiving environment which like the sea has many traps for the careless or ignorant voyager. From this statement, the importance of knowledge, when flying can be appreciated. Once knowledge is gained the appropriate skills can be developed more quickly and in an atmosphere of safer airmanship.

Before proceeding further it is advisable to point out that the Civil Aviation Authority is the responsible body for deciding the privileges of those who hold a Private Pilot Licence. It is also responsible for deciding the type and amount of training which a person must undertake before receiving these privileges. In the case of the Microlight Pilot these privileges are defined in relation to the Aircraft Rating which is an integral part of any type of pilot licence. Microlight aircraft are all classified under Group "D" in the Aircraft Rating.

The Civil Aviation Authority has stated that it will be regulating Group "D" aircraft and the pilots who fly them with a 'light touch' and therefore a minimum of regulations and restrictions will apply to microlight operations. Nevertheless, because you will be operating in the airspace over the United Kingdom, often adjacent to other types of airspace users, e.g. military, commercial and light aircraft you will still have to learn a number of regulations in order that you are able to safely operate in this environment and so not be a hazard to yourself or others.

The CAA in accordance with its 'light touch' policy and its wish to keep regulatory costs to a minimum with regard to the operation of microlight aircraft has conferred to the British Microlight Association the responsibility of co-ordinating microlight activities within the United Kingdom. The BMAA is therefore an Association which represents your interests and conducts a regular dialogue with the CAA in connection with your pilot training and ultimate privileges.

The Syllabus of training which you undertake to obtain your Private Pilot Licence has been produced by the BMAA and has the approval of the CAA. The detailed application of this syllabus is however, normally undertaken by the individual Microlight Training Organisations, therefore the training you receive lies in the hands of those individuals who have a particular knowledge and experience in the training of microlight pilots.

In order to keep costs of microlight activities to a reasonable level it is vital that the BMAA have the ability to communicate and advise all microlight pilots on any aspect of microlight operation, and therefore it is essential that anyone concerned in the Microlight Movement should belong to this Association.

Membership of the BMAA brings with it the assurance that your interests are properly represented and protected, and a copy of the Association's Magazine "Flight Line" is sent to all members at two monthly intervals to ensure that all latest developments and safety aspects are communicated to microlight pilots for the benefit of the movement as a whole.

The contents of the previous paragraphs make clear that the responsibility for the Microlight activity in this country is not just placed in the hands of one body or individual, it is spread amongst the CAA, the BMAA, your Training Organisation, your instructor and ultimately yourself. Remember however, in the final analysis, it is your knowledge, your skills and your judgement which will result either in a safe enjoyable flight, one made within your limitations and experience or an unpleasant or hazardous event... one suffered by you and perhaps others, because these essential qualities were lacking.

This Manual is specifically written to assist in your training and before delving into the pages which follow you must appreciate that the knowledge required by a microlight pilot embraces several subjects, not only because a pilot must have a sound understanding of operating his particular type of aircraft but also of the environment in which it is operated.

Although microlight aircraft at the present stage of their development have a restricted operational use they do form an integral part of the Private Flying movement in this country and in order to operate safely in an environment used by other types of aircraft the CAA has decided that all microlight pilots must have a certain minimum level of knowledge in the subjects of Air Legislation, Aviation Law, Flight Rules and Procedures, Air Navigation and Meteorology.

In order to ensure that this level of knowledge is established prior to the issue of a licence the microlight pilot will have to pass the current standard Private Pilot written examinations in these subjects. Therefore this Manual includes information which at first sight may appear to be inappropriate to the operation of microlight aircraft, however if this information is not included in your training programme you will have problems in passing the necessary examinations as well as lacking certain knowledge which is fundamental to the safe operation of aircraft generally.

The manual is written with this in mind and it also conforms to the syllabus produced by the BMAA and Approved by the CAA for the issue of a Private Pilot Licence with a Group "D" Rating. This syllabus covers a wider area than just handling the controls of an aeroplane and therefore to simplify and direct a student's task, the necessary items of knowledge have been placed in a manner which follows the syllabus yet contains each subject within its own section. A further facet of the Manual is that it contains a Progress Test section composed of multiple choice type questions which will allow you to monitor and self examine your learning coverage simply and efficiently.

It would also be relevant at this stage to point out that learning is achieved in various ways, but generally two methods are paramount. One, in which reading, thinking and resolving problems plays the primary part, and the other where the person practices and develops physical skills. In flying training you will find that both these methods of learning are employed, however, whereas learning is the act of acquiring knowledge, the purpose of it is to obtain a skill or acquire experience.

Therefore, the knowledge gained through studying this manual must be related to understanding those factors which concern the practical operation of an aircraft. If this fact is borne in mind whilst reading this book, an important and necessary step towards your pilot competence will result.

In order to organise training time efficiently, it will be necessary for you to know the depth of knowledge expected in each of the subject areas, and therefore in the following pages an attempt has been made to embrace both the coverage and depth of the information which is considered essential for you to understand, in order to develop the necessary skills and judgement required of a safe competent pilot. However, in a Manual of this nature, it would not be amiss to cover briefly the best way of tackling your learning programme.

In this respect, it is a basic fact that your memory retention will be significantly improved by using an organised 'review technique'. This is based upon the fact that most people forget some 80% of the information they have received within 24 hours of a learning session. Therefore correct review technique can result in an enormous reduction in the amount which is normally forgotten. For example, a first review of the subject matter learned should take place about 10 minutes after a learning session and this review should be some 10 minutes in length. The following day, a second review of the subject matter learned should be completed and this should last about 5 minutes.

A third and fourth review of 5 minutes at a time should be carried out within one week and this should be followed by a final 5 minute period one month later. After these reviews, most of the knowledge gained will be implanted into your long term memory and can then be recalled in the same manner as a person can recall the address of his previous home although several years may have elapsed since he lived there.

It must also be realised that although this type of review sequence may seem an unnecessary chore, its most significant benefit lies in its accumulative effect upon the activity of learning, thinking and recall. A person who does not find time to correctly review what he has learned, will continually waste most of the effort he has put into the learning task. On the other hand, a person who has developed good memory recall will be far more likely to arrive at the correct decision at the correct time when the circumstances require it, and as such, he will be able to demonstrate the essential qualities of good airmanship.

SECTION ONE

AIR LEGISLATION

AIR LEGISLATION

INTRODUCTION

As individuals, we are required to live in an organised society and although we may dislike many of the regulations which govern our activities, it is clear that without some form of legislation chaos would occur. This is particularly true of aviation where humans and complex products of technological engineering come together and operate as one unit in a common environment.

The airspace system is an environment without physical fences or barriers and as such large and fast jet aircraft and small and slow aircraft in the shape of microlights have to be protected from one another and because of this some form of clear and precise legislation is a must. Through this legislation stems the many regulations which pilots have to learn and understand in order to safely control their aircraft and prevent hazards to one another.

The Governments of most counties have organisations to implement and regulate for Aviation Safety and in the United Kingdom it is the task of the Civil Aviation Authority to protect the safety and the interests of those who fly as well as the general public.

To a person with a non-legal turn of mind the Statutory Instruments which cover what we can and cannot do in the field of aviation are often very difficult to understand. This is because they are written in legal language, however, quite simply our aviation legislation stems from the Civil Aviation Act as approved by Parliament. This Act gives powers to the various legislative documents which affect us as pilots and it would therefore be useful to cover them briefly as an introduction to this section.

THE LEGISLATIVE DOCUMENTS

The main statutory documents which cover the privileges of aircraft pilots, and the regulations concerning the safe operation of aircraft are the:

Air Navigation Order

Air Navigation (General) Regulations

Rules of the Air and Air Traffic Control Regulations

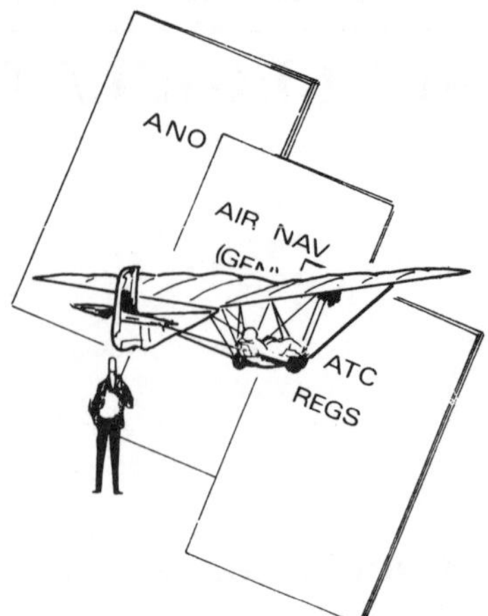

The Air Navigation Order (ANO) is the legal document which contains the written law enacted by Parliament. It contains a large number of Orders known as "Articles" which relate to flight crew licensing and the operations of aircraft registered in, or operated within, the United Kingdom.

The ANO also contains a section of "Schedules" which, where necessary, amplify (usually in tabular form) details relating to the respective Articles.

The Air Navigation (General) Regulations is another legal document enacted by Parliament and it contains regulations of a general nature which in the main relate to Public Transport operations, e.g. the carriage of fare paying passengers. Nevertheless, some of the regulations contained in this document are applicable to private pilots who fly fixed wing aircraft.

The Rules of the Air and Air Traffic Control Regulations is a document which has the same status as the aforementioned Orders and contains the detailed information indicated by its title.

Other publications which to a large extent precis the regulations contained in the above three documents are issued by the Civil Aviation Authority and these are listed below:

CAP 53

This contains information relating to licensing and the privileges of Student and Private Pilots.

CAP 85

This booklet contains information on Aviation Law e.g. Rules of the Air and Air Traffic Control Regulations.

All private pilots should obtain a copy of these last two publications. However the main statutory documents contain considerably more information than microlight pilots need to know, and therefore to simplify your learning task the areas which are important to you are extracted and outlined on the following pages. The information required from the Air Navigation Order is considered first.

THE AIR NAVIGATION ORDER

Certain of the information contained in this document varies with the class of aircraft so it would be helpful to first see how the various aircraft are classified and where the microlight aircraft fits into the picture.

CLASSIFICATION OF AIRCRAFT

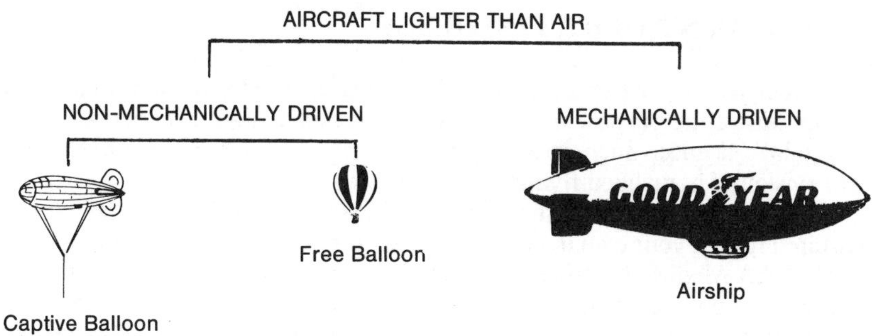

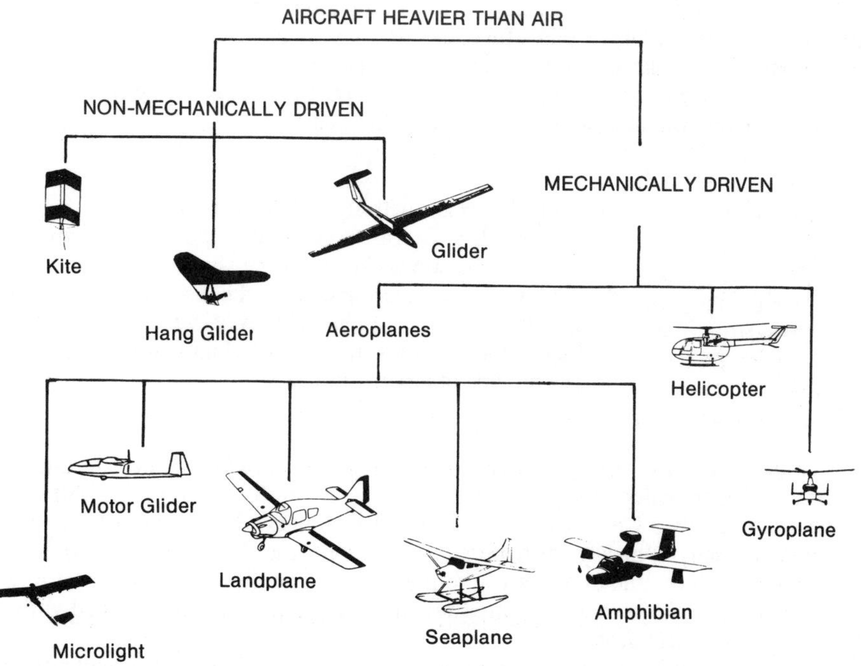

Fig. 1—1

The contents of this manual relate to the operation of those aircraft which are heavier than air and which fall into the classification of 'Aeroplanes'. Microlight aircraft fall within the classification of aeroplanes and as such they must be registered with the CAA, and show their registration marks as clearly as possible.

THE STUDENT PILOT'S PRIVILEGES

A student pilot's privileges are limited to being able to fly as pilot 'in command' of an aircraft for the purpose of obtaining the necessary flight experience for the issue of a pilot's licence. Such flying must be carried out under the authorisation and supervision of a qualified flying instructor.

If you decide to train for the Group "D" Rating (microlight aircraft) you will be required to visit your own doctor or a CAA Authorised Medical Examiner, who will sign a CAA Medical Certificate or a Declaration of Health upon satisfying himself that you are not suffering from any of the following conditions:

Epilepsy, fits, severe head injury, recurrent fainting, giddiness or blackouts, high blood pressure, coronary artery disease, insulin controlled diabetes, any psychiatric disorder. Additionally your colour vision must be normal. You will also have to sign the certificate to declare that you are not suffering from any of the above limiting conditions.

The reverse side of the Medical Certificate or Declaration of Health states the privileges of the microlight pilot, these are:

Provided the holder of the Certificate is 17 years old or more he/she may act as pilot in command of a microlight aircraft for the purpose of becoming qualified for the grant or renewal of a pilot's licence provided that:

(a) Such flights are within the United Kingdom.
(b) This Medical Certificate is valid at the time of flight.
(c) No other person is carried in the aircraft.
(d) He/She acts in accordance with the instructions given by a person holding a pilot's licence which includes an Instructors Rating entitling the holder to give instruction on the type of aircraft flown.

If at any stage you wish to obtain the privileges of a student or private pilot in aircraft which are categorised in the Group "A", "B" or "C" Ratings you will need to be examined by a CAA Authorised Medical Examiner. A large number of such doctors are geographically distributed throughout the UK and your training organisation will be able to direct you to the nearest Examiner. Providing you meet the higher medical standards required for these Ratings, you will be issued with a Class 3 Medical Certificate.

In relation to either of the medical certificates mentioned above you will also be required to renew them at set intervals if you wish to maintain you pilot privileges. The period between renewals will depend upon your age at the time, as shown on the next page.

Civil Aviation Authority

MEDICAL CERTIFICATE:
MICROLIGHT AEROPLANES (GROUP D) & BALLOONS

LICENCE NUMBER

I hereby declare that to the best of my knowledge and belief I am in good health. I am not receiving medical care and so far as I am aware I do not suffer from any of the conditions listed overleaf. I further understand that if at any time hereafter I know or suspect that I have contracted any of the conditions listed in para A overleaf I shall inform the Civil Aviation Authority in writing. If my physical or mental condition renders me unfit to fly I will cease to fly until I have obtained medical opinion.

Applicant's Name: ______________________
(Block Letters)

Signature: ______________________ Date: __________

I am a CAA Authorised Examiner*/the applicant's regular general practitioner and I understand that he/she wishes to fly as a pilot in microlight aircraft or balloons. I am not aware of any reason why it should not be safe medically for him/her to fly, nor I am aware that he/she suffers from any of the conditions listed overleaf.

Doctor's Signature: ______________________ Date: __________

Full Name: ______________________ AME Stamp: ______
(if applicable)

Address *(Block Letters)*: ______________________

____

A **A Medical Certificate *cannot be issued* to any person suffering from the following conditions:**

epilepsy, fits, severe head injury, recurrent fainting, giddiness or blackouts, high blood pressure, coronary artery disease, insulin controlled diabetes, any psychiatric disorder or any other disorder liable to cause incapacitation.

B **Colour vision must be normal (this requirement is not necessary for a balloon licence).**

If the doctor doubts that it would be safe medically for any applicant to fly because he/she suffers from a particular condition he should refer the case to CAA Medical Department, 45—59 Kingsway, London WC2B 6TE.

If you normally wear spectacles for distant sight you should always carry a readily accessible spare pair. In the case of spectacles for reading a suitable pair should be available.

Any minor injury, medically prescribed drugs, dental anaesthesia, blood donation may make you temporarily unfit to fly. You should seek medical advice before resuming flying. Attention is drawn to the Air Navigation Order 1980, Article 19(8).

This Medical Certificate is renewable as follows:

(1) up to and including age 39 – every 5 years;

(2) age 40 to 49 – every 2 years;

(3) age 50 to 69 – annually;

(4) age 70 and over – every 6 months.

The renewal date is calculated from the last day of the month in which the Certificate was signed by the medical practitioner.

PRIVILEGES OF A STUDENT PILOT

This Certificate permits the holder, provided he/she is 17 years or more, to act as pilot in command of a microlight aircraft or balloon for the purpose of becoming qualified for the grant or renewal of a pilot's licence provided that:

(a) such flights are within the United Kingdom;

(b) this medical certificate is valid at the time of flight;

(c) no other person is carried in the aircraft; and

(d) he/she acts in accordance with the instructions given by a person holding a pilot's licence which includes an Instructor's Rating entitling the holder to give instruction on the type of Aircraft flown.

Fig. 1–2

aged under 40 years	5 years	aged 50 to 70	1 year
aged 40 to 50	2 years	aged over 70	6 months

Note: A Medical Certificate or a Declaration of Health for a PPL or a student pilot issued before the applicant's fortieth birthday will only remain valid until the applicant's forty-second birthday.

The renewal date in either case is calculated from the last day of the month in which the certificate is signed.

Notwithstanding the existence of a valid medical certificate you must remain aware of your day to day physical condition and if you suffer an injury or illness you must not attempt to fly as pilot in command until you are fit and well again. In any case of doubt, it is your responsibility to consult your doctor and obtain a clearance prior to further 'in command' flights.

In relation to the above paragraph the ANO states:

1. A person shall not be entitled to act as a member of the flight crew of an aircraft registered in the United Kingdom if he knows or has reason to believe that his physical or mental condition renders him temporarily or permanently unfit to perform such function or to act in such capacity.
2. Every holder of a medical certificate issued under the Articles of the ANO should inform the CAA as soon as possible if he suffers:

   A personal injury involving incapacity to undertake his functions as a member of the flight crew, or

Suffers any illness involving incapacity to undertake those functions through a period of 20 days or more; or

In the case of a woman, has reason to believe that she is pregnant.

Legislation of this nature is no more than the application of common sense which is the fundamental basis of good operating practices.

THE PRIVATE PILOT'S LICENCE

United Kingdom Civil Aviation Authority

PRIVATE PILOT'S LICENCE-AEROPLANES

Licence No 00007/PP880A

Name Ian William Flywell

Nationality British Date of Birth 1.10.57

Issued in accordance with the provisions of the Civil Aviation Act, 1949, and of Annex 1 to the Convention of International Civil Aviation signed on 7th December, 1944, and subject to the terms and conditions of the Air Navigation Order for the time being in force, the holder is entitled to exercise the privileges of a Private Pilot's licence-Aeroplanes.

Date and Stamp

Signature of Issuing Officer........................
For the Civil Aviation Authority.

Signature of Holder........................

In order to obtain the licence a student pilot will have to sit and pass the written examinations and when sufficient flight training has been completed he will have to undergo the flight test.

The ground examinations will consist of three written tests of the multiple choice type in the following subjects:

1. Aviation Law
2. Navigation and Meteorology
3. Aircraft Technical Part 1 (General)
   Part 2 (Specific type — oral questions)

In the case of Microlight pilots the "Aircraft Technical" examination is one which relates directly to those subjects concerned with the operation of Microlight aircraft and includes questions on Principles of Flight, Flying Controls, Microlight Engines and Instruments, etc.

The flight test is a two part examination in which the candidate will be required to demonstrate his standard of competence in handling the aircraft on the ground and during flight as well as answering oral questions relating to pre-flight preparation, and the specific type of aircraft used during training.

When the ground examinations and flight test have been satisfactorily completed the licence when issued will be made up of a basic licence (or title page), a medical certificate and the aircraft Rating. The basic licence page indicates the class of licence, e.g. Private Pilot Licence, and the name of the holder together with his date of birth and nationality.

The licence itself will be non-expiring but the privileges it contains will lapse unless the medical certificate is renewed at the appropriate time and the holder carries out a minimum of 5 hours of flight during the 13 months following its issue.

The medical certificate can be renewed by making the necessary arrangements for a further examination from your doctor, and the 5 hours flight experience must be certified in the holder's log book by an approved Private Pilot Licence examiner. Full details on the method of logging these 5 hours is given later under the heading of 'Licences and Ratings — Renewal'.

The Rating included in the Private Pilot Licence is appropriate to the Group(s) of aircraft which the holder is permitted to fly. These Groups are defined below:

Group 'A' All types of single engined aeroplanes of which the maximum total weight authorised does not exceed 5700 kg.

Group 'B' All types of aeroplanes which have two or more engines of which the maximum total weight authorised does not exceed 5700 kg.

Group 'C' Individual types of aeroplanes of which the maximum total weight authorised exceeds 5700 kg or are considered to be of a complex nature.

Group 'D' 'Microlight aeroplane' means an aeroplane having a maximum total weight authorised not exceeding 390 kg, a wing loading at the maximum total weight authorised not exceeding 25 kg per square metre, a maximum fuel capacity not exceeding 50 litres and which has been designed to carry not more than 2 persons.

A licence cannot be issued without including a Certificate of Test and an aircraft Rating for at least one of the above groups of aeroplanes. Once a group or type has been entered in an aircraft Rating it will not normally be removed, but the entitlement to fly an aeroplane and exercise the privileges of a private pilot within the group, or of the type listed, will be dependent upon a certain minimum flight time being carried out by the holder of the licence in that group or in the case of Group 'C' in the specific type.

Additional Ratings which extend the licence privileges can be obtained by satisfactorily completing specific courses of training and passing appropriate examinations. Although these Ratings are not applicable to Microlight operations at the time of publication of this manual they are nevertheless included in summary form on the basis of general information.

The Night Rating This Rating permits the holder to carry passengers at night.

The IMC Rating The Instrument Meteorological Rating extends the privileges of a Private Pilot's Licence to undertake flights in conditions of reduced visibility.

The Instrument Rating This Rating gives the private pilot specific additional privileges in relation to flight in controlled airspace.

The privileges of the Private Pilot Licence are covered in detail in the ANO and these are summarised as follows:

The holder of a Private Pilot's Licence may fly as pilot in command of an aeroplane of any of the types specified in the licence. However, he shall not fly as pilot in command of an aeroplane:

1. On a flight outside controlled airspace:

(a) When the visibility is less than 1.5 nautical miles (nm), or

(b) When any passenger is carried and the aeroplane is flying either above 3000' above mean sea level (amsl) in Instrumental Meteorological Conditions (IMC) or when flying at or below 3000' amsl in a flight visibility of less than 3 nm.

(c) When out of sight of the surface.

2. He shall not fly on a Special VFR flight in a control zone in an flight visibility of less than 5 nm unless a special clearance is obtained from the appropriate Air Traffic Control Unit.
3. When any passengers are carried he shall not fly as pilot in command of an aeroplane at night.
4. A private pilot must not fly an aeroplane for the purpose of public transport or aerial work and he shall not receive any remuneration for his services as a pilot.

Fig 1-3 shows a graphic illustration of these privileges with regard to weather limitations i.e. flight visibility and proximity to cloud and in relation to flights conducted with or without passengers above, at or below 3000' amsl and outside controlled airspace.

BASIC PRIVATE PRIVILEGES FOR FLIGHT IN UNCONTROLLED AIRSPACE

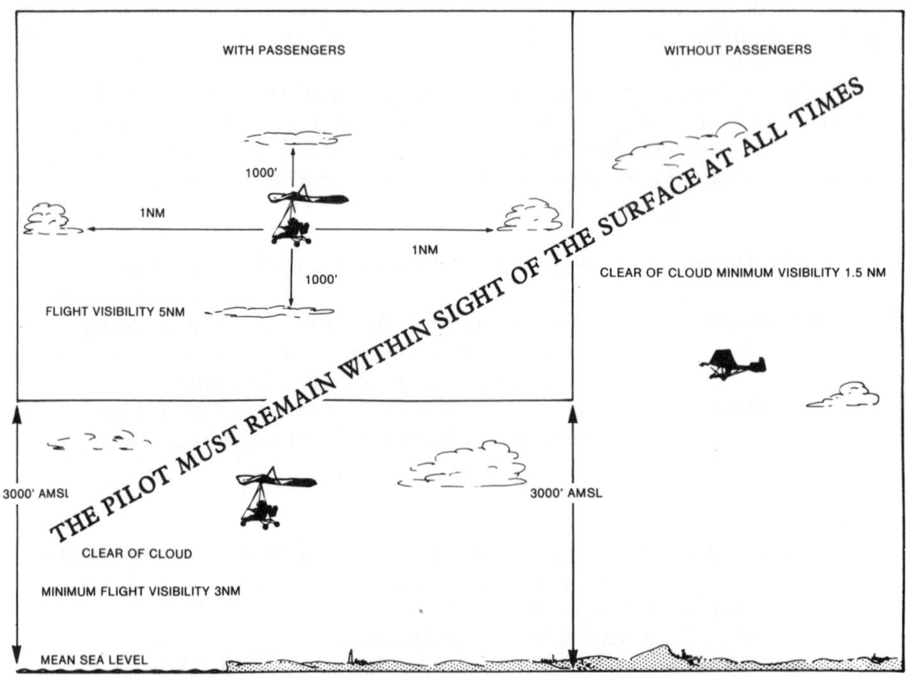

No Public Transport..No Remuneration..No Flying by Night with Passengers

Fig. 1–3

LICENCE AND RATING — RENEWALS

Apart from the requirement to hold a current medical certificate the privileges of the Private Pilot's Licence will last for a statutory period of 13 months from the date of the initial flight test. This date will be shown on the Certificate of Test which is included in the licence.

Any subsequent Certificates of Test will be entered in the licence holder's log book.

Certificate of Experience

Following the issue of the licence the privileges can be renewed by carrying out a minimum of 5 hours flying in the following 13 months and then obtaining a stamp and a signature in the holder's log book from an authorised Private Pilot Group 'D' examiner. The 5 hours required may be obtained by carrying out the following:

5 hours in command, or in the case of aircraft in which dual training can take place, at least 3 hours in command plus sufficient dual flying with a qualified instructor to make the total up to 5 hours.

When the PPL examiner has inspected the log book and is satisifed that the flying hour requirements have been met, he will stamp and sign the log book which will then extend the holder's PPL privileges for a further 13 months.

NOTE: It is the personal responsibility of all pilots to ensure that their licences and privileges are valid, during any flight they undertake as pilot in command.

PERSONAL LOG BOOK

Any person who engages in flying for the purposes of qualifying for the grant or renewal of a licence or rating, or who acts as a pilot or other member of flight crew during flight must keep a personal flying log book.

Evidence of flying time is needed when applying for a licence or a rating and also when you wish to obtain the stamp and signature to renew your certificate of experience. The ANO requires that the following particulars are shown in a pilot's log book:

Personal Details:

The name and address of the holder.

Particulars of the holder's licence.

Particulars of all flights made as a member of the flight crew, including:

The date, duration and places of arrival and departure of each flight.

The type and registration marks of the aircraft.
The capacity in which the holder acted during the flight.
Particulars of such special conditions under which the flight was conducted, e.g. night flying or instrument flying.

Recording of Flight Tests:

Any flight test required to be conducted for the issue or renewal of a licence or rating must be recorded in the pilot's personal log book.

There are several types of log book available for the pilot to purchase and Fig 1-4 shows a page from the log book designed and produced by the British Microlight Association. Your instructor will explain the method of entering the above particulars in your log book.

YEAR...... Total Flying time brought forward Remarks

Date	Aircraft type & No.	Engine	Place of take off	Pilot	Hrs Mins	Purpose of flight, weather, distance, landing place etc.

Fig. 1–4

Instructor's Endorsements of Flight Times

All log book entries should be made in ink for obvious reasons and you should also obtain your instructor's signature against all training flights to ensure corroboration of the flight time and other details.

You are also advised to take care over your entries, making them clearly legible and ensuring that the totals in the columns are added up accurately. At the end of your private pilot course and any training for subsequent ratings your Chief Flying Instructor should stamp and sign your log book before it is sent, together with an application form and appropriate fee to the CAA.

INSTRUCTION IN FLYING

The CAA regulations require that the student pilot is given sufficient flying training in order to attain the level of competence compatible with the privileges allowed to a private pilot.

Definition of Flying Instruction

Whenever the ANO calls for instruction to be given as a part of a course for a pilot licence or rating the instruction must be given by a qualified flying instructor who holds a current flying instructor's rating, and who is entitled to give instruction on the type of aircraft being used for the training.

Once a private pilot is qualified there is no requirement for instruction to be undertaken in a type of aircraft which is within the Group held on his aircraft rating. However, private pilots would be advised to obtain the services of a flying instructor when converting onto a different type of microlight aircraft.

Requirement for Flying Training to be Given

The minimum flying experience required by a student pilot before a licence can be granted is 25 hours. Of this at least 10 hours must have been solo flight. This latter requirement has to be specified in this way because there are 'solo' single seat microlights and 'dual' two seat microlights and either of these may be used for your training. The specific details of the type of training and practice flying relative to solo or dual type aircraft is covered in the BMAA syllabus and the Flight Section of this Manual.

AIRCRAFT OPERATION

The Air Navigation Order contains a large number of Articles and Schedules which cover much of the Legislation concerning the operation of aircraft, however a large part of the Order is not relevant to the operation of Microlights. Therefore, and to simplify the student's task the Articles listed in the Private Pilot Licence Syllabus for Group "D" aircraft are covered on the following pages of this Section.

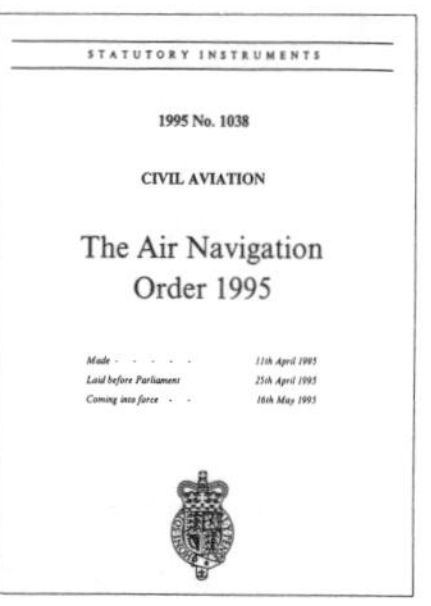

STATUTORY INSTRUMENTS

1995 No. 1038

CIVIL AVIATION

The Air Navigation Order 1995

Made - - - - - -	*11th April 1995*
Laid before Parliament	*25th April 1995*
Coming into force - -	*16th May 1995*

PRE-FLIGHT ACTIONS BY COMMANDER OF AIRCRAFT

When a pilot abides by the principles of good airmanship then the requirements of safety are present. This cannot be done by just sitting in the pilot's seat and operating the controls, to achieve it the pilot will require to exercise a strong sense of personal discipline and responsibility towards his passengers and others.

This cannot begin to be demonstrated unless adequate pre-flight preparation has been carried out. The ANO broadly lays down the pre-flight actions that should be covered prior to every flight and although many of your training flights will not require all these actions to be accomplished in detail they nevertheless indicate those actions which should be reviewed prior to any flight.

The commander of an aircraft registered in the UK must satisfy himself before the aircraft takes off:

That the flight can safely be made, taking into account the latest information available as to the route and aerodromes to be used, the weather reports and forecasts available, and any alternative courses of action which can be adopted in case the flight cannot be completed as planned, e.g. diverting to an alternate airfield or turning back to the departure airfield.

That all the equipment required for the flight (including radio if applicable) is carried and in a fit condition for use.

That the aircraft is in every way fit for the intended flight.

That the load carried by the aircraft is so distributed and secured that it may safely be carried on the intended flight.

That sufficient fuel, oil (and where applicable engine coolant) are carried and that a safe margin has been allowed for such contingencies as getting lost, or having to divert.

That due regard has been observed in relation to the aircraft's performance in respect of being able to safely take off and land within the available distance at the departure and destination airfields (including selected alternate(s) and to maintaining a safe height on the intended or alternate route.

A pilot who before flight does not check the weather at destination and the general forecast concerning the likely weather en-route, or who does not plan for an alternate route or an alternate aerodrome (when either are available) would be acting contrary to the requirements of the ANO and the principles of good airmanship.

The same would apply if for example, a map appropriate to the route was not carried, or where an adequate pre-flight inspection of the aircraft has not been conducted.

With regard to the weight and balance of the aircraft used during training flights, it will often be known from past experience that the particular aircraft's actual weight is not in excess of the all-up weight authorised and that the balance will be within limits. However whenever an aircraft is going to be flown with a greater load than usual a weight and balance calculation must be undertaken.

In a similar manner, most pilots will know from their experience of operating a particular aircraft in certain conditions from known airfields, (or take-off and landing strips, etc.) that an adequate distance will be available for take-off or landing, but when any combination of such conditions as light winds, a heavily laden aircraft, long grass or soft surfaces and similar circumstances which will reduce aircraft performance occur, then a sensible and safe pilot will carry out performance calculations during his pre-flight preparation.

CARRIAGE OF MUNITIONS

Due to obvious national and international implications and the dangers of inadvertent discharge of such items in an aircraft the law of the UK expressly forbids the carriage of weapons and munitions of war.

This law does not prevent the carriage of articles such as Verey Pistols or similar equipment used to discharge cartridges or flares for making the signals required by the Rules of the Air and Air Traffic Control Regulations. Nevertheless extreme care must be exercised when handling this equipment and it must be kept unloaded unless required for immediate use.

DROPPING PERSONS OR ARTICLES

It is an offence to drop persons, animals or articles from an aircraft in flight. However this rules does not apply when an emergency situation has occurred and the commander authorises such action in order to save life or prevent damage to property, or in any of the following circumstances:

The dropping of articles for the purpose of saving life.

The jettisoning, in cases of emergency, of fuel or articles in the aircraft.

The dropping of ballast in the form of fine sand or water.

The dropping of articles for the purpose of navigation, e.g. flares etc.

The dropping of articles for the purpose of agriculture, horticulture, forestry or public health.

The dropping of parachutists when authority has been given to do so.

CARRIAGE OF DANGEROUS GOODS

In addition to munitions and weapons there are regulations which restrict the carriage of othe dangerous articles unless certain stringent precautions are taken.

Dangerous goods which may be carried in reasonable safety by other forms of transportation can present extreme hazards when contained in an aircraft hold or cabin. This is due to the fact that the aircraft occupants will be unable to leave the confined space of an aircraft until it has landed.

Pilots must, therefore, learn to appreciate the potential hazards presented by certain articles which may be carried in an aircraft and goods which can be classified as dangerous for this purpose include such items as:

Explosives of any nature.

Flammable liquids and solids including such items as paint removers, liquid flavouring extracts, paints and varnishes, rubber cement, alcohol, matches etc.

Oxidising materials, e.g. nitrates that yield oxygen readily, which may in turn stimulate combustion.

Corrosive liquids, such as battery acids, certain cleaning compounds and similar agents.

Compressed gases including most household type sprays.

Poisons, apart from the more obvious poisons this heading includes such commonplace items as pesticides.

Radio-active materials.

To appreciate the care which is necessary in determining which goods are dangerous one has only to consider the potential effects of two very commonly used household materials, fertilizer compounds and aerosol cans.

Fertilizer compounds if not packaged properly could leak or spill into an area which if dampened by moisture will produce an oxidising agent which will quietly eat into a structural component or control cable and this may not be recognised until too late.

Aerosol cans or any other item which is packaged under pressure represent a positive hazard when carried in an aircraft due to the effect of the outside air pressure lowering substantially with increase of altitude. The effect of this could result in the aerosol cannister exploding and the contents catching fire.

Another point to be borne in mind is that magnetized materials, while not inherently dangerous in the ordinary sense, must nevertheless be regarded as hazardous when carried on board an aircraft, because of their potential for adversely affecting radio navigation equipment and certain flight instruments.

With these examples in mind, it is as well to remember that it is the pilot in command of an aircraft who is ultimately responsible for compliance with the regulations and the safety of any flight.

IMPERILLING SAFETY OF AIRCRAFT

"A person must not wilfully or negligently act in a manner likely to endanger an aircraft, or any person therein".

This statement from the ANO is terse and to the point, but it covers a multitude of circumstances, from a lack of pre-flight planning to such positive violations of the code of safety as deliberately flying at very low heights.

It is not intended to spell out here the manifold instances which could constitute a breach of this Article but rather to bring the regulation to the attention of all student pilots and point out that the application of simple common sense, together with a serious approach to their responsibilities as pilots, will ensure that the principle underlying this regulation is met.

IMPERILLING SAFETY OF ANY PERSONS OR PROPERTY

"A person shall not wilfully or negligently cause or permit an aircraft to endanger any person or property"

In a sense this Article of the ANO is directly linked with the previous regulation. It is nevertheless spelt out in this manner to emphasise the fact that an aircraft like a car can be a dangerous tool in the hands of a foolhardy person, and can if operated without care and regard for others, create hazards to the public at large and their property, whether by intent, or neglect of the pilot in command.

DRUNKENNESS IN AIRCRAFT

"A person shall not enter any aircraft when drunk, or be drunk in any aircraft"

In relation to the consumption of alcohol and piloting an aircraft the ANO goes on to say that no person may act as a member of the flight crew if the influence of alcohol or drugs impairs his ability.

Clearly the consumption of either, must have an effect upon a person's judgement skill and reactions, and the amount consumed and the time it was consumed in relation to the flight departure will have an important bearing upon anyone's fitness to fly.

Because of these factors and the varying effects that alcohol has on different people it is impossible to give hard and fast rules to meet every case. Pilots must understand that even small amounts of alcohol in the blood produce a measurable deterioration of performance of skilled tasks. Recent in-flight research has confirmed that even in small uncomplicated aircraft blood alcohol concentrations of 40 milligrammes per 100 millilitres (i.e. half the legal driving limit) are associated with substantial and highly significant increases in the errors committed by both inexperienced and experienced pilots. From this it is clear that even a single alcoholic drink can produce a positive loss of performance although the individual may not consider himself affected.

It is equally important to remember that the effects of alcohol remain for a considerable time after it has been consumed. Pilots should therefore, not fly for at least eight hours after taking relatively small amounts of alcohol, while larger amounts need an even longer recovery period.

Advice on taking medicinal drugs can be considered separately in that if there is a physical or mental need for them to be taken, the person concerned must clearly be unfit to pilot an aircraft and any pilot who attempts to fly when he is medically unfit will be placing himself, his passengers and the general public at serious risk.

When a pilot enters an aircraft he becomes an integral part of a 'man-machine system' he is just as essential to a successful flight as the aircraft control surfaces. Therefore to ignore one's physical fitness during pre-flight planning would be as senseless as failure to inspect the control surfaces or any other vital part of an aircraft prior to flight.

SMOKING IN AIRCRAFT

"Notices indicating when smoking is prohibited shall be exhibited in every aircraft registered in the UK, so as to be visible from each passenger seat therein. A person shall not smoke in any compartment at a time when smoking is prohibited by the aircraft commander".

Whether or not it is considered safe to smoke in an aircraft is initially decided upon by the CAA Airworthiness Division and if smoking is permitted this will usually be evidenced by the siting of ashtrays in appropriate positions in the cabin.

When smoking is totally prohibited in an aircraft it is a requirement to clearly exhibit 'No Smoking' signs.

In those aircraft where smoking is permitted the ultimate decision as to when smoking can be allowed is vested in the aircraft commander who will in any event forbid smoking to take place during take-off and landing or at such other times as he thinks fit.

AUTHORITY OF COMMANDER OF AIRCRAFT

"Every person in an aircraft registered in the UK shall obey all lawful commands which the commander of that aircraft may give for the purpose of securing the safety of the aircraft and of persons or property carried therein, or the safety, efficiency or regularity of air navigation"

This authority vested in the aircraft commander must not however be abused and the basis of all such commands must relate to reasons of safety or efficiency and regularity of the flight.

Such flight begins when the aircraft first moves under its own power and the intent is to take-off until such time as the aircraft becomes stationary again, immediately prior to engine shut down.

DOCUMENTS TO BE CARRIED

"An aircraft shall not fly unless it carries the documents which it is required to carry under the law of the country in which it is registered"

In relation to flights other than public transport or aerial work, e.g. private flights, there are two circumstances of flight which relate to whether or not aircraft documents must be carried in the aircraft.

Domestic Flights:
Any flight in which the aircraft departs from and lands at an aerodrome within the UK and which does not include passage over any other country is termed a 'domestic flight' and when it is conducted for private purposes no aircraft documents need to be carried.

International Flights:
Any flight to or from any other country is termed an 'international flight' and in these circumstances the following documents should be carried:

The Certificate of Airworthiness.

The Certificate of Registration.

The Radio Licence in respect of the aircraft radio station.

The Licences of the members of the flight crew of the aircraft.

It will also be advisable to carry the aircraft insurance policy or a copy of this document as many countries insist upon seeing this during aircraft arrival and departure procedures.

Note: The Channel Islands and the Isle of Man are considered to be part of the UK. for the purposes of this regulation.

PRODUCTION OF DOCUMENTS AND RECORDS

"The commander of an aircraft, shall within a reasonable time after being requested to do so by an authorised person, caused to be produced to that person:

The Certificate of Registration and the Certificate of Airworthiness in force in respect of the aircraft.

The Licences of its flight crew.

Such other documents as the aircraft may be required to carry during flight under the regulations of the ANO.

The requirements of this regulation shall be deemed to have been complied with in relation to the licences of the flight crew if they are produced at a police station in the UK. within 5 days from the date of the request.

The time taken to produce such documents as are required to be kept in the aircraft or kept at an aerodrome, is considered in a different way, and is specified in the ANO as 'within a reasonable time'. This is because of the practical difficulties which may arise in producing documents of this nature within a specific time.

The requirement to produce the aircraft documents when called for by an authorised person apply equally to the operator of the aircraft as well as the commander, and any member of a flight crew must also abide by this regulation in respect of his licence, rating or any certificate of validation which may be part of his licence.

Finally a similar regulation applies to the producing of personal flying log books within a reasonable time, however the pilot is not bound to produce entries made earlier than two years prior to the request.

REVOCATION, SUSPENSION OR VARIATION OF CERTIFICATES, LICENCES OR OTHER DOCUMENTS

The Civil Aviation Authority has power to suspend, vary, or revoke any licence, certificate, or similar document which it has issued. This action can be taken pending or after any enquiry, or during consideration of the case, and in these circumstances the holder of the licence, certificate or document must surrender it to the CAA.

Whether or not a licence, certificate, or document, has been suspended varied or revoked, a breach of any condition subject to which the document was issued will result in it becoming invalid during the continuance of that breach.

OFFENCES IN RELATION TO DOCUMENTS AND RECORDS

The Air Navigation Order states:

1. A person shall not with intent to deceive -

   (a) Use any certificate, licence approval, permission, exemption or other document issued or having effect or required by or under this

Order which has been forged, altered, revoked, or suspended, or to which he is not entitled; or

(b) lend any certificate, licence, approval, permission, exemption or other document issued or having effect or required by or under this Order to or allow it to be used by, any other person; or

(c) make any false representation for the purpose of procuring for himself or any other person the grant, issue, renewal or variation of any such certificate, licence, approval, permission or exemption or other document.

2. A person shall not wilfully mutilate, alter or render illegible any log book or other record require by or under this Order to be maintained or any entry made therein, or knowingly make, or procure or assist in the making or, any false entry in or material omission from any such log book or record or destroy any such log book or record during the period for which it is required under this Order to be preserved.
3. All entries made in writing in any log book or record referred to in paragraph 2 shall be made in ink or indelible pencil.
4. A person shall not wilfully or negligently make in a load sheet any entry which is incorrect in any material particular, or any material omission from such a load sheet.
5. A person shall not purport to issue any certificate for the purposes of this Order or the Regulations made thereunder unless he is authorised to do so under this Order.
6. A person shall not issue any such certificate as aforesaid unless he has satisfied himself that all statements in the certificate are correct.

POWER TO PREVENT AIRCRAFT FLYING

If it appears to the CAA or to any authorised person that an aircraft is intended or likely to be flown:

"In such circumstances that the flight would be in contravention of any provision of the ANO or any regulations made thereunder and be a cause of danger to any person or property whether or not in the aircraft, the CAA or that authorised person may direct the operator or the commander of the aircraft that he is not to permit the aircraft to make the particular flight or any other flight of such description as may be specified in the direction, until the direction has been revoked by the CAA or by an authorised person, and the CAA or that authorised person may take such steps as are necessary to detain the aircraft".

In order to determine whether the intended flight will be in contravention of the ANO or any regulation made thereunder, a representative of the CAA or any authorised person may enter upon and inspect the aircraft.

SECTION TWO

AIR TRAFFIC RULES AND SERVICES

AIR TRAFFIC RULES AND SERVICES

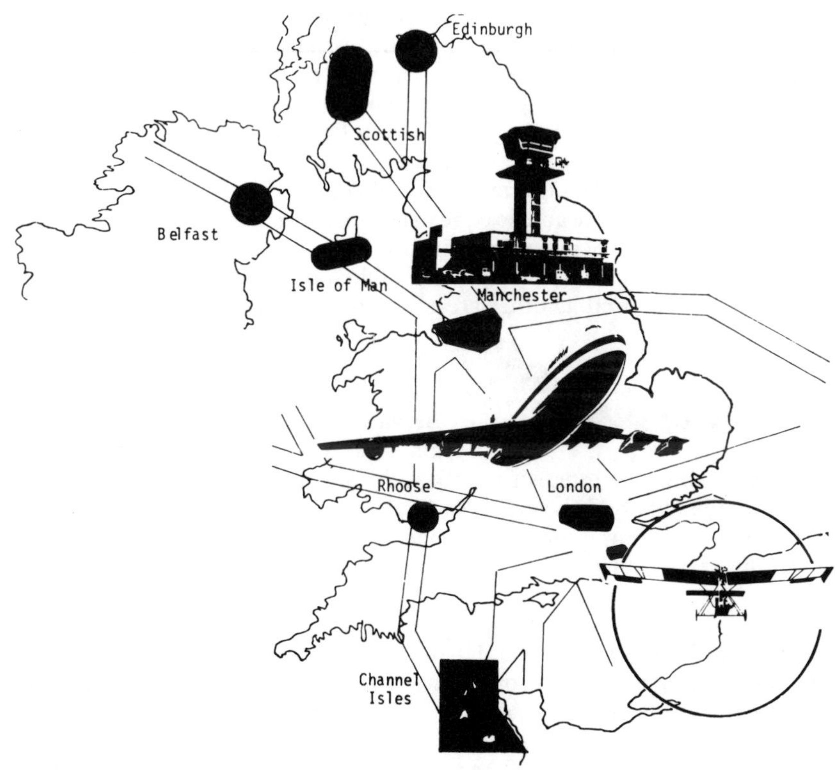

INTRODUCTION

During the early years of aviation the safe passage of aeroplanes depended upon pilots armed with a simple set of rules of the air and a navigation chart which covered the intended route to be flown.

These operations were normally conducted in reasonable good weather and in conditions where the pilot could 'See and Avoid'. Letting down through cloud to accomplish a landing was generally considered an unsafe procedure due to the lack of any aids other than that provided by outside visual references.

Therefore in the main, aviation safety was achieved due to limitations placed upon pilots through the lack of navigation and landing aids, and the slow speed of their machines. These low speeds, incidentally applied to most aircraft of that period whether they were small trainers or larger passenger carrrying aircraft.

In more recent years the scene has changed completely and today we have considerable numbers of aircraft operating in the skies above most countries. Further to this there has been a notable change in the relative sizes, speeds and performance of aircraft. Within the present airspace system, small and slow aircraft, e.g. microlights and light trainers now have to co-exist in the same environment as very large high performance airliners and military aircraft, having performance capabilities which permit them to travel at very high speeds and in some cases well above the speed of sound.

The pilots of light fixed wing aircraft and helicopters, by virtue of the equipment they carry, e.g. radio, etc. are able to cope in this environment and stay clear of large and fast air traffic. Pilots of microlight aircraft however, will not normally have this advantage and so must be especially aware of the problems and keep well clear of regulated airspace as well as other areas which are hazardous to flight.

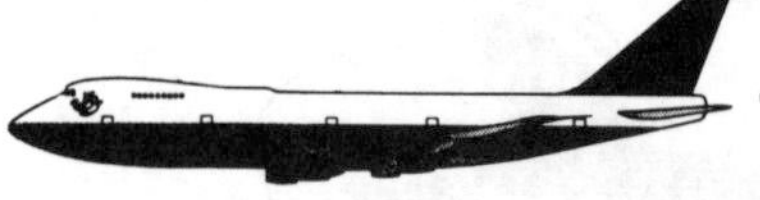

Because of the various changes over the years and in order to separate different classes of aircraft in the interests of safety, the sky over most countries has been gradually divided up, both horizontally and vertically into different types of airspace with varying sets of rules.

Together with this further subdivision of the airspace, has grown a larger number of rules, regulations and operating procedures not all of which will need to be understood by the private pilot. He will, however need to know the procedures and regulations which govern his own type of activity and he will also need to understand that there are areas of the airspace system into which he is not allowed to go unless he acquires additional ratings and privileges.

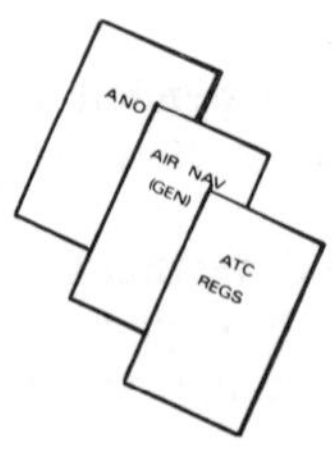

The regulations governing the movement of aircraft at aerodromes and in flight are laid down partly in the Air Navigation Order, and in greater detail in the statutory document entitled ‘The Rules of the Air and Air Traffic Control Regulations’.

**THE RULES OF THE AIR
AND AIR TRAFFIC CONTROL REGULATIONS 1985**

INTRODUCTION

The text included in this section is taken from SI No. 1985/1714.

The Secretary of State for Transport in exercise of his powers under Article 64(1) of the Air Navigation Order 1985[a] (hereinafter referred to as 'the Order'), and of all other powers enabling him in that behalf, hereby makes the following Regulations:—

1 These Regulations may be cited as the Rules of the Air and Air Traffic Control Regulations 1985, and shall come into operation on 1 December 1985.

2 The Rules set forth in the Schedule hereto are hereby prescribed as the Rules of the Air and Air Traffic Control.

3 (i) Subject to the following provisions of this Regulation, the following Regulations are hereby revoked, that is to say:

The Rules of the Air and Air Traffic Control Regulations 1981[b];

The Rules of the Air and Air Traffic Control (Amendment) Regulations 1981[c];

The Rules of the Air and Air Traffic Control (Second Amendment) Regulations 1983[d];

The Rules of the Air and Air Traffic Control (Third Amendment) Regulations 1985[e].

(ii) (a) These Regulations shall apply to or in relation to any licence or other document issued or granted under any Regulation revoked by these Regulations as they apply to a licence or other document issued or granted under these Regulations.

(b) Any licence or other document issued or granted under any Regulations revoked by these Regulations in force at the date of the coming into operation of these Regulations shall, subject to the provisions of Article 59 of the Order, remain in force and shall have the effect for the purposes of these Regulations as if it had been issued or granted under the corresponding provisions thereof:

Provided that any such document which is expressed to remain in force for a definite period shall remain in force, unless renewed, only until the expiration of that period.

Fig 2-1

This document is amended from time to time and at periodic intervals a new edition is issued. The copy shown at fig 2-1 for example, relates to the regulations which came into operation in 1985.

The contents of 'The Rules of the Air and Air Traffic Control Regulations' are divided into eleven sections which are fairly wide ranging and cover the following aspects and procedures:

Section I

Interpretation (Definitions).

Section II

*Application of Rules to Aircraft.
*Misuse of Signals and Markings.
Reporting Hazardous Conditions.
*Low Flying.
Simulated Instrument Flight.
Practice Instrument Approaches.

Section III

Lights and Other Signals to the shown or made by aircraft.

Section IV

General Flight Rules:
*Weather Reports and Forecasts.
*Rules for Avoiding Aerial Collisions.
Aerobatic Manoeuvres.
*Right Hand Traffic Rule.
Notification of Arrival.
Flight in 'Notified' Airspace.
Choice of VFR or IFR.

Section V

*Visual Flight Rules:
- Outside Controlled Airspace.
- Within Controlled Airspace.

Section VI

Instrument Flight Rules:
- Outside Controlled Airspace.
- Within Controlled Airspace.
- Minimum Height to Fly.
- Quadrantal and Semi-Circular Rule.
- Flight Plans and Air Traffic Control Clearances.
- Position Reports.

Section VII

Aerodrome Traffic Rules:
*Visual Signals.
*Access to, and Movement on the Manoeuvring Area.
*Right of Way Rule.
*Dropping of Glider Tow Ropes.
*Aerodromes Without ATC Units.
*Aerodromes With ATC Units.
*Special Rules for Certain Aerodromes.

Section VIII

Special Rules for Low Level Cross-Channel Traffic.

Section IX

Special Rules for Air Traffic in the Upper Flight Information Regions.

Section X

Aerodrome Signals and Markings.
Distress, Urgency and Safety Signals.

Section XI

Air Traffic Control.

The items which are of specific concern to microlight pilots are marked in the above list with an asterisk, however certain questions will be asked in the PPL written examination which cover other aspects, and information relating to these has therefore been included under the appropriate headings on the following pages.

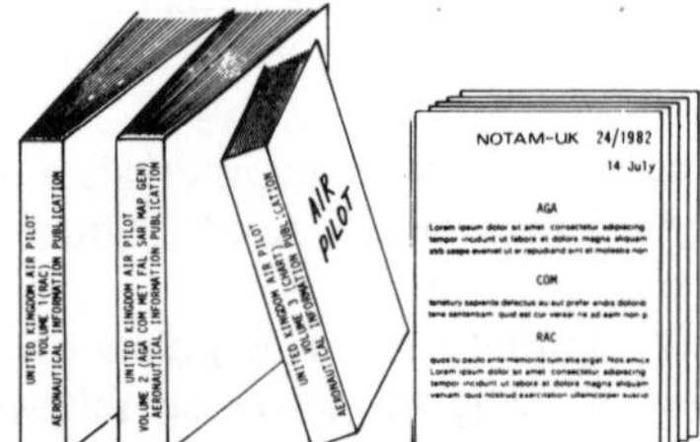

Additional detailed information in relation to Air Traffic Rules, Services and Procedures to be adopted during flight operations in the different types of airspace and at particular aerodromes, is contained in the UK Air Pilot and Notices to Airmen (NOTAMS). These documents are touched upon later in this section.

First it would however be of value to review how the airspace above the UK is divided up as this knowledge will then enable a microlight pilot to have a basic understanding of the various differences which occur in the airspace system and to know which areas he should keep clear of and also the best way to route any cross country flight he undertakes.

DIVISION OF AIRSPACE IN THE UNITED KINGDOM

The airspace above the UK and the surrounding waters is divided into two large areas known as 'Flight Information Regions' (FIR's). They are the London FIR, and the Scottish FIR. Fig 2-2 shows these regions in plan view together with the names of the adjacent Continental FIR's.

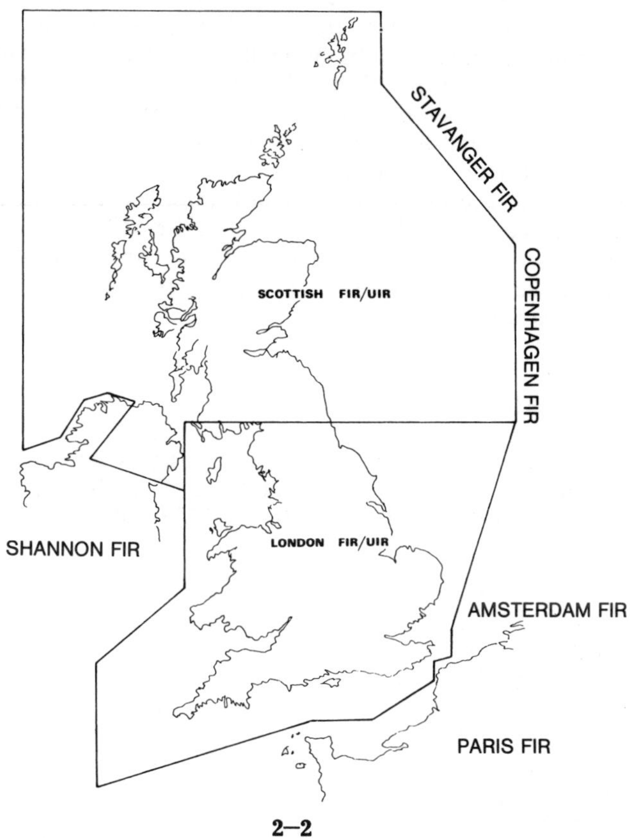

2–2

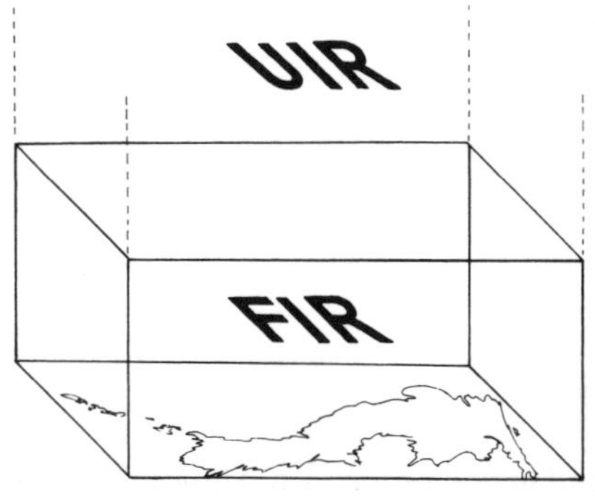

The London and Scottish FIR's extend upwards from mean sea level to approximately 24.500 feet. Above this level and covering the same geographic areas there are two Upper Information Regions (UIR's) and within them additional rules apply, e.g. within this airspace it is mandatory for aircraft to carry radio equipment unless otherwise authorised.

Certain areas within the FIR's are classified as Controlled Airspace, Special Rules Airspace, Aerodrome Traffic Zones and Military Traffic Zones. All civil and military aerodromes have an Aerodrome Traffic Zone of a standard horizontal and vertical extent of 2000 feet vertically and 1.5 nm horizontally from the boundary of the aerodrome but at certain military aerodromes where the air traffic activity is heavy an increased size and shape of protected airspace is added and this is known as a Military Aerodrome Air Traffic Zone.

The existence and specific dimensions of Controlled Airspace, Special Rules Airspace and Military Traffic Zones is notified in the AIP (UK Air Pilot) and are also clearly shown on 1:500.000 Topographical Aeronautical Charts. The 1:250.000 Topographical Chart however only shows Controlled Airspace below 3000 feet above mean sea level.

CONTROLLED AIRSPACE

Controlled airspace is further subdivided into three types of areas, 'Control Zones' (CTR's), 'Airways' and 'Terminal Control Areas' (TMA's). Fig 2-3 shows the disposition of the Control Zones existing in the UK including the Channel Islands and the Isle of Man.

Control Zones existing in the UK at the date of publication of this Manual.

Fig 2—3

These Control Zones are established around major airports from ground level to specific altitudes in order to give the passenger carrying airliners and other commercial air traffic added protection during flight in these areas.

This is achieved by restricting the movements of some aircraft into this airspace unless the pilot holds the additional privileges of an Instrument Rating, a qualification which is obtained by more rigorous training than that required for a basic licence.

AIRWAYS

In order to expedite and protect the flow of passenger carrying aircraft on public transport operations between major airports., Control Areas known as Airways have been established. These Airways are normally 10 nm wide and extend vertically from a specific lower limit to an upper limit which is usually in the region of 25.000' above mean sea level (amsl). Fig 2-4 shows an illustration of an Airway, and fig 2-6 shows how these Airways criss cross the UK.

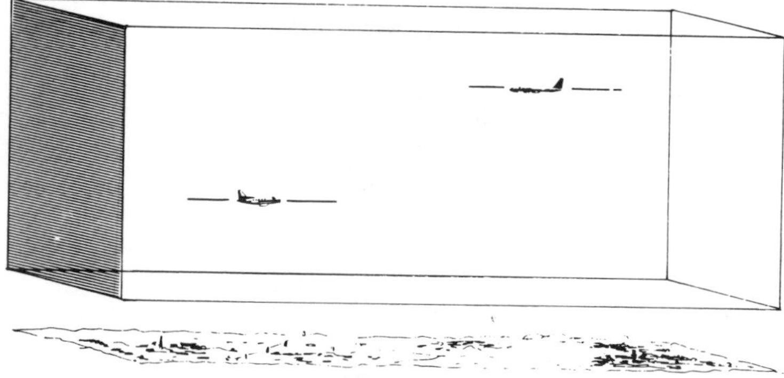

Fig 2—4

Those portions of Airways which are adjacent to Control Zones will often have lower bases than the en-route sections. This is to afford protection to aircraft using Airways and which are climbing up from, or descending outside the limits of the particular Control Zone. Reference fig 2-5.

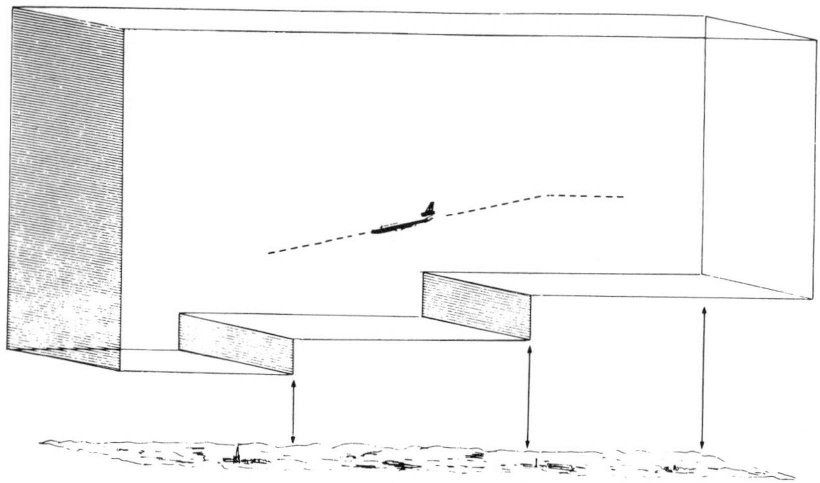

Fig 2—5

Individual Airways are identified by a colour code and number system which is sometimes supplemented by the description, East, West, North or South, e.g. Red One, Red One North. These identification codes are shown on topographical charts but in an abbreviated form, e.g. Red One South will appear as R1S followed by the numerals which relate to the base and top of the Airway. An example of the approximate airways structure in the UK is shown in fig 2-6.

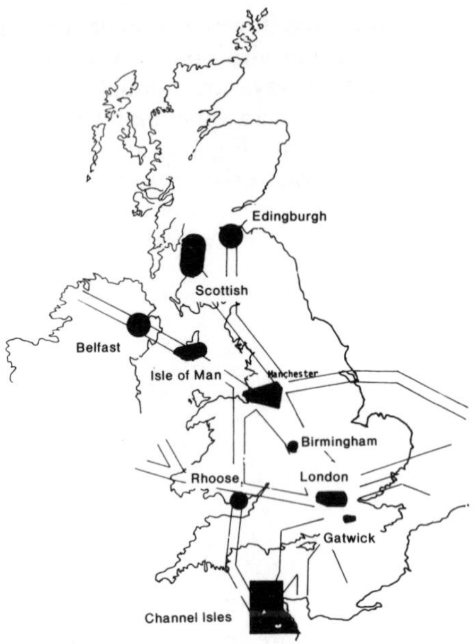

Fig 2—6

TERMINAL CONTROL AREAS

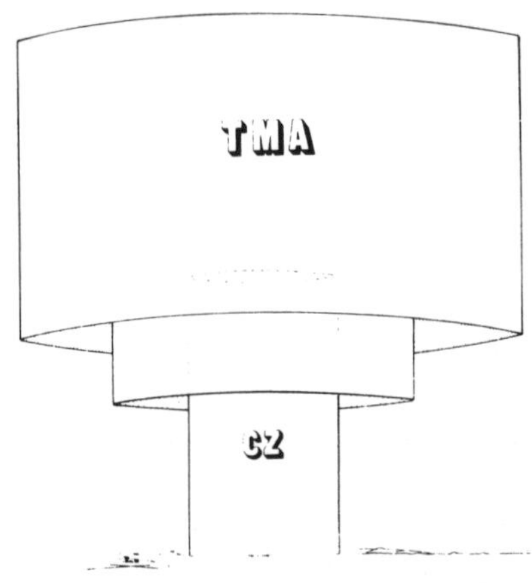

Fig 2—7

Where Airways intersect in the vicinity of Control Zones, additional controlled airspace known as Terminal Control Areas (TMA's) are established, the geographic dimensions of which are larger than the associated Control Zones.

However it is not normally necessary for a TMA to extend down to the surface and a descriptive picture of the vertical shape which may apply to a TMA is shown at fig 2-7

It will be seen that the base of the TMA is stepped up as it extends outwards from the associated Control Zone, this permits a greater area of uncontrolled airspace to exist in the lower levels and thus allows light aircraft, e.g. small fixed wing aircraft, microlights, etc, to operate under the TMA and into and out of other airfields or take-off and landing strips which may be situated close to a Control Zone without the pilots having to hold an Instrument Rating or the aircraft to be fitted with additional instrumentation or radio equipment.

Further to this and when circumstances permit, cut outs may be incorporated in the TMA (as shown in fig 2-8) to permit even greater flexibility of light aircraft movements to take place within the uncontrolled section of airspace.

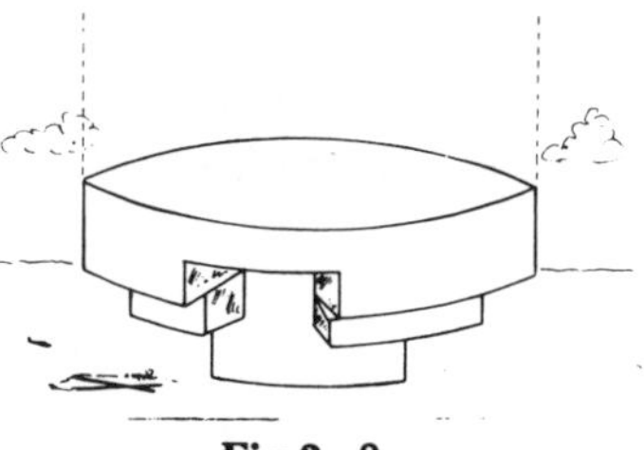

Fig 2–8

An illustration of how TMA's are established throughout the UK is shown below in fig 2-9.

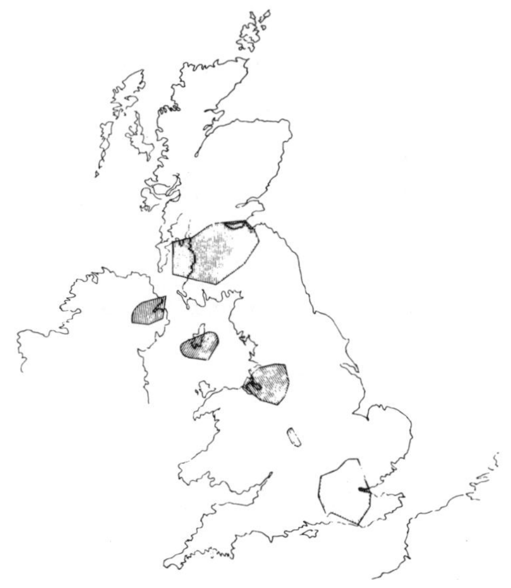

Fig 2–9

TMA's existing in the UK at the date of publication of this Manual. Dimensions and details of TMA's change and must be verified from the UK Air Pilot/Notams.

SPECIAL RULES AIRSPACE

Special Rules Airspace is established within the FIR's when it is considered necessary to assist the orderly flow of air traffic. The microlight pilot will be mainly concerned with knowing where the Special Rules Zones (SRZ's) and Special Rules Areas (SRA's) are established in order that he can give such areas a clear berth.

The basic purpose of Special Rules Zones or Areas is to afford additional safeguards to air traffic movements in the vicinity of those specified aerodromes which do not have air traffic movements of an intensity or type which would warrant the establishment of a Control Zone (together with its attendant restrictions) but for air traffic safety reasons do need added protection in the form of procedures additional to those normally considered necessary at less busy airfields.

In the broader sense these Zones and Areas can be considered as mini Control Zones and Terminal Areas in so far as their horizontal and vertical structure is concerned. For example a Special Rules Zone is an area of specific geographic dimensions around a particular airfield which extends from the surface to a specified level. A Special Rules Area has specific geographic dimensions which extend from a specified altitude above the surface with a specified top level.

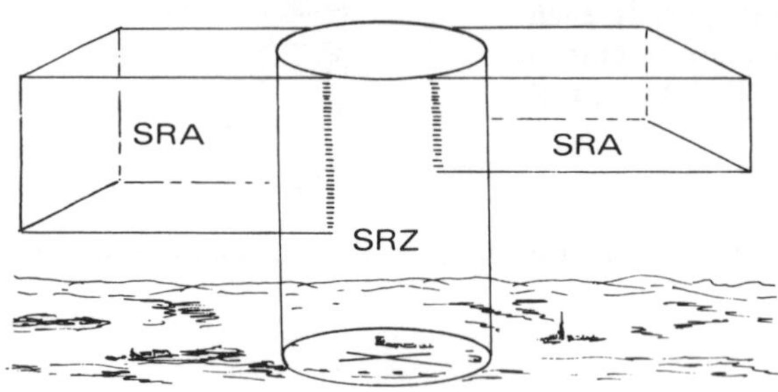

Fig 2—10

Fig 2—10 shows how a SRZ/SRA may be constructed, but it should be noted that:

the vertical and geographic dimensions vary with the particular SRZ/SRA.

The top of a SRA may not be at the same level as the top of its associated SRZ.

MILITARY AERODROME TRAFFIC ZONES

At certain military aerodromes, zones have been established to afford added protection to military air traffic departing from or arriving at those airfields.

These zones known as MATZ normally comprise the airspace within 5 nm radius of the particular aerodrome and extend upwards from the surface to 3000' above aerodrome level.

To further protect aircraft on the final approach path of the main runway used at the airfield it is often necessary to have a projection of one or more 'stub' areas. extending some 5 nm outwards from the MATZ boundary and encompassing the area 2 nm either side of the approach path centre line. The stub areas normally extend from 1000' above the surface to 3000' above the aerodrome level. Fig 2—11 shows a typical 'single stub' MATZ in elevation.

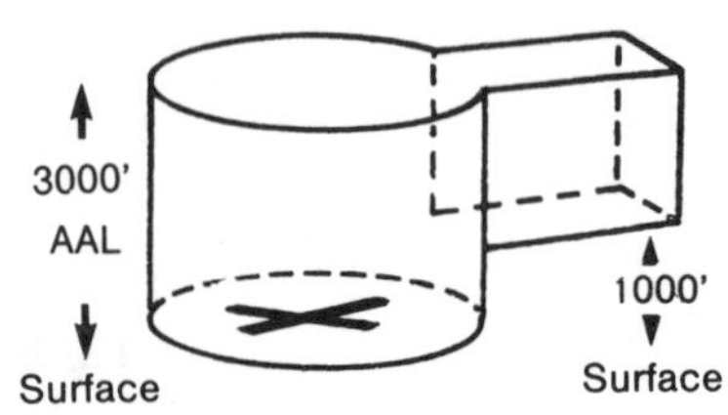

Fig 2—11

METEOROLOGICAL CONDITIONS - VMC AND IMC

The weather governs the ability for pilots to see the ground and navigate visually and also see other aircraft during flight. Therefore it is natural for the basic regulations pertaining to aircraft operation to be based upon the weather conditions in the vicinity of the aircraft and because of this fact the Rules under which pilots fly their aircraft are related to two types of meteorological conditions - these are Visual Meteorological Conditions (VMC) and Instrument Meteorological Conditions (IMC).

Flights conducted in VMC are carried out in accordance with the Visual Flight Rules (VFR).

Flights conducted in IMC must be carried out in accordance with the Instrument Flight Rules (IFR).

NOTE: All flights within the UK must be conducted in accordance with either the Visual Flight Rules or the Instrument Flight Rules.

The Visual Flight and Instrument Flight Rules are covered in the Rules of the Air and Air Traffic Regulations and this document also defines the circumstances under which VFR or IFR can be conducted.

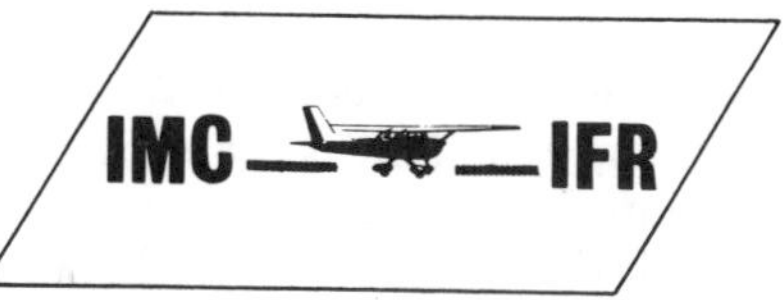

What are the Visual Flight Rules?

These are all the normal Rules applicable to flight, e.g. right of way rules, Rules for avoiding aerial collisions, low flying Rule, etc. These Rules are covered in detail later in this Manual.

What are the Instrument Flight Rules?

In addition to any of the normal flight Rules which may apply at the time there are 4 additional Rules which make up the Instrument Flight Rules, these are:

Rule 25 The Minimum Height Rule.

This requires the aircraft to be flown at a height not less than 1000' above the highest obstacle within 5 nm of the aircraft. However there are certain exceptions to this rule, i.e.

(a) When the aircraft is flying at or below 3000' amsl and in sight of the surface.

(b) When the aircraft is taking off or landing.

(c) When the aircraft has been authorised by a competent authority to fly lower than this.

Rule 26 The Quadrantal and Semi Circular Rule.

This rule is covered in detail later on in this manual but in summary it means that above 3000' amsl the aircraft must be flown at an altitude (expressed as a 'flight level') and in accordance with its **magnetic track** over the ground.

Rule 27 Flight Plan and Air Traffic Control Clearance.

This rule is only applicable for flight within Controlled Airspace.

Rule 28 Position Reports.

This rule is also only applicable to flight within Controlled Airspace.

It therefore follows that two additional rules, the minimum height rule and the quadrantal rule will apply to flight in uncontrolled airspace above 3000' amsl and when flight is being conducted below this altitude only rule 25 will apply and then only if the aircraft is not in sight of the surface.

Having summarized the Visual and Instrument Flight Rules the next step is to consider what constitutes VMC and IMC. The Visual Meteorological Conditions will vary depending upon whether the aircraft is being flown above or below 3000' amsl. At and below 3000' amsl the conditions will also vary depending upon the indicated airspeed of the aircraft.

VMC above 3000' amsl.

The basic weather conditions which relate to VMC above 3000' amsl are such that the pilot must be able to see a distance of 5 nm and remain 1000' vertically and 1 nm horizontally clear of cloud. If the prevailing weather conditions in the vicinity of the aircraft are such that the above conditions are less than stated then the flight conditions are considered as IMC.

VMC at or below 3000' amsl.

When any aeroplane is flying at an indicated airspeed of 140 knots or less the minimum flight conditions to maintain VMC are, an in flight visibility of at least 1 nm with the aircraft clear of cloud and in sight of the surface.

Although indicated airspeeds of more than 140 knots are not relevant to microlight aircraft at the present time it should nevertheless be noted that at these higher speeds the conditions for VMC change to:

> The aircraft must remain 1000' vertically and 1 nm horizontally from cloud and in a flight visibility of at least 3 nm.

Fig 2-12 illustrates the weather conditions in relation to indicated airspeed and altitude which are applicable to the maintenance of VMC.

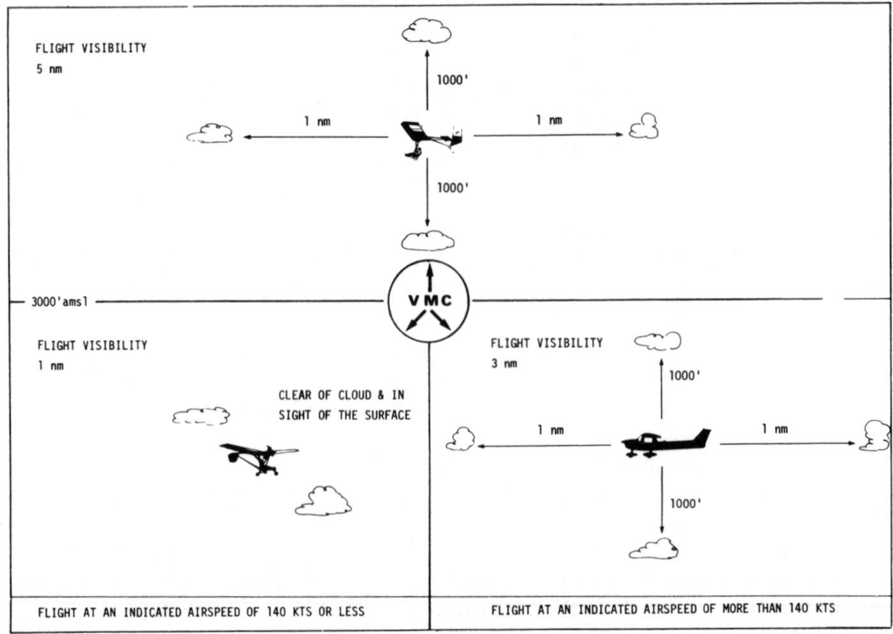

Fig 2–12

Because of the statutory nature of the Air Navigation Order and the Rules of the Air and Air Traffic Control Regulations they are couched in legal terms and as a result it is not always easy to understand them. This is aggravated by the fact that although the basic Private Pilot privileges and the conditions for VMC/IMC are separate entities in the statutory documents they do become related during any flight. In consequence it would be sensible at this stage to review the private pilot privileges and then relate them to flight in Visual and Instrument Flight Conditions. For the purpose of simplification only those privileges which apply to flight by day in uncontrolled airspace need to be considered as follows:

> The holder of a Private Pilot's Licence may fly as pilot in command of an aeroplane of any of the types specified in the licence. However he **shall not** fly as pilot in command of an aeroplane on a flight outside Controlled Airspace:
>
> (a) When the visibility is less than 1·5 nautical miles, or
>
> (b) When any passenger is carried and the aeroplane is flying either above 3000' amsl **in IMC** or when flying at or below 3000' amsl in a flight visibility of less than 3 nm.

Conditions for Flight in Accordance with VFR

From these privileges and the information shown in fig 2-12 it can be seen that when passengers are not carried the Private Pilot can legally fly in a visibility down to 1·5 nm and this will apply regardless of altitude. In the case of a flight when passengers are carried the minimum visibility is raised to 3 nm when flying at or below 3000' amsl and 5 nm when flying above 3000'. This latter visibility minimum is derived from the fact that when carrying passengers above 3000' amsl the pilot must remain in Visual Meteorological Conditions and you will recall that one of the requirements for VMC above 3000' amsl is that the visibility must be 5 nm.

Therefore to summarize the relationship between pilot privileges and VFR/IFR it can be seen that if a pilot who does not hold an IMC or an Instrument Rating is flying in VMC above 3000' amsl and is carrying passengers he should operate in accordance with the Visual Flight Rules. If he is carrying passengers and the weather is less than VMC then his privileges will not allow him to conduct such a flight.

If the weather conditions are VMC or IMC above 3000' amsl and he is not carrying passengers it will be within his privileges to conduct the flight but he must do so in accordance with the Instrument Flight Rules.

Conditions for Flight in Accordance with IFR

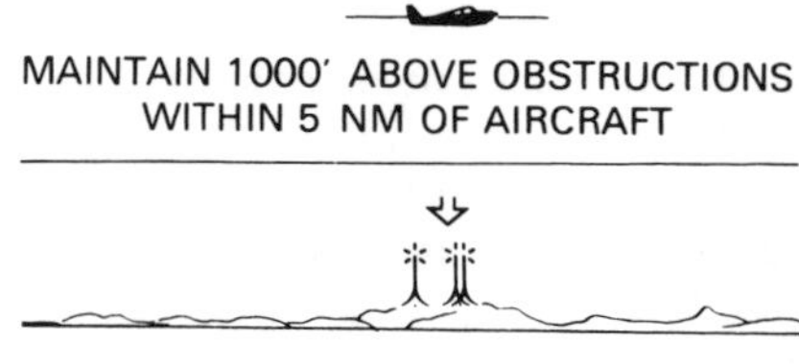
MAINTAIN 1000' ABOVE OBSTRUCTIONS
WITHIN 5 NM OF AIRCRAFT

When operating outside Controlled Airspace under IFR the pilot must abide by Rules 25 and 26 of the Rules of the Air and Air Traffic Control Regulations.

Rule 25 states that 'the aircraft must not be flown at a height of less than 1000' above any obstruction which is within 5 nm of the aircraft'.

Rule 26 states that aircraft operating under IFR outside Controlled Airspace and above 3000' amsl shall be flown at a level appropriate to their magnetic tracks, in accordance with a Table laid down by this Rule. The basis for this requirement lies in the fact that when aircraft operate in weather conditions which are less than VMC a greater risk of collision between them exists.

In order to reduce this risk standard separation rules have been established and these rules known as the Quadrantal and Semi-Circular Rule require that the aircraft altimeter be set to a standard datum of 1013 millibars (mb) and the cruising level be selected according to the magnetic track of the aircraft in relation to the Table shown in the Rules of the Air and Air Traffic Control Regulations.

For example, when an aircraft is flying on a magnetic track which lies between 360 degrees and 089 degrees an 'odd' cruising level must be chosen such as 3000', 5000' etc.

Aircraft which are following magnetic tracks which lie in the reciprocal sector, i.e. between 180 to 269 degrees must fly at 'even' cruising levels such as 4000', 6000' etc.

Fig 2-13 illustrates this principle and if will be seen that aircraft on reciprocal tracks will have a separation of 1000' and those on crossing tracks a vertical separation of 500'. This is known as the 'Quadrantal Rule' and it is illustrated more fully in the following Table.

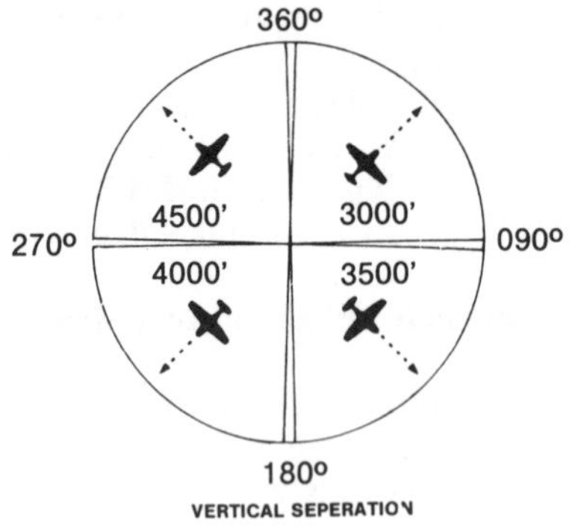

Fig 2—13

Magnetic Tracks Degrees	Cruising Level
000 TO 089	ODD THOUSANDS OF FEET E.G. 3000ft., 5000ft., 7000ft., ETC.
090 TO 179	ODD THOUSANDS OF FEET + 500ft. E.G. 3500ft., 5500ft., 7500ft., ETC.
180 TO 269	EVEN THOUSANDS OF FEET E.G. 4000ft., 6000ft., 8000ft., ETC.
270 TO 359	EVEN THOUSANDS OF FEET + 500ft. E.G. 4500ft., 6500ft., 8500ft., ETC.

24,000'

Above 24.000' the quadrantal rule no longer applies and is replaced by a second rule known as the 'Semi-Circular Rule', but as flight at these altitudes is not applicable to small aircraft such as microlights this rule is not detailed in this manual.

Although it is mandatory to operate at cruising levels selected in accordance with the foregoing table when the flight is conducted under IFR, it is not so when flying en-route under VFR.

This is because the basic private pilot privileges only permit flight which is clear of cloud at all times. If cloud is present at or in the close vicinity of the selected cruising level and the pilot were to maintain that level he would be exceeding his privileges and breaking the law.

Different rules apply for flight in accordance with IFR outside and inside Controlled Airspace. Private pilots are not normally permitted to operate under IFR in Controlled Airspace unless they hold an Instrument Rating, nevertheless they are allowed to enter such airspace on certain occasions and under certain conditions.

Therefore all pilots should have an understanding of the application of Instrument Flight Rules within Controlled Airspace so that they may appreciate and anticipate the movement of IFR traffic if operating in these areas.

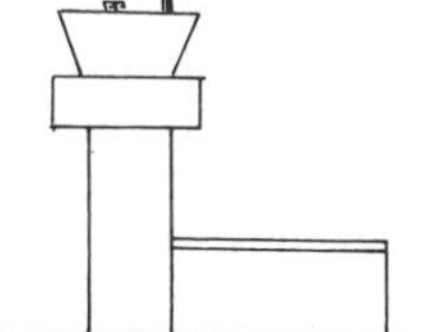

Aircraft operating under IFR within Controlled Airspace will be subject to Rule 25, and additionally Rules 27 and 28. Rule 27 concerns the 'Filing' of flight plans and Rule 28 applies to the making of 'Position Reports' additional to those normally used in the vicinity of aerodromes.

Rule 26 (the quadrantal rule) does not apply as aircraft cruising levels within Controlled Airspace will be governed by ATC clearances which are based upon achieving safe separation standards compatible with the current movements of air traffic which may be descending, climbing or in transit through these areas.

Rule 27 requires a Flight Plan to be filed, and an ATC clearance to be issued prior to entering or taking off from any point within the Controlled Airspace. The pilot must abide by the flight clearance in respect of altitudes, cruising levels and routes so that the Air Traffic Control unit knowns exactly where the aircraft is at all times, and thus ensuring a safe and smooth flow of air traffic within the area.

Rule 27 will apply within Controlled Airspace regardless of whether IMC or VMC obtains, however certain relaxations may be applied to the departure and letdown phases of flight during Visual Meteorological Conditions.

Rule 28 is linked in with Rule 27 in that 'Position Reports' must be made by the pilot in accordance with his flight clearance instructions or as otherwise directed by the relevant ATC unit. (In this case the carriage of two way radio equipment is required).

Special VFR Flight

Those who use the airspace system have varying operational requirements and because of the nature of some flight operations, restrictions must be placed upon others in the interests of their collective safety.

However these restrictions can sometimes be relaxed without infringing their underlying principles, thus although the regulations in relation to Controlled Airspace are primarily designed to protect IFR traffic operating within these areas, certain relaxations can be made from time to time without lowering the standards of flight safety. Any relaxation of the basic regulations will however be dependent upon, the existing weather, volume of air traffic movements, and pilot competence.

Because a private pilot may not be able to operate in much of the Controlled Airspace unless he holds an Instrument Rating, the concept of 'Special VFR Flight' has been incorporated in the regulations.

Special VFR Flight is normally only applicable to Control Zones and some Special Rules Airspace, thus permitting the private pilot access to aerodromes situated within them. It does not apply in any circumstances to Airways.

Permission for this type of flight will usually be given on those occasions when reasonable good weather exists and when air traffic movements are not too dense. However on those occasions when the visibility is less than 5 nm an Instrument Meteorological Conditions (IMC) Rating must be held by the pilot, in which case and provided circumstances allow he will be permitted to conduct Special VFR Flight down to a visibility of not less than 1.5 nm.

Note: An IMC Rating is an additional rating which can be obtained by a private pilot after he has acquired a certain number of flying hours and completed a course of instrument flying and radio navigation training.

Although it is not necessary to file a Flight Plan for a Special VFR Flight, a prior clearance to carry out the proposed flight must be obtained from the appropriate Air Traffic Control Unit.

It must be stressed that Special VFR Flights are concessions which can only be granted when the number of air traffic movements in relation to the existing weather conditions permit.

An authorisation to make this type of flight into a Control Zone absolves the pilot from complying with IFR and also one other Rule which relates to the minimum operating height for aircraft over built up areas, i.e. a sub section of Rule 5 of the Rules of the Air and Air Traffic Control Regulations states:

"An aeroplane shall not fly over a city, town or settlement below a height of 1500 feet above the highest fixed object within 2000 feet of the aircraft".

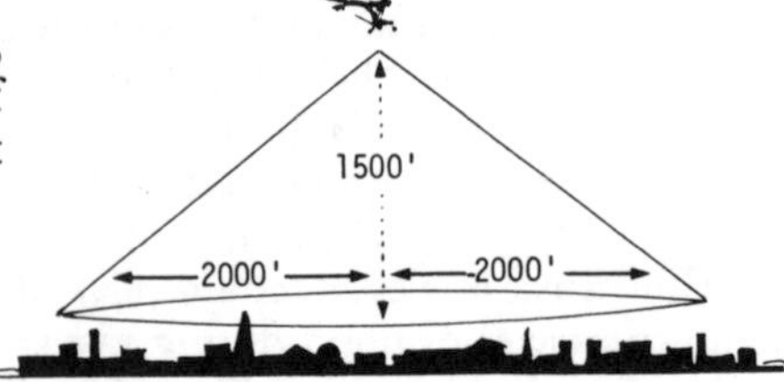

It must be appreciated that in order to maintain reasonable separation from IFR traffic, Special VFR Flight will normally be conducted in the lower levels of a Control Zone. This may therefore make it impossible for a pilot to comply with this sub section of Rule 5. The pilot however is only absolved from this Rule if the height given to him by ATC makes compliance with this 1500' requirement impossible. **The pilot must nevertheless operate at a height sufficient for him to glide clear of built up areas in the event of engine failure.**

Throughout a Special VFR Flight the pilot will be responsible for complying with all ATC instructions and ensuring that the flight conditions, such as, forward visibility and clearance from cloud, will enable him to determine his flight path and remain clear of all obstructions. The flight visibility should be at least 5 nm unless the pilot holds an IMC Rating.

In order to give greater flexibility to private pilot operations many aerodromes within Control Zones have Entry/Exit Lanes established to enable aircraft to operate from them in IMC without having to comply with full IMC procedures and in most cases without having to obtain ATC clearance or carry radio. These Entry/ Exit Lanes are promulgated in the UK Air Pilot and also shown on topographical charts.

An extract from the Air Pilot showing an example of the Entry/Exit Lanes in the Manchester Control Zone is shown below. The information depicted should however not be used for flight planning purposes as it is subject to change, therefore an up to date reference can only be obtained through the Air Pilot or a current topographical chart.

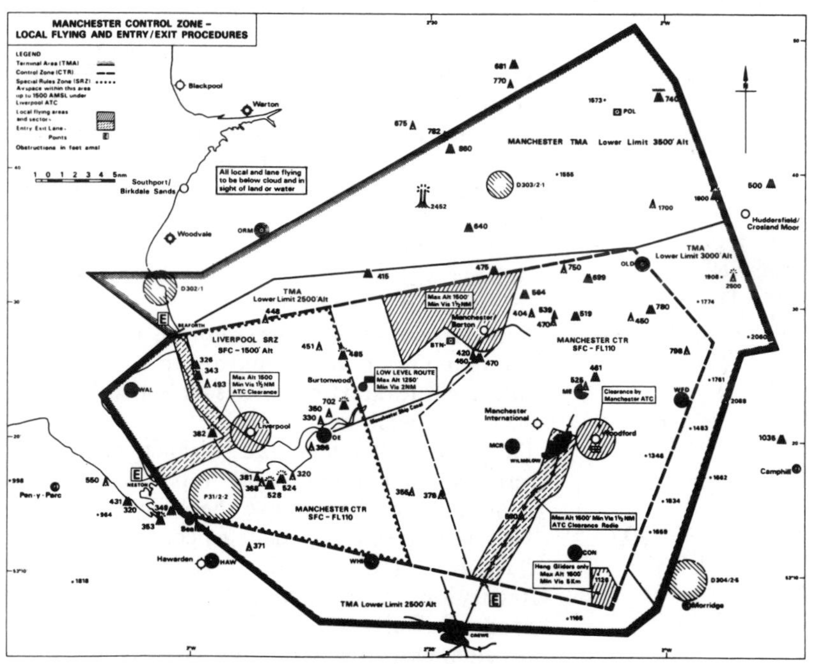

Fig 2–14

TYPES OF AIR TRAFFIC SERVICE UNITS

Within the UK, Air Traffic Services are available in many forms and the UK Air Pilot is the main document through which these services are promulgated.

In addition to this, a service is provided in the form of Notices to Airmen (NOTAMS) which are used to inform pilots of recent or temporary changes in the services which affect the flight operations of aircraft, e.g. aerodrome runway unserviceability, withdrawal or changes in aviation facilities such as radio frequencies etc.

The UK Air Pilot and NOTAMS are normally available at Air Traffic Control on most airfields, and training schools.

Although at the present time a microlight pilot is unlikely to require a detailed knowledge of the Air Traffic Services, or the contents of the Air Pilot and NOTAMS he should be aware of their existence and the type of service and information obtained by reference to them. A student pilot will, of course, also need to answer any questions on these documents which may be set in his written examinations. Therefore a brief summary of the Air Pilot and NOTAMS is included here.

The Air Pilot is divided into three volumes which collectively have a total of nine sections:-

Volume	Section	Contents
1.	RAC	Rules of the Air and Air Traffic Services.
2.	GEN	This section covers references to the Civil Aviation Legislation and Air Navigation Regulations together with such information as the dimensional units used in flying. It also contains information on the nationality and registration marks of aircraft and the time system used in aviation reporting procedures.
	AGA	This section contains detailed information on airfields within the UK together with their hours of operation and similar items.
	COM	This section gives information on the aeronautical telecommunication system, together with details of radio facilities and frequencies for both RTF and radio navigation equipment.
	MET	This section covers the various meteorological services which are available to pilots, together with information on how to use these facilities.
	FAL	This section covers such aspects as Immigration, Customs and Public Health requirements. Regulations relating to the import and export of goods, the Rules and Regulations governing the use of airfields and the fees and charges for en-route navigation services and landing charges.
	SAR	This section covers the Civil Search and Rescue Organisation and the facilities and procedures which are used.
	MAP	The CAA publishes a wide range of aeronautical maps and charts for use by civil pilots. Details of these are given in this section of the Air Pilot.
3.	CHARTS	This volume contains information relating to the airfield instrument approach charts which are published by the CAA.

Air Traffic Service Units (ATS) are dispersed throughout the country at various aerodromes and Control Centres. Details of the types of ATS units available and information on their facilities can be found in the UK Air Pilot Volume 1 RAC section.

There are two types of NOTAM; Class I and Class II:

Class I NOTAMS contain information which has to be disseminated quickly and are therefore sent out using the Aeronautical Fixed Telecommunication Network (AFTN).

Class II NOTAMS contain information which is not of an urgent nature and are dispatched through normal postal services.

ALTIMETER SETTING PROCEDURES

In order to determine distance above the earth's surface aircraft are equipped with pressure sensitive altimeters which are calibrated in feet and operate through the pressure changes in the atmosphere.

Aircraft altimeters have an adjustable knob which permits the pilot to set a desired reference datum in millibars (units of the dyne scale). This adjustable datum facility is necessary to cater for the normal changes in atmospheric pressure at the earth's surface and for other reasons outlined in the following text.

The datums which are normally used are:

Mean Sea Level Pressure.

Aerodrome Surface Pressure.

International Datum Level known as the Standard Setting of 1013 millibars (mb).

When the pressure is set to the pressure prevailing at sea level, the altimeter will indicate altitude above sea level (QNH). Whenever the QNH is set on the datum scale the term 'altitude' is used.

Whenever the datum is set to the pressure existing at the surface of the particular aerodrome (QFE) the altimeter is said to be measuring 'height'. An altimeter set to QFE will read zero when the aircraft is on the surface of the particular aerodrome.

Where the datum pressure used is the International Standard pressure setting, i.e. 1013.2 mb (QNE), the altimeter will indicate 'flight level'. The pilot must understand the significance of the terms, height, altitude and flight level in order to operate his aircraft safely as well as to fly in accordance with any instructions issued by ATC.

In relation to VFR flight and the private pilot, the QFE is normally used for take-off, landing and all flights within an aerodrome circuit. However, the earth's surface is irregular and ground level varies according to geographic location, therefore during those flights conducted away from the aerodrome it will be necessary to set the QNH value in order to assess the aircraft's clearance from the surface.

Terrain Clearance

Aeronautical maps and charts show the heights of surface contours and obstructions relative to mean sea level, therefore provided the QNH value (which relates to the mean sea level datum) is used, a pilot will be able to determine the altitude necessary to maintain a safe terrain clearance throughout the period of his flight.

When operating below TMA's the pilot will have to set the altimeter datum to the QNH of any airfield below the particular TMA.
This is necessary in order to remain clear of the base of such Controlled Airspace.

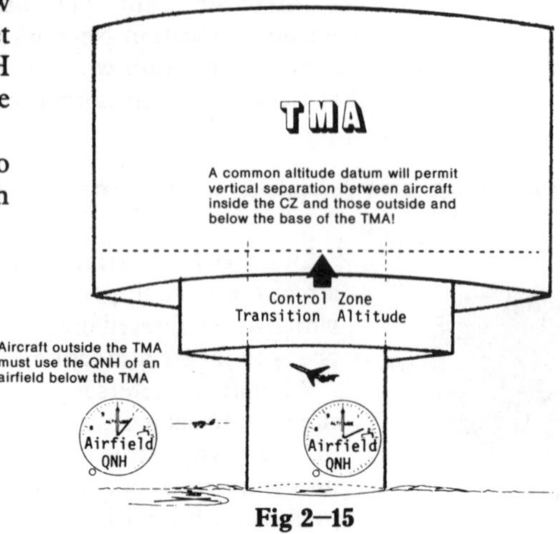

Fig 2—15

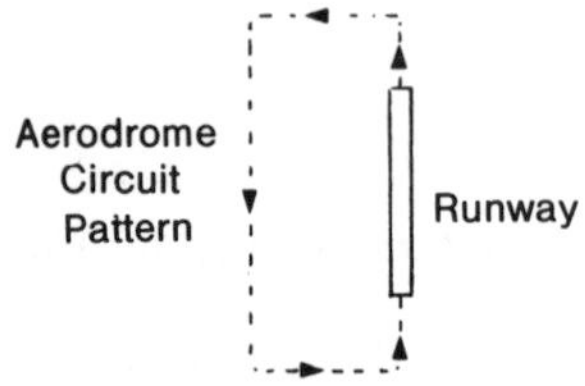

When operating within an aerodrome circuit pattern the use of QNH or QFE is optional, however as circuit heights are quoted in relation to aerodrome level pilots will normally find it more convenient to set the aerodrome QFE prior to take-off or before descending into an aerodrome circuit pattern.

Flight Separation

The use of the quadrantal rule has already been covered in the application of the Visual and Instrument Flight Rules and the use of this system is to ensure a safe means of flight separation between aircraft on opposing tracks in uncontrolled airspace when Instrument Flight Conditions are experienced above 3000' amsl.

The Standard Setting of 1013.2 mb is used as the datum for the application of both the Quadrantal and Semi-Circular Rules. When the altimeter is set to this standard datum the term 'flight level' is used instead of 'altitude'. The following table illustrates the relationship between flight level 'numbers' and the altimeter indications when 1013.2 mb is set on the datum scale.

Flight Level Number	Altimeter Indication (feet QNH).
30	3,000
35	3,500
40	4,000
45	4,500
100	10,000
150	15,000

F.L 45 F.L 30
F.L 40 F.L 35

4500' 3000'
4000' 3500'

When operating at flight levels a pilot must ensure during flight planning that the flight level(s) chosen are sufficiently high for him to maintain a safe terrain clearance en-route.

The reason for this statement lies in the fact that with the Standard datum set a pilot will not immediately be able to determine his altitude in relation to the surface below or ahead. Therefore prior to those occasions when it is intended to operate at flight levels additional care must be used to calculate a safe flight level.

To appreciate this point more fully assume the minimum safe altitude to fly is 3000' amsl and the Area QNH is 1001 mb. It must also be understood that a change in height of 30 feet in the lower levels of the atmosphere corresponds to approximately one millibar. Referring to fig 2-16 a pilot using a QNH of 1001 mb will upon reaching 3000' and adjusting the altimeter datum to 1013 mb increase his altimeter reading to 3360'. (12 x 30 = 360').

In these circumstances it would be inadvisable to use 'flight level' 30 as a cruising level because this would place him below 3000' (altitude) and in this case the lowest safe flight level would be 35.

Another term used in relation to flight levels is 'Transition Altitude'. This is defined as the altitude in the vicinity of an aerodrome at or below which the vertical position of an aircraft is controlled by reference to altitude, i.e. with the aerodrome QNH set upon the altimeter.

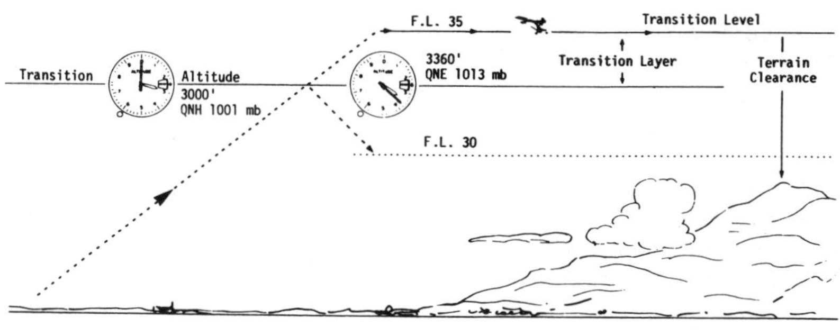

Fig 2—16

The lowest flight level available for use above the Transition Altitude is known as the 'Transition Level', and the vertical distance between 3000' in terms of altitude and the Transition Level is known as 'Transition Layer'. It can therefore be seen from this that the lowest flight level which can safely be used will depend upon the prevailing QNH value.

The standard Transition Altitude for civil aerodromes outside Controlled Airspace is 3000' on the aerodrome QNH. Aerodromes situated within Control Zones have specific Transition Altitudes laid down and these are promulgated in the UK Air Pilot.

In addition, certain military aerodromes available for civil use have a Transition Altitude above 3000' for terrain or operational reasons,. When using such aerodromes civil pilots must conform to military procedures by setting the aerodrome QFE upon which vertical separation from military aircraft below Transition Level is based.

Another point regarding altimeter setting procedures is that when operating within Military Air Traffic Zones whether for the purpose of transit or landing the QFE of the particular military aerodrome should normally be used.

However microlight pilots should avoid these MATZ as normally they would be unable to communicate by radio with the Air Traffic Controller and in any case they would be transitting an area in which high speed military traffic will be operating in some numbers.

FLIGHT AT AERODROMES

Although most microlight activity is normally arranged to occur away from normal aerodromes the environment and changing circumstances of any flight such as weather or possible emergency situations may create situations in which a microlight pilot may have to fly close to active airfields or avail himself of the services which they offer. Because of this all pilots no matter what type of aircraft they fly, must have a good appreciation of the procedures used at aerodromes. This is of especial importance when one considers the number of air traffic movements which can be taking place in the immediate vicinity of such areas. Questions are also asked in the Private Pilot examinations and which concern aircraft movements on and around aerodromes.

An aerodrome is an area of land (or water) which is designed, equipped and set aside for the purpose of affording facilities for the landing and departure of aircraft.

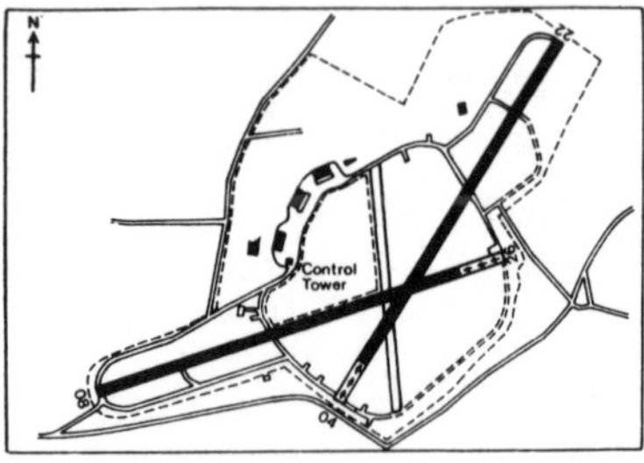

Within the UK a large number of aerodromes are available to the private pilot. These vary from large airports which daily handle hundreds of aircraft,

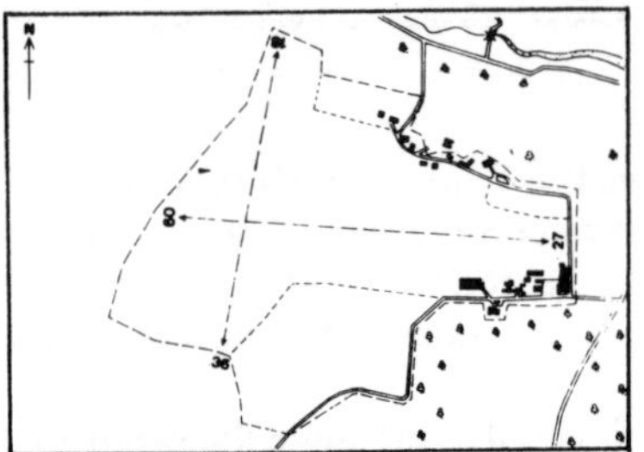

to small grass airfields where aircraft movements may be few.

Additionally a number of private landing areas in the form of grass or tarmac strips are also available, and although these may be technically considered as aerodromes they are commonly referred to as ‘Landing Strips’.

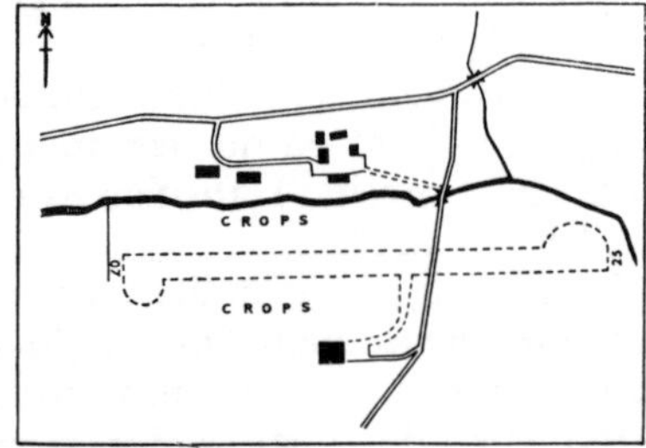

When using Landing Strips the pilot's common sense coupled with the basic Rules of the Air will largely apply, however at normal aerodromes there are specific rules which must be observed by all pilots.

The area upon which aircraft movements take place for the purpose of manoeuvring prior to and during take-off, or for landing and taxying to the parking area is designated the 'Manoeuvring Area' and on this area aircraft have the right of way over all other vehicles and persons.

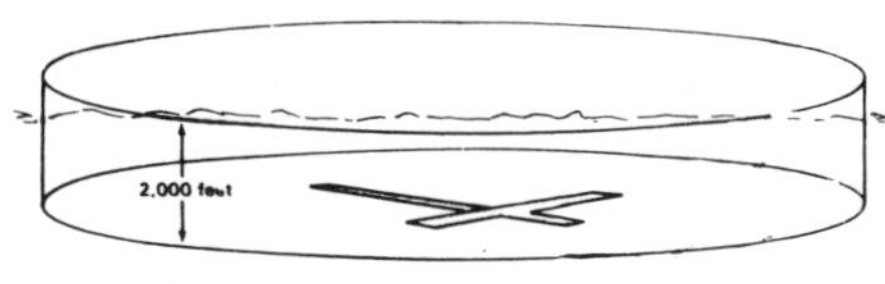

All aerodromes are established with an 'Aerodrome Traffic Zone'. This is an area surrounding the aerodrome and extending from the surface to 2000 feet above aerodrome level and contained within a circle centred upon the mid point of the longest runway and having a radius of 2 nm where the runway length is 1850 metres or less and 2.5 nm where the length is greater than 1850 metres.

When an aerodrome is not equipped with ATC facilities, or radio is not carried particular caution must be displayed when entering the Aerodrome Traffic Zone. When an ATC unit is available it will co-ordinate aircraft movements by Radiotelephony (RTF) or where applicable by signalling lamp or ground signals.

Aircraft movements on the Manoeuvring Area or within the Traffic Zone are controlled by ATC and pilots must comply with the directions issued by ATC unless they consider it would be unsafe to do so.

In the case of military aerodromes and of civil aerodromes licensed for private use it will be necessary to obtain permission to land from the authority of the aerodrome concerned.

Permission to use military aerodromes must be obtained prior to departure and the use of such aerodromes by civil aircraft is restricted to the normal hours of watch of the particular ATC unit and then only to aircraft on flights within the UK.

Not all military aerodromes are available for use by civil aircraft (apart from an emergency) but those which can be used are listed in the AGA section of the UK Air Pilot.

At unlicensed aerodromes permission to land must be obtained from the owner or person in charge. The method of obtaining this permission will be either by telephone, in writing or when available by RTF. It should be noted that landing strips also fall into this category. When prior permission is a requirement to land at any aerodrome listed in the Air Pilot, it will be indicated by the annotation PPR.

LIGHTS AND PYROTECHNIC SIGNALS

When radio communication is not available between an aircraft and an aerodrome ATC unit a system of standard light and pyrotechnic signals has been devised. The following tables shows the different visual signals employed and their respective meanings when used by an ATC unit or an aircraft.

Signals From The Ground

LIGHT	FROM AERODROME CONTROL TO:	
	AIRCRAFT IN FLIGHT	AIRCRAFT ON THE GROUND
Steady Green	Cleared to Land	Cleared for Take-Off
Steady Red	Give Way to Other Aircraft and Continue Circling	Stop
Green Flashes	Return for Landing*	Cleared to Taxy or You may Move on the Manoeuvring Area
Red Flashes	Do Not Land, the Aerodrome is not Available for Landing	Move Clear of the Landing Area
White Flashes	Land at this Aero-drome and proceed to the Parking Area*	Return to the Starting Point on the Aerodrome
Red Pyrotechnic	Do Not Land, Wait for Permission	

* Clearances to Land and Taxy will be given in due course.

Signals From An Aircraft

(a) A red pyrotechnic light or flare means - 'Immediate Assistance is Requested'

§ (b) White flashes, switching On and Off landing and/or navigation lights means - 'I am compelled to land'

§ When navigation lights are being used for this signal they should be switched ON and OFF in an irregular manner to avoid confusion with those navigation light systems which automatically flash ON and OFF at short regular intervals.

GROUND SIGNALS USED AT CIVIL AIRFIELDS

The following ground signals and markings are used at civil airfields in the UK. They are either displayed in or adjacent to a part of the airfield surface known as the 'Signals Area' and which is set aside for this purpose. Some signals will nevertheless be placed on other positions of the airfield as indicated in the following text.

The signals area is usually laid out in the vicinity of the Air Traffic Control building and marked by white strips in the form of a large square which is clearly visible to pilots flying overhead.

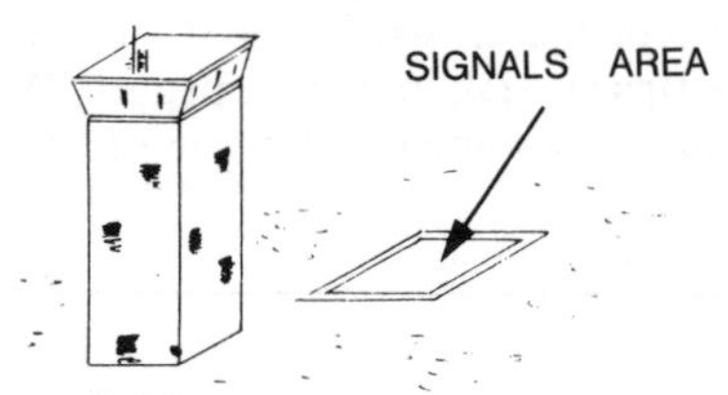

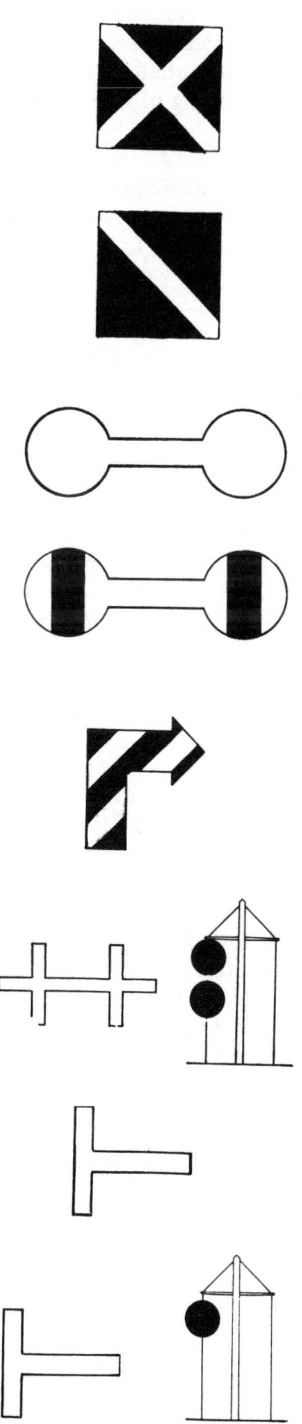

Prohibition of Landing:

A red square panel with a yellow strip along each diagonal signifies that the airfield is unsafe for the movement of aircraft and that landing on the airfield is prohibited.

Special Precautions:

A red square panel with a yellow strip along one diagonal signifies that the state of the manoeuvring area is poor and that pilots must exercise special care when landing.

Use Hard Surfaces Only:

A white dumbell signifies that movements of aircraft and gliders on the ground shall be confined to paved, metalled or similar surfaces. The superimposition of black strips in each circular portion of the dumbell, at right angles to the shaft signifies that aircraft and gliders taking off or landing shall do so on a runway but that movement on the ground is not confined to paved, metalled or similar hard surfaces.

Right Hand Circuit:

A red and yellow striped arrow placed along two adjacent sides of the signals area and pointing in a clockwise direction signifies that a right hand circuit is in force.

Gliding:

A double white cross and/or two red balls suspended from a mast one above the other signify that glider flying is in progress at the airfield. A yellow cross indicates the tow rope dropping area.

Direction of Take-Off and Landing:

A White T signifies that aircraft and gliders taking off or landing shall do so in a direction parallel with the shaft of the T and towards the cross arm, unless otherwise authorised by the appropriate air traffic control unit.

A white disc displayed alongside the cross arm of the T and in line with the shaft of the T signifies that the direction of landing and take-off do not necessarily coincide. This may also be indicated by a black ball suspended from a mast.

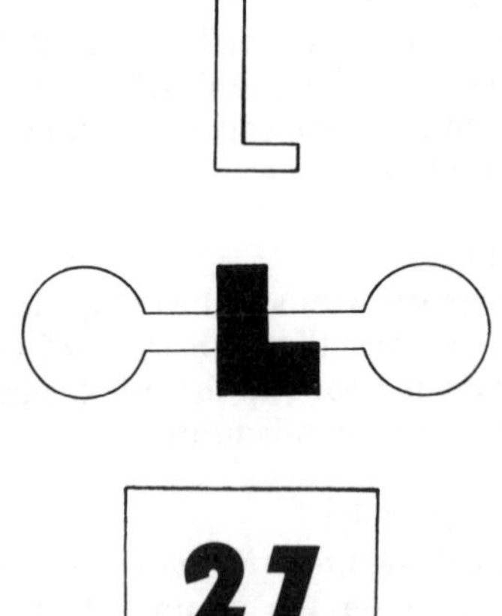

Landing Area for Light Aircraft:

A white letter L indicates a part of the manoeuvring area which shall be used only for the taking off and landing of light aircraft.

A red letter L displayed on the dumbell signifies that light aircraft are permitted to take-off and land either on a runway or on the area designated by a white letter L.

Runway Indication:

Black numerals in two figure groups, and where parallel runways are provided the letter or letters L (left), LC (left centre), C (centre), RC (right centre) and R (right), placed against a yellow background, indicate the direction for take-off or the runway in use.

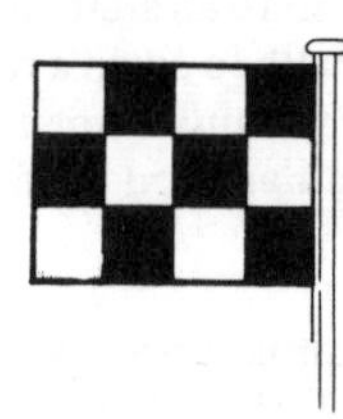

Airfield Control in Operation:

A checkered flag or board containing 12 equal squares, coloured red and yellow alternately, signifies that aircraft may move on the manoeuvring area and apron only in accordance with the permission of the ATCU at the airfield.

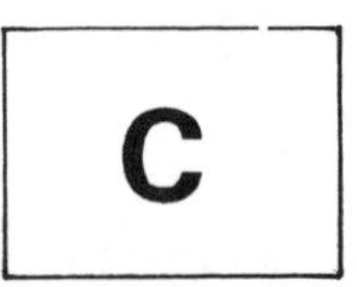

Reporting Point:
A black letter C against a yellow background indicates the position at which a pilot can report to the ATCU or to the person in charge of the airfield.

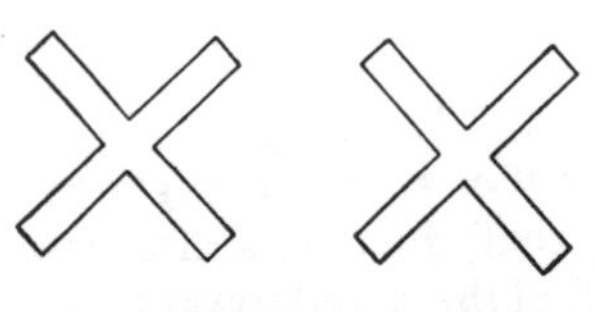

Unserviceable Portion of Runway or Taxiway:

Two or more white crosses displayed on a runway or taxiway with the arms of the crosses at an angle of 45° to the centreline of the runway or taxiway at intervals signify that the section marked by them is unfit for the movement of aircraft.

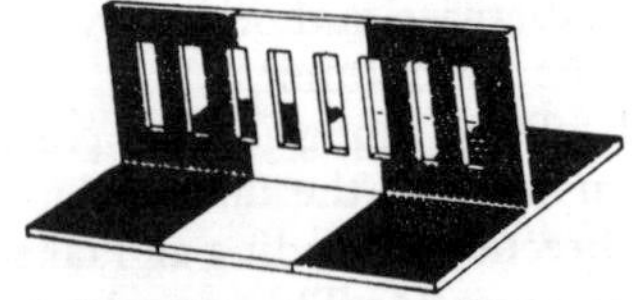

Orange and white markers as illustrated, spaced not more than 15 metres apart, signify the boundary of that part of a paved runway, taxiway or apron which is unfit for the movement of aircraft.

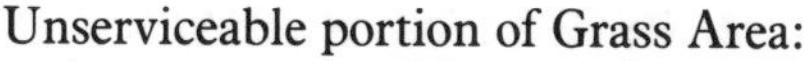

Unserviceable portion of Grass Area:

An unserviceable portion of a grass manoeuvring area is indicated by markers with orange and white stripes alternating with flags showing equal orange and white triangular areas.

Landing Dangerous:

A white cross displayed at the end of a runway shall indicate that landing is dangerous and that the airfield is used for storage purposes only.

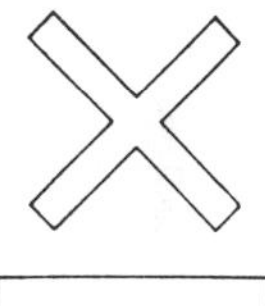

Emergency Use Only:

A white cross and a single white bar displayed at the end of a runway at a disused airfield indicates that the runway is fit for emergency use. Runways so marked are not safeguarded and may be temporarily obstructed.

Land in Emergency Only:

Two vertical yellow bars on a red square on the signals area indicate that the landing areas are serviceable but the normal safety facilities are not available. Aircraft may land in emergency only.

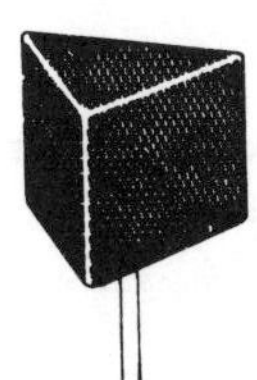

Unserviceable Areas:

An alternative signal to mark unserviceable areas on an airfield is a solid orange triangle.

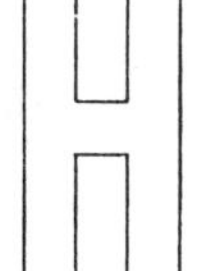

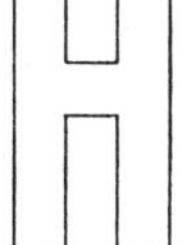

Helicopter Operations:

A white letter H indicates the area to be used by helicopters.

Light Aircraft:

A single red L shall indicate that light aircraft may land on a special grass area which is delimited by white corner markings; taxying of light aircraft on grass is permitted.

MARSHALLING SIGNALS

These signals are devised to enable a form of communication to exist between the pilot and the groundcrew directing the aircraft's movements on the ground. They are laid down in detail in "The Rules of the Air and Air Traffic Control Regulations" and are also shown in "The United Kingdom Air Pilot". Although pilots of Microlight aircraft may consider them irrelevant, all pilots must become conversant with these signals in order to control the aircraft safely when being directed and manoeuvring in parking areas.

Examples of the more common marshalling signals detailed in the Rules of the Air and Air Traffic Control Regulations are shown below:

Description of Signal	Meaning of Signal	In Daylight	By Night
A circular motion of the right hand at head level, with the left arm pointing to the appropriate engine.	Start engines.		
Arms down, the palms facing outwards, then swung outwards.	Chocks away.		
Raise arm, with fist clenched, horizontally in front of the body, then extend fingers.	Release brakes.		No Equivalent Signal
Arms repeatedly moved upward and backward, beckoning onward.	Move ahead.	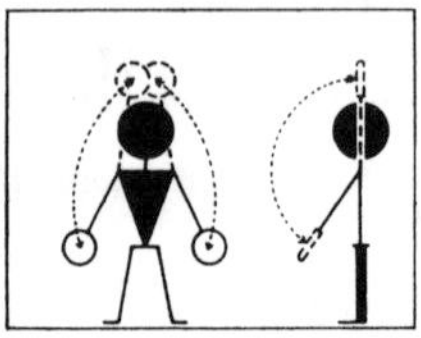	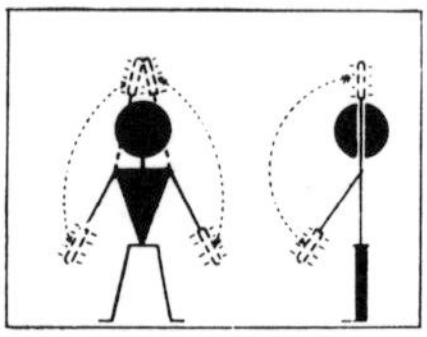
Right arm down, left arm repeatedly moved upward and backward. The speed of arm movement indicates the rate of turn.	Open up starboard engine or turn to port.		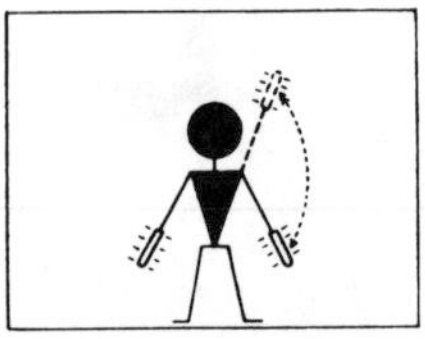

Description of Signal	Meaning of Signal	In Daylight	By Night
Left arm down, the right arm repeatedly moved upward and backward. The speed of arm movement indicates the rate of turn.	Open up port engine or turn to starboard.		
Right or left arm down, the other arm moved across body and extended to indicate position of the other marshaller.	Proceed under the guidance of another marshaller.		
The right arm raised at the elbow, with the arm facing forward.	All clear: Marshalling finished		
Arms placed above the head in a vertical position.	This bay or area for parking.		
Arms placed down, with the palms towards the ground, then moved up and down several times.	Slow down.		

Description of Signal	Meaning of Signal	In Daylight	By Night
Arms placed down, with the palms towards the ground, then either the right or left arm moved, up and down indicating that the engines on the left or right side as the case may be should be slowed down.	Slow down engines on indicated side.		
Arms Repeatedly crossed above the head. The speed of arm movement indicates the urgency of the stop.	Stop.	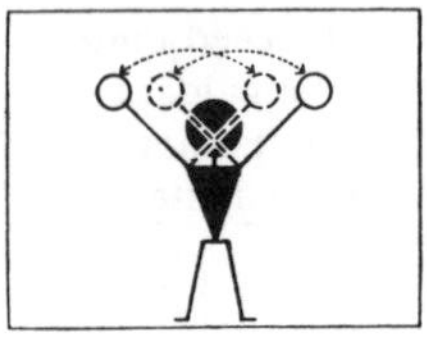	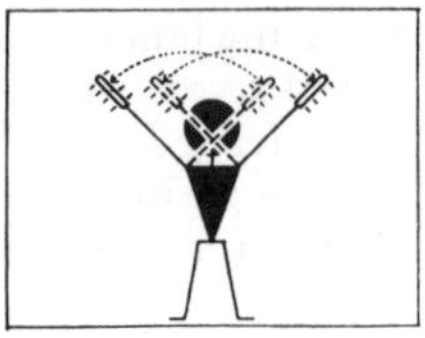
Raise arm and hand, with fingers extended horizontally in front of the body, then clench fist.	Engage brakes		No Equivalent Signal
Arms extended, the palms facing inwards, then swung from the extended position inwards.	Chocks inserted.		
Either arm and hand placed level with the chest, then moved laterally with the palm downwards.	Cut engines.		

FLIGHT PLANS

Although the filing of a flight plan for a microlight flight may appear to be inappropriate there are certain occasions when it may be necessary. For this reason and also because questions on this subject may be asked in the Private Pilot examination a brief outline is included in this manual.

Pilots intending to make a flight from an aerodrome with an Air Traffic Control Unit must either inform ATC giving brief details of the proposed flight or file a "Flight Plan". The first method is known as 'Booking Out' and is a local procedure which is simpler than that used for filing flight plans.

However there are certain occasions when a pilot must file a flight plan and these are covered in the following paragraphs. Flight plan details are entered on a standard flight plan form (CA 48) which is published by the CAA and available from the aerodrome Air Traffic Control unit. When the flight plan is completed it should be passed to ATC who will then relay the details via the Aeronautical Fixed Telecommunication Network (AFTN) to the destination aerodrome.

It is essential that the details entered on the form are written as accurately as possible and instructions are attached to each flight plan folder to ensure that pilots can complete this action without ambiguities occurring. Flight plans must be filed with the relevant ATCU at least 30 minutes prior to requesting taxi clearance.

Private pilots may, if they wish, file a flight plan for any flight but they are not mandatory for flights undertaken within uncontrolled airspace covered by the UK Flight Information Regions. Nevertheless it will be advisable to do so whenever possible if the pilot intends to fly more than 10 nm from the coast during overwater flights, or over stretches of sparsely populated or mountainous areas. This is to ensure that appropriate search and rescue action can be taken with a minimum of delay if an accident occurs away from populated regions.

A pilot is required to file a flight plan:

1. For a flight conducted under Instrument Flight Rules within Controlled Airspace.
2. For flight in certain Special Rules Zones/Areas irrespective of weather conditions. This requirement will be promulgated in the UK Air Pilot for the Special Rules Zone/Area concerned.
3. If he wishes to take advantage of an Air Traffic Advisory Service.
4. For any flight which crosses an International Boundary.

If for any reason a pilot who has filed a flight plan diverts or lands at any aerodrome not specified in his flight plan it is his responsibility to ensure that the planned destination aerodrome is informed within 30 minutes of landing.

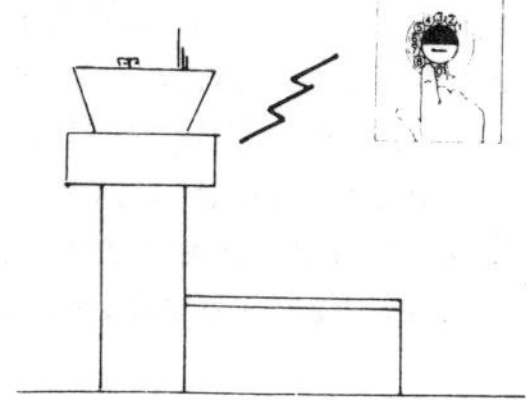

If this is not done, search and rescue action will be put into effect and cause considerable inconvenience, expense and wasted effort which might be required for an actual emergency.

Flight in Special Rules Zones and Areas
Pilots wishing to fly within Special Rules Zones or Areas must comply with the following procedures during the hours of watch of the appropriate aerodrome ATCU.

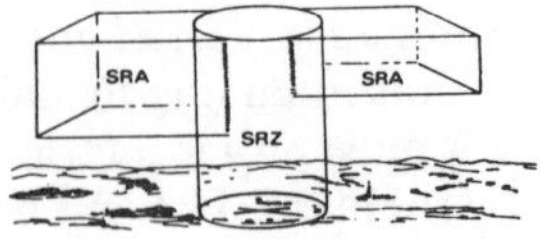

1. Prior to entering the relevant airspace, obtain the permission of the ATCU at the aerodrome upon which the Zone or Area is based and inform them, on the notified radio frequency, of the aircraft position, level and track.
2. Whilst flying within the relevant airspace, maintain a continuous watch on the notified radio frequency and comply with any instructions which the ATCU may give.

An exemption from the above requirements may be given to non-radio aircraft which remain at least 1 nm horizontally and 1000' vertically clear of cloud and in a flight visibility of not less than 5 nm and which have obtained prior permission from the ATCU.

Note: Different Special Rules Zones and Areas will have different rules and procedures and the above information represents the general rules which apply. It will therefore be necessary to consult the RAC Section of the UK Air Pilot to determine the exact procedures which exist in individual Special Rules Zones and Areas.

Flight in Airways
With the exception of certain portions which lie within TMA's or CZ's, Airways are Control Areas in which permanent Instrument Flight Rules apply and therefore they cannot be used unless the pilot holds an Instrument Rating and the aircraft carries certain mandatory radio and navigation equipment.

AIRMISS REPORTING PROCEDURES

On occasions during flight, aircraft may inadvertently come sufficiently close to one another so as to create a serious risk of airborne collision. In order to investigate and if possible to avoid repetition of such circumstances an Airmiss reporting procedure has been laid down.

Whenever a pilot considers that his aircraft may have been endangered by the proximity of another aircraft during flight within UK airspace to the extent that a defininte risk of collision existed, such an incident should be reported as an 'Airmiss Report'.

If radio is carried, the initial report of the incident can be made by RTF to the ATCU with which the aircraft is in communication at the time, or by telephone or other means immediately after landing.

Whichever method is used to make the initial report, it must be confirmed in writing by the pilot within 7 days of the incident. Form CA 1094 should be used for this purpose and an example of the front side of this form is shown on the next page at fig 2-17.

The official investigation which takes place following such a report may indicate a prima facie offence under military or civil law and a pilot reporting an Airmiss may be required to make a formal statement to one of the police authorities. He may also be required to give evidence at military or civil legal proceedings.

When the investigation is complete, the pilot, and where appropriate the operating company of the aircraft concerned in the incident, will be advised officially of the findings and of any action that it has been possible to take to avoid a similar occurrence. When a Company is informed, a copy of the information will be sent to the pilot.

An Airmiss which takes place within the airspace of another State will not be investigated by the UK authorities. A pilot of a UK registered aircraft involved in such an incident should consult the Aeronautical Information Publication of that State and follow its National reporting procedure.

Civil Aviation Authority

AIRMISS REPORT – PILOTS

INSTRUCTIONS FOR USE

UNITED KINGDOM FIR, UIR OR SHANWICK OCEANIC AREA

1 **Pilots reporting an Airmiss.** This form should be used by Pilots to confirm and/or supplement details given in initial reports when such reports have been made by radio or telephone to an ATSU. This form should be used also by Pilots reporting an Airmiss if and when it has not been possible to make an initial report. When completed this *form must be sent direct* to Joint Airmiss Section, Hillingdon House, Uxbridge, Middlesex UB10 0RU (Uxbridge 57300 ext 444).

2 **Other Pilots.** This form should be used by other Pilots involved in Airmisses to provide information as requested by the Joint Airmiss Section.

3 Detailed information on Airmiss Reporting Procedures is promulgated in the UK Air Pilot.

4 Shaded areas indicate items to be included in an initial report by radio.

5 Details may be expanded in a separate narrative report.

ALL OTHER AIRSPACE

1 **Pilots reporting an Airmiss.** This form may be used in the absence of a State's form or a CAA approved Company form to confirm and/or supplement details given in initial reports when such reports have been made by radio or telephone to an ATSU. At the same time as submitting the report to the Authority involve a copy of the report should be sent to the CAA Safety Data Unit, Brabazon House, Redhill, Surrey RH1 1SQ.

2 Detailed information on Airmiss Reporting Procedures should be found in the appropriate State's AIP.

3 Shaded areas indicate items to be included in an initial report by radio.

	A	AIRMISS REPORT
1 Name of pilot in command 2 Flight deck crew complement	B	1 2
Operator	C	
Aircraft registration marks/colour scheme	D	
Aircraft type	E	
1 Radio call sign 2 In communication with 3 Frequency 4 SSR Code; (Was Mode 'C' operating?)	F	1 2 3 4
Aerodrome of departure	G	
Aerodrome of first intended landing	H	
Type of flight plan	I	*IFR/VFR/None
1 Position of Airmiss 2 Aircraft heading 3 True airspeed	J	1 .... (Lat and Long) 2 .... *True/Magnetic 3 .... knots
1 Flight level, Altitude or Height 2 Altimeter setting 3 Aircraft attitude 4 Phase of flight	K	1 *FL ....../............/.................... ft 2 .... mb(*standard/REG.QNH/QNH/QFE) 3 *Level/Climbing/Descending/Turning (*Right/Left) 4 *Take-off, Initial climb, En route climb, Cruise, En route descent, Holding, Final descent, Landing, Circuit, Overshoot, Aerobatic, Trg or Mil manoeuvres
Flight weather conditions at time of Airmiss	L	1 *IMC/VMC 2 Distance .... ft *Above/Below *Cloud/Fog/Haze 3 Distance .... *km/NM horizontally from cloud 4 In *Rain/Snow/Sleet/Fog/Haze/Cloud/Between layers 5 Flying *into/out of sun 6 Flight visibility .... *km/NM 7 *Day/Night/Twilight
Date and Time (GMT) of Airmiss	M	
Description of other aircraft if relevant 1 Type, high/low wing, number of engines 2 Radio call sign, registration 3 Markings, colour, lighting 4 Other available details	N	1 2 3 4

Fig 2—17

AIRSPACE RESTRICTIONS AND HAZARDS

The airspace considered under this heading in as far as it is applicable to the UK, is basically divided into six types of area over which civil aircraft operations may for one reason or another be restricted, either temporarily, or permanently, on the ground of safety. The six types of areas which represent a primary hazard to aircraft in flight are:

1. Danger Areas
2. Prohibited Areas
3. Restricted Areas
4. Military Flight Training Areas
5. Bird Sanctuaries
6. High Intensity Radio Transmission Areas

In addition there are several other areas or locations which present additional hazards or within which it is advisable to restrict aircraft movements.

7. In-Flight Refuelling Areas
8. Areas of Intense Air Activity
9. Gilder Launching Sites
10. Hang Glider Sites
11. Disaster Areas
12. Certain Airspace (Outside Danger Areas) in which Pilotless Aircraft are manoeuvred
13. Target Towing Areas
14. Areas where Parachute Training Balloons are Flown
15. Locations where high obstructions are sited

All of these areas and locations together with detailed information relating to them are promulgated in the RAC section of the UK Air Pilot. Additionally items 1 to 7 are also shown on the 'Chart of United Kingdon Airspace Restrictions'. NOTAM and Aeronautical Information Circulars (AIC's) are also used to alert pilots to any changes which may occur in relation to their period of activity.

Danger Areas:

These areas are captive balloon flying areas and weapon ranges, the latter including test and practice ranges for all types of weapons (guns, bombs, aircraft cannon and rocket etc.). It is emphasised that only the type of activity most likely to be encountered is listed. Pilots should, therefore, take every precaution to avoid infringing the boundaries of active danger areas regardless of the type of activity expected within the area. Pilots should also be aware that in the immediate vicinity of those Danger Areas in which military aircraft operate, many of these aircraft fly pre-set range patterns, and some may be towing targets with cable lengths which, although normally 6000 ft may extend to 24,000 ft with the target up to 2,500 ft below the towing aircraft and therefore the combination of towing aircraft, cable and target will present a considerable hazard. Pilots of aircraft flying close to Danger Areas should therefore keep an especially sharp lookout for such aircraft and take any necessary avoiding action as early as possible.

The UK Air Pilot only contains details of those danger areas within the UK Flight Information Regions which have an upper limit in excess of 500' above the local surface level (i.e. 500' above ground level or mean sea level as applicable).

The attention of all pilots is drawn to the fact that there are many ranges, rifle small arms etc. with upper limits of 500' agl/amsl or less. Pilots should therefore satisfy themselves that they are clear of such activity if forced to fly below 500 feet.

Danger areas are of two types, Permanent (Scheduled) or Notified. Scheduled Areas are operational for laid down fixed periods which do not vary, for example these periods may be:

24 Hours of every day (H24)
24 Hours from Monday to Friday (H24 M-F)
Day only
Day only from Monday to Friday
For specified hours and days

Note: In relation to Danger Areas 'Day' means the period between 0800 to 1800 Local Time.

Scheduled Danger Areas are coded and shown on Topographical Charts and the 'Chart of UK Airspace Restrictions' with a solid red outline to indicate their geographic dimensions.

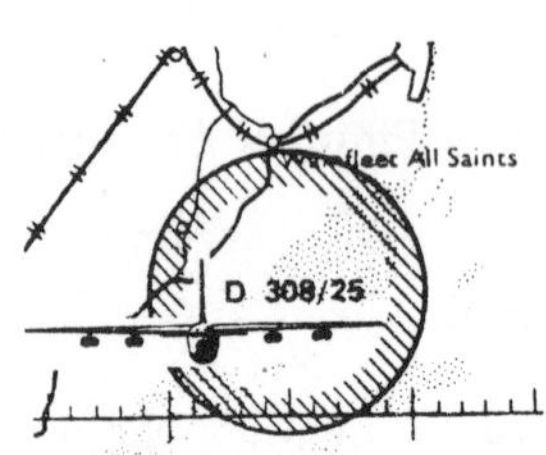

Because the UK Danger Areas are situated within the latitudes 49N to 59N a simple code designation has been arranged in that the first number e.g. 3 in the illustration on the left, shown the area is situated in the geographic region between 53N and 54N, if the first number had been 4 then this would indicate that it was situated in the region between 54N and 55N.

The letter and numbers (adjacent) is the identification code of the particular Danger Area. The numbers 25 after the oblique stroke give the upper limit in thousands of feet above mean sea level, i.e. 25.000'.

Notified Danger Areas are those whose operational periods vary and information relating to their operational activity is given by NOTAM. The code figures of these areas have the same meanings as for Permanent (Scheduled) Danger Areas but the geographic boundaries are shown on Topographical Charts and the 'Chart of UK Airspace Restrictions' by a broken red outline.

Prohibited and Restricted Area

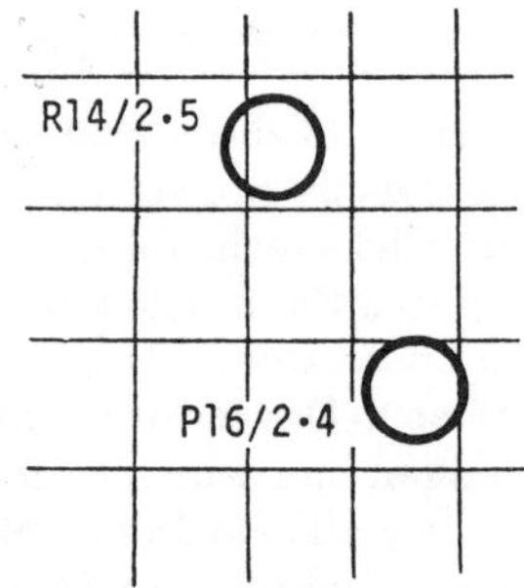

These areas normally relate to the airspace within the immediate vicinity of Atomic Energy or Security Establishments. They are promulgated in the UK Air Pilot and on the Chart of UK Airspace Restrictions which also shows their vertical and geographic dimensions.

Prohibited Areas are indicated on maps and charts by the letter P and are permanent H24 throughout the year. Pilots must at all times avoid flying within these areas. Certain Atomic Energy or Security Establishments are situated in the close vicinity of the approach paths of airfields and in these circumstances a modification to the rules is made and the area is designated a Restricted Area.

Within Restricted Areas, aircraft may only operate for the purposes of entry/exit to the particular airfields. Nevertheless a minimum height restriction may apply. Restricted Areas are depicted on maps and charts with the letter R.

Military Flight Training Areas

These are areas of Upper Airspace (above flight level 245) of defined dimensions within which intense military flying training takes place. Such areas are normally above the levels used by private pilots and reference to them in this manual is for general information only.

There are however similar areas known as "Areas of Intense Aerial Activity in which either civil or military flying takes place on an intensive basis. These areas may extend from the surface upwards and are shown on topographical charts in the following way . . . Isle of Wight AIAA SFC -6500 ALT, the name of the AIAA will apply to the particular area and the vertical limits vary. In the example given the vertical limits are from the surface to 6500'.

There are also many Low Level Routes along which military high speed flying takes place. The UK authorities do not publish information concerning the whereabout of such routes because of Air Defence Regulations. Pilots must therefore be especially vigilant when operating below 1000' outside aerodrome traffic zones.

Bird Sanctuaries

These are particular areas in which large colonies of birds are known to breed. They normally extend from ground/sea level up to 4000' and information relating to their geographic and vertical limits is shown on topographical maps and the Chart of UK Airspace Restrictions. The figure 4 shown in the adjacent illustration indicates a top limit of 4000'.

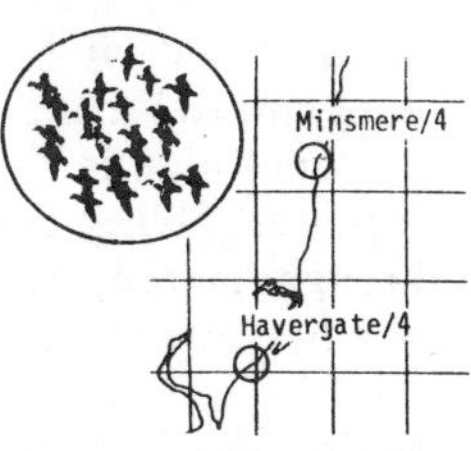

Pilots are specifically requested to avoid these areas, especially during any stated breeding season. Apart from the ecological nuisance of aircraft flying within these areas there also exists a very high risk of aircraft bird strikes with attendant hazards to aircraft in flight. Information on bird migration and areas of bird concentrations is given in the UK Air Pilot and when large concentrations of bird movements are known to be taking place 'Bird Warning Movement Messages' are promulgated in NOTAMS.

High Intensity Radio Transmission Areas (HIRTA)

There are a number of these areas within the UK. The installations based within them emit radio energy of an intensity which may cause interference to and sometimes damage to aircraft radio equipment as well as possible harmful bodily effect if the aircraft remains in the vicinity for an appreciable period.

The vertical dimensions which such interference can reach vary from 1000' to above 10.000' amsl so they must be treated with respect and avoided whenever possible.

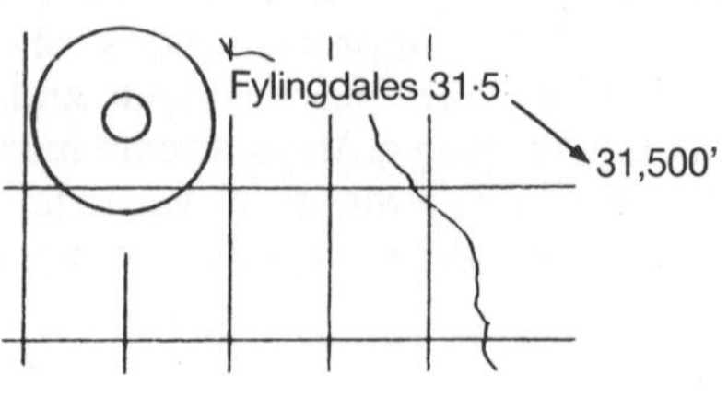

Some of these areas are not shown on topographical charts and reference will need to be made to the UK Air Pilot or Chart of UK Airspace Restrictions during flight planning operation.

Additional Hazards to Aircraft in Flight

The areas which are listed as 'additional hazards to aircraft in flight' are all clearly defined in the UK Air Pilot and (with the exception of No's 7, 11, 12 and 13) also shown on topographical charts. Consideration will need to be given to these areas during pre-flight planning.

Above the UK and surrounding waters there are a number of In-Flight Refuelling Areas. Normally these are above flight level 110 (11,000') but at the time this manual was published one area adjacent to Great Yarmouth had a lower level of 2000', therefore pilots must be aware of the variations in altitude limits which occur from time to time.

At the present time there are also over 400 gliding, hang gliding and parachuting sites in the UK. Gliding sites may have winching cables extending up to 1500' above the surface, and additionally tug aircraft carrying towing cables may be operating up to considerable altitudes. The sport of Free Fall Parachuting has also increased considerably over recent years and parachutists may be dropping from up to 10.000' and above. All three of the above sites are clearly shown on topographical maps and charts.

A final note is that temporary areas such as those used during Military Air Exercises, Flying Displays, Air Races etc., will be established for short periods throughout the year. The geographic and vertical dimensions of these areas together with their times of operation will be promulgated by NOTAM.

Navigation Obstructions

In the United Kingdom an 'Air Navigation Obstruction' is defined as any building or work, including waste heaps, which attains or exceeds a height of 300' above ground level (agl). Details of those obstructions of which the CAA has been informed, are listed in the RAC Section of the Air Pilot. Additionally obstructions within 4 nm of an aerodrme reference point are listed in the AGA Section.

Whenever obstructions are listed in the Air Pilot their exact positions are shown together with their heights above ground level and above sea level. In the case of tall masts, the position of the centre of the mast is given but it should be noted that the stays or guys may spread out for a considerable distance.

In cases where a number of buildings, works or masts form the obstruction the approximate centre of the site is given.

Those air navigation obstructions which are 500' or more above ground level are lighted. Lighting is in the form of a red obstruction light or lights, positioned on or near the highest point of the obstruction. Additional lights may be positioned at different heights on the obstruction. Details of unserviceability and return to serviceability, when notified to the CAA, will be promulgated by Class I NOTAM.

Air navigation obstructions between 300' and 500' agl are sometimes lighted as noted above but details of unserviceabilities of lights on these obstructions will not normally be promulgated.

Details of all air navigation obstructions known at the date of the chart's preparation are shown on the topographical maps published by the CAA. This information will indicate whether or not the obstruction is normally lighted.

Royal Flights

Flights by Her Majesty the Queen and certain other members of the Royal Family are classified as 'Royal Flights'. When these flights are made in fixed wing aircraft and in order to reduce the risk of collision with other aircraft, Royal Flights are conducted where possible within existing controlled airspace. Where this is not possible temporary controlled airspace in the form of a 'Purple Airway' or 'Zone' will be established to cover the Royal route.

Irrespective of the weather conditions all controlled airspace used for this purpose, whether of a permanent or temporary nature, will be notified as being IFR. Details of Royal Flights will be promulgated by a Special RF NOTAM.

When a Royal Flight is made in a helicopter, no special ATC procedures are employed, but the route(s) being used (including times) will be promulgated by a RF Notam and pilots flying in the vicinity of these routes are requested to keep an especially alert lookout for the aircraft.

Disasters in the UK FIRs-Restriction of Flying

In the event of a disaster occuring on land or at sea within the UK FIRs, the Emergency Controlling Authority (ECA), normally a representative of one of the following agencies: Home Office; Department of Energy; HM Coastguard Headquarters; Edingburgh RCC or Plymouth RCC, may find it necessary for the safety of life and property and particularly for the protection of those subsequently engaged in Seach and Rescue action, to inhibit flight in the vicinity of the disaster by aircraft not directly engaged with emergency action.

On receipt of a request from the ECA, the initial action will normally be to establish by NOTAM Class I a temporary Danger Area around the scene of the incident. If the temporary Danger Area fails to achieve the objective 'Restriction of Flying-Disaster-Regulations', which will make it an offence for an aircraft to be flown in the designated area without the permission of the ECA, will be brought into operation by NOTAM Class I.

Subject to any overriding considerations of safety, requests for overflight in the designated area from governmental and other official agencies, such as the Nature Conservancy Council, are to be given priority over requests from en-route traffic, company aircraft, the press and television.

AERODROMES

Information relating to aerodromes in the UK is promulgated in the Air Pilot which is amended at regular intervals and additionally NOTAMS are used to promulgate changes of a temporary nature, or items which are considered too important to wait for the next issue of the Air Pilot amendment service.

The AGA Section of the Air Pilot gives details of all major airports and licensed aerodromes. It also contains information of unlicensed and military aerodromes available for use by civil aircraft.

Information relating to private landing strips is not given in the Air Pilot but details of a large number of such landings areas as well as licensed and unlicensed aerodromes can be obtained from the 'Air Touring Flight Guide' which is published by Airtour Associates International Ltd., Elstree Aerodrome, Herts. London. This guide is published annually and is valid for one year. An amendment service is also provided Microlight pilots would be well advised to purchase a copy of this publication as it is a mine of useful information on aerodromes, landing strips, gliding sites etc. in the UK.

Pooley's Flight Guide
United Kingdom & Ireland
Produced with the assistance of the
CIVIL AVIATION AUTHORITY
1990

AERODROME GROUND LIGHTS

These are installed at various civil and military aerodromes within the United Kingdom and are of the following two main types:

Identification Beacons

These exhibit a two letter morse group at speed equivalent to 6 to 8 words a minute every 12 seconds. When installed at civil aerodromes their colour is green and when installed at military aerodromes their colour is red.

Aerodrome Beacons

These are not normally provided at aerodromes where an Identification Beacon is installed. Aerodrome Beacons emit a flashing white/green light but a few aerodromes in the UK have Beacons which only flash white.

Time of Operation

Any of these beacons may be operated in daylight hours during conditions of poor visibility, and at other times during the ATC hours of watch e.g. during any period when night flying operations are being conducted at the particular aerodrome.

Royal Air Force and Royal Navy Master Aerodromes

Certain RAF and RN aerodromes are designated 'Master Aerodromes'. These are operational throughout 24 hours each day, and at these aerodromes identification beacons will operate continuously throughout the hours of darkness.

Other Royal Air Force and Royal Navy Aerodromes

At these aerodromes the operation of Identification Beacons will depend upon military flying commitments and as such they may be switched on at any time during the day or night.

UK AIR PILOT-AERODROME INFORMATION

For those microlight pilots intending to use normal aerodromes it would be pertinent to point out that the Air Pilot (AGA Section) contains information relating to special instructions, restrictions, warnings, obstructions, times of operation, etc. which apply to specific aerodromes in the UK. This type of information is promulgated in the manner shown at figs 2-18, 2-19 and 2-20.

AERODROME DIRECTORY

Local Flying Regulations, Warnings and Lighting etc.

Additional to any given in the Aerodrome Directory column 24.

Abingdon — **Warnings**

1 Caution is necessary on approach to Runway 26. Houses and television aerials form an obstruction, height 30 ft agl, 457 metres from touch-down.

2 Aircraft inbound to Abingdon are to call Benson Approach or Abingdon at least 5 nm before the boundary of Benson/Abingdon MATZ or be under control of London Military.

3 There is no control of traffic on the public road which crosses the approach to Runway 18.

Andrewsfield — **Warning**

1 Aerodrome is located on Southern edge of Wethersfield MATZ and 2 nm East of Stansted SRZ.

Audley End — **Local Flying Regulations**

1 All circuits are to avoid over-flying Saffron Walden.

2 Aircraft approaching from the North or South must contact Stansted on 125·55 MHz.

☞ **Barra** — **Warnings**

1 The landing and take off areas may be considerably ridged by hard sand and contain pools of standing water. These are potential hazards to aircraft.

2 Prior permission for the use of the aerodrome is essential in order to obtain information on surface conditions, in addition to other information.

Bembridge — **Warning**

1 Manufacturer's demonstration flights and aerobatics may take place without notice at any time including weekends, during daylight hours, within 1·5 nm of the aerodrome boundary and up to 3 000 ft agl. Visiting aircraft must be prepared to remain clear of this area until cleared to approach for landing.

Benson — **Warnings**

1 Aircraft inbound to Benson are to call Benson Approach on 120·9 MHz at least 5 nm before the boundary of the Benson/Abingdon MATZ or be under control of London Military Radar or Cotswold Radar.

2 Intensive MATZ crossing traffic at all times. Regular glider and helicopter activity in the MATZ.

Bodmin — **Warnings**

1 Rifle range bearing 085°T, distance 1·4 nm. Safety height 1 000 ft agl.

2 Use of the aerodrome is limited to aircraft below a maximum AUW of 2 490 kg (5 500 lbs).

3 The maximum elevation of the manoeuvring area is located at the approximate intersection of the runways and there is no line of sight from the downwind to the upwind end of the runways.

Fig 2—18

UK AIP (30 Jul 81) AGA 3-4-1

AERODROME DIRECTORY (contd.)

Aerodrome Obstructions

Aerodrome Obstructions. Details are given of obstructions within 4 nautical miles of the centre of the aerodrome—exceptionally beyond 4 nautical miles. The datum point from which the distances and bearings are quoted is the Aerodrome Reference Point (ARP) or, where no official ARP is established, the approximate centre of the landing area. The co-ordinates of the ARP or datum point are given in column 1 of the Schedule of Aerodromes. The heights of obstructions above aerodrome level are all related to the aerodrome elevation. All bearings are in degrees True.

Obstruction information is limited to significant obstacles: the lists are not comprehensive nor do they necessarily include all shadowed obstacles. For detailed and comprehensive data, in particular that necessary for compliance with the weight and performance requirements of the current Air Navigation (General) Regulations, consult the aerodrome operator.

Obstructions at Airports listed in AGA 2. Details are not included in this tabulation but are given for the individual airport in AGA 2.

Abbreviations

aal — Above aerodrome level
agl — Above ground level
amsl — Above mean sea level
Ad — Aerodrome
L — Lighted
nm — Nautical miles

Andrewsfield

Take-Off and Climb Area—Obstructions

Obstruction	Dist Beyond Start of TORA (m)	Dist R or L of Extended RCL (m)	Elevation amsl (ft)
Runway 09 → Vehicles on road	765	Across RCL	295
Runway 27 → Vehicles on road	860	Across RCL	291

BELFAST/Harbour

Chimney (gas flare)	169 ft aal	184 ft amsl	0·68 nm	358°
3 Chimneys (L)	168 "	183 "	0·60 nm	350°
Spire	189 "	204 "	1·67 nm	043°
Mast (L)	668 "	683 "	1·47 nm	086°
Spire (L)	218 "	233 "	0·92 nm	184°
Gasholder	263 "	278 "	2·30 nm	225°
Spire (L)	155 "	170 "	1·64 nm	225°
Chimney	215 "	230 "	1·81 nm	228°
Chimney	343 "	358 "	3·06 nm	232°
Travelling crane (L)	308 "	323 "	1·42 nm	233°
Travelling crane (L)	344 "	359 "	1·03 nm	239°
TV mast (L)*	1,739 "	1,754 "	5·20 nm	251°
Grain silo	186 "	201 "	1·48 nm	257°
TV mast (L)	1,683 "	1,698 "	4·80 nm	260°
Chimney (L)	206 "	221 "	1·03 nm	289°

Fig 2-19

AGA 5-2 (11 Feb 82) UK AIP

AERODROME 1	AERODROME AVAILABLE FOR USE WINTER PERIOD 2	AERODROME AVAILABLE FOR USE SUMMER PERIOD 3	SERVICE PROVIDED BY AERONAUTICAL GROUND STATION 4
*ABERDEEN/Dyce	0700-2150	0600-2050	ATC
☞ Alderney	0830-1745 (Extensions restricted to Scheduled Services only)	0700-1745 (Extensions restricted to Scheduled Services only)	ATC
*Andrewsfield	0900-SS (and by arrangement)	0800-SS (and by arrangement)	A/G
*BARROW/Walney Island	**0800-1700 Mon-Fri	**0700-1600 Mon-Fri	A/G
*BEDFORD/Castle Mill	HJ	HJ	NIL
*BELFAST/Aldergrove	H24	H24	ATC

Fig 2-20

FLIGHTS ABROAD-CUSTOMS REQUIREMENTS

When an aircraft leaves or enters the National Boundaries of the United Kingdom the pilot must arrange Customs Clearance at a notified Customs Airport.

It must however be appreciated that some Customs Airports are not available throughout 24 hours each day and it is the responsibility of the pilot who is entering or leaving the UK to ensure that he lands at an airport at which Customs facilities are available.

The aerodromes in the United Kingdom which have been designated as Customs and Excise Airports by the Department of Trade with the concurrence of the Commissioners of Customs and Excise are shown in the following list:-

ABERDEEN/Dyce
BELFAST/Aldergrove
Biggin Hill
Birmingham
Blackpool
BOURNEMOUTH/Hurn
BRISTOL/Lulsgate
Cambridge
Cardiff
Coventry
East Midlands
Edinburgh
Exeter
Glasgow
GLOUCESTER AND CHELTENHAM/Staverton
Humberside
ISLE OF MAN/Ronaldsway
Kirkwall
Leeds and Bradford
Liverpool
LONDON/Gatwick
LONDON/Heathrow
LONDON/Stansted
Luton
Lydd
Manchester International
Manston
Newcastle
Norwich
PLYMOUTH/Roborough
Prestwick
Southampton
Southend
Sumburgh
Tees-side
Valley

Customs and Excise attendance at these airports is provided according to the needs of regular air traffic and details of 'hours of availability' for each airport are given in the Air Pilot (FAL Section).

Private Flights, Documentary Requirements

Flights abroad which are of a private and temporary nature will need to meet the following simple documentary procedure:

The pilot will have to present to the Customs Officer, either a Carnet de Passages en Douane, or a Customs Form No. XS 29A in duplicate. The Carnet or duplicate copy of the completed Form XS 29A will be retained by the pilot, and presented to the Customs Officer on the aircraft's return to the UK.

It must be appreciated that aircraft are liable to Customs duty and all aircraft arriving in the UK from abroad are prima facia liable to Customs duty but this will not apply provided the above procedure has been carried out.

Customs Requirements

Aircraft flying to or from places abroad may cross the UK coastline at any point subject to the requirements of any regulations in force. All persons leaving or entering the UK must produce their baggage and articles carried with them for examination by the Customs Officer.

Flights to the Channel Islands and the Isle of Man are considered as flights abroad. When visiting the Isle of Man the first point of landing must be at Ronaldsway Airport, however inbound flights from the Isle of Man to the UK need not land at a Customs Airport if the goods being carried have the same 'duty equivalent' as UK values.

After an aircraft has been cleared outbound from a UK Customs Airport it must not land in the UK again other than at a Customs Airport. If for any reason a pilot has to force land after receiving Customs clearance outbound, or before receiving Customs clearance inbound, he must report the occurrence as quickly as possible either to the Customs authorities or to the local police.

He must also produce upon demand the documents relating to the flight and ensure that his passengers and any goods unloaded are kept in close vicinity to the aircraft unless it is necessary to move them for reasons of health, safety or preservation of life or property.

Public Health Requirements

The Health laws of the United Kingdom permit an Airport Medical Officer to examine any crew member or passenger entering the UK:-

> 'Who is suspected of suffering from, or been exposed to an infectious disease or is suspected of being verminous'

He may also examine any person intending to depart from the UK if there are reasonable grounds for believing that person is suffering from a (quarantinable) disease within the International Health Regulations.

A Medical Officer may require the crew or passengers to produce a valid international certificate of vaccination against 'Smallpox' if they have entered the UK from certain countries or areas. If a valid certificate of vaccination cannot be produced the person concerned may be offered vaccination and may be placed under health surveillance or in isolation for an appropriate period.

SEARCH AND RESCUE

Search and Rescue is a life saving service provided for the safety of aircraft passengers and crew. The United Kingdom and surrounding waters within the FIRs and the Shanwick Oceanic Area (OCA) are divided into two regions for this purpose. Pilots of microlight aircraft who will normally not be carrying radio equipment should understand how the Search and Rescue facilities are organised and also how to display and interpret the standard distress signals.

Responsibility and Organisation

The responsibility for co-ordinating seach and rescue action lies with a joint Civil/ Military Organisation which has a Rescue Co-ordination Centre in each region.

When the location of a civil aircraft which has crashed on land is known and no air search is necessary, responsibility for dealing with the incident devolves upon the civil ground organisation. A CAA Air Traffic Control Centre (ATCC), upon becoming aware of an aircraft in distress and knowing the position of its emergency landing, will notify the local police in the area who will then alert fire, ambulance and hospital services as appropriate.

At some places arrangements are made for the fire service to be notified directly in order to save time in bringing this service into operation. Should the first report of an accident be given by a member of the public to the police, that force will immediately alert the fire and other services including the ATCC who will be informed of the rescue action being taken and given all relevant details.

The Rescue Co-ordination Centres can call upon a large number of resources whenever a 'Search and Rescue' operation is implemented, some examples of these are:

The Royal Air Force;
- Fixed Wing and Helicopter Aircraft
- Mountain Rescue Units

Royal National Lifeboat Institution
Ocean Station Vessels
Royal Navy Helicopters and Ships
HM Coastguard Service

When radio equipment is carried the Aeronautical Emergency Service on RTF frequency 121.5 MHz should be used for distress communications. Distress and Diversion (D&D) ATC units of the Royal Air Force maintain a continous listening watch on this frequency.

In the event of an aircraft having to force land in the sea, or sparsely populated or mountainous areas, the difficulties of the SAR operation will be increased and it is therefore a responsibility of all General Aviation pilots to ensure that when flights are planned over such areas, they carry appropriate survival equipment and file a flight plan, particularly if the aircraft is not equipped with radio.

Aircraft not equipped with Radio

A pilot of an aircraft not equipped with radio is strongly advised to file a flight plan if he intends to fly more than 10 nm from the coast or over sparsely populated or mountainous areas as this will assist rescue action should the aircraft be reported overdue.

Pilots should particularly note that flight plans can only be delivered to destinations which are on or linked to the Aeronautical Fixed Telecommunication Network (AFTN) and that prompt search action can only be initiated if an aircraft is reported overdue by the destination aerodrome.

Microlight pilots will not normally be flying to destinations which have an AFTN facility and should therefore advise a responsible person at the destination of the intended flight and arrange for that person to notify the ATS authorities in the event of non-arrival. This action is particularly important when the route of the flight takes the aircraft over areas which are considered to be difficult from a Search and Rescue aspect. These areas in the UK are as follows:

Scotland
Hebrides, Orkneys and Shetlands
Pennine Range
Lake District
Yorkshire Moors
Welsh Mountains
Peak District of Derbyshire
Exmoor
Dartmoor

VISUAL DISTRESS AND URGENCY SIGNALS

The visual Distress, Urgency and Safety Signals which are internationally established for use by aircraft are shown on pages 2-49 and 50

In addition to these signals a set of International Ground/Air Visual Signals are laid down for the use of survivors and search parties. These signals are shown in fig 2-21 below

Ground-Air Visual Code for use by Survivors

1	REQUIRE ASSISTANCE	**V**
2	REQUIRE MEDICAL ASSISTANCE	**X**
3	NO OR NEGATIVE	**N**
4	YES OR AFFIRMATIVE	**Y**
5	AM PROCEEDING IN THIS DIRECTION	**↑**
If in doubt use International Symbol for Distress SOS		

Fig. 2–21

In the event that such signals have to be made the procedures outlined in the next few paragraphs should be followed where applicable:

Lay out these symbols by using strips of fabric, pieces of wood, stones or any other available material. Endeavour to provide as big a colour contrast as possible between the material used for the symbols and the background against which the symbols are exposed.

Symbols should be at least 2 to 3 metres in height and larger if possible. Care should be taken to lay out the symbols exactly as depicted in order to avoid confusion.

In addition to using these symbols, every effort should be made to attract attention by means of radio, flares, smoke, or any other available means.

If the ground is covered with snow, signals can be made by dragging, shovelling or trampling the snow. The symbols thus formed will appear to be black when seen from the air.

Survivors should also use any of the following methods to attract attention when aircraft, surface craft or search parties are heard or seen:

Make the aircraft as conspicuous as possible by spreading material (if available) over the wings and fuselage.

Use smoke or fire. A continuously burning fire is recommended with material ready to hand to cause it to smoke at short notice. A quantity of green branches or leaves, or oil, or rubber from the aircraft should produce the desired result. Three fires in the form of a triangle make a very good signal particularly at night.

Fire distress flares or cartridges.

Use some object with a bright flat surface as a heliograph.

Fly anything in the form of a flag and, if possible, make the international distress signal by flying a ball, or something resembling a ball, above or below it.

At night, flash torches or lights.

PROCEDURES AND SIGNALS EMPLOYED BY RESCUE AIRCRAFT

During the day the pilot of the search aircraft will rock his wings to indicate that the survivors have been spotted. Certain rescue aircraft carry survival equipment which can be dropped by parachute.

The following technique is used when RAF aircraft are searching for survivors at night:

The search aircraft will fire a single green pyrotechnic a intervals of 5 to 10 minutes.

Survivors should then allow 15 seconds after they see the signal (so that the search aircraft can pass out of the glare). If the survivors have pyrotechnics available they should then fire a red pyrotechnic, followed after a short interval, by a second.

The survivors should fire additional pyrotechnics if the search aircraft appear to be getting off track, and when it is overhead, so that an accurate position can be obtained.

All pilots must have an understanding of the procedures to be followed during flight emergencies. Although there is no legislation applicable to the carriage of emergency equipment for private flights, a pilot's pre-flight planning should reflect his awareness of the possibility of emergency situations developing in unexpected circumstances, e.g.

Overwater flights not only demand the carriage of lifejackets but also require a passenger briefing on their operation and additionally, practice in wearing them whilst inside the aircraft.

When flight over sparsely populated territory is planned, it would be wise to carry some warm clothing and if possible to have some flares or smoke candles available and stowed in a secure position away from the cabin area where smoking may take place.

Only by paying attention to the possible consequences of a forced landing or ditching will the pilot meet the requirements of a good aircraft captain, and give his crew or passengers the best chance of survival.

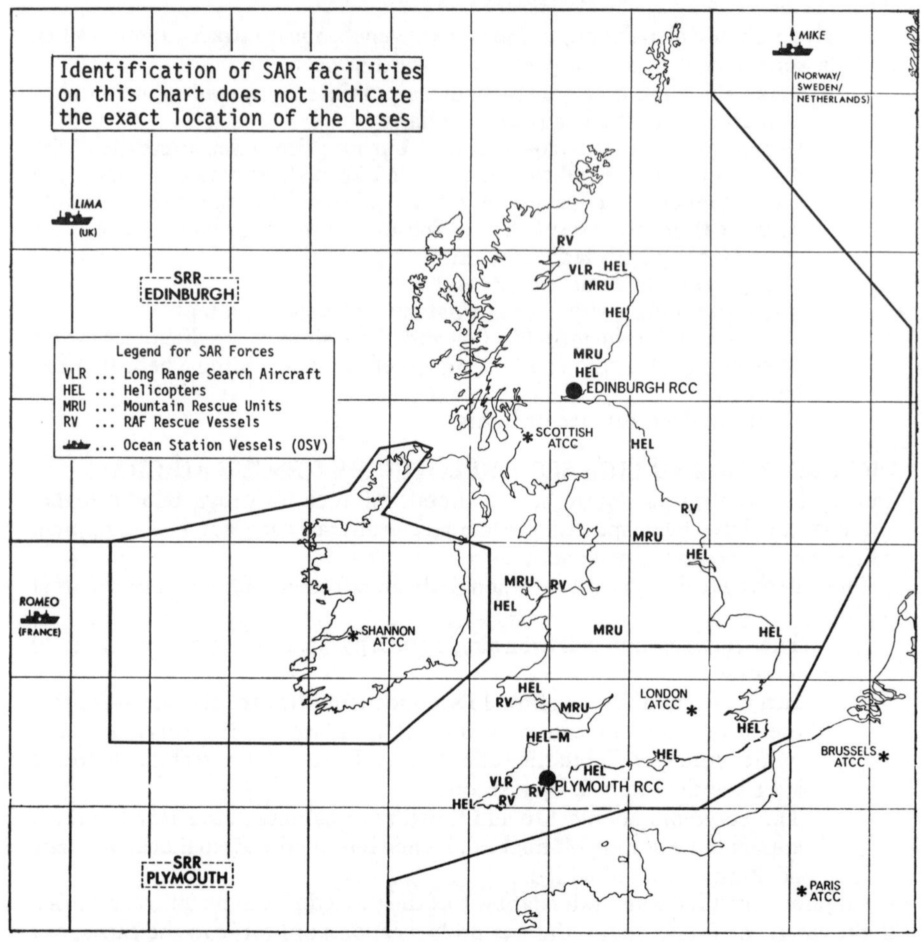

Fig 2—22

DISTRESS, URGENCY AND SAFETY SIGNALS

DISTRESS

The following signals given, either together or separately, before the sending of a message, signify that an aircraft is threatened by grave and imminent danger and requests immediate assistance.

By RTF	The Spoken Word 'MAYDAY'
By Visual Signalling	The Signal SOS - Morse Code A Succession of pyrotechnic Lights Fired at Short Internals each Showing a Single Red Light. A Parachute Flare Showing a Single Red Light.
By Sound Signalling (Other than RTF)	The Signal SOS - Morse Code A Continuous Sounding with any Sound Apparatus.

URGENCY

The following signals given together or separately, indicate that the commander of the aircraft has an urgent message to transmit concerning the safety of a ship, aircraft, vehicle or other property or of a person on board or within sight of the aircraft from which the signal is given.

By RTF.	The Spoken Word 'PAN'
By Visual Signalling	The Signal XXX - Morse Code
By Sound Signalling (Other than RTF)	The Signal XXX - Morse Code

SAFETY

The following signals, given either together or separately, before the sending of a message, signify that the commander of the aircraft wishes to give notice of difficulties which compel it to land but that he does not require immediate assistance.

By RTF	No RTF Signal Designated
By Visual Signalling	A Succession of White Pyrotechnic Lights, or The Repeated Switching On and Off of the Aircraft Landing Lights, or, The Repeated Switching On and Off of the Aircraft Navigation Lights (in an Irregular Manner).

Warning Signals to Aircraft in Flight

In the United Kingdom, by day or by night, a series of projectiles discharged from the ground at intervals of ten seconds, each showing, on bursting, red and green lights or stars, shall indicate to an aircraft that it is flying in or about to enter a danger area or an area concerning national defence or affecting public interest and is required to take such action as may be necessary to leave the area or change course to avoid the area.

If the commander of an aircraft becomes aware that his aircraft is flying in one of the above mentioned areas he must leave the area by flying to the least possible extent over such area and not begin to descend until clear of the area, or comply with any instructions given by radio or visual signals from the appropriate air traffic control unit or a commissioned officer of Her Majesty's naval, military or air forces.

DISASTERS IN THE UK FIRs — RESTRICTION OF FLYING

In the event of a disaster occurring on land or at sea within the UK FIRs, the Emergency Controlling Authority (ECA), normally a representative of one of the following agencies: Home Office; Department of Energy; HM Coastguard Headquarters; Edinburgh RCC; or Plymouth RCC, may find it necessary for the safety of life and property and particularly for the protection of those subsequently engaged in search and rescue action, to inhibit flight in the vicinity of the disaster by aircraft not directly engaged with emergency action.

On receipt of a request from the ECA, the initial action will normally be to establish by NOTAM Class I a temporary danger area around the scene of the incident. If the temporary danger area fails to achieve the objective, 'Restriction of Flying — Disaster — Regulations', which will make it an offence for an aircraft to be flown in the designated area without the permission of the ECA, will be brought into operation by NOTAM Class I.

Subject to any overriding considerations of safety, requests for overflight in the designated area from governmental and other official agencies, such as the Nature Conservancy Council, are to be given priority over requests from en-route traffic, company aircraft, the press and television.

EXTRACTS FROM THE RULES OF THE AIR AND AIR TRAFFIC CONTROL REGULATIONS.

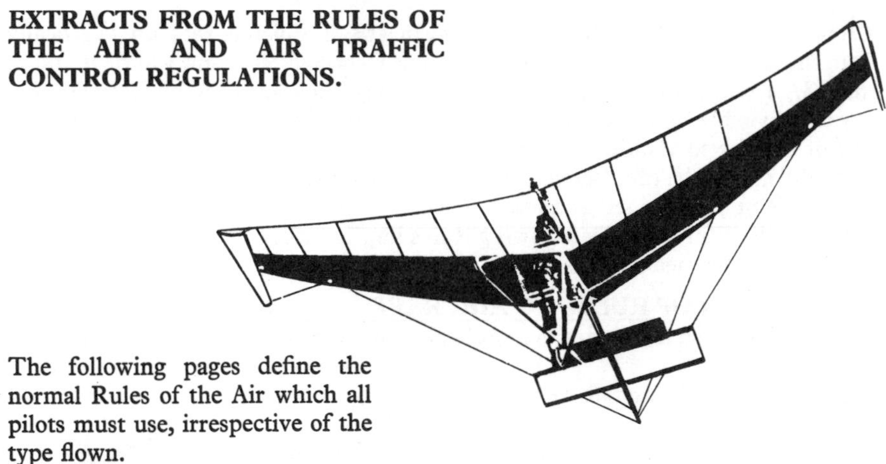

The following pages define the normal Rules of the Air which all pilots must use, irrespective of the type flown.

INTERPRETATION

The statutory document which covers these Rules and Regulations commences with an introductory paragraph defining some of the expressions used in the body of the document. This will permit the contents to be understood more clearly.

Many of these definitions have already been covered in the preceding paragraphs of this section but to avoid any misconceptions when reading the following pages they are repeated below.

'Air Traffic Control Clearance' means authorisation by an Air Traffic Control Unit for an aircraft to proceed under conditions specified by that unit.

'Anti-Collision Light' means a flashing red light showing in all directions for the purpose of enabling the aircraft to be more readily detected by the pilots of distant aircraft.

'Apron' means the part of an aerodrome provided for the stationing of aircraft for the embarkation and disembarkation of passengers, the loading and unloading of cargo and for parking. This area is often called the 'Parking Area'.

'Ground Visibility' means the horizontal visibility at ground level.

'IFR Flight' means a flight conducted in accordance with the Instrument Flight Rules.

'Manoeuvring Area' means the part of an aerodrome provided for the take-off and landing of aircraft and for the movement of aircraft on the surface, excluding the apron and any part of the aerodrome provided for the maintenance of aircraft.

'The Order' means the current Air Navigation Order (as amended)

'Runway' means an area, whether or not paved, which is provided for the take-off or landing of aircraft.

'VFR Flight' means a flight conducted in accordance with the Visual Flight Rules.

'Cloud Ceiling' in relation to an aerodrome means the distance measured vertically from the notified elevation of that aerodrome (Notified elevation will be found in the AGA section of the Air Pilot and on air navigation maps) to the lowest part of any cloud visible from the aerodrome which is sufficient to obscure more than one half of the sky so visible.

'Night' means the time between half an hour after sunset and half an hour before sunrise being determined at surface level.

Unless the context of the following Rules implies otherwise they shall have the same respective meanings as in the Air Navigation Order.

APPLICATION OF RULES TO AIRCRAFT

These Rules, in so far as they are applicable in relation to aircraft, shall apply to:

1. All aircraft within the United Kingdom.

2. All aircraft registered in the United Kingdom, wherever they may be.

The application of this Rule has several purposes, two example of which are:

To ensure as far as possible that foreign registered aircraft operating within the UK airspace system do so in a manner which conforms to the UK Air Traffic Regulations.

UK registered aircraft equipped to comply with these Rules and flying overseas may not always be equipped to meet certain requirements contained in foreign air legislation, therefore some basis must be laid down to permit the aircraft to continue its passage.

LOW FLYING

In as far as aeroplanes are concerned this Rule clearly states:

(a) An aeroplane shall not fly over any congested area of a city, town or settlement:

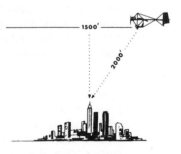

(i) Below such a height as would enable it to be flown clear of the area and land without incurring danger to persons or property in the event of engine failure; or

(ii) Below a height of 1500' above the highest fixed object within 2000' of the aircraft,

whichever is the higher.

(b) An aircraft shall not fly:

(i) Over, or within 3000' of, any assembly in the open air of more than 1000 persons who are assembled for the purpose of witnessing or participating in any organised event except with the permission in writing of the CAA and in accordance with any condition therein specified and with the consent in writing of the organisers of the event; or

(ii) Below such a height as would enable it to alight clear of the assembly in the event of engine failure.

Clearly it would be difficult for a pilot to determine the number of persons forming such an assembly unless he has prior information, and because of this it is unlikely that a pilot would be prosecuted for breaking this Rule, providing he can prove that he was maintaining a reasonable height during the en-route phase of his flight, and that prior information regarding the existence of such an assembly was not promulgated.

(c) An aircraft shall not fly closer than 500' to any person, vessel, vehicle or structure.

500′

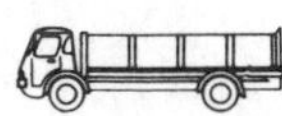

Due to the practical difficulties of definition, animals are not included in this Rule, but clearly cattle and horses etc., should be considered by a sensible pilot and he should keep well clear of them whenever possible.

Nothing in this Rule shall prohibit an aircraft from flying in such a manner as is necessary for the purpose of saving life. It should also be noted that (a) (ii) will not apply during that stage of any flight in which the pilot is acting according to a Special VFR Clearance, or along any route notified for the purposes of this Rule, e.g. Entry/Exit Lanes.

Further to this (c) will not be applicable if the aircraft is taking off or landing at an aerodrome in accordance with normal aviation practice. Nevertheless unless in emergency conditions the approaches to land must be confined to the airspace customarily used for this purpose.

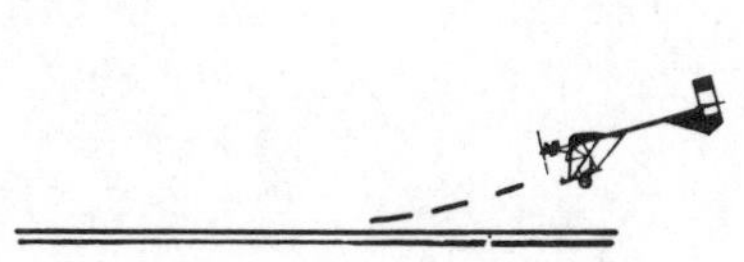

LIGHTS AND OTHER SIGNALS TO BE SHOWN OR MADE BY AIRCRAFT

All aircraft must display a minimum system of external lights when taxiing or flying at night. These lights together with the appropriate colours are clearly laid down in Rule 9 of the Rules of the Air and Air Traffic Control Regulations.

In the interests of safety during night operations pilots must be able to distinguish between powered aircraft, gliders and balloons and for this reason, there are differences in the lighting systems of the varying classes of aircraft. These differences are shown in fig. 2–23 and expanded in the following text.

Display of Lights by Aircraft

By night an aircraft shall display such of the lights specified in the Rules as may be appropriate to the circumstances and shall not display any other lights which might obscure of or otherwise impair the visibility of, or be mistaken for, such lights. Provided that nothing in this paragraph shall prevent the display of an anti-collision light.

Flying Machines

A flying machine registered in the UK having a maximum total weight authorised of 5.700 kg or less, should when flying at night display the following system of lights:

(a) (i) A green light of at least 5 candela showing to the starboard side through an angle of 110° from dead ahead in the horizontal plane;

(ii) A red light of at least 5 candela showing to the port side through an angle of 110° from dead ahead in the horizontal plane, and

(iii) A white light of at least 3 candela showing through angles of 70° from dead astern to each side in the horizontal plane, all being steady lights; or

(b) The lights specified in paragraph (a) and including an anti-collision light; or

(c) The lights specified in paragraph (a) but all being flashing lights flashing together.

Note: Other lighting systems are mentioned in the Rules of the Air and Air Traffic Control Regulations, but these are not covered in this manual as they mainly concern large aircraft.

Flying Machines on the Ground

A flying machine on a land aerodrome in the UK at which aircraft normally land or take-off at night shall, unless it is stationary on the apron or part of the aerodrome provided for the maintenance of aircraft, display by night either the lights which it would be required to display if it were flying, or such other lights as may be specified in the Rules of the Air and Air Traffic Control Regulations.

Failure of Navigation Lights

In the United Kingdom, in the event of the failure of any light which is required by the Rules to be displayed in flight, if the light cannot be immediately repaired or replaced the aircraft shall land as soon as in the opinion of the commander of the aircraft it can safely do so, unless authorised by the appropriate Air Traffic Control Unit to continue its flight.

Although anti-collision lights or strobe lights are not a requirement for small aircraft the use of such additional lighting systems will enhance safety. However when using these lights and flying close to or in cloud it is advisable to switch them off to avoid possible distractions or even spatial disorientation to the pilot.

Gliders

A glider while flying at night shall display either a steady red light of at least 5 candela, showing in all directions or lights in accordance with paragraph (a) page 2-54

Free Balloons

A free balloon while flying at night shall display a steady red light of at least 5 candela showing in all directions, suspended not less than 5 metres and not more than 10 metres below the basket, or if there is no basket, below the lowest part of the balloon.

Captive Balloons and Kites

(1) A captive balloon or kite while flying at night at a height exceeding 60 metres above the surface shall display lights as follows:

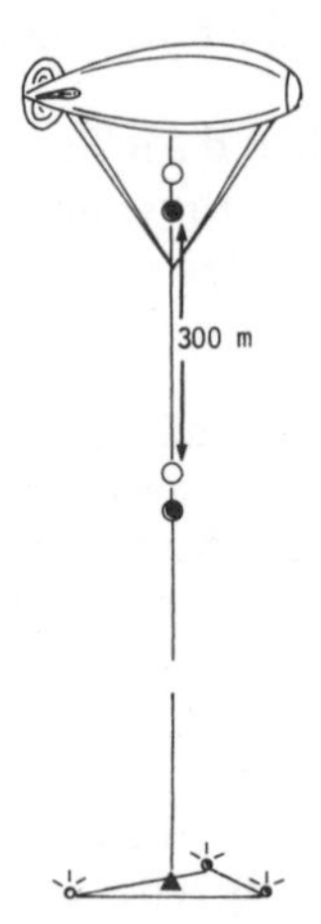

(a) A group of two steady lights consisting of a white light placed 4 metres above a red light, both being of at least 5 candela and showing in all directions. The white light being placed not less than 5 metres or more than 10 metres below the basket, or if there is no basket, below the lowest part of the balloon or kite.

(b) On the mooring cable, at intervals of not more than 300 metres measured from the group of lights referred to in sub-paragraph (a) of this paragraph, groups of two lights of the colour and power and in the relative positions specified in that sub-paragraph, and, if the lowest group of lights is obscured by cloud, an additional group below the cloud base; and

(c) On the surface, a group of three flashing lights arranged in a horizontal plane at the apexes of a triangle, approximately equilateral, each side of which measures at least 25 metres; one side of the triangle shall be approximately at right angles to the horizontal projection of the cable and shall be delimited by two red lights; the third light shall be a green light so placed that the triangle encloses the object on the surface to which the balloon or kite is moored.

(2) A captive balloon while flying by day at a height exceeding 60 metres above the surface shall have attached to its mooring cable at intervals of not more than 200 metres measured from the basket, or, if there is no basket, from the lowest part of the balloon, tubular streamers marked with alternate bands of red and white.

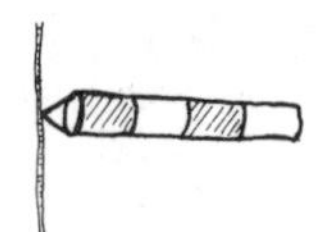

(3) A kite flown in the circumstances referred to in paragraph (2) of this Rule shall have attached to its mooring cable either:

(a) Tubular streamers as specified in paragraph (2) of this Rule, or

(b) Streamers at not more than 100 metre intervals measured from the lowest part of the kite.

Airships

(1) Except as provided in paragraph (2) of this Rule, an airship while flying at night shall display the following steady lights:

(a) A white light of at least 5 candela showing through angles of 110° from dead ahead to each side in the horizontal plane;

(b) A green light of at least 5 candela showing to the starboard side through an angle of 110° from dead ahead in the horizontal plane;

(c) A red light of at least 5 candela showing to the port side through an angle of 110° from dead ahead in the horizontal plane; and

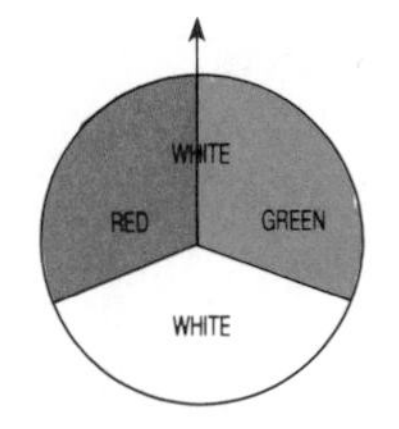

(d) A white light of at least 5 candela showing through angles of 70° from dead astern to each side in the horizontal plane.

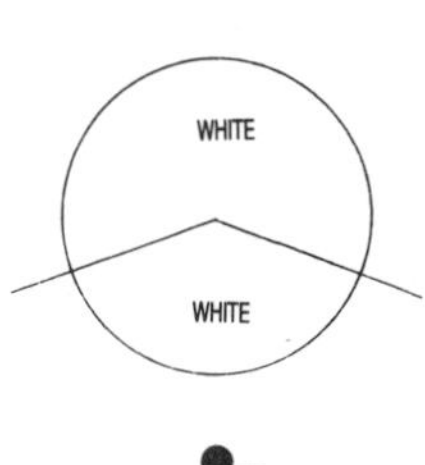

(2) An airship while flying at night shall display, if it is not under command, or has voluntarily stopped its engines, or is being towed, the following steady lights:
(a) The white lights referred to in paragraph (1) (a) and (d) of this Rule;
(b) Two red lights, each of at least 5 candela and showing in all directions suspended below the control car so that one is at least 4 metres above the other and at least 8 metres below the control car; and
(c) If the airship is making way but not otherwise, the green and red light referred to in paragraph (1) (b) and (c) of this Rule:

RED

Provided that an airship while picking up its moorings, notwithstanding that it is not under command, shall display only the lights specified in paragraph (1) of this Rule.

(3) An airship, while moored within the UK by night, shall display the following lights:

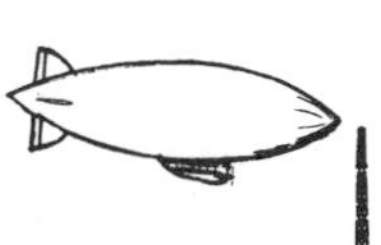

(a) When moored to a mooring mast, at or near the rear a while light of at least 5 candela showing in all directions;
(b) When moored otherwise than to a mooring mast:
(i) A white light of at least 5 candela showing through angles of 110° from dead ahead to each side in the horizontal plane;
(ii) A white light of at least 5 candela showing through angles of 70° from dead astern to each side in the horizontal plane.

(4) An airship while flying by day, if it is not under command, or has voluntarily stopped its engines, or is being towed, shall display two black balls suspended below the control car so that one is at least 4 metres above the other and at least 8 metres below the control car.

(5) For the purposes of this Rule:
(a) An airship shall be deemed not to be under command when it is unable to execute a manoeuvre which it may be required to execute by or under these Rules;
(b) An airship shall be deemed to be making way when it is not moored and is in motion relative to the air.

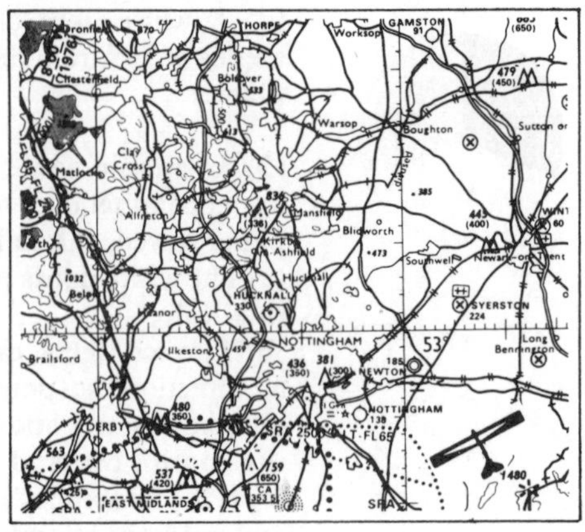

GENERAL FLIGHT RULES

Knowledge of the actual weather and forecast weather conditions en-route and at destination is of vital concern to the pilot and he is responsible for obtaining such weather information whenever practical before setting off on a planned flight.

The General Flight Rules lay down the following:

WEATHER REPORTS AND FORECASTS

(1) Immediately before an aircraft flies the commander of the aircraft shall examine the current forecasts and reports of the weather conditions on the proposed flight path, being reports and forecasts which it is reasonably practicable for him to obtain, in order to determine whether Instrument Meteorological Conditions prevail or are likely to prevail during any part of the flight.

(2) An aircraft which is unable to communicate by radio with an air traffic control unit at the aerodrome of destination shall not begin a flight to an aerodrome within a control zone if the information which is reasonably practicable for the commander of the aircraft to obtain indicates that it will arrive at that aerodrome when the ground visibility is less than 5 nautical miles or the cloud ceiling is less than 1500 feet, unless the commander of the aircraft has obtained from an air traffic control unit at that aerodrome permission to enter the aerodrome traffic zone.

RULES FOR AVOIDING AERIAL COLLISIONS

For the same reasons that road traffic have to obey certain rules, e.g. they must be driven on a particular side of the road, so aircraft must abide by the same principles and follow specific rules adapted to their environment.

(1) **General**
(a) Notwithstanding that the flight is being made with air traffic control clearance it shall remain the duty of the commander of an aircraft to take all possible measures to ensure that his aircraft does not collide with any other aircraft.
(b) An aircraft shall not be flown in such proximity to other aircraft as to create a danger of collision.
(c) Aircraft shall not fly in formation unless the commanders of the aircraft have agreed to do so.
(d) An aircraft which is obliged by these Rules to give way to another aircraft shall avoid passing over or under the other aircraft, or crossing ahead of it, unless passing well clear of it.

Note: The reason for Rule (d) is to avoid situations where pilots of opposing or converging aircraft simultaneously attempt to climb up or dive down in their attempts to remain clear of the other aircraft.

(e) An aircraft which has the right-of-way under this Rule shall maintain its course and speed.
(f) For the purpose of this Rule a glider and a flying machine which is towing it shall be considered to be a single aircraft under the command of the commander of the towing flying machine.

(2) **Aircraft which are Converging:**
(a) Subject to the provisions of paragraphs (3) and (4) of this Rule, an aircraft in the air shall give way to other converging aircraft as follows:
(i) Flying machines shall give way to airships, gliders and balloons;
(ii) Airships shall give way to gliders and balloons;
(iii) Gliders shall give way to balloons.
(b) Subject to the provisions of sub-paragraph (a) of this paragraph, when two aircraft are converging in the air at approximately the same altitude, the aircraft which has the other on its right shall give way:
Provided that mechanically driven aircraft shall give way to aircraft which are towing other aircraft or objects.

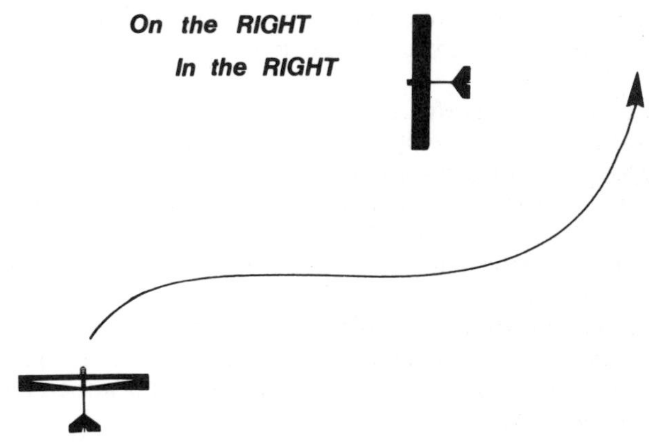

(3) **Aircraft Approaching Head-On**

When two aircraft are approaching head-on or approximately so in the air and there is danger of collision, each shall alter course to the right.

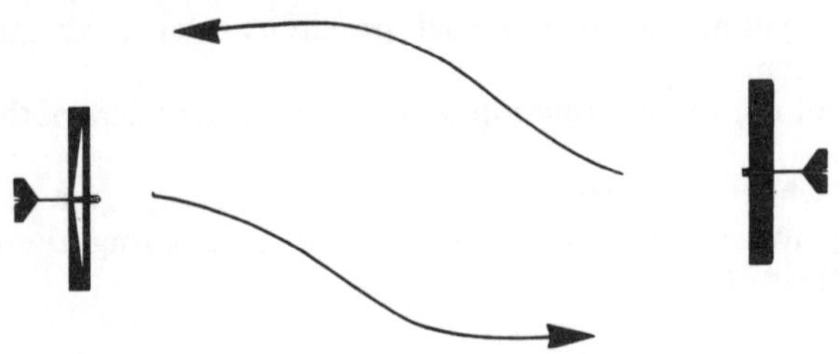

(4) **Aircraft Overtaking**

An aircraft which is being overtaken in the air shall have the right-of-way and the overtaking aircraft, whether climbing, descending or in level flight, shall keep out of the way of the other aircraft by altering course to the right, and shall not cease to keep out of the way of the other aircraft until the other aircraft has been passed and is clear, notwithstanding any change in the relative positions of the two aircraft.

Provided that a glider overtaking another glider in the United Kingdom may alter its course to the right or left.

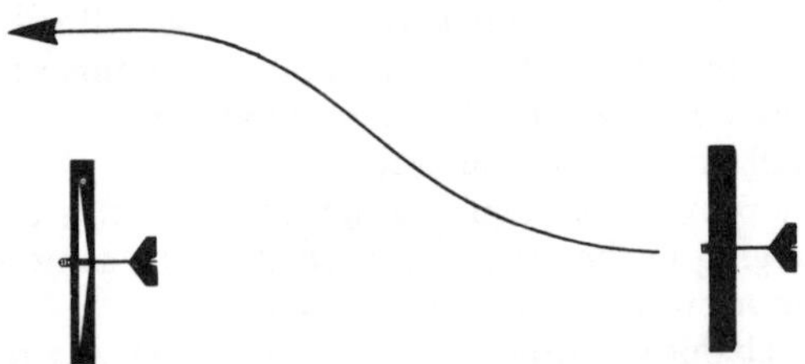

(5) **Aircraft Landing**

An aircraft while landing or on final approach to land shall have the right-of-way over other aircraft in flight or on the ground or water.

(6) **Two or more Aircraft Landing**

In the case of two or more flying machines or gliders approaching any place for the purpose of landing, the aircraft at the lower altitude shall have the right-of-way, but it shall not cut in front of another aircraft which is on final approach to land or overtake that aircraft. Provided that:

(a) When an air traffic control unit has communicated to any aircraft an order of priority of landing, the aircraft shall approach to land in that order, and

(b) When the commander of an aircraft is aware that another aircraft is making an emergency landing, he shall give way to that aircraft, and at night, notwithstanding that he may have received permission to land, shall not attempt to land until he has received further permission to do so.

AEROBATIC MANOEUVRES

An aircraft shall not carry out any aerobatic manoeuvre:

(a) Over the congested area of any city, town or settlement; or

(b) Within controlled airspace except with the consent of the appropriate air traffic control unit.

CLEAR OF TOWNS

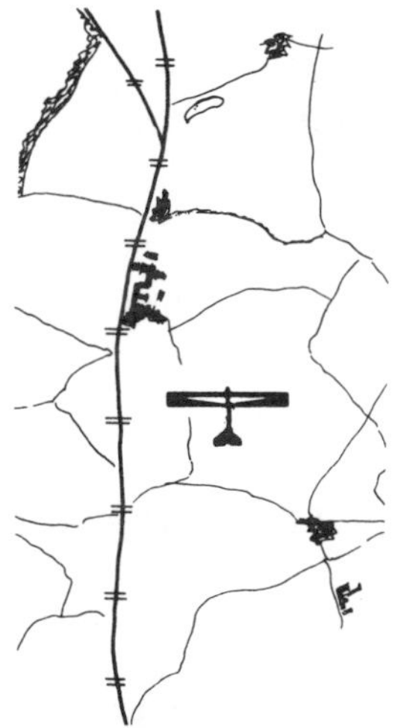

RIGHT HAND TRAFFIC RULE

An aircraft which is flying within the United Kingdom in sight of the ground and following a road, railway, canal or coastline, or any other line of landmarks, shall keep such line of landmarks on its left.
Helicopters following certain landmarks may sometimes be exempt from this rule.

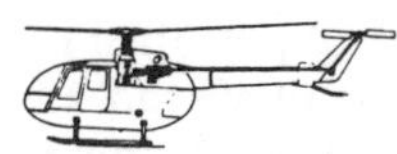

NOTIFICATION OF ARRIVAL

(1) The commander of an aircraft entering or leaving the United Kingdom on any flight for which a flight plan has been submitted shall take all reasonable steps to ensure upon landing that notice of the arrival of the aircraft is given to the aerodrome of departure.
Provided that notice of arrival need not be given upon completion of a flight between the United Kingdom and the Republic of Ireland or any other country in Europe or in or bordering on the Mediterranean Sea, unless an air traffic control unit at the aerodrome of departure has required it to be given, or unless the aircraft lands at an aerodrome other than its intended destination when it began the flight.

(2) The commander of an aircraft who has caused notice of its intended arrival at any aerodrome to be given to the air traffic control unit or other authority at that aerodrome shall ensure that the air traffic control unit or other authority at that aerodrome is informed as quickly as possible of any estimated delay in arrival of 45 minutes or more.

AERODROME TRAFFIC RULES

In order to ensure the safe and expeditous movement of aircraft at aerodromes certain Rules applicable to flying machines are established. These Rules must also be observed (whenever practical) by pilots of all other types of aircraft.

VISUAL SIGNALS

The commander of a flying machine on, or in the traffic zone of, an aerodrome shall observe such visual signals as may be displayed at, or directed to him from the aerodrome by the authority of the person in charge of the aerodrome and shall obey any instructions which may be given to him by means of such signals.

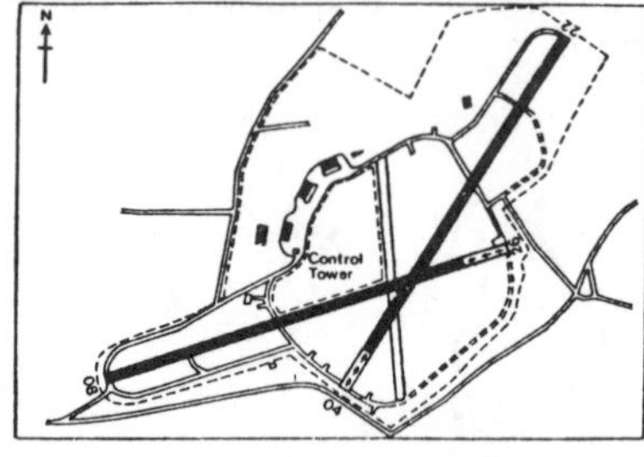

Provided that he shall not be required to obey Marshalling Signals if in his opinion it is inadvisable to do so in the interests of safety.

ACCESS TO AND MOVEMENT ON THE MANOEUVRING AREA AND OTHER PARTS OF THE AERODROME USED BY AIRCRAFT

(1) A person or vehicle shall not go onto any part of an aerodrome provided for the use of aircraft and under the control of the person in charge of the aerodrome without the permission of the person in charge of the aerodrome, and except in accordance with any conditions subject to which that permission may have been granted.

(2) A person or vehicle shall not go or move on the manoeuvring area of an aerodrome having an air traffic control unit without the permission of that unit, and except in accordance with any conditions subject to which that permission may have been granted.

(3) Any permission granted for the purposes of this Rule may be granted either in respect of vehicles or persons generally, or in respect of any particular vehicle or person or any class of vehicle or person.

RIGHT OF WAY ON THE GROUND

(1) This Rule shall apply to: (a) Flying Machines. (b) Vehicles.
Such flying machines and vehicles being on any part of a land aerodrome provided for the use of aircraft and under the control of the person in charge of the aerodrome.

(2) Notwithstanding any air traffic control clearance it shall remain the duty of the commander of an aircraft to take all possible measures to ensure that his aircraft does not collide with any other aircraft or with any vehicle.

(3)(a) Flying machines and vehicles shall give way to aircraft which are taking off or landing.
(b) Vehicles, and flying machines which are not taking off or landing, shall give way to vehicles towing aircraft.

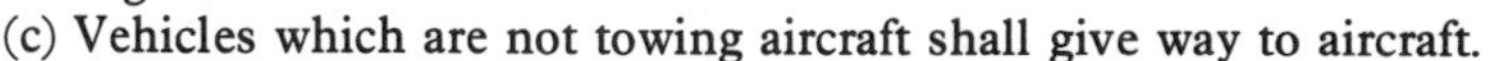

(c) Vehicles which are not towing aircraft shall give way to aircraft.

(4) Subject to the provisions of paragraph (3) above, in case of danger of collision while taxying between two flying machines:

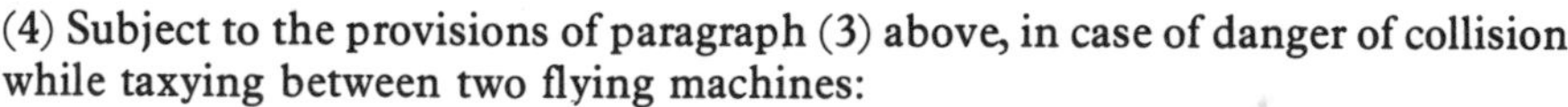

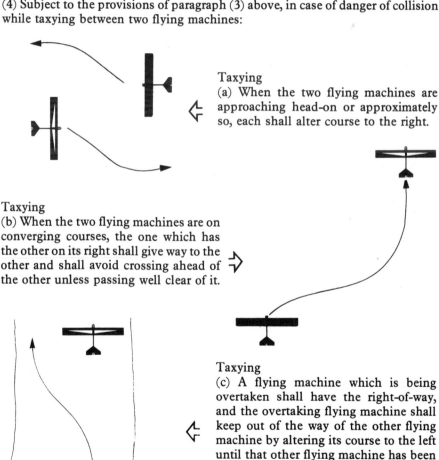

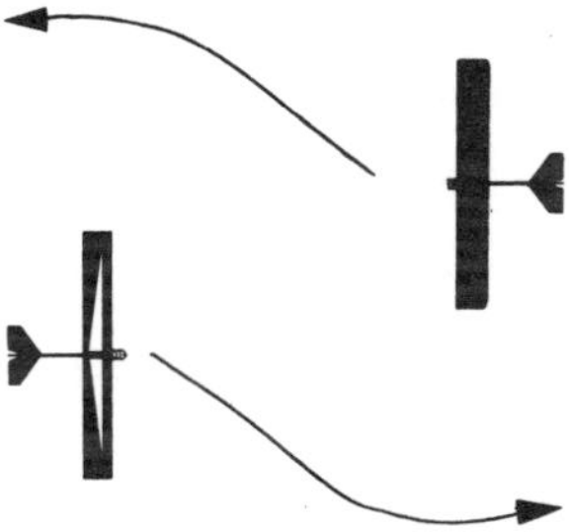

Taxying
(a) When the two flying machines are approaching head-on or approximately so, each shall alter course to the right.

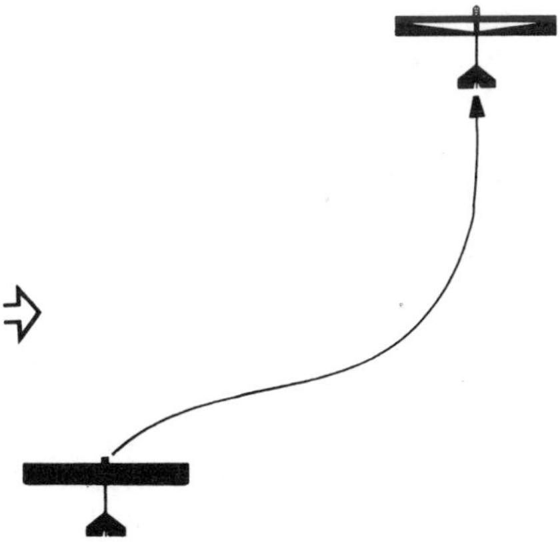

Taxying
(b) When the two flying machines are on converging courses, the one which has the other on its right shall give way to the other and shall avoid crossing ahead of the other unless passing well clear of it.

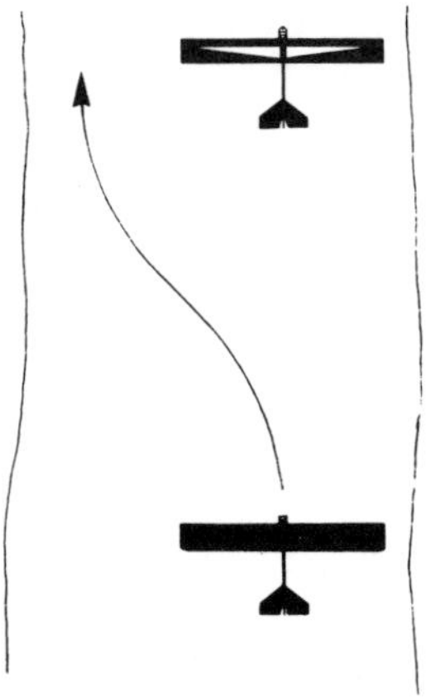

Taxying
(c) A flying machine which is being overtaken shall have the right-of-way, and the overtaking flying machine shall keep out of the way of the other flying machine by altering its course to the left until that other flying machine has been passed and is clear, notwithstanding any change in the relative positions of the two flying machines.

(5)Subject to the provisions of paragraph (3) (b) of this Rule a vehicle shall:
(a) Overtake another vehicle so that the other vehicle is on the left of the overtaking vehicle.
(b) Keep to the left when passing another vehicle which is approaching head-on or approximately so.

DROPPING OF TOW ROPES

Tow ropes, banners or similar articles towed by aircraft shall not be dropped from aircraft except at an aerodrome and:
(a) In accordance with arrangements made with an air traffic control unit at the aerodrome or, if there is no such unit, with the person in charge of the aerodrome, or
(b) In the area designated by the marking shown here (a yellow cross), and the ropes, banners or similar articles shall be dropped when the aircraft is flying in the direction appropriate for landing.

AERODROMES NOT HAVING AIR TRAFFIC CONTROL UNITS

(1) (a) An aircraft shall not fly within a zone which the commander of the aircraft knows or ought reasonably to know to be the aerodrome traffic zone of an aerodrome where no air traffic control unit is for the time being notified as being on watch, except for the purpose of taking off or landing at that aerodrome or observing the signals in the signals area with a view to landing there, unless he has the permission of the person in charge of the aerodrome.

(b) An aircraft flying within such a zone for the purpose of observing the signals shall remain clear of cloud and at least 500' above the level of the aerodrome.

Note: Good operating practice dictates that whenever an aircraft has to be flown overhead an aerodrome for the purpose of interpreting the signals area, it should be flown at or above 2000' above the aerodrome level. However the prevailing cloud base may make this impractical and the above rules must therefore make provision for the aircraft to be flown at a lower height. Nevertheless this action should be considered the exception and not established as a practice.

(2) The commander of an aircraft flying in such a zone or moving on such an aerodrome shall:
(a) Conform to the pattern of traffic formed by other aircraft, or keep clear of the airspace in which the pattern is formed.
(b) Make all turns to the left unless ground signals otherwise indicate; and
(c) Take-off and land in the direction indicated by the ground signals or, if no such signals are displayed, into the wind, unless good aviation practice demands otherwise.

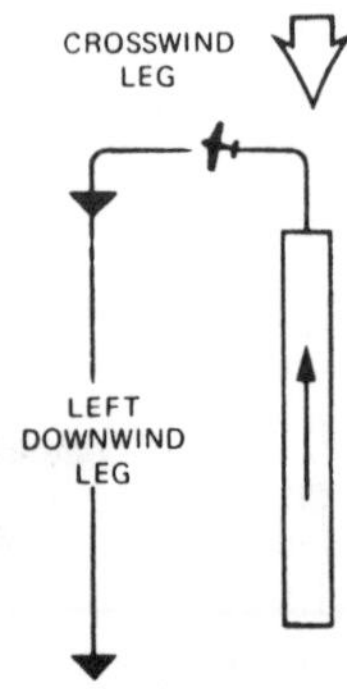

(3)(a) A flying machine or glider shall not land on a runway at such an aerodrome unless the runway is clear of other aircraft.

(b) Where take-offs and landings are not confined to a runway -

(i) A flying machine or glider when landing shall leave clear on its left any aircraft which has already landed or is already landing or is about to take-off; if such a flying machine or glider is obliged to turn, it shall turn to the left after the commander of the aircraft has satisfied himself that such action will not interfere with other traffic movements; and

Note: In the circumstances of (b) (i) above a pilot of a high wing aircraft would be advised to stop and raise the aircraft flaps prior to turning left after landing. This will permit a greater field of vision behind him.

(ii) A flying machine about to take-off shall take up position and manoeuvre in such a way as to leave clear on its left any aircraft which is already taking off or about to take-off.

(4) A flying machine after landing shall move clear of the landing area in use as soon as it is possible to do so.

AERODROMES HAVING AIR TRAFFIC CONTROL UNITS

(1) An aircraft shall not fly within a zone which the commander of the aircraft knows or ought reasonably to know to be the aerodrome traffic zone of an aerodrome where an air traffic control unit is for the time being notified as being on watch, except for the purpose of observing any signals at that aerodrome with a view to landing there, unless he has the permission of the appropriate air traffic control unit.

(2) The commander of an aircraft flying in the aerodrome traffic zone of an aerodrome where an air traffic control unit is for the time being notified as being on watch or moving on such an aerodrome shall -

(a) Cause a continuous watch to be maintained on the appropriate radio frequency notified for air traffic control communications at the aerodrome, or, if this is not possible, cause a watch to be kept for such instructions as may be issued by visual means;

(b) Not taxi on the apron or manoeuvring area or take-off or land anywhere in the zone except with the permission of the air traffic control unit;

(c) Comply with the provisions of the rule concerning 'Aerodromes not having Air Traffic Control Units' paragraphs (1) (b), (2), (3) and (4), unless he has the permission of the air traffic control unit at the aerodrome, or has been instructed by that unit, to do otherwise.

(3) Without prejudice to the provisions of the rules relating to 'Notification or Arrival' and 'Flight Plans and Air Traffic Control Clearances'. the commander of an aircraft shall, immediately upon arrival at, or prior to departure from, an aerodrome within the United Kingdom having an air traffic control unit, ensure that such unit is informed of the flight which he has made or which he is about to undertake.

SPECIAL RULES FOR CERTAIN AERODROMES

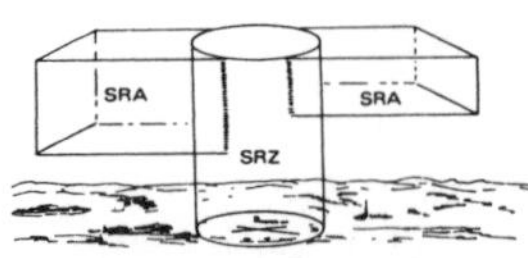

Certain aerodromes within the United Kingdom have air traffic movements of an intensity and type which in the interests of flight safety require protection greater than that afforded by the provision of an aerodrome traffic zone, yet which the requirement for a Control Zone or Terminal Area is not deemed to be necessary.

Such aerodromes are established with a Special Rules Zone usually accompanied with a Special Rules Area. Information on this type of airspace has already been covered on pages 2–9 and 2–10.

The Rules of the Air and Air Traffic Control Regulations and the UK Air Pilot contain a list of aerodromes at which these Special Rules apply. The procedures to use in each case are also detailed in these two documents. It can however be noted here that the following procedures will apply in all cases.

(1) For the purpose of these special rules for certain aerodromes, 'Special VFR Clearance' means a clearance given by the appropriate air traffic control unit to an aircraft for flight within this special airspace. Such clearance will require that the aircraft remains clear of cloud, in sight of the surface and flown in accordance with any special instructions given by that unit.

(2) Unless otherwise authorised by the air traffic control unit at that aerodrome -
- (a) An aircraft shall not, during the notified hours of watch of the air traffic control unit at that aerodrome, fly within the notified airspace unless the commander of the aircraft, before so flying, obtains the permission of the air traffic control unit at the aerodrome and informs the air traffic control unit, on the notified radio frequency appropriate to the circumstances, of the aircraft's position, level and track; and
- (b) While an aircraft is within the notified airspace at any time during the notified hours of watch the commander of the aircraft shall cause a continuous watch to be maintained on that frequency and comply with any instructions which the air traffic control unit at that aerodrome may give in the particular case.

> The Rules of the Air and Air Traffic Control Regulations contain approximately 50 Rules of concern to pilots. This Manual does not define all these Rules in detail but the general contents of these Rules has been covered in this Section.

FLIGHT SAFETY
Extracts from:

CIVIL AVIATION (INVESTIGATION OF ACCIDENTS) REGULATIONS 1989
AIR NAVIGATION (INVESTIGATION OF COMBINED MILITARY AND CIVIL AIR ACCIDENTS) REGULATIONS 1988

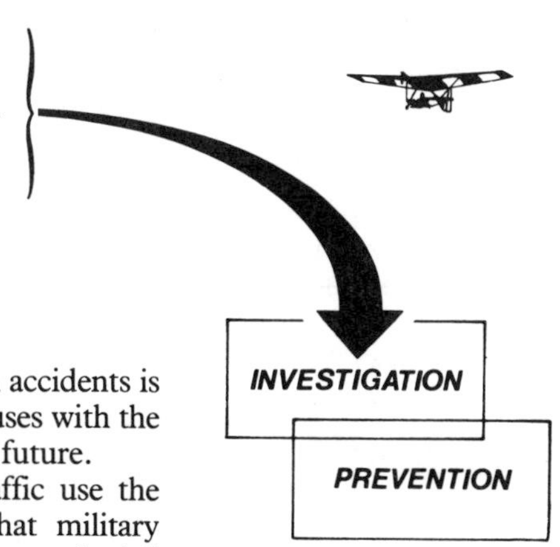

The main purpose of investigating aviation accidents is to determine the circumstances and the causes with the objective of avoiding such accidents in the future.

Because both military and civil air traffic use the national airspace system and the fact that military aircraft may use certain civil aerodromes and civil aircraft are permitted to use certain military aerodromes, a number of investigations may occur where it is necessary to obtain evidence from both civil and military personnel. For this reason a separate statutory document as referred to in the heading of this section has been enacted.

Both the Civil Aviation Investigation of Accidents and the Combined Military and Civil Air Accident Regulations have many common areas and the following regulations apply to both.

NOTIFIABLE ACCIDENTS

An accident shall be notified if, between the time when any person boards an aircraft with the intention of flight and such time as all persons have disembarked from the aircraft:

(a) Any person suffers death or serious injury whilst in or upon the aircraft or by direct contact with the aircraft or anything attached thereto, or
(b) The aircraft receives substantial damage.

Note: Substantial damage includes any damage or structural failure which adversely affects the structural strength, performance or flight characteristics of the aircraft and which would normally require the major repair or replacement of the affected component.

When a notifiable accident occurs it is the duty of the aircraft commander to furnish a report but in the event of the commander being killed or incapacitated this report must be made by the operator of the aircraft.

The report must be communicated to the Department of Trade Accident Investigation Branch by the quickest means available and when the accident occurs within the UK the local police authorities must also be informed.

The report should commence with the identifying abbreviation 'ACCID' and must contain (as far as possible) the following information:

Type, model, nationality and registration marks of the aircraft.
Name of the owner, operator and hirer, if any, of the aircraft.
Name of the commander of the aircraft.
Date and time (Greenwich Mean Time) of the accident.

Last point of departure and the next point of intended landing.
Position of the aircraft with reference to some easily defined geographical point.
Number of persons on board the aircraft at the time of the accident.
Number of those persons killed as a result of the accident.
Number of those persons seriously injured as the result of the accident.
Number of persons killed or seriously injured elsewhere than on the aircraft.
Nature of the accident and brief particulars of the damage to the aircraft as far as is known.

FLIGHT SAFETY INFORMATION

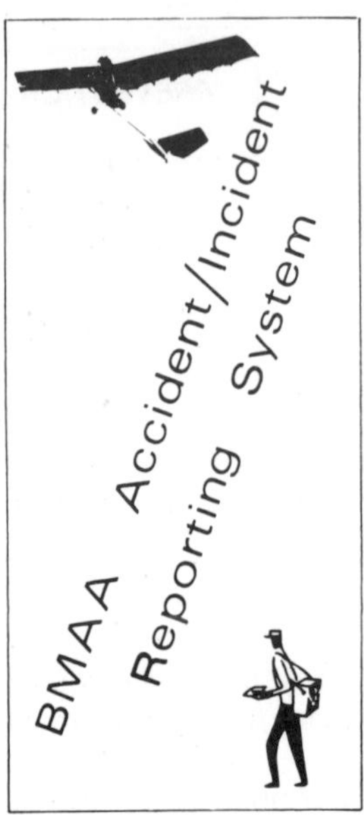

The British Microlight Aircraft Association has a reporting system in which an incident/accident report form is completed and sent to the BMAA Safety Officer. The information on the circumstances of the incident/accident is then recorded and disseminated via the BMAA Magazine so that microlight pilots can obtain this information and as a result will be able to avoid these casual factors in their future flying. The system relies heavily on the responsibility of the pilots involved completing and sending in the forms but the results of this action are naturally of great importance to improving the 'safety factor' in the Microlight Movement.

There are various publications available which contain useful information relating to aircraft accidents and pilots should make every effort to read these in order to obtain an understanding of how aircraft incidents and accidents occur. These various publications are reviewed in summary form below.

FLIGHT SAFETY BULLETIN

This bulletin is issued quarterly by the General Aviation Safety Committee to all owners of UK registered aircraft and to Flying Training Organisations.

It contains useful information relating to the avoidance of accidents and should be read by all student and private pilots.

GENERAL AVIATION SAFETY INFORMATION LEAFLETS

These are issued monthly by the Safety Promotion Section of the CAA.

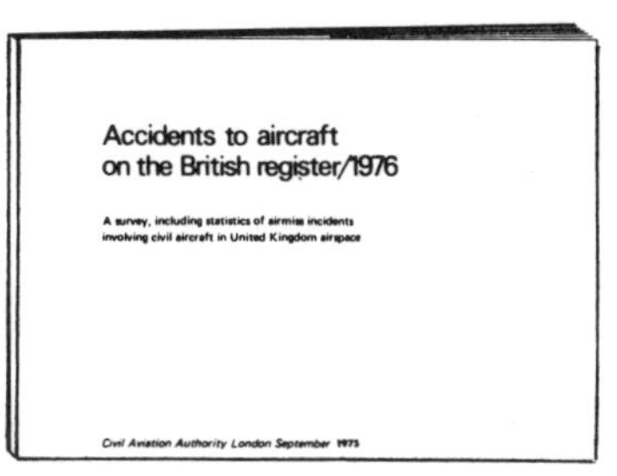

Accidents to aircraft
on the British register/1976

A survey, including statistics of airmiss incidents involving civil aircraft in United Kingdom airspace

Civil Aviation Authority London September 1975

ACCIDENTS TO AIRCRAFT ON THE BRITISH REGISTER (CAA ANNUAL PUBLICATION)

The CAA publishes an annual survey, which includes statistical information together with short briefs on the aircraft accidents which occurred during the particular year.

The information published in this survey is divided into 'classes of aircraft' operation and includes the accidents which occurred to aircraft being used in Club, Group and Training activities.

AIB BULLETINS

The Accident Investigation Branch of the Board of Trade produce a monthly summary of aircraft accidents in the form of specific information concerning the type of aircraft, date and time of accident, type of flight, damage and/or injuries sustained by the occupants. Short summaries of individual accidents are also included.

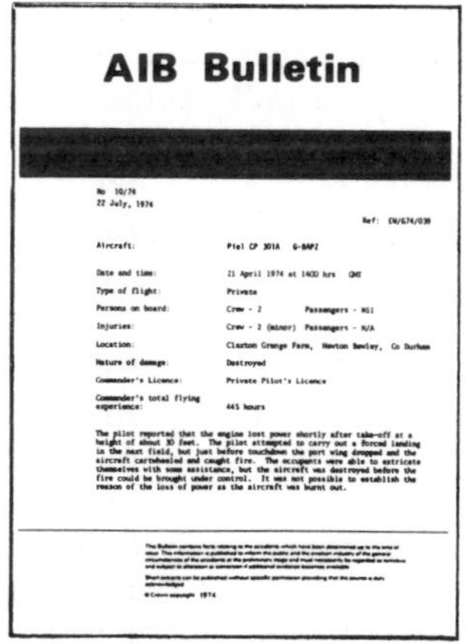

AIB Bulletin

No 10/74
22 July, 1974

Ref: EW/G74/039

Aircraft:	Piel CP 301A G-BAPZ
Date and time:	21 April 1974 at 1400 hrs GMT
Type of flight:	Private
Persons on board:	Crew - 2 Passengers - Nil
Injuries:	Crew - 2 (minor) Passengers - N/A
Location:	Claxton Grange Farm, Newton Bewley, Co Durham
Nature of damage:	Destroyed
Commander's Licence:	Private Pilot's Licence
Commander's total flying experience:	445 hours

The pilot reported that the engine lost power shortly after take-off at a height of about 30 feet. The pilot attempted to carry out a forced landing in the next field, but just before touchdown the port wing dropped and the aircraft cartwheeled and caught fire. The occupants were able to extricate themselves with some assistance, but the aircraft was destroyed before the fire could be brought under control. It was not possible to establish the reason of the loss of power as the aircraft was burnt out.

CIVIL AVIATION AUTHORITY

AERONAUTICAL INFORMATION CIRCULAR
UNITED KINGDOM

Aeronautical Information Service (AIS 1)
Tolcarne Drive, Pinner, Middlesex, HA5 2DU
Phone: 01-866 8781 Ext. 259
Ext. 271 (Distribution)

47/1977
18th April

FLIGHT WITHOUT THE BENEFIT OF RADIO
CODE OF PRACTICE

Pilots who fly an aircraft without radio, or who operate in a mixed radio/non-radio environment, can encounter difficult or dangerous situations unless a range of fundamental good airmanship practices are borne in mind.

2. The Civil Aviation Authority, the National Air Traffic Services, and the General Aviation Safety Committee have recently co-operated to produce a Code of Practice. All pilots flying outside Controlled or Special Rules Airspace are strongly urged to comply with this Code, particularly in situations where either the aircraft is not equipped with radio, or there is no radio at the local or destination airfield. The Code of Practice-which is reproduced at Appendix A - does not supersede the requirements of the air navigation legislation, nor the practices taught from a CAA approved syllabus; its aim is to highlight aspects of good airmanship and certain associated legal requirements. A list of some of the more important of the relevant provisions in the legislation is attached at Appendix B. A thorough knowledge of the Rules and the Code of Practice should help enhance the safety of aircraft operations.

Pink Aeronautical Information Circulars

The Aeronautical Information Service distributes aviation circulars covering many aspects of aircrew licensing and aircraft operations. The circulars which directly concern matters relating to aviation safety are coloured pink.

These circulars are available to all pilots and are obtainable from **AIS, Tolcarne Drive, Pinner, Middlesex, HA5 2DU**

Summary

If pilots are to conduct safe and efficient flight operations, they must be made aware of all the factors which affect flight safety. Such factors range from those which concern the physical and psychological aspects of flying, the mechanical aspects of the aircraft and the environment in which both aircraft and pilots operate.

Only by keeping himself up to date in these three areas can a pilot expect to function safely and efficiently. It is therefore the responsibility of all aircrew to read and absorb the various facts concerning how accidents have occurred as well as following the advice given in the relevant publications.

The CAA has implemented a mandatory incident reporting system to ensure widespread dissemination of information which could be of value to pilots. The occasions when such reports should be made, together with the appropriate forms, can be obtained from most Flying Training Organisations.

In addition to the mandatory incident reporting system, each issue of the GASC Flight Safety Bulletin contains an Aircraft Occurrence Report Form and should a pilot experience an occurrence which in his opinion adversely affects flight safety he should complete and post this form to the General Aviation Safety Committee. This action will ensure that the information is received by those whose primary interest is to protect the safety of all aircraft and those who fly in them.

Pilots, Owners and Operators will find it useful to know where to report various events; if the appropriate form is not available, the following table shows the addresses (at the time this Manual was printed) against the Accident or type of Incident, details should be sent by letter.

Accidents	By the quickest means available to Accidents Investigation Branch, Kingsgate House, 66-74 Victoria Street, London SW1E 6JS (Phone: 01 212 5852, Telex: 811074 AFTN EGGCYL) and forthwith in the UK to the local police authority.
Airmisses	Immediate radio reports to ATS Unit with which the pilot is in communication, or if this is not possible by phone or other means to any UK ATS unit but preferably to an ATCC.
UK Airspace	Form CA1094 to Joint Airmiss Section, Hillingdon House, Uxbridge, Middlesex UB10 0RU
Foreign Airspace	Form CA1094 to relevant Foreign Authority with a copy to CAA Safety Data & Analysis Unit, Brabazon House, Redhill, Surrey RH1 1SQ

(See UK Air Pilot 3-1-8 Section 7 and AIC 92/1978—Airmiss Reporting).

Reportable Occurrences (including human factors, engineering, flight handling & ATC incidents in UK airspace) should be made on Form CA1673 to CAA Safety Data & Anaylsis Unit, Brabazon House, Redhill, Surrey RH1 1SQ.

ATC Incidents (Foreign Airspace)should be made on Form CA1673 to relevant Foreign Authority with a copy to CAA Safety Date & Analysis Unit, Brabazon House, Redhill, Surrey RH1 1SQ.

Wake Turbulence reports should be made to Civil Aviation Authority, TRD3, CAA House, 43-59 Kingsway, London WC2B 6TE.

SECTION THREE

PILOT NAVIGATION

PILOT NAVIGATION

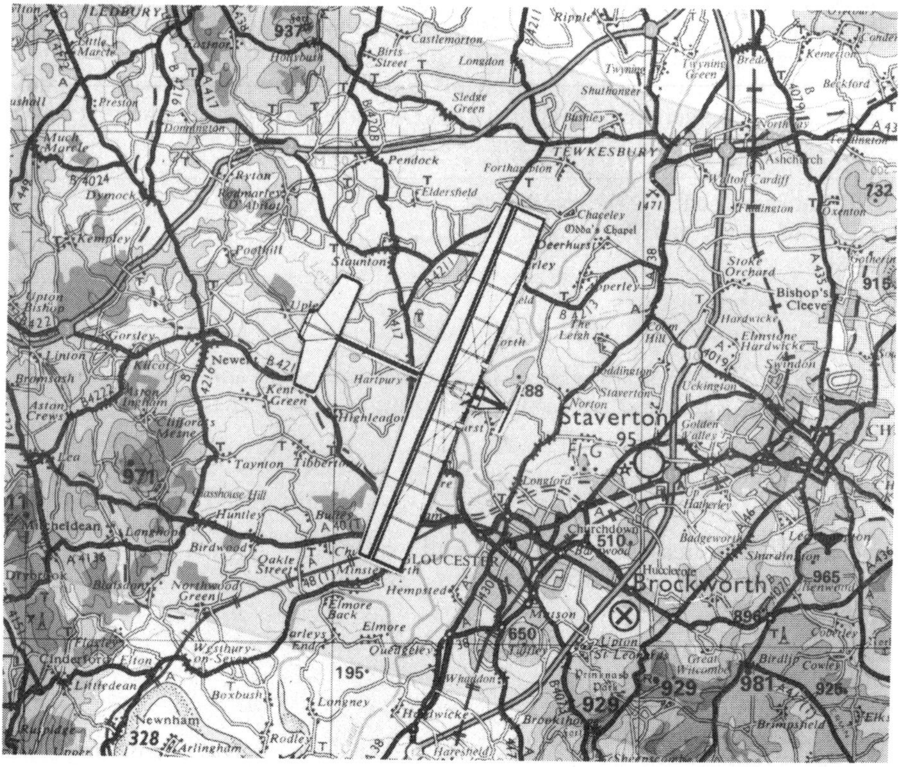

INTRODUCTION

In its widest interpretation Air Navigation can involve complicated mathematical procedures and the use of highly sophisticated technological aids to assist aircraft crews to move over the surface of the earth with great accuracy in varying weather conditions with a high degree of safety. This manual however is solely concerned with the knowledge and methods of navigation which, over the years, have been developed to enable a pilot to navigate with safety whilst, at the same time, coping with all the other facets of flying single handed. It is for this reason known as Pilot Navigation.

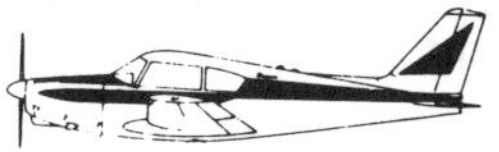

Although a microlight is a very basic aircraft when compared with the more conventional 2 to 4 seat fixed wing aircraft used in the Private Flying Sector, the pilot of a microlight will have to face up to many of the problems experienced

by pilots of larger and faster aircraft whilst at the same time lacking the various sophisticated aids and personal comforts. Therefore when studying the information given on the following pages you will need to keep in mind that the objective in all navigation is to get from one place to another with safety regardless of the type of aircraft you are flying. This requires you to develop a reasonably good understanding of basic navigation principles and there are no short cuts to achieve this. Your learning task will therefore involve an understanding of the following items:

1. How wind effects the path and speed of an aircraft flying over the earth's surface.

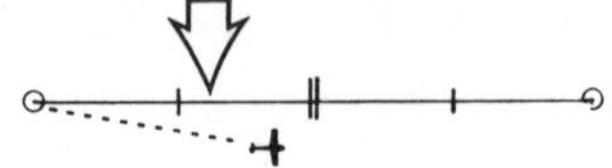

2. A knowledge of the magnetic compass and how to measure a required track on an aeronautical map or chart.

3. How to measure distances and calculate groundspeeds in order to arrive at the time a particular flight will take.

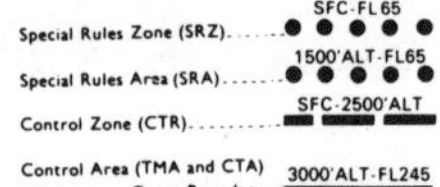

4. Map reading and interpreting the overprinted aeronautical information relating to Controlled and regulated Airspace, Danger Areas etc.

5. How to calculate fuel consumption and how wind will effect the amount of fuel used on any particular flight.

6. Weather knowledge and the likely conditions to be met with on any particular flight.

7. What to do when uncertain of your position or when lost.

Pilot Navigation is not dependent upon extreme accuracy, and most of it may be described as 'rule of thumb', it does however rely to a great extent upon the elimination of errors at the ground planning stage and therefore careful pre-flight planning will be an essential part of safe navigation. Some of the material which follows may appear to have little relevance to microlight flying as it is currently practised, but bearing in mind the need to have a good grasp of navigation principles and the fact that a microlight pilot will have to pass the standard navigation examination applicable to all Private Pilots it will be seen that an understanding of the following material will be essential.

MAPS AND CHARTS

Before dealing with the types of maps and charts used in air navigation it would be of benefit to refresh your memory on a few essential points relating to the method of how the position of places on the earth's surface is determined.

Apart from the use of geographic and cultural features, the basic method used is to superimpose imaginary lines over the surface of the earth and then duplicate these lines on maps and charts. These lines are then used for reference purposes in navigation. A pilot needs to know this method as it will assist him to understand what he is measuring in terms of angles and distances.

Meridians of Longitude and Parallels of Latitude

The basic method mentioned above of constructing imaginary lines over the Earth's surface is conducted in such a manner that they represent a graticule. The graticule lines run from North to South and East to West and are known as Meridians of Longitude and Parallels of Latitude. Fig 3-1 shows the disposition of these lines.

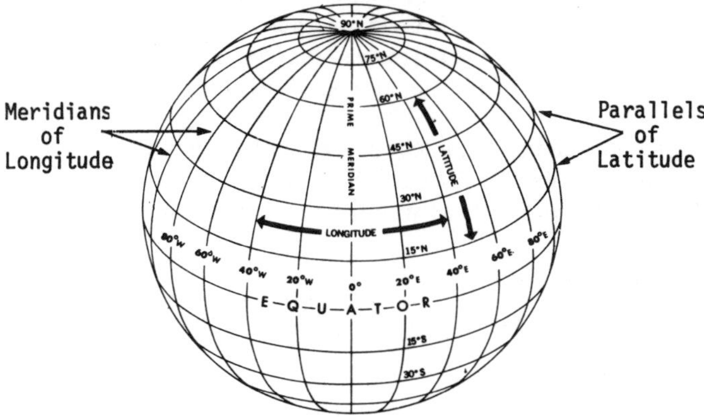

Fig. 3—1

Meridians of Longitude are circles passing through the North and South Poles and whose common centre is the Earth's centre. One of these meridians is given the value of 0/180° and this is used as a datum against which longitude is measured numerically, as an angle to this line.

By convention a circle is divided into 360 degrees, and therefore longitude is measured up to 180 degrees West and 180 degrees East from the 0 Meridian of Longitude which is called the Prime Meridian. By international agreement the Prime Meridian is established so that it passes through the Greenwich Observatory in London.

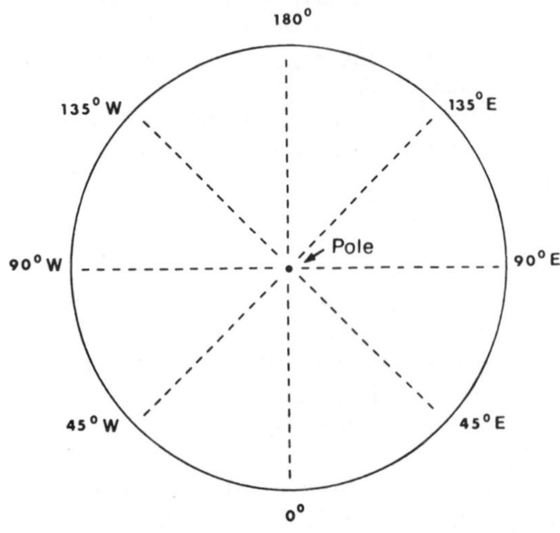

Fig. 3–2

Parallels of Latitude are imaginary circles whose planes lie parallel to the Equator which is used as a datum from which their numerical values are measured. Parallels of Latitude can be visualized as lines encircling the Earth which are numbered from 0 degrees at the Equator to 90 degrees at the North and South Poles.

A Parallel of Latitude in the Northern Hemisphere would be identified by its number in degrees followed by the letter N, i.e. 30° N. In the Southern Hemisphere the equivalent Parallel of Latitude would be identified as 30° S.

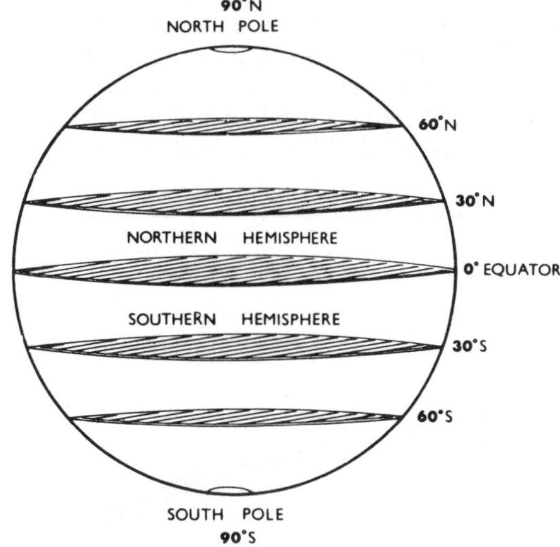

Fig. 3–3

The areas covered by each degree of latitude and longitude are divided into 60 equal angular segments which are called minutes, and these in turn are also divided into 60 equal angular segments called seconds. This allows very accúrate position to be plotted on the geographical grid covering the surface.

Each minute of latitude is on average 6080 feet long or one nautical mile at the earths surface, so that the 10 degree parallel either North or South will be 600 nautical miles from the equator (or 691 statute miles). From this it can be appreciated that distance in nautical miles can be measured on a chart along the latitude scale. Fig 3-4 shows an example of this and it can be seen that the distance from the equator to 40 degrees south is 2400 nm.

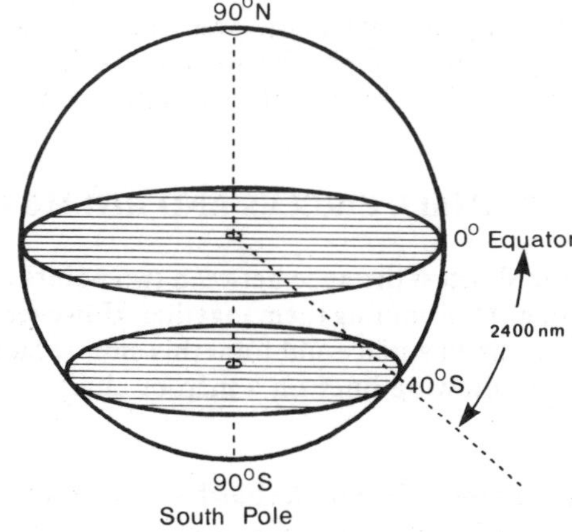

Fig. 3–4

Fig 3-5 shows an illustration of how a point on the earths surface can be identified by using the graticule formed by meridians of longitude and parallels of latitude. As the graticule is depicted on the earths surface the lines are curved, but when plotting the same position on a map or chart the lines forming the graticule will of course be straight, since the chart will be flat. In the example shown the position at 'A' is located 52° 23' North of the Equator and 0° 37' West of the Prime Meridian.

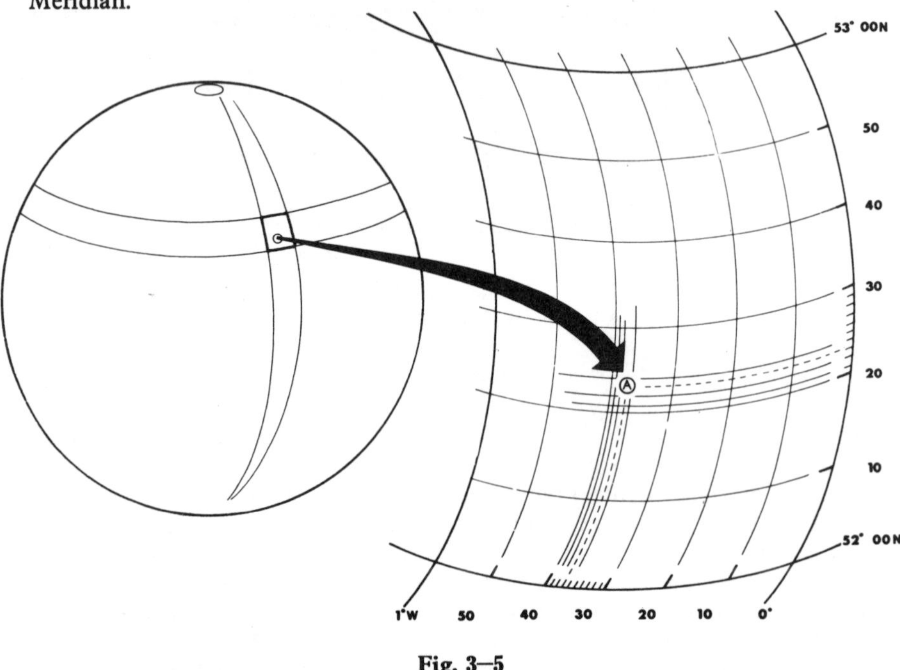

Fig. 3—5

Geographical co-ordinates are normally used during pre-flight planning as they permit greater accuracy in navigation preparation, however when using pilot navigation techniques during flight the aircraft position is usually estimated by a bearing and distance from a known place or landmark.

GREAT CIRCLES, SMALL CIRCLES AND RHUMB LINES

The measure of the shortest distance between two points on the Earth's surface is the length of a straight line joining them together. However it is impossible to draw a straight line on a curved surface and from this simple fact three definitions arise which are related to drawing lines on a map or chart.

1. Great Circle:
This is a circle superimposed upon the Earth's surface whose centre and radius are those of the Earth itself. The plane of a great circle therefore passes through the centre of the Earth, cutting it into two equal parts.

It follows therefore, that all Meridians of Longitude are semi great circles. Fig 3-6 shows several illustrations of great circles.

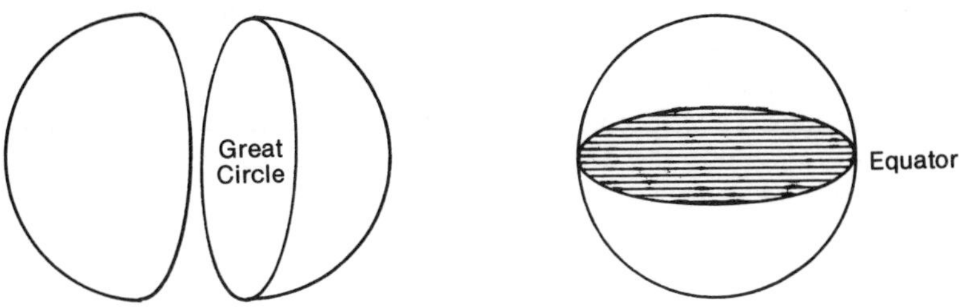

The Equator is also a Great Circle.

Fig. 3—6

Only one great circle can be drawn through two places which are not diametrically opposed to one another. The shortest arc of a great circle which joins two places together is called the great circle distance.

2. Small Circle:

Any circular line superimposed on the Earth's surface whose centre and radius are not those of the Earth is known as a small circle.

The plane of a small circle will not pass through the centre of the Earth, therefore it follows that with the exception of the Equator all Parallels of Latitude are small circles.

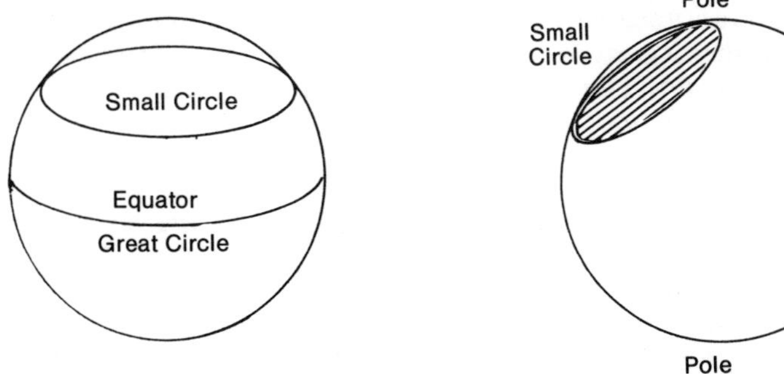

Fig. 3—7 **Fig. 3-8**

3. Rhumb Line:

Any line which crosses all Meridians at a constant angle is known as a rhumb line.

A rhumb line will appear as a curved line on the surface of a sphere as shown in fig 3-9.

A rhumb line represents the path an aircraft will follow when its heading is maintained through the use of a compass. The Meridians of Longitude and the Parallel of Latitude at the Equator are the only lines which are both great circles and rhumb lines. Therefore if two places are not on the Equator or on the same Meridian of Longitude the distance along a rhumb line will not be the shortest distance between them.

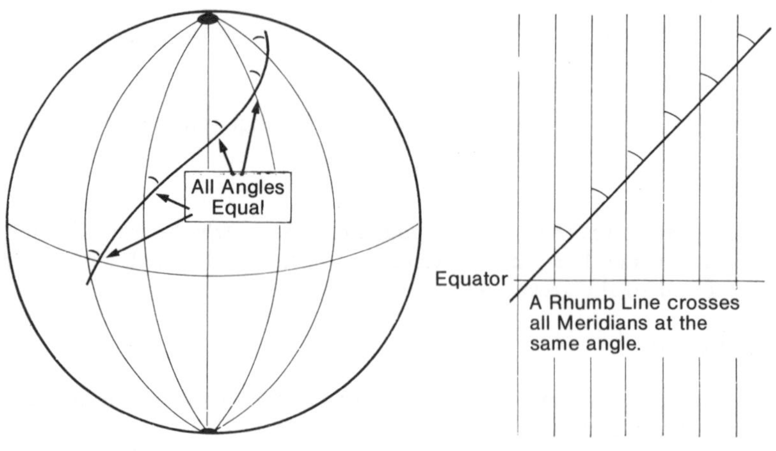
All Angles Equal
Equator
A Rhumb Line crosses all Meridians at the same angle.

Fig. 3—9

But because map design generally arranges for direction to remain constant along rhumb lines, they are easier to fly and are often more convenient and practical to use than a great circle along which direction will continuously change. In pilot navigation it will be rhumb lines that we shall normally use on our maps and charts.

Further to this and under certain conditions the difference between great circle tracks and rhumb line tracks is fairly small, these conditions are as follows:

1. Over short distances a rhumb line track and a great circle track almost coincide.
2. A rhumb line track between two points on the same Meridian will be coincident with a great circle track.
3. The lower the latitude i.e. the nearer the Equator, the more closely a rhumb line approximates a great circle and even in the latitudes of the United Kingdom a rhumb line distance from the East coast to the West coast will only be greater by some 2 to 3 miles at the halfway point.
4. The most common maps used in pilot navigation are the 1:500,000 and 1:250,000 topographical charts and provided the track direction is measured approximately half way along the track line the error is reduced to negligible proportions for practical navigation.

MAPPING OF THE EARTH'S SURFACE

The primary tool used for visual navigation is a suitable map or chart of the Earth's surface. It should however be appreciated that the difference between the definitive terms 'map' and 'chart' lies mainly in that charts were originally designed to show sea areas and maps were used to portray land areas of the Earth's surface. Therefore to the pilot maps and charts really represent the same thing, something by which he can visually navigate his aircraft whether looking for information relating to coastlines, lightships or sea areas or attempting to identify towns, forests or similar topographical features.

Maps, or charts are designed to portray parts of the Earth's surface upon a flat sheet. The manner in which the graticule made up of the lines of latitude and longitude is presented, and the accuracy of the overprinted information in the form of geographic and cultural features will depend upon the purpose for which the map is intended.

However it must be appreciated that it is not possible to accurately portray the surface of a sphere upon a flat sheet of paper. One has only to visualize the effect of attempting to flatten a segment of orange peel to realise it cannot be done without wrinkling, distortion or tearing.

Although it is impossible to make a flat chart of any part of the Earth's surface without suffering some distortion it is nevertheless possible to minimise those errors which are most detrimental to the integrity of any type of chart, in other words the chart-maker has a choice as regards which qualities of the Earth's spherical surface he wishes to depict most accurately.

The cartographer, therefore has to decide which properties of the chart will be the most important for its purpose. For example, although he can arrange to depict the exact shape of a wood or lake this may prevent angles or distances from being measured accurately, and as a result the map or chart would be unsuitable for navigational purposes.

Apart from the more obvious requirement of clarity in presentation of information, some of the important properties a pilot would like to have accurately portrayed on a map, or chart used for pilot navigation are shown below:

***Conformality or Orthomorphism**
Angles on the chart should be accurately presented in relation to those on the Earth's surface.

Scale
The distance on the chart between one place and all other places should bear a constance ratio to the true distance on the Earth.

Equivalence
The presentation of area on the chart should be in correct proportion to that on the Earth.

*Either of these words are commonly used to express 'correct angular representation'.

Great Circle
Because the shortest distance between two places on the Earth's surface is along a great circle it would be convenient to have great circles appearing as straight lines.

Rhumb Line
This will be the path followed by an aircraft in flight when maintaining a heading measured against a True North datum, therefore it would be convenient if this also appear as a straight line on the chart.

In view of the previous statements concerning the presentation of a spherical surface on a flat sheet it is clear that a pilot will have to accept certain compromises between these various ideals. It would therefore be of value to evaluate their importance to one another and to examine the need to construct a suitable chart which will be of practical value to the pilot.

This can be done by examining each requirement in turn as follows:

Conformality:

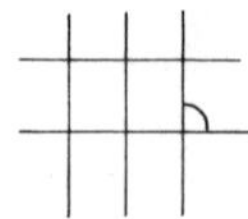

Accurate navigation cannot be achieved if bearings or angles are not correctly presented on the chart, so this property is an absolute requirement.

Scale

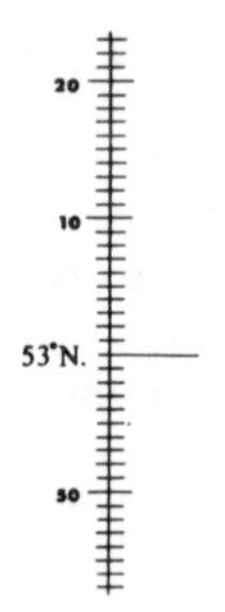

Correct scale is impossible to achieve, due to the inevitable distortion which will occur when presenting the Earth's surface on a flat sheet. The problem of scale revolves around how much variation can be considered as acceptable without the chart losing its practical value. There are two basic methods of handling this problem, one, is to provide the chart with a scale line measurement overprinted on the sheet or along the edges so that the pilot can measure distance on the chart against the adjacent section of the scale line, or two, arrange for the scale to be substantially constant by using a particular chart construction suitable for this purpose.

Equivalence

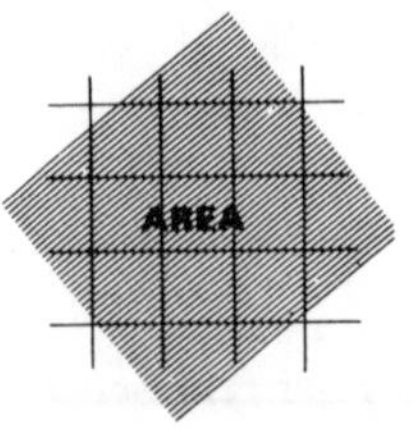

The presentation of correct area is possible but in achieving this, the requirement of conformality cannot also be obtained. Therefore small errors in the presentation of area have to be accepted. Provided these errors are small the practical value of the chart for map reading purposes during flight will be satisfactory.

Great Circles

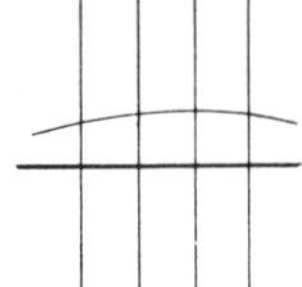

Although the ability to follow a great circle track will keep the distance travelled to a minimum, the actual distance saved will depend upon the total distance to be travelled. The distance travelled by most light aircraft on any one flight is relatively small. Therefore the facility of being able to measure a great circle track in one operation and hold one heading when airborne to maintain it, is more a matter of convenience to pilot navigation rather than an essential requirement. It need therefore only be retained on a chart used for pilot navigation if it did not interfere with other more important requirements.

Rhumb Lines

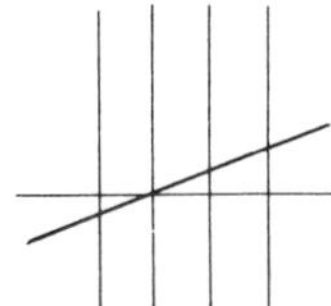

These are the easiest routes to follow because the datum used in air navigation is True North. Nevertheless the facility of having rhumb lines presented as straight lines is not essential and can therefore be subordinate to, for example, Conformality.

To sum up, the most important property an aeronautical chart should have is the portrayal of accurate angles and bearings and whilst the other factors mentioned above are also important some degree of inaccuracy in their presentation can be accepted.

The most widely used maps for pilot navigation are the:
1:500,000 scale topographical chart based upon a projection known as Lambert Conformal.
1:250,000 scale topographical chart based upon a projection known as the Transverse Mercator.

Lambert Conformal Chart

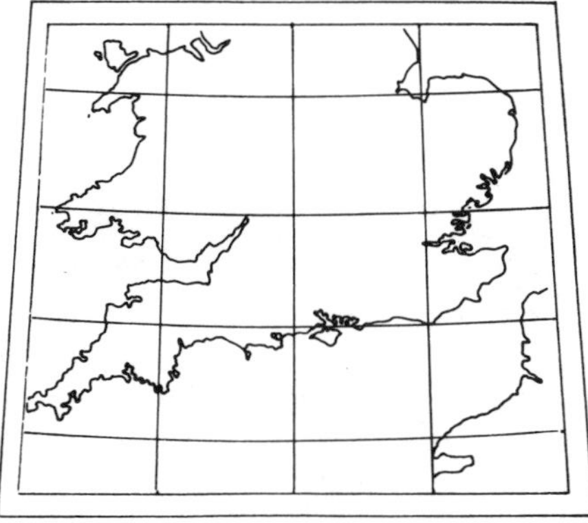

Fig. 3—10

On this chart the meridians of longitude appear as straight lines converging towards the nearer pole and the parallels of latitude are presented as concentric circles centred on the nearer pole. It is not intended to cover the mathematics of map construction in this Manual but it can be simply stated that the results achieved in the Lambert Conformal Conic projection produce a great circle which for all practical purposes is a straight line, (Ref fig 3-10).

Other properties of a Lambert Conformal chart are:

Conformality

The chart is made conformal by mathematical construction and therefore all angles and bearings are accurately portrayed.

Scale

Although scale varies slightly, contracting inside the Standard Parallels and expanding outside them, the scale over the whole chart can be taken for all practical purposes as constant.

Equivalence

The chart can be regarded as having the property of equal area. Therefore the shapes of woods, lakes etc., will appear the same as those on the Earth's surface.

Great Circles

These can be considered to be straight lines on the chart

Rhumb Lines

With the exception of the meridians, rhumb lines will appear as curved lines concave towards the nearer pole.

Transverse Mercator Chart

On this chart the meridians of longitude converge towards the top of the chart whilst the parallels of latitude are depicted as curved lines which are convex to the equator, refer to fig 3-11.

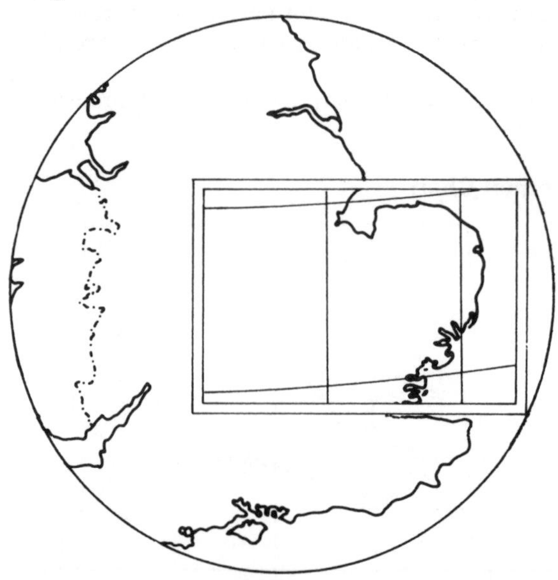

Fig. 3—11

Other properties of the Transverse Mercator are:

Conformality
The chart is made conformal by mathematical construction and therefore all angles and bearings are accurately portrayed.
Scale
The scale is correct at the central meridian which is used as the datum. Either side of this it expands, however due to the relatively small area covered on individual charts in this series the extent of the expansion is quite small.
Equivalence
Area becomes distorted either side of the datum meridian.
Great Circle
Although over large distances great circles become complex curves, the use of a Transverse Mercator projection for topographical charts is confined to fairly small areas over which great circles can be considered as straight lines.
Rhumb Lines
These can generally be considered as curved lines which are concave to the nearer pole.

The Transverse Mercator projection is used for topographical charts generally covering small areas. It is also used to produce strip charts for use along selected routes. Many Ordnance Survey maps are based upon this projection.

Magnetic Variation
The maps and charts used in pilot navigation use True North as a reference datum. However an aircraft heading is selected and maintained by reference to a magnetic compass which uses Magnetic North as its datum. Because of this a pilot must understand the basic principles of a magnetic compass and how to calculate the difference between True and Magnetic headings. This difference is known as 'Magnetic Variation'.

The surface of the Earth is covered by a weak magnetic field which culminates at two Magnetic Poles which are situated near the North and South Geographic (True) Poles. This terrestrial magnetism is irregular in both direction and strength, the amount experienced at any one place depending upon its geographical position in relation to the Magnetic Pole, and the influence of local magnetic disturbances set up by geological conditions.

Information obtained from world wide geological surveys is produced in chart form and shows the lines of equal magnetic variation and their value in relation to latitude and longitude. These lines, known as 'Isogonals', are overprinted on pilot navigation maps to show the pilot the amount of variation he has to allow for when calculating headings from True to Magnetic.

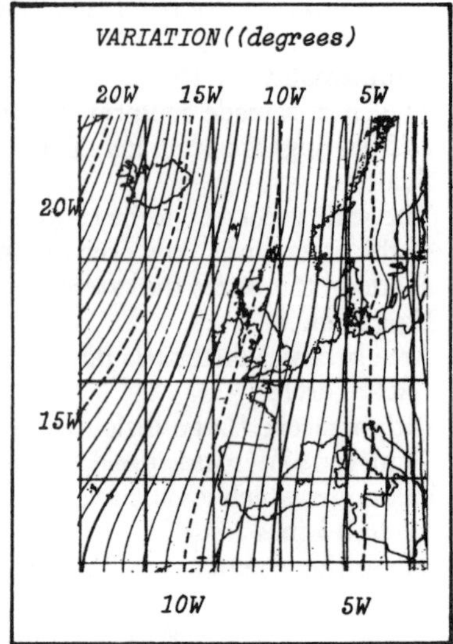

Fig. 3—12

Although the amount of variation at a given place on the Earth's surface will vary, the change is relatively small (at the present time over the UK it averages about .1 of a degree annually) and an aeronautical chart will become obsolete for many other reasons long before significant changes in variation occur.

Variation can be defined as being the angular difference between the direction taken up by an aircraft compass needle (when influenced only by terrestial magnetism) and the direction of True North.

It is said to be Easterly variation if the Magnetic North Lies to the East of True North and Westerly variation if the Magnetic North lies to the West of True North.

Depending upon the aircraft position in relation to the True Pole the variation at that place will therefore be westerly or easterly. On those occasions when the aircraft position is in line with both the True and Magnetic Poles the variation will be zero. Lines of zero variation are known as 'Agonic Lines'. Fig 3-13 illustrates how variation changes in relation to the position of the aircraft.

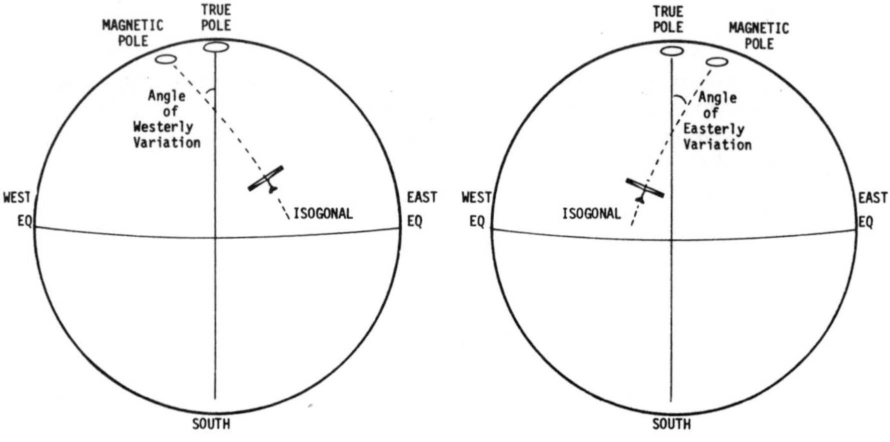

Fig. 3—13

The path followed by an aircraft over the surface is called its track, and because the track to be flown is measured on charts which use True North as a datum for angular measurement the true direction must be converted into a magnetic direction for the purpose of flight.

This conversion is made by adding or subtracting the value of the variation as notified in the geographical areas of the track to be flown. This heading is then known as the 'Magnetic Heading'.

When there are only a few degrees between the values of the isogonals in the vicinity of the intended track a mean variation can be used for pilot navigation purposes, however if the route length covers several hundred miles it will be advisable to calculate a mean variation value for different segments of the route.

Application of Variation

Fig 3-14 shows two planned navigation legs in relation to lines of magnetic variation. To determine the magnetic track it will be necessary to measure the track true and then apply the value of the mean variation. Westerly variation is added to the true track to arrive at the magnetic track and Easterly variation is subtracted.

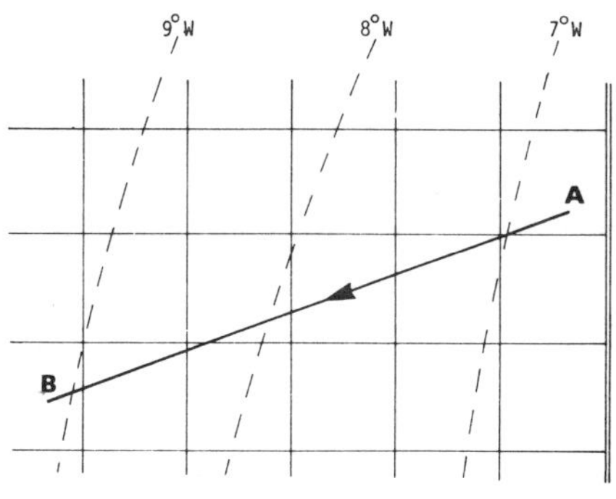

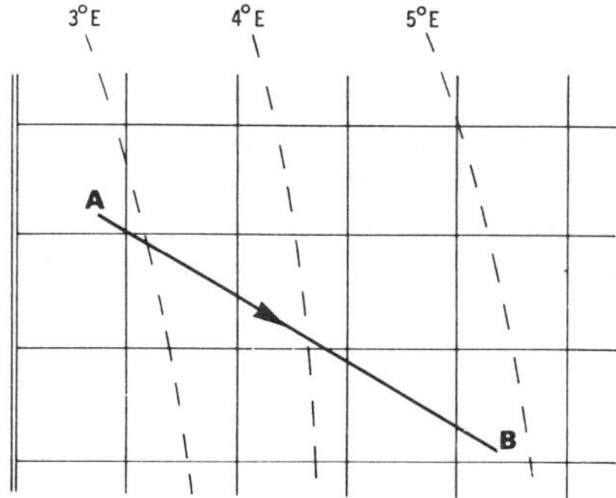

Fig 3-14

Track to be flown = 250° True (T)
Mean variation en-route = 8° W
250° + 8° = 258°
Magnetic Track = 258°

Track to be flown = 120° True (T)
Mean variation en-route = 4° E
120° - 4° = 116°
Magnetic Track = 116°

Therefore when variation is Westerly the magnetic track will be more than the true track and when the variation is Easterly it will be less. This leads to a simple aide memoire which can be used to apply the value of variation:

VARIATION WEST – MAGNETIC BEST

VARIATION EAST – MAGNETIC LEAST

Note: When calculations are made which involve establising True Track from Magnetic Track the value of variation must be reversed.

Compass Deviation

Important Note:
The installation of a magnetic compass is not a universal feature of all microlights, but it should be appreciated that any form of proper navigation will require the use of a compass. Therefore you are strongly advised not to attempt any serious navigation away from the area of your take-off and landing site unless you have one fitted and know how to use it.

Due to local magnetic influences within the aircraft e.g. electrical circuits, magnetized metal components etc., an inherent error known as 'Compass Deviation' will exist in any magnetic compass installed in an aeroplane.

This error will vary between aircraft and will also vary when a particular aircraft is on different headings, and where different items of electrical equipment are in operation.

Therefore the direction taken up by a compass needle in an aircraft will not only be influenced by the Earth's magnetic field but also by the magnetic forces existing within the aircraft. Fig 3-15 shows an example of how one local magnetic field, in this case the aircraft engine, can affect the compass needle.

In the case of Example 1 the particular magnetic field selected is in line with the compass needle and magnetic north, and this field would therefore have no influence on the normal direction taken up by the compass needle.

In the case of Example 2 the aircraft is on a different heading, and it can be seen that this localised magnetic field is no longer in line with the compass needle and magnetic north, therefore it will tend to pull the compass needle away from its natural direction, i.e. a deviation will occur.

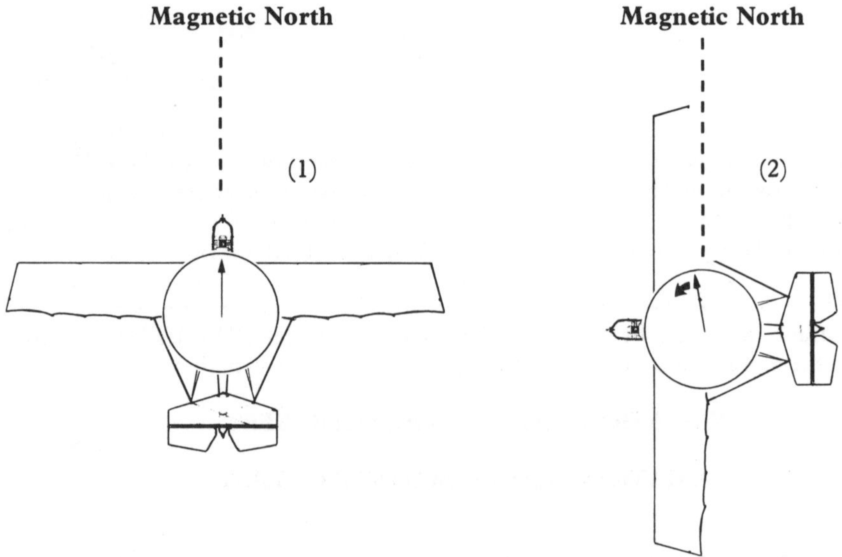

Fig. 3—15

In other words, when there is deviation present, if an aircraft were heading directly towards magnetic north, the compass needle would not be indicating this, and the amount by which the compass needle is in error would be the value of the deviation.

The amount of deviation present is measured by 'Swinging the Compass' which is a procedure carried out on the ground at periodic intervals. This procedure will involve checking the aircraft compass against a hand held compass which is positioned away from the aircraft and other magnetic disturbances.

Although deviation values are unlikely to be recorded for microlight aircraft the following information will be necessary for the Private Pilot written examination.

On conventional aircraft the residual errors are shown at 30° intervals on a compass deviation card (see fig 3-16) fitted adjacent to the aircraft compass or other convenient position in the cockpit.

For Magnetic	N	030	060	E	120	150	S	210
Steer Compass	0	027	058	091	122	148	180	207

Fig. 3—16

Deviation may therefore be defined as the angular difference between Magnetic North and Compass North. It is termed Easterly if compass north is to the East of magnetic north and Westerly if the compass north lies to the West of magnetic north.

Application of Deviation

After applying the value of variation and obtaining the Magnetic Heading to steer to make good a particular track over the ground it will then be necessary to apply the appropriate deviation value to this figure in order to find the Compass Heading.

Assuming the required Magnetic Heading is 030 degrees and using the deviation card shown at fig 3-16 it will be seen that the Compass Heading to steer will be 027°. When applying the value of deviation to a Magnetic Heading to obtain a Compass Heading, Westerly deviation has a plus sign and Easterly a minus, for example:

MAGNETIC HEADING	DEVIATION	COMPASS HEADING
210°	3°W	213°
150°	1°E	149°

Fig. 3—17

Note: When calculating a Magnetic Heading from a given Compass Heading the signs for deviation should be reversed.

TYPES OF TOPOGRAPHICAL CHARTS

The range of topographical charts available for Pilot Navigation is as follows:
ICAO World Aeronautical Chart Series - (1:1000.000)
Individually these charts cover very large areas and are particularly useful for flight planning purposes when long routes are planned.
Practical Use:

Although they can be used for pilot navigation they suffer one disadvantage, in that, because of their small scale a large amount of cultural, geographical, and overprinted aeronautical information appears very close together. This can often be difficult to interpret during flight and would be unsuitable for navigating in microlight aircraft.

ICAO Aeronautical Chart - (1:500.000)
This series covers the whole of the UK on four separate sheets.
Practical Use:
They are based upon Lambert's Conformal Conic Projection and are most suitable for pilot navigation techniques as the scale used permits clarity and definition of cultural and geographic features.

Danger and other similar areas are clearly shown, and easily identified. However the overprinted information depicting such items as Controlled Airspace in the form of Control Zones and Control Areas, does become congested in certain areas of the UK, e.g. the London area.

These charts are most commonly used in aircraft which have cruising speeds of approximately 100 knots or more. In the case of microlight aircraft with much lower speeds a pilot may find it more suitable to use the 1:250,000 topographical series.

Topographical Air Charts (1:250,000)
This series is based on a modified version of the 1:250.000 Ordnance Survey, constructed on a Transverse Mercator Projection.
Practical Use:
Due to the larger scale this series shows considerably more surface detail than is normally required for pilot navigation in aircraft which travel at speeds of over 100 knots. However they are admirably suited for slow moving aircraft such as gliders and microlights. Nevertheless they do have a basic disadvantage in that aeronautical information relating to Controlled Airspace whose lower limit is above 3000' amsl is not shown, so care must be used to ascertain this type of information before flight when altitudes above 3000' amsl are intended to be flown.

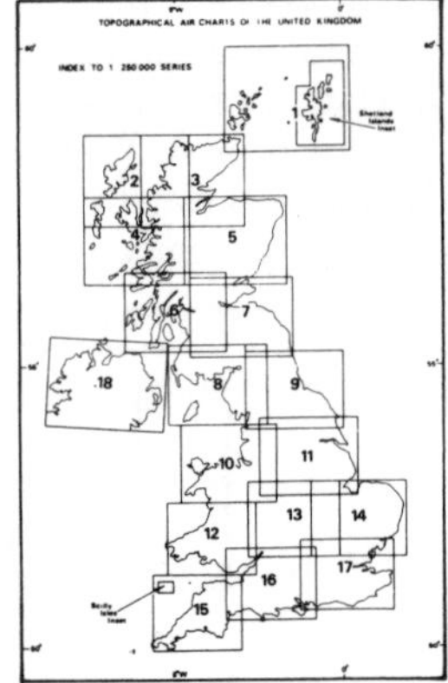

MAP REFERENCE INFORMATION

The series of topographical charts available for aeronautical purposes portray a considerable amount of reference information designed to assist the pilot navigator. This information includes identification codes for individual sheet numbers, the position of isogonals, topographical information relating to natural geographic and hydrographic features, and symbolic presentations of cultural features, e.g. aerodromes, towns, railways, roads etc.

In addition to the above information a large amount of overprinted detail concerning areas of airspace such as TMA's, Control Zones, Airways, Special Rules Airspace, Danger and Prohibited Areas, etc is shown in order to assist the pilot during his pre-flight planning procedures and in-flight navigation.

Chart Sheet Codes

The UK Air Pilot (MAP) section lists the types of charts available for use in the UK and also other countries. This list includes the identification codes of the particular types of charts.

For example the 1:500.000 series topographical chart which covers the southern part of the UK up to 53° N is identified as 2171CD.
This is illustrated in fig 3-18

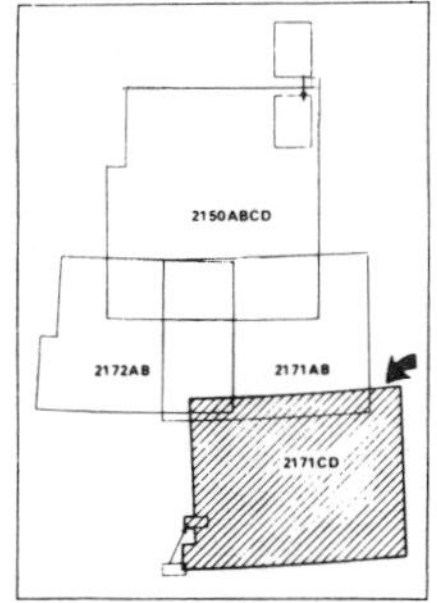

Fig 3—18

The 1:250.000 series charts are identified by a series and sheet number as shown in fig 3-19

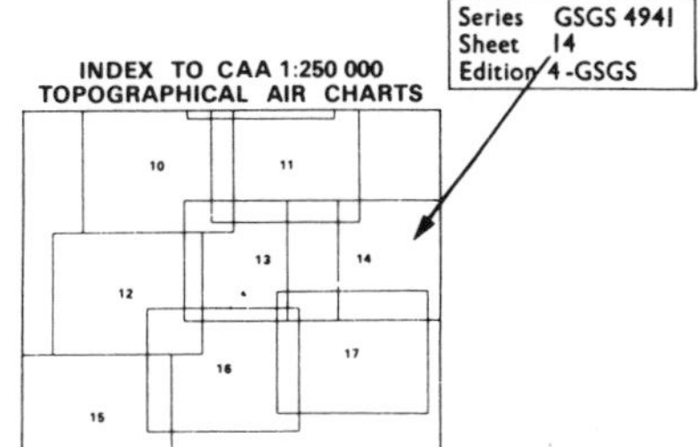

Fig. 3—19

Latitude and Longitude

This is shown by a graticule. The degrees and minutes of latitude and longitude are numbered along the outer edges of the charts and in other suitable locations. In the 1:500.000 series it is the basic graticule, but in the latest 1:250.000 series the basic graticule is the national grid, with latitude and longitude depicted in a secondary sense.

Fig 3-20 shows a graticule with the divisions in degrees and minutes. There are 60 minutes to each degree and the measurement of a position in terms of latitude and longitude is a straightforward task.

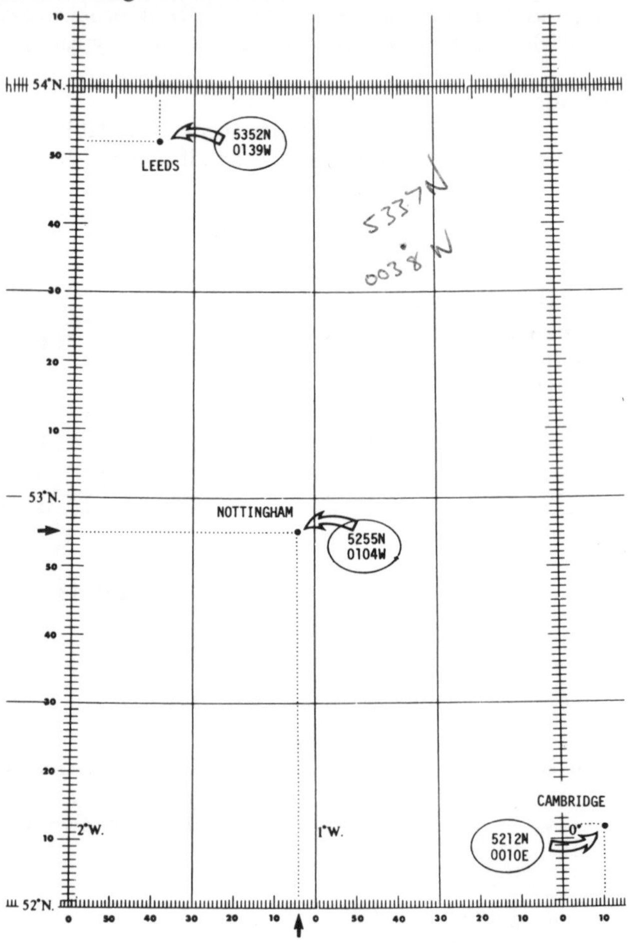

Fig 3-20

The above illustration shows the position of three airfields, Cambridge, Leeds and Nottingham, by simple measurement it can be seen that the locations of these airfields in terms of latitude and longitude are as follows:

Cambridge..	52°	12'N..	00°	10'	E
Leeds..	53°	52'N..	01°	39'	W
Nottingham..	52°	55'N..	01°	04'	W

Isogonals

Lines of equal variation (Isogonals) are shown on aeronautical charts by a dashed line. Because the amount of variation at any place gradually changes it is computed annually for chart presentation and the actual amount of variation and its year of validity is displayed adjacent to the appropriate isogonal.

Additionally, the mean annual change for the area covered by the chart will be displayed in the chart margin. Fig 3-21 shows how isogonals are presented.

Isogonals run from the top to the bottom (normally diagonally) of the chart and the amount of variation and the year for which it is valid are printed at the top and bottom ends of the lines.

Topography

There are several methods used to bring ground contours into relief when seen on a topographical map or chart. The combined use of several methods including colour is usually employed to further emphasize the variation of ground height in relation to the surrounding surface and sea level.

Fig. 3—21

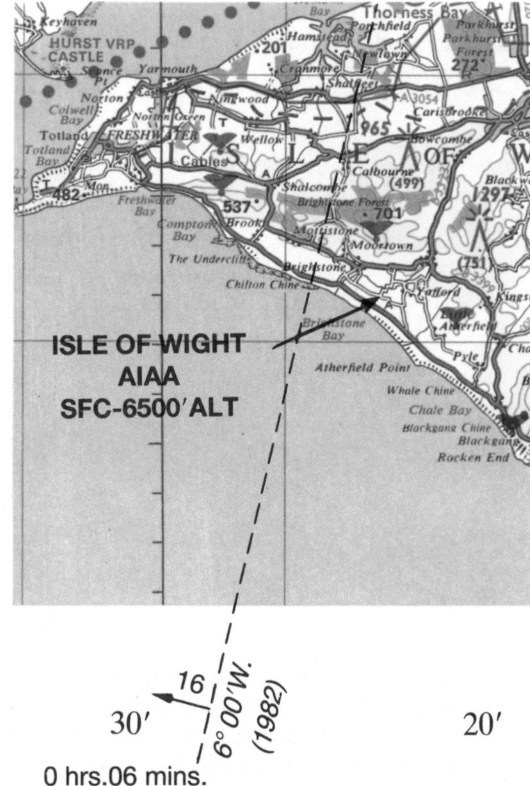

Relief Portrayal

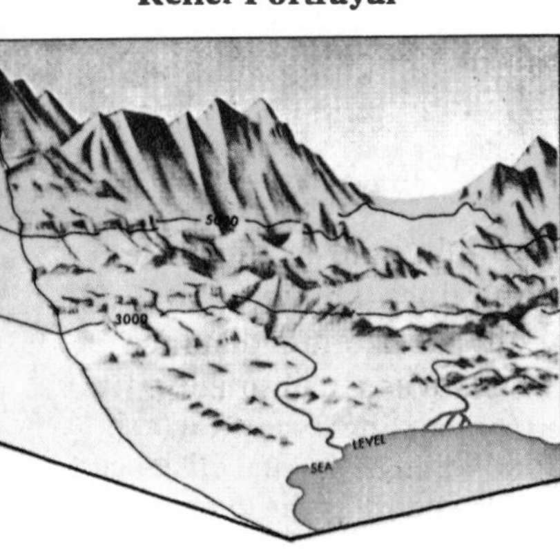

Relief

The generally used methods are:

Contours (or form lines)
Spot Heights
Layer Tinting (use of colour)
Hachuring
Hill Shading

Contours, spot heights and layer tinting form the basis of presenting relief on UK topographical charts. Hachuring is not normally used on topographical charts as it does not stand out very clearly against the mass of geographic and cultural detail shown on such charts. The use of hachures is mainly confined to plotting charts which lack the topographical detail of those maps which are used for pilot navigation.

Hill shading is employed on the latest charts in the UK Topographical Series 1:250.000. It is also used extensively on the ICAO World Aeronautical Chart Series 1:1000.000 and many other topographical charts produced by other European countries.

Contours

A contour is a line drawn on a chart which joins together places of equal height above a specified datum (normally sea level). Contour lines indicate gradient and shape as well as height.

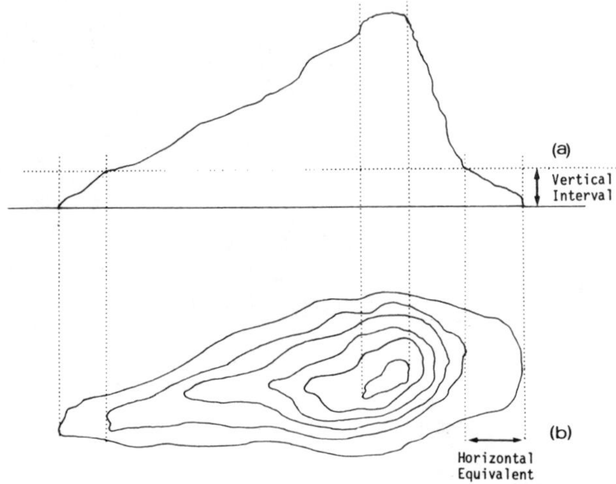

Fig. 3—22

Fig 3-22 shows the principle of constructing contours on a map to illustrate varying ground levels. The vertical distance between contour lines (shown at (a) in the diagram), is known as the 'vertical interval' and the horizontal distance between contour lines (shown at (b) in the diagram), is known as the 'horizontal equivalent'.

The 1:500.000 topographical charts show contour lines at heights of 500' intervals up to 1000' amsl, thereafter the contour lines are shown for 1000' intervals. It should be noted that no contour lines are shown for ground heights of less than 500' amsl. In the 1:250.000 series, contour lines commence at 200' amsl and continue at 200' intervals until 1000' amsl. Above this height and up to 2000' contour lines are shown at 400' intervals.

Ground height is extremely important to the pilot who must maintain a safe altitude above the surface at all times. With practice, contour lines can be interpreted quickly and become a useful adjunct to map reading.

Spot Heights

These are shown on topographical charts by a black dot with adjacent numerals. Such heights have been measured accurately and are normally used to show local peaks which are significantly higher than the adjacent highest contour line.

The position and height of the highest elevation is normally printed on the margin of the particular chart and the spot height of the highest elevation on that chart is shown in large numbers against a white background outlined in black. Fig 3-23 refers.

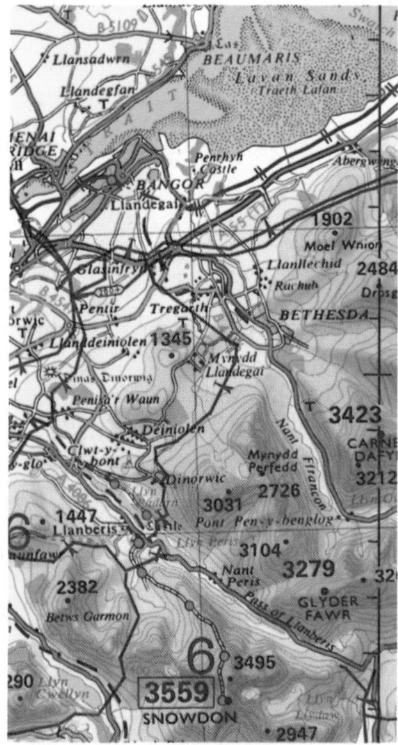

Fig 3—23

Layer Tinting

Aeronautical topographical charts also use colour tinting in addition to contour lines. The colour code is shown in the chart legend (see fig 3-24)

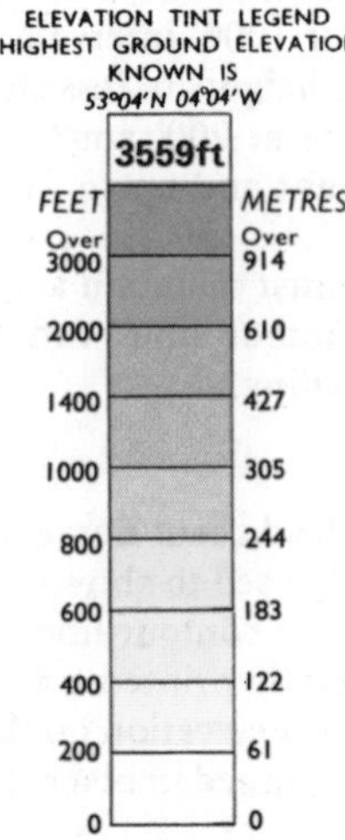

HIGHEST GROUND ELEVATION DOES NOT INCLUDE THE ELEVATIONS OF AIR NAVIGATION OBSTRUCTIONS. SEE AIR INFORMATION

Fig. 3–24

These shades get darker with increase in ground elevation. The colour coding is arranged to be coincidental with a change in contour line and therefore give a clear indication of relief.

Ground which lies below the lowest contour line on the 1:500.000 or 1:250.000 series topographical charts is not coloured and appears as white.

Hachuring

This method consists of short lines which radiate from the high ground. Numerals indicating the height will appear inside the pattern so made. Fig 3-25 is an example of hachuring and the heights shown in this case are in metres.

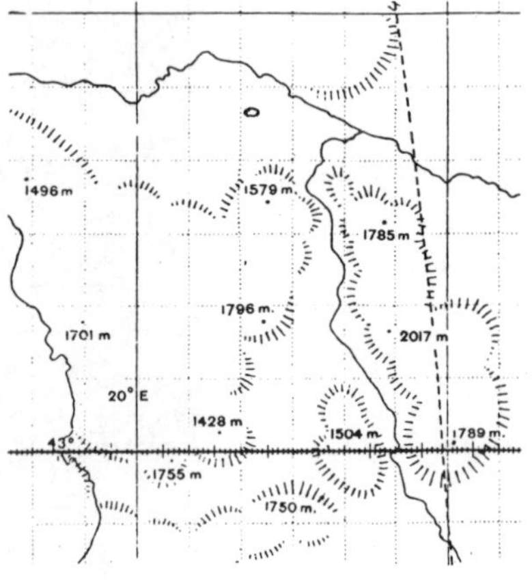

Fig 3–25

Hill Shading

Commonly used on Continental charts this method is based upon the principle of a bright light shining obliquely across the surface so that shadows fall on the low side of the high ground.

It can be used quite successfully to give a three dimensional effect to the chart in which the high ground, and in particular the higher peaks, are brought into contrasting relief. Fig 3–26 is an illustration of this effect.

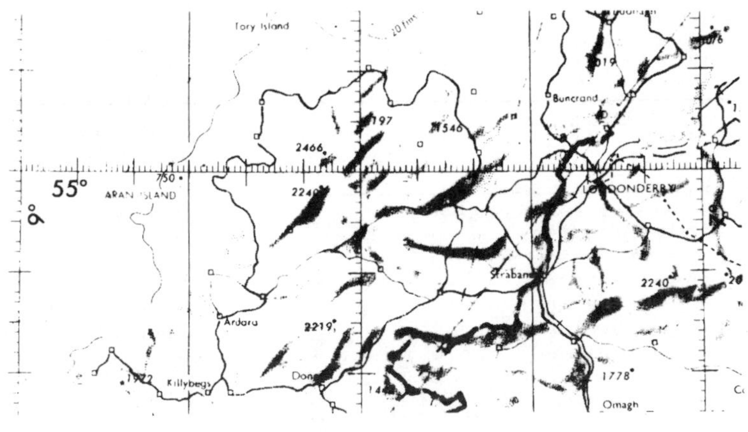

Fig 3–26

Hydrographic Features

Hydrographical features are portrayed by the use of blue colour to indicate water in the form of seas, inland water areas, rivers and canals.

When reservoirs are under construction, hatched blue lines are used instead of a solid blue colour. On some charts, rivers and canals which are prone to dry up during periods of drought are indicated by broken blue lines.

Cultural Features

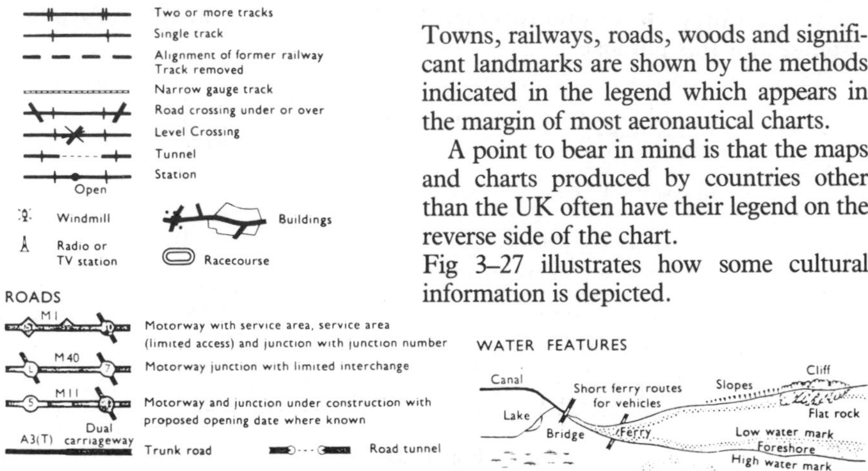

Towns, railways, roads, woods and significant landmarks are shown by the methods indicated in the legend which appears in the margin of most aeronautical charts.

A point to bear in mind is that the maps and charts produced by countries other than the UK often have their legend on the reverse side of the chart.

Fig 3–27 illustrates how some cultural information is depicted.

Fig. 3—27

Aeronautical Symbols

Included on the chart margin are a range of aeronautical symbols which are considered essential information when planning a navigation flight.

AERODROMES

Field limits with hard runway pattern.................................... Howes 168 (M)

Howes-Name 168-Elevation (M)-Military, (C)-Civil, (J)-Joint

Aerodrome Traffic Zone (ATZ)..

Circle 2·0 or 2·5 NM radius (See UK AIP RAC 3-2-10).

Minor aerodromes with runway pattern unknown.............................
or not portrayable.

Disused or abandoned aerodromes..

Heliports (M)-Military, (C)-Civil, (J)-Joint......................................

Customs Aerodromes are distinguished by a pecked line around the name of the aerodrome.................................... Manston

Glider Launching Site (See UK AIP RAC 5-1-3)

a. Primary activity at locations..

b. Additional activity at locations..

Parascending Site (See UK AIP RAC 5-1-8)

a. Primary activity at locations..

b. Additional activity at locations..

Hang-Gliding Site (See UK AIP RAC 5-1-7)..

Free-fall Parachuting Site, DZ circle 1·5NM radius............................

Site of Intensive Microlight Flying..

(Intensive Microlight activity also takes place at certain Licenced and Unlicenced Aerodromes. See UK AIP RAC 5-1-7)

Instrument Approach Procedure (IAP)........

(Outside regulated airspace, the existence of an IAP is indicated by the symbol aligned to the **Main** Instrument Runway. Other IAPs may also exist).

These symbols are used to identify types of aerodromes, e.g. military or civil, and areas such as gliding sites and parachute dropping zones. Figs 3-28 and 3-29 show the types of symbols which are used and because of their importance to safe navigation, pilots should develop the ability to interpret them at a glance.

Surface obstructions which reach or exceed a height of 300' above the surface are considered as hazards to air navigation and symbols are used to show their positions. These symbols will indicate whether they are lighted or unlighted, and also whether they are exceptionally high. Fig 3-29 illustrates the types of symbols employed for this purpose.

Exceptionally High Obstruction (Lighted)
Single, Multiple
1000ft. or more AGL *1950* (1720) *1536* (1300)

Obstruction (Unlighted) *530* (323)

Group Obstruction (Lighted) *560* (425)

Numerals in italics indicate height of top of obstruction above Mean Sea Level.

Numerals in brackets indicate height of top of obstruction above Local Ground Level.

Cables joining Obstructions ....

SYMBOLS ARE NOT SHOWN ON THIS CHART FOR LAND-SITED OBSTRUCTIONS LESS THAN 300FT ABOVE LOCAL GROUND LEVEL. PERMANENT OFF-SHORE OIL AND GAS INSTALLATIONS ARE SHOWN REGARDLESS OF HEIGHT CATEGORY.

Fig. 3—29

Aeronautical Information

In order to assist the pilot in his task of navigating an aircraft through the UK Airspace System a topographical chart must display information relating to Controlled Airspace, Special Rules Airspace, Military Aerodrome Traffic Zones, Danger Prohibited and Restricted Areas etc.

This is done by overprinting the chart with information relating to the horizontal and vertical dimensions of Controlled Airspace and similar areas of importance to safe navigation.

Fig 3-30 shows the symbols used on the 1:250.000 topographical chart series for the UK. It should be noted that slight variations exist in the manner of presenting reference information between the 1:500.000 and 1:250.000 series. However these differences will present no problems to the pilot because in each case the methods of presenting such information is clearly shown on the lower margins of both charts.

Aeronautical Charts become obsolete more quickly than most other maps or charts, because the overprinted information in relation to such items as Danger Areas and Controlled Airspace is often subject to change within a few months of the chart's publication. It will therefore be important to check the information in the margin, which relates to the period of chart validity, so ensuring that the chart being used is current for air navigation purposes.

The issue of a new chart published by the CAA will automatically cancel the previous edition without further notification. Information relating to the issue of new charts will be notified by an Aeronautical Information Circular.

REFERENCE TO AIR INFORMATION

Special Rules Zone (SRZ) SFC-FL65

Special Rules Area (SRA) 1500'ALT-FL65

Control Zone (CTR) SFC-2500'ALT

Control Area (TMA and CTA)
Outer Boundary 3000'ALT-FL245
Inner Boundary 1500'ALT-FL245

Control Area (Airway) R 3 2500'ALT-FL245

FIR Boundary

Low Level Corridor or Special Route 500'-4500'ALT

Radar Advisory Service Zone or area
(See UK AIP RAC 3-6-3)

Area of Intense Aerial Activity (AIAA)
(See UK AIP RAC 5-1-2)

Military Aerodrome Traffic Zone (MATZ) MATZ
MATZs have the following vertical limits. SFC to 3000ft AAL within circle and 1000ft AAL to 3000ft AAL within stub. Controlling Aerodromes are marked with an asterisk within a circle

Visual Reporting Point (VRP) ASHFORD VRP

Special Access Lane Entry/Exit E

(Indicates centre of lane, see UK AIP for conditions of use) E

Altimeter Setting Region CHATHAM PORTLAND

Bird Sanctuary
Areas shown with name/effective altitude (in thousands of feet AMSL)

High Intensity Radio Transmission Area,
Areas shown with name/effective altitude (thousands of feet AMSL)

Gas Venting Station (See UK AIP RAC 5-1-7)
Areas are shown with effective altitude (in thousands of feet AMSL).

Airspace Restrictions D308/11

Prohibited 'P', Restricted 'R', and Danger Areas 'D', are shown with identification number/vertical limits in thousands of feet AMSL.
Areas activated by NOTAM are shown with a broken boundary line.
For those Scheduled Danger Areas whose upper limit changes at specified times, only the higher of the upper limits is shown on the chart.
Danger Areas whose identification numbers are prefixed with an asterisk* contain airspace subject to Byelaws which prohibit entry during the period of Danger Area Activity. See UK AIP RAC 5-1-1.

Fig. 3—30

Finally it must be stressed that the most meticulous approach to pre-flight planning calculations will be of little value if the chart being used is not current at the date of planning the flight, therefore it is the responsibility of the pilot to ensure that the charts he uses in his navigation operations are up to date. The cost of the current chart is insignificant when compared to the problems and possible hazards of attempting to navigate an aircraft when using incomplete or incorrect information.

Conversion of Units (Distance and Height)
Normally the Navigation Computer is used for the conversation of units but there may be occasions when reference to the following conversion factors will prove useful.

Distance: When necessary, the conversion of units used in distance measurements can be carried out using the following values:

To Convert	Into	Multiply By
Nautical Miles	Statute Miles	1.1515
Nautical Miles	Kilometres	1.853
Statute Miles	Nautical Miles	0.8684
Statute Miles	Kilometres	1.60932
Kilometres	Nautical Miles	0.540
Kilometres	Statute Miles	0.62137

Note: In the UK, the flight visibility is officially given in kilometres or metres, but distance (apart from relatively short distances such as those relating to aerodromes, e.g. runway length) is still referred to in units of nautical or statute miles.

Height: The two units of height used in altitude calculations are feet and metres. Conversion factors for these two units are shown below:

To Convert	Into	Multiply by
Feet	Metres	0.3048
Metres	Feet	3.2808

A conversion table for feet and metres is printed in the margin of many aeronautical charts and the adjacent illustration shows how this is presented on the 1:500.000 topographical series.

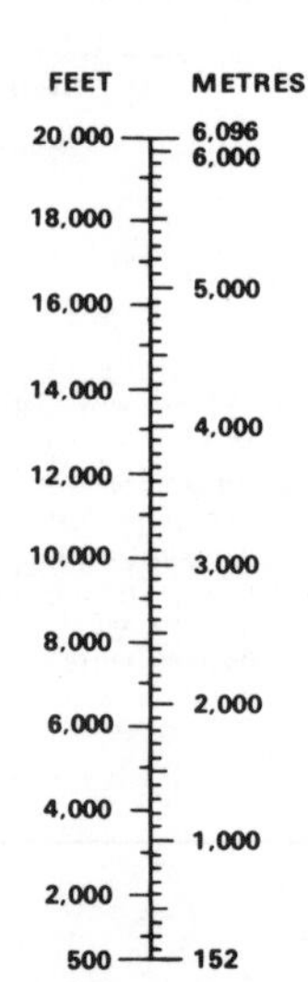

Chart Scale

The ratio between a given length on the chart and the actual distance it represents on the Earth is called the scale of the chart. This applies regardless of the type of projection used in the chart construction.

Scale can be expressed as:

$$\text{Scale} = \frac{\text{Chart Length}}{\text{Actual Distance on Earth's Surface}} \quad \text{Expressed in the same units}$$

Scale can be shown in one or more of three ways on a chart as follows:

Representative Fraction:

This indicates the ratio of a unit length on the chart to its corresponding number of similar units on the Earth.

Thus 1:500.000 means that one unit on the map is equivalent to 500.000 such units on the Earth.

Statement in Words:

This will express the relationship between a given chart length and its corresponding distance on the Earth.

This could be stated using different units, for example, 1 inch to 10 nm or 1 cm to 5 km.

Graduated Scale Line:

These scale lines are normally displayed in the bottom margin of topographical charts and usually include distance measurements in nautical miles, statute miles and kilometres.

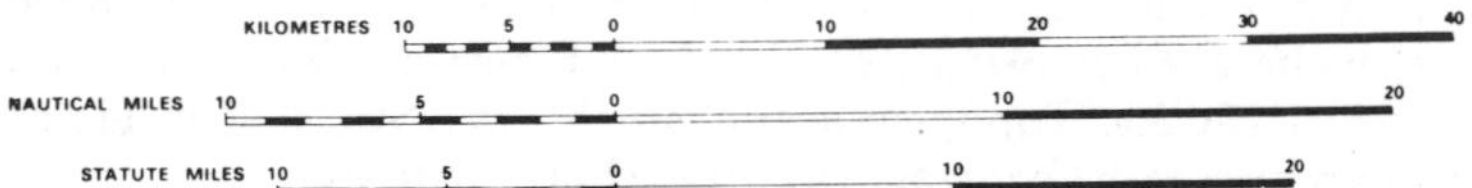

In addition to the graduated scale lines the topographical series also have distance scales in nautical miles incorporated along a number of meridians and parallels as shown below.

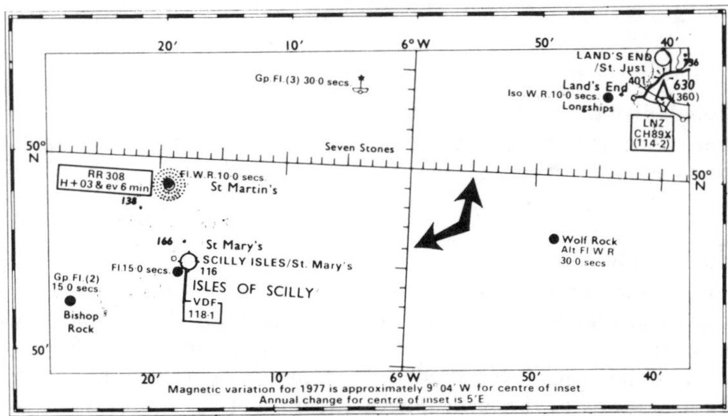

Fig. 3—31

Measurements (Distance and Height)

The measurement of distance on a chart can be made by using the units of statute miles (st.m), nautical miles (nm) or kilometres (km). The most convenient scale in aeronautical navigation is nautical miles as this is the length of one minute of latitude. However the aircraft airspeed indicator may be calibrated in statute miles (mph), nautical miles (knots) and occasionally in kilometres. In this latter case the scale appropriate to the airspeed indicator will probably be the most practical to use.

Statute Mile:
This represents a length on the Earth's surface of 5280 feet.

Nautical Mile:
This is equivalent to one minute of latitude and represents a distance on the Earth's surface of 6046 feet at the equator and 6108 feet at the poles. The figure of 6080 feet is generally used as mean length to represent one nautical mile for navigation purposes.

Kilometre:
This is the length of 1/10.000th part of the average distance between the equator and either pole. It is equivalent to 3280 feet. Kilometres are widely used on Continental charts but in addition, the scales for both statute and nautical miles are also usually shown.

A suitably calibrated rule or a pair of dividers may be used to measure distance on a map or chart. When using a Lambert's or Transverse Mercator chart, i.e. the 1:500,000 or 1:250,000 Topographical chart the scale can be considered for all practical purposes to be constant over the whole chart area.

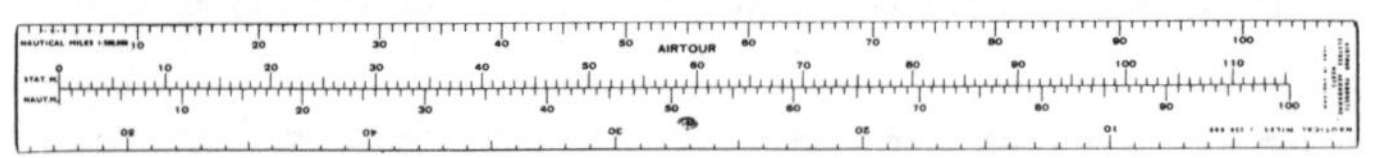

Although distances are usually estimated by eye during flight it is nevertheless essential to be meticulous in measuring distance during pre-flight planning operations as this will reduce errors in other calculations.

Height/Altitude

Apart from horizontal distance measurements the pilot will need to have immediate information in relation to the altitude of the aircraft above the surface. Aeronautical maps and charts portray surface elevations and obstruction heights in relation to mean sea level, therefore provided a pilot uses an altimeter setting which corresponds to the atmospheric pressure at sea level (at the time of the flight) he will be using a datum which is common to both his altimeter reading and the ground elevation and obstruction heights marked on his chart, i.e. he will be able to determine the vertical distance his aircraft is above the ground and/or any surface obstructions.

Units of Height

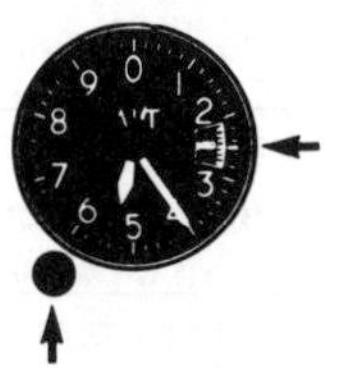

The altimeters fitted in UK registered aircraft are calibrated in feet, and when the altimeter sub-scale is set to the mean sea level pressure existing in the immediate area of the aircraft, this setting is known in aviation terms as the QNH and once set the altimeter will indicate the aircraft distance above mean sea level. As mean sea level is constant this datum is used for the en-route phase of a flight.

In the case of microlight operations it will not always be possible for the pilot to obtain the existing sea level pressure for the area in which he is operating. However, provided the pilot knows the height above sea level of his take-off point he can set this height on his altimeter and this will give him the approximate sea level pressure on the instrument datum, and his approximate height above sea level during flight.

It should be noted that certain charts produced in Europe and elsewhere use metres to show height of ground above sea level. Metres may also be used to indicate the height of obstructions above ground level and mis-reading these figures as units of feet could have disastrous consequences, for example, a pilot mistakenly reading a ground elevation on the chart of 1500 metres for 1500 feet could place himself and the aircraft in a very dangerous situation. (1500 metres represents 4920 feet).

PRINCIPLES OF NAVIGATION

During air navigation the pilot will be concerned with the effect of wind, the aircraft's speed, the passage of time and the combined effect of these factors upon the aircraft's position in relation to the surface.

The underlying principles of navigation calculations will be just as much the concern of a microlight pilot as it is to pilots of larger and faster aircraft. Many of the calculations used in navigation are based upon the "Triangle of Velocities" and all pilots should have an elementary understanding of the construction and application of this vector triangle as the solution of problems which are an integral part of navigation procedures depends upon its use.

Before outlining the procedures involved in solving navigation problems the following definitions should be reviewed:

Wind Velocity

This term concerns both the direction and speed of the prevailing wind. When the wind is blowing from the North to the South at 20 knots it will be expressed as 360/20k. Information on winds prevailing during the period of the flight is obtained from the weather forecasts issued by the meteorological office.

True Airspeed (TAS)

The air speeed indicators fitted to aircraft usually suffer from a 'position and installation error'. In conventional aircraft this error can be determined by the manufacturer and an airspeed correction table will be included in the aircraft manual. This corrected figure is known as RAS (rectified airspeed). The aircraft's TAS is obtained by taking the RAS and correcting it for the density effect of altitude. However in the case of microlight aircraft which use very basic air speed indicators installed in positions of convenience the position and installation error is unlikely to be known, so for all practical purposes TAS will be the indicated airspeed corrected for density error. Aditionally and because microlight aircraft fly at low airspeeds and relatively low altitudes the effect of density will be very small and on many flights of little practical significance. Nevertheless the Private Pilot Navigation Examination will include questions on determining TAS so microlight students will have to learn how to carry out this type of calculation, therefore information regarding RAS and TAS has been included in the following pages.

Groundspeed (G/S)

This is the actual speed of the aircraft over the ground. It is the TAS corrected for wind effect and is calculated prior to take-off and revised as necessary during flight.

Track True (Tr T)

This is the intended path of the aircraft over the ground. During pre-flight planning the track will be the line marked on the chart joining the point of departure to the destination or the line(s) joining turning points en-route.

Heading (Hdg)

This is the actual heading in degrees steered by the pilot during flight. It can be measured from True, Magnetic or Compass North. Heading is normally calculated initially from True North, following which Variation and Deviation are applied to find the actual compass heading to steer.

Track Made Good (TMG)

This is the actual path of the aircraft over the surface as distinct from the intended track to be flown.

Drift

This term is used to express the angular difference between the track and the heading required to maintain the track. It is stated as Port (left) or Starboard (right) in relation to the heading.

Track Error

This is the angular difference between the track required and the actual track made good. It is expressed as Port or Starboard in relation to the track required.

IAS, RAS and TAS

A vital calculation in pilot navigation is the actual speed of the aircraft over the ground as distinct from its speed through the air. The groundspeed is arrived at by calculating the effect of the wind direction and speed upon the aircraft's TAS.

However before the TAS can be determined, two computations have to be made and to understand the reason for making these computations the following facts must be appreciated.

The direct reading of airspeed obtained from the airspeed indicator is known as the Indicated Airspeed (IAS), and, as mentioned on page 3-32 the 'position and installation error' must be taken into account before the Rectified Airspeed can be determined. A point to note in respect of terminology is that in the USA RAS is called Calibrated or Corrected Airspeed (CAS) therefore the Owner's Manual of an American produced aircraft will refer to CAS instead of RAS.

Having converted IAS into RAS a second computation will need to be made to arrive at the TAS. The reason for this is due to the fact that airspeed indicators are calibrated to show the correct or true airspeed under conditions known as the International Standard Atmosphere (ISA). This assumes the following conditions at mean sea level:

An atmospheric pressure of	...	1013.25 mb
An air temperature of	...	15°C
An air density of	...	1225 grammes per cubic metre
A temperature lapse rate with increase in height of	...	1.98°C per 1000'

When these conditions exist the RAS at sea level will be the same as the TAS at sea level. However these assumed conditions will rarely occur in practice, and because the density of air decreases with increase of altitude a further error known as 'Density Error' occurs. Therefore because the air speed indicator is calibrated to measure the airspeed assuming a constant density the IAS in practice will invariably differ from the TAS.

At all times the only airspeed visible to the pilot will be that which is directly read from the air speed indicator (IAS). Any large discrepancies between this speed and the true airspeed will be important in navigation as it will be reflected immediately in the accuracy of the groundspeed. The method used to convert IAS into TAS is covered in a later section of this manual under the heading "The Navigation Computer". However at the speeds which microlight aeroplanes normally use it is unlikely that any large errors will occur save those which result from density variations as altitude is gained.

Wind, Heading and Groundspeed

If the air surrounding the Earth was completely motionless, air navigation would be relatively simple. The pilot would only need to measure the angle of his required track from a suitable chart, apply a correction for variation and deviation and steer this computed heading. The track over the ground would then coincide with the measured track on the chart.

The Earth's atmosphere however is constantly undergoing variations in pressure which in turn sets up air mass movements in different directions and speeds. This movement of the air is called 'wind' and it affects all aircraft during flight. Therefore any object which is free from contact with the Earth will be affected by the direction and speed of the wind. In the case of an aeroplane, the lighter its weight and the slower it flies the greater will be the influence of the wind upon it, therefore with microlight aircraft the effect of wind can be very considerable.

Wind is measured in degrees and knots, i.e a wind which is blowing from due North to South at 20 knots is expressed as 360/20k, and in such a wind an inert object like a balloon floating in the air would, in one hour, be blown 20nm to the South of its original position.

When direction and speed are expressed together they are known as 'Velocity', therefore 360/20k is known as the wind velocity. Graphical representation of a velocity is called a vector and this 'measure' plays an important part in understanding the principles of air navigation.

For example the aircraft in fig 3-32 on a heading of 090° with a wind blowing abeam its heading would be continously blown sideways. This effect is called 'drift'.

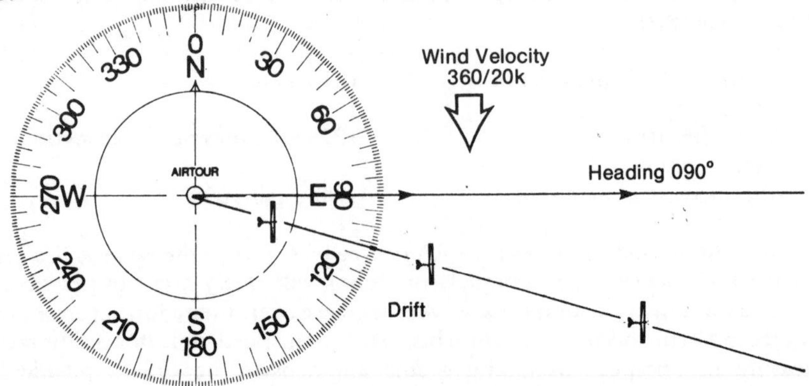

Fig. 3—32

In connection with making allowances for the effect of the wind it is important to note that all windspeeds quoted in meteorological forecasts and reports are given in knots (nautical miles per hour). Although most air speed indicators used in conventional aircraft are calibrated in knots, those used in microlight aircraft are commonly calibrated in miles per hour. If you are using one of these air speed indicators it will be necessary to convert the wind speed to miles per hour before placing any figures on the computer or calculating wind effect.

Naturally the speed of an aircraft must be affected by the wind velocity and direction. To take the simple case of a microlight aircraft flying at 50 knots indicated airspeed into a 20 knot headwind (fig 3-33). The actual speed over the ground (Groundspeed) would be 30 knots. Conversely at the same IAS but with a tailwind of 20 knots, the groundspeed would be 70 knots.

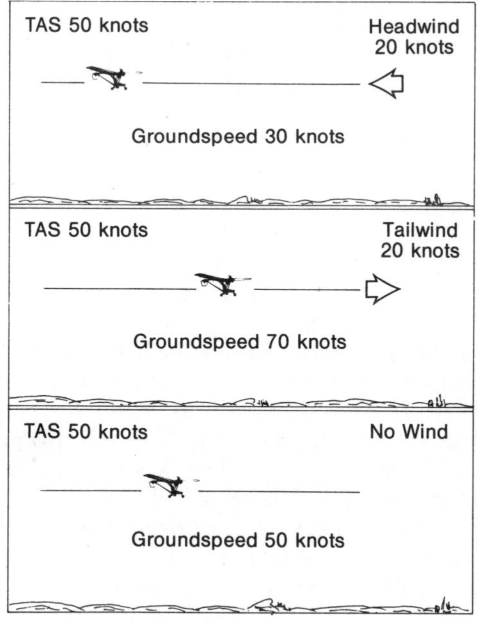

Fig. 3—33

To sum up, both the direction and strength of the prevailing wind play an important part in navigation calculations, and because wind direction is usually at an angle to the intended track it will be necessary to make certain calculations to ascertain the correct heading to fly as well as to establish the aircraft's speed over the ground.

Calculation of Heading and Groundspeed

Referring to fig 3-34, if an aircraft is heading 090° at 50 knots and no wind exists it will arrive at 'B' after one hour, however if a wind is blowing from 360° at 20 knots it will follow the path shown between 'A' and 'C' and at the end of one hour it will be 20 nm to the South of 'B'.

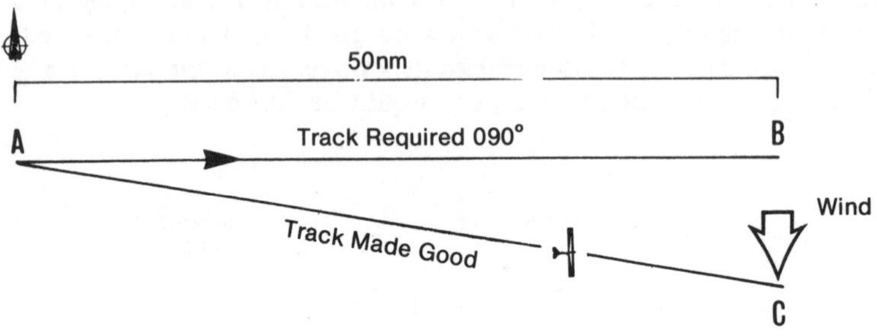

Fig. 3—34

In order to arrive at 'B' the pilot would therefore have to allow for the effect of drift and establish a heading which in this case will be less than 090°.

Normally the calculations necessary to find the correct heading and groundspeed are made on a navigation computer and this procedure is covered later in this Manual. However a pilot who takes the trouble to grasp the basic principles involved in these calculations will also be in a position to reduce the possibility of making major errors when using such a computer.

The direction in which an aircraft is pointing is called its heading but the actual path it follows over the ground will be a combination of the speed of the aircraft and the motion of the air in which it is flying. This in effect is the 'track made good'. The angle between the aircraft's heading and its track is termed the 'drift angle' (ref fig 3-35).

Provided the pilot knows the wind velocity and the aircraft's true speed through the air he can calculate the drift angle and make an allowance for its effect, i.e. in the above case by altering heading by a number of degrees to the left. From this it can be seen that if the wind is blowing from the left of the intended track line the heading must be to the left of the track line and if the wind is blowing from the right the aircraft must be headed to the right of the intended track line. Fig 3-36 (a) shows an illustration of the effect of drift and fig 3-36 (b) shows the correction needed to maintain a given track.

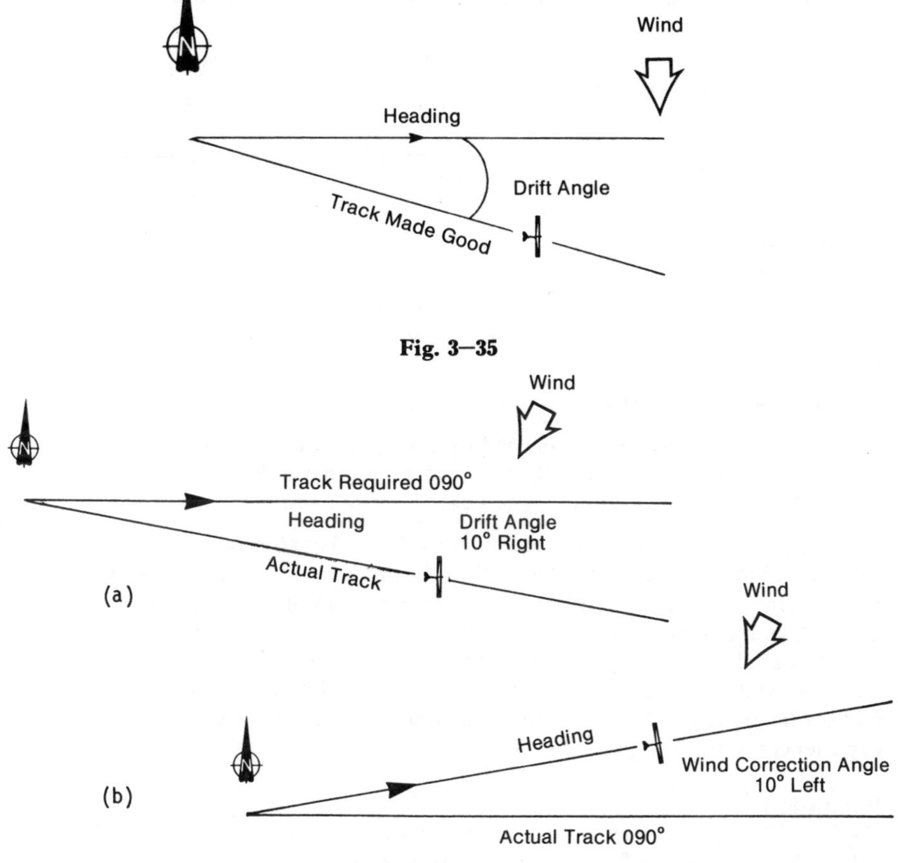

Fig. 3—36

The Triangle of Velocities

This is simply a method of determining graphically the effect of wind upon an aircraft in flight. Calculations concerning the effect of wind on an aircraft's passage through the air during pilot navigation can be limited to the following six variables:

- Wind Direction and Speed
- Aircraft Track and Groundspeed
- True Airspeed and True Heading

A vector triangle can be used to solve many problems relating to air navigation. For example, an aircraft in flight will be subject to two velocities, the wind speed and direction, and the aircraft heading and airspeed. These two velocities will interact and give as a result the aircraft's track and speed over the ground. Fig 3-37 shows an example of a vector triangle using the appropriate variables.

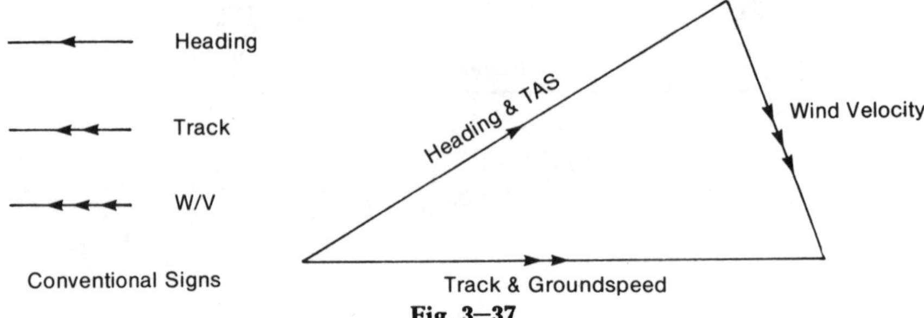

Fig. 3—37

It should be noted that:

- The true airspeed and heading go together on one side.
- The wind speed and direction form another side.
- The track and groundspeed complete the third side.

A knowledge of any four of these six variables will enable the pilot to determine the value of the other two. Further to this, the unknown two, do not need to be part of the same side, e.g. given the wind direction and speed, TAS and track, the heading and groundspeed can be found.

Although there are many variables which can be solved by this method, the pilot navigator will primarily be concerned with finding the heading and groundspeed and occasionally the finding of heading and airspeed, or the wind velocity being experienced during flight.

Example 1

Fig 3-38 illustrates the method of finding 'Heading and Groundspeed' when the TAS, Wind Velocity (W/V) and Track are known.

Track required 090°T
TAS .... 40 knots
W/V .... 360/20 knots

Step 1.
Draw in the wind vector from a direction of 360° and of a length equal to 20 units.
Step 2.
Draw in the track line of 090° from the upwind end of the wind vector 'A'.
Step 3.
Open out a pair of compasses to a scale distance of 40 units. Centre one end of the compasses at the downwind end of the wind vector 'B' and draw an arc to locate 'C' on the track line (a rule could also be used for this purpose).
Step 4.
Measure the direction from 'B' to 'C' to obtain the heading required = 060°.
Step 5.
Measure the length 'A' to 'C' to establish the groundspeed which in this case is 34 knots.

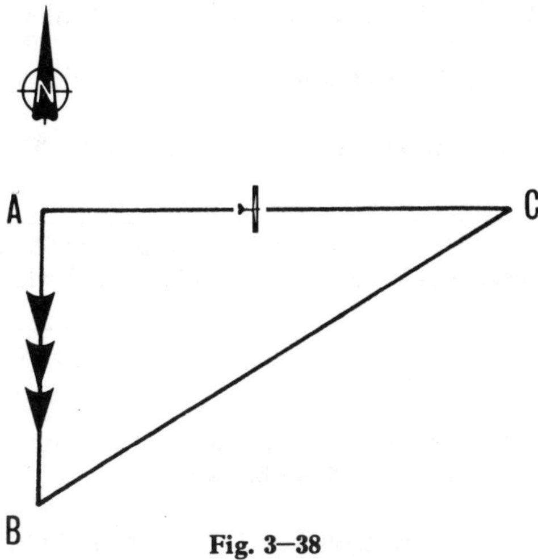

Fig. 3—38

Example 2.
Fig 3-39 illustrates the method of finding the aircraft heading and TAS when the track, groundspeed and wind velocity are known.

Track	....	045°T
Groundspeed	....	60 knots
Wind Velocity	....	180/25

Step 1.
Drawn in the wind vector from a direction of 180° and of a scale length of 25 units.

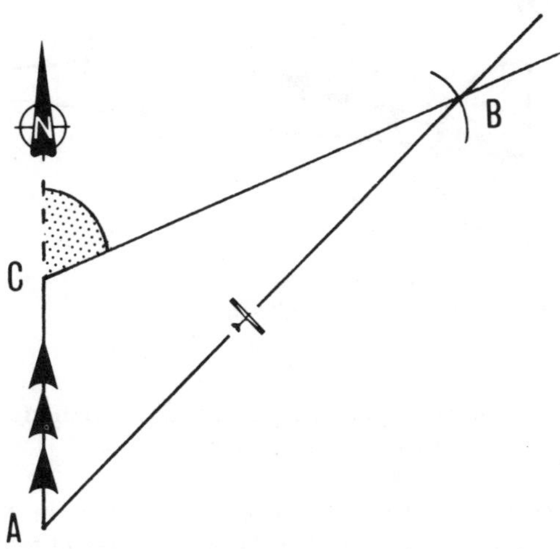

Fig.3—39

Step 2.
Draw in the track line of 045° from the upwind end of the wind vector 'A'.
Step 3.
Mark off 60 units along the track line.
Step 4.
Draw in a line from the downwind end of the wind vector 'C' so that it intersects the track line at 'B'.
Step 5
Measure the angle 'C' to 'B' to determine the heading = 067°.Then measure the length of the line between 'C' and 'B' to establish the IAS which in this case = 46 knots.

Example 3

Fig 3-40 illustrates the method of finding the wind velocity when TAS, heading, track made good and groundspeed are known.

TAS	... 50 knots	Track Made Good ...	270°T
Heading	... 260°T	Groundspeed ...	25 knots

Step 1.
Draw in the direction of the track made good to a length equal to the groundspeed 'A' to 'B'.
Step 2.
Draw in the heading from 'A' to a length equal to the TAS 'A' to 'C'.

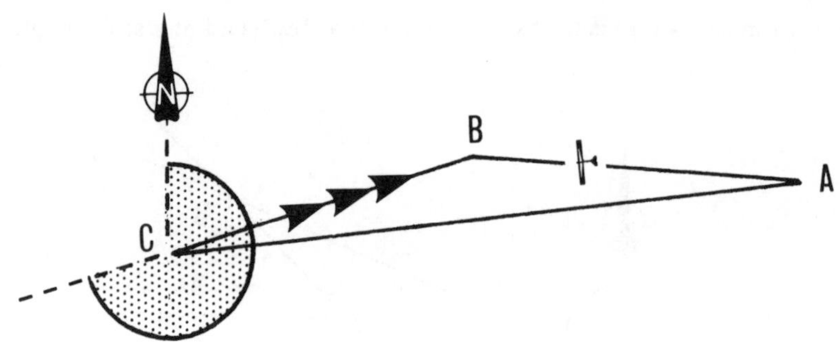

Fig.3—40

Step 3.
Join up 'C' to 'B' and measure the direction = 251°, then measure the length of the line 'C' to 'B' to determine the wind speed = 25k.

NOTE: The foregoing examples are used again later in this Manual when discussing the 'Navigation Computer' and it may be useful to cross refer to these examples at that time.

Dead Reckoning

This term, usually annotated 'DR' is used to describe the estimated position of the aircraft after a period of time, e.g. the DR Position. In effect the process of solving the triangle of velocities will give a DR estimate of the aircraft's position after any selected period of time.

The basis of all DR calculations must nevertheless stem from a known position. This will be either the departure point or a 'Fix' established en-route. Dead reckoning is therefore used to forecast where the aircraft will most probably be at some time ahead, or where it was assumed to have been at some specific time in the past.

Fig. 3—41

The process of dead reckoning will inevitably afford opportunities for miscalculation particularly as the components used, e.g. wind velocity, groundspeed and heading can change or vary during flight.

Bearing this in mind it will also be appreicated that during flight the magnitude of any error in assessing a DR position ahead, will grow larger with the passage of time since the last fix. Therefore the pilot must be very careful in his calculations and estimating procedures.

The difficulty of accurate DR navigation is increased in microlight aircraft due to their lack of navigational equipment and their low speed and weight, hence the pre-planning of a cross country flight needs to be as accurate as possible if errors are to be reduced to acceptable levels.

Measurement of Angles, Tracks and Bearings

In relation to the practical aspect of measuring angles, tracks, or bearings, the pilot will normally use one of two methods. The particular method will depend on whether he is carrying out pre-flight planning operations, or making angular assessments during flight.

Pre-flight planning will involve the use of a protractor placed on the chart in relation to the meridians and the track to be flown, but when in flight this method may become impractical and therefore a pilot will have to practice and develop the ability to make reasonably accurate estimations of angles in relation to bearings from landmarks on the surface, and checkpoints or features on the chart.

Occasionally alterations to track may be necessary due to circumstances which could not be planned, e.g. weather deterioration etc., and in such circumstances the new track to be flown will also have to be estimated by eye.

Measuring Angles and Tracks

During flight planning the pilot will need to select the appropriate chart and provided there are no hazards or similar factors which present a direct track from being followed he will need to draw a line joining up the place of departure with his destination point. This line represents the aircraft's intended track which is expressed in degrees from true North.

Fig 3-42 shows an example of a single track drawn from the airfield of departure (Enstone) to the airfield of destination (Long Marston). For the sake of clarity in presentation the normal topographical information shown on charts used for pilot navigation is not shown in this diagram.

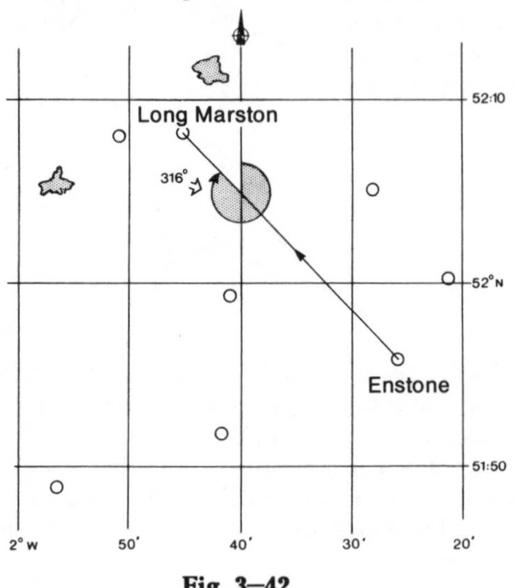

Fig. 3–42

The angle of the track between Enstone aerodrome and Long Marston aerodrome must be measured using a navigation protractor as shown in fig 3-43. The protractor should be placed so that its central North-South line is superimposed over the meridian which is closest to the middle of the intended track with its centre over the intersection of the track line and the meridian. This method will permit the track angle to be measured accurately and in this case it is 316°.

This angle represents the track which is required to be followed, and as meridians are displayed in relation to True North it is known as the True Track, more commonly written as Track (T).

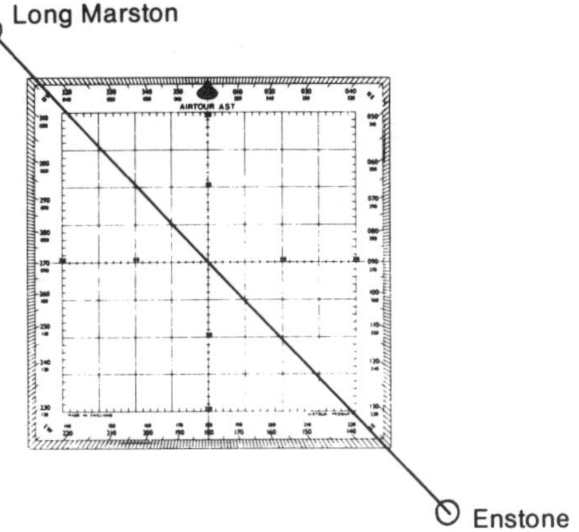

Fig. 3—43

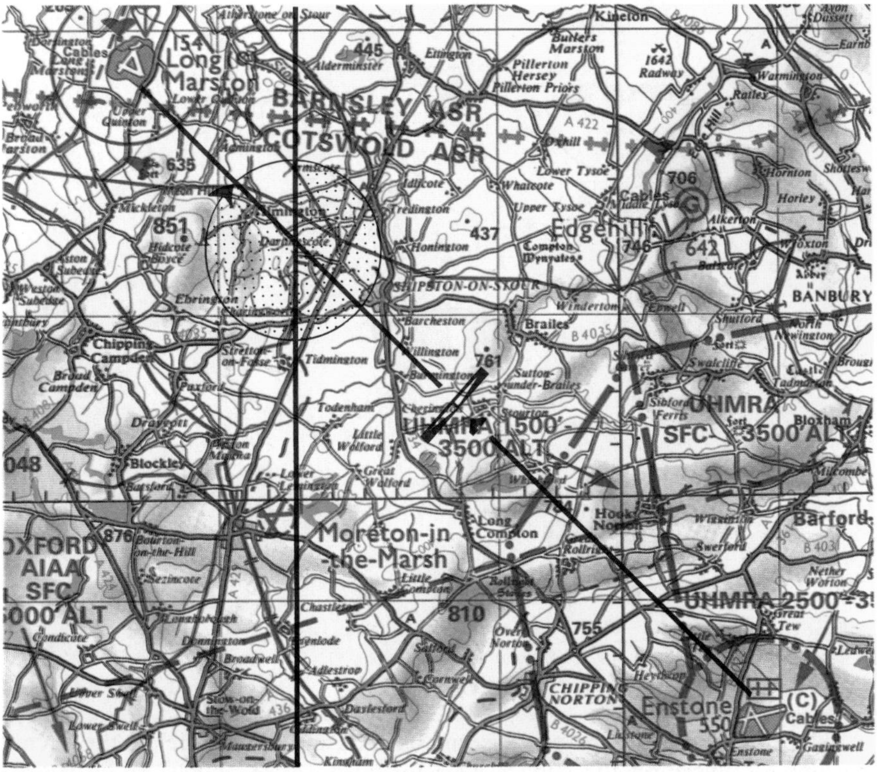

Fig. 3—44

The 1:250,000 Topographical chart will normally be used by microlight pilots and on this projection all meridians converge towards the poles. Therefore when using this chart (and unless the track runs approximately North-South) the point to measure the track should be approximately midway between the departure and the destination points but in this case the nearest convenient meridian is two thirds of the way along the track line. Nevertheless using this will for all practical purposes give a sufficiently accurate track angle.

Fig 3-44 shows the previous example using a 1:250.000 topographical chart. In this illustration the topographical detail adjacent to the track line has been suppressed to show the track more clearly. The return track (normally called the reciprocal) from Long Marston to Enstone will be 136°(T).

Measuring Bearings

The direction of one place from another is called its 'bearing' and like other directions used in navigation it may be expressed in relation to True, Magnetic or Compass North.

However the term bearing when applied to pilot navigation is often used to denote the angle at which a place lies relative to the aircraft's fore and aft axis (relative bearing). Such bearings are not directly related to the aircraft's compass heading.

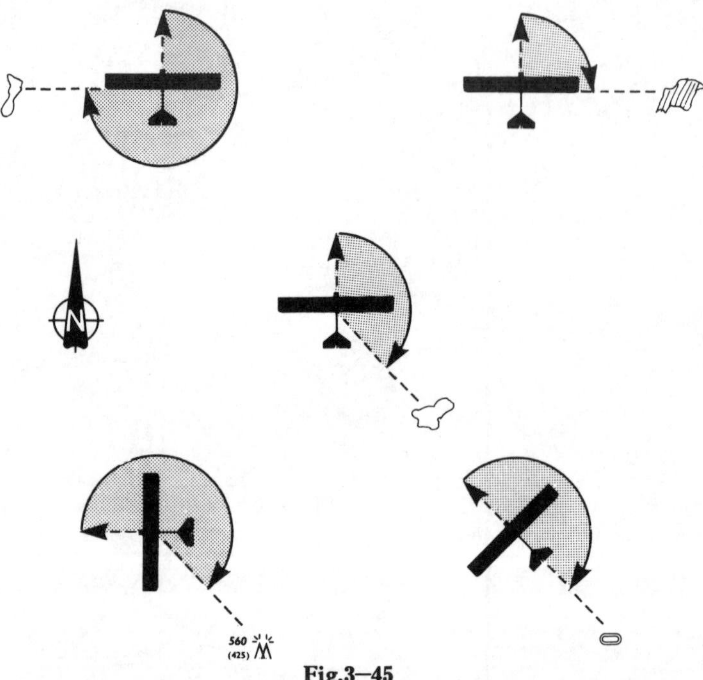

Fig.3—45

Relative bearings are most commonly used during flight to relate the aircraft position to places on the surface. Due to the practical difficulties of using a protractor with any degree of accuracy whilst at the same time flying an aircraft and attending to the many other aspects of pilot navigation, relative bearings are usually obtained by making a visual estimation rather than accurately measuring from a chart. Nevertheless, with practice a pilot will soon be able to achieve a sufficient degree of accuracy from this method to permit a satisfactory standard for pilot navigation techniques.

Relative bearings are measured from the nose of an aircraft in a clockwise direction and fig 3-45 shows some examples of this procedure.

Bearings - True, Magnetic and Compass

Tracks and bearings can relate to True, Magnetic or Compass North. When measuring an angle between two places on a chart for the purpose of plotting a track the initial measurement will be related to the geographical or True North datum.

This must then be converted to magnetic by calculating and applying variation. Following which the compass deviation must be applied in order that a compass heading can be flown. It will be recalled that variation and deviation may be Westerly or Easterly and when converting bearings, tracks or headings from True to Compass, Westerly variation and deviation is given a plus sign and Easterly a minus.

The following examples illustrate the method of calculating a Compass heading from a True heading.

True Heading	Variation W+	Magnetic Heading	Deviation E-	Compass Heading
040°	10°W	050°	3°E	047°

Note: The variation and deviation signs must be reversed if doing a calculation in the reverse direction, i.e. from Compass to True.

Compass	Deviation E+	Magnetic W-	Variation W-	True
047°	3°E	050°	10°W	040°

It should be noted that from a practical viewpoint the deviation for a conventional aircraft will already be calculated and displayed on a Compass Card in the cockpit as already explained in the paragraphs relating to deviation, however this facility will not normally be available in Microlight Aircraft.

MAP READING

Map reading, whereby the aircraft position is determined in relation to surface features is the essential basis of pilot navigation. In order to achieve this, a pilot must remain in weather conditions which permit him a reasonable view of the surface ahead of the aircraft and which in turn will enable him to interpret the many different physical and cultural features and so form a mental picture of how map features will look when they are observed on the surface from an aeroplane in flight.

A crude method of navigation may be to follow roads, railway lines or similar features between the departure and destination points, it should however be appreciated that this method has severe limitations in that within the UK there exists a confusion of roads which when viewed from the air may well lead to difficulties of identification.

Although identification of particular roads etc. may be successfully achieved within the locality of the commonly used take-off site the wider use of such features could easily lead to a pilot becoming lost. A microlight pilot should therefore take all reasonable steps to develop the ability to navigate through the use of the well proven conventional methods as outlined on the following pages rather than rely on following line features alone.

Map Analysis

The essential requirements to successfully reading a map and establishing the position of an aircraft during a cross country flight are summarised below:

The pilot must be able to:

- Recognise ground features (reading from the ground to the map) and relate them to the features and symbols used on pilot navigation maps.
- Be capable of intuitively appreciating the scale of the chart being used and thus automatically relate distances between chart features to the actual distances on the ground.
- Appreciate the relative merits between different ground features and be able to select the most appropriate ones for use during a navigation flight.
- Absorb the information presented by any combination of ground features and form an overall picture of how they will look on the map.
- To relate the speed of the aircraft to the passage of time and thus assess the approximate distance covered over the ground for any interval of time.

Maps and charts cannot be made with 100% accuracy and on occasions map reading can become a difficult task, particularly when flying over featureless terrain, or over areas where ground features are so numerous that unavoidable congestion occurs when portraying them on a topographical chart.

Although every effort is made by the cartographer to use map symbols which have a distinctive relationship to features on the ground he is nevertheless limited in scope. The pilot therefore has to learn how to discriminate between different types of map scale and presentation in order to be able to choose the one most suitable for the terrain over which he is flying, and one appropriate to the cruising speed of his aircraft.

In addition to this he must also be able to select the type of map most suited to his method of navigation, e.g. in this case, for pilot navigation using visual fixes.

Permanent Features

These consist of general coastlines, terrain features in the form of hills, valleys and mountains, together with towns, cities and most large inland stretches of water such as lakes, reservoirs etc. Most of the main railway lines, motorways and trunk roads can also be considered as features which are of a permanent nature.

Coastlines are in the main easily recognisable from the air, however on occasions certain stretches of coastline will be lacking in bays and inlets. On such occasions the best identification method will be to relate the general direction in which the coastline runs to that shown on the map.

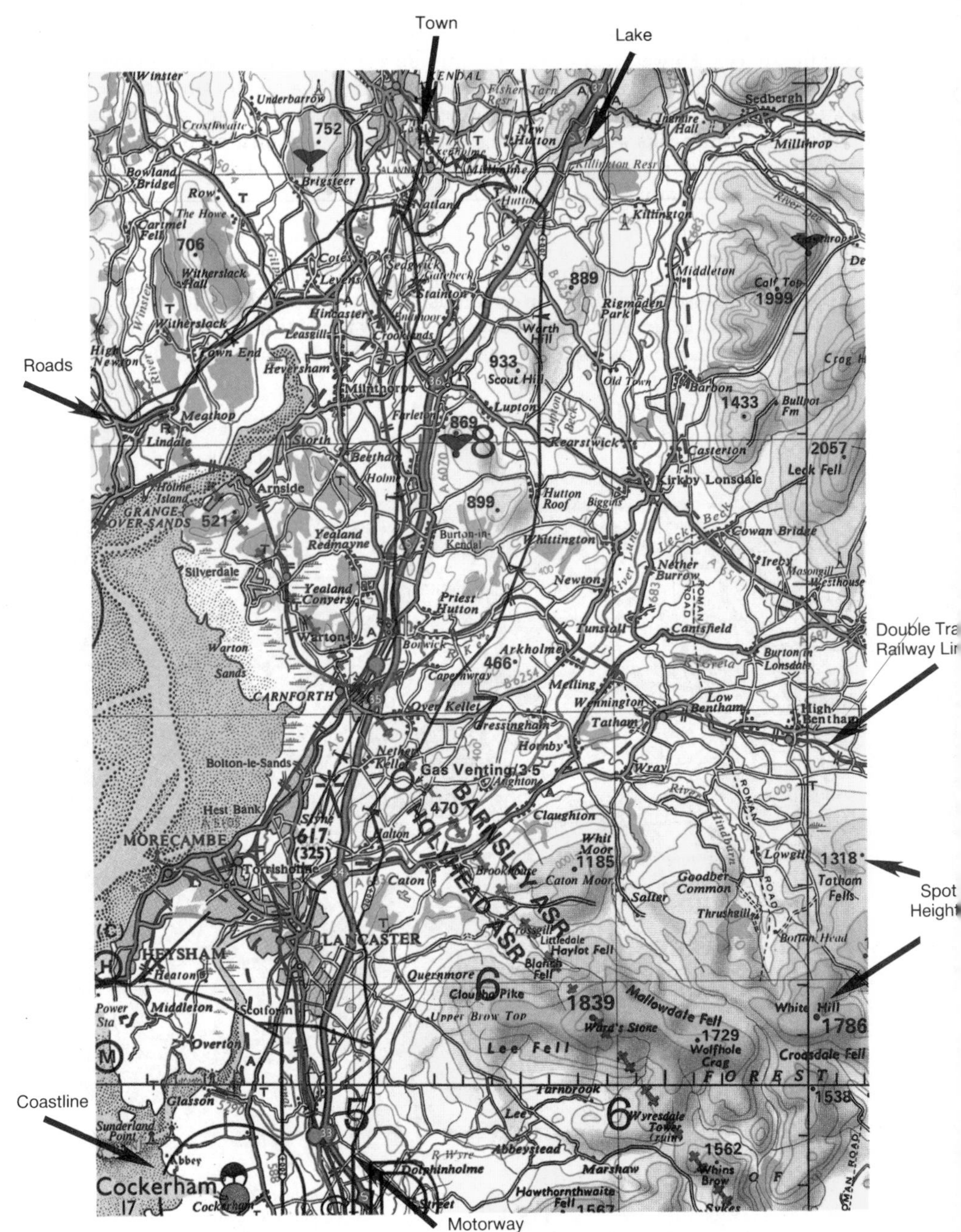
Town
Lake
Roads
Double Tra
Railway Li
Spot
Height
Coastline
Motorway

Fig 3-46

Relief

The general shape of high ground can often be used to obtain an approximate position check. However, the cruising altitude at which the aircraft is flying will play an important part in the value of this method as the greater the altitude the flatter these features will appear when viewed from above. Ranges of mountains and outstanding peaks will nevertheless show up fairly well on most occasions and can often be used in association with other features to give a reasonable check of the aircraft's position.

Line features

Coastlines, railway lines and motorways are all good line features which will assist the pilot navigator. Nevertheless a pilot must not place too much importance upon the value of railway lines and motorways when they travel through heavily built up areas as they can easily become relatively insignificant and thus difficult to identify.

GOOD FIX

1. Circular Lake
2. Town
3. Rising Ground to North

POOR FIX

1. Town and Roads with no other confirming feature.

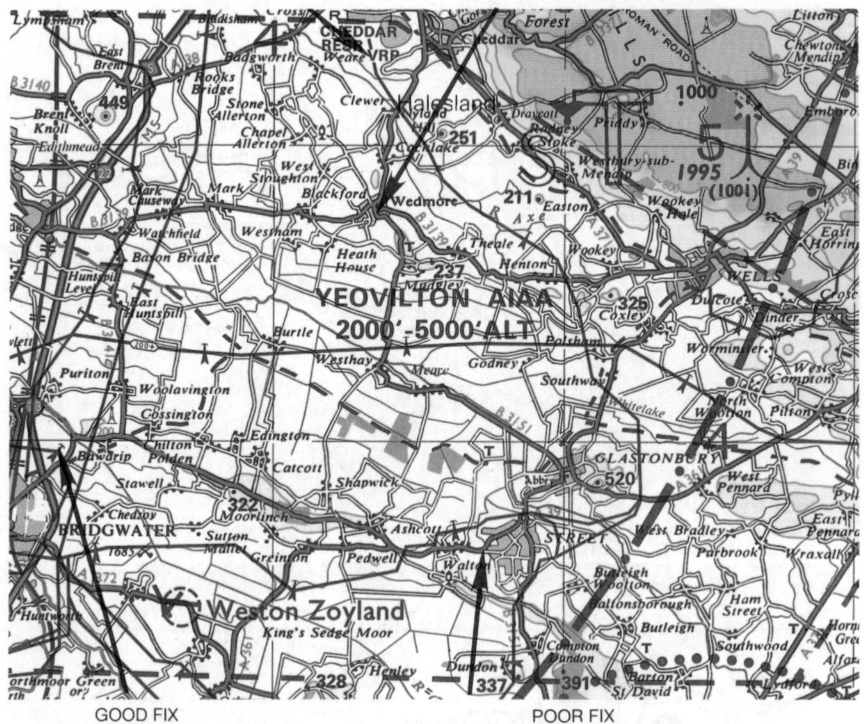

GOOD FIX

1. Railway Line
2. Motorway
3. River
4. Town to South

Fig 3–47

POOR FIX

1. Town and Roads with no confirming Features

In order to establish the position of the aircraft with reasonable accuracy, it will be necessary to use a landmark or feature which is prominent, or alternatively to use at least two features, e.g. a railway line crossing a river or a town from which railways trunk roads or rivers emerge in different directions. Fig 3-47 shows some typical examples of suitable and unsuitable features in relation to map reading.

Spot Features

As mentioned previously a single feature has to be prominent in the surrounding countryside to be a dependable method of obtaining a position check unless it combines with some other suitable and easily recognisable feature.

For example a town in close proximity to another town can easily be mis-identified, but a built up area which is set out well away from other areas of habitation may offer a reasonable position check. It will nevertheless have to be used with discrimination, and a second check should be sought within a short time in order to obtain confirmation.

Roads are normally too abundant to be of much value in map reading except when flying over sparsely populated areas. Small rivers can also be difficult to identify particularly when close to one another.

Unique or Special Features

Success at map reading lies in being able to select the most prominent or easily recognisable feature along or adjacent to the track to be followed. Many areas of coastline can be considered as unique, equally a particularly isolated high spot in a surrounding flat area may also possess this quality. Figs 3-48 and 3-49 show two examples of individual prominence.

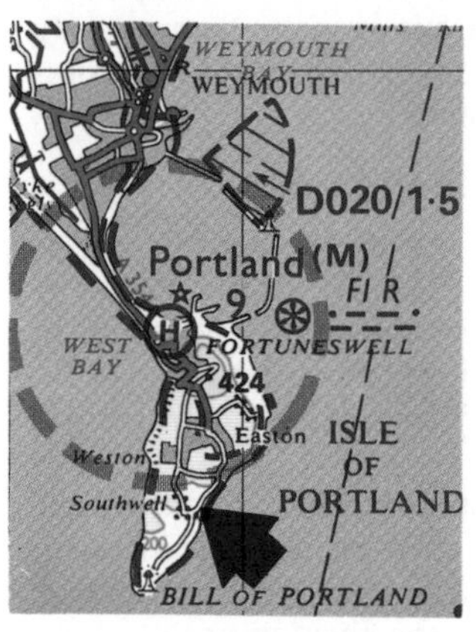

Fig. 3–48

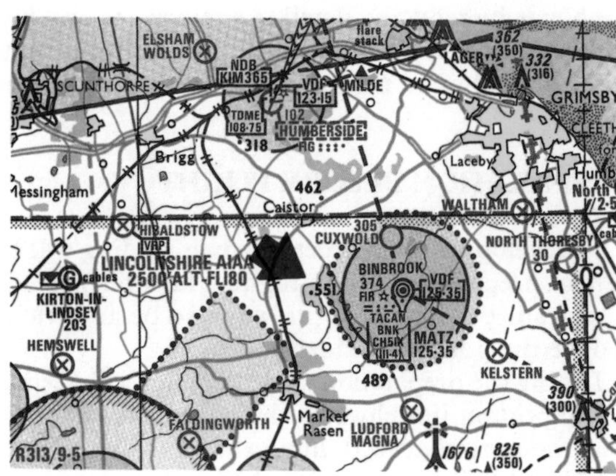

Fig. 3–49

Features Subject to Change

Over the last few years many railway lines have been abandoned and the land they occupied handed over for other uses, e.g. agriculture and building projects. It will however take some time for the removal of railway lines from aeronautical charts, and the pilot must be prepared for those occasions when a feature marked on the chart no longer exists on the ground. Nevertheless it often takes some years before the path left by a dismantled railway line disappears and this can sometimes be used as an additional line feature.

Tall masts and other man made obstructions are shown on topographical charts when their height above the surface attains or exceeds 300'. Masts which do not quite attain 300' will nevertheless often be seen from the air, and this may sometimes cause confusion in map reading.

Further to this, information regarding the erection of navigation obstructions may not always be received by the CAA in time to be incorporated in a new chart issue. Similarly the dismantling of such structures may not always be known at the time a new chart is prepared.

A large number of disused airfields exist in the UK as an aftermath of the 1939-1945 war. Many of these airfields are gradually being absorbed back into agriculture and others are being built upon. Therefore the existence of a disused aerodrome symbol on a chart must not automatically be taken to indicate that the aerodrome is still recognisable as such from the air.

Finally the outline shape of towns and wooded areas may undergo changes during the periods between cartographical surveys, therefore the outlines of these features should be used with caution.

Effects of Seasons

The two major reasons for marked changes in the appearance of the surface are flooding and snowfall.

In abnormal conditions, such as flooding or widespread heavy snowfall, students are reminded that much of the detailed information shown on a navigational chart will be obliterated. While in some cases this could serve to ease navigational problems by reducing detail to a minimum, and highlighting major features only, for the most part abnormal conditions can only make navigational problems more difficult, and extra planning and caution will be essential.

PREPARATION BEFORE FLIGHT

The development of successful map reading will be considerably speeded up by careful preparation before flight. The ability to anticipate the appearance of the next feature along the route will also be an invaluable asset and one which will reduce the pilot's workload.

During the preparation stage the pilot will need to study the intended route and if any portion lies close to the edge of his chart, he must ensure he carries the neighbouring chart with him in order to insure against the possibility of being 'off track' and flying over areas which are not covered by the chart in use.

The track line must be clearly drawn so that it stands out from the topographical detail and overprinted information shown on the chart. A soft lead pencil is preferable for this purpose and it can also be rubbed out more easily after the flight.

There are several methods used in marking distance lines on the chart and your instructor may recommend any of the following:

1. Time Scale - 5 or 10 minute marks made along the track line and representative of the distance covered at the calculated groundspeed.
2. Distance Scale - Marks made at specific distances, usually at 5 mile intervals.

3. Proportionate Division - The track can be marked out in 1/4, 1/2 and 3/4 intervals. This permits quick and simple calculations of revised 'Estimated Times of Arrival' (ETA) at the next division mark and destination.

Note: All charts should be checked to ensure that they are still current for navigational purposes.

The construction of most microlight aircraft creates a situation where the pilot is exposed to the elements with little or no facilities to stow navigation equipment, e.g. flight logs, maps, pencils, etc. In most cases it will however be possible to fold the required map into a clear plastic cover and attach it to a kneeboard strapped to a leg.

In the case of microlights in which the pilot is totally exposed to the oncoming wind it would be more practical to use overalls in which a clear plastic pocket is stitched to each leg above the knee.

The map can then be folded and inserted into the pocket so that the route is visible through the plastic section. A flight log can be slipped into the opposite pocket in a similar manner.

Due to the difficulties of using a paper and pencil during flight all calculations must of necessity be as simple as possible to perform. Therefore the "Proportionate Division" method of marking off distance on a map may be the easiest one to use as it requires only simple mental calculations to be made during flight. This method is covered in greater detail later.

Checkpoint Features and Selection

The route must be studied with the object of selecting features which will make suitable checkpoints (fixes) at intervals along the track. These checkpoints do not necessarily have to be on the track itself but they must be within reasonable sighting distance compatible with the expected visibility conditions.

The basic principle governing the selection of the best checkpoints available is the ease with which they can be identified. When choosing checkpoints during the preparation stage the pilot must ensure they are sufficiently distinctive to be recognisable from their immediate surroundings and not easily confused with adjacent similar landmarks.

Most checkpoints should lie within a few miles either side of the track line. Selecting checkpoints at greater distances can cause difficulties if the visibility decreases during flight. The student pilot will not normally be sent on a solo cross country flight unless the visibility conditions are forecast to remain at least 8 km (5nm). To select checkpoints at a greater range from track than this would therefore not be very sensible. Added to this is the fact that the further the checkpoint is away from the aircraft, the more difficult it will be to assess distance and consequently the possibility of large errors in a pilot's estimations can increase.

A cautionary note in relation to the selection of checkpoints is that it is not necessary to select every available checkpoint along the route. Discrimination is required or the pilot will find that his total effort is spent in locating and identifying ground features.

It will be appreciated therefore that good navigation practice will require that the pilot studies the route and selects only the number of checkpoints which are compatible with navigating the aircraft competently and safely by locating its position, and calculating where it will be in the immediate future.

In the case of microlights which generally have groundspeeds in the order of 30 to 50 knots it would normally suffice to plan on obtaining a fix every 5 to 10 minutes. Any attempt to fix the position of the aircraft at shorter intervals of time will usually occupy the pilot's attention unnecessarily, and is likely to prevent him from making other vital calculations and planning ahead.

Fig 3-50 shows a track plotted on a 1:250.000 topographical chart and a number of checkpoints have been enumerated to give guidance in assessing the type of features to use. It should be understood however that in order to discuss all the suitable checkpoints which could be used, no consideration has been given to selecting a suitable distance or time period between checkpoints.

Checkpoint 1.

The two large lakes situated either side of track will be clearly visible and form an excellent fix. The rising ground shown by the map contour lines, together with the surface elevation spot height of 1065' to the right of the intended track will give a good guide to the aircraft's general position whilst proceeding to checkpoint No.2.

Checkpoint 2.

The small town of Cheddar with its associated lake to the left of the track line could be a useful checkpoint. However both the town and lake are situated on low ground at the base of high ground, and they will not come into view until the high ground has been cleared.

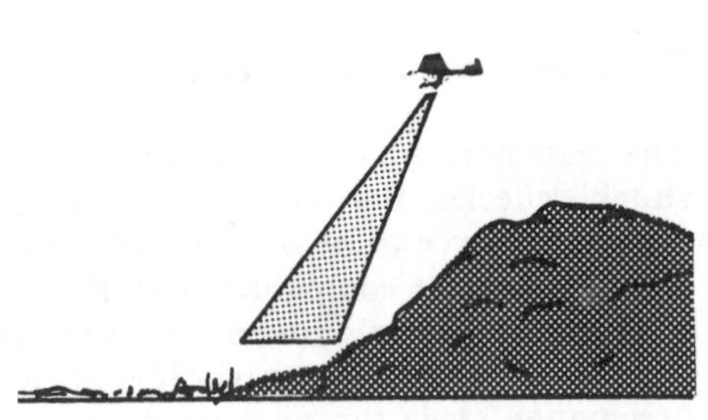

This means that the time available for seeing and identifying the checkpoint would be relatively short, and if the aircraft was slightly to the right of track the features might be missed altogether as the aircraft would pass directly overhead.

Checkpoint 3.

The map shows that the ground between checkpoint 2 and the town of Bridgewater contains no suitable checkpoints close to track. The small town at "A" has no positive identification features and in this situation the town of Burnham on Sea which lies some 5 nm to the West of the track could be used provided the visibility is good. It lies on a coastline with a small estuary immediately to its South. Additionally a railway line and motorway, both running North/South come together on the East side of the town. The railway line and the motorway can be considered as unique line features as there are no others in the area. However caution must be used not to put too much reliance on seeing the railway and motorway if flying at altitudes below 2000' amsl. This is because of the oblique angle of sight.

An accurate position fix can be made when Burnham lies directly abeam the right wing as shown by the arrow in the illustration.

Fig. 3—50

Checkpoint 4.

The town of Bridgwater has three good features which provide positive identification, a large river, a railway line, and a motorway.

Because of the collective uniqueness of the features already mentioned and bearing in mind that in the UK roads can often be confusing features the main roads which run out of Bridgwater in different directions can be ignored in this case.

Checkpoint 5.

The town of Taunton would be the next good checkpoint to use. It has similar confirmation features as checkpoint 4.

After passing over the railway line which runs East/West through Taunton a running fix will be available for the next 10 miles or so by using the railway line which runs approximately parallel and to the West of the trackline and the motorway coming in from the East and crossing the track at point "B".

Folding the Map for Use

There are various methods used in folding aeronautical charts for use in the cockpit. The first priority is that the method used enables the pilot to survey the complete track coverage on the minimum number of folds.

Further to this and when possible, the chart should be folded so that the track line lies in a position which allows the maximum area either side of the track line to be visible without having to unfold the chart while in flight.

METHODS OF MAP READING

There are four basic factors involved in sensible map reading procedures, these are as follows:

1. The selection of suitable checkpoints.
2. A knowledge of the aircraft's direction and groundspeed.
3. The assessment of distances.
4. The obtainment of accurate fixes.

The selection of checkpoints has already been discussed but, in relation to the factors shown at 2 and 3 it can be stated that knowledge of direction and the groundspeed together with the ability to assess distances, enables a pilot to think ahead and anticipate when checkpoints will appear. This will permit him to allocate his time properly between flying the aircraft, making calculations, and searching for the next checkpoint along the route.

The 4th factor is achieved by the pilot using three simple steps:

(a) The selection of a good checkpoint feature some distance ahead of the aircraft's position.

(b) The confirmation of the distance to be flown to reach it, which in conjunction with a known groundspeed will enable him to estimate with accuracy the time he will arrive in its locality.

(c) Anticipating the time the checkpoint will come into view, identifying it and noting the time he was over or abeam of it.

Map Orientation

To facilitate recognition between map features and ground features it is advisable to orientate the map so that the track drawn on it is coincident with the track direction and in line with the fore and aft axis of the aircraft. Thus resulting in the track line on the map approximately pointing in the direction in which the aircraft is travelling. This should be borne in mind when inserting the map into a plastic cover attached to a kneeboard. This will ensure that when the aircraft is on track the features which appear on the left of the track line on the map will appear on the left of the aircraft's track and similarly for those on the right.

However this arrangement may not be possible in a microlight aircraft when multiple tracks are flown on a single cross country flight. This is due to the difficulty of re-arranging the position of the kneeboard during flight.

The use, where possible, of the procedure described in the previous paragraph may make it a little more difficult to read names or numerals shown on the map, but this disadvantage is generally outweighed by the natural presentation of relative bearings between the aircraft and ground features, and ensuring that degrees of the compass seen relative to the map, are the same relative to the aircraft.

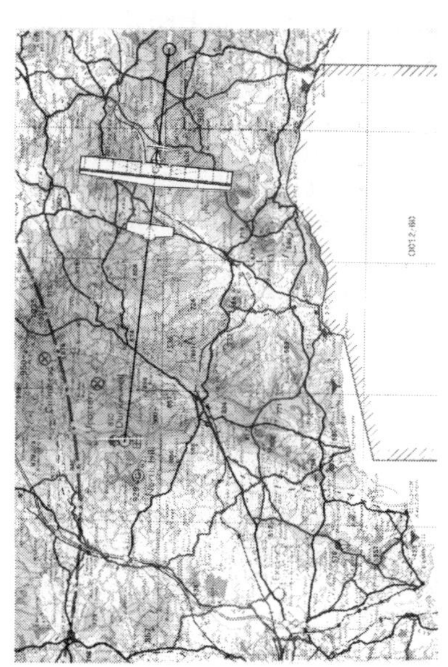

Fig. 3—51(a)

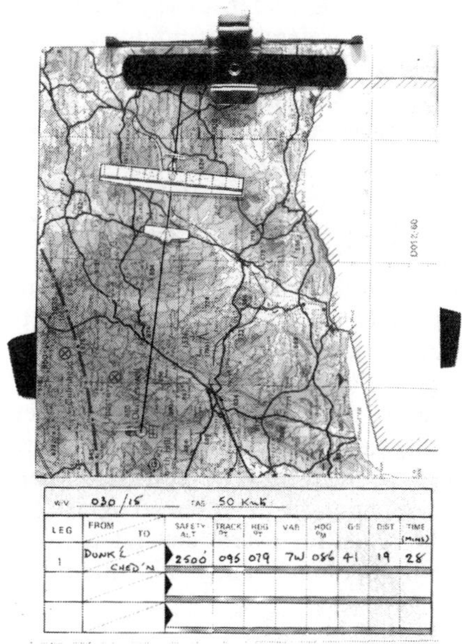

Fig. 3—51(b)

Anticipation of Checkpoints

The need to anticipate checkpoints is a primary requirement in pilot navigation, but this process can be affected by varying flight conditions.

For example, although a student will not normally be sent on a solo cross country flight unless the visibility is at least 8 km and suitable cloud conditions prevail, the weather in the UK can often change unexpectedly and be contrary to that which is forecast. This in turn can affect the time available for anticipation or even cancel it altogether.

Continuous Visual Contact

When good visibility exists and cloud base remains above the flight planned altitude, the time available to a pilot in searching for checkpoints, will be subject only to the constraints of flying the aircraft and making other essential navigational calculations. Therefore a pilot will normally be able to plan his workload to enable him to reasonably anticipate identification of the ground features he has chosen during his pre-flight preparation.

Restricted Visual Contact

Sometimes the visibility deteriorates during flight and this will bring additional problems. Reduction in visibility is usually caused by haze produced from smoke or other particles in the atmosphere, precipitation, or occasionally thick bands of smoke drifting downwind from industrial areas.

In these conditions, consideration must be given to the advisability of turning back or diverting. Such considerations are discussed later under the heading of 'Flight Planning', and the comments which follow merely relate to the difficulties of map reading under these conditions.

It may be preferable in circumstances of reduced visibility to shorten the period between obtaining each fix, but this will however be dependent upon the number of additional checkpoints which are available along the route.

The decision to use an increased number of checkpoints must be balanced against the progress of the flight so far. For example, if the aircraft has remained on track and checkpoints have been appearing at the pre-determined times, there will be less need to increase the navigation workload by selecting additional checkpoints at that time.

Flight conditions may however change in a manner which could prevent the pilot determining his position at a selected checkpoint. This may be due to smoke, or rain showers obscuring the checkpoint area. When this happens it is particularly important that a pilot is able to accurately assess his groundspeed, and therefore gauge the time at which the next selected checkpoint should appear.

If the flight has been proceeding according to plan and previous checkpoints have been arrived at on schedule, there will be no immediate need to become worried about the failure to recognise a selected fix. If conditions however change to the situation where several consecutive checkpoints have been missed, a condition of 'uncertainty' will undoubtedly exist.

Uncertain of Position - Procedure

When a pilot has flown for an appreciable time without obtaining a fix it will be necessary as a first step to assess the distance that could have been travelled since the last identified checkpoint.

The map should be carefully studied to ascertain the presence of suitable checkpoints within an area of at least 10 nm either side of the original track. It is usually best to read from the map to the ground when in this situation, but no hard and fast rules can be laid down, as a wide range of different conditions may apply. For example, a good feature may be seen on the ground and if it can be related to the map, an immediate fix will have been obtained and normal navigation can be continued.

Full details of the procedure to adopt should the situation change from being only uncertain of position, to becoming lost, is covered later under the heading of 'Practical Navigation'.

THE NAVIGATION COMPUTER

Earlier in this Manual the triangle of velocities and its application to pilot navigation was discussed. However pilots, do not have to plan their cross country flights by first constructing such triangles to determine the information they require. Instead, a device known as the 'Navigation Computer' has been designed to simplify this task, and there are many sizes and designs of computers on the market which are available for this purpose.

It is not intended to go through step by step operation of using a navigation computer in this manual, however the contents of the next few pages will give you some idea of the way a navigation computer can be used to solve certain navigational problems. Regardless of what follows, it must be clearly understood that due to the different types of computers available you should study the specific directions issued with the computer you may decide to use.

Notwithstanding the previous comments, many of the computers currently available have not been designed to cater for the low airspeed of Microlight aircraft. Therefore when working out problems involving the triangle of velocities it will be more convenient and practical to follow the methods shown in the examples an pages 3-60 to 3-64 providing the type of computer being used is suitable for this purpose. One such computer (described in the following text) is the Airtour CRP-1 model which is produced and sold by Airtour International Ltd at Elstree Aerodrome. This type of computer is widely used in the UK by private pilots and has two elements. One is constructed for use in solving problems which involve the triangle of velocities, and the other comprises a circular slide rule which can be used to solve numerous arithmetical problems, e.g. the finding of TAS, time-distance, conversion of units, fuel calculations etc.

NOTE: You will be required to answer questions relating to the above items during your written navigation examination for the issue of your private pilot's licence.

Problems Involving the Triangle of Velocities

Fig 3-52 shows an illustration of the vector triangle side of the computer, and provided certain facts are known it can be used for finding such information as heading, track, drift, groundspeed and wind velocity. In fact, anything that can be found through the use of the previously discussed triangle of velocities, can be easily and quickly solved by computer.

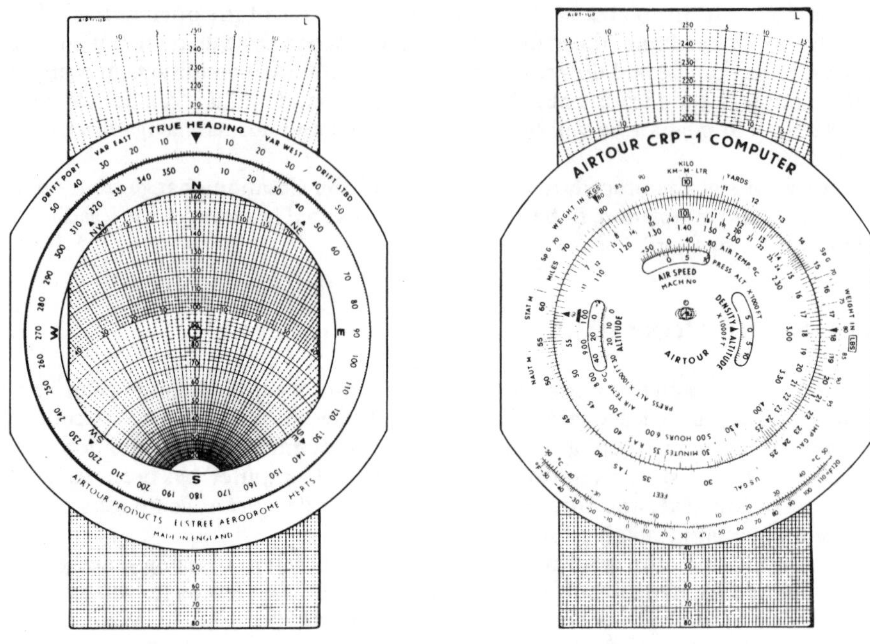

Fig. 3—52

Bascially the vector side of the computer consists of a rotatable compass rose with a clear plastic circular window, a drift scale, and a sliding plastic sheet upon which is superimposed curved speed lines and angled drift lines. The clear plastic window, is provided to draw on any of the elements used in the vector triangle, e.g. wind velocity, track, heading etc.

To find heading and groundspeed, the TAS, W/V and track, must first be established. The required track is measured from the chart and the W/V is obtained from the Area Meteorological Forecast. The TAS will however have to be calculated by selecting an appropriate IAS converting it to RAS, and then compensating for the pressure and temperature (density) at the altitude it is intended to fly. The conversion of RAS to TAS is undertaken by using the circular slide rule on the other side of the navigation computer, as shown in fig 3-53. Although it has already been stated that the indicated airspeed as measured by the air speed indicator will be the one most likely used for practical purposes when flying a microlight aircraft you will be required to demonstrate your ability to carry out calculations from IAS to TAS during your written examination. Studying the following examples will therefore be of value to you. The first airspeeds shown are more typical of light aircraft rather than microlights but the principles and methods used are the same regardless of the actual airspeeds used.

Determination of TAS using the Airtour CRP-1 Computer.
When using the calculations for conventional aircraft the RAS is established by referring to the Owner's/Flight Manual/Pilot's Operating Handbook, the circular slide rule of the computer should then be referred to and the following steps taken:

Using the window marked 'Airpseed' set the altitude to be flown against the forecast temperature for that height. The temperature is obtained from the Meteorological Forecast used for flight planning.

Note: The temperature scale is divided into 'plus' and 'minus' temperatures so be sure to use the right one for the calculation, temperatures are also clearly marked (+) or (-) on the Meteorological Forecast.

Example 1.
Assume the following:
RAS 120 kts
Pressure Altitude 3000'
Temperature +11° C
1. Set +11°C against 3000' in the airspeed window.
2. Read off from the RAS 120 on the inner scale the number 126 on the outer scale.
Answer TAS = 126 kts.

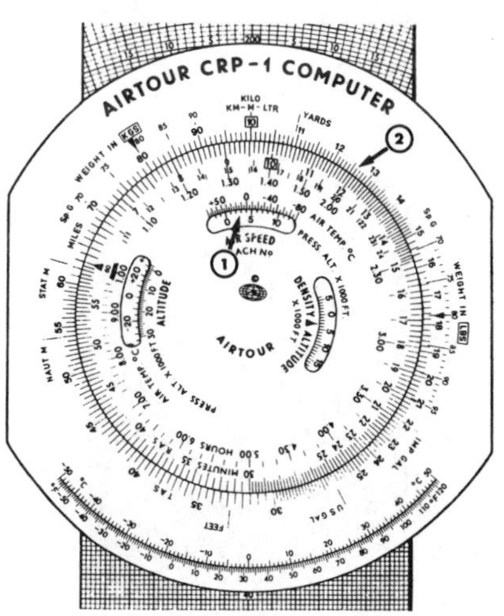

Fig 3-53

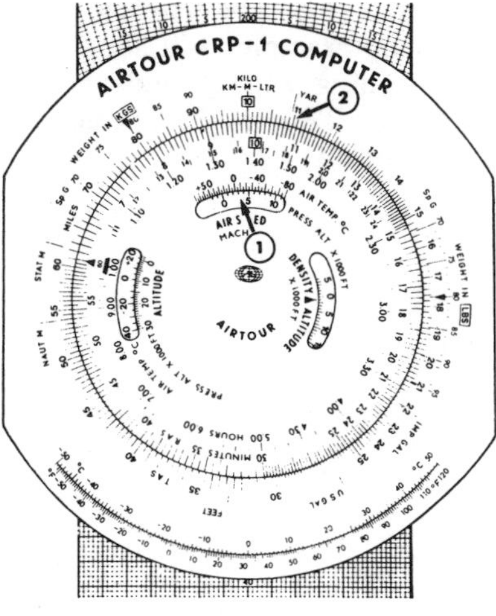

Fig. 3—54

Example 2. (Ref fig 3-54)
Assume the following:
RAS 110 kts
Pressure Altitude 3000'
Temperature -5°C
Answer TAS = 112kts.
In the two examples shown it will have been seen that the difference between RAS and TAS was relatively small but at higher altitudes the difference between RAS and TAS can increase considerably.

Determination of Heading and Groundspeed

Having established the TAS, the W/V can be obtained from the Area Meteorological Forecast. However, before using the vector side of the computer it would be of value to explain the principle of its construction.

Fig 3-55 shows the basic construction in which the point of origin is omitted from the computer so that a large range of speeds can be shown on the slide. The vertical arrow 'A' represents the TAS and the tip of this arrow is positioned by setting the speed circle representing TAS under the centre of the circle which is marked on the pastic window of the computer.

The wind arrow 'B' is drawn from the same point, and its length which represents wind speed, will show the amount of drift 'C' experienced, and thus the heading required can be ascertained.

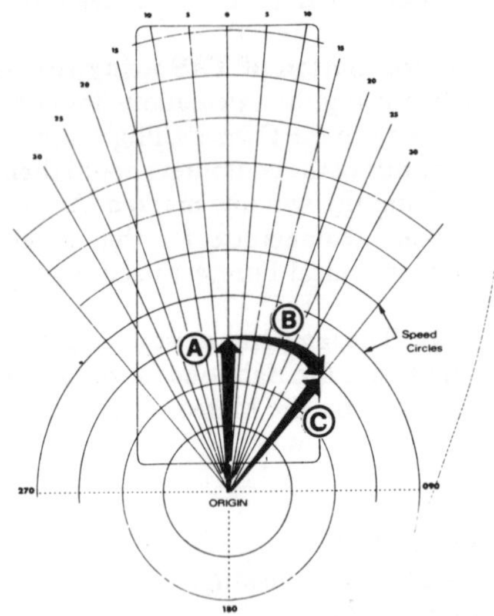

Fig. 3—55

Fig 3-56 shows how the triangle of velocities would appear if superimposed over the computer slide.

The TAS is 120 kts, W/V is 270/30 and the required track is 360°.

Drift in this case is 14° starboard.

The following examples will show how the true heading and groundspeed is obtained when TAS, W/V and track required are known.

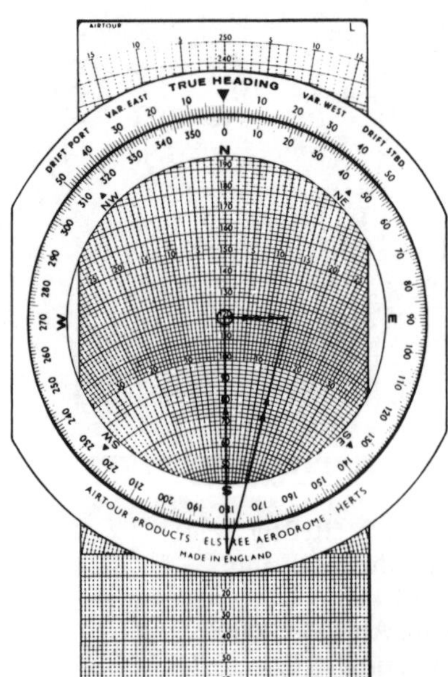

Fig. 3—56

In the following examples the same figures are used as in the examples shown in fig. 3-38, 3-39 and 3-40 when discussing the 'triangle of velocities'. You might therefore, find it helpful to cross refer to these earlier diagrams when studying the following 3 computer problems, based upon airspeeds compatible with microlight aircraft.

Example 1.
Find the True Heading and Ground-speed when:
TAS is 40 knots
W/V is 360/20 knots
Track Required is 090°T

Step 1.
Set wind direction under the True Heading pointer.

Step 2.
Mark wind velocity up from the centre (each division = 2 units) make a small pencil mark at this point.

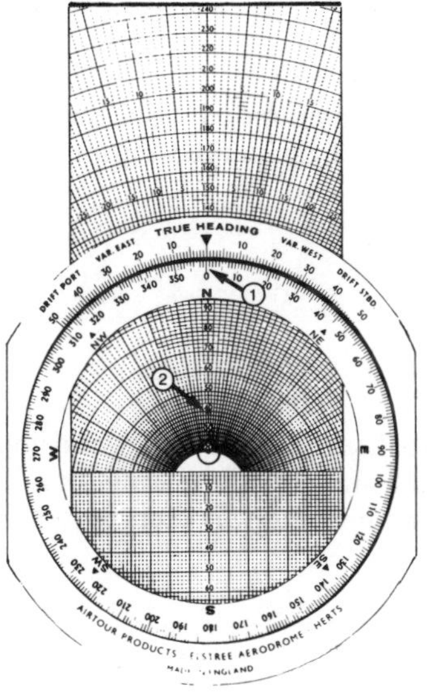

Fig 3—57

Step 3.
Place track required 090° under the True Heading pointer.

Step 4.
Slide cursor so that the wind velocity point is over the TAS curve.

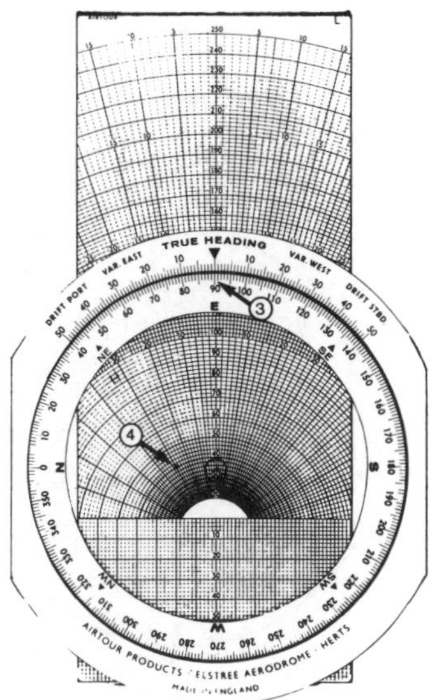

Fig. 3—58

Step 5.
Read the groundspeed under the centre circle of the plastic window, i.e. 34 knots.

Step 6.
Read the amount of drift that will be experienced against the appropriate drift line, i.e. 30°.

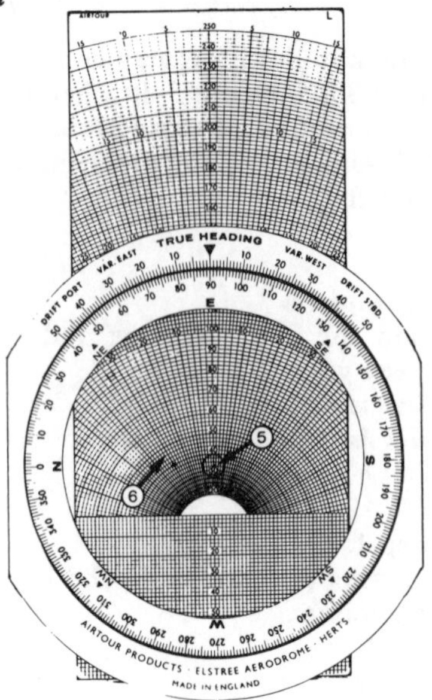

Fig 3—59

Visualise the effect of the wind upon an aircraft travelling East and it will be seen that the aircraft will be drifted to the right, therefore apply the 30° into the wind and the heading will then need to be 090° minus 30° = 060°.

Example 2
Find the True Heading and TAS when:
Track is 045°T
Groundspeed is 60 knots
W/V is 180/25 knots.

Step 1.
Rotate the bearing scale until the wind direction of 180° is under the True Heading pointer.

Step 2.
Mark in the wind strength by making a pencil mark of length 25 knots above the centre circle of the plastic window.

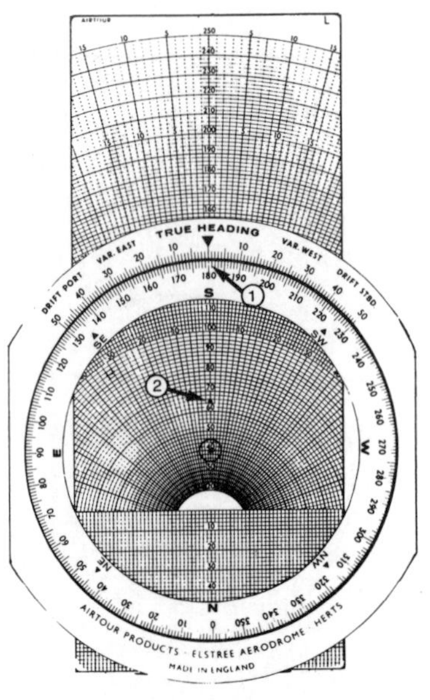

Fig. 3—60

Step 3.
Rotate the bearing scale until the track of 045° appears under the True Heading pointer.

Step 4.
Adjust the slide so that 60 knots is located under the centre circle of the plastic window.

Step 5.
Note the drift angle of 22°.
The wind is coming from the right of track so in this case subtract 22° from the track angle = heading 067°.
The TAS is measured at the end of the wind line = 46 knots.

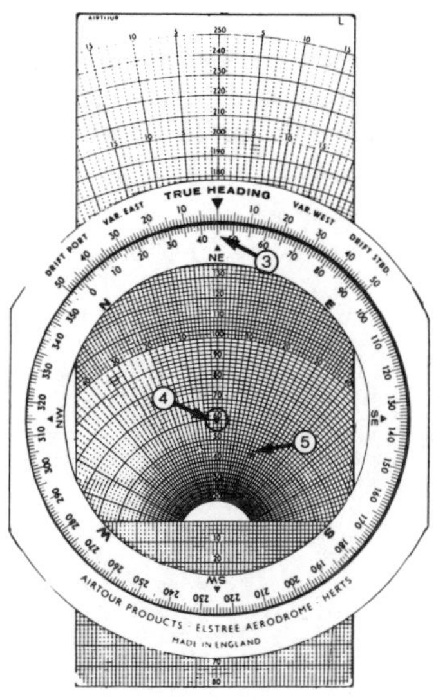

Fig. 3—61

Example 3.
Find the wind velocity when
TAS is 50 knots
Heading is 260°
Track Made Good is 270°
Groundspeed is 25 knots

Step 1.
Rotate the bearing scale until the true heading is against the True Heading pointer.

Step 2.
Adjust the slide so that the TAS of 50 knots is in the centre of the circle on the plastic window.

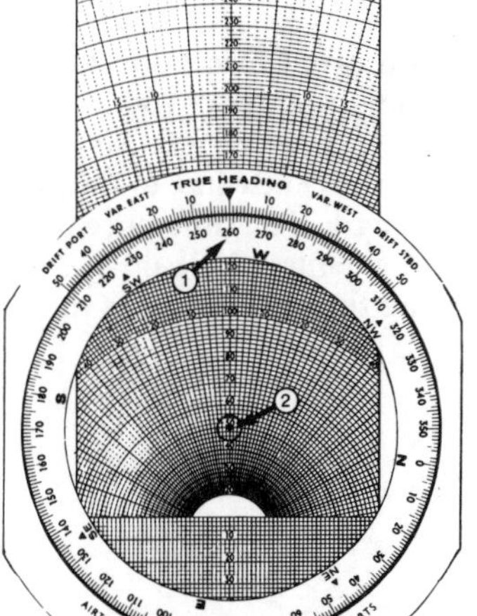

Fig. 3—62

Step 3.
Mentally determine the drift angle by comparing the heading with the track made good - in this case it is 10° to the right.

Step 4.
Make a pencil mark at the intersection of the 10° starboard drift line and the groundspeed arc of 25 knots.

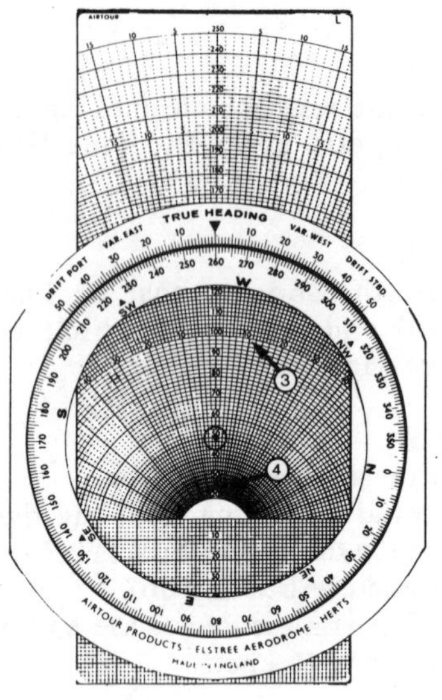

Fig. 3—63

Step 5.
Rotate the bearing scale until the pencil mark is directly below the centre circle.

Step 6.
Read off the wind direction against the True Heading pointer = 250°.

Read down the centre line to the point of the pencil mark. The difference in speed between the centre circle on the plastic window and the pencil mark is the windspeed = 25 knots.

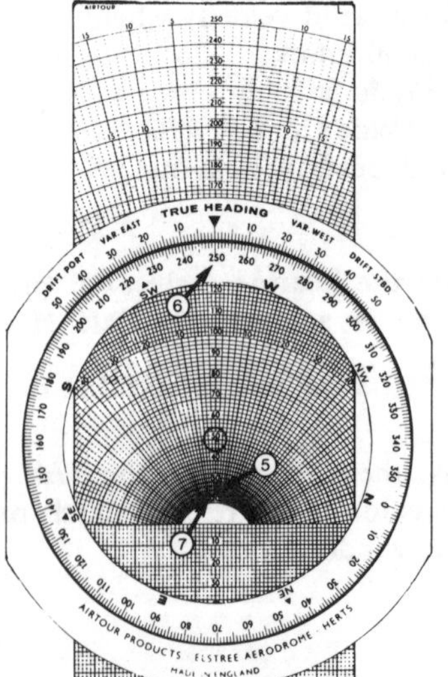

Fig. 3—64

Circular Slide Rule

This side of the computer can be used to solve many types of arithmetical problems particularly those which are specifically used in navigation, such as:

- TAS Calculations.
- Time - Distance - Speed Problems.
- Conversion Calculations involving Metric, British and US Units, e.g.
- Distances, Lengths, Liquid Measures, etc.
- Fuel Consumption Calculations.
- Pressure, Density and True Altitude Calculations.

The circular slide rule consists of one fixed and one rotary scale, both of which are marked with numerical divisions. A transparent rotatable cursor which is engraved with a red 'hair line' facilitates the setting and reading of the numerical scales.

Note: The unit value of the numerical scales on the circular slide rule change at specific intervals and a particular note should be made of this point in order to avoid errors in calculations.

The fixed outer scale carries additional markings in specific positions around the rim. These marks are used for various conversions, e.g. statute miles to nautical miles or kilometres, Imperial gallons to US gallons or litres, yards to feet, etc. The rotary inner disc also has a circular scale marking in the form of hours and minutes as well as small windows which form additional scales which are used when converting RAS to TAS, or calculating such items as Density Altitude etc.

The simplest way of learning how to use the calculator side of the navigation computer, is to carry out some specific examples of typical navigation problems. Note: As with all slide rule calculations the position of the decimal point will have to be determined by inspection, from the values being used.

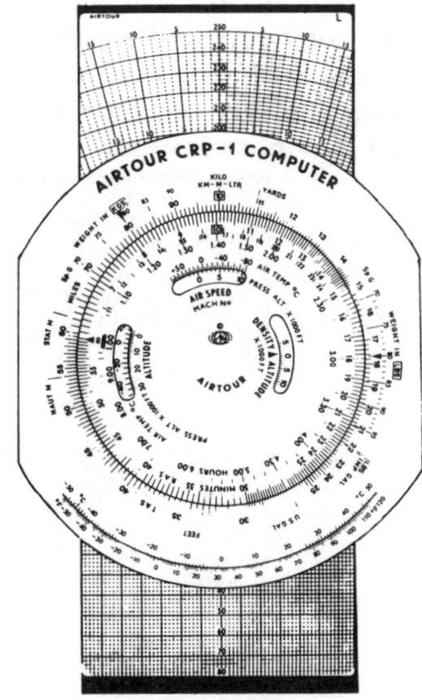

Fig. 3—65

Time, Speed and Distance Problems:

It can be stated that:
Time x Speed = Distance
Distance ÷ by Time = Speed

The following pages give examples of how the calculator side of the computer is used to solve a few of the typical problems associated with navigation.

Example 1. Time x Speed = Distance

If an aircraft travels for one hour 20 minutes at a groundspeed of 45 kts what is the distance it will cover?

Step 1.
Rotate the inner scale until ▲ (60 minutes = 1 hour) is against 45 on the outer scale.

Step 2.
1 hour 20 minutes = 80 minutes therefore read off against 80 on the inner scale, the figure of 60 on the outer scale. Mentally consider the problem, 45 kts in one hour will equal 90 nm in 2 hours, therefore the distance travelled in 1 hour 20 minutes at this speed must be 60 nm.

Note: Immediately adjacent to 80 on the inner scale appear the numerals 1.20, this represents one hour and twenty minutes and it will usually be more convenient to use this direct reading of hours and minutes rather than reducing the time to minutes and then converting it back to hours and minutes.

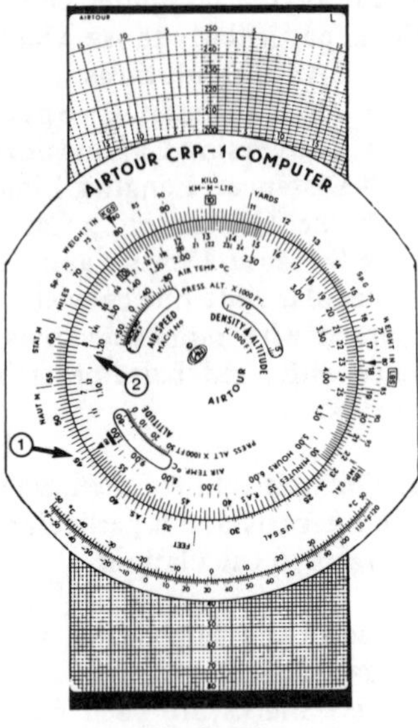

Fig. 3—66

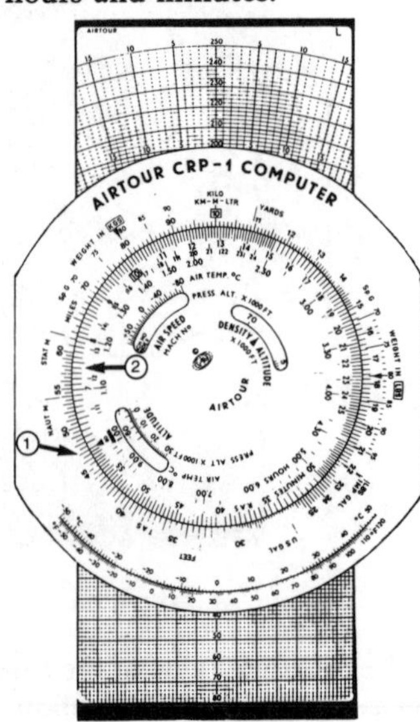

Fig. 3—67

Example 2. Distance ÷ Speed = Time

If an aircraft travels at a groundspeed of 47 kts for a distance of 58 nm how long will it take?

Step 1.
Set ▲ on the inner scale against 47 on the outer scale.

Step 2.
Read off against 58 on the outer scale, the figure of 74 on the inner scale.
Answer 74 minutes.

Example 3. Distance ÷ Time = Speed
If an aircraft covers a distance of 58 nm in 1 hour 14 minutes what is its groundspeed?

Step 1.
Set 74 on the inner scale against 58 on the outer scale.
Step 2.
Against the speed index on the inner scale read off 47 on the outer scale.
Answer: 47 kts.

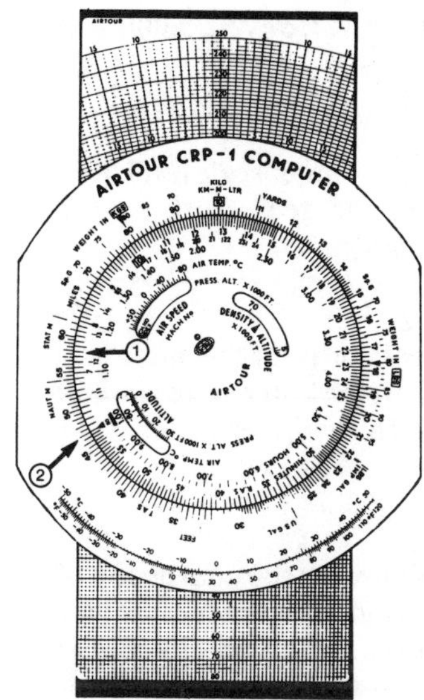

Fig. 3—68

Conversion Calculations

The rim of the outer scale has various marks which are labelled, Nautical Miles, Statute Miles, Kilometres, Metres, Yards and Feet. These index marks are used to solve conversion problems in relation to distance. Fundamentally all conversions commence by setting the value to be converted on the inner scale against the appropriate 'unit mark' on the outer scale. The answer is then read off from the inner scale against the index mark of the unit required.

Example 4. How many nautical miles is 35 statute miles?

Step 1.
Rotate the inner scale until 35 is set again the statute mile mark on the outer scale.

Step 2.
Read off from the nautical miles mark on the outer scale the figure of 30.4 on the inner scale.

Note that in this band each small division on the inner scale equals a 1/2 unit.

Answer: 30.4 nm.

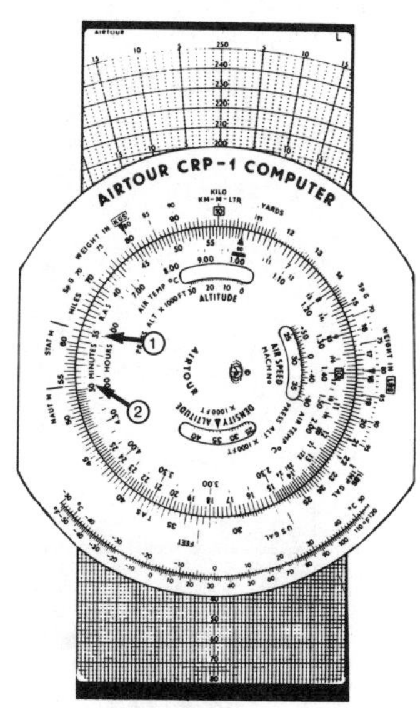

Fig. 3—69

Example 5. Convert 5.000 feet to metres.

Step 1.
Rotate the inner scale until 50 is against the 'feet' mark on the outer scale.

Step 2.
Against the 'm' of the index km-m-ltr on the outer scale read off 15.24 on the inner scale.
Answer: 1524 metres.

To cater for the conversion of pounds to kilogrammes or vice versa, lbs and kgs marks appear on the outer scale of the calculator side of the navigation computer. The procedure for conversion of these units of weight is similar to that used in the previous examples.

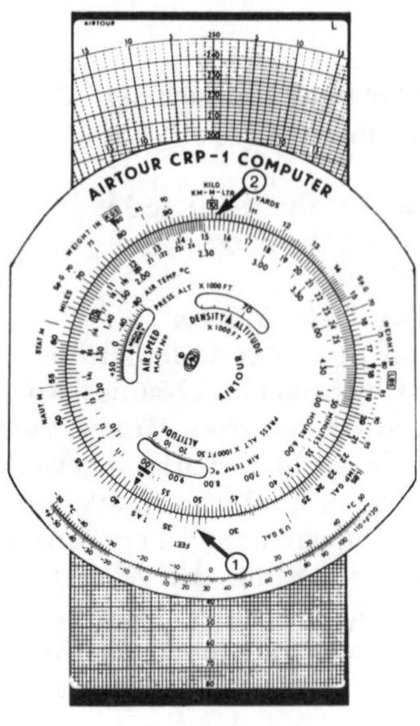

Fig. 3—70

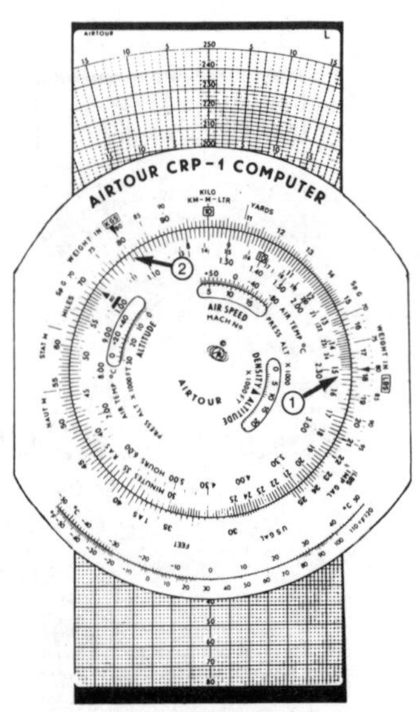

Fig.3—71

Example 6. Convert 1500 lbs to kgs.

Step 1.
Rotate the inner scale until 1500 lbs appear against the lbs mark on the outer scale.

Step 2.
Read off against the kgs mark on the outer scale the figure of 680 on the inner scale.

Answer: 680 kilogrammes.

Fuel Calculations

Fuel management is an integral part of safe flight operations, therefore fuel consumption calculations form a necessary part of proper pre-flight planning. Such problems are resolved quite simply on the calculator side of the computer.

First, it will be necessary to establish the aircraft's fuel consumption per hour from reference to the Aircraft/Engine Handbook. Then determine the estimated flight time from the point of departure to the destination and then use the calculator to find out how much fuel will be required for the trip.

Example 7. If the fuel consumption is 1.5 Imperial gallons per hour (ghp) and the flight time en-route is 1 hour and 20 minutes how much fuel will be used?

Step 1.
Rotate the inner scale until ▲ is against 1.5 (gph) on the outer scale.

Step 2.
Read off against 8 (1hour 20 minutes) on the inner scale the amount of fuel required.

Answer: 2.0 gallons.

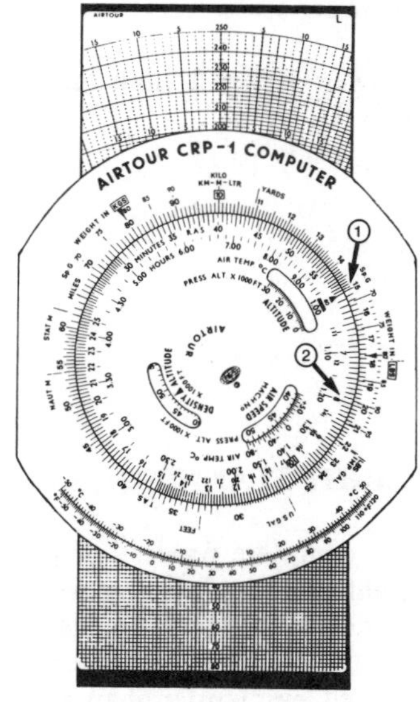

Fig. 3–72

This procedure will give the fuel required for the en-route phase only and an allowance should also be made for the fuel used during taxying, take-off, the climb to planned altitude and the circuit and landing at destination. This allowance will vary, being dependent upon the actual fuel consumption of the aircraft being used.

Additionally, an allowance must also be made to cater for any reduction in the en-route groundspeed due to unfavourable headwinds, and for other unplanned circumstances such as becoming lost, and/or diverting to an alternate aerodrome. The minimum allowance for this in the case of microlight aircraft should be at least 30 minutes fuel consumption at cruising power.

Example 8. If the fuel consumption is 1.4 gph and the total useable fuel carried is 2.5 gallons, what is the maximum duration of flight?

Step 1.
Set ▲ on the inner scale against 14 on the outer scale.

Step 2.
Read off against 25 on the outer scale the time in minutes from the inner scale.

Answer: 107 = 1 hour and 47 minutes.

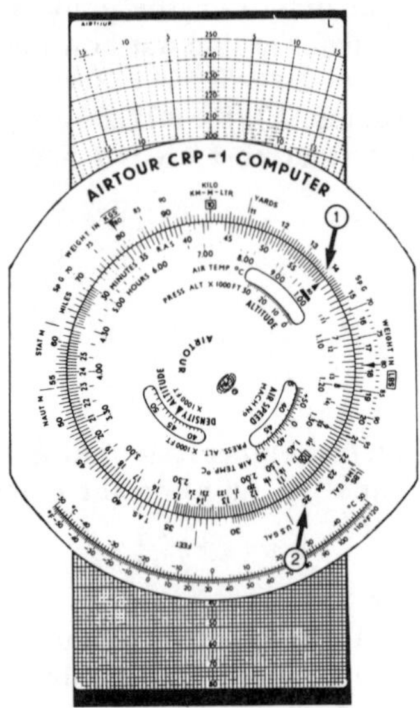

Fig. 3—73

FLIGHT PLANNING

The complete process of pre-flight preparation involving navigation is called 'flight planning' during which a number of factors must be borne in mine. In relation to the legal aspects of a flight the pertinent paragraphs of the Air Navigation Order can be summarised as follows:

The Commander of an aircraft shall satisfy himself before the aircraft takes off that:

The flight can safely be made, taking into account the latest information available as to the route and aerodrome to be used, the weather reports and forecasts available, and any alternative course of action which can be adopted in case the flight cannot be completed as planned.

The equipment (including radio apparatus) required by the Order to be carried in the circumstances of the intended flight is carried and in a fit condition for use. The aircraft is in every way fit for the intended flight and the certificates relating to airworthiness, maintenance etc, are in force and will continue to remain in force during the intended flight (A similar requirement exists in relation to pilot licences and ratings).

The load carried by the aircraft is of such weight, and is so distributed and secured that it may safely be carried on the intended flight.

A sufficient quantity of fuel and oil is carried for the intended flight, and that a safe margin has been allowed for contingencies, i.e. becoming lost or having to divert to an alternate aerodrome.

Having regard to the performance capability of the aircraft in the expected conditions of the intended flight (including any obstructions at the places of departure, along the intended route and at the intended destination), it is capable of safely taking off, reaching and maintaining a safe height thereafter, and making a safe landing at the place of intended destination.

Although not all of the items above are applicable to microlight operations, it can be appreciated that the factors spelled out in the above paragraphs cover points of a practical nature applicable to any type of aircraft operation. They do in fact form the basis of any type of pre-flight planning and it is pertinent to note that many aircraft accidents are attributed to the pilot's neglect of these factors.

Therefore in order that pilots can fulfill these responsibilities and ensure the safety of the flight, it is necessary that they have adequate knowledge of those elements which are involved in the process of pre-flight planning. This process will also need to include those factors which affect the take-off and landing stages of the flight.

CAUTION
AIR INFORMATION CURRENT THROUGH
4th MARCH 1982
Consult NOTAMS, UK Air Information Publications and Chart of UK Airspace Restrictions for latest air information. NOTE. The portrayal of aerodromes does not imply any right to use.
UK Military Low Flying System
For geographical detail, consult Chart of Intense Aerial Activity & Military Low Flying System (see UK AIP RAC 5-1-2)

Fig.3—74

A basic element of pre-flight preparation requires the use of current navigation charts from which the pilot can review the intended route in relation to items such as Controlled Airspace, Danger Areas etc.

The use of an outdated chart could result in the pilot inadvertently entering Controlled Airspace and/or creating circumstances which may hazard himself, his passengers, or other aircraft and their occupants. Using the correct information contained on current charts will on the other hand enhance the pilot's ability to complete the flight with greater confidence, and safety.

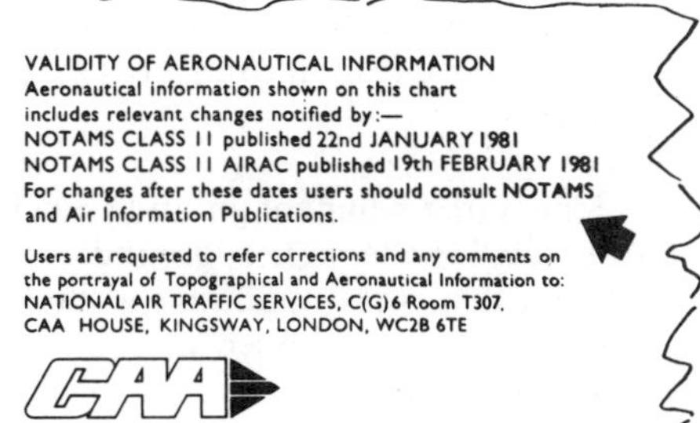

VALIDITY OF AERONAUTICAL INFORMATION
Aeronautical information shown on this chart
includes relevant changes notified by:—
NOTAMS CLASS II published 22nd JANUARY 1981
NOTAMS CLASS II AIRAC published 19th FEBRUARY 1981
For changes after these dates users should consult NOTAMS and Air Information Publications.
Users are requested to refer corrections and any comments on the portrayal of Topographical and Aeronautical Information to:
NATIONAL AIR TRAFFIC SERVICES, C(G)6 Room T307,
CAA HOUSE, KINGSWAY, LONDON, WC2B 6TE
CAA

Fig. 3—75

A further point to bear in mind is that whenever the intended route (or part of it) is close to the edge of a chart, the adjacent chart should be studied during pre-flight planning and also carried during the flight. Otherwise in the event of an unplanned route change due to bad weather or other circumstances, the pilot may arrive over terrain which is not covered by the primary chart, leaving him without the necessary topographical and overprinted aeronautical information upon which the successful outcome of the flight is so dependent.

Plotting the Route

Although the shortest distance between two points is a straight line, this principle may not always be safely applied when drawing in the route between departure and destination.

The chart will need to be studied to determine the effect of such items as the geographical dimensions and height limitations of Controlled Airspace. The geographical dimensions and activity of Danger Areas, the position of airfields en-route, the physical characteristics of the surface to be overflown, e.g. mountainous areas, water areas etc and other items. Because of these varying considerations the pilot will often find it necessary or judicious to draw in more than one track in order to safely circumnavigate areas into which he is nor allowed or those which could result in unnecessary hazards.

Selection of Altitude

During training the student will find that the selection of an en-route altitude will be made according to the recommendations of his Flying Training Organisation or his instructor.

Once qualified he will be expected to assess any particular situation himself and decide upon the best altitude to fly to maintain a safe clearance from the surface, obstructions and Controlled Airspace etc.

Normally private pilot navigation is conducted between approximately 2000' and 3000' amsl. Use of this altitude band is brought about because of the lower limits of Controlled Airspace, the upper limit of Aerodrome Traffic Zones, and the general cloud ceilings which exist in the UK through the year.

Notwithstanding the foregoing considerations, it is essential to examine the elevation of the surface and obstructions along and on either side of the track line to establish a minimum safe altitude below which the pilot should not descend during the en-route phase.

There are several methods used in calculating a safe altitude to fly, however in relation to navigation conducted by private pilots a commonly used method is as follows:

Review the height of ground and obstructions within 5 nm either side of track. Add 1000' to the highest ground/obstruction which lies within this 10 nm band and use this as the minimum atltitude acceptable for safe en-route navigation. In the case of very low speed aircraft such as microlights the figure of 1000' could be reduced to 500'.

The practical purpose of determining Minimum Safe Altitudes for the route during the preparation stage is to be able to immediately assess the minimum altitude at which it will be safe to fly if lowering cloud is encountered during the en route phase of the flight. This information will then be used by the pilot in deciding whether it is safe to continue, or whether to divert to another place or turn back.

Having determined the Minimum Safe Altitude a pilot will be in a better position to make a positive and correct decision in the event of weather deterioration. It must be stressed that a pilot must avoid any tendency to fly lower than this altitude particularly if the decision to continue is based on the premise that the weather will improve. Clearly a pilot who is not trained in instrument flying must remain clear of cloud and he should bear in mind that a lowering cloud base en-route will be most likely indicative of a continuing trend and that incorrect and impulsive decisions are among the most common causes of aviation accidents.

Selection of Alternate Landing Places

Even though care has been taken to obtain an adequate weather forecast, and one which indicates that VMC will prevail along the intended route during the period planned for the flight, it must be appreciated that unpredicted weather changes can often occur.

On these occasions, deteriorating weather can present problems to the pilot who will be faced with the need to make a positive decision as to whether it will be safe to continue or whether it will be necessary to turn back to the departure point or to divert to an alternative landing site. The possibility of this type of situation occuring must therefore be considered during the pre-flight planning stage.

A review of the available alternates should therefore be made in relation to the planned track(s) and the relative position of any Controlled Airspace or similar feature noted together with the possibility of having to amend the planned Safety Altitude if a diversion has to be made.

Airspace Restrictions in the United Kingdom

Over the UK there exists a number of areas in which civil aircraft operations may for one reason or another be restricted or prohibited, either temporarily or permanently, on the grounds of safety.

These Airspace restrictions have been covered in section two of this manual and the reader should review this information as part of his Navigation Training.

Fig. 3–76

Fig. 3–77

Weather Forecasts and Reports

The weather in the UK can change significantly within a short time and also over relatively short distances. Microlight aircraft are particularly vulnerable to certain types of weather, e.g. strong winds, gustiness, turbulence and reduced visibility. It is therefore essential that a pilot obtains weather information prior to setting off on any navigation flight.

Without such information a pilot cannot reasonably ensure that he will be able to conduct the flight in weather conditions which are compatible with the privileges of his licence or even to determine that the flight can be safely undertaken.

The Aviation Weather Forecasting Service

An essential requirement for any safe flying operation, whether conducted in large passenger carrying airliners or small private aircraft is the availability of a weather information service.

To meet the needs of civil aviation, an adequate, reliable and fast weather information service has been set up by the UK Meteorological Office. This comprises a complex and highly sophisticated weather reporting system through which actual and anticipated weather conditions over large areas are passed to the Aviation Weather Service at Bracknell in Berkshire.

This information is then processed by skilled forecasters, following which, weather forecasts applicable to particular areas or routes are issued. Nevertheless this vast technological network can only be of practical value where individual pilots utilise it correctly.

The following list itemises the various methods which can be used by pilots to obtain aviation weather information:

Area Forecasts
The UK General Aviation Visual Flight Forecast Service
Route Forecasts
Aerodrome Weather Forecasts
Aerodrome Weather Reports
VHF 'In-Flight' Weather Reports
Prestel 'Aviation Weather Information'

Fig. 3–78

Area Forecasts

Area Forecasts are issued to aerodromes from the appropriate Area Meteorological Office. This type of forecast is available to all aerodromes with ATC units and can be obtained for other aerodromes on request.

An Area Forecast is normally issued every 6 hours commencing from 0001 hours. Fig 3-79 shows an example of an Area Forecast which covers a radius of 60km. from a stated datum, in this case Luton Airport.

Particular points of note are:

That time is expressed in GMT and care must be taken to ensure the period of the Forecast is current for the time of the flight.

A synopsis of the general weather situation is given together with its anticipated movement.

The wind velocity is given in degrees (T) and knots, and normally only specified for selected altitudes. If a flight is planned at an altitude between those shown on the Forecast, it will be necessary to interpolate the wind velocity for that altitude.

It will also be necessary to interpret the forecast weather and visualise the actual conditions which may be experienced during the flight in terms of wind, visibility, cloudbase etc.

Metform 2324A
(Revised March 1968)

METEOROLOGICAL OFFICE.

A.(1) SERIAL No. .... B. AREA FORECAST for Cranfield & 60 kms radius Luton

C. FOR THE PERIOD FROM 0600 HOURS 16/8/ 1982 TO 1400 HOURS 15/8/ 1982

ALL HEIGHTS IN THE FORECAST ARE ABOVE SEA LEVEL. ALL TIMES ARE GMT

D. SPECIAL FEATURES OF THE METEOROLOGICAL SITUATION:

NE'ly airstream covers the area with a region of thundery rain moving slowly into the area from the SW later in the day.

E. WINDS (Deg. TRUE and Knots) AT:		**TEMPERATURES (DEG. C.)**
SURFACE	ENE 10 - 15 kts	
2 ,000 FT	100 15 kts	+14
,000 FT		
5 ,000 FT	090 10 kts	+ 8
,000 FT		
10 ,000 FT	VBL 10 kts	0
,000 FT		
18 ,000 FT	250 15 kts	-16
,000 FT		
24 ,000 FT	250 25 kts	-28
,000 FT		
30 ,000 FT	230 35 kts	-41

CLOUD

F. OVC St base 300' - 600' covering hills, tops 1200', breaking midmorning and dispersing later.

G. BKN Sc base 2000' tops 3000'. Cloud bec generally midmorning on, BKN Cu base 2500' tops 9000' and OCNL tops 16.000'.

H. BKN Ac/Cs above 10.000' from the SW late in period.

J. SURFACE VISIBILITY:

1000 mtrs - 3000 mtrs and locally 500 mtrs or less, slowly improving to 5 - 8 kms, but 3 -5 kms in showers.

K. WEATHER

Fog and hill fog patches until midmorning, Showers later, Cloudy.

L.(1) HEIGHT OF 0 DEG. C. ISOTHERM: 9000'

L.(2) AIRFRAME ICING: Moderate, locally severe.

S. TROPOPAUSE: .... **FT** .... **DEG. C**

T. CONTRAIL LEVELS BETWEEN: .... **FT AND** .... **FT.**

W. REMARKS, WARNINGS, TURBULENCE ETC. **BAROMETRIC CHANGES:**

Fog and hill fog. Falling

Y. FURTHER OUTLOOK: To 2000z

Thundery rain from the SW.

METEOROLOGICAL OFFICE Heathrow. .... FORECASTER

Issued at .... hours .... 196....

Fig. 3–79

Having explained the content of an Area Forecast it must also be appreciated that these forecasts will probably only be available at microlight training schools and aerodromes. Nevertheless there are other methods whereby weather information can be obtained and one which has been specifically set up for the private pilot is the AIRMET forecast service. It consists of pre-recorded forecasts from a published telephone number.

This facility provides routine area forecasts for designated areas of the United Kingdom between the surface and 10,000 feet, for pilots planning flights at low level, particularly those intending to fly under VFR. Its main purpose is to enable pilots flying on a non-scheduled basis, at lower altitudes than those normally used by scheduled air transport and mainly outside controlled airspace, to obtain an overall description of the weather situation in the lower levels of airspace when planning their flight(s).

The Service is available only on the public telephone network (Automatic Answering System or ATAS) from outlets at West Drayton and Manchester, and is produced in a standard format to facilitate transcription on to a form produced for the purpose.

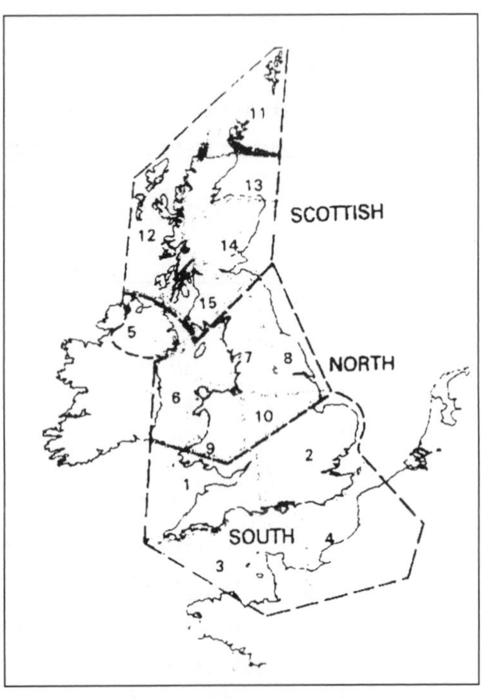

Fig 3–80

1	FORECAST REGION	AIRMET TEL. NOS. (0530 – 2300L)	0001 – 0800 FCST (2300 – 0530L)	AMENDMENTS (1930 – 0530L)	CONSULTATION; TAFS/METARS
	SOUTH	0898-500-693	BRACKNELL 0344-860488		
	NORTH	0898-500-692	MANCHESTER 061-429-0927		
	SCOTTISH	0898-500-691	GLASGOW 041-221-6116		

2	PERIOD OF VALIDITY			
	From		on	
	To		on	

TAFS/ METARS ONLY		
	ABERDEEN	0224-722331 Ext 5176
	ALDERGROVE	08494-23275
	BIRMINGHAM	021-782-6241
	CARDIFF	0222-390492
	LEEDS	0532-457687

AIRMET forecasts are available by telephone for three regions in the UK, as shown on the map on page 3–76. The telephone broadcasts are read in conversational English, at a moderate dictation speed. They can be obtained on the following numbers:

AIRMET SOUTH region (which includes parts of Northern France)	:	0898-500-693
AIRMET NORTH region (which includes Northern Ireland)	:	0898-500-692
AIRMET SCOTTISH region	:	0898-500-691

All three forecasts are renewed routinely four times daily, to give the following periods of validity:

0600–1400 local time*,	with outlook to	2000 the same day
1200–2000	"	0200 the following day
1800–0200	"	0800 the following day
0001–0800**	"	1400 the same day

Each forecast becomes available about half an hour before the start of the period of validity.

The Pilots Proforma is self-explanatory and allows the recorded information to be copied down in the same sequence in which it is recorded. It also contains a map of the British Isles, showing the geographical disposition of the weather areas used in the broadcast. It should be noted that comments on the Service can be made at any time; the address to send them to is included in the preliminary details at the top of the Proforma.

Procedure for obtaining forecasts for GA flights
By telephoning the appropriate number shown at the head of the Proforma, a recording will be heard of the current appropriate low-level forecast for the Scottish, northern or southern group of areas as shown on the map on the Proforma. This is read out at dictation speed in the same sequence as on the Pilots Proforma, to enable the forecasts to be copied directly on to the appropriate parts of the Proforma. When completed, the form gives a general description of the low-level weather (surface/10,000 feet) in the respective areas, enabling pilots to plan flights through these areas. It should be noted that all heights given in the Proforma, and in the recordings, are above Mean Sea Level (amsl).

A copy of the Pilots Proforma is a basic pre-requisite to making use of this Service. The Proforma is obtainable free of charge on request to:

The Technical Secretary
Aircraft Owners and Pilots Association
British Light Aviation Centre
50a Cambridge Street
London SW1V 4QQ — Telephone Number: 071-834-5631

provided a stamp, self-addressed envelope is included with the request.

Further developments are currently being made to improve the dissemination of meteorological information to private pilots.

MINIMUM WEATHER CONDITIONS ACCEPTABLE TO SAFETY

Whenever a pilot exceeds his own and/or his aircraft limitations, the basis of an accident will inevitably be present. Past and present records show, that most people involved in accidents induced by deteriorating weather are not irresponsible pilots, but ordinary normally careful and responsible private pilots who have been momentarily forgetful of the need to obtain a weather forecast and assess it in relation to their own limitations.

Additionally, on those occasions when the weather deteriorates en-route, a form of compulsion often engulfs such individuals, and instead of returning to the place of departure or diverting to an alternate aerodrome or landing strip until the weather improves, they carry on until the inevitable occurs, 'a frightening' experience or worse.

The training you receive is designed to reduce the possibility of hazardous situations occurring due to poor preparation, or a disregard to the rules of flight safety. Weather forecasts and reports are always available, and considerable sums of money are spent in providing this service to pilots. It will therefore be your responsibility to ensure that you make the best use of this service both during pre-flight preparation, and when making decisions prior to and during flight.

The limitations of student pilots and qualified private pilots will inevitably vary because of differences in their experience and the type of aircraft being flown. Any form of safe navigation will demand that many requirements be met, but in particular, visual navigation techniques demand that two basic requirements are met at all times, these are, a sufficient degree of visibility to ensure that practical visual navigation can be maintained and, a minimum cloud base for the route to ensure that a safe clearance above terrain and obstructions can be achieved.

What follows are some simple rules which when adopted by the pilot, will give him and his passengers a reasonable assurance of completing a safe and pleasant flight.

Pre-Flight Preparation

Obtain and assess the weather forecast for the route and time for which the flight is planned.

Visualise the weather likely to be experienced, and assess its effect upon the visibility and the minimum safe altitude which the route requires.

Visibility requirements are such, that any sensible private pilot without instrument flying capability will need a minimum of 5 km to ensure a successful visual navigation flight. If the forecast indicates that such a visual requirement cannot be met throughout the period of the flight...
'Do Not Go'.

The forecast must indicate clearly that the minimum safe altitude required for the flight can be maintained along all segments of the route. The general rule for establishing a minimum safe altitude is that it must be possible to remain clear of cloud and above 1000' over all terrain and obstructions en-route within 5 nm of the aircraft. This figure should be increased to 1500' and preferably 2000' when the flight passes over or in the vicinity of mountainous terrain. If the forecast indicates that this requirement is unlikely to be met, assess whether an alternative route is feasible and if not ...
'Do Not Go'.

Although visibility and cloud base are primary factors which apply to the conduct of all flights, there are other aspects to consider and the instruction you receive from your Flying Training Organisation will cover these and many others. For example, precipitation in the form of rain, drizzle, and snow, will be vital factors to consider during flight planning. Other considerations are the probability of strong winds, gustiness, turbulence, thunderstorm activity or the formation of fog, all of which are hazardous to microlight operations.

PRACTICAL NAVIGATION

The following pages cover the practical factors to be considered and the steps to be taken prior to and during a navigation flight. They are based upon the fact that a microlight pilot will be required to navigate his aircraft with only limited aids, and yet it must be possible for him to conduct his pilot navigation in safety. The most important aspects will therefore be in his preparation before flight, in his understanding of the basic principles involved in map reading and in applying simple 'dead reckoning' techniques.

An essential requirement to a successful navigation flight will be thoroughness in pre-flight planning, tackled in such a way that the pilot's workload during the flight is organised in a methodical manner. In this way the flight can be conducted more efficiently in relation to handling the aircraft and in maintaining an adequate lookout for checkpoints and other aircraft.

When a trip is well planned with due consideration to the essential aspects of weather information, care in calculations, and the observance of good operating practices, its outcome will normally be successful. However inattention to standard planning procedures will increase the workload during flight and commonly lead to situations where the pilot becomes lost.

The working plan for any navigation flight will be the "Flight Log Sheet". In the case of navigating in microlight aircraft it will be advisable to keep this as simple as possible in its format, but in view of its dual purpose, i.e. to assist in flight preparation as well as using it as a reference during flight it will need to contain those essential items of information such as, tracks headings distances, the selected altitude(s), minimum safety altitude and estimated times for each leg of the route to be flown. Provision on the flight log for some form of fuel calculation would be advisable even it only to act as an aide memoire that fuel is a very important consideration at all times and particularly when navigation flights are planned.

Your flying instructor will no doubt have his own ideas on the format of a flight log, but fig. 3-83 shows an example of how the information could be laid out in a convenient manner to assist your pre-flight planning calculations.

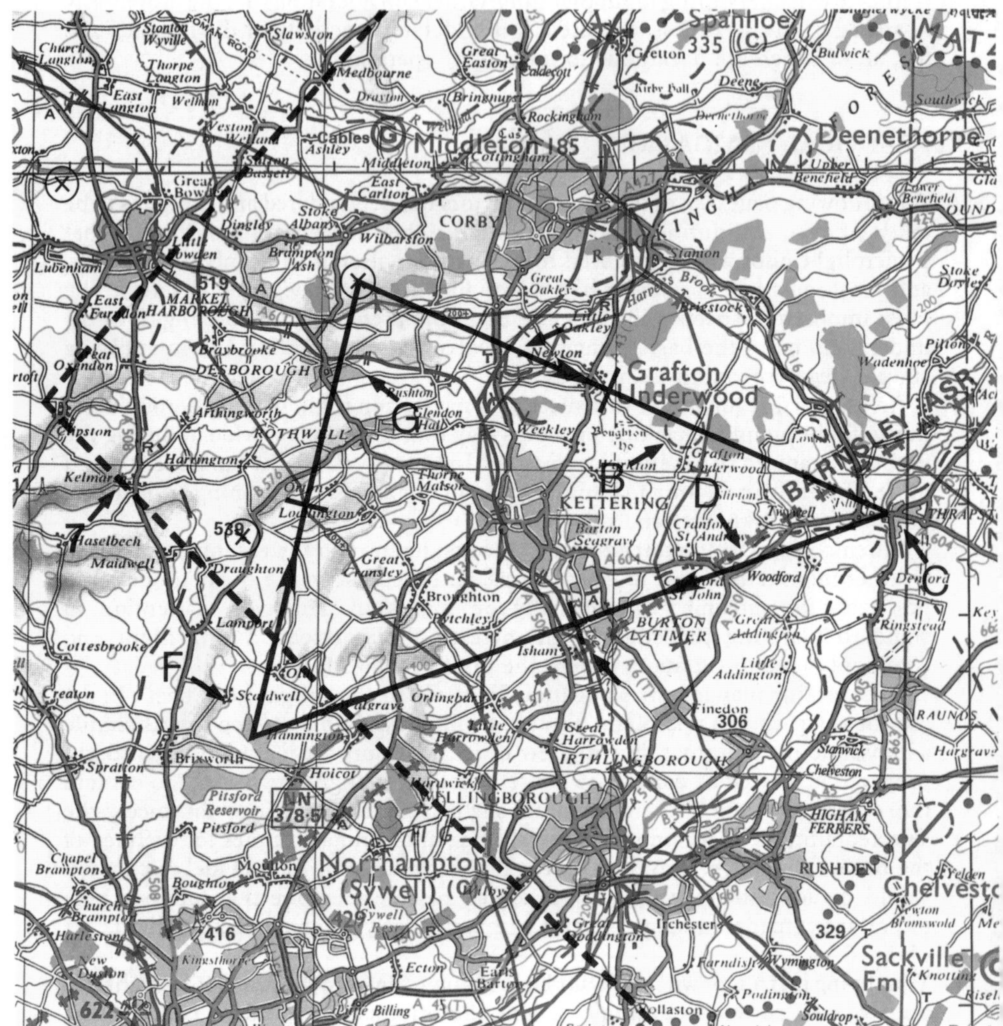

Fig. 3—82

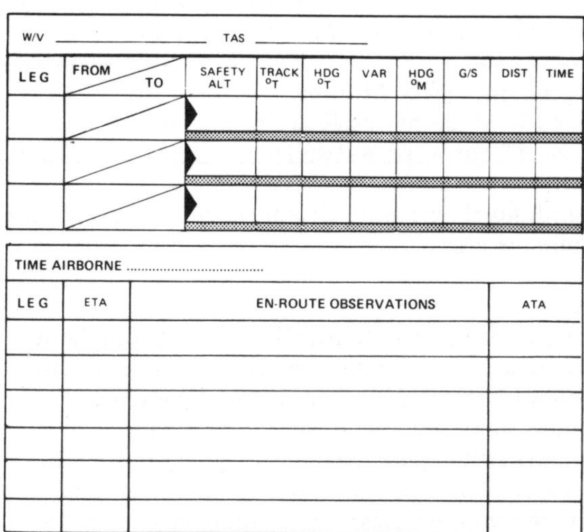

W/V ______________ TAS ______________

LEG	FROM / TO	SAFETY ALT	TRACK °T	HDG °T	VAR	HDG °M	G/S	DIST	TIME

TIME AIRBORNE ....

LEG	ETA	EN-ROUTE OBSERVATIONS	ATA

Fig. 3—83

Measurement of Tracks

Fig. 3-82 shows the route of a typical practice triangular cross country flight. The first step will be to determine the track angles (°T). These should then be entered in the flight log in the appropriate column. See fig. 3-84. Following this the distance between the respective turning points can be measured and these too will need to be entered.

W/V ______________ TAS ______________

LEG	FROM / TO	SAFETY ALT	TRACK °T	HDG °T	VAR	HDG °M	G/S	DIST	TIME
1	DES' / THRAP'		113					10	
2	THRAP' / PITSFORD		251					12	
3	PITSFORD / DES'		015					8	

Fig. 3—84

The protractor should be placed so that the central vertical line is over a meridian of longitude which is approximately half way along the track line. When measuring the distance for the first leg it will be noted that this is 10.5 nm, however for the purpose of practical pilot navigation this should be rounded off to 10 or 11 nm for the log entry.

The Altitude to Fly

Apart from such weather conditions as cloud base there are four factors to be considered when determining the altitude which should be used for the flight. These are:

- The Minimum Safety Altitude.
- The need to abide by the Rules of the Air.
- The base of Controlled or Regulated airspace in the vicinity of the route to be flown.
- The additional ground clearance to be given when flying over mountainous areas.

Safety Altitude

Bearing in mind the need to maintain a safe altitude throughout the flight in case of any deterioration in visibility, a minimum safety altitude should be decided upon. Using the formula of a minimum height of 1000' above all obstructions within 5 nm of the aircraft's intended flight path it will be necessary to scan the area 5 nm either side of the route to be flown. This scan should take into account the contour lines and any spot heights shown.

Refering to fig 3-82 it will be seen that the contour lines in the vicinity of Desborough reveal the ground to be approximately 400' above sea level. Looking further ahead towards Thrapston (the first turning point) it can also be seen that the contour lines drop down to 200' amsl. A spot height can be seen some 4 nm east of Thrapston but as this is lower than the ground in the vicinity of Desborough the 400' contour line should be used as a basis for determining the safety altitude for this leg will be 1400' amsl.

A survey of the area either side of the second leg reveals a spot height of 416' and another of 622' which is just outside the 5 nm distance, but a third spot height of 519' at Harrington is within a 5 nm distance of track. This third spot height should therefore be used to calculate the safety altitude for the second leg. 519 + 1000 = 1519 (say 1500) therefore the safety altitude for the second legs will be 1500' amsl. A review of the area either side of the third leg shows spot heights of 519', 613' and 519'. The spot height of 613 is just outside the 5 nm distance so the safety altitude for this leg can remain as 1500' amsl. If however the spot height of 613' was significantly higher it should be used to decide the safety altitude because of its close proximity to the 5 nm distance either side of our track.

For convenience it would be sensible to use 1500' amsl as the safety altitude for the whole route and this can be entered in the flight log for reference purposes during flight. This does not however mean that the total flight can be conducted at 1500', the reason being that whilst a minimum safety altitude allows for a margin of safety should the visibility deteriorate, there are other factors such as the minimum height which a pilot is permitted to fly over towns, the need to allow sufficient height to avoid serious downdraughts when flying over mountainous areas and the requirement to avoid penetration of controlled or regulated airspace and other areas.

Rules of the Air - Considerations

In relation to towns the Air Traffic Control Regulations and Rules of the Air require a pilot to remain at least 1500' above built up areas which are within 2000 feet of the aircraft, or at such height that he can glide clear of the built up area in the event of the engine failing, whichever is the higher.

Referring to fig. 3—82 it will be seen that this 1500' rule will apply to the first leg at Thrapston, on the second leg at Burton Latimer and on the third leg at Desborough. Additionally the town of Rothwell (two-thirds along the third leg) is very close to track and it would be advisable to include this when calculating the altitude to fly.

A survey of the map contour lines relative to these towns shows that Thrapston is below the 200' contour level, Burton Latimer is on the 200' contour line and both Rothwell and Desborough are on a 400' contour area. Therefore the pilot should add 1500' to these figures to arrive at the minimum altitude to fly in the vicinity of these towns. In considering the whole route it would seem that 2000' amsl would therefore be a suitable en-route altitude.

A further important point occurs in relation to contour lines and obstructions. This is the fact that the white areas on topographical charts indicate areas below the level of the first contour line depicted on the chart. The first contour line on the 1:250,000 series begins at 200' amsl and on the 1:500,000 series it is 500' amsl. On either type of map the ground height below these contour lines is not shown, and this means that a pilot could unknowingly be flying over ground which is nearly 200' amsl or in the case of the 1:500,000 series map, nearly 500' amsl.

A similar situation exists in relation to the marking of obstructions in that these are not necessarily shown unless they are at least 300' above the surface. A combination of these two factors could produce a situation where, for example an obstruction of 299' could be sited on ground which is 199' amsl, i.e. reaching a height of 498' amsl and a pilot would be unlikely to be able to determine this from the information given on a 1:250,000 series map.

To sum up, whenever using a 1:250,000 series map you should start your safety altitude calculations from a minimum basis of 500', this means that the minimum safety altitude would never be lower than 1500' amsl. In the case of the 1:500,000 series map it will need to be at least 1800' amsl.

A final note in relation to height, altitude and the use of the altimeter is that some of the simple types of altimeter used on microlight aircraft may not have a pressure setting facility. Additionally, as most microlight operations are conducted away from normal aerodromes the current sea level pressure will not often be available.

A practical solution to this, is for the pilot to set the height of the ground on the main dial of the altimeter prior to take-off. This will permit a pilot to assess with reasonable accuracy his height above the surface by cross referring to his altimeter and the ground contours and spot heights shown on his map.

For example, referring to fig. 3—85 the pilot at "A" sets 300 feet on his altimeter at a ground level of 300 feet above sea level. After take-off he will be flying at a height which has sea level as a datum, this is known as 'altitude'. Topographical charts show the ground contours at their respective heights above sea level so by checking the reading of the altimeter and comparing it with the contour heights over which he is flying the pilot will know what his ground clearance is during the en-route phase of the flight. When it comes to landing the pilot will need to note the height of the landing ground above sea level, again this can be established (approximately) from his map. In the case of fig. 3—85 this will be 500 feet, therefore in order to carry out a 500' circuit he will need to fly at 1000' on his altimeter and must remember that when the altimeter reads 500' he will be at ground level.

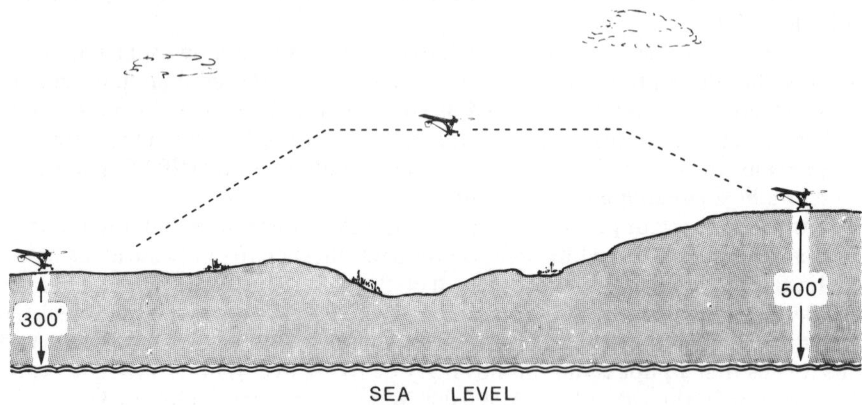

Fig. 3—85

Controlled Airspace, Danger Areas, Aerodromes, Etc.

During the review of the route a note should be made relating to such areas as Controlled Airspace, Danger and Prohibited Areas, etc, and where necessary the route must be re-planned to avoid these areas. The pilot should also note whether his route will take him close to civil and military aerodromes and if so he should ensure that he keeps a reasonable distance from their Air Traffic Zones unless he has obtained prior permission from the appropriate Air Traffic Controller. In the case of the route planned in fig. 3—82 the dashed lines shown at (7) indicate that nearly all the route lies within an Area of Intense Military Activity and the pilot must therefore bear in mind that fast military aircraft may be flying at relatively low heights in this area. An extra careful lookout must therefore be kept throughout the whole flight.

The only active civil aerodrome shown in the vicinity of the intended route is Sywell aerodrome which lies two nm south of track towards the end of the second leg. However it should be remembered that flying activities often take place at disused airfields and a careful lookout should be kept for such activity in the vicinity of Grafton Underwood and Harrington, both of which are marked as disused airfields.

In relation to Sywell it should be borne in mind that the radius of an aerodrome Traffic Zone is 1.5 nm from its boundary and the vertical limit reaches up to 2000' above the aerodrome level. The pilot will have to be careful not to drift to the south of track in the region of Sywell aerodrome as he will be flying at 2000' amsl. This

altitude is below the vertical limit of the Traffic Zone which is based upon the height of the aerodrome, e.g. 429 feet plus 2000', and the upper limit of the Sywell aerodrome Traffic Zone is therefore 2429' amsl.
A mental note should be made of the 3 MATZ's situated one below each other on the eastern side of the map. If the pilot overshoots Thrapston he could find himself penetrating the stub portion of the Matz just to the east of his turning point. The base of a stub section of a MATZ is 1000' above the surface.

Having surveyed the route, selected the altitude to fly and determined that the tracks do not conflict with Controlled or Regulated airspace, etc. the wind velocity at 2000' will not be needed in order to compute the true headings and also the groundspeeds. Assuming a TAS of 40 knots and a W/V of 360/15 the following true headings and groundspeeds will apply.

Heading	Groundspeed
Leg 1. 093°	43 knots
Leg 2. 271°	42 knots
Leg 3. 007°	26 knots

These figures can now be entered in the flight log, ref. fig. 3—86 item 1. The variation in the area of the flight is 6°W so this should be entered together with the magnetic headings for each leg. ref. fig. 3—86 item 2.

W/V 360/15 TAS 40 Kts (1)

LEG	FROM / TO	SAFETY ALT	TRACK °T	HDG °T	VAR	HDG °M	G/S	DIST	TIME
1	DES' / THRAP'	1500'	113	093	6W	099	43	10	
2	THRAP' / PITSFORD	1500'	251	271	6W	277	42	12	
3	PITSFORD / DES'	1500'	015	007	6W	013	26	8	

(2)

Fig. 3—86

Groundspeed, Distance and Time

The distance along each leg has already been entered in the log and at this stage the time for each leg can be computed by using the calculator side of the navigation computer and applying the particular groundspeed for the individual distances. These figures should be rounded off to the nearest minute and then entered in the time column of the flight log, (see item 1 of fig. 3—87).

Selection of Checkpoints and Time/Distance Marks

Referring to the cross country route shown at fig. 3—82 as an example, it can be seen that the halfway marks on each leg can be used in conjunction with suitably selected checkpoints to ascertain the aircraft position and the progress of the flight in relation to the estimated time. In fig. 3—82 the most suitable checkpoints to use for this cross country are shown at "A" to "G". It will be necessary to revise the estimated times of arrival at the turning points and destination in accordance with the actual times that the aircraft arrives at checkpoints.

Leg 1. After taking off from Desborough the aircraft can be climbed on track or via a climbing turn to pass directly overhead Desborough on track for the first turning point at Thrapston. Assuming the second method is used the time of setting course overhead Desborough can be noted and for the purpose of the following paragraphs it will be assumed that set course time was 1101 hours. Adding the estimated time en-route to Thrapston i.e. 14 minutes, will now give an ETA at Thrapston of 1115 hours.

The first suitable checkpoint after leaving Desborough will be the railway line at A in fig 3—83. The next will be a combination of Grafton Underwood airfield and the woods immediately to the north. It should be appreciated that disused airfields are often very poor features particularly if much of the original site has been converted back to agriculture.

The halfway point is approximately 1 nm short of Grafton Underwood airfield, this fact coupled with the position of the woods on and to the north of track will give the pilot a good visual reference of the half way position, and at this stage the time should be noted. If the pilot had set heading from overhead Desborough and at the flight planned altitude the length of time taken from Desborough to the half way point will also be the length of time taken between the half way point and Thrapston.

If the pilot were to note the time at the half way stage was 1108 then the ETA of 1115 at Thrapston will hold good. However if the length of time between Desborough and the half way point had been, say, 9 minutes then 9 minutes will need to be added to the current time at the half way point in order to obtain a revised ETA for Thrapston. It should therefore be appreciated that using your watch and noting times is one of the fundamental requirements in navigation.

The third checkpoint will be the town of Thrapston at the end of the leg. Although small towns by themselves are not good identification features the lake just to the north of the town will combine to make a reasonable checkpoint. The black dashed line running north east - south west either side of the town indicates an old railway line with its track removed and this may still be visible to give an additional identification feature.

W/V 360/15 TAS 40 Kts (1)

LEG	FROM / TO	SAFETY ALT	TRACK °T	HDG °T	VAR	HDG °M	G/S	DIST	TIME
1	DES' / THRAP'	1500'	113	093	6W	099	43	10	14
2	THRAPS' / PITSFORD	1500'	251	271	6W	277	42	12	17
3	PITSFORD / DES'	1500'	015	007	6W	013	26	8	18

Fig. 3—87

When turning through a large number of degrees to take up a new heading as will be the case at Thrapston, it is usually preferable to turn the long way round as shown in the adjacent diagram. This is because a turn to the right through some 180 degrees (as in this case) will drift the aircraft significantly to the south of the intended track line, because during the turn the wind will be behind the aircraft.

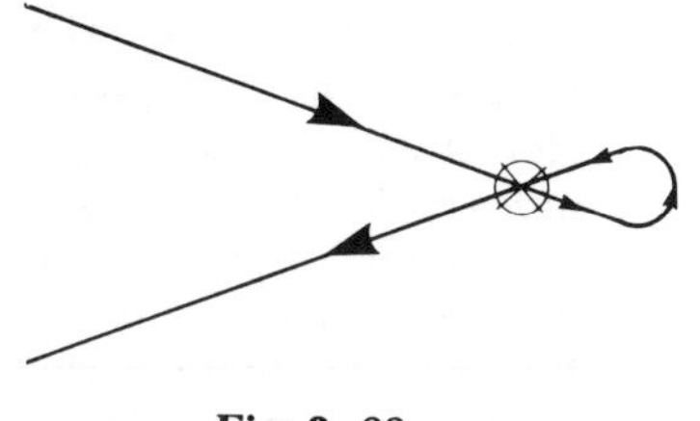

Fig. 3–88

Leg 2. Referring to fig. 3–82 a railway line(D) which commences two nm west of Thrapston runs more or less parallel with the track line and this could be used as a running fix until arriving at Burton Latimer (E).

A good checkpoint is available at this stage, it is formed by the towns of Burton Latimer and Kettering and also the railway line running out of Kettering to the south which intersects the required track at the half way point. The time should be noted when crossing this railway line and used to confirm or revise the ETA at the end of the second leg.

The end of the second leg is at Pitsford Reservoir (F) and this water feature will be a unique checkpoint, and one which in normal conditions will be clearly visible.

Pitsford Reservoir

Leg 3.

After turning onto the third leg there will be little in the way of ground features to identify position until reaching the town of Desborough. Nevertheless it may be possible to identify the two small lakes (G) two miles to the east of track at the half way point. It may also be possible to identify the disused airfield of Harrington but the pilot should not place too much reliance on this as an identification feature. The town of Rothwell has no associated features and this also should not be relied upon to any great extent.

Slightly further north is the town of Desborough with an associated railway line running east west. The presence of the railway line will make Desborough a reasonable checkpoint and one which will not be confused with Rothwell. In view of the lack of a good checkpoint until two-thirds of the way along this leg it will be quite possible for the pilot to drift to the right or the left of track. If he drifts to the right the two small lakes adjacent to the half way point should come into view and as there are no similar lakes to the immediate west of track they can be used to establish the aircraft's position with a fair degree of certainty.

If the aircraft drifts to the left of track the pilot will eventually see the railway line between Desborough and Market Harborough. This line feature crosses the intended track and will give the pilot a good idea of how far he has travelled along this leg. He will not however know for sure whether he is to the right or left of track because the general direction of the railway lines is more or less the same either side of Desborough town. In this event the pilot could turn left or right in an attempt to return to track overhead Desborough. If he turns left he will soon come to the larger town of Market Harborough which can be identified by the change in direction of the railway, i.e. it takes up a northerly direction. From this it can be seen that the general direction of a railway line in association with other features will form a very useful aid to visual navigation.

The aerial photographs which follow show how the possible checkpoints along this leg will look when seen from the air.

Checkpoint A

Checkpoint D

Sywell Aerodrome

Revisions to Headings

Having dealt with a simple method of revising ETA's on the previous pages the next consideration will be how to revise headings when the aircraft drifts 'off track' due to changes in the wind velocity during flight.

There are two methods which are commonly used in pilot navigation, these are known as the 'closing angle method' and the 'one in sixty method'. The former is porbably the easiest to use in microlight navigation, but because questions are asked about the one in sixty method in the Private Pilot Licence written examinations both methods have been included in this manual.

The Closing Angle Method

The first step will be to draw in drift lines' on your map as shown in fig. 3—89. In the case of short tracks, say, 20 nm or less it would simply suffice to draw in the drift lines from the destination back towards the departure point.

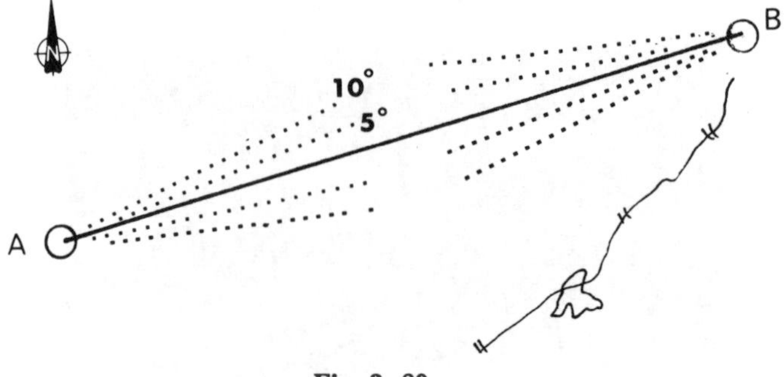

Fig. 3—89

Before showing a practical example of how these lines can be used to assess the degree of heading change required, an explanation of the principle of this method will be valuable. For example:

Assuming an aircraft has drifted to the left of track as shown by position C in the illustration at fig. 3—90.

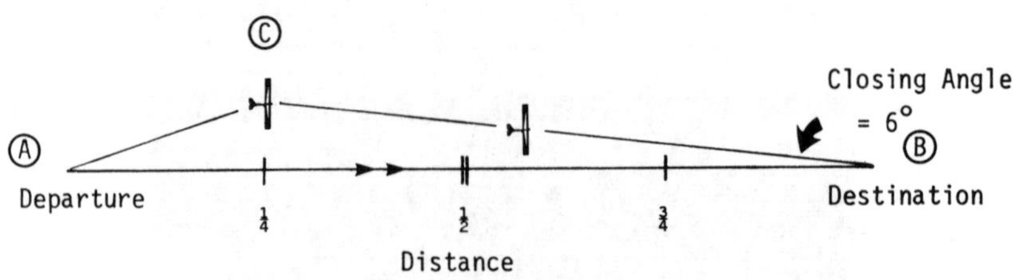

Fig. 3—90

First estimate the closing angle required and then apply the following calculation:

Proportion of Track Flown = Heading Alteration Required to Reach Destination
e.g. If closing angle is 6° and the aircraft has flown one quarter of its track distance then:
6° divided by ¼ = $\frac{6}{1}$ X $\frac{4}{1}$ = 24°

Therefore an alteration to heading of 24° to starboard will bring the aircraft (approximately) back onto track at destination.

The first difficulty which is apparent is how to estimate the closing angle?, and this is where the drift lines drawn on the map will prove invaluable.

By marking in these lines at 5° and/or 10° either side of the track line the amount of drift experienced can be more accurately and easily assessed during flight, and an estimation of the closing angle can now be made with sufficient accuracy for the calculations to be effective.

By referring to fig. 3—91 it will be seen that an aircraft which has drifted to the right of track (position A) will be 10° off track at the half way point. This equals a closing angle of 10°.

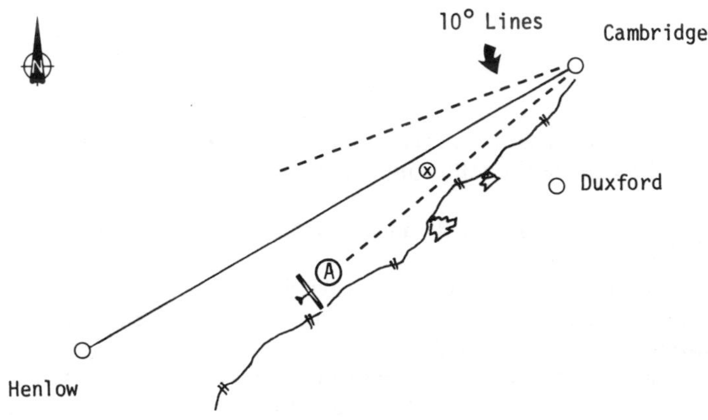

Fig. 3—91

$\frac{\text{Closing Angle}}{\text{Proportion of Track Flown}}$ = The heading alteration to be flown to reach destination.

Closing Angle = 10° Therefore 10 divided by ½ = $\frac{10}{1}$ X $\frac{2}{1}$ = 20°

A heading alteration of 20° to port is required to reach Cambridge.

The 1:60 Method of Heading Correction

This method of assessing and correcting track errors and revising estimated arrival times is also known as the '1 in 60 Rule'. The basis of this method is the fact that one nautical mile subtends an angle of one degree at a distance of approximately sixty nautical miles.

Whereas calculations can be carried out in relative ease whilst on the ground when distractions or limitations on the time available do not interfere, their use during flight must be kept as simple as possible. An example of this simplification is to state the 1:60 rule as follows:

A heading error of 1° will result in the aircraft being 1 nm 'off track' after flying 60 nm, e.g. 6° equals a track error of 6 nm in 60 nm (see fig. 3—92).

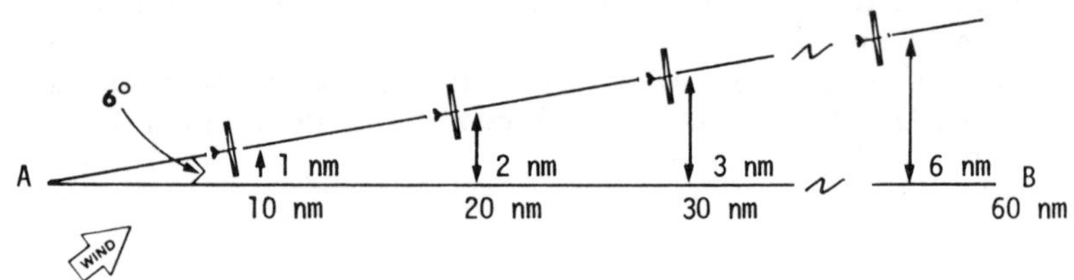

Fig. 3—92

Therefore given the distance 'off track' and the distance flown, the track error can be calculated by using the following simple formula:

$$\frac{60}{\text{Distance Flown}} \text{ X Distance Off Track} = \text{Track Error (Degrees)}$$

Doubling this error and applying it to the heading (towards the required track) will result in the aircraft regaining the planned track at a distance ahead which is equal to the distance already travelled.

Fig. 3—93 is an illustration of this method and in this case the error was determined at the halfway point, therefore application of the correction will bring the aircraft back onto track at the same time as it reaches its destination.

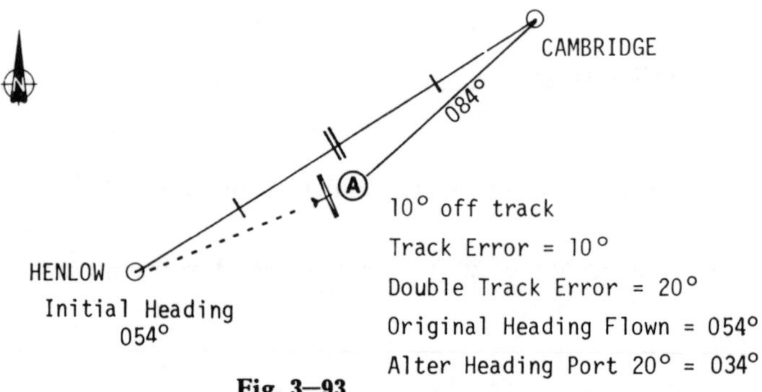

Fig. 3—93

The application of this procedure will be satisfactory as long as the alteration to heading is carried out at or before the half way position along the leg, after this it will result in the aircraft arriving back on a line which is an extension of the required track beyond the actual destination.

Therefore when insufficient distance remains for the aircraft to return to the required track before the destination another procedure will be needed as follows: Original Track Error (established by the previous method) plus:

$$\frac{60}{\text{Distance to Go}} \times \text{Distance Off Track} = \text{Heading Alteration (Degrees) or Closing Angle}$$

An illustration of this procedure is given at fig. 3—94, in this example the aircraft position is fixed at B.

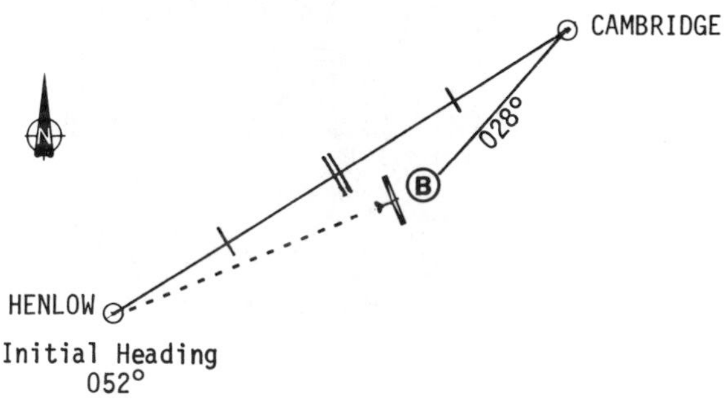

Fig. 3—94

$$\text{Original Track Error } \frac{60 \text{ X Distance Off Track}}{\text{Distance Gone}} = \frac{60 \times 2}{14} = 9^{\circ} \text{ (to the nearest whole degree)}$$

$$\frac{60 \text{ X Distance Off Track}}{\text{Distance to Go}} = \frac{60 \times 2}{7} = 17^{\circ} \text{ (to the nearest whole degree)}$$

Correction to Reach Destination 9° + 17° = 26° to Port
Original Heading 052° New Heading to Steer for Cambridge = 026°

Note:
It must be clearly understood that the 1:60 method of revising headings can only be used with reasonable accuracy providing heading alterations are less than 20°. Above this figure the method becomes increasingly inaccurate.

USE OF THE MAGNETIC COMPASS

The magnetic compass utilises the inherent qualities of magnetism to indicate direction. If is a simple self-contained instrument which has a single or multiple bar magnet freely suspended to allow it to rotate in the horizontal plane. The bar magnet will assume a position in which one of its ends points towards the Earth's Magnetic Pole. This is known as the North seeking pole of the magnet. A common type of compass used in microlight aircraft is shown at fig. 3—95.

Fig. 3—95

Construction and Function

The instrument consists of a liquid filled bowl containing a pivoted float element to which the bar magnets are attached. The liquid is normally an acid free white kerosene which is used to dampen the oscillations of the float assembly during flight and also to decrease the friction of the pivot and support some of the weight of the compass heading card or ring.

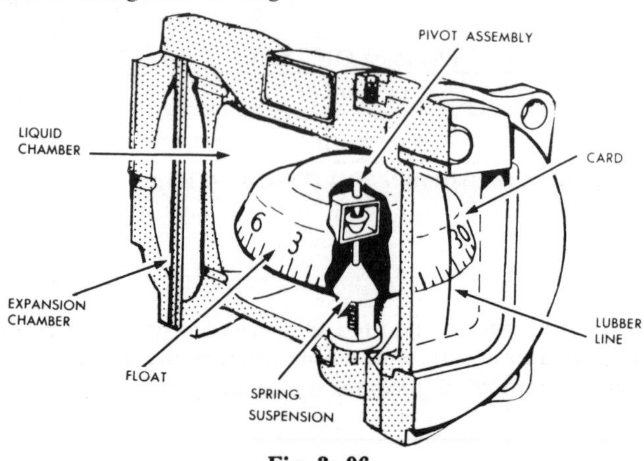

Fig. 3—96

In order to provide for contraction and expansion of the fluid during temperature changes, an expansion chamber is an integral part of the assembly.

The Angle of Dip

In its attempt to point to magnetic north the compass will attempt to point downwards at an angle relative to its position from the North Pole. For example, if an aircraft were flying over the North Pole the compass needle would attempt to tilt vertically downwards, whereas at the equator this 'angle of dip' would be much less. The problem of minimising the effect of this angle is of more concern to the instrument manufacturer than the pilot. However, even though the instrument manufacturer is able to construct a reliable compass in which the effect of the dip angle is minimised, the secondary effect of compensating for this leads to two basic errors in the instrument and the pilot will have to appreciate these effects during flight.

Turning Errors

Turning error is the most pronounced of the in-flight errors to which the magnetic compass is prone. This occurs because when an aircraft is banked, the compass heading ring and needle are also banked, and the angle of dip caused by the vertical component of the Earth's magnetic field causes the end of the compass needle to dip to the low side of the turn giving an erroneous indication.

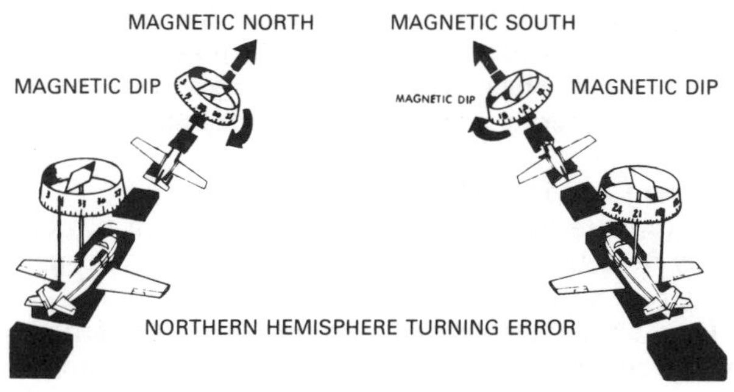

Fig. 3—97

When making a turn onto North, the resultant indication is a lead into the direction of heading change and this will apply when turning through East or West onto a Northerly heading. The correction is applied by rolling out of the turn when the compass reading is stil some 30° from North, when operating in latitudes covered by the United Kingdom. This correction is however based upon the aircraft making a rate 1 turn (bank angle approximately 15°)

When turning onto a Southerly heading the error is reversed in relation to the readings of the compass card and the correction will be to roll out some 30° after the compass has indicated a Southerly heading. Turning error is maximum when turning onto North or South and nil when using a rate 1 turn onto East or West. Therefore if the heading required is 045° or 315° the turn error correction will be approximately 15°.

Acceleration and Deceleration Errors

This occurs on Easterly and Westerly headings, and when accelerating on East or West an apparent turn towards North will be indicated when the aircraft is actually maintaining a constant heading. When decelerating on Easterly or Westerly headings the apparent turn will be in the opposite direction, i.e. to the South.

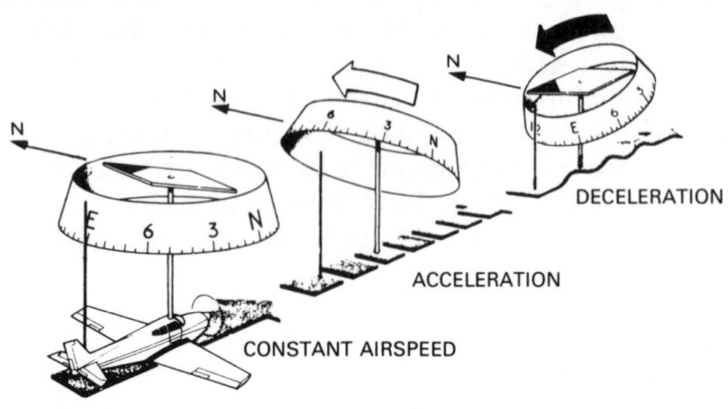

Fig. 3—98

The acceleration or deceleration forces which occur under normal circumstances in microlight aircraft are relatively small but whenever a positive acceleration or deceleration effect does occur the aircraft should be kept on a steady heading by reference to ground features. Although there is little practical point in memorizing the direction of the errors which occur due to changes of speed you may well be asked a question on this during your written PPL examination.

Precautions When Carrying "Magnetic Goods"

A pilot must take care to keep any magnetic materials which may be carried in the aircraft well away from the magnetic compass or large erroneous readings may occur during navigation flights.

The effect of large unpredictable errors produced by the carriage of magnetic materials near the compass can easily lead to a pilot becoming lost, therefore particular care must be taken to avoid placing metal pens, clipboards etc. near the compass during the flight.

Pilot's Serviceability Checks

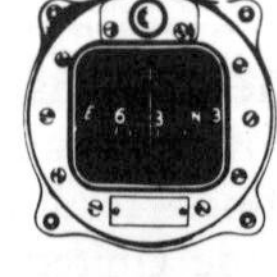

Before flight, the compass should be inspected for security of installation, and that it can be easily read. The liquid should be free of discolouration and bubbles, and the glass should be secure and uncracked.

A check should be made to ensure that it is indicating an approximately correct direction and this can be done by comparing the compass reading with a known magnetic direction at the take-off and landing site. When operating from aerodromes, the compass can be checked against runway direction. Runways, it may be recalled, are always numbered according to the magnetic direction to which they are aligned.

During taxying, the aircraft can be turned to the left and right to check that the compass responds in the correct direction.
An important practical problem relating to the use of the compass during flight is that it cannot be damped sufficiently to overcome the fluctuations which will inevitably occur when air turbulence is present. This will result in oscillations and consequent difficulty for the pilot to maintain a steady heading. Therefore once the required heading is established the pilot should where possible note the position of a distant ground feature and use this, in conjunction with the compass, to hold a heading.

IN-FLIGHT PROCEDURE TO REACH AN ALTERNATE AIRFIELD OR LANDING PLACE

The reasons for diverting to an alternate aerodrome would usually be due to aircraft unserviceability or deteriorating weather, coupled with a decision that a return to the departure airfield would not be a safe or sensible procedure.
Having determined the particular alternate airfield or landing site to use, an estimated track and heading will have to be mentally calculated, together with the distance to run, groundspeed and ETA. The minimum safe altitude may often be the same as for the original navigation leg, but it will be necessary to review this again at the time.
If a return to the point of take-off is decided upon, remember that the drift will have to be applied from the opposite direction.

Uncertainty of Position Procedure

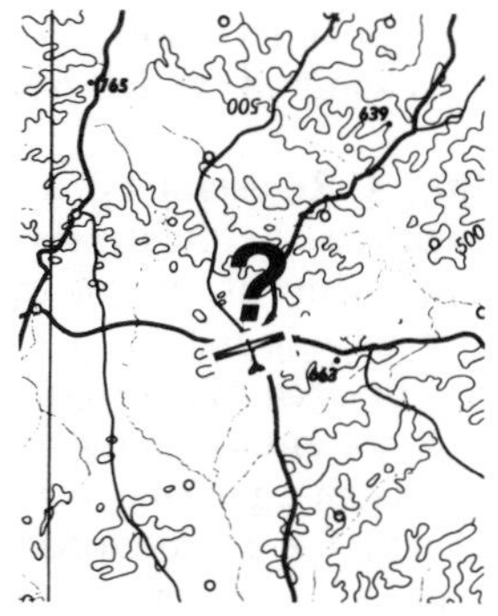

During any form of navigation (as distinct from map reading) there will be times when a pilot will not be able to fix his exact position by reference to his map and the ground features being overflown. This is a perfectly normal situation and one which must not give immediate cause for concern.
Navigation calls for the maintenance of accurate headings and identification of ground features, i.e. checkpoints at pre-determined intervals, and if a particular checkpoint is not identified on time it may be due to a number of reasons.
Providing previous checkpoints have been appearing satisfactorily the pilot should initially assume that the missing checkpoint has been overflown, and he should continue to maintain his heading until the next anticipated checkpoint is identified.
In the event that the next checkpoint does not appear at the expected time, then the pilot must consider the situation to have deteriorated into an 'Uncertainty of Position' phase. It is at this stage that the pilot must follow the initial steps outlined on the following pages under the heading of 'Lost Procedure'.

LOST PROCEDURE

Within the UK, it can normally be stated that when a pilot has not been able to establish his position for some 20 to 30 minutes, it can be assumed that the situation has changed from one of being uncertain of position, to becoming lost. If this occurs it will be important to carry out a sequence of positive actions rather than to continue aimlessly wandering about the sky in the hope that a ground feature will eventually be identified, and the aircraft's position re-established. Although it is not possible to detail the order of checks and procedures to be carried out in all circumstances, the following list of actions represent a general guide to be followed in the event of becoming lost.

Step 1. Safety Considerations:
An immediate check should be made of the fuel state, daylight hours remaining, weather situation, and a general check on the map of the area being overflown to ascertain the possibility of having to re-assess the safety altitude and to ascertain whether there is any chance of Controlled Airspace being inadvertently penetrated.

Step 2. Re-check the Headings Flown
Re-check the entries in the flight log to ensure whether the correct headings have been flown.

Step 3. Re-check the Time Flown
Double check any in-flight calculations and re-assess the ETA's for the checkpoint(s) which have been missed.

Step 4. Re-establishing Position
Estimate the most probable DR position and around this visualize a circle of uncertainty of a radius equal to approximately 10% of the distance flown since the last reliable fix.

The circle of uncertainty represents the probable bounds of the aircraft position, and the aircraft is most likely to be somewhere within this circle.

Assuming visual contact with the ground, search for an identifiable feature within the circle of uncertainty, reading from the ground to the map.

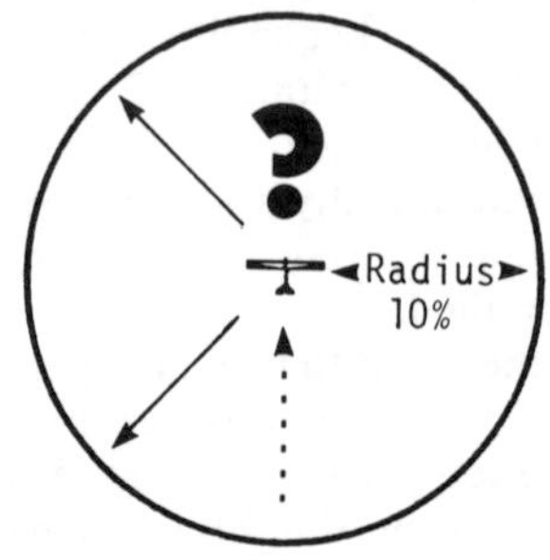

Once a fix has been established it will be necessary to estimate a heading and ETA for a return to the original track or to the destination.

If after approximately 10 to 15 minutes no fix has been established maintain a frequent check on the fuel state, daylight hours and weather.

Step 5. Increase the Search Area
If no fix has yet been established, fly in a direction which will give the greatest opportunity of finding a line feature or a fix. If a line feature appears before a fix is obtained use this as a heading to follow.

Line features e.g. railway lines, motorways or coastlines will eventually lead to towns and the pilot should then be able to obtain a fix. However is is important to bear in mind that following unidentified line features may also lead the pilot into Controlled Airspace, such as Control Zones, TMA's and Special Rules Zones which usually encompass large towns or cities.

General Points

The most common causes of becoming lost can be listed as follows:

- A marked change in wind velocity, which has gone unnoticed.
- Mis-reading the heading to fly or the time calculations in the flight log.
- Incorrect identification of a previous checkpoint.
- Weather deterioration involving reduced visibility and/or increased cockpit workload.
- Unscheduled diversions from the original track.

Taking these factors into account, a systematic check should be made to establish which of the above items was the reason for becoming lost and an estimate then made of the track which has actually been followed and as already stated, the radius of the circle of uncertainty should then be based upon 10% of the estimated track distance covered since the last positive fix.

Finally, in a "Lost Situation" where all else has failed to provide a remedy, the best course of action will be to maintain a steady heading in the safest direction and search for a suitable landing site. A safe landing can then best be made before the situation is compounded by running out of fuel.

Arrival Procedures

These procedures will vary depending on whether a landing is intended at a normal aerodrome where conventional aircraft are operating or on a microlight landing site. The procedures to adopt are covered briefly in the Flight Training section of this manual and will be fully demonstrated by your instructor.

SECTION FOUR

AVIATION METEOROLOGY

AVIATION METEOROLOGY

INTRODUCTION

The weather and its changing patterns has always been of interest to man. However the degree of importance attached to it varies considerably between individuals, and even within the same person on different occasions, depending upon whether a simple picnic or a long journey is planned.

Additionally, there are those whose safety and well-being are more closely related to a knowledge of the weather because it is of vital importance to their functions and tasks. Aviation, is one area in which weather conditions probably play the most vital role of all.

If aviation operations are to be safely planned, a knowledge of the anticipated weather conditions is a basic requirement and because weather forecasts cannot be guaranteed, either in their accuracy or availability, the pilot must develop a basic understanding of the elements involved in weather prediction, so that he can make sensible decisions prior to or during flight.

At this stage it is relevant to the intentions of this Manual to quote an extract from one of the UK General Aviation Safety Committee's Bulletins:

'Aviation is so much less forgiving of any carelessness or neglect than almost any other form of transport, so it is often vital to the safety of one's friends as well as one-self that an aeroplane is not treated like a boat or a car. It is the realisation of this fact that puts the hallmark of competence on the aviator, be he amateur or professional, novice or expert'.

A microlight is an aeroplane and it operates in the environment of the air just like any other aircraft, it is therefore essential that a microlight pilot is aware of the problems which result from deteriorating weather and has a basic understanding of how changes in weather conditions can effect his operations.

This does not mean that pilots have to be meteorologists, but rather they must have a basic knowledge of the weather elements and how they interact to produce good or bad flying conditions. They will also need to know the limitations of the weather forecasting services and be familiar with the methods of obtaining weather reports and forecasts.

Although it is the responsibility of the Meteorological Office to provide weather information to pilots in the form of forecasts and reports, it will always remain the pilot's individual responsibility to make wise decisions in respect of whether a planned flight can safely be made. To the pilot, Aviation Meteorology could be summed up as consisting of four basic elements:

Visibility.
Cloud Base.
Precipitation.
Wind Velocity.

However a pilot's role in relation to safe flight operations cannot be achieved unless he is conscious of how these elements may affect his own limitations, and those of his aircraft. Therefore although the information in the following pages is part academic, and part practical, it must be understood by any pilot if he is to become capable of assessing the hazards associated with various weather phenomena. Ignorance of this, will lead to him taking chances, which in turn can easily result in the occurrence of dangerous 'In-Flight' situations.

THE ATMOSPHERE

The atmosphere which surrounds the Earth forms an elastic layer of air with a varying depth which has aptly been described as an 'Atmospheric Engine'. This graphic description is well chosen, as all the weather which affects mankind occurs within this layer.

Composition and Structure

This invisible ocean of air is formed from a mixture of gases which exert a pressure, have measurable weight, and can be compressed. It is composed of several chemical elements which remain substantially constant and fig 4-1 shows the proportions which are contained in any given volume of dry air.

However, air is never completely dry, and always contains water vapour in varying amounts, from 5% in most tropical areas, to almost 0% in regions of intense cold and at great heights. The amount of moisture held in the air is called humidity.

The vertical structure of the atmosphere is divided into several regions. The lowest layer is known as the 'Troposphere' and this extends from the surface to an average altitude of 7 miles.

Because air is matter which has weight, it also has density. This density decreases with increase of altitude and has a marked effect upon the amount of oxygen which enters our lungs each time we breathe. Above 10.000' the effect of reduced density is that we need the assistance of extra oxygen to maintain a correct balance in our body's respiratory system.

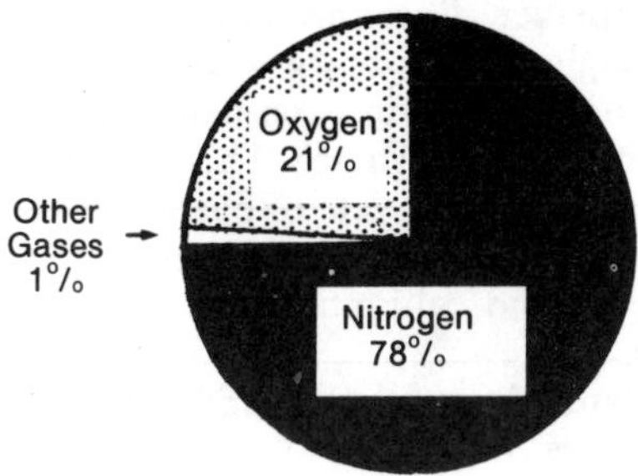

Fig. 4—1

This reduction of density with altitude also affects aircraft performance, and as altitude is increased the power available from an aero engine decreases; which has a significant effect upon the aeroplane's performance. Air temperature also decreases with altitude and this is known as 'Lapse Rate'. The average decrease in temperature per 1000' increase of altitude, is approximately 2°C.

It has already been stated that the element of humidity varies, and that the quantity of water vapour held in the atmosphere is relatively small. However without this moisture most life as we know it would not exist. In meteorology, the moisture content in the atmosphere plays a significant part in the formation of clouds, precipitation, and fog.

Above the Troposphere there are other regions which are divided by order of altitude into the Tropopause, the Stratosphere and several others. The Troposphere is the region within which the weather is most active, and for this reason we are concerned primarily with that area in this Manual. This region is lowest at the poles (about 20.000' amsl) and highest at the equator (about 65.000'), (fig 4-2).

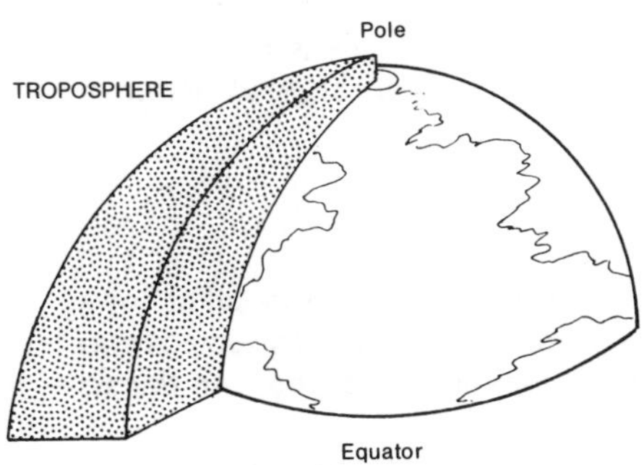

Fig. 4—2

The Standard Atmosphere

Due to the continual fluctuations of pressure, density, and temperature, certain problems occur when engineers and meteorologists have to measure or calibrate instruments or aircraft performance. Therefore in order to establish a universal standard, the conditions throughout the atmosphere at all latitudes, altitudes and seasons, have been averaged out to result in a standard condition which is known as 'The International Standard Atmosphere'. This has a specified sea level pressure and temperature, and a specific rate of change of temperature with an increase of altitude. This Standard Atmosphere serves as an arbitrary datum for measuring aircraft performance and calibrating recording instruments used in aeroplanes and meteorology.

The International Standard Atmosphere (ISA) assumes the following atmospheric conditions at sea level:

Pressure..	1013.25 mb
Temperature..	+15°C
Density..	1225 grammes per cubic metre

and a temperature lapse rate of:

1.98°C per 1000' of altitude until a temperature of -56.5°C is reached at 36.500' (11 km) after which it is assumed constant.

In the natural atmosphere all these conditions vary from day to day, and sometimes considerable changes will occur anywhere over the Earth within a few hours.

Pressure, Density and Effect of Altitude

Atmospheric pressure is the force per unit area exerted by the weight of the atmosphere. Since air is not solid it cannot be weighed with conventional scales. Instead it is measured by means of either a mercury barometer or an aneroid barometer.

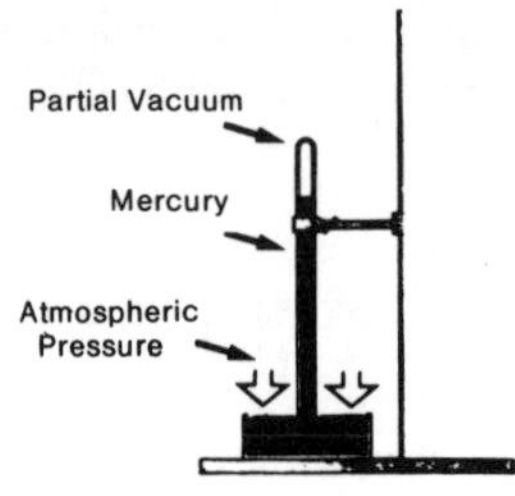

Fig. 4—3

In the mercury barometer the pressure of the air is balanced against the weight of a column of mercury inside a glass tube. The mercury barometer is a very accurate recording instrument but is also bulky and therefore, to suit situations where mobility is required, or where space is restricted, for example an aircraft altimeter, the aneroid barometer is used.

The aneroid barometer consists of a flexible metal bellows which is sealed after most of the air has been extracted from it. The bellows contracts or expands in response to the air pressure exerted on it.

The unit of pressure now in general use in meteorology is the millibar (mb), and a pressure of one millibar is equivalent to a force of 1000 dynes acting upon a square centimetre.

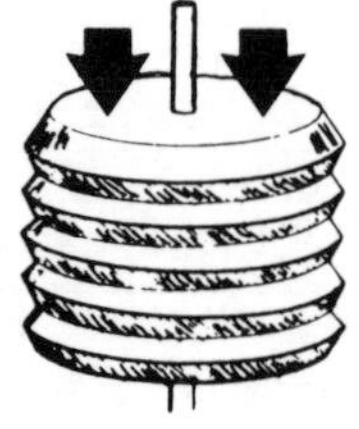

Fig. 4—4

Atmospheric pressure varies with both altitude and temperature as well as with the horizontal movements of air mass systems. Moving upwards through the atmosphere results in the weight of air above becoming less and less. Within the first few thousand feet, the pressure decreases fairly rapidly and corresponds to a drop of 1 mb per 30 feet. At higher levels the rate of pressure drop decreases, for example at 20.000' a drop of one millibar is equal to 50 feet.

These pressure variations are based upon standard temperatures in accordance with the Standard Atmosphere, however in the natural atmosphere, temperatures are seldom standard. In relation to volume, air expands as it becomes warmer and contracts as it cools.

Air Density

Air density is defined as the mass of a unit volume of air and the thin rarefied air at higher altitudes is lighter and therefore less dense than air near the surface. If one was to take a box with a small hole in the top it can be seen that the greater the atmospheric pressure, the more air will be forced through the hole into the box, and therefore the mass of air it contains will be greater, i.e. the density will be increased. If the atmospheric pressure is reduced air will pass outwards through the hole and the air density will be reduced. Air density is thus directly proportional to atmospheric pressure.

With change in temperature a similar airflow will occur, and if the air within the box is heated it will expand and pass outwards through the hole, the higher the temperature the less will be the amount of air contained within the box. Conversely, if the air in the box is cooled its contents will contract, and more air will be drawn in, thus increasing the density, i.e. the lower the temperature the greater the air density. From this it can be seen that, air density is inversely proportional to the temperature.

Whenever an aircraft climbs, the air pressure decreases because there is a lesser weight of air above. Therefore, density which is proportional to pressure also decreases with increasing altitude.

ALTIMETER SETTINGS

The purpose of an aircraft altimeter is to measure distance above the surface and this distance is referred to by the use of three different terms, altitude, height, and flight level. Each term is defined in relation to a different datum as follows:

Altitude

This is the vertical distance of a level, point, or object, measured from mean sea level and is related to a datum setting known as QNH.

Height

This is the vertical distance of a level, point, or object, measured from an airfield surface. This datum is known as the aerodrome QFE.

Flight Level

This is a level measured in relation to a constant atmospheric pressure datum known as the Standard Setting or QNE.

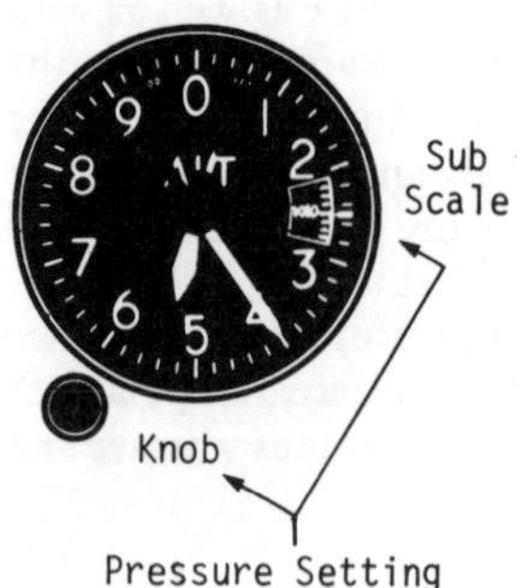

In each of the above cases a different millibar reference datum is used, and when obtained, this reference datum is set on the sub-scale of the altimeter by means of the pressure setting knob.

When the millibar setting is increased the altimeter reading will increase, and when the millibar setting is decreased the altimeter reading is decreased.

An aircraft altimeter is essentially an aneroid barometer in which the scale is constructed to indicate increments of height or altitude in feet, rather than units of pressure. It must nevertheless be appreciated that its principle is based upon the measurement of atmospheric pressure.

In other words if an aircraft is maintaining an indicated altitude of 4000' the pilot will be following the horizontal atmospheric pressure which gives this indication. Atmospheric pressure is measured in millibars, and lines of equal pressure are known as 'Isobars'. These can be depicted in plan form as shown on Surface Weather Charts, or horizontally as illustrated in fig 4-5.

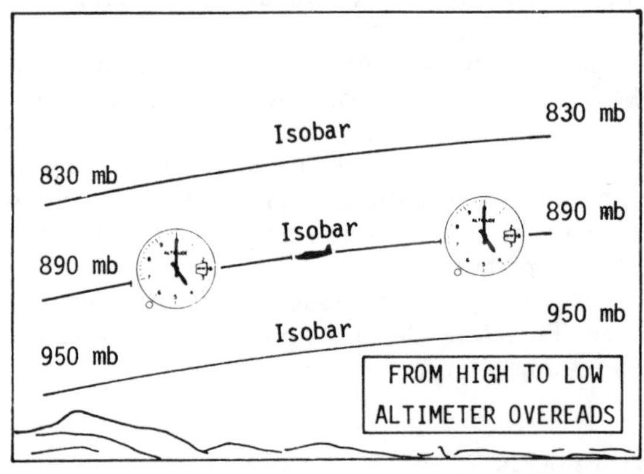

FLYING TOWARDS LOW PRESSURE

Fig. 4—5

By studying this illustration it can be seen that if the pressure variation is such that it decreases along the aircraft flight path a pilot maintaining a reading of 4000' on his altimeter will actually be following a descending path in relation to the Earth's surface. This clearly indicates the need for understanding the principles of 'Altimetry' and its importance to safe flying operations.

Although altitude may seem a simple term used in indicating distance above the Earth's surface it can have several meanings as follows:

True Altitude

This is the aircraft's actual altitude above mean sea level, but since the conditions existing in the real atmosphere are seldom in accordance with the International Standard Atmosphere (ISA), the altimeter will seldom indicate the true or actual altitude above mean sea level.

Indicated Altitude

When the datum pressure changes from that originally set on the altimeter sub-scale the altimeter indication will no longer show the correct height or altitude. This effect can be allowed for by obtaining the new value and setting it on the sub-scale. However there is no method for adjusting the instrument to counteract for changes of temperature experienced in flight.

The atmospheric temperatures and pressure changes which occur between places within the UK are normally relatively small, and therefore altitude errors from these causes are also small. This often leads to the impression that knowledge of these errors is unimportant to navigation flights undertaken in VMC conditions, because in these circumstances the ground would be clearly visible to the pilot and he would soon become aware of any significant reduction in his true altitude relative to the surface.

Nevertheless, pilots must be aware that many flights do not go exactly to plan and any weather deterioration en-route may often be caused by a lowering pressure which together with any associated reduction in visibility will, even it if is only temporary, cause planned safety altitudes to be violated. Worsening weather could then lead to a hazardous situation.

Pressure Altitude

This is the altitude indicated by an altimeter when the Standard Setting of 1013.2 mb is set on its datum scale. This standard datum is an arbitrary level based upon the International Standard Atmosphere.

As atmospheric pressure changes occur, this datum level may be below, at, or above mean sea level. Its basic purpose is the provide a fixed pressure setting for the application of flight levels to the Quadrantal or Semi-Circular Rules.

Density Altitude

This is the pressure altitude corrected for non-standard temperature conditions. When ISA conditions are present, the pressure altitude and the density altitude will be the same.

The application of density altitude relates to the performance of an aircraft and its pressure instruments. Whenever the density of air is reduced the performance of an aircraft is also reduced.. The efficiency of both the engine and the wings are affected. An aero engine works at peak efficiency when the fuel/air mixture fed to it is in the correct proportion. If the density of the air fed to the engine is less than ISA, then the ratio will be disproportionate, and the engine will develop less power for any given throttle setting.

An aircraft depends upon the air passing over the wings to give it lift. All other things being equal, thinner less dense air will develop less lift for any given set of circumstances than thicker denser air.

TEMPERATURE

The movements and changes which occur in the lower levels of the atmosphere involve the use of large quantities of energy. The source of this energy is the sun which constantly supplies a radiant beam to the Earth's surface equivalent to 1·5 kilowatts per square metre. This energy when measured in terms of horsepower is equal to 4 million hp per square mile. Such terms graphically describe the enormous heat potential which is received into the Earth's atmosphere as a result of the sun's rays.

This solar energy is absorbed in part by the higher levels of the atmosphere above the tropopause and results in temperature variations at very great heights. Within the troposphere (the lower level of the atmosphere) part of the heat energy is reflected back into space by the dense air and clouds. The remainder continues to Earth where it is absorbed by the surface which warms up and re-radiates its heat back into the troposphere. For this reason the Earth's surface does not continuously heat up, and a balance occurs whereby the atmosphere loses to space as much heat as it received from the sun.

Because the Earth is a sphere, is tilted on its axis and revolves around the sun, the amount of heat energy received by different parts of its surface will vary with latitude and season.

It can be seen from fig 4-6 that when the sun is directly overhead any part of the Earth's surface the heat energy is concentrated into a smaller area than if an angular deflection is involved. This effect can more easily be appreciated by visualizing a torch beam firstly pointing directly at a surface and secondly pointing to the surface at an oblique angle. In the second case the beam will be more widespread and cover a greater area.

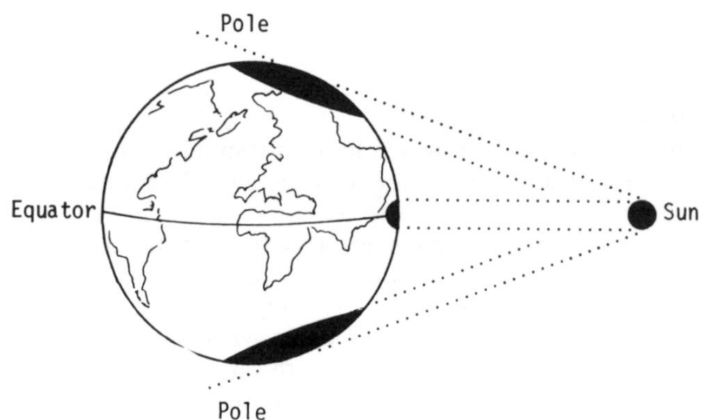

Fig. 4—6

As a result of this uneven heating of the surface a vertical circulation pattern of air movement occurs which forms the basis of the world's weather.

An illustration of this vertical circulation is shown at fig 4-7 on the following page.

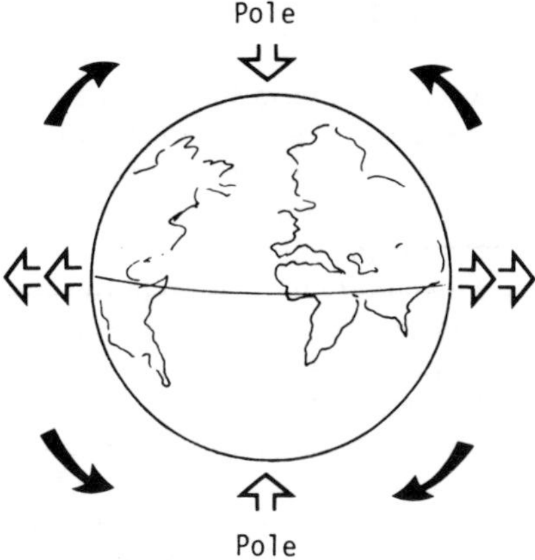

Fig. 4—7

Abiabatic Cooling and Heating

Whenever air is compressed its temperature rises and this effect can easily be seen when using a bicycle pump, the lower end gets very warm when inflating a tyre. The opposite effect, expansion, can again be evidenced by the release of pressure inside a fire extinguisher, an action which will produce a covering of frost around its nozzle. These effects are known as adiabatic temperature changes.

In the atmosphere adiabatic changes in temperature occur when air descends (subsidence) and is heated by compression, or when warm air rises to a higher level and cools due to expansion as a result of the lower pressure.

Since the atmosphere is heated from below the temperature normally decreases with increase of altitude throughout the troposphere. The rate of temperature decrease is known as the 'Lapse Rate' and although variations in this lapse rate occur it can be stated that the average figure is 2°C per 1000'.

It should also be noted that there are occasions when the temperature remains constant throughout several thousand feet of altitude change and sometimes it may actually increase with an increase of altitude. When this latter condition occurs it is known as an 'Inversion'.

From a practical viewpoint, the temperature changes in the atmosphere are caused by various factors as shown below:

Atmospheric Heating	**Atmospheric Cooling**
Radiation - from the ground by convection and mechanical turbulence. The latter being produced by vertical changes in air movement caused by surface irregularities (buildings, mountains etc).	Radiation - contact of air with a surface which has been cooled by radiation.
Advection - horizontal air mass movement over a warm surface.	Advection - the horizontal movement of an air mass over a cold surface.
Adiabatic - the compression of air (normally due to subsidence).	Adiabatic - the expansion caused when air rises.

STABILITY AND INSTABILITY

In relation to flying an aeroplane the term stability is an important one to the pilot. A stable aeroplane, when disturbed from a given attitude, will tend to return to this attitude of its own accord, thus making it easier to control. An unstable aeroplane once disturbed from its original attitude continues to move away from it and therefore creates difficulties for the pilot.

The terms stability and instability in relation to the atmosphere have the same meanings as when applied to an aeroplane. When a stable atmosphere exists it will resist any upward or downward movement, but an unstable atmosphere will encourage vertical disturbances to develop.

Apart from the atmospheric turbulence which vertical air currents produce they also have a significant effect upon the weather itself. Whenever air rises it expands due to decreasing pressure, and this expansion causes it to cool, and if sufficient moisture is present clouds will form. The converse occurs whenever air settles downwards.

Air contains invisible water vapour in varying quantities, which when sufficient cooling takes place, will condense into visible water droplets, e.g. clouds or fog. When air contains the maximum amount of water vapour which it can hold in an invisible state, it is known as 'Saturated', and in this condition the slightest cooling will cause condensation to occur. Therefore if saturated air rises the temperature drop will cause cloud to form, and when this happens the rate of cooling will be reduced due to the latent heat released through the process of condensation.

EFFECT OF DRY AND MOIST AIR UPON DENSITY

The moisture content in the atmosphere not only influences the production of cloud, fog, precipitation or icing, but also affects the performance of an aircraft Water vapour weighs less than dry air. Therefore when water vapour is present in the atmosphere, the resulting mixture has a lower specific weight or density than dry air.

Due to this, air which has a high water vapour content will cause a significant reduction in the power output of an internal combustion engine. When water vapour enters the induction system the amount of air available for combustion is reduced, and an enrichment of the fuel/air ratio occurs, which results in the reduction of the heat energy produced.

When large amounts of water vapour are present in the air, its density is reduced by approximately 3%, but the resultant power loss from an aero piston engine could be as high as 12%. Additionally when the density is decreased both the lift and drag of an aeroplane are decreased. Therefore the combined effect of low density on the lift producing surfaces, and on the power output of an aircraft can be especially significant during take-off, as a longer run will be required to get the aircraft off the ground.

Whereas this effect may not be noticeable when operating from large or medium sized aerodromes, where available take-off distances are normally well beyond those required by light aircraft, it could be much more critical, perhaps even dangerous, when taking off from a small airfield or landing strip.

PRESSURE AND WIND

It was not until the seventeenth century that man began to understand 'pressure' and its influence on air and liquids. Until that time they simply believed that 'Nature Abhorred a Vacuum'. Torricelli, finally provided the answer by reasoning that when water was raised from shallow wells by the use of vacuum pumps, the vacuum created did not draw in water, but rather did the weight of the atmosphere upon the surrounding water in the well force water up the evacuated pipe.

The subject of air pressure is important to the pilot not only because of its effect upon the altimeter but also because the pressure distribution and its continous changes in the atmosphere controls the winds and to a large extent the occurrence of cloud, precipitation, fog etc.

A basic understanding of how changes in atmospheric pressure influence the weather, is an essential part of a pilot's knowledge in order that he can better appreciate the contents of weather forecasts, and also anticipate changes in the existing weather conditions.

Vertical Motion of the Atmosphere

The chief factor which disturbs the normal equilibrium of atmospheric pressure is the uneven heating of the Earth's surface. This occurs due to the Equator receiving more direct radiation from the sun than the polar regions, and as a result a wide scale vertical and horizontal circulation of air is set up.

Fig 4-8 shows the idealised circulation pattern which would occur if the Earth did not rotate. Air in the vicinity of the Equator would rise due to heating and expansion would take place. This air then flows towards the cooler polar regions, descends, compresses, and then flows back towards the Equator.

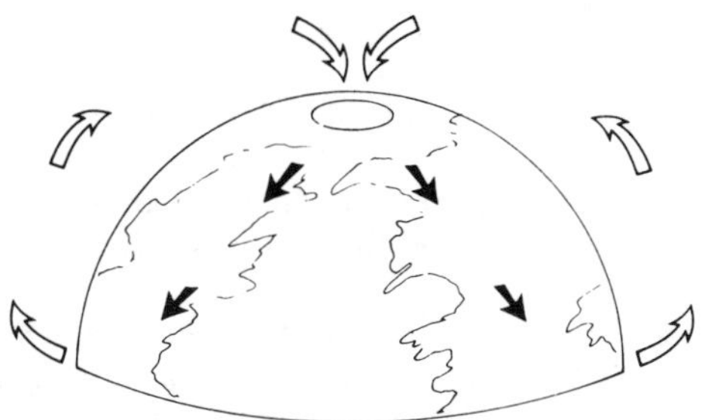

Fig. 4—8

This convective circulation is however not simply between the tropics and the polar regions. The Eather's rotation and the distribution of mountains, plains and oceans, complicate this movement of air, and in the natural environment a far more complex circulation pattern occurs.

In nature the inward flow of the sun's heat energy to the Earth maintains a fairly consistent pattern, but the outward flow of terrestial radiation is vastly more complex. This occurs because of the continual changes in the distribution of air temperature, water vapour content, and a large scale cloud formations, which are brought about as a result of the distribution of land areas with differing topography and the existence of large sea areas. The fact that the Earth rotates about its axis also further complicates the situation.

Horizontal Motion of the Atmosphere

The wind direction and strength is governed by two main forces, the heat from the sun and the rotation of the Earth, but it is now necessary to introduce two other factors in order that a better understanding of wind velocity can be achieved. These other factors are, Pressure Gradient and Coriolis Force.

The wind strength is a direct product of the pressure gradient which exists when two regions of the atmosphere have different pressures. The air in the region of the higher pressure moving towards the region of lower pressure.

Pressure differences are shown on weather maps by isobars which depict lines of equal pressure. Fig 4-9 shows an illustration of a High and Low pressure area together with their associated isobars.

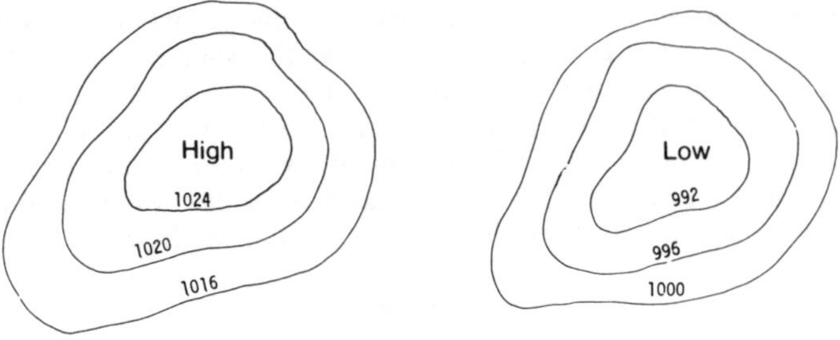

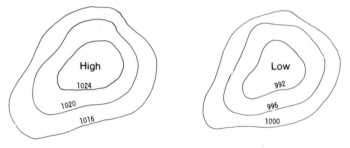

Fig. 4—9

From this diagram it can be appreciated that isobars are similar in principle to the contour lines shown on a map, and the presure gradient is similar to the vertical interval between contour lines.

By referring to fig 4-10 it will be seen that a pressure gradient will exist between the High and Low pressure areas, and if it were not for the fact that the Earth rotates, the movement of air would be directly from the High pressure area to the Low.

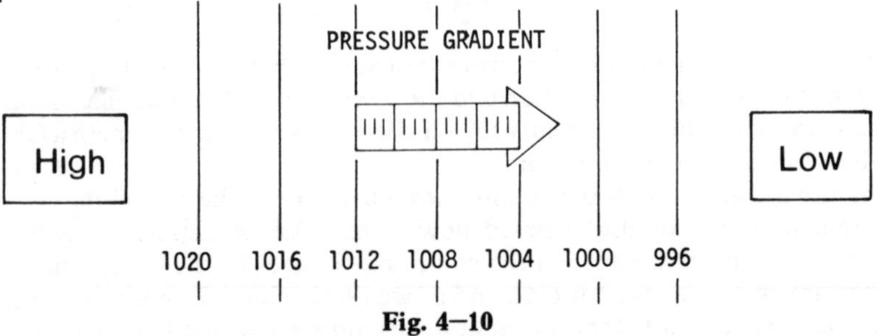

Fig. 4—10

However due to the Earth's rotation a force known as 'Coriolis' exists, and whenever a particle of air moves, this force will deflect its direction of movement to the right in the northern hemisphere, and to the left in the southern hemisphere. A detailed explanation of how this coriolis force works is fairly complex and outside the scope of this manual.
The resultant wind velocity is known as the 'Geostrophic Wind', i.e. the wind which blows parallel to the isobars.

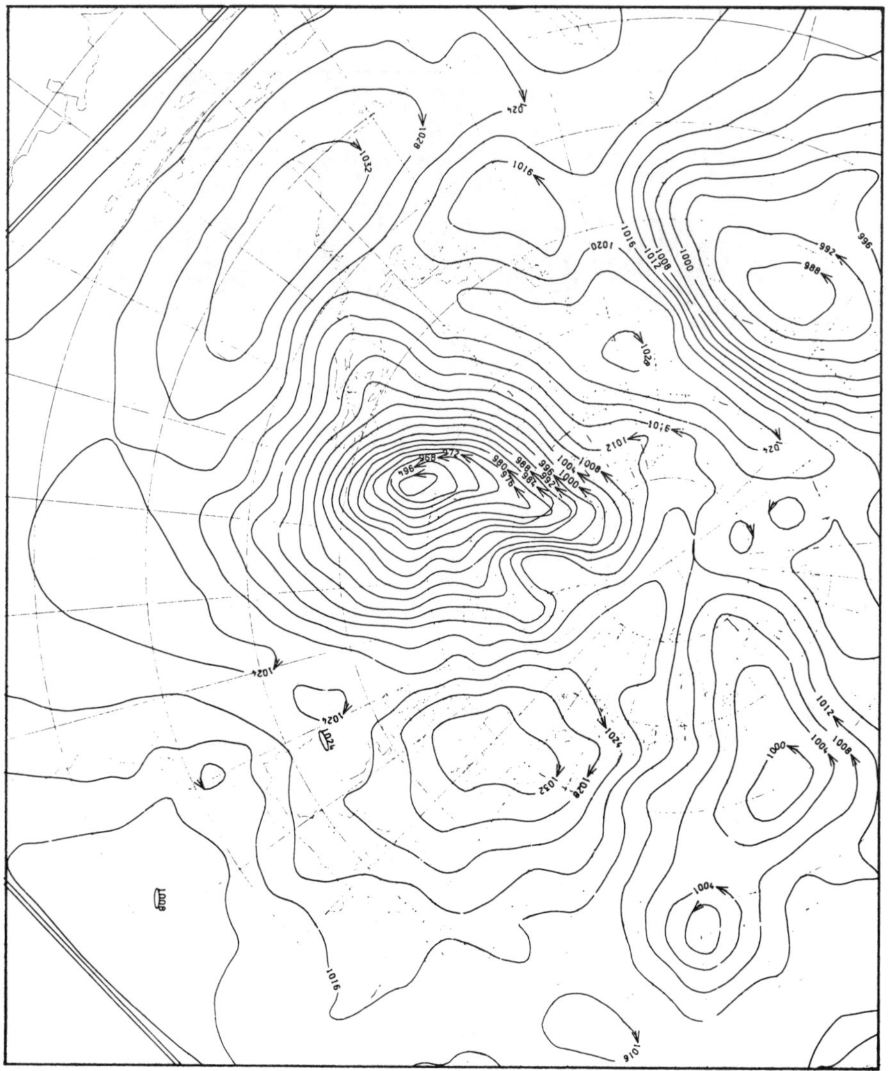

Fig. 4—11

The determination of High and Low pressure areas are extremely important in the forecasting of weather. In general, low pressure areas are indicative of the type of weather conditions which are very often outside the capabilities of private pilots. High pressure areas are indicative of stable weather conditions, but this may not necessarily guarantee good weather, as will be seen later under the heading of "Anticyclones".

A simple rule which can be used to determine the relative position of low pressure and high pressure areas was first propounded by the Dutch meteorologist Buys Ballot. This rule has become to be known as 'Buys Ballot's Law' and can be summarised as follows:

In the northern hemisphere a person standing with his back to the wind will have high pressure on his right and low pressure on his left. In the southern hemisphere this situation is reversed.

Fig. 4—12

To a pilot this law will indicate that an aircraft in flight with a prevailing drift to the right will be flying towards an area of low pressure (as shown in fig 4-13 and therefore two important considerations will be brought to his attention:

- The altimeter will gradually start to over read unless the datum setting is corrected.
- Lowering pressure is associated with deteriorating weather, which could mean reducing visibility, lowering cloud bases and the occurrence of precipitation.

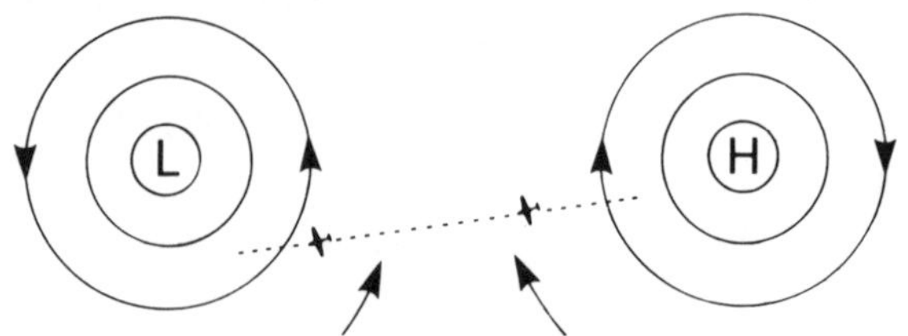

Fig. 4—13

Variation in Surface Wind

Near the Earth's surface, friction occurs and the wind speed is reduced. The more irregular the terrain the greater will be this effect.

The net result of friction is to slow down the speed of the wind in the lower levels and also to cause the air to blow at an angle across the isobars, and towards the area of low pressure. The greater the effect of friction the more the wind speed is reduced and the greater the angle at which it blows across the isobars, (fig 4-14)

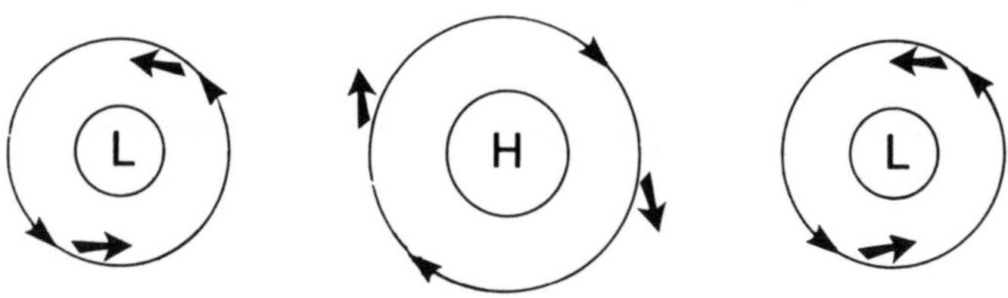
Winds at 2000' follow the Isobars
L
H
L
Winds below 2000' are slowed down by surface friction and incline accross the Isobars towards the Low Pressure

Fig 4-14

Frictional effects are normally confined to 1500' - 2000' above the surface and so in general the wind over the sea where friction is minimal blows at an angle of approximately 10° to the isobars, whereas over land surfaces this angle may reach up to 40°. At approximately 2000' the wind will conform to the general direction of the isobars.

Veering and Backing

In meteorological observations and reports the wind direction is always stated in degrees true. If the wind changes direction in a clockwise manner it is said to have 'Veered' and if it changes direction in an anticlockwise manner it is said to have 'Backed', (ref fig 4-15)

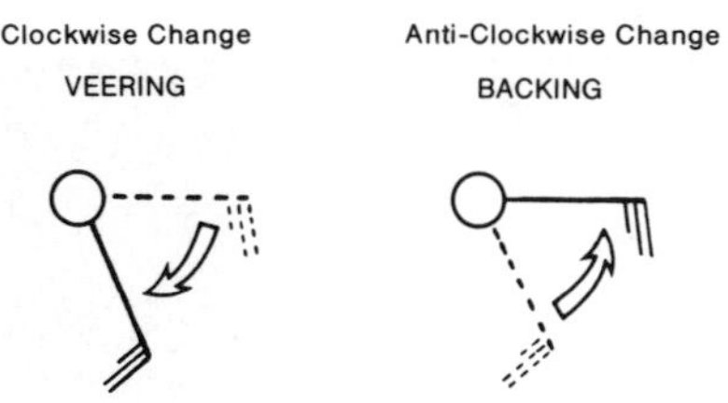
Clockwise Change
VEERING
Anti-Clockwise Change
BACKING

Fig 4-15

Diurnal Effects

During the day surface heating causes vertical air currents to occur and the air in the lower levels will rise and mix with the air above. As the surface cools during the night this mixing action is diminished or dies out completely. Fig 4-16 illustrates this effect.

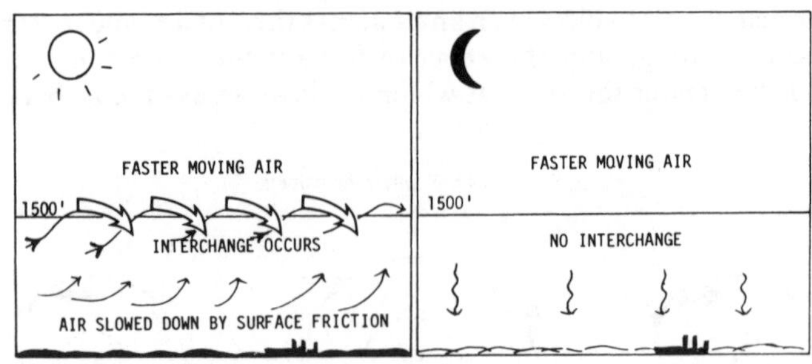

Fig. 4—16

The diurnal effect on the wind direction in the lower layers can therefore be summarised as follows:

By Day	Surface winds veer and increase in strength.
By Night	Surface winds back and decrease in strength.

Land/Sea Breezes

Another effect of diurnal variation is the land and sea breezes which occur along coastlines. During the day the land warms more rapidly than the sea. Therefore, during the day the air over the land surface rises, the pressure lowers, and the air over the land is replaced by cooler more dense air from the adjacent sea area. This action creates a cooling wind blowing from the sea to the land and is known as a Sea Breeze.

At night the reverse may occur when the air which cools more rapidly over the land becomes colder and more dense than that over the sea. This causes the wind to flow from the land to the sea and is known as a 'Land Breeze'.

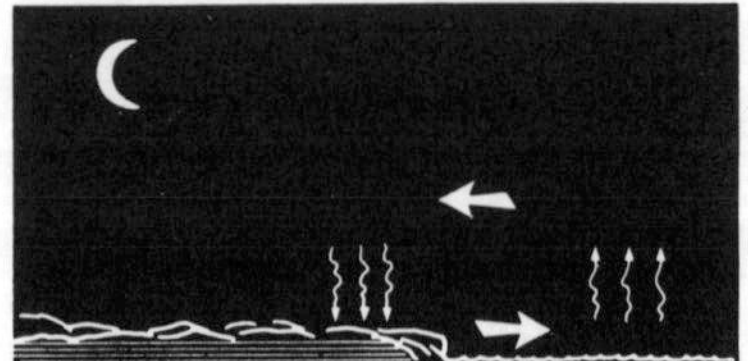

Fig. 4—17

Land and sea breezes occur in coastal districts mainly during settled weather conditions with sunny days and cloudless nights. They are mainly localised and rarely penetrate more than 10 to 20 miles inland or exceed 10 knots in strength. The effect of either breeze is usually limited to within 1000' of the surface.

During the development stages of these breezes the wind normally blows more or less at right angles to the coastline (directly from high to low pressure), but after a short while the effect of coriolis causes the wind to be deflected and blow at an angle to the coastline.

Sea breezes may suddenly develop during the late morning or early afternoon and can become of significance to aircraft taking off or landing at aerodromes near to the coast. If fog or haze conditions exist over the sea when sea breezes develop, it is likely to be brought in over the land causing a sudden reduction to visibility and making a safe landing difficult or even impossible.

Katabatic Winds

These are local winds which are also created by radiation effects. When air is cooled during the night, its density increases and in mountainous or hilly areas the air adjacent to the terrain is chilled by contact with the cold surface, and so becomes more dense that air at the same level away from the slope. This increase in density causes the air in the upper levels to flow down the slope and displace the warmer air below.

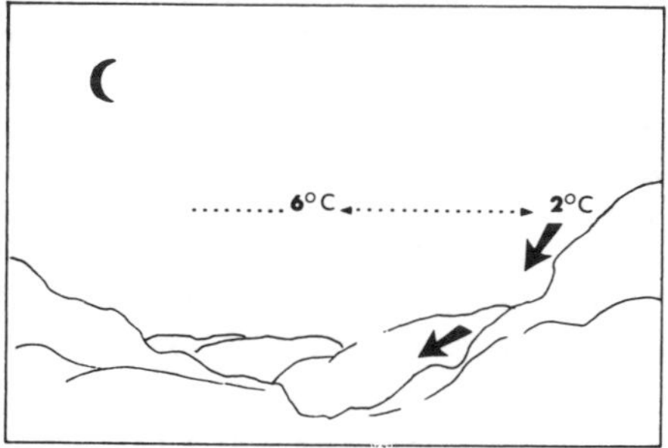

Fig. 4—18

Katabatic wind is of particular significance when operating in mountainous areas and many local names are used to describe this effect. A few examples are the Bora off the North Mediterannean, the Mistral from the Alps in Southern France, and the Chinook on the Eastern side of the Rocky Mountains.

Other Topographical Effects

Mountain ranges will often act as barriers and deflect the direction of the general wind. Valleys often produce a 'Funnel Effect' in that the wind may change its direction and flow through narrow passes in hill or mountain ranges, sometimes considerably increasing in speed.

Wind gusts abound in areas where the local topography is irregular or man made obstructions are sited. These gusts may produce significant local variations in wind speed, and sharp changes of wind direction. They can therefore create hazards, particularly to Microlight Aircraft, during the take-off or landing stage of a flight.

Fig 4-19 shows an example of gusts which may occur when moderate or strong winds prevail in the region of a landing area.

Fig. 4–19

Wind Gradient/Wind Shear

It has already been pointed out that the frictional effects of the Earth's surface slow down the wind speed and alter the wind direction in the layer of the atmosphere adjacent to the Earth's surface. These effects are usually (but not always) small when the winds are light, but become greater when the winds are strong. Added to this is the effect of mechanical turbulence which produces horizontal and vertical gusts, resulting in up and down draughts. Downdraughts can cause a sudden decrease in the aircraft's rate of climb immediately after take-off, or a sudden increase in the rate of descent during the approach phase.

The possibility of meeting such conditions creates a need for all pilots to be aware of the hazards associated with these variations of wind velocity during the take-off and landing stages of a flight. Any variation of airflow velocity, whether it be horizontal or vertical, produces a shearing action between layers of air, hence the term 'Wind Shear'

The effects of wind gusts and associated turbulence can be appreciated fairly easily, but changes in the horizontal wind speed and/or direction will require more explanation. For example, lift is the force which overcomes weight, and an aeroplane obtains this lift from the angle of attack at which the wings are presented to the airflow and the speed at which it is flown. The higher the speed at which the airflow passes over the wings, the greater is the lift. Therefore any sudden change in the wind speed or its direction relative to the aircraft will affect the lift being produced.

It can be seen from fig 4-20 that an aircraft descending through layers of air where the wind speed is decreasing rapidly will be penetrating a region of wind shear, the effect of which will temporarily lower the airspeed, less lift will be produced and the aircraft will descend more quickly.

When the wind shear is gentle the pilot will have no difficulty in lowering the nose of the aircraft to regain its original airspeed, but if the wind shear is rapid and pronounced he will need to act very quickly to re-adjust the aircraft attitude, and also increase engine power.

Sometimes the effects of mechanical turbulence, thunderstorm activity, or an inversion, can create the effect shown in fig 4-21. In this case the wind direction has become temporarily reversed near the ground, leading to the need for very quick reactions from the pilot, during the take-off or landing phase.

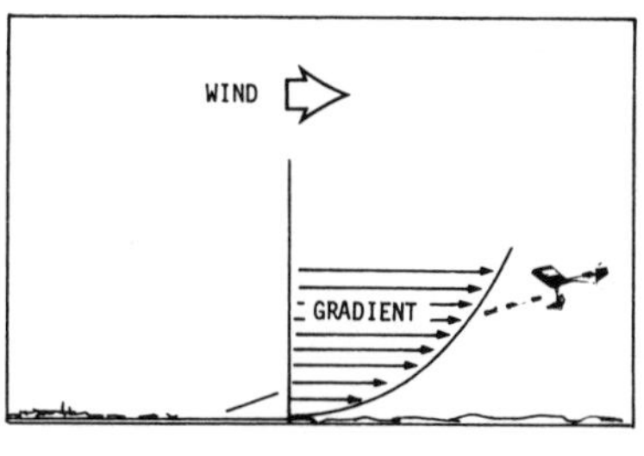

Fig. 4—20

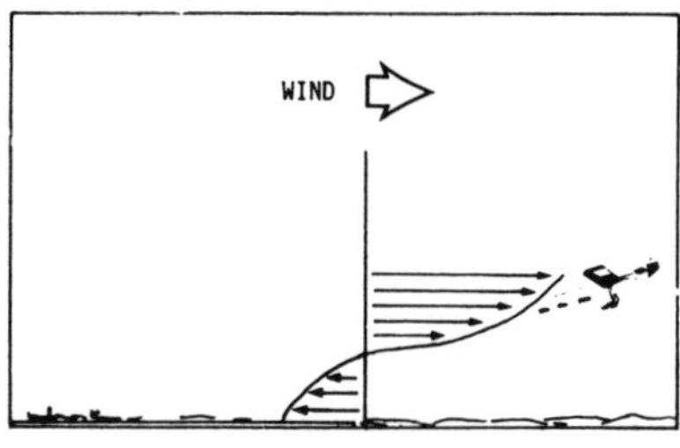

Fig. 4—21

A change in wind speed relative to an aircraft can also be caused by a sudden change in the horizontal direction of the wind as shown in fig. 4-22. It can be seen in this example that the aircraft is flying in a wind of 35 kts on a heading which gives a 30 kt headwind component. The horizontal wind shear as shown, will result in a sharp drop in airspeed of 20 kts.

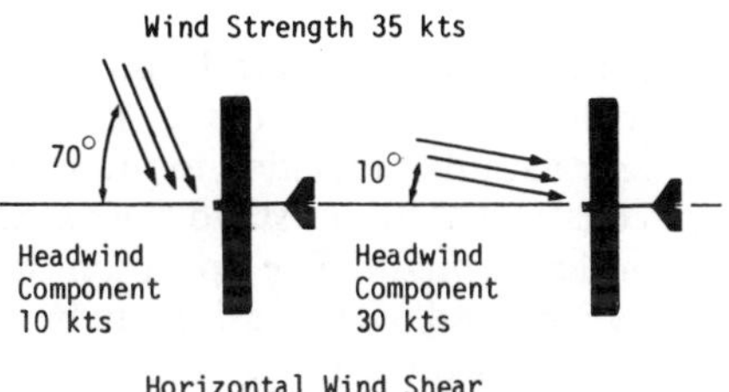

Fig. 4—22

Wind shear is a particularly common occurrence during thunderstorm activity and can be met with on any side of such an area. The wind shift line (or gust front) can precede a storm by up to 15-20 miles, consequently, when thunderstorms are within this distance of an aerodrome wind shear hazards must be anticipated at any time during take-off or landing.

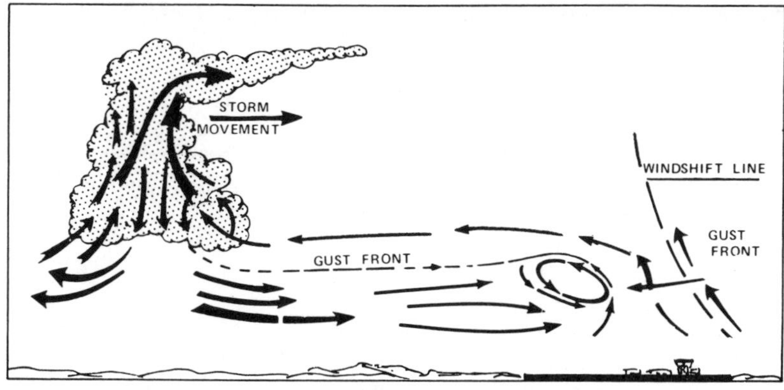

Fig. 4—23

A further note in relation to wind shear is that it is not necessarily associated with strong winds. For example, when a temperature inversion exists, a common situation is for very light or zero wind conditions to be present at the surface although winds just above the inversion layer may be moderate to strong.

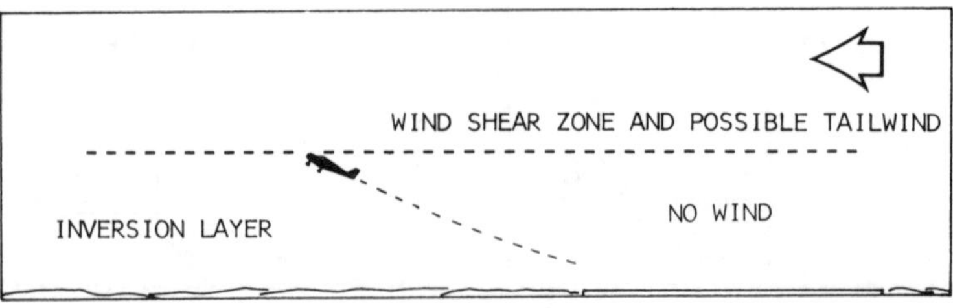

Fig. 4—24

Flight in Turbulent Conditions

Apart from the discomfort to the passengers and pilot, turbulence can induce inflight hazards in relation to the stresses imposed upon the airframe. All aircraft are constructed to withstand reasonable load factors which may be imposed upon them during flight. The operation of any aircraft is subject to specific strength limitations, and overstressing can be created by the powerful influences of nature, as well as by the physical actions of the pilot.

The effect of vertical gusts is an important factor in relation to structural stresses in that they cause rapid changes to the 'angle of attack' of an aircraft in flight, in just the same way as the pilot can by suddenly applying a appreciable back pressure to the control column.

When a sudden backward pressure is applied to the control column the aircraft will respond by a change in attitude, but inertia will prevent it from altering its flight path until a few moments have elapsed. During this time, the angle of attack will have been increased and with it the load factor. Fig 4-25 shows the effect of a vertical gust in relation to changing the relative angle of attack.

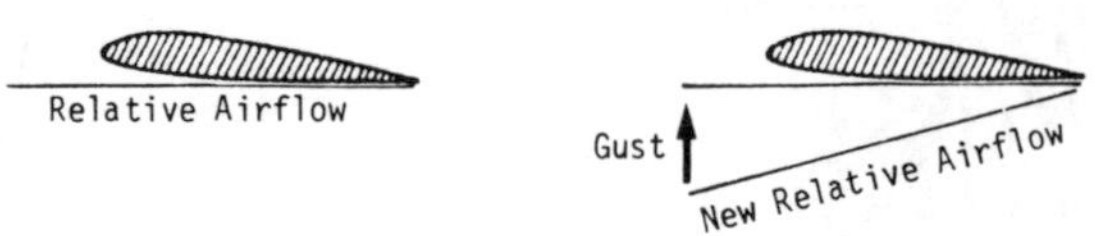

Fig. 4—25

With the exception of thunderstorms or line squalls, the effects of turbulence are usually greatest near the surface or just below large cumulus clouds. These regions can normally be avoided during en-route flight. However the altitude band in which small aircraft operate is somewhat restricted, and additional care will need to be exercised when mountains or high hills have to be traversed. In these regions, very strong up and down currents are often present and they can produce considerable hazards.

Mountain Waves

When unstable air flows across a topographical barrier such as a range of mountains or high hills, it spills down the leeward slopes and produces strong downdraughts. The rate of sink in such a downdraught may exceed the maximum rate of climb of a microlight aircraft. Although this effect is fairly localised it could nevertheless give rise to a hazardous situation. (Ref fig 4-26).

Therefore in these circumstances, a minimum safe altitude should be selected which gives a clearance of at least 2000' above the highest ground. Additionally, the aircraft heading should be such that it traverses the high ground at an angle of 90 degrees, so that it is in the downdraught area for the shortest possible period.

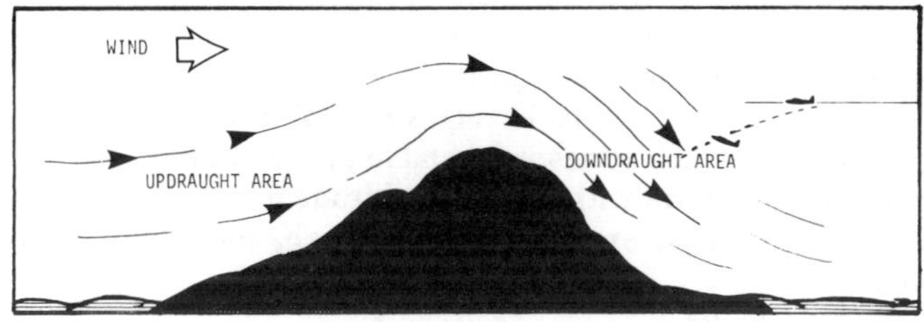

Fig. 4—26

Another situation occurs when stable air flows across a line of high hills or a mountain range, where air flowing up the windward side of the ground barrier is relatively smooth, and the airflow is therefore laminar, i.e. it tends to flow in layers. The barrier formed by the ground may set up waves in these smooth layers in a similar manner to waves developing upon a disturbed water surface. In addition to this, large scale eddies may occur which give strong vertical currents and turbulence.

This condition has been given the name 'Mountain Wave', and the wave pattern remains essentially stationary, but can extend a considerable distance downwind from the mountain range. Extreme turbulence can be produced in the vicinity of the 'roll cloud' on the leeward side, and the presence of mountain waves can sometimes be recognised by the formation of 'Lenticular' (lens shaped) clouds,as shown in fig. 4—27.

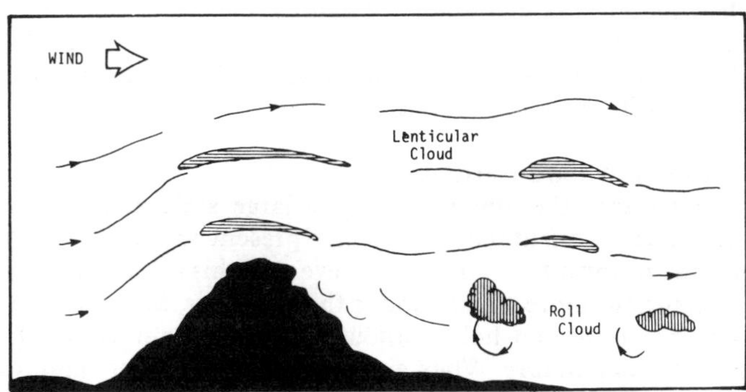

Fig. 4—27

Considerable caution must be exercised by pilots overflying mountain ranges when conditions conducive to mountain wave formation exist, and particular attention to this possibility must be given during examination of the weather forecast if the flight is over or in the vicinity of mountain areas.

FORMATION OF CLOUD AND PRECIPITATION

Unlike temperature and pressure changes, cloud formation can be clearly seen, representing aerial signposts from which the pilot can obtain significant information. Clouds enable him to visualize the actual weather conditions, and so assist him in anticipating how the weather might affect his flight.

Clouds are classified into many different types but initially they can be considered as taking two distinct forms:

Stratus - which forms in relatively stable air conditions.

Cumulus - which forms in unstable air conditions.

Because cloud types form within general altitude bands they are also identified by altitude families. These are, Low, Middle, High, and clouds of large vertical development.

Stratus Clouds

The term stratus means stratified or layered. Stratus is characterised by a fairly level sheet of uniform appearance often several thousand feet thick and covering a wide area. Clouds of this type are divided into a number of categories each with its own particular name. Most of them are associated with smooth flying conditions.

Cumulus Clouds

The term cumulus means accumulation or heap, and this name is given to those clouds which form isolated heaps or towers with a marked vertical development. They may take the form of a large towering mass of isolated clouds extending upwards to 40.000' or more, and several miles across, or form locally and in association with stratus cloud sheets.

All cumulus clouds are associated with a degree of atmospheric instability which may vary from conditions of minor turbulence, to violent vertical air currents on a wide scale.

A third category is 'Nimbus', or the prefix 'Nimbo' and the suffix 'Nimbus', meaning rain bearing. These are used in association with stratus or cumulus clous, for example, cumulo-nimbus or nimbo-stratus.

Cloud amounts are reported in "Oktas", or the number of eighths of sky covered by cloud. An okta is easily estimated if one imagines the sky is cut into 4 quadrants - each quadrant will represent 2 oktas.

General Causes of Cloud Formation

Water evaporates into the atmosphere on a large scale and becomes an ever present but variable constituent. The water present in any part of the Earth's atmosphere may be invisible to the human eye, and this is known as water vapour.

Warm air can hold more water vapour than cold air, therefore the amount of water vapour which air can hold without condensing out as cloud or fog will depend upon its temperature. When air contains all the water vapour it can hold without releasing it into visible form, it is said to be saturated and will have reached what is called the 'Dew Point'.

There are two ways that saturated air will release water vapour into the form of minute water droplets, these are:

1. When additional water vapour is absorbed beyond the saturated state, or
2. By lowering the air temperature and thus 'squeezing out' the excess water vapour into cloud or fog.

The latter of these two methods is by far the most common cause of cloud formation, but to interpret the conditions which lead to the formation of cloud or fog in the atmosphere it will be necessary to understand three commonly used meteorological terms which relate to humidity, these are:

1. Dew Point Temperature
   This is the temperature at which the air would become saturated (with no change in pressure or moisture content).
2. Relative Humidity
   This is the term used to express the relationship between the water vapour actually present in the air, to the amount of water vapour which could be held in the air (at the same temperature and pressure) without condensation occurring.
   It is usually expressed as a percentage, for example, if the air at a certain temperature contains all the invisible water vapour possible at that temperature it is said to be saturated and the Relative Humidity will be 100%. If the air contains only one half as much water vapour as it could at that temperature, then the Relative Humidity will be 50%.
3. Absolute Humidity
   At any moment of time, the air contains a certain quantity of water per unit volume, a quantity which will vary from place to place. The actual amount of water per unit volume is termed the Absolute Humidity.

Aviation weather reports usually include the dew point temperature so that a pilot can compare it with the actual temperature to determine for example, whether, (if other conditions are suitable), fog will form. Meteorologists also use this information to forecast the possible cloud base level.

In addition to this there are many other minute hygroscopic particles such as sulphur, the by-products of combustion etc, all of which abound in the Earth's atmosphere. The type and amount of such nuclei affect the commencement of the condensation process which in turn causes cloud or fog to form at slightly different temperatures than that of the Dew Point. For example, if sufficient hygroscopic particles are present the condensation process can begin in humidities as low as 85%.

When the visible water droplets which make up clouds become larger for any reason, the air can no longer support their weight and precipitation in the form of rain, drizzle, sleet, snow or hail occurs. Bearing in mind that clouds give the pilot certain information as to what weather conditions are likely to be met en-route, it will be of interest to note the connection between cloud type and cause.

The following table gives a broad indication of the principal classes of clouds together with the four major reasons for the air reaching its dew point temperature:

CAUSAL ACTION Temperature Changes Due To	GENERAL TYPE OF CLOUD FORMATION	CLOUD NAME	SURFACE CHART SYMBOL	PRECIPITATION TYPE If Cooling is Sufficient
Widespread Ascent of Air Mass	Multilayer Clouds	Cirrus Cirrostratus Altostratus Altocumulus Nimbostratus		Prolonged Moderate Rain, Sleet or Snow
Widespread Irregular Mixing of Air	Low Level Layers or Shallow Layers of Fog or Cloud	Stratus Stratocumulus		Drizzle, or Possible Light Snow
Local Convection Currents	Cumuliform	Cumulus Cumulonimbus		Showers of Rain, Snow, or Hail. Possible Thunderstorm Activity
Local Orographic Disturbances	Lenticular or Wave Cloud	Lenticularis		Occasionally, an Increase in Existing Precipitation

Widespread Ascent of an Air Mass
This type of vertical motion is normally associated with frontal activity and is covered under the heading 'Depressions and Fronts' later in this manual.

Widespread Irregular Mixing of Air
This is a result of air moving over the Earth's surface and creating irregular vertical and horizontal eddies as shown in fig 4-28.

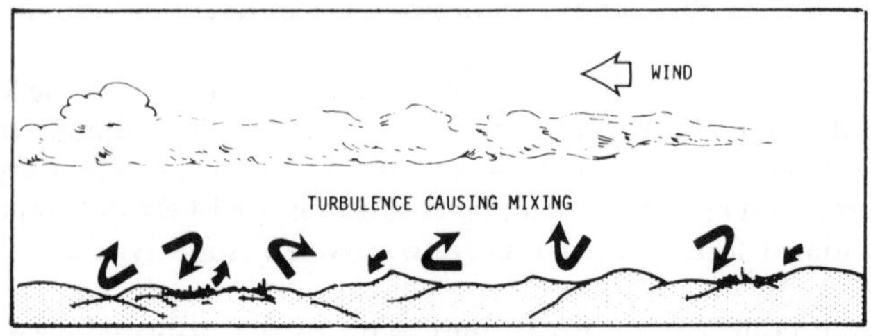

Fig. 4—28

This mechanical turbulence causes mixing between layers of the atmosphere and sometimes results in certain layers reaching a state of saturation and the formation of stratus, or stratocumulus cloud, depending upon the local conditions.

Local Convection Currents

These can bring abut an unstable situation and if saturation takes place the rising parcels of air will produce relatively flat based cumulus cloud. The height of the tops will depend upon the height at which a stable condition occurs.

When the temperature differential between the ascending air and the surrounding air is small, the resulting cumulus cloud will not normally extend more than a few thousand feet. This type of cumulus is known as 'Fair Weather Cumulus', Fig 4-29 illustrates this.

Fig. 4–29

However on those occasions when instability continues with increase of altitude the vertical currents are vigorous and reach greater altitudes, producing large cumulus clouds of considerable vertical extent, with the likelihood of precipitation. Such conditions can often be the springboard from which thunderstorms develop.

Large Orographic Disturbances

These are associated with large irregularities of the Earth's surface in the form of hills and mountains. Air flowing over the surface must follow the terrain, so resulting in vertical displacement. Air which encounters these physical barriers will undergo orographic lifting and depending upon the resultant cooling the air temperature may drop below its dew point and cloud will form.

When stable conditions exist, a wave cloud called 'Lenticularis) ref fig 4–30) forms in the vicinity of the high ground, sometimes resting at surface level and sometimes occurring at different levels in the air above.

When atmospheric instability results from this orographic lifting, clouds may build up on the windward side of the barrier. The rising air will initially cool at the DALR until cloud forms, thereafter cooling will occur at the SALR and precipitation may fall from the cloud, (fig 4–31).

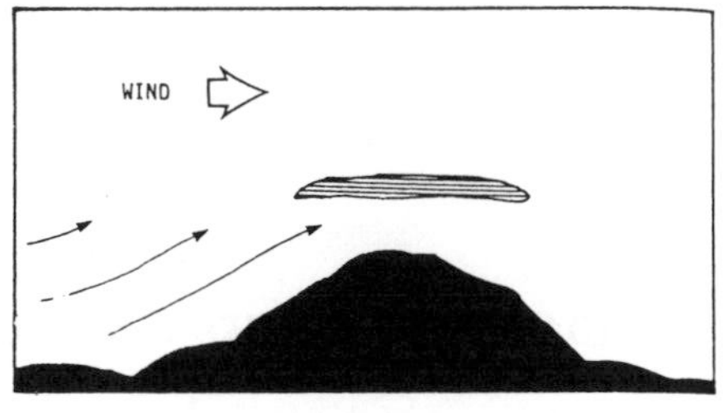

Fig. 4–30

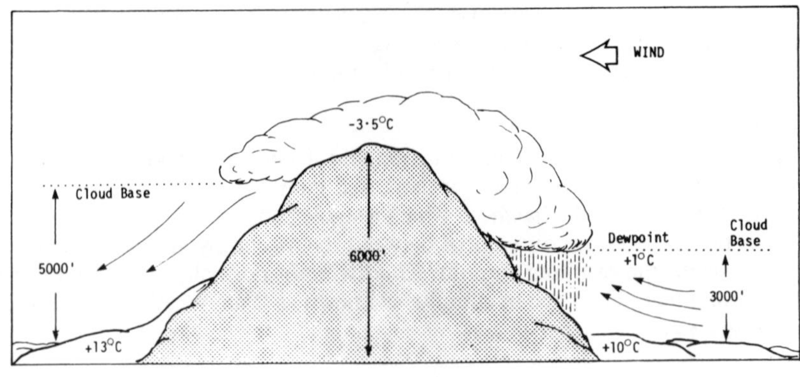

Fig. 4—31

As shown in the above diagram this situation often produces higher temperatures on the leeward side of the mountain range.

PRECIPITATION, RAIN, SNOW AND HAIL

The subject of precipitation is rather complex, and a detailed analysis of how it is formed is outside the scope of this manual. Suffice to say, that in the first place some nuclei (dust, smoke or other minute particles having an affinity to water) must be present in the air for cloud particles to become visible. Following this, and when conditions are right, precipitation in the form of rain, snow or hail may develop.

Put simply, precipitation occurs due to the coalescence of small cloud particles which then form water droplets. Alternatively, at lower temperatures cloud particles may attach themselves to minute ice particles which form the nuclei from which the water droplets, snow or hail can form. As these droplets grow in size the surrounding atmosphere is unable to support their weight and they fall, either reaching the surface or evaporating during their downward path.

To summarise precipitation is the final result of a series of events in the physical chemistry of the atmosphere., the degree of intensity of the precipitation, and whether rain, snow or hail is formed, will depend upon the amount of moisture available, the rate of cooling which takes place, the degree of instability, and the range of ambient temperatures involved.

Stratus cloud formations can produce continuous periods of rain which may vary in intensity from light to heavy, and under certain conditions, cumulus clouds can produce heavy showers, possibly hail, which reduce in-flight visibility to almost nil.

AVOIDANCE OF FLIGHT THROUGH OR NEAR THUNDERSTORMS

Although the chemistry involved in the formation of a thunderstorm is extremely complex, the advice to pilots regarding flight through or in the immediate vicinity of these violent forms of weather can be summed by the corruption of two simple words:

DON'T

This is the simplest and safest policy for all pilots of microlights and small General Aviation aircraft, and the following list sums up the 'DO NOT' points where thunderstorms are concerned...

Don't—Attempt to fly underneath a thunderstorm area, even though you can see through to the other side. The lower levels of the cloud and that region immediately below is an area of intense turbulence.

Don't—Get too close to any form of active thunderstorm activity. A good rule of thumb when deciding how close a light aircraft can be safely flown to such an area is as follows:-

'Allow one mile clearance for every 2000' of its vertical development'.

Don't—Attempt to fly through or below a Line Squall. These intense weather areas may produce violent turbulence, and lightning, and can extend a long a line of considerable length. They can therefore be difficult to circumnavigate, and it is usually advisable to turn back or land at the nearest available aerodrome or landing site until it is safe to continue. Remember Line Squalls move rapidly and sweep across an area quickly.

Don't—Assume that thunderstorms move in the direction of the general wind, thunderstorms often generate their own winds and on occasions have been known to move precisely in the opposite direction to the general wind prevailing at the time.

Don't—Assume that any thunderstorms will be of light intensity. They can reach the mature stage with remarkable speed, and an incorrect decision can leave a pilot trapped inside an area of intense and violent weather activity.

Don't—Attempt to climb over the tops of large and rapidly building cumulus cloud, such formations often rise more quickly than the maximum rate of climb of a small aircraft.

In addition to the above list of Don'ts there are also some very important Do's, for example:

When operating in areas of strong turbulence or whilst circumnavigating thunderstorm activity. DO ensure that loose articles are firmly stowed and all safety belts or harnesses are tightly secured.

DO remember that intense turbulence can be experienced many miles away from the location of a storm, this distance will usually be greatest when a line of thunderstorms are developing.

DO avoid flying below the overhang area of cloud, ahead of the storm region, it may contain large hailstones.

ICE ACCRETION ON AIRCRAFT

Whenever an aircraft is flown through cloud or rain at temperatures below 0°C there is a possibility that airframe icing will occur. Although microlights are not cleared to fly into cloud this does not in itself prevent inadvertent cloud penetration taking place nor does it prevent situations where the pilot finds himself flying below clouds and in rain.

To sum up, the accretion of ice upon the exposed surfaces of an aircraft, needs a low temperature and a supply of moisture. This moisture is normally in the form of cloud particles or rain. The type of icing so formed is related to these two factors in such a way that a number of specifically different and recognisable airframe ice formations can occur.

Types of Airframe Icing

Aircraft in flight encounter a wider variety of icing conditions than those found on the ground and this results in a greater number of forms (or types) of ice. The two basic processes which directly affect the type of ice formed are:

1. Ice formed directly from water vapour without passing through a liquid stage, i.e. Direct Sublimation.
2. Ice formed by the freezing of liquid droplets.

Ice which forms on the ground is generally defined as Hoar Frost and Rime Ice. Additionally when raindrops, which may themselves be supercooled, strike a cold ground surface, the ice so formed is called Glazed Frost (sometimes known as Glaze Ice or Clear Ice).

Hoar Frost

This is a white crystaline formation that can cover the surfaces of an aircraft. It is formed by the process of direct sublimation, i.e. conditions when moist air comes into contact with freezing temperatures and the water vapour freezes into ice crystals without first appearing as visible water droplets.

Hoar Frost can form when aircraft are parked in the open on clear cold nights when radiation from the upper surfaces causes the metal to cool below 0°C. It can also occur during flight when an aircraft which has been flying in sub-freezing temperatures, descends into warmer moist air. In this situation hoar frost can form on the windscreen surface and completely obscure forward vision until the aircraft surfaces warm up and the ice melts.

Rime Ice

This is an opaque, granular type of ice which can form on the leading edges of the wings, propeller blades, etc. It is usually brittle in character, being formed when the surfaces are at temperatures below 0°C and supercooled water droplets are present. It normally forms during flight through clouds composed of small water droplets, i.e. stratus, and these small drops freeze immediately upon coming into contact with the aircraft surfaces.

In these conditions a droplet freezes instantaneously and before another droplet hits the same spot, therefore air is trapped between the successive drops and makes the ice formation brittle. Although ice of this nature only causes a little additional weight on the aircraft it does significantly affect the aerodynamic flow over the wing surfaces, altering the lift values. Its formation can also block the air intake(s) to the engine(s).

Clear Ice

This is sometimes called 'Glazed Ice' and consists of a transparent glossy ice which forms, often unevenly over the aircraft surfaces, including the propeller etc. Ice of this type forms when conditions are such that relatively large water droplets are not significantly below 0°C. Initially only a small portion of the droplet freezes on impact, this action releases latent heat to the rest of the droplet which flows back along the surface and gradually freezes in the process.

Clear ice can also form when an aircraft descends into or flies through an area of falling rain when the aircraft surfaces are below 0°C. In this case the formation is often severe and builds up rapidly.

Rime ice and clear ice represent the two types of icing which form on aircraft flying in cloud or rain, but as the ambient temperatures over which either may form range from 0°C to -40°C, intermediate types of icing may occur. These types of icing are known as Mixed or Cloudy Ice. In summary it can be stated that the smaller the water droplets are, the more likely it is that Rime Ice may form, and that the larger the water droplets, the more likely it is that Clear Ice will form.

EFFECTS OF ICING UPON AIRCRAFT PERFORMANCE

Any type of ice which forms on the aircraft wings will adversely affect the production of lift and increase the drag. Clear ice in particular, because of its compact formation, will produce a significant increase in weight. When any type of ice forms on the propeller blades, and on or around the engine air intake, thrust will be reduced.

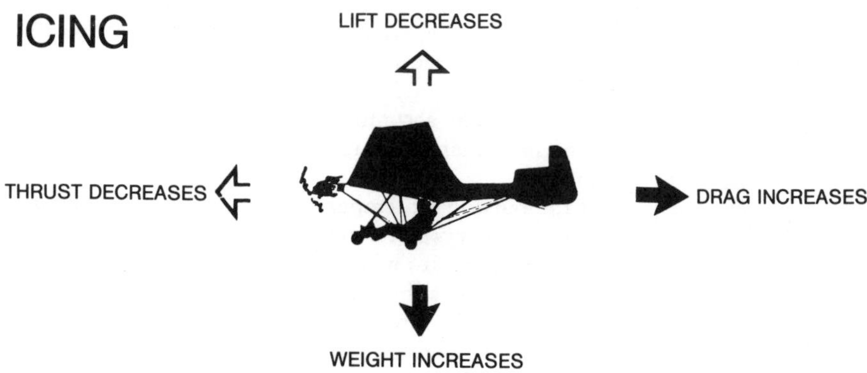

PERFORMANCE DECREASES

Further to this, if the aircraft continues to fly through the same conditions for any period of time the ice will continue to build. The effects of ice are cumulative, and the performance of an aircraft may be so impaired that level flight becomes impossible.

Precautions, and Preventions, and Avoidance

When VFR flight can be conducted there will normally be no problem of ice forming on the aircraft unless flying through rain at temperatures below 0°C, or after descending rapidly into warm moist air after flying at levels where sub-zero temperatures exist. Prevention can therefore be ensured by avoiding flight through cloud or rain, whenever the ambient temperature is at 0°C or below.

Types of Engine Icing

Airframe icing which occurs over the engine intake will produce a reduction, or possibly a complete loss of power. Another situation which can produce a significant loss of power is the ingestion of large water droplets into the air intakes or carburettors. This can affect the fuel/air mixture ratio, and cause power loss, but when temperatures in the engine induction system are at or below 0°C, these water droplets can freeze on the internal surfaces of the system and form carburettor ice.

This type of icing is caused during moderate to high humidity conditions in conjunction with the temperature drop due to the evaporation of fuel and the expansion of air as it passes through the carburettor. In small aero engines this temperature drop can be as much as 20°C. Water vapour contained in the air is condensed by the cooling and if the temperature in the carburettor reaches 0°C or below, moisture is deposited as frost or ice on the inside of the carburettor passages and the throttle butterfly valve.

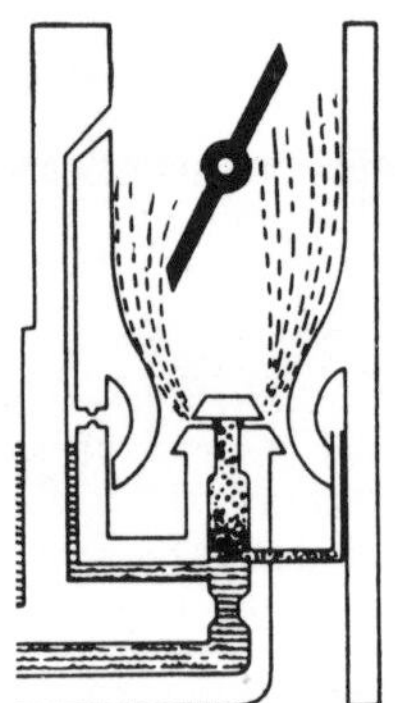

Even a slight accumulation of this deposit will reduce power and in larger amounts may lead to complete engine stoppage.

If the outside air temperature is much lower than about minus 6°C any water droplets will condense directly into minute ice particles which will pass through the induction system without adhering to the inside of the carburettor passages. Most modern conventional aircraft have an outside air temperature gauge fitted inside the cockpit, and the outside air temperature can be monitored from this instrument.

It must be appreciated that unlike airframe icing (with the exception of Rain Ice) carburettor icing is just as likely to occur whether flying in, or clear of cloud.

Due to the variations in fuel flow at different power settings, and the consequent differences in temperature drop within the carburettor system plus the variation in the humidity of the ambient air, it is impossible to lay down a hard and fast outside air temperature at which carburettor icing will occur. Therefore a pilot must be alert for the formation of this type of icing at any time during a flight.

Dry days, or days when the outside air temperature is well below freezing, are conditions not conducive to carburettor icing, but when the outside air temperature is about -6°C to +20°C with high humidity, carburettor icing risks will be high. In temperature latitudes it can be generally stated that the higher the humidity - the greater are the risks of carburettor icing.

Precautions and Prevention and Clearance of Carburettor Icing
In conventional light aircraft, a carburettor heat system is installed so that the pilot can prevent or remove ice. Guidance on how to operate such systems is contained in the aircraft manual for the specific type.

In general the remedial actions when engine icing occurs are as outlined below:

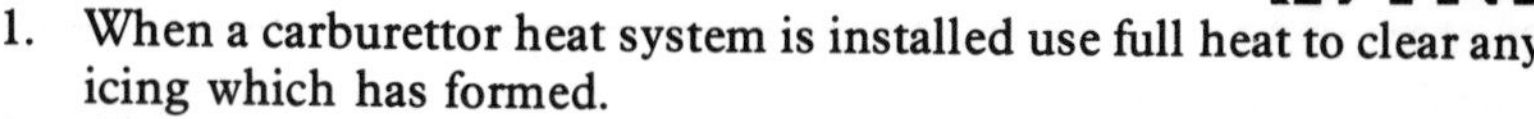

1. When a carburettor heat system is installed use full heat to clear any icing which has formed.
2. Alter the power setting or if applicable use mixture control. The evaporation of fuel normally accounts for some 70% of the temperature drop in the carburettor and therefore a power change can often have a positive effect upon the internal temperature of the carburettor. The greatest change in temperature will usually be made by increasing the power above that being used for cruising flight.
3. Alter the altitude at which the aircraft is flying, this however is usually a rather restricted remedy as the temperature change is only approximately 2°C per 1000'.

Note: When full hot air is being used the pilot must bear in mind that the engine power output is reduced and the fuel consumption rate is increased.

VISIBILITY

Visibility is measured as the furthest distance along a specified direction at which a person with normal sight can readily distinguish and identity a known object.

In the case of the basic private pilot with no formal instrument flying training the loss of visual reference whilst in flight can be disastrous. The ability to see ahead of the aircraft is vital to the safe conduct of a flight, whether taking off or landing, or using visual navigation techniques. During any flight the visibility may vary from conditions of VMC to situations where smoke, cloud or fog may give rise to temporary or more persistent difficulties to navigation or landing.

The training a private pilot receives during his basic course of instruction will normally school him to avoid clouds and cope with transient atmospheric changes such as smoke banks or haze, but it will not provide for flight in seriously deteriorating visibility. Pilots must therefore be alert to any possibility of worsening visibility and have an understanding of when such conditions are likely to occur.

Formation of Fog and Mist
The formation of fog or mist present a most hazardous condition for take-off or landing, therefore all pilots must be capable of interpreting aviation weather reports and forecasts as well as in-flight signs which indicate the possibility of this hazard.

By definition, fog is composed of small visible water droplets (or ice crystals) which reduce the visibility at the Earth's surface to less than 1000 metres. Mist is defined as a visibility condition of between 1000 and 2000 metres.

The relative humidity is generally about 100% in fog and at least 95% in mist, therefore a fairly fine distinction occurs between them. Clearly, with such a delicate balance of relative humidities, mist can very quickly degenerate into fog. When fog occurs over high ground, it is commonly given the name 'Hill Fog' which is usually cloud formed by orographic lifting or the saturation of air at the surface during frontal conditions.

Radiation, Advection and Frontal Fog

Apart from cloud forming on high ground, fog is most usually the result of condensation produced as a result of a relatively cold surface cooling the air immediately above it. There are three distinct types of fog as follows:

Radiation Fog
This is caused primarily by the loss of heat during the evening and night.

Advection Fog
This occurs when moist air moves over a relatively colder surface.

Frontal Fog
When precipitation and/or low cloud occurs at the surface in association with a warm front or warm occlusion.

Radiation Fog—The conditions favourable for the formation of radiation are:
Clear skies to allow sufficient cooling.
High relative humidity
Light winds to ensure a shallow mixing level.

This type of fog forms mostly during the evening, night or near daybreak. Radiation cools the ground, which in turn cools the air in contact with it and if the air is cooled to its dewpoint, fog can occur.

When all other conditions are suitable for fog formation but no wind is present the water vapour in the atmosphere will condense out as dew and fog will not occur. However on some occasions when no wind is present the gentle turbulence caused by the sun heating the surface at daybreak will be sufficient to create the right amount of mixing and radiation fog can form rapidly.

If the wind strength is more than about 5 knots the mixing effect will occur throughout a deeper layer leading to a reduction in the rate of cooling in the lower layers. This can result in the formation of low stratus, or it may prevent condensation from occurring in any form.

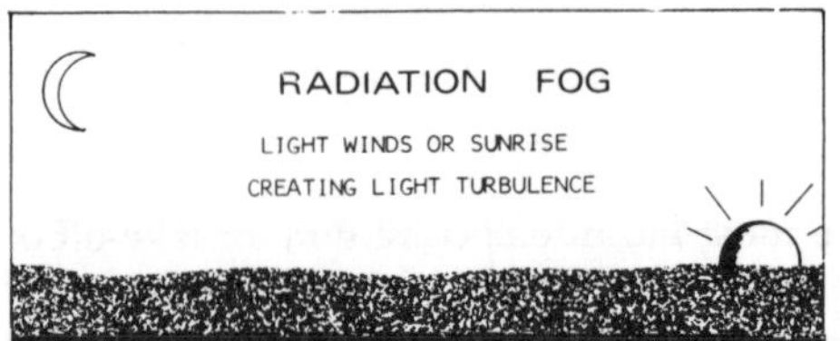

Fig. 4—32

Radiation fog generally clears during the day due to surface heating. The turbulent mixing associated with surface heating assists this effect, and leads to a breakdown of the inversion process.

During days when cloud cover reduces surface heating the fog may persist all day or for many days at a time. The advent of moderate to strong winds will dissipate radiation fog as a result of turbulence lifting the air close to the surface and mixing it with the drier layers above.

Advection Fog—This type of fog forms when moist air moves over a colder surface and when the temperature at the surface is below the dew point temperature of the moving air. It is most common along coastal areas but sometimes develops inland.

Overland, advection fog is most likely to occur in the winter months after a cold spell, when a warmer air mass arrives from the sea. The air which will have had a relatively long sea track will be extremely humid and may have become almost saturated, so that cooling by the land surface will often produce fog or drizzle.

Due to its method of formation advection fog can form and remain in existence even though moderate winds are prevailing. This means that when banks of fog form at sea close to the coast and an inshore wind is prevailing, the fog can drift over the land and create hazards for aircraft intending to land in that vicinity. If strong winds prevail the fog usually lifts into low stratus with very poor visibility underneath. In either form it will present a considerable hazard to pilots, often covering a wide area and persisting for long periods.

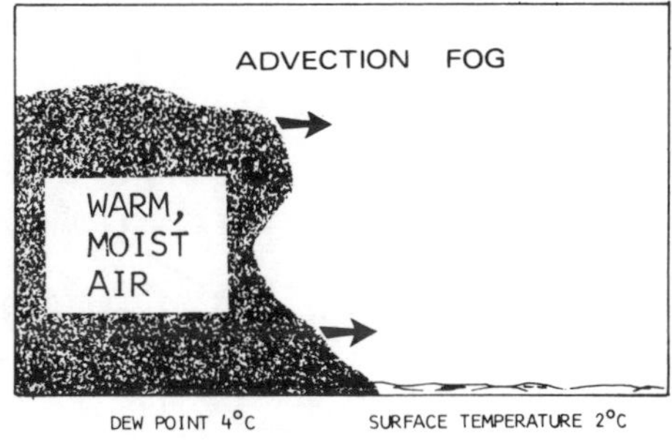

Fig. 4—33

Frontal Fog—The formation of frontal fog is associated with the interaction of two separate types of air mass. It can occur in one of two ways, either of which can produce a belt of fog or cloud at the surface for some hundreds of miles in length and a similar distance in breadth.

Often it is in the form of cloud slowly lowering to the surface during the passage of a weather front. This occurs more usually over high ground. Alternatively it may form because the air at the surface becomes saturated during the continuous rainfall associated with the passage of a warm front or warm occlusion. The onset of frontal fog unlike that formed by radiation and advection, is usually slower and so ample warning is given to pilots because the weather deteriorates over a relitively long period.

In assessing the probability of this situation giving difficulty during flight, consideration will often have to be given to whether large industrial areas are in the vicinity of the route. It should be appreciated that smoke and dust can exist many miles downwind of these areas. A further point to bear in mind is that haze or smoke can often be avoided by climbing to a higher altitude and/or routing well to the leeward of an industrial area.

In the UK persistent haze can exist over a wide area for many days during anticyclonic conditions (regions of high pressure) which produce an easterly air-flow. The incoming air from the continent of Europe can be heavily impregnated with smoke, dust and sand particles. It must be appreciated that flying into sun can aggravate poor visbility due to haze etc, whereas when flying down sun the visibility may be quite good.

Hazards of Flight in Reduced Visibility

By now the reader will be able to appreciate the hazards created by restricted visibility for whichever reason. Neverthless a pilot should also be aware that a distinction exists between hroizontal visibility and, oblique air to ground visibility. This difference occurs due to the slant range involved when looking at the ground some distance from the aircraft.

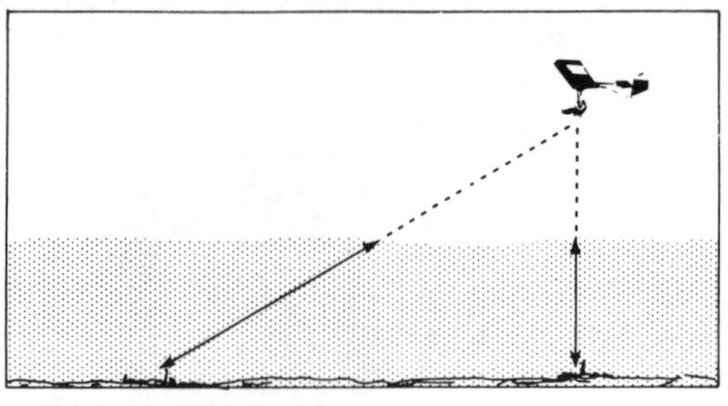

Fig. 4—34

Fig 4-34 shows this effect and although there are many occasions when the ground directly below the aircraft can be recognised, upon looking ahead at a distant surface the same facility will not be available because the pilot will be looking through a thicker layer of haze or mist.

A further important fact is that flying at low altitude during poor visibility in order to improve visual contact with the surface leads to greater hazards in relation to high ground and obstructions, as well as making map reading more difficult. (Refer to fig 4-35).

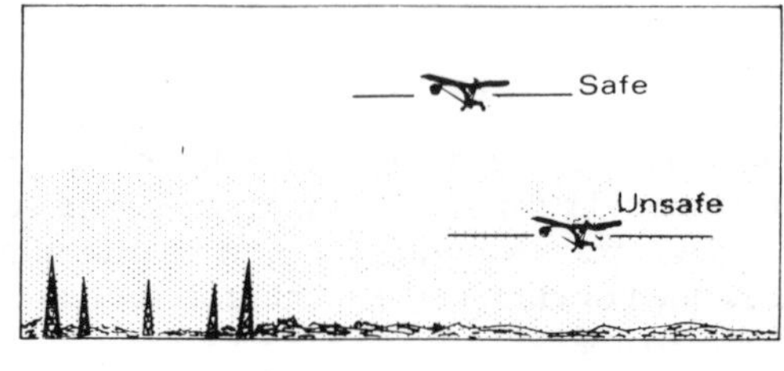

Fig. 4—35

Approaching to land in poor visibility. Initially the ground and features on the approach path may be visible, but as the aircraft descends closer to the ground the increased density of water particles in the lowest layers can cause the landing area to become obscured. Fig 4-36 shows an illustration of this effect.

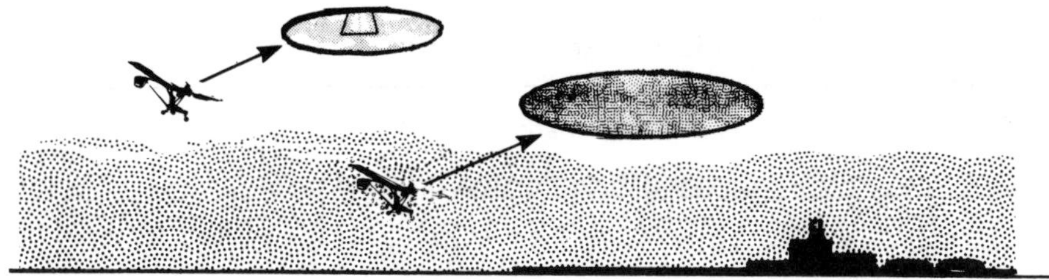

Fig 4–36

Another point to be aware of is the amount of daylight present during a particular flight. On many occasions when the flight continues into the late afternoon or evening, the degree of visibility will worsen for no other reason than the reduced strength of the daylight.

This effect is usually fairly insiduous and the pilot can suddenly find himself in a situation where he can no longer navigate the aircraft visually. It must further be appreciated that whilst the sun may have already set at ground level, it will still be reasonably light at altitude.

Note: Whenever the air temperature and the dew point are close together— **BEWARE** of fog formation, particularly during the early morning and evening.

DEPRESSIONS AND FRONTS

Having covered the basic principles of temperature, pressure and humidity, and their effect upon the weather, it will now be necessary to spend a short period discussing the characteristics of Air Masses and how their movements interact to produce what are known as Weather Fronts.

Air Masses

The term air mass is given to a very large mass of air (perhaps many hundreds or thousands of miles in width and length) with fairly uniform properties of temperature and moisture content through their horizontal extent.

These huge masses of air are created by the air aloft slowly sinking and coming more or less to rest over a large area of ocean or land. The air takes on the characteristics of the underlying surface, e.g. moist or dry, warm or cold. The longer the air remains in such an area the more it will become modified by the nature of the underlying surface.

In the Earth's restless and changing atmosphere where large variations of temperature and pressure occur this more or less stationery condition cannot remain indefinitely, and eventually the air mass being continually fed from above will become too large, and immense bubbles of air will break away, carrying their acquired temperature and humidity characteristics with them.

This is basically the way in which cold air moves South, warm air moves North, and moist air moves from the oceans to the land. Air Masses are classified as two basic types:

1. Cold, dense air masses which form in the polar or arctic regions.
2. Warm, less dense air masses, which form in temperate or tropical regions.

Depending upon whether their source region was the sea (maritime) or the land (continental) these two types may be moist or dry. Hence the following descriptive terms which are used to describe a particular air mass.

GENERAL DESCRIPTION OF AIR MASSES

TROPICAL MARITIME	WARM AND MOIST
TROPICAL CONTINENTAL	WARM AND DRY
POLAR MARITIME	COLD AND MOIST
POLAR (OR ARCTIC) CONTINENTAL	COLD AND DRY

The above is only a brief description of the principal air masses and it must be appreciated that the location of their source areas, their temperature and humidity, together with their speed and direction of movement may cause changes within them, and therefore to the weather which they produce during their travel.

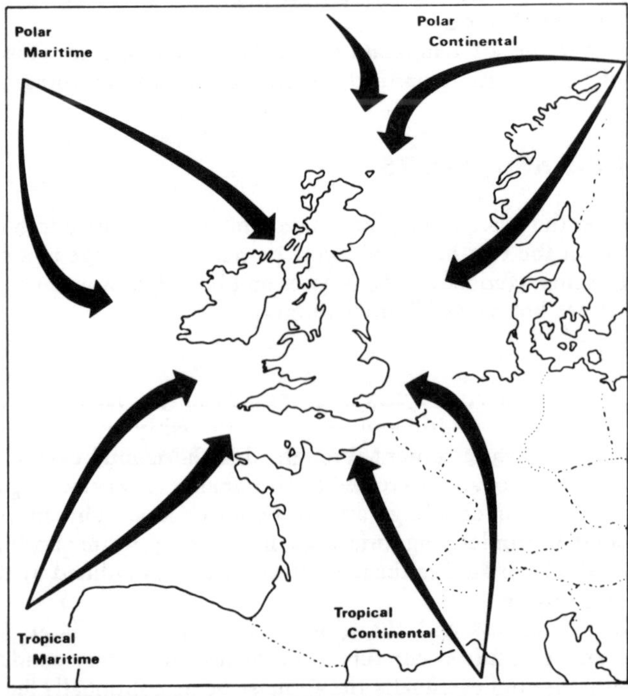

Fig. 4—37

Formation of Depressions

Depressions are areas of the atmosphere where the pressure is low. They appear on surface weather charts as a series of closed isobars, approximately oval or circular in shape, and with the lowest pressure occurring in the centre.

Depressions vary in size from a diameter of a few hundred metres (Tornadoes) to a thousand miles or more. When the pressure at the centre is very much less than the perimeter it is said to be deep and when only a small pressure difference occurs, the depression is said to be shallow. Depressions have alternative names such as, Lows and Cyclones, though the term cyclone more properly belongs to intense depressions such as Tornadoes.

Various theories are put forward as to how depressions occur, but these are outside the scope of this manual. Therefore what follows is a summary only of how Frontal Depressions form.

When a pressure drop occurs in the transition region between two air masses of distinctly different temperatures, the colder air bulges southwards, and the warmer air northwards. Fig 4-38 shows a plan view of 3 stages of air movement during the initial growth of a frontal depression.

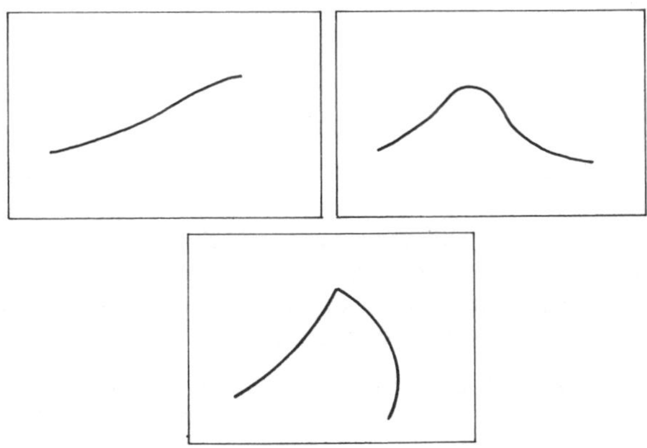

Fig. 4—38

Formation of Warm and Cold Fronts

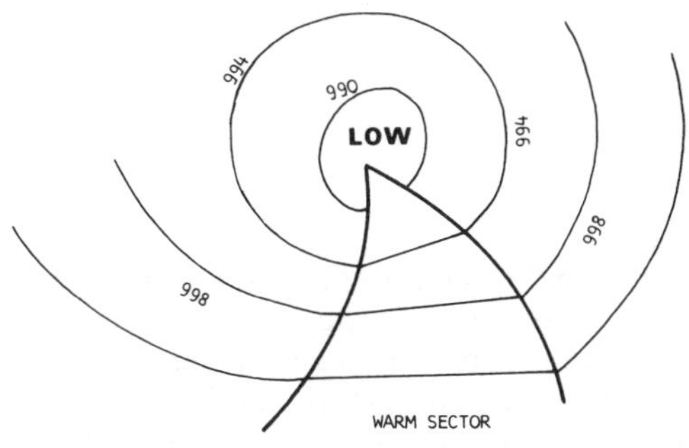

Fig. 4—39

Following the initial development of a frontal depression and during the deepening process the pressure continues to drop and the boundaries between the two air masses take up the pattern shown in fig. 4—39.

Although like most weather phenomena the formation and life cycle of fronts is a complex process, an idea of the typical weather situations associated with their passage can be gained by the following simple and basic explanations. The two principal types of front are the Cold Front and the Warm Front:

The Cold Front

This is the leading edge of an advancing cold air mass overtaking and replacing warmer air. It should be appreciated however, that the temperature difference between the cold and warm air can be relatively small. Cold fronts move at about the same speed as the geostrophic wind.

Cross section of a Cold Front.

Fig. 4—40

Cold Front as shown on a weather chart.

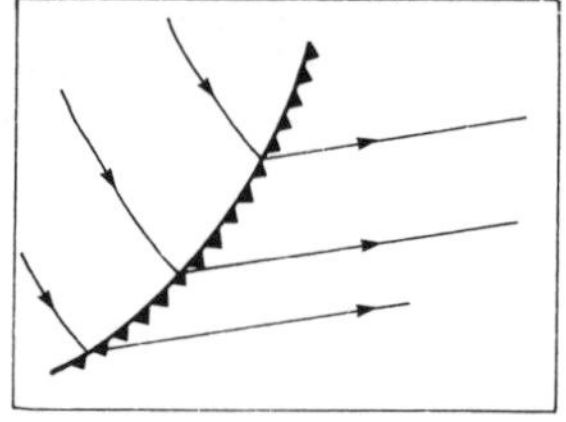

Fig. 4—41

The Warm Front

This is the leading edge of the warm sector which is replacing the cold air in the direction of frontal passage. Since the cold air ahead of the warm sector is more dense, the warm air gradually slides up and over the cold air forming a shallow frontal slope at a markedly smaller angle than that of the cold front.

Cross section of a Warm Front

Fig. 4—42

Warm Front as shown on a weather chart

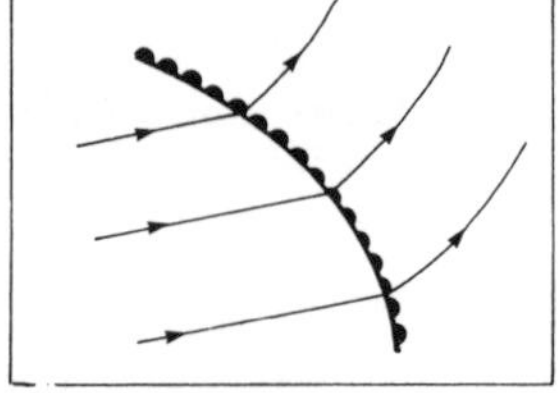

Fig. 4—43

The weather associated with the passage of warm and cold fronts is shown in the following cross section of an idealised developed frontal depression.

Well ahead of the warm front cirrus cloud appears and as the frontal line gets closer to the surface the cloud type changes through cirrostratus to altostratus and then to nimbostratus. Precipitation in the form of rain or snow falls from the higher altostratus but usually evaporates before reaching the ground.

Fig. 4—44

As the frontal line gets closer to the surface the cloud becomes lower and thickens, and the precipitation heavier, and eventually it reaches the ground. Continuous rain occurs until the warm front has passed after which the clouds usually take the form of low stratus.

The wind veers and the temperature and dew point rise. The pressure normally falls steadily ahead of the front and then remains steady or falls at a slower rate. The cold front brings weather of the unstable variety, i.e. cumulus or cumulo-nimbus clouds, squall lines or thunderstorms.

The passage of a cold front is liable to a wide variation of weather conditions, but normally the wind will veer, temperature drops rapidly, the dew point lowers, and after the front has passed there is a rapid rise in pressure.

All the foregoing conditions are common to most frontal activity but it must be stressed that there are many variations to the classic situation.

Occlusions

When a cold front catches up with a warm front, the two of them close together and form what is known as an occlusion. During this stage the centre of the low becomes almost stationary and signifies the final period in the life of a frontal depression.

During the occluding stage the weather can be a mixture of warm and cold front conditions with the possibility of active cumulonimbus embedded in stratus. The weather therefore, can be severe during the initial period of the occluding process, but shortly afterwards the weather will usually improve.

Cross section of an Occlusion

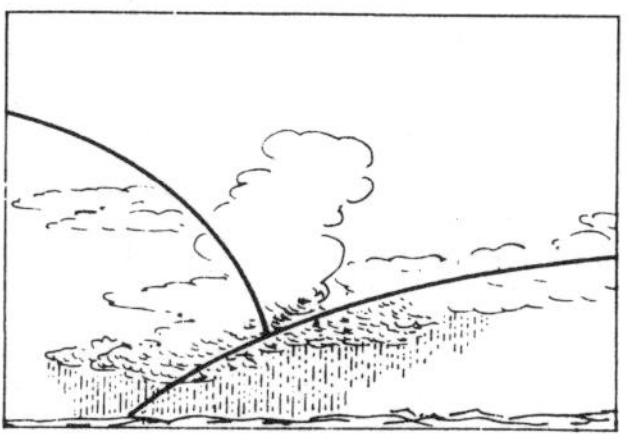

Fig. 4—45

Occlusion as shown on a weather chart

Fig. 4—46

Formation of Troughs

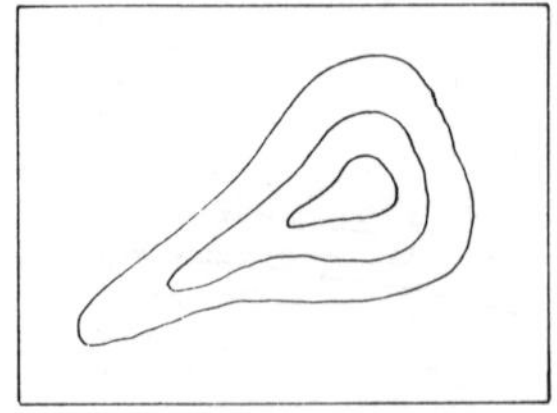

Fig. 4—47

Sometimes a pressure drop occurs which produces isobars in the shape of a V or a U. These are called Troughs of Low Pressure, and they can occur regardless of whether frontal conditions exist or not. Sharply marked troughs in the shape of a V usually occur in association with fronts and U shaped troughs are normally associated with non-frontal conditions.

Either of these are the result of a pressure drop, leading to convergence and rising air. Such conditions are a natural step to the formation of cloud and often precipitation and strong winds will be present.

Flight Conditions Associated with Depressions and Fronts.

Wind:

Strong winds can be expected during the passage of cold fronts and in either cold or warm frontal conditions a marked veer in wind direction can occur, leading to the possibility of the aircraft being blown well off track unless fairly frequent fixes are obtained.

Cloud:

The general cloud base will gradually lower over a large area during the passage of a warm front. The base of the cloud can reach the ground and form fog. Stratus clouds are associated with warm fronts, but when the occluding process is occurring, stratus cloud may mask cumulonimbus cloud and thunderstorm activity which will not easily be recognised until the aircraft has penetrated these conditions.

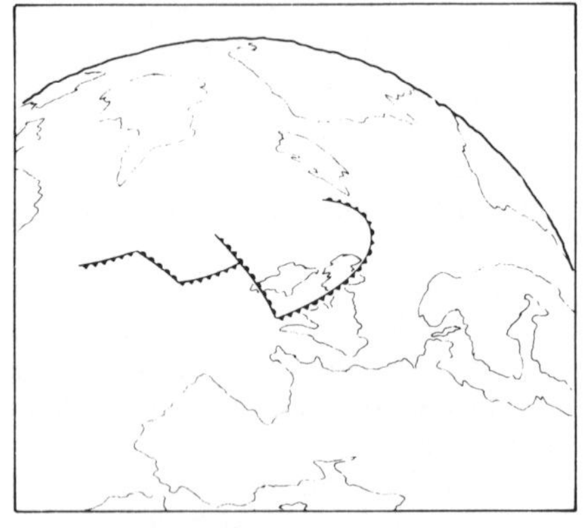

Fig. 4—48

Cold fronts, usually move at a moderate or rapid speed, and the frontal weather is generally less than 50 miles in depth. Large cumulus or cumulonimbus clouds are usually present and line squalls and thunderstorm activity may also occur.

Turbulence:

Strong turbulence is not normally associated with the passage of warm fronts, but intense turbulence can be experienced in the region of a cold front, whether or not large cumulus clouds are present.

Precipitation:
This can be encountered throughout a large altitude band and is most heavy along the frontal line near the surface. When flying through warm frontal conditions, the advent of very heavy precipitation can usually be taken as an indication that thunderstorm activity is present.
Icing:
Apart from the normal airframe icing risk when flying in cloud and rain in temperatures which are at or below 0°C, a condition may arise where rain falls from warm air into the colder region existing below a warm front surface. When this rain makes contact with the surfaces of an aircraft which have been cooled below 0°C, a type of clear ice will form. This is known as Rain Ice, and it can present an extreme hazard due to its rapid rate of accretion.

Recognition of Deteriorating Weather
Flight towards either warm or cold frontal conditions will be associated with a marked wind change in the lower levels. This change in wind direction is such that in all cases, alterations to starboard will be required to maintain a constant track.

When flying in the vicinity of a cold front the general visibility is good outside the areas of heavy precipitation, and so recognition of deteriorating weather is usually not difficult. In the vicinity of a warm front however, the visibility is usually poor, and extends over a much wider area, so making the identification of further weather deterioration much more difficult.

ANTICYCLONES

These are regions of high pressure which when shown on the surface weather chart consist of a pattern of isobars more or less circular in shape with the highest pressure in the centre.

Formation of High Pressure Areas
Normally anticyclones are areas where the pressure gradient is small and consequently the isobars are fairly widely spaced indicating the existence of the light winds which are normally associated with such regions.

The basic difference between high and low pressure areas (anticyclones and depressions) is that whereas in the latter the vertical movement of the air is upward, leading to expansion, cooling, clouds and precipitation, the former are regions in which the exact opposite occurs.
Due to the general influx of air from aloft the air sinks and subsidence occurs due to outflow near the surface. This causes compression, warming and a drying out of the atmosphere leading to a general lack of cloud. In anticyclones the winds follow the isobars in a clockwise direction.

Ridges and Cols
These names given by the meteorologist to particular pressure patterns which form within an air mass.

A Ridge of high pressure may extend outwards from an anticyclone in any direction and is generally an area of passive weather which is usually fine and clear, particularly when it occurs following the passage of a frontal depression.

The adjacent diagram shows a typical ridged shape pattern of isobars.

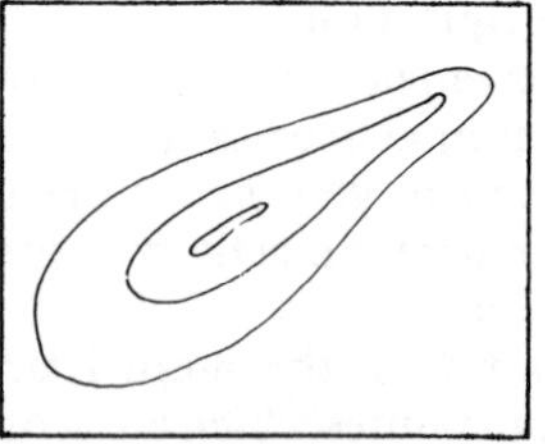

Fig. 4—49

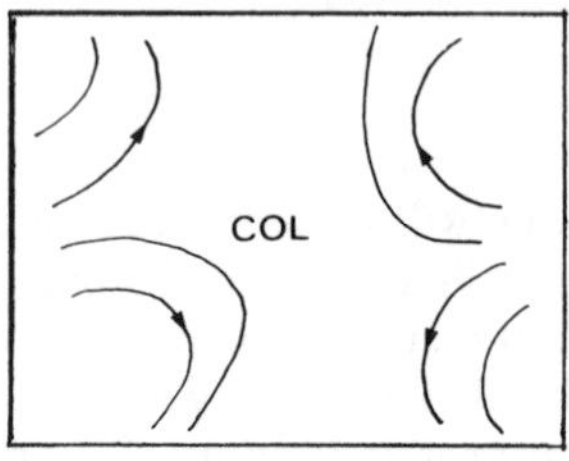

Fig. 4—50

A Col is distinguished on weather charts by a saddle shaped formation of the isobars between high and low pressure areas. Winds do not circulate around a col but flow towards and away from it.

The weather associated with col regions can vary significantly. These conditions may consist of high winds or nil wind, good visibility or poor visibility, fine weather or the formation of thunderstorms.

Flight in Anticyclonic Conditions

It will now be appreciated that the characteristics of anticyclones are stable weather, usually producing conditions which are good for flying operations. For example, over inland regions the development of an anticyclone following the passage of a frontal depression will usually result in good visibility, little cloud, and light winds.

There will, nevertheless, be occasions when the effect of subsidence will trap dust and smoke particles in the lower layers of the atmosphere and so lead to poor visibility. High pressure regions are also conducive to the formation of fog, particularly over Europe in winter. Therefore anticyclonic weather may more aptly be described as quiet rather than good.

The movement of anticyclones is generally slow and irregular, and they can remain over the same area for days or weeks at a time. The actual weather which occurs in these regions will be influenced by the type of air mass, the surface over which it has travelled and the season of the year.

Because anticyclones tend to be slow moving, conditions are often influenced by local effects and during the autumn and winter they are areas where radiation fog can quickly form during the evening and night.

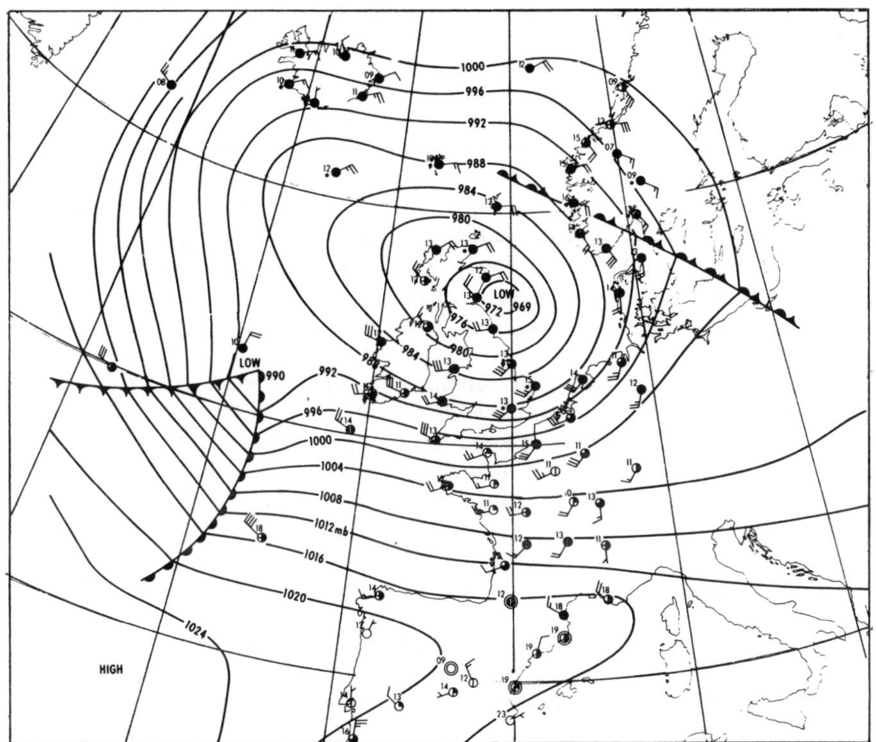

Fig. 4—51

The abridged weather chart shown above gives an illustration of a well defined cold and warm front, an occlusion and the relationship of these to areas of low and high pressure.

FORECASTING AND REPORTING

In order for a pilot to determine whether a flight can safely be made within his own limitations and those of his aircraft, he will need information regarding the existing weather and its trend in the near future.

In relation to aviation, a pilot may need to know what the weather is doing in the vicinity of a particular aerodrome in order to decide if it is suitable for local flying, or he may need to know what the weather situation is further afield, prior to making a decision relating to a navigation flight.

In the first case his own observations of the weather at the particular aerodrome may be all that is required to enable him to make a correct decision, although he should still consult the area forecast, and note for example, whether strong wind warnings or a rapid deterioration of the weather is forecast.

In the second case he will undoubtedly need more information than can be gained by simply studying the sky in the vicinity of the departure aerodrome. An important consideration in cross country flying is that the weather can vary a great deal, depending upon the type of air mass prevalent, the season of the year, and the geographic area over which the flight is to be conducted

Therefore although pilots need to learn many basic principles in relation to weather formation, this knowledge must be used in conjunction with weather reports and weather predictions made by skilled observers and forecasters. **Sensible pilots will avoid the mistake of flying off into unknown weather conditions and instead they will take the trouble to interpret the information which is made available in current weather reports and forecasts prior to embarking on any cross country flight, no matter whether it is to be of long or short duration.**

A point to bear in mind when obtaining weather forecasts is that when an aerodrome weather 'report' is contained in the forecast it will indicate the weather expected only during a one hour period following the time of origin of the report.

An aerodrome weather report obtained from a specific aerodrome will be a report of the weather conditions being experienced at that aerodrome at that time.

In Conclusion...

The pilot in command has the final responsibility for the safety of his aircraft and the occupants. This responsibility is his and his alone, no matter what advice he may have been given, and regardless of any pressures imposed upon him to complete the flight as intended.

Such a responsibility demands a high level of discipline and common sense if a flight is to be safely conducted. Therefore it is certain that occasions will arise when the weather situation is such, that a responsible pilot will delay, or even cancel, a planned flight, regardless of the inconvenience or personal frustration which may be incurred to himself or others.

By the same reasoning there will also be occasions when a pilot in-flight will, in exercising these responsibilities, divert or turn back to his point of departure, and none of these decisions should ever be considered as abnormal.

SECTION FIVE

PRINCIPLES OF FLIGHT

PRINCIPLES OF FLIGHT

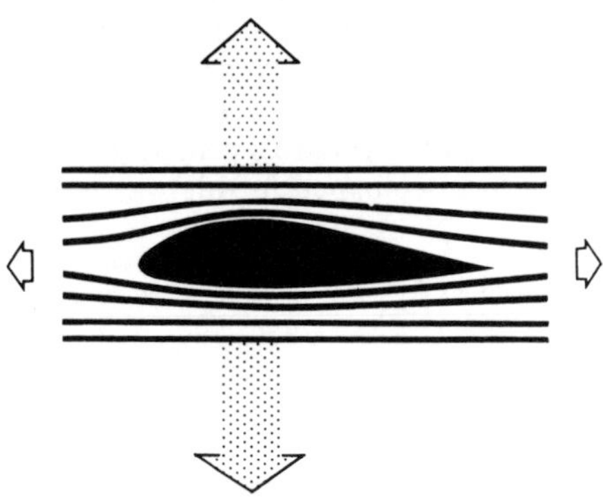

INTRODUCTION

Air is a mixture of gases, and can be defined as a fluid, that is to say, a substance which can be made to flow and change its shape when pressure is applied to it.

Aerodynamics is the science which involves a study of the action and interaction of forces which act upon a body in motion through the air, however, the contents of this section are intended to explain some of the basic aspects of aerodynamics as applicable to an aircraft in flight, or put more simply the Principles of Flight.

Although a pilot does not need to obtain a profound knowledge of aerodynamics, it must nevertheless be appreciated that his ability to control an aircraft and arrive at correct decisions during the many and changing flight conditions to which he will be exposed will benefit considerably from a basic understanding of certain aerodynamic principles. Hence this subject has been included in the microlight training syllabus.

PHYSICS AND MECHANICS

In order to comprehend more easily some of the terms which are used in this manual, the first few pages have been devoted to a brief review of those areas of physics and mechanics which are related to the principles of flight.

Bernoulli's Principle

The science of aerodynamics involves the natural pressures exerted by the atmosphere and the pressures which originate through technology. An aeroplane is able to fly as a result of producing lift. This lift is achieved by creating a differential pressure around an aircraft wing (or aerofoil).

This is produced by giving a wing a certain shape and moving it through the air. As a result of this, the pressure above the wing is slightly reduced and the pressure below the wing is slightly increased. The reason why this occurs is found in the principle expounded by Daniel Bernoulli and can be explained by considering the case of fluid moving through a tube:

> Providing the mass flow of fluid remains constant, any restriction in the diameter of the tube will cause the fluid to increase its speed and its

pressure will drop. If the mass flow through the tube is increased the pressure drop at the restriction will increase.

A commonplace effect which demonstrates this principle occurs when a door is left slighty ajar. When the volume of air passing through the gap moves fast enough, the door will close on its own accord. This is because the air flowing through the narrow gap suffers a sharp drop in pressure. Fig 5-1 shows an illustration of Bernoulli's principle when using a tube which is constricted at the centre. A tube shaped in this way is known as a 'Venturi'.

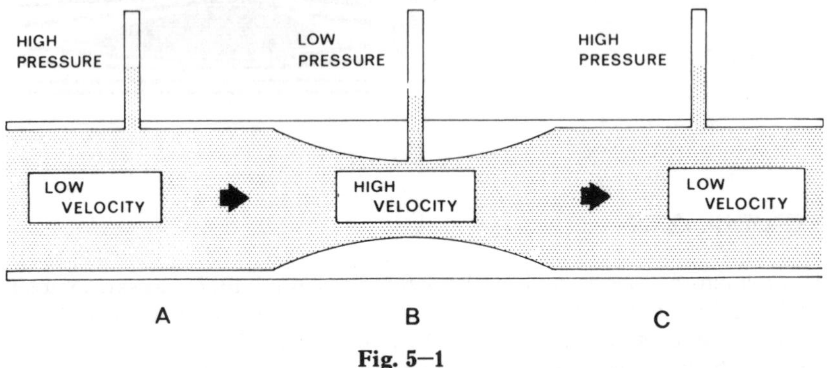

Fig. 5—1

The three small vertical tubes shown in the illustration indicate the change of fluid pressure as it passes through the venturi. In the portion of the venturi at A and C the fluid velocity is low and is at, say, normal pressure. However, to maintain the same rate of flow at each end of the tube, the flow through the narrow section at B has to speed up and in so doing, it creates a lower pressure.

The shape of an aircraft wing is designed to create this type of pressure change and it can be seen from fig. 5-2 that it is similar in shape to one half of a venturi tube, i.e. air passing over the type of a wing is forced to speed up, thereby creating a low pressure area and in consequence "Lift".

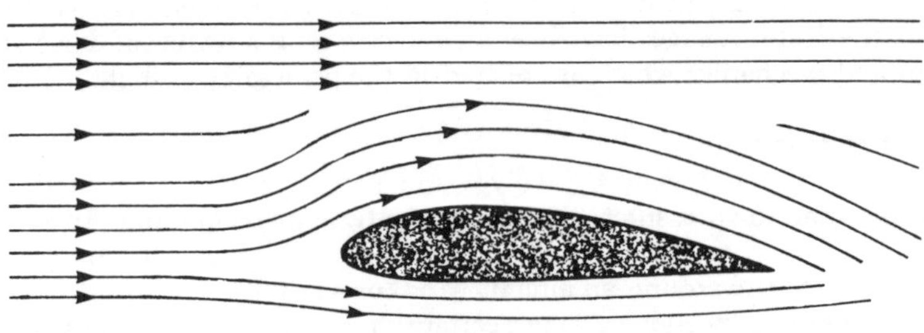

Fig. 5—2

When a wing is directed through the airflow at an angle as shown in fig. 5-3, both the pressure below the wing and the speed of the air passing over the wing are increased, thus creating a greater pressure differential between the top and bottom surfaces, and generating increased lift.

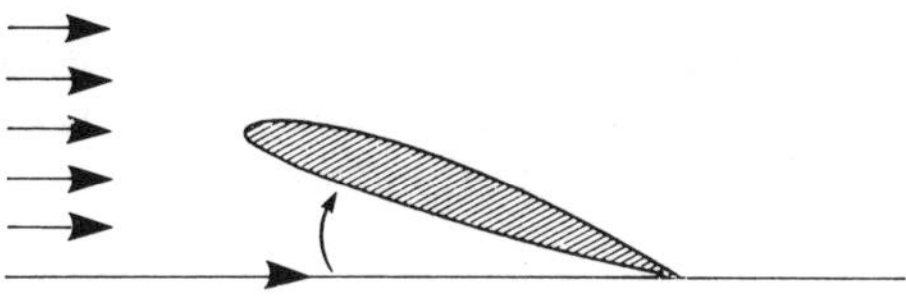

Fig. 5—3

Figure 5-4 relates the increased wing angle to the previously explained venturi effect. Increasing the angle at which the wing is passed through the air (angle of attack) is in a sense the equivalent of increasing the size of the restriction in a tube and therefore creates a greater drop in air pressure.

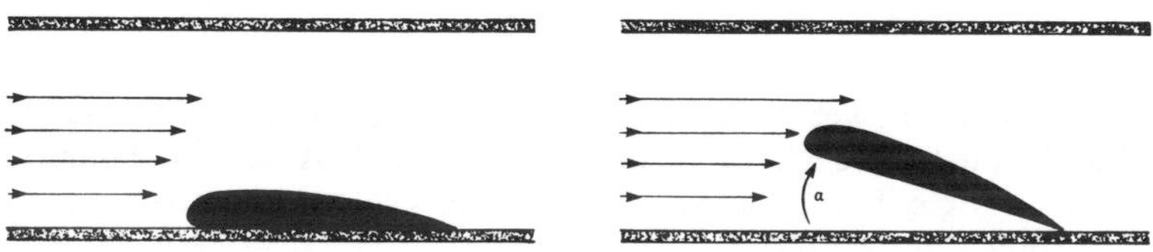

Fig. 5—4

Although the pressure differential created about an aircraft wing by this method is relatively small, the total effect is considerable when integrated over the complete area of the wing surface.

For example, a typical weight and wing area of a conventional light aircraft could be 2500lb. and 175 square feet. This means that each square foot of wing must support 14.28lbs. Dividing 14.28 by the number of square inches in a square foot (144) reveals that a pressure difference of only .099lb per square inch is necessary to support the weight of the aircraft.

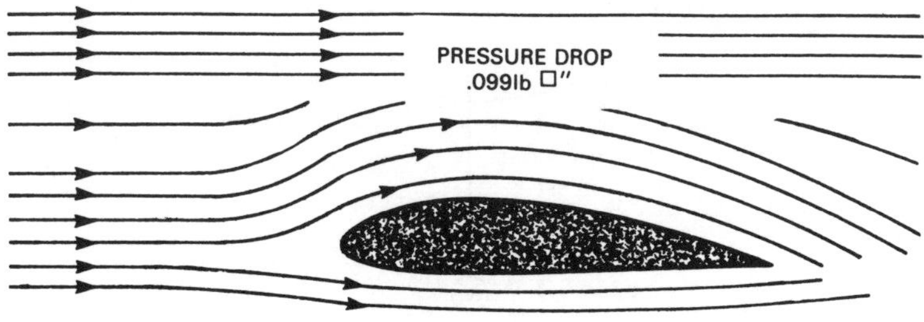

Fig. 5—5

Action and Reaction

Newton's third law of motion is commonly called the law of action and reaction. It states: for every action, there is an equal and opposite reaction. For example, if the propeller of an aircraft pushes a mass of air backward with a force of 625lbs, the air pushes the blades forward with a force of 625lbs.

Another term used when discussing principles of flight is Total Reaction and this can be explained by taking an example from everyday life and considering the forces involved in pushing a lawn mower. Initially, the only force exerted is the weight of the mower which acts vertically downwards.

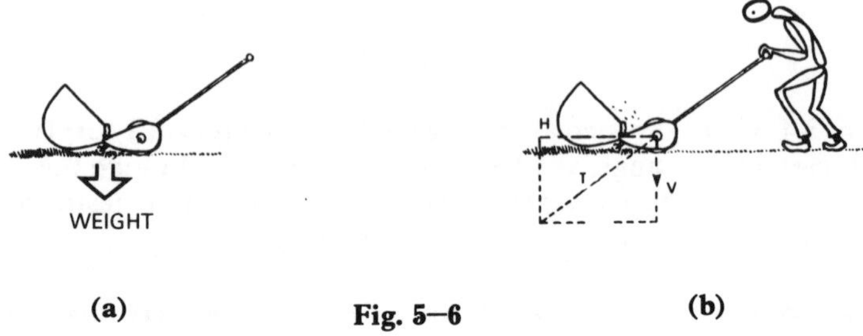

(a) **Fig. 5–6** **(b)**

When the lawn mower is pushed, the action is to set up a horizontal forward force, but the push force will be forwards and downwards due to the handle being inclined at an angle. This inclined force T can be resolved into two components H and V as shown in fig.5-6(b)

A further example of this can be applied to the lifting force required by an aeroplane. This lifting force is obtained by the wings when they are presented at an angle to the airflow. This causes the pressure over the top of the wing to decrease whilst the pressure below the wing is slightly increased. The resultant force or total reaction will be approximately perpendicular to the wing chord line. (Ref. fig 5-7).

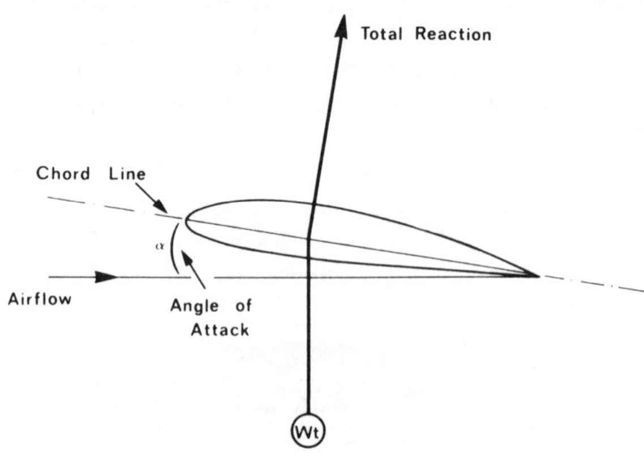

Fig. 5–7

An aerodynamicist however, requires to know how much vertical (lifting) force is required to overcome the weight of the aircraft and support it in the air. This can be calculated by resolving the total reaction into two components as shown in fig.5-8.

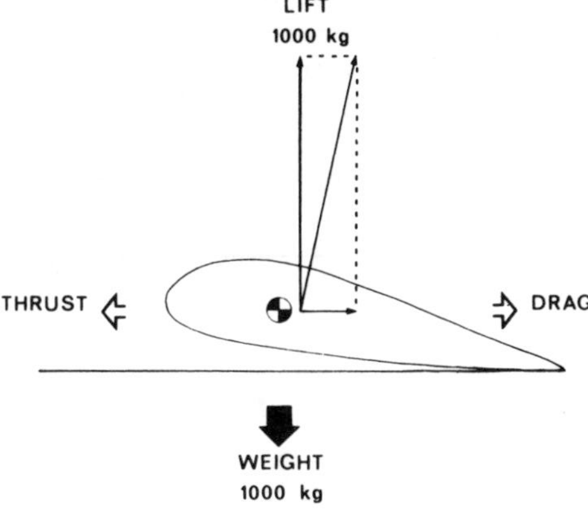

Fig. 5—8

The lift force of 1000kg will balance the weight and provided the thrust force is equal to the drag produced by the aircraft as it moves through the air, the forces of lift and weight, and thrust and drag will be in equilibrium, i.e. the aeroplane will remain at a constant altitude and airspeed.

So far, only the effect of forces which act through the same point have been discussed, but if the forces do not act through the same point they can create a turning effect. This turning action has to be considered in relation to the disposition of the four basic forces of Lift, Weight, Thrust and Drag, all of which act on an aeroplane during flight. These turning forces are also important to the distribution of the weight carried.

The application and use of forces to provide a turning action is a common practice in engineering, for example, the force applied to the pedals of a bicycle. The turning effect of any force will depend upon the amount of force used and the distance from the turning point at which the force is applied. This is called a simple lever.

Fig.5-9 shows this simple principle through the action of balancing a beam on a fulcrum and placing weights upon it.

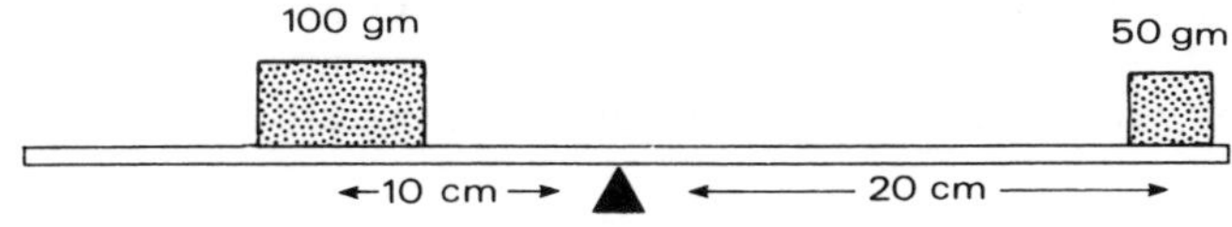

Fig. 5—9

A heavy weight positioned nearer the fulcrum on one side of the lever could be balanced by a smaller weight positioned further from the fulcrum on the other side of the lever. This is an illustration of the effective moment of a force

i.e. 100gm x 10cm = 1000 units or 50gm x 20cm = 1000 units.

Therefore, 1000 units is the effective turning force which exists either side of the fulcrum and this is known as a moment of force. To define this expression more clearly, the moment of force about a point is equal to the product of the magnitude of the force, and the perpendicular distance between the point and the line of action of the force.

The relationships of such moments of force are very important when arranging for the stability and balance of an aircraft, because it would be rare to achieve an ideal situation where the centre of lift (known as the Centre of Pressure) is exactly aligned with the aircraft's Centre of Gravity.

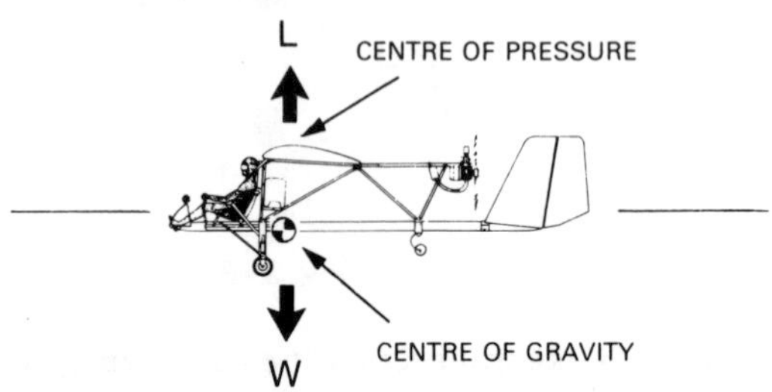

Fig. 5—10

Although, theoretically it would be possible to design an aircraft in which the weight and lift forces are arranged as shown in fig.5-10, it would be impractical to maintain this relationship during flight. For example, as fuel is used up, the weight will decrease and the position of the centre of gravity will usually change. Therefore to reduce the lift and so prevent the aircraft from climbing, the pilot will have to adjust the attitude of the aircraft in order to reduce the angle at which the wings meet the relative airflow. This angle is known as the Angle of Attack.

This change in the angle of attack of the wings will also move the position of the centre of pressure. From this, it can be appreciated that any change in the centre of pressure or centre of gravity will result in the two forces of weight and lift no longer acting through the same point.

Therefore, a turning force (or couple effect) will be created between the two forces as shown in fig.5-11.

The magnitude of this couple when W = L will be Wa when a is the perpendicular distance between the centres of gravity and pressure and W is the weight of the aircraft.

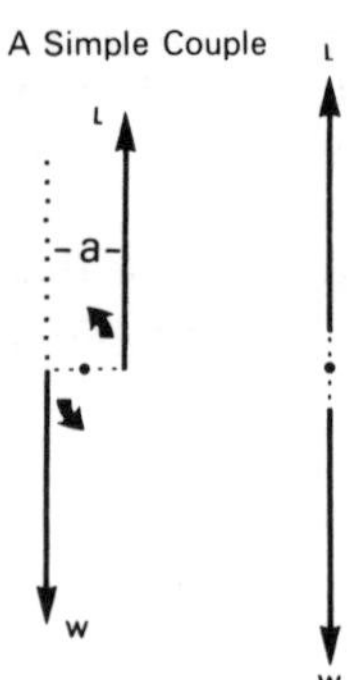

The opposing forces will tend to pull themselves into alignment.

Fig. 5—11

In a conventional aircraft this turning force is controlled by placing a tailplane at the rear of the fuselage. With minimum aircraft, such as microlights different methods are often used. The principles involved in the aspects of tailplane operation are covered later under the heading of **"Stability"**.

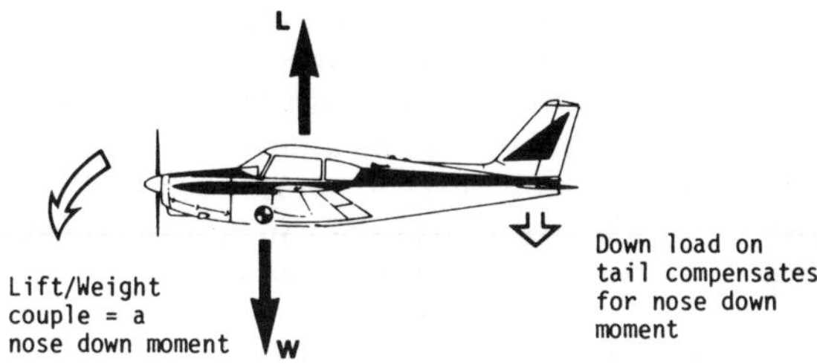

Fig. 5—12

AEROFOILS, LIFT AND DRAG

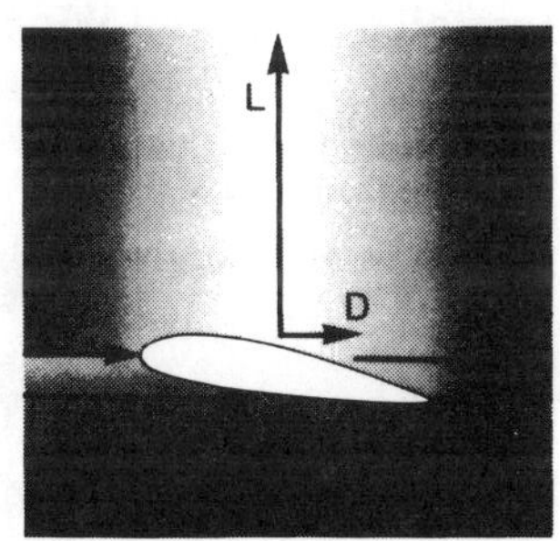

An aerofoil is any shape or surface which is constructed so that its movement through the air achieves a reaction which provides a lifting force. This movement through the air will also produce a resisting force called Drag.

Air Resistance and Air Density
Whenever an aerofoil is moved through the air, a total reaction will be produced which may be resolved into two force components, these are known as lift and drag. The greater the surface area of the aerofoil which is presented to the air at a given angle of attack and the faster it moves relative to the air, the greater these two forces will become.

It is therefore apparent that the density of the air will also play a vital part in aerodynamics, for without some density, the lift and drag forces could not exist. Therefore, if all other factors were to be held constant, the value of the air density would itself control the amount of lift and drag produced from an aerofoil.

Air density is simply the mass of air per cubic foot or metre of volume, and it is a direct measure of the amount of matter in a unit volume of air. In Standard Atmospheric conditions, the density of air at the earth's surface is approximately .0765lb per cubic foot, or, expressed in metric units 1.225kg per cubic metre. The actual value will however be affected by the air temperature and pressure in accordance with the following rules:-

(i) Density varies in direct proportion with the pressure.
(ii) Density varies inversely with the absolute temperature.

i.e. The greater the pressure the higher the density, and the lower the temperature the higher the density.

Aircraft fly at varying altitudes, and since both temperature and pressure decrease with altitude, it might be thought that the air density remains constant regardless of the altitude flown. However, because pressure drops more rapidly than temperature when altitude is increased, the net result will always be a lowering of air density. Changes of density will affect the performance of an aircraft, but if the propulsive thrust value can be maintained, an aircraft will fly faster when the air is less dense.

If the humidity (amount of water vapour in the air) increases, the density will decrease, for example, water vapour weighs approximately 5/8ths as much as dry air. If the temperature and pressure remains constant, the density of air will vary inversely with the humidity, therefore the lift produced from the wings will become less with increase of humidity.

Aerofoil Shapes and Wing Plan Forms

A flat plate placed at an angle to a moving airstream could be used to obtain a reaction similar to lift by creating a higher pressure below the plate, fig.5-13.

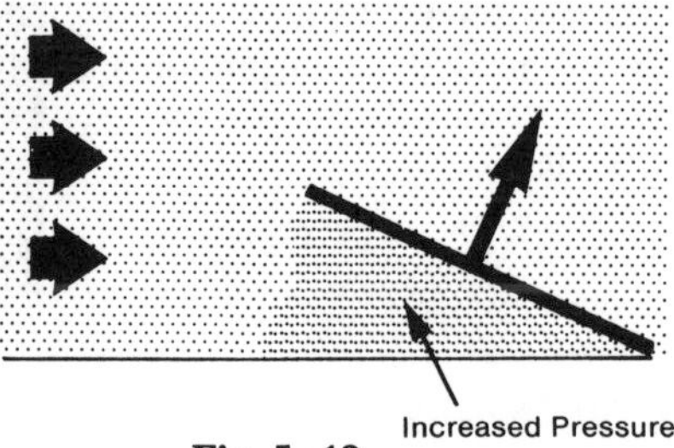

Fig. 5—13

However, the properties of reaction to movement of air can be utilised more efficiently in relation to the energy expended in moving such a plate through the air, if its shape is changed to that shown in fig.5-14.

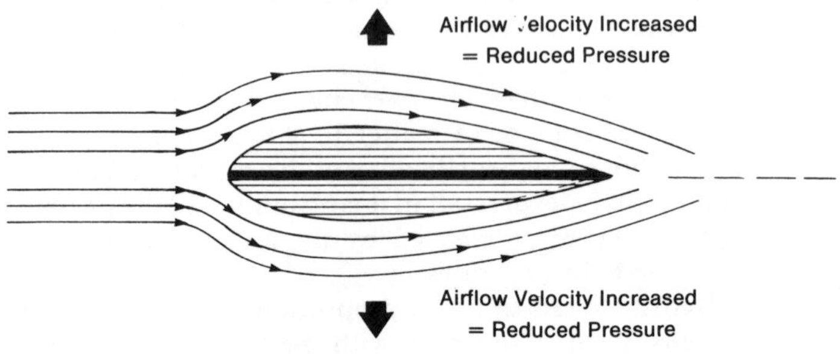

Fig. 5—14

In this example, the contours of the top and bottom surfaces are symmetrical and therefore air flowing below and above the wing would speed up an equal amount (Bernoulli's principle). This would result in an equal pressure change above and below the wing with the result that no net force would be produced. If, however, the aerofoil were to be placed at an angle to the relative airflow as shown in fig.5-15, a pressure differential between the top and bottom surface would exist and an upward force opposing the weight would be produced.

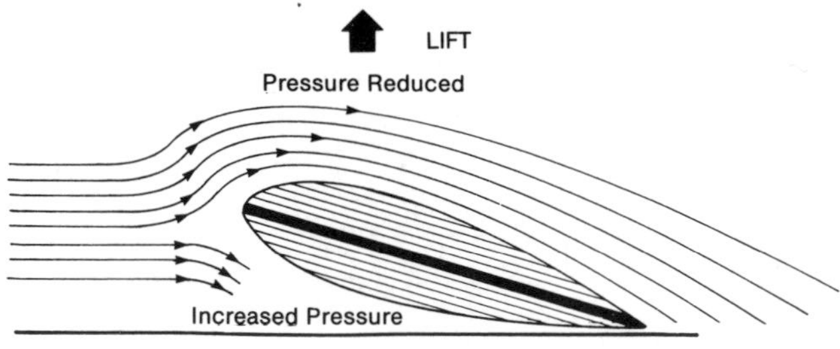

Fig. 5—15

By modifying the aerofoil section to the shape shown in fig.5-16 i.e. by giving it an asymmetric shape in which the top surface has a greater curvature than the bottom, the aerofoil will produce lift even when placed at a zero angle of attack to the airflow.

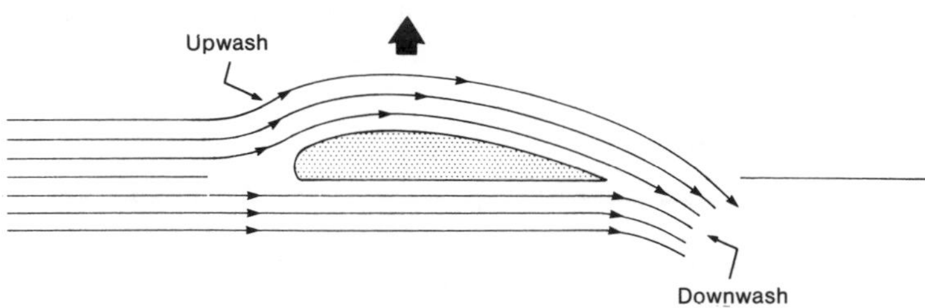

Fig. 5—16

In this illustration, the downwash effect of the air leaving the trailing edge after passing over the curved surface of an aircraft wing is shown. Downwash has a significant effect in relation to lift, drag and the angle at which the airflow meets the aircraft tailplane, however, the importance of this is discussed later under the heading of Induced Drag and Aspect Ratio.

Since the shape of an aerofoil and its inclination to the airflow are important to the distribution of pressure, the terminology used when referring to it should be known and this is illustrated in fig.5-17.

> The chord line is a straight line connecting the leading and trailing edges of the aerofoil and the chord of an aerofoil is the length of this line. The actual curvature of the aerofoil is known as camber and the thickness of the aerofoil at any point of its profile is known as its depth of

section. The greater the thickness ratio, the greater will be the displacement of air passing over it.
At the most efficient angle of attack the Total Reaction or Resultant Force acts approximately at 90° to the chord line. The lift force is measured at 90° to the relative airflow.
The angle of attack is the angle between the chord line and the relative airflow. Angle of attack is given the short notation of α (Alpha).

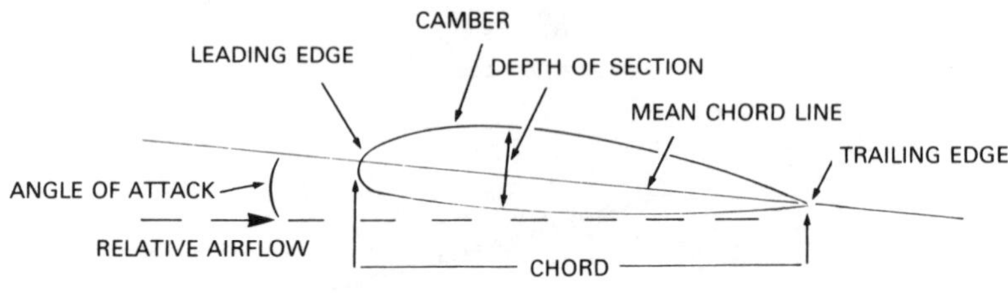

Fig. 5—17

Because aircraft are built for different purposes, the many variables involved by their range of operational requirements has led to a large number of different wing sections. Although it is not the intention in this manual to go into a detailed explanation of the various reasons for the derivation of these wing section, it could be stated as a general example, that thin aerofoils (low thickness ratio) are employed for high speed aircraft, and thick aerofoils are commonly used for those aircraft which operate in the lower speed range.

Fig. 5—18

It will be recalled that in the preceding Physics and Mechanics section that (ignoring design shape) the lift force over an aerofoil is achieved by two basic factors, speed of airflow and angle of attack. It can therefore be seen that high speed aircraft can utilise a relatively thin wing section whereas slow speed aircraft will require a thicker wing section to create the necessary differential pressure about the wing.

Although a non symmetrical cambered wing i.e. one having a greater camber over the top surface, can produce a positive lift force at an angle of attack of 0°, the most efficient angle i.e. the one which gives the greatest lift for the least drag, is somewhere between 2° and 6° depending upon wing plan, wing section etc.

Therefore, in order to minimise fuselage drag at normal cruising speeds, the wing is attached to the fuselage at a fixed positive angle of between 2° and 6° (normally between 2° and 3° for light aircraft) this angle is known as the angle of incidence.

Lift and Drag

Whenever a body is moved through the air, it meets a resistance which varies with its size, and the speed of movement, and the density of the air.

In aerodynamics, this resistance is known as drag, and in relation to an aircraft wing it is also affected by the angle at which the wing meets the airflow. For example, increasing the angle of attack also increases the frontal surface area presented to the airflow, hence its resistance to movement is increased.

This can be illustrated by constructing a parallelogram of forces showing how the total reaction from the aerofoil's movement can be resolved into vertical and horizontal forces. (fig.5-19).

Angle of Attack

Figure 5-19 shows an aerofoil being passed through the air where the resultant force acts at 90° to the chord line. By resolving this total reaction (TR) into perpendicular and parallel components to the airflow, the amount of the lift force (L) can be determined. Resolving the basic force in this manner also indicates the amount of drag, force (D), which is acting against the forward movement of the aerofoil.

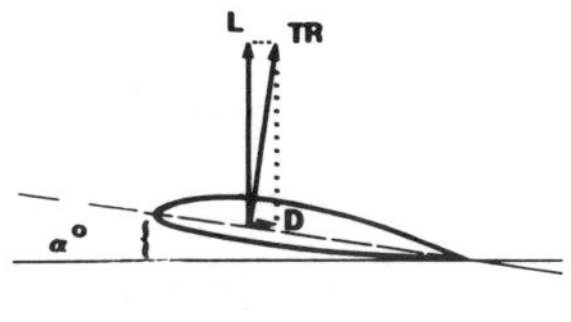

Fig. 5—19

In fig. 5-20 the aerofoil is passing though the air at an angle of attack of 8°. In fig.5-20(b) the aerofoil is at an angle of attack of 20° and the total reaction is therefore greater. Resolving this reaction into the lift and drag components, it can be clearly seen how increasing the angle of attack will also increase the values of lift and drag.

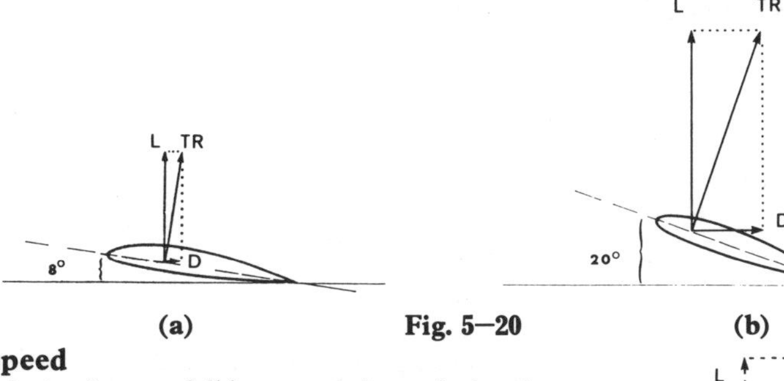

Fig. 5—20

Airspeed

The faster the aerofoil is passed through the air, the greater will be the total reaction obtained, and therefore the greater the lift and drag produced.

The value of lift increases by the square of the speed and fig.5-21 illustrates how the amount of lift is obtained at 50 Knots and 100 Knots varies. It can also be seen from this illustration that the effect of speed also affects the drag.

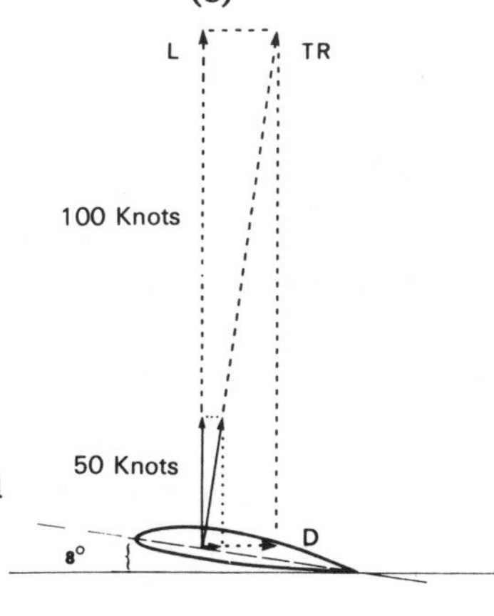

Fig. 5—21

An important point in relation to the angle of attack is that as it is increased a point will be reached on any wing where the smooth flow of air about the wing will become disrupted. When this occurs a sudden and large decrease in lift is experienced, this is known as a 'Stall' and is covered in greater detail in the Flight Training section of the Manual.

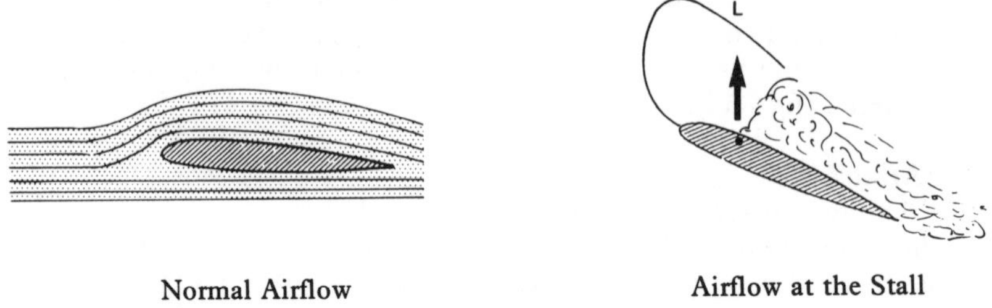

Normal Airflow Airflow at the Stall

Fig. 5—22

Slats, Slots and Spoilers

Another method of increasing the lift over a wing is to use Slats or Fixed Slots. The principle involved in either case is the same, in that their use delays the occurrence of flow breakaway at the higher angles of attack, and therefore reduces the stalling speed.

Slats

Slats are moveable control surfaces fitted to the leading edge of the wing, which are controlled by the air pressure or the pilot. When the slat moves forward, a slot is created between the slat and the wings actual leading edge (fig. 5-23).

Fig. 5—23

This effectively introduces high energy air into the boundary layer over the top of the wing with the result that lift increases and the stalling speed decreases.

Fixed Slots

Another method of achieving the same results is to integrate fixed slots into the wing structure as shown in fig. 5-24.

When fixed slots are used they are normally integrated in the leading edge section of the main wing, but sometimes these are incorporated in stabilators in order to maintain a smooth flow of air around this type of control surface at the higher deflections necessary during low airspeed operation.

Spoilers are used to reduce lift, and in some aircraft, they can often be used more effectively in place of ailerons to cause asymmmetric lift along the wing span.

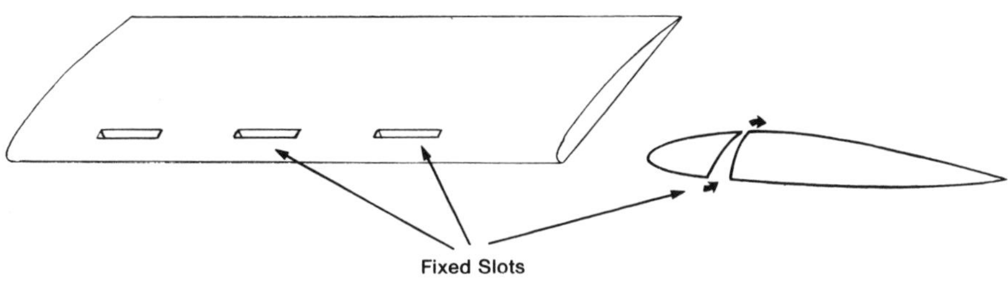

Fig. 5—24

Centre of Pressure

In considering the basic shape of an aerofoil, it must be appreciated that the speed of airflow passing about the wing will vary with the depth of section over which it passes. In other words, the amount of lift created will vary from the leading to the trailing edge. Fig. 5-25 illustrates this point. The aerofoil in fig. 5-25 (a) has a greater depth of section than that in fig. 5-25 (b), therefore, at the same airspeed and angle of attack, the thicker aerofoil will produce more lift.

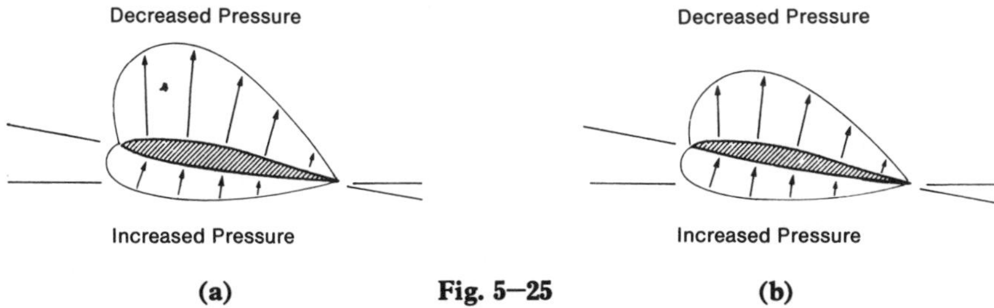

(a) **Fig. 5—25** **(b)**

To simplify discussion in relation to lift, it is normal to show a line vector representing the sum of the lift forces produced over the entire aerofoil chord. The position of this line is called the Centre of Pressure, and is analogous to the term Centre of Gravity.

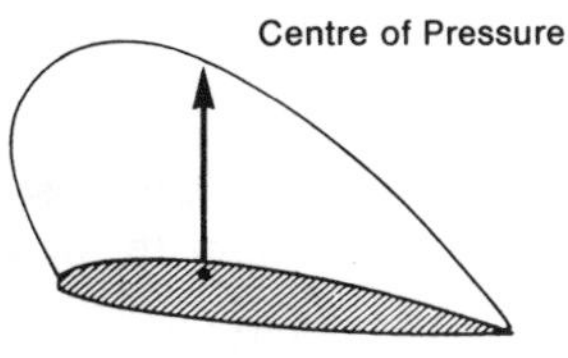

Fig. 5—26

Throughout most of the aircraft's speed range the Centre of Pressure moves forward as the angle of attack is increased and rearwards as the angle of attack is decreased.

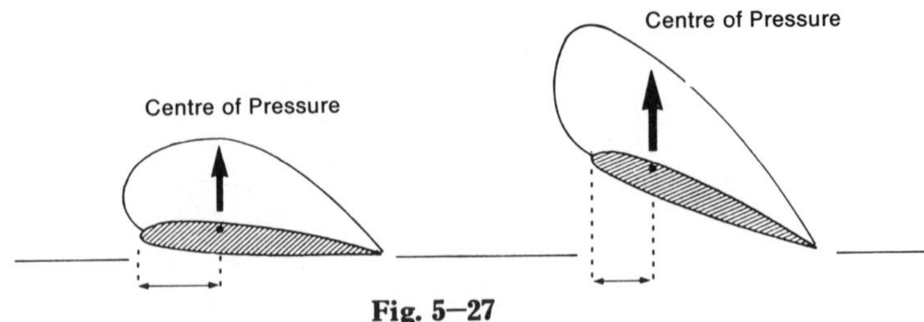

Fig. 5—27

Any movement of the Centre of Pressure creates a turning moment leading to a pitching action which has to be taken into account by the designer when considering the aircraft's longitudinal stability.

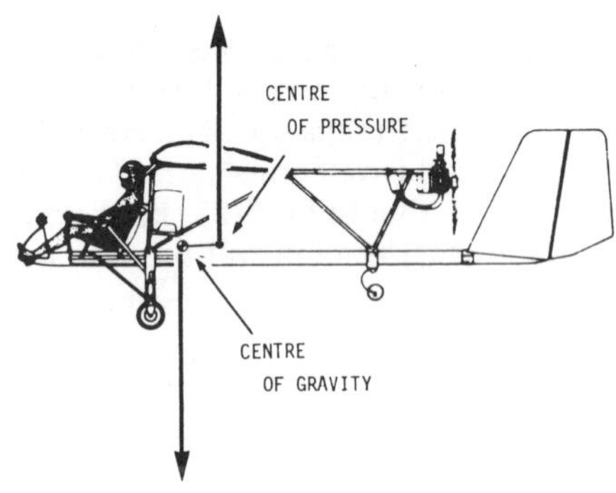

Fig. 5—28

Drag—Parasite and Induced

For the purposes of aircraft performance computations, drag is divided into two classes Parasite and Induced. Parasite drag applies to any type of drag which is not a direct consequence of the production of lift.

The three basic types of parasite drag are:-

Form Drag
Skin Friction Drag
Interference Drag

Form and Skin Friction Drag are often collectively referred to as Profile Drag.

Form Drag

This is produced by a body in motion, and is most clearly seen by visualizing the effect of moving a flat plate at right angles to the airflow as shown in fig. 5-29

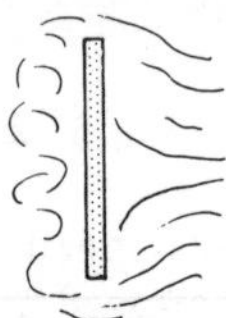

Fig. 5—29

A high pressure is built up in front and a low pressure at the rear. This effect can be seen in everyday life by noting the action of water spray thrown up from a wet road behind a lorry. The reduced pressure area at the rear acts as a retarding force which tends to pull against the motion of a body.

Fig. 5—30

This type of drag can be reduced by giving the plate a rounded shape as shown in fig. 5-31(a) and can be reduced even further by a bullet type configuration illustrated in fig. 5-31(b).

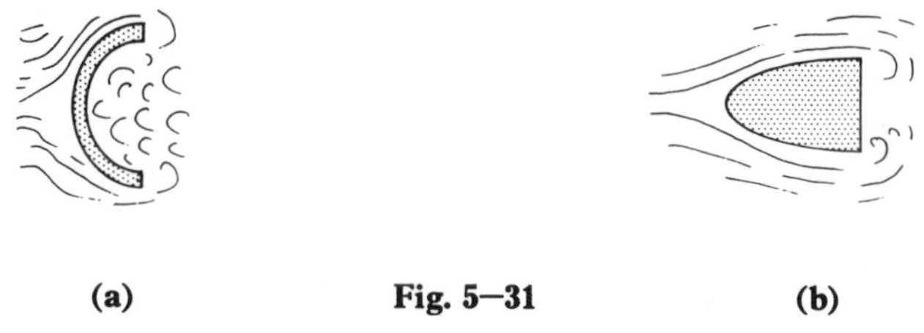

(a) **Fig. 5—31** **(b)**

By adding a tapered section at the rear, a completely streamlined shape can be constructed which will reduce the drag, still further. (fig. 5-32).

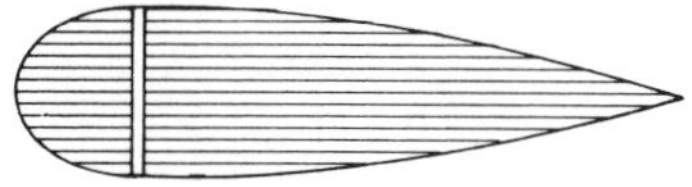

Fig. 5—32

The term streamlined body is used to describe the shape of a body which produces a very low coefficient of drag. Such a body will be capable of movement through the air with a minimum of resistance. Thus, it is clear that form drag is a direct consequence of the form or shape of a body.

Skin Friction Drag

When air is passed over a surface, friction between the surface and the air will always be present. For example, a wing upon which a layer of dust has settled will retain this layer of dust even though it is moved at high speed through the atmosphere. This molecular attaction between the surface of an aerofoil and the molecules of air creates a region over the wing known as a Boundary Layer.

In this layer, the laminae of air are slowed down from the free stream velocity, until, at points of contact with the surface, the relative velocity of the air actually becomes zero. Above these points of contact with the surface, each lamina of air will travel a little faster until it reaches the free stream where the air is outside the frictional influence of the aerofoil surface. Therefore it is important to keep the surface of an aerofoil as smooth as possible to keep the skin friction drag to a minimum.

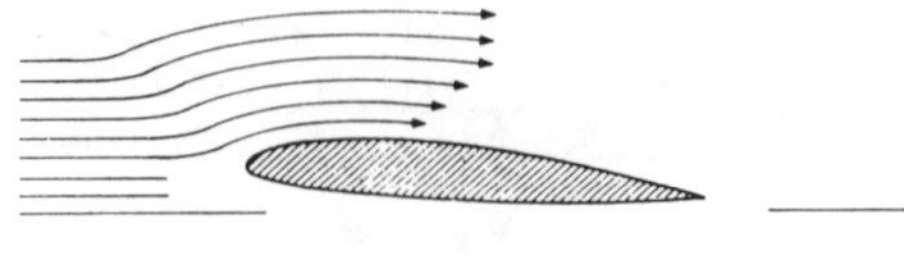

Fig. 5—33

A term often used to express the sum of form and skin friction drag is profile drag, and it will apply to any component or body attached to an aircraft wing or fuselage. Examples of such components would be the landing gear, struts, aerials or similar objects, and whenever possible, these items are given a streamlined shape to reduce the drag effects.

Interference Drag

The total drag of the wings, fuselage and other components cannot be taken as the sum of the drag of the individual components. This is because the airflow in passing over the joining points of the various aircraft components causes a mixing of the air (turbulence) and therefore creates additional drag. (fig. 5-34).

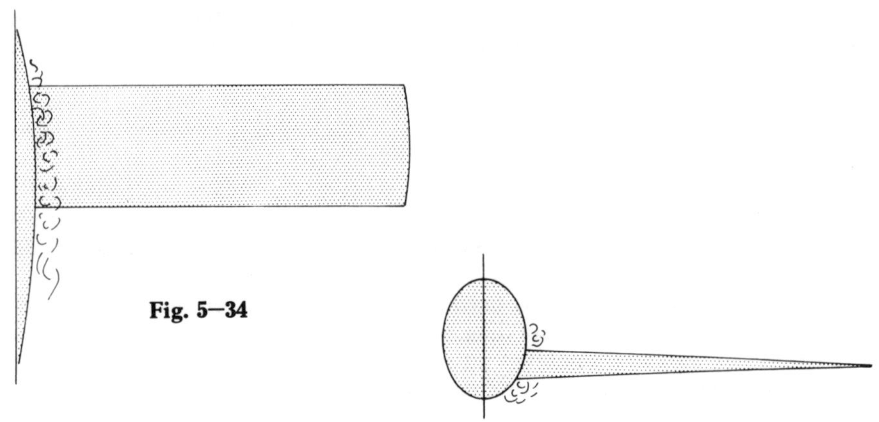

Fig. 5—34

Fig. 5—35

This type of drag which is known as interference drag can be kept to a minimum by the employment of fairings and fillets which are suitably shaped to minimise interference effects.

It is nevertheless of interest to note that by careful contouring of the associated surfaces, such as between a wing tip and fuel tank, a reduction in the total drag of the two components can sometimes be achieved.

The other class of drag is that which results from the production of lift about a wing of finite length. The information which has been covered so far relates to the lift and drag specifically about an aerofoil section in a two dimensional flow, i.e. tantamount to an aerofoil of infinite span in which the airflow effects about the ends are not considered.

However, when an aerofoil is used to provide a wing for a specific aircraft, a significant difference will occur in that it will have a limited (or finite span), and so a third dimensional aerofoil characteristic around the wing must therefore be taken into account. This is induced drag. (Sometimes referred to as Vortex drag).

Induced Drag

During flight, a reduction of pressure above the wing and an increase of pressure below the wing is produced, and the pressure differential will attempt to equalise at the tips. In consequence, there will be spanwise movement of the high pressure air below the wing, which spills out and over the tip, thus producing three dimensional flow.

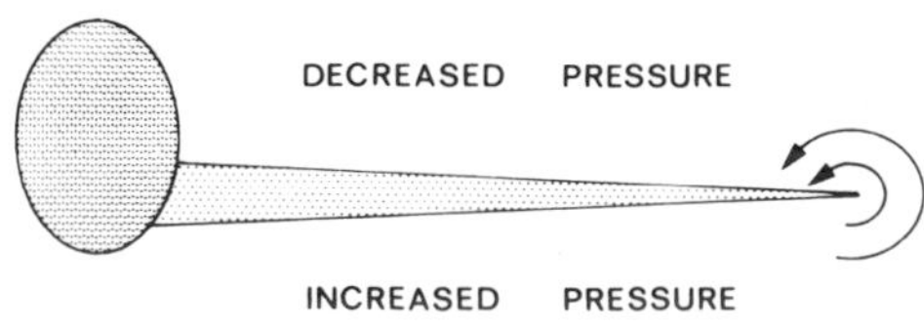

Fig. 5—36

The net result being to deflect air downwards at the wing tip and changing the average direction of the relative airflow along the span. Thus the strong downwash effect at the wing tip modifies and reduces the actual angle at which the airstream passes the wing.

One way of illustrating vortex drag is presented in fig. 5-37. This shows that the effect of air spilling over the wing tip area results in a lateral cross flow along the wing.

The air moving along the bottom of the wing tends to flow as indicated by the dotted lines in fig. 5-37 and the air moving along the top of the wing will tend to follow the path shown by the unbroken lines. This action causes a series of vortices to form at the trailing edge.

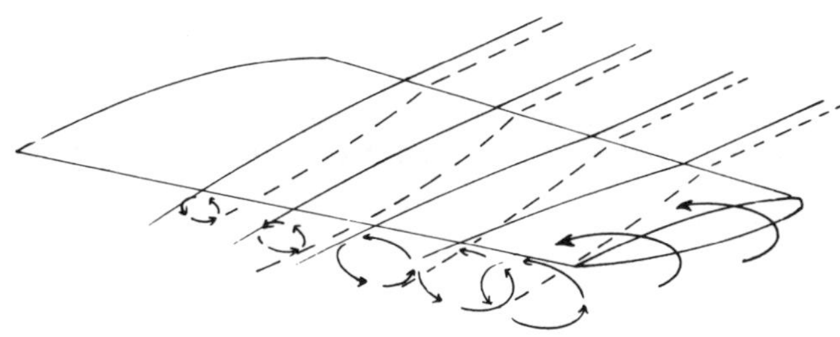

Fig. 5—37

The strength of the vortices produced along a wing from the tip to the root will be governed by the wing section and chord, the span, and the angle of attack. Increasing the angle of attack will increase the size of the vortices and therefore the induced drag.

It can be seen from fig. 5-38 that the greater the downwash angle, the greater is the induced drag and as the downwash angle is increased with increasing angle of attack, the induced drag will be greatest at high angles and least at low angles of attack.

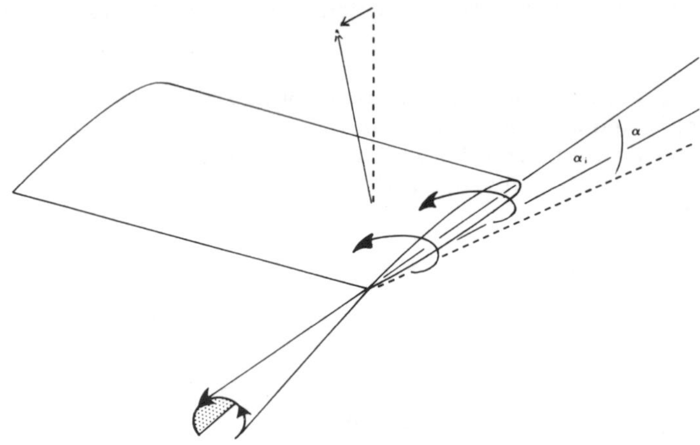

Fig. 5–38

Bearing in mind that lift is produced by a combination of aircraft speed and angle of attack, it can be appreciated that a particular value of lift can be obtained either at a high angle of attack and low speed (high induced drag), or at a high speed and low angle of attack, (low induced drag). So, whereas parasite drag increases with the square of the speed, induced drag varies inversely with the square of the speed.

Increasing the length of the wing span in relation to the wing chord (aspect ratio) will reduce the induced drag, and if it were possible to have an infinite aspect ratio the induced drag would of course be zero.

When an aircraft takes off or lands it will for a short period be flying very close to the ground. The proximity of the ground to the wings causes a change to the flow pattern about the wings. This change is brought about by the influences of the ground on the angle of downwash and the nearer the wing is to the ground, the greater will be the ground effect.

Referring to fig. 5-40, it can be seen that close to the ground the downwash angle is modified, thereby reducing the induced angle of attack and in consequence, the induced drag.

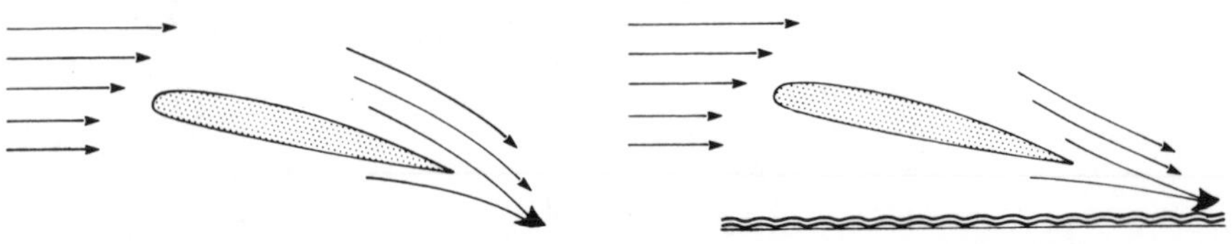

Fig. 5–39 **Fig. 5–40**

Bearing in mind that during the lift off or landing phase of a flight, the induced drag may account for over 80% of the total drag, any significant decrease in induced drag at this stage could have an appreciable effect upon the aircraft's acceleration immediately following lift off, and its deceleration during the float period prior to landing.

Lift/Drag Ratio

The lift drag ratio is the ratio of the amount of lift to drag produced from an aerofoil and is a direct measure of aerodynamic efficiency. When the data for lift and drag for a specific aerofoil section is produced, the ratio of the lift to drag coefficient can be determined for each specific angle of attack.

Fig. 5-41 shows an example of how the lift coefficient of a wing may vary for different angles of attack and fig. 5-42 shows a similar graph in relation to the change in drag coefficient.

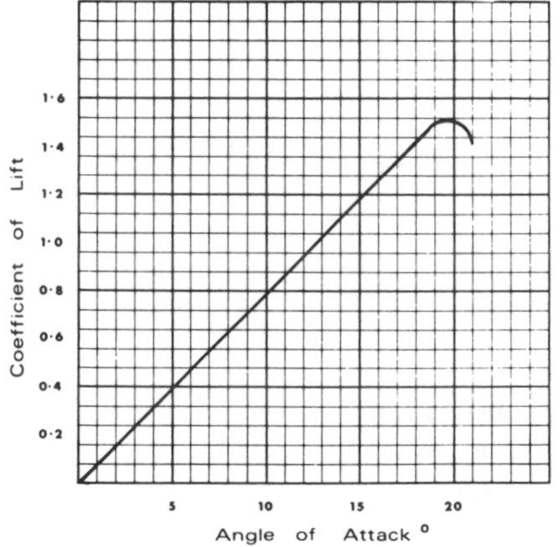

Fig. 5—41

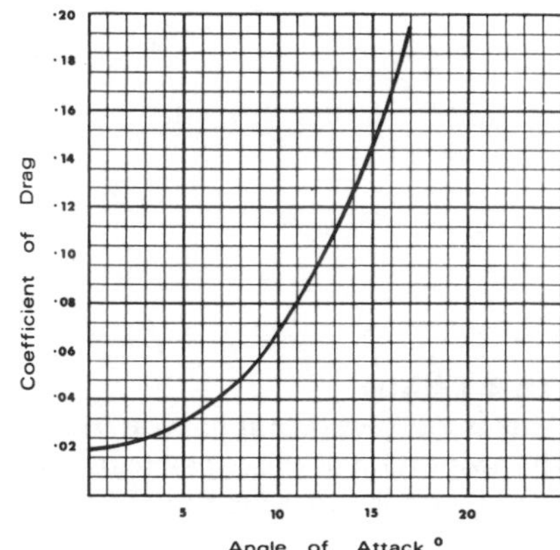

Fig. 5—42

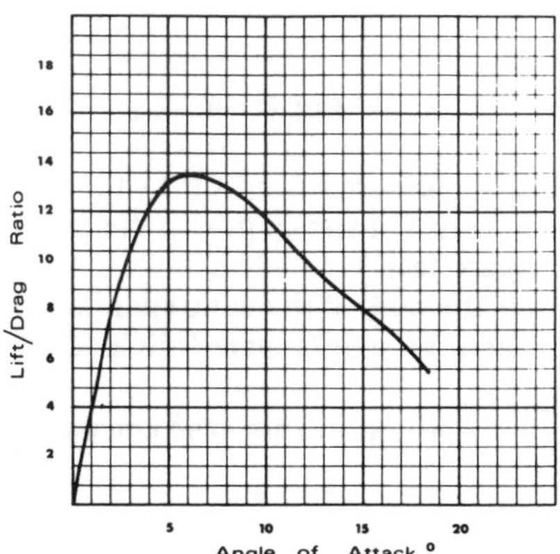

Fig. 5—43

The information gained from the graphs, fig. 5—41 and fig. 5—42, will permit the construction of a graph measuring L/D ratio as shown in fig. 5-43.

In the case of the example aerofoil sections used, the maximum lift/drag ratio is approximately 13.5, and this is achieved at an angle of attack of 6.5°.

Another interesting point about L/D ratio is that by examining the forces acting on the aircraft during a glide, (the drag in this case being of the complete aircraft and not just the wing) it can be seen that the glide ratio or distance flown to height lost, is equal to the ratio of lift to drag. In other words, an aircraft having an overall lift/drag ratio of 10:1 would (in still air) travel 10,000 feet forward for every 1000 feet of altitude lost.

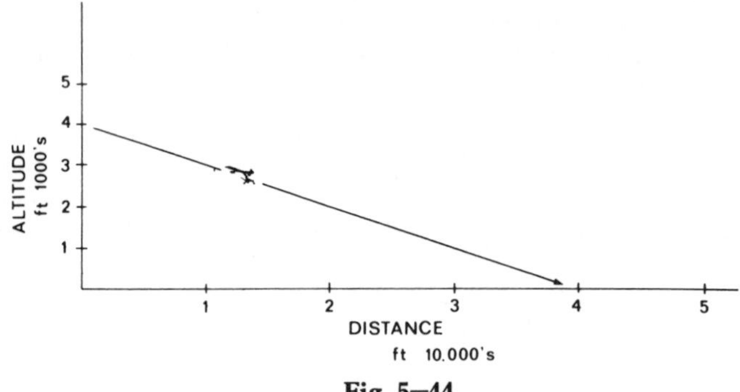

Fig. 5—44

Aspect Ratio

This is another common term used in relation to aircraft wings, it is a measure of the proportion of wing span to mean chord, i.e. aspect ratio is equal to span ÷ mean chord, and is illustrated in the following diagram.

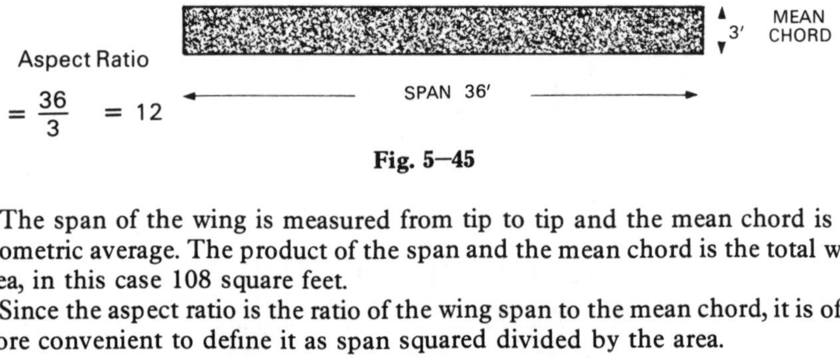

3′ MEAN CHORD

Aspect Ratio

$= \frac{36}{3} = 12$

SPAN 36′

Fig. 5—45

The span of the wing is measured from tip to tip and the mean chord is the geometric average. The product of the span and the mean chord is the total wing area, in this case 108 square feet.

Since the aspect ratio is the ratio of the wing span to the mean chord, it is often more convenient to define it as span squared divided by the area.

i.e. aspect ratio $= \frac{(\text{Span})^2}{\text{Area}}$ which in this case equals

$$\frac{36^2}{36 \times 3} = 12$$

The main importance of aspect ratio is its relationship to induced drag. For example, it can be seen that the two wings in fig. 5-46 have the same lifting area i.e.

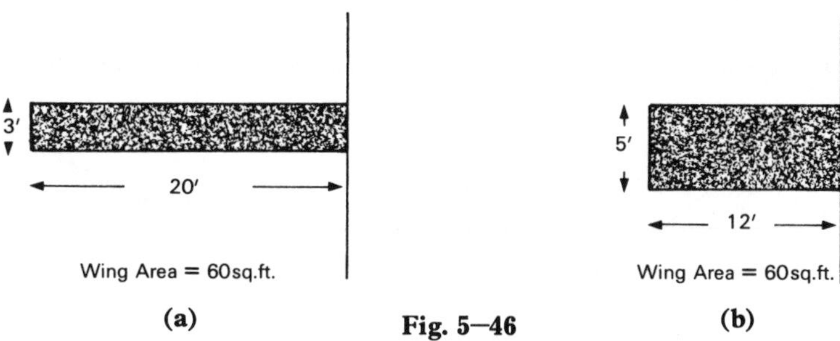

(a) **Fig. 5—46** **(b)**

In fig. 5—46(b) the chord is almost twice that in (a), thus, the effect of the spill over of pressure at the tip will be greater in (b) than in (a) and therefore the induced drag effect will be greater. To sum up, the lower the aspect ratio of the wing, the higher will be the induced drag. Bearing in mind that anything which reduces drag during flight will lead to greater efficiency, a designer will incorporate the highest aspect ratio wing which structural strength and other requirements will permit.

Wing Loading
This is the weight of the aircraft divided by the wing area and is usually defined in lbs per square foot and occasionally in kg/m^2. For example, an aircraft which weighs 330lbs and has a wing area of 165 square feet would have a wing loading of 2 lbs. per square foot.

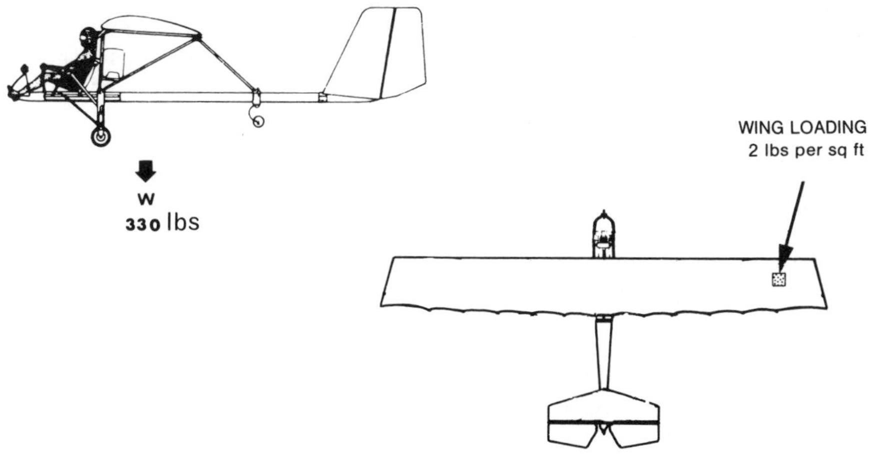

Fig. 5—47

As will be seen later during the flight training exercise "Stalling", wing loading has an important bearing on the stalling speed of an aircraft.

STABILITY AND CONTROL

An aeroplane, has the ability to move about three axes as shown in the following diagram.

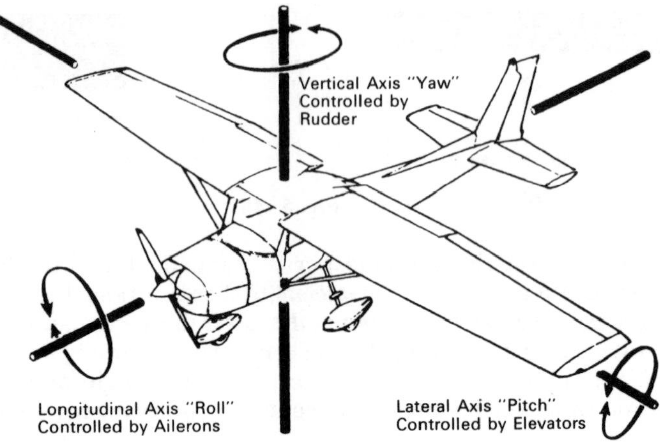

Fig. 5—48

The pilot can control the aircraft about these three axes but the designer has to ensure that the aircraft is designed with a certain stability in relation to movement about these axes.

Local changes in air temperature and pressure, or irregularities in the Earth's surface cause air turbulence. These changing conditions create gusts and air currents which can vary the speed and direction of the airflow relative to the aircraft. Thus the speed of the airflow relative to the aircraft and the angle of attack will tend to vary during flight and so disturb the aircraft about any one or all of its axes.

Although the pilot can overcome the effects of gusts etc. by use of the flying controls, this could become a very tiring business if the aircraft were not designed with some inherent stability to cause it to tend to return to its original condition if displaced during flight.

Before going into the subject in more depth, it can be stated that an aircraft is designed to have a certain degree of the following three qualities:

(1) Stability
(2) Manoeuvrability
(3) Controllability

In relation to an aeroplane, the term stability can be summarised as that characteristic which tends to cause the aircraft to fly (hands off) in a steady attitude along a constant path. A body is defined as stable, if after disturbance, it has a natural tendency to return to its original state of equilibrium. Manoeuverability is the measure of the ability of an aircraft to be directed along a certain flight path, and to withstand the stresses imposed upon it by the manoeuvre. Controllability is the quality of the aircraft's response to the pilot's operation of the controls.

From these statements, it can be seen that the degree of stability of an aircraft has an important bearing upon its operation. For example, an unstable aircraft would be difficult to control, whereas too much stability would make it difficult to manoeuvre.

Aircraft stability in any form applies to the state or quality of equilibrium which the aircraft can achieve during flight, and therefore relates to the aircraft's horizontal, lateral and vertical axes.

It is however necessary to appreciate that there are two basic forms of stability, these are static and dynamic.

Static Stability

When an aircraft is in a state of equilibrium, the sum of all the forces acting upon it is equal to zero. Therefore an aircraft in equilibrium is experiencing no accelerations other than that of gravity and will thus continue its movements through the air in a state of steady flight.

Any gust, or turbulence or deflection of the flying controls will disturb this state of equilibrium and the associated force or acceleration will unbalance the steady state moments and forces.

Three types of static stability apply and are separately defined as, static stability, neutral static stability or static instability. An explanation of these terms can be given as follows.

If an object is disturbed and then returns to a state of equilibrium, a condition of positive stability is said to exist, for example, if a ball bearing is placed in a concave receptable, it will, if disturbed, return to its original position without any external influences. (fig. 5—49).

Fig. 5—49

Fig. 5—50

When an object is disturbed and has neither the tendency to return to its original position or to continue its displacement, it is said to have neutral static stability. An example of this would be a ball placed on a level surface as shown in fig. 5—50. Having once been disturbed, it could come to rest but in a different place to its original position.

If however, an object is disturbed and continues in the direction of the disturbance, it will have a negative static stability. This characteristic can be seen by referring to fig. 5—51. In this diagram, the ball bearing has been placed on the top of a convex surface and it can be seen that any disturbance will therefore cause the ball to continue its movement.

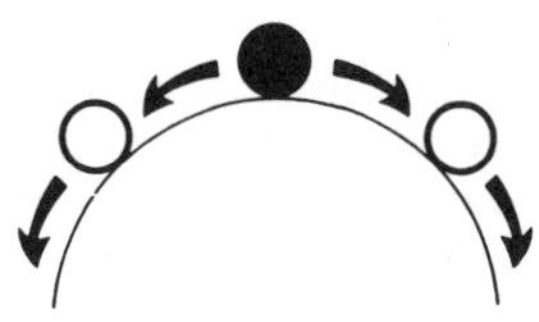

Fig. 5—51

Dynamic Stability

Although an aircraft may be statically stable in that, it has the tendency to return to its original position of equilibrium, it may also have a tendency to overshoot the original position during its return movement and a series of oscillations may occur before the original state of equilibrium is once again achieved. In the terminology of aerodynamics, this type of oscillation is known as phugoid.

Providing the phugoid motion damps out, the aircraft will have a degree of dynamic stability. If the movement persists without any increase or decrease in its rate of movement, a condition of neutral dynamic stability will exist, but if the amount of its original oscillation increases, the aircraft will be dynamically unstable. Fig. 5—52 illustrates the difference between these three types of dynamic stability.

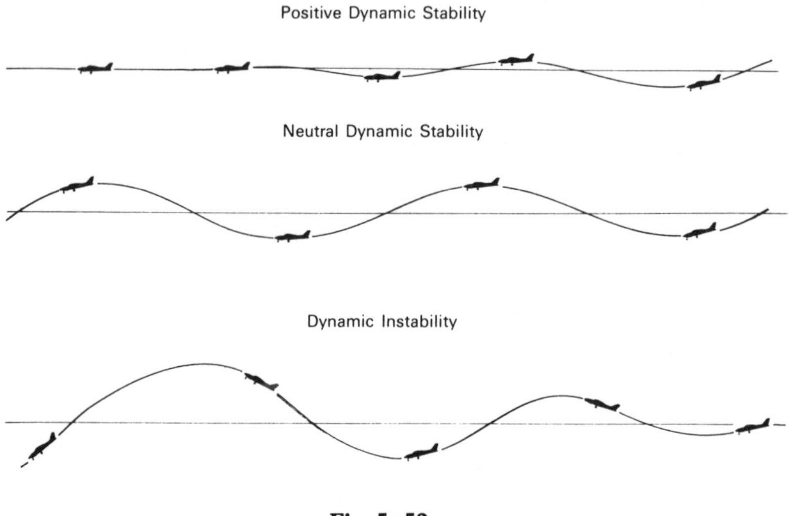

Fig. 5—52

The various methods of achieving stability about the three axes are covered later under the heading of Straight and Level Flight.

Mass Balance

It has already been explained that for an aircraft to remain in steady flight, the forces acting upon it must be in a state of balance. A similar requirement applies to the flying controls, in that without some form of balance, they will tend to oscillate about their pivot points. When the amplitude of these oscillations continues to get larger, this is then known as flutter.

For example, it can be seen from fig. 5-53 that the pivot point of the control surface is well forward of its centre of gravity, therefore a condition of static unbalance exists.

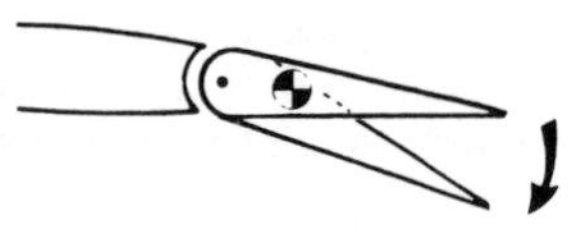

Fig. 5—53

The consequence of this during flight can be seen by taking as an example the effect that this unbalance has with respect to the ailerons. An aircraft wing cannot be made completely rigid and during flight it will flex as a result of changing air loads as shown in fig. 5-54.

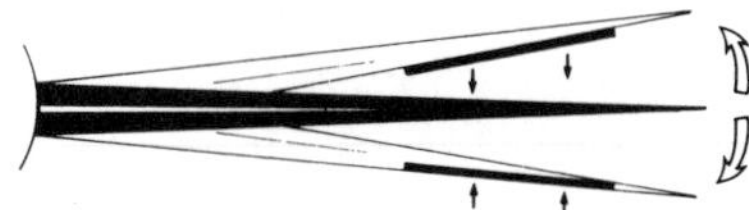

Fig. 5–54

The effect of this upward and downward movement of the outboard wing sections will cause the ailerons to float up and down, i.e. as the wing flexes upwards, the aileron tends to lag behind. This out of balance condition can cause the conrol surface to flutter during flight and create difficulties for the pilot in controlling the aircraft.

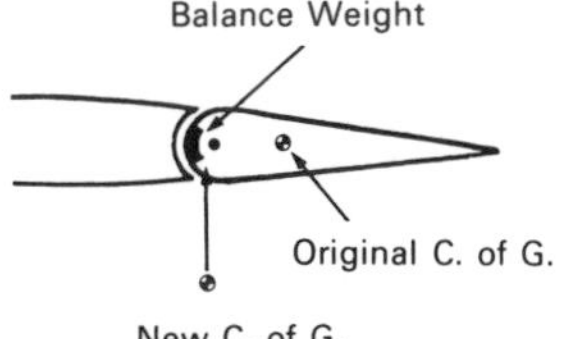

Fig. 5–55

To reduce this effect, it is normal in light aircraft to add weights inside or along the leading edge of the particular control surface to bring its centre of gravity forward of the hinge line and thereby achieve a state of balance to the control itself. (fig. 5-55)

Another method is to mount a weight further ahead of the leading edge as shown in fig. 5-56. The length of the resulting arm so produced, means that the balance weight can be smaller and lighter, yet produce the same effect. Either method will assist in reducing the moments of intertia, lessen the stresses on the aircraft structure, and make control easier for the pilot.

Fig. 5–56

Aerodynamic Balance

In order to reduce the force required from the pilot in moving the flying controls, they are normally also balanced aerodynamically. This is achieved by arranging for a portion of the control surface ahead of the hinge line to protrude into the path of the airflow.

A common example of this is given in fig. 5-57. From the plan view, it can be seen that a portion of the wing is ahead of the hinge line and this area is increased towards the tip so producing a horn shape.

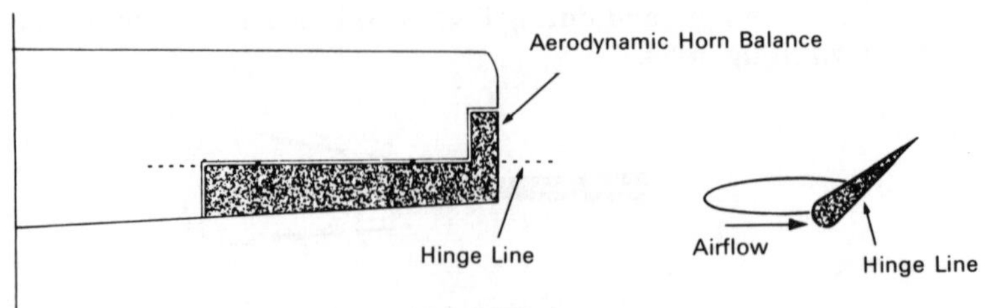

Fig. 5–57

When the control surface is raised or lowered, the forward portion protrudes into the oncoming air and a force will be present, which in the example shown above, can be seen to assist in raising the control surface and so reduce the force required from the pilot.

SECTION SIX

MICROLIGHT ENGINES AND INSTRUMENTS

MICROLIGHT ENGINES AND INSTRUMENTS

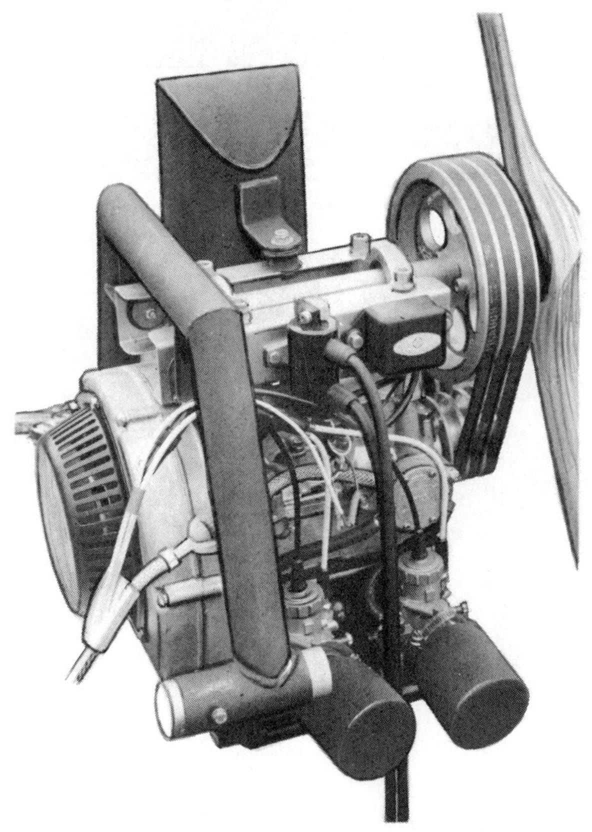

INTRODUCTION

In all types of powered aircraft the engine is perhaps the most critical item of the necessary equipment, without it we cannot hope to stay airborne for very long, and on certain occasions failure of this component can be most dangerous. In many respects the worst results of a power plant failure are cushioned by a very light-weight aircraft, coupled with low forward speed and rate of descent, however since we are much safer with an engine than without one, it behoves us to understand and care for the engine and in this respect you are advised to carefully read and abide by the manufacturers instructions in the particular engine handbook. This section of the manual cannot deal with the many individual power plants which are in use on microlight aeroplanes, and it will therefore concern itself with general considerations which apply to most if not all these engines.

Fig. 6-1 A Typical Single Cylinder Two Stroke Engine

Since weight must be our paramount consideration it is unlikely that the choice of engine will be anything other than a two stroke petroil design, since its simplicity and ruggedness make it most versatile for a variety of applications. There are few if any two stroke engines which have been specifically designed for use in a light airframe, so most engines will have been modified in some way to power a propellor. In this respect the choice must be carefully made if the airscrew is to be fitted to the end of the crankshaft direct, since the stresses on the crankshaft bearings would be beyond the design limitations resulting in early failure or low life in the bearing. Broadly speaking the greater the diameter of the crankshaft the stronger it will be, but it is always best to check with the manufacturers to obtain their recommendations. In any event it is not difficult to rig a simple reduction gear to ease the load on the crankshaft bearings as we shall see later in this section.

The Crankshaft Assembly

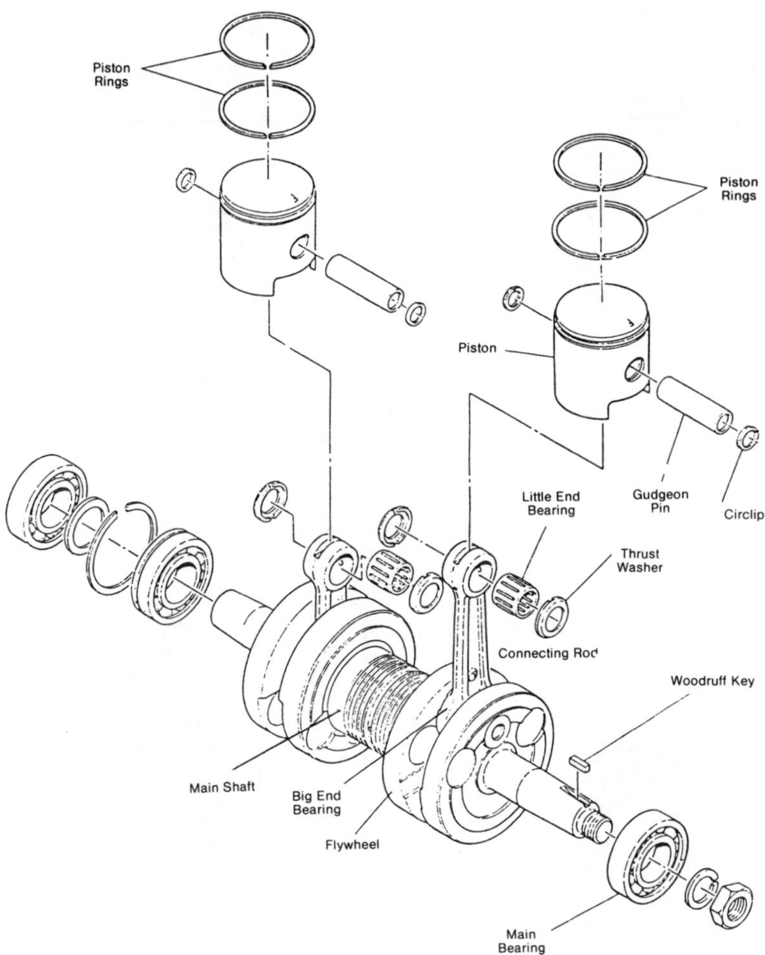

Fig. 6–2

The two stroke engine has none of the mechanical complications of the conventional four stroke engine. It does not require valves, so therefore it does not need a camshaft to operate the valves, nor will it need push rods of belts or chains so the saving in weight is obvious.

The following diagrams show the differences between the four stroke and two stroke cycles.

THE FOUR STROKE WORKING CYCLE

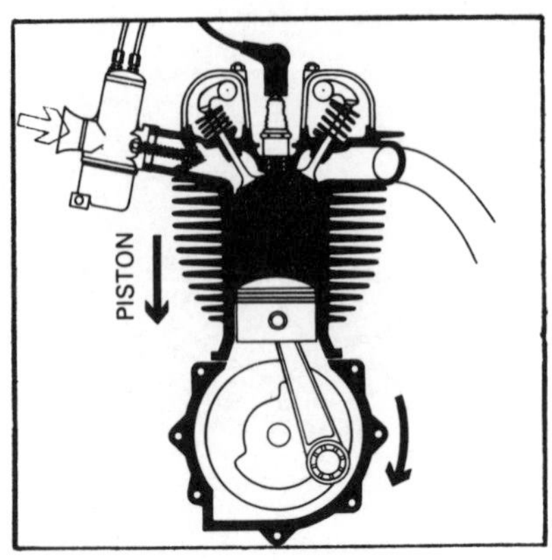

1 INDUCTION
At the beginning of the stroke both valves are shut but as the crankshaft turns the piston moves down the cylinder, the inlet valve opens and the petrol/air mixture is sucked into the cylinder.

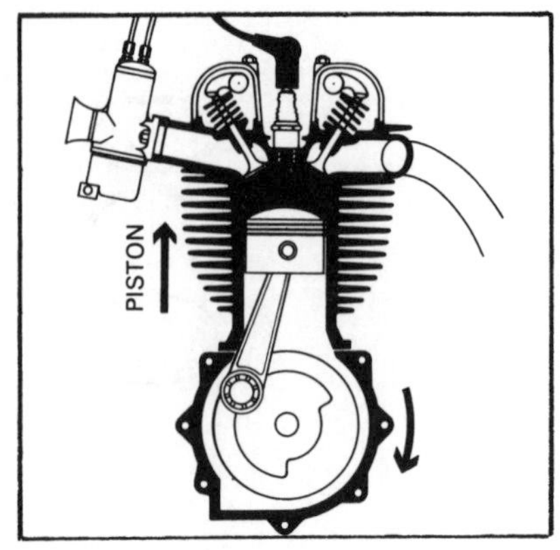

2 COMPRESSION
When the piston reaches BDC (bottom dead centre) the inlet valve shuts, the crankshaft continues to turn and the piston moves up, compressing the mixture. Both valves remain shut during this stroke.

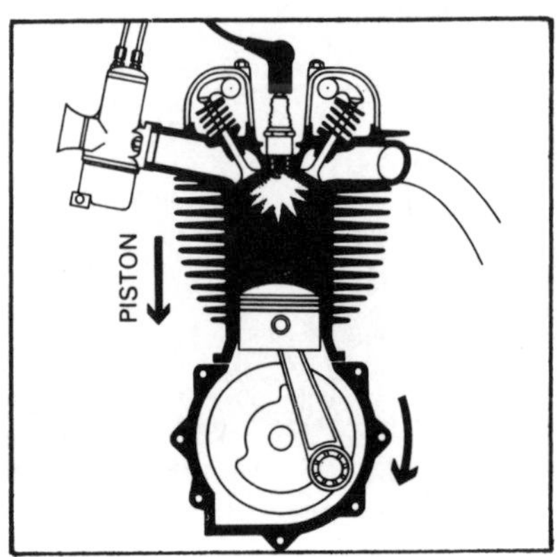

3 POWER
As the piston reaches TDC (top dead centre) the sparking plug fires the compressed mixture, the gas expands rapidly and forces the piston down the cylinder. Again both valves remain shut during this stroke.

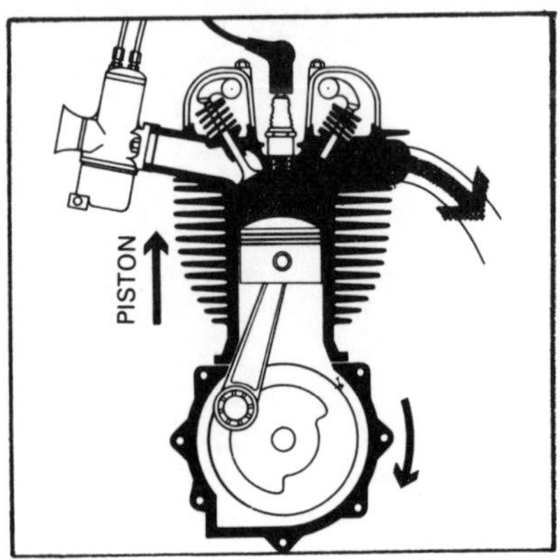

4 EXHAUST
At BDC the exhaust valve opens and as the piston rises the spent gases are forced out. As the piston approaches the top of its stroke, the exhaust valve closes, and at TDC both valves are shut. The crankshaft is still turning so another cycle begins.

Fig. 6—3

THE TWO STROKE WORKING CYCLE

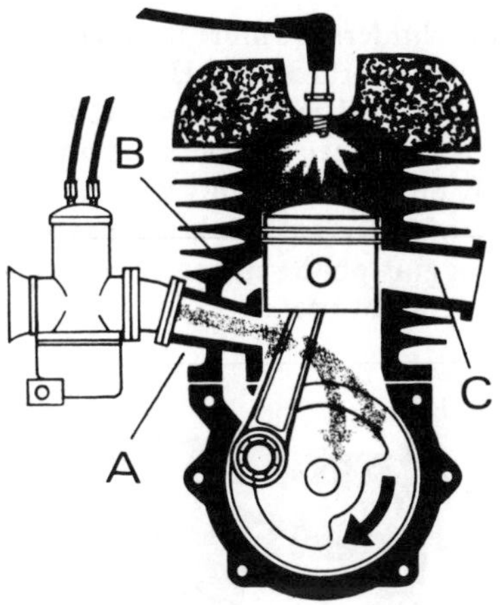

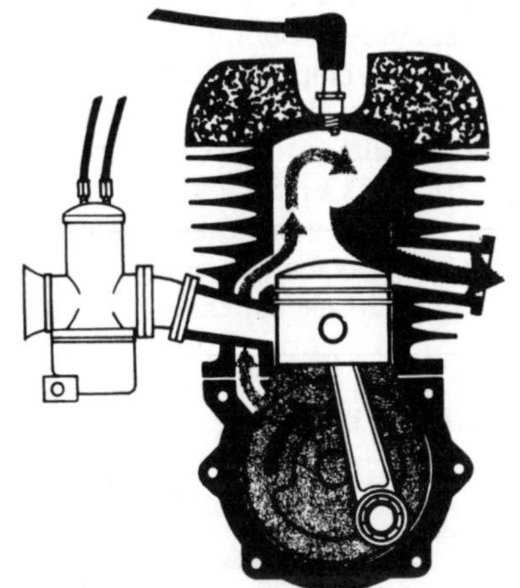

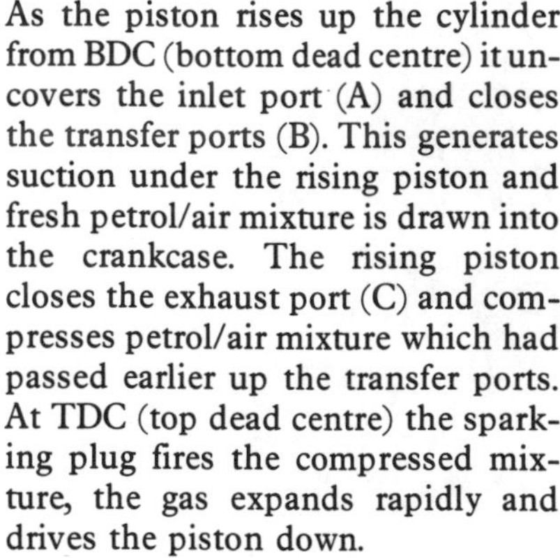

As the piston rises up the cylinder from BDC (bottom dead centre) it uncovers the inlet port (A) and closes the transfer ports (B). This generates suction under the rising piston and fresh petrol/air mixture is drawn into the crankcase. The rising piston closes the exhaust port (C) and compresses petrol/air mixture which had passed earlier up the transfer ports. At TDC (top dead centre) the sparking plug fires the compressed mixture, the gas expands rapidly and drives the piston down.

The descending piston skirt closes the inlet port (A) and compresses the gas in the crankcase. The piston then uncovers the exhaust port (C) and expanding burnt gas rushes down the exhaust pipe. It next uncovers the transfer ports (B) and the mixture trapped in the crankcase is forced up the transfer passages—usually two or more in number—into the space above the piston. The piston finally reaches BDC when the cycle is complete, and starts over again.

Fig. 6–4

So what are the disadvantages of the two stroke engine? there have to be some, or there would't need to be four stroke engines. Well, to start with they are a great deal noisier than four strokes for two major reasons:-

1. They develop the power through very high revolutions.
   (On some advanced engines these may be as high as 12000 rpm)
2. If the silencing is carried too far the power developed by the engine is significantly reduced, so they are noisy.

Then there is a fuel complication since the petroil mixture is as its name implies a mixture of lubricating oil and petrol in the correct proportions which vary with different engines. The correct mixture is critical for best performance and easy starting.

Finally there is the reduced engine life due to high stresses which result from the necessarily high rpm.

Two stroke engines may be single cylinder or twin cylinder, and in rare instances even triple cylinder.

Generally speaking the greater the number of cylinders the more the power that will be developed, and the smoother will be the power delivery. However there must nearly always be a weight penalty with increased numbers of mechanical components, so most engines are a compromise between the possible and the practical. As a microlight pilot you will normally be concerned only with single or twin cylinder two stroke engines up to a capacity of 250 cc's as this is the maximum size which is really practical for single handed rigging on the airframe. This is not to say there are not engines of larger capacity in current use.

EXHAUST

Fig. 6—5 A typical Two Stroke Exaust System

The exhaust on a two stroke engine is more critical than its counterpart on a four stroke engine as the exhaust gases in the two stroke carry a much higher quantity of unburnt oil. This clogs the passages and drillings in the silencer and eventually causes a build up of back pressure which may seriously reduce the power output of the engine. For this reason the exhaust on some two stroke engines can be dismantled for cleaning and it is prudent to do this at regular and frequent intervals.

The exhaust or muffler is specifically designed for each individually designed engine, and any changes in dimensions, or shape, will almost certainly affect the performance. Do nothing without first consulting the manufacturers or you will most certainly invalidate any guarantee and irreparable damage might well occur.

Use of the correct grade of oil (as per manufacturers recommendations), and the correct proportions of petrol and oil will do much to reduce the worst problems inherent in the two stroke engine exhaust system.

THE PROPELLER (Airscrew)

Take a section through a typical propeller and it will bear a remarkable resemblance to a typical aerofoil section, this similarity is no accident for this is exactly how a propeller is designed. The propeller or airscrew generates lift in the direction of flight and so has all the built in advantages and disadvantages of a normal aerofoil, ie it also develops drag which in effect tends to hold back our forward progress.

Fig. 6–6

If the factors affecting the lift generated by an aerofoil are now reviewed it will be apparent how very complicated the design of a propller has to be.

Factors affecting lift

Angle of attack or PITCH
Speed through the air REVOLUTIONS OF PROPELLER
Aerofoil shape PROPELLER DESIGN
Density of the air.

Since the airscrew pivots around a central shaft it is not difficult to see that the speed of each individual aerofoil section must vary from shaft to propeller tip, in some cases the tip speed approaches the speed of sound, with a drop in efficiency and a vast increase in noise. Unless therefore the angle of attack of the aerofoil section is changed along the length of the propeller blade to develop the same amount of lift the stresses on a propeller would be unacceptable. Examination of a typical propeller shows that as a result of the need for a varying angle of attack the propeller blade twists from the boss towards the tip, with the maximum blade angle being developed at very near the boss and the smallest angle at the tip. In this way the structural load is reduced to acceptable limits, although of course the stresses are still very high and can be generally described as follows.

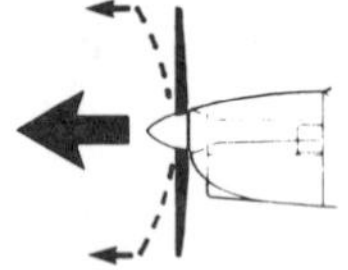

Propeller blades undergo very high centrifugal, twisting and bending forces.

The twisting forces come from the aerodynamic and centrifugal moments:

The aerodynamic twisting moment is a consequence of the centre of pressure of the blade, acting ahead of the centre of twist of the blade section. Thus during its rotation, there is a tendency for the blade to twist about the hub axis, thereby exerting a force which tries to turn the blade to a higher angle.

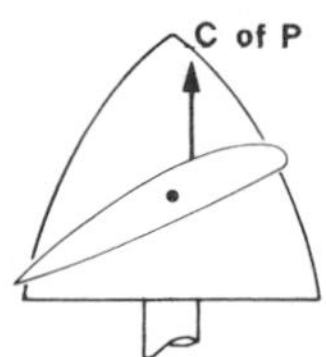

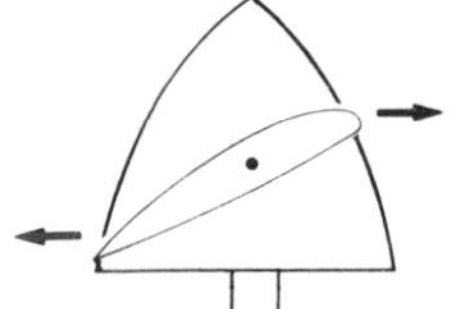

The centrifugal twisting moment is a consequence of the centrifugal force tending to untwist the blades i.e. twisting the blades towards a lower blade angle.

The consequence of these twisting moments and centrifugal force is to induce fairly high stresses within the material of the propeller blade. Because these stresses will multiply if there is any propeller imbalance or surface defects, it is important to inspect the propeller carefully before flight.

Although modern propellers are generally considered to be very durable and relatively maintenance free, in-flight breakage can occur when minor damage in the form of nicks, dents, scratches etc. which have been incurred by the propeller vortex picking up stones and other debris from the ground.

To guard against this type of incident, pilots should examine the condition of the propeller during pre-flight inspections. It is also advisable to lightly run one hand along the whole of the blades, as nicks and cuts can often be more easily felt than seen.

These structural stresses can be reduced by the simple expedient of slowing down the speed of rotation which also gives increased efficiency and less noise, but as the slower turning propeller has to be larger there are of course the usual penalties of greater weight and more drag (torque). In any event the size of the propeller is usually decided by the ground clearance and structural limitations. Slowing down the speed of rotation is achieved by a simple reduction gear provided through a belt drive to pulleys on the crankshaft of the engine, and on the shaft of the propeller, although of course in a conventional aircraft the reduction gearing will be more sophisticated than this.

Fig. 6—7

Like most things to do with aviation the propeller is in the end the best compromise that can be designed, but all the skills of the manufacturer and designer can be ruined if the propeller is incorrectly aligned and/or poorly balanced. There should be less than 1/64 of an inch difference between the path of one tip and the other, and this alignment can be usually corrected by adjusting the propeller mounting bolts, ensuring that the locking wire is replaced after the adjustment has been carried out.

The correct positioning of the engine and propeller has a significant bearing upon aircraft performance and personal safety, and the sections of this manual which are devoted to stability and preparation for flight should therefore be vary carefully read and clearly understood.

Finally propellers may be mounted on engines which sit directly behind the pilot and which push the aircraft through the air, and which are not unnaturally called pushers! Alternatively the propeller may be mounted on a forward facing engine fitted in front of the pilot and which pulls the aircraft behind as it 'screws' its way through the air. This is called a tractor propeller.

Fig. 6—8 A Pusher Propeller

THE IGNITION SYSTEM

The ignition system supplies the very considerable electrical charge which gives the spark which ignites the mixture in the cylinders and so gives us the power to stay in the air. This alone serves to illustrate the importance of this part of the engine, however there is more to it than this. In addition to supplying electrical charge for the spark, it is necessary for this spark to occur in the correct place in the cycle of things. If the spark occurs too soon in the cycle the combustion will occur when the piston is still rising and damage will result. Conversely if it occurs too late then much of the "punch" will be lost and the engine will lack power. It is not inappropriate to mention at this point that according to recent surveys made by the leading motoring organisations troubles in the ignition system were the major cause of breakdowns and failures. Clearly it behoves microlight aviators to pay careful attention to the components which provide the electrical power to the ignition.

There are two main types of ignition system, both do exactly the same thing but in different ways. Most motor vehicles for instance are fitted with the coil ignition, and the coil boosts the current to the high value necessary to cause the spark. If the battery fails then there is no electrical current – no sparks – no power! So there has to be a component to keep the battery charged which as most of us know is either an alternator or a dynamo. This system is therefore a weighty package, and there is no provision for a backup should failure occur, and for this reason this system is not normally in use in aircraft power plants.

The other system utilises rotation of the engine to generate the electrical current necessary to provide the spark, and so long as the engine continues to function, and always barring mechanical failure of the component, the ignition system will funcation efficiently. No coil, no battery, no alternator or dynamo. Clearly the simplicity and saving of weight make this system a must for piston type aircraft engines. In most cases there is a second separate magneto to provide an adequate safety margin for aircraft systems. This system is called the magneto type and in its basic form the impluse necesssary to rotate the engine to provide the power for the spark is achieved by swinging the propeller or by using a recoil starter. Whilst this is fine for the average microlight pilot, it is not adequate for modern light aeroplanes so it is necessary to add a battery to power a starter motor, and an alternator or generator to keep the batter charged, so we are nearly back to the weight and complication of a coil ignition system – save for one very important thing, the magneto is retained.

Whether we have a coil ignition system or a magneto it will require regular inspection and some simple maintenance which we can only neglect at our peril.

Most modern two stroke engines have a flywheel magneto which is rugged reliable and simple. The only maintenance required is to check the ignition timing from time to time, and to adjust the magneto points and keep the points themselves in good condition. See fig. 6–9. Your engine handbook will give you all the necessary information to keep this unit in good working order.

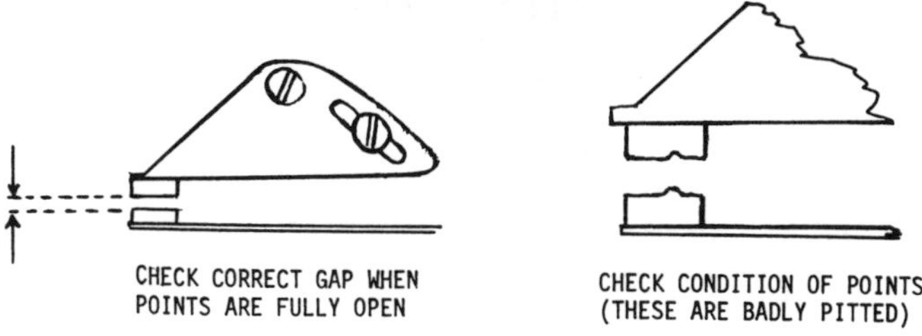

CHECK CORRECT GAP WHEN
POINTS ARE FULLY OPEN
CHECK CONDITION OF POINTS
(THESE ARE BADLY PITTED)

Fig. 6–9

If you are lucky enough to have a modern engine such as the Fuji/Robin, then you will escape the chore of servicing the magneto, because the engine does not use one. Instead it has a unit called a C.D.I. (Capacitor Discharge Igniter) which serves the same function but more reliably and simply.

No matter what ignition system your engine uses, it will have an aversion to oil or grease in the wrong places, so keep the unit clean and free from unnecessary lubricant.

A significant development by Nicklow Engineering of Buckingham, is a form of dual ignition which provides two separate sparking plugs per cylinder. Whilst not technically a dual magneto system with each magneto firing a sparking plug or plugs each unit independent of the other; this two plug system gives a greater margin of safety and a better rate of combustion than that given by a single spark plug system. See fig. 6–10.

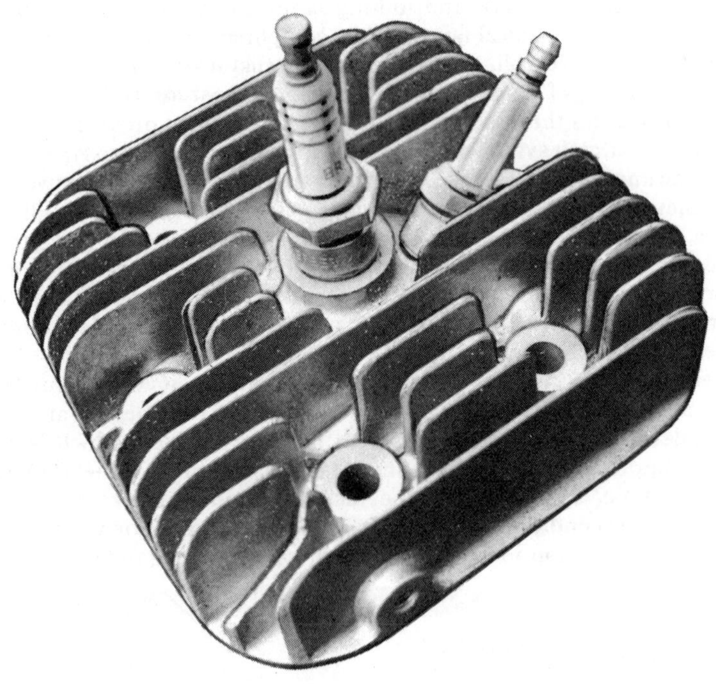

Fig. 6–10

SPARK PLUGS

The sparking plug may seem to be one of the simplest parts of an engine, but it is very much more than a piece of thick wire covered with an insulating ceramic material, attached to a threaded boss. If you remember that a plug may have to give a clean spark up to 50 times a second, you will see why it is important to use the correct type for your engine.

What Happens at the Plug Points

The voltage required to produce a spark varies with the condition of the plugs and the load on the engine but may be as much as 12,000 volts in normal operation, which means that a 6-volt ignition system has to multiply the voltage 2,000 times. Also it means that every volt lost at the contact breaker points will be 2,000 less at the plug, which is why it is important to eliminate any voltage losses in the low-tension circuit.

Contact breaker gap is most important for two reasons; firstly the gap setting has been calculated to produce optimum output from the system, and secondly varying the gap will change the ignition timing. Contact breaker neglect is the most frequent single cause of poor starting.

Plug gap is equally important. It if is too big the ignition system may not be able to produce enough voltage to create a spark, and if it is too small the spark may not be strong enought to ignite the mixture.

Plug Performance

Plugs are designed to work within a specific temperature range. If the electrodes fall below the lower limit (around 450 deg C) they carbon-foul and eventually misfire. At the other end of the scale, if the temperature gets above 850 to 1000 deg C, they can cause pre-ignition, rapid electrode wear and eventually piston damage.

Fouling can be caused by low temperatures and over-rich mixtures, or both. At higher temperatures there is a region in which the plug will tolerate rich mixtures without fouling, but neither will it self-clean. Deposits formed previously will stay put and can mislead anyone trying to "read" the plug.

Above 500 deg C, with correct air-fuel mixtures, the plus will self-clean. If it runs at higher temperatures, 600 deg C, or more, it will tolerate very rich mixtures and still stay clean.

Plug temperature tends to reach a maximum at the correct air-fuel ratio.

How Can You Help

Always use the recommended grade of plug. If problems occur while using this, it almost certainly means that something is incorrectly adjusted or the engine is worn.

When fitting new or serviced plugs the seating area must be clean; this is best achieved by brushing (or blowing with an airline) round the plug when partly removed. With new plugs, screw down fingertight, then a further quarter turn with a spanner will compress the gasket correctly. Serviced plugs, or those with a taper seating, should be screwed down fingertight, and then gently pinched secure, with a plug spanner.

Do not over-tighten plugs. No performance is gained, and if your engine has an alloy head, the threads may be stripped. If this happens, a steel insert can be fitted.

Keep the insulator clean, also the suppressor (if fitted), and the plug cap, inside as well as outside. Check for a good electrical contact between the plug lead and the terminal. If you have an ohmmeter, you can check the value of the suppressor element, which should be no more than 20,000 ohms.

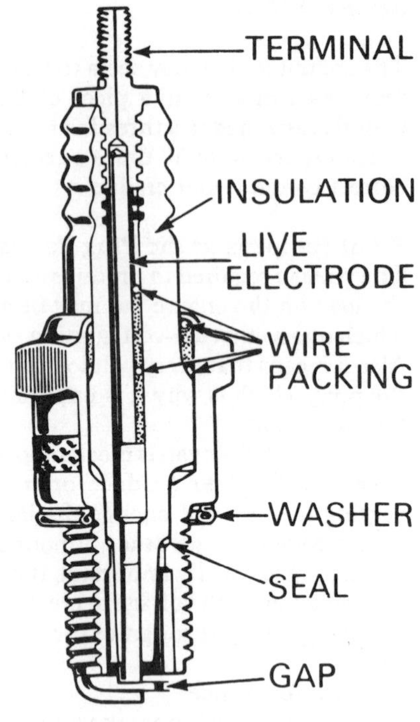

Fig 6–11

Plug servicing

Plug life depends on the type of use, but follow the particular engine manual and in this respect if you have any doubt as to the serviceability of a plug, play safe, throw it away. A new plug is less expensive than an accident.

Plug servicing should only be required once, halfway through the plug's life as given above.

The only satisfactory method of cleaning plugs is to use an abrasive machine; most garages have these and make only a nominal charge for the job. Oil-fouled plugs must be degreased, by using white spirit, before abrasive cleaning.

Restoring clean flat surfaces to the electrodes is most important. Open the gap enough to use a small magneto file to dress the end of the centre electrode and the facing surface of the other. Then reset the gap by bending the side electrode; never distort the centre electrode.

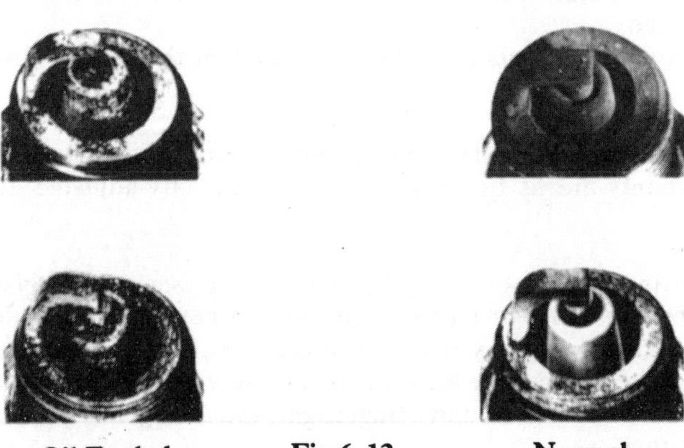

Oil Fouled **Fig 6–12** **Normal**

CARBURETTOR

There is nothing complicated about a two stroke engine carburettor it is a case once again of rugged simplicity. The mixture is delivered into the float chamber by gravity or by pump, and it is metered to the cylinder through an orifice in a casting known as a jet, in this case the main jet. The amount of mixture fed into the cylinder is controlled by a tapered needle which fits into the orifice in the jet. The tapered needle is moved in or out of this orifice by the throttle which may be a lever or twist grip thus increasing the engine revolutions or decreasing them as required. There may be secondary jets in the system to allow for starting or idling but these work independently of the needle and are rarely integral with the main jet. The holes in each jet are numbered as is the taper of the needle, and care must be exercised if the jets are replaced to get the correct size. It is a favourite occupation by enthusiasts to change the jet and needle sizes to find increased performance, but this should not be done without first seeking expert advice. It is perhaps expedient to point out here that there is no provision for negative G in this type of carburettor, if the unit is subject to this the engine will stop, or at best lose power.

There is usually a form of strangler or choke to close off the greater part of the air delivered into the cylinder to give a rich mixture for cold starting, and this is normally manual and progressive and operated by a lever and cable, or a direct push pull arrangement on the carburettor body according to the application for which the engine is required.

When the aircraft is not going to be flown for several days, it is a good practice when shutting down the engine to close the fuel cock (if one is fitted). Thereby cutting off the fuel and allowing the engine to run until it stops from fuel starvation. The reason for this is that if fuel remains in the float chamber for a period, the petrol can evaporate and leave the lubricating oil thus causing blocked jets and sometimes difficulty in starting.

Some high performance engines have two carburettors, and in recent years the motor cycle world has become used to triple and quadruple installations. A typical twin carburettor unit appears below. See fig. 6—13.

Fig. 6—13

Once again it will be necessary to consult your engine handbook to ascertain what adjustments can be made and how, and for instructions regarding maintenance.

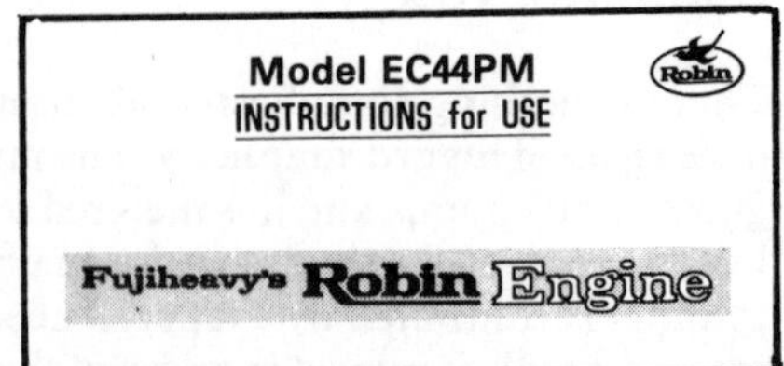

Model EC44PM
INSTRUCTIONS for USE
Robin
Fujiheavy's Robin Engine

Typical Carburettor

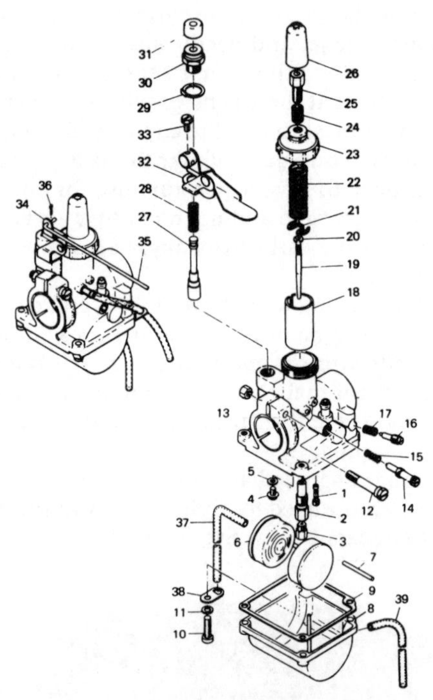

1. Pilot jet
2. Main nozzle
3. Main jet
4. Valve seat assembly
5. Valve seat washer
6. Float
7. Float pivot shaft
8. Float chamber body
9. Float chamber gasket
10. Pan head screw
11. Spring washer
12. Body fitting screw
13. Nut
14. Throttle stop screw
15. Throttle stop screw spring
16. Pilot air screw
17. Pilot air screw spring
18. Throttle valve
19. Jet needle
20. Jet needle clip
21. Clip retainer
22. Throttle valve spring
23. Mixing chamber top
24. Cable adjusting spring
25. Cable adjusting screw
26. Cap
27. Starter plunger
28. Plunger spring
29. Starter lever plate
30. Plunger cap
31. Plunger cap cover
32. Starter lever, left
33. Rod screw
34. Starter lever, right
35. Starter lever rod
36. Cotter pin
37. Air vent pipe
38. Plate
39. Overflow pipe

Fig. 6–14

FUEL

Most small two stroke engines including the highly developed Japanese makes are normally designed to run on a mixture of lubricating oil and regular grade (2 Star) petrol, although some engines may need premium grade fuel (4 Star). Your operating handbook will make this quite clear. In respect of fuel the microlight aviator is more fortunate than his compatriot in the light aircraft world, since he can obtain his fuel from any garage or filling station. It is however vital that the correct petrol/lubricating oil mixture is used, since it will ensure easier starting and smoother running to say nothing of cleaner sparking plugs and a less troublesome exhaust system. Any change in the recommended mixture ratio should only be made after consultation with the engine manufacturers or the guarantee will be invalidated and worse still there may be early failure of the bearings and perhaps total engine seizure. The mixture ratio is usually expressed as so many parts of petrol to so many parts of oil ie :20 : 1, although your handbook will tell you what the correct mixture ratio is. A very rich mixture would be 20 : 1, and a very lean mixture 100 : 1. Usually a non detergent oil of SAE 30 grade is used for your mixture, but follow the manufacturers recommendations in this respect. It is essential to continue to use the same oil in the petrol mix through the life of the engine, and no benefit whatever will accrue from using different oils according to convenience.

Fuel System

The fuel system will inevitably be one of two types:-

a) Gravity fed
b) Pump fed

If a fuel pump is used it will be driven by the engine to draw fuel from the fuel tank and deliver it in the right quantity and at the right pressure to the carburettor. This pump may work by mechanical linkage or pressure differential (Autovac system) and it has the following advantages.

1. Fuel is delivered according to the demands of the engine in all configurations regardless of "G" forces (though unfortunately the carburettor may not be similarly unaffected by "G" forces)
2. The fuel tanks can be fitted according to convenience providing always that the pump has the lifting capacity and the power.

A typical installation is shown in the following illustration.

Fig. 6—15

If the system is gravity fed it will of course not require a pump and the fuel tanks will therefore be mounted above the level of the carburettor otherwise the fuel will not flow. Quite clearly this system will be affected by "G" forces which may arrest or diminish the fuel flow with consequent engine problems.

Fuel Tanks

Fuel tanks must be as light as possible since total fuel weight is a significant part of the load the aircraft will have to carry and so naturally will affect the performance. It goes really without saying, that the fuel tanks and pipework should be kept clear of the exhaust pipe or muffler.

The Recoil Starter

Once again a rugged simple and generally trouble free unit which when correctly used will function without difficulty for long periods of time. It will be necessary however to follow the correct starting drill otherwise difficulty will be experienced and as a result of the frenzied muscular activity which usually follows, there will be accelerated wear of this unit with perhaps an early malfunction. The correct starting drill is as follows:-

a) Set throttle to start or idle
b) Pull out choke
c) Gradually pull out the starting handle until it becomes heavy – continue pulling lightly until it feels slack, then let the handle return fully to its normal position.
d) Now PULL THE HANDLE FORCIBLY avoiding pulling the whole length of the rope out.
e) Reset in normal position as soon as the engine has started.

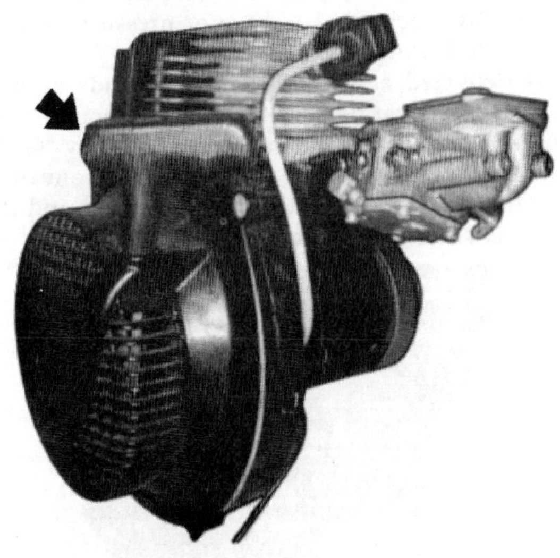

Fig. 6–16 The Recoil Starter

Effect of Temperature on Engine Performance

Warm air is less dense than cold air and since the amount of fuel at a given throttle setting does not vary significantly, warm air will result in a richer mixture and therefore a drop in engine performance. In warm weather the take off run will be increased and the rate of climb reduced.

Effect of Altitude on Engine Performance

As altitude increases the density of the air is reduced and since fuel delivery stays fairly constant at a fixed throttle setting, the mixture will become richer the higher the aircraft climbs.

In microlight aeroplanes it is unlikely that much can be done by the pilot to ameliorate the above effect, but since the effects are significant they must be appreciated by all pilots.

Checking the Engine Condition (Fuji/Robin)

The following information is supplied by Nicklow Engineering Ltd. and gives a good practical example of how to check the condition of a Fuji/Robin engine.

Before starting the engine always check the condition of transmission belts, all nuts and bolts for tightness in alliance with the propeller. Check the condition of the propeller for chips or cracks. These can cause an out of balance condition and the future failure of some moving part. To assess the condition of bearings check the amount of tip movement of the propeller. If the engine has done some 10 hours running in or flying time, check the condition of the fuel filter as this can be important to your mixture readings. Before starting the engine you should ensure you are using 4 star petrol, using a petrol/oil mix ratio of 32:1 or 40:1, depending upon the grade of oil used, e.g. in the case of Filtrate it should be 32:1.

NGK 9ES plugs should be used in mild weather and NGK 10EV for hot weather. Having ensured the fuel is primed to the carburettors, operate full choke and pull the starting cord. The engine should start on the 2nd or 3rd pull, if not a slight amount of throttle can be used. Run the engine for some 5 minutes to get up to the operating temperature whilst checking the engine and exhaust for any unusual noise. If everything is satisfactory set the engine idle between 1200 rpm and 1500 rpm. This setting can be altered with the 'tick over' screw on the side of the carburettor.

If you are satisfied that everything is secure at this stage place the engine under full load by opening up to full throttle for 5 minutes. This is to check the main fuel jet and the plug readings. You should also be listening for any jangling or tinkling sounds in the engine as these will tell you that the engine is detonating. If these noises are not present, continue to run the engine for the 5 minutes at full throttle. At the end of this time, stop the engine quickly and remove the sparking plugs. The centre electrode of the plug(s) should be a golden brown to a dark straw colour with the shroud a dark grey if a perfect mixture is being achieved.

To correct any error in plug colour, the main jet should be altered in stages of tens, higher to richen and lower to weaken. All plug readings should be on new or cleaned plugs. The necessity to check the mixture is that high performance two strokes are very susceptible to barometric pressure changes and therefore plug checks should be made at regular intervals when weather conditions change.

MICROLIGHT INSTRUMENTS

Although it is possible to fly small microlight aircraft without the aid of any instruments, the flight safety of microlight operation is enhanced by equipping the aircraft with some means of determining such items as airspeed, altitude, rate of climb or descent, magnetic heading, and engine performance.

At the present time there are available a number of simple instruments which can be bought for these purposes, and although they would be considered as rather crude for use in conventional aircraft they are quite satisfactory for use in microlight operations. These instruments are made by different manufacturers and vary in their design and construction but the general principles of operation as considered on the following pages are very similar.

The Air Speed Indicator

These essentially consist of a flexible capsule mounted in an instrument case. One end of the capsule is fixed to the case and the pressure of the surrounding air (static pressure) is exerted on the exterior of the capsule via an inlet tube. Another tube allows the pressure which is exerted as the aircraft moves through the air to be fed into the capsule which will then expand. The faster the aircraft moves through the air, the greater will be this impact pressure and the more the capsule will expand. The expansion is measured via a linkage system and shown on a calibrated dial in miles per hour or knots.

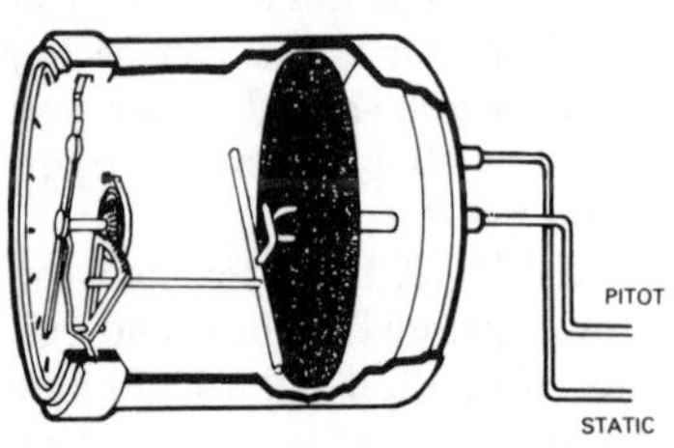

Fig. 6–17

Another extremely simple arrangement for the measurement of airspeed is constructed from a plastic tube which has an aperture into which the impact air enters. Inside the tube is a small plastic disc which rises up the tube by an amount equal to the impact pressure being received. The tube is calibrated to show the airspeed by a number of lines marked around the outside of the tube. The position of the disc relative to these lines therefore indicates the aircraft speed through the air.

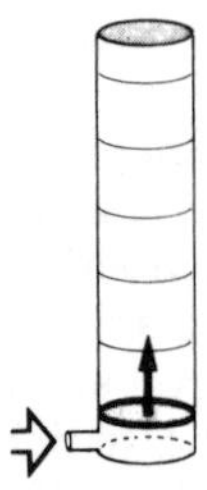

THE ALTIMETER

This instrument is required in order to show the pilot his height or altitude.

It is similar to an aneroid barometer in that it utilises a stack of two or three pressure responsive capsules which expand or contract with the pressure changes in the atmosphere.

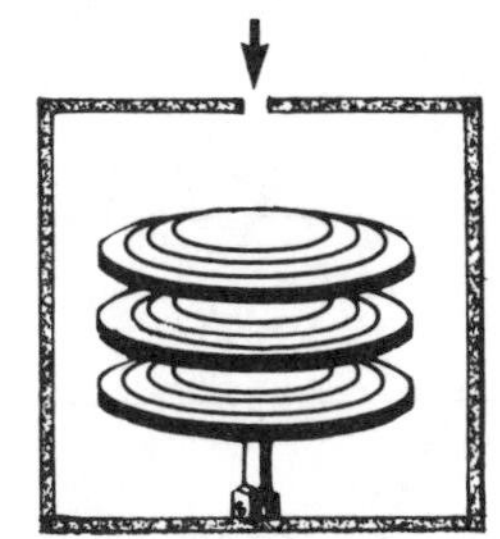

The instrument case is sealed except for a connection with a static tube. Any changes of static pressure surrounding the aircraft therefore affects the capsule stack.

The expansion or contraction of the aneroid capsule actuates a linking mechanism of levers and gears which indicates the movement by pointers moving around a dial calibrated in feet or metres. Altimeters used in U.K. registered aircraft are calibrated in feet.

A barometric pressure scale (which in the UK is graduated in millibars) is located at one side of the instrument face. This scale can usually be adjusted to give any pressure datum within a range from 950—1050mb.

Since atmospheric pressure continually changes it will be necessary to set the required datum pressure e.g. sea level (QNH) or aerodrome level (QFE) as required in order to measure the aircraft's vertical distance from sea level or the aerodrome surface. Increasing the barometric pressure setting scale will increase the indicated altitude by approximately 30ft. for every millibar.

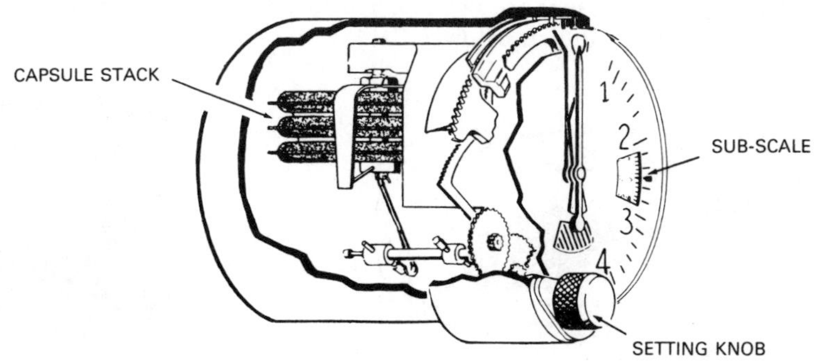

Fig. 6—18

Two types of altimeter presentation commonly used in microlight aircraft are shown below.

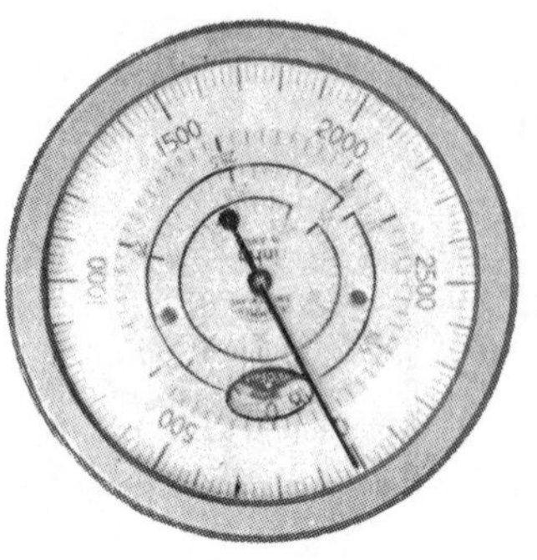

Fig. 6—19

VERTICAL SPEED INDICATOR (Variometer)

This instrument is mainly used to determine the aircraft's rate of climb or descent. However, when flight conditions are calm and the aircraft is in level flight, it can also be used as a trend instrument due to the vertical speed indicator needle being generally more sensitive and so responding more quickly to any variation of altitude.

A vertical speed indicator is essentially a sensitive differential pressure gauge which is connected to the static tube to indicate rate of change in static pressure. A capsule inside the sealed case of the instrument is directly fed with the static air pressure surrounding the aircraft. The static pressure is also fed into the case but through a restricted passage which acts as a metering unit. When the aircraft remains at a constant pressure level the static pressure inside the capsule and the case balance out and cause the indicator needle to show zero on the calibrated dial. A conventional VSI is shown below.

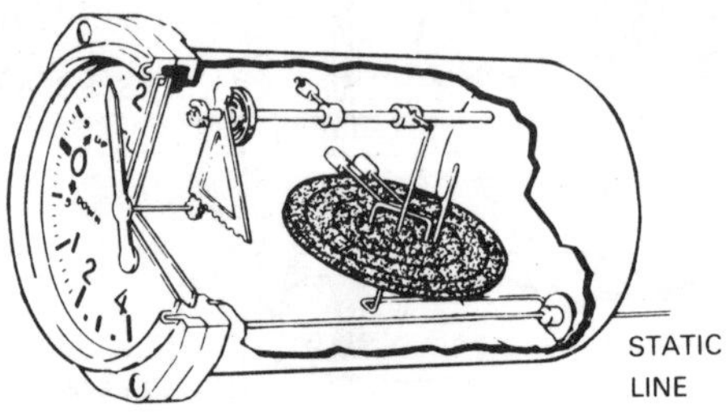

Fig 6—20

If the aircraft changes altitude the new static pressure is immediately felt inside the capsule but the change of pressure inside the case is delayed due to the action of the metering unit. Therefore whenever the aircraft climbs, the pressure in the case will remain slightly higher that that within the capsule and the indicating mechanism will cause the pointer to indicate a rate of climb. When the aircraft descends the pressure in the case will remain a little less than that within the capsule and the mechanism causes the pointer to show rate of descent.

The adjacent illustration shows the face of a typical variometer used in microlight aircraft.

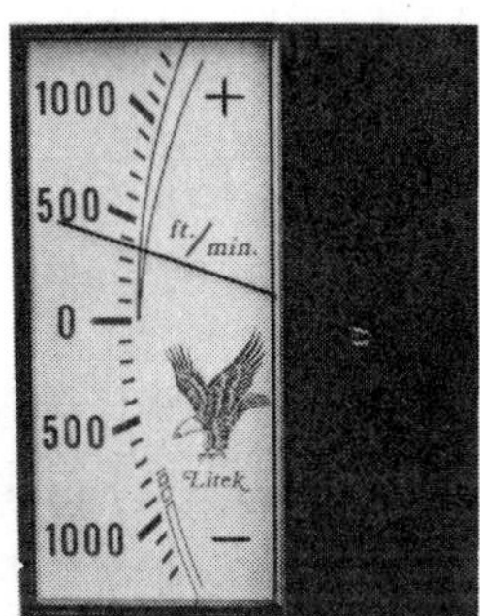

Some microlights may be fitted with an instrument designed to indicate the rate at which an aircraft is turning and these instruments also incorporate a type of spirit level which shows whether the aircraft is slipping, skidding or in a state of balance. There are several different ways of presenting this information and fig. 6—21 shows two common types of turn indicator. The picture at (a) shows an instrument with a needle which moves across a dial painted with calibrated marks to indicate the rate of turn and (b) shows a display used in a similar instrument known as a turn co-ordinator and on which an index aircraft is used in place of a needle.

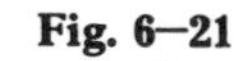

(a) **Fig. 6—21** **(b)**

The most common type of balance indicator in use today consists of a curved glass cylinder filled with kerosene in which is placed a small agate stone, common ball bearing, or some other suitable spherical and dense material. The fluid provides a damping action and so ensures smooth and easy movement of the ball.

A small vertical projection at one end of the glass tube (not visible to the pilot) contains a small bubble of air to compensate for expansion of the fluid during changes in temperature.

The glass container is curved so that when no yaw forces are present the ball will settle at the lowest point. (Fig. 6–22a.) During turns, the ball will also settle in the centre of the tube when the centrifugal force is equal to the horizontal component of the lift force i.e. when the forces are in balance. If the aircraft is "slipping in" during the turn, the ball will move from the centre of the tube and in the direction of the turn (Fig. 6–22b.) When the aircraft is "skidding", the ball will move from the centre towards the outside of the turn. (Fig. 6–22c.)

The older types of balance indicator use a needle presentation in conjunction with a dial which is marked in degrees of slip or skid.

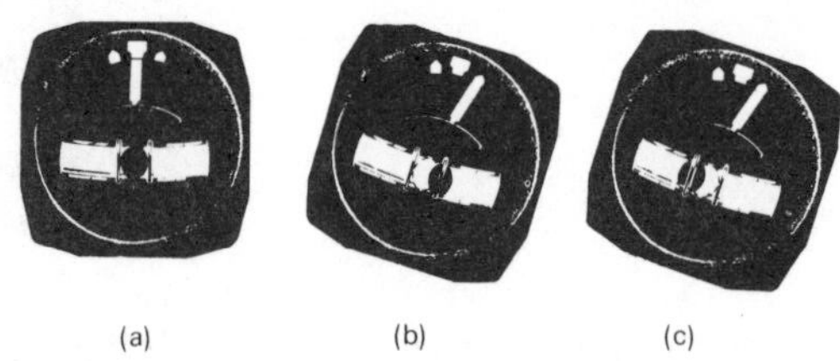

(a) (b) (c)

Fig. 6–22

MAGNETIC COMPASS

This has been covered in Section 3 Navigation.

ENGINE INSTRUMENTS.

The serviceability of the engine is undoubtedly a vital consideration for safe flight, and although an engine does not require instruments in order to operate properly, a pilot will need some form of instrumentation to know that it is working as it should. One primary information instrument is the tachometer (RPM gauge) and through the use of this instrument a pilot can determine whether the engine is developing the correct rated static RPM at full throttle or whether the idling RPM are remaining constant. If not then the tachometer will be indicating that all is not well. It may be that the plugs are becoming fouled, the carburation needs adjustment or some more serious fault is developing.

A Tachometer can have either a mechanical or electrical means of operation and a commonly used RPM indicator is shown in the adjacent illustration.

Another useful instrument is the Cylinder Head Temperature Gauge. Engine manufacturers determine optimum operating temperatures for your engine and if these are exceeded, the engine could be damaged. Although engines can stand extremes of heat and cold they can be damaged by sudden changes in temperature from one extreme to another, therefore the use of a cylinder head temperature gauge will also be of benefit to a pilot during descents when the engine will cool fairly rapidly. Monitoring this instrument will enable a pilot to know when to open the throttle to warm the engine during a descent and so prevent it from becoming too cold.

Typical cylinder head temperature gauges as used in microlight aircraft are shown below.

Fig. 6—23

SECTION SEVEN

FLIGHT TRAINING

FLIGHT TRAINING

INTRODUCTION

Due to the variations in design of microlight aircraft and the different methods which are used to control them, e.g. from weight shift through to 3 axis control systems, it is not possible in a manual of this nature to be specific in relation to the aircraft handling techniques which will be used in your training. Added to this is the fact that your sequence of instruction will vary depending upon whether you are learning on single seat (solo type) aircraft or two seat (dual type) aircraft.

In the case of single seat aircraft being used for your training there will also be differences in the sequence and methods of training used by different schools. One method which has been widely used in many countries since the inception of microlight aircraft is for the student to first learn how to taxy following which he carries out a number of short straight runs at ever increasing speeds until they develop into airborne hops which last longer and get higher each time. This method however often lacks continuity due to the need for very light wind conditions and as a result several other methods have been devised. For example, some schools will use conventional light aircraft to introduce you to the environment of the air and to give you practice in handling the flying controls. Others use towing methods whereby the microlight aircraft is towed by a land vehicle adapted for this purpose. The instructor sits in the vehicle and talks to his student through the medium of two way radio. Yet other schools use a combination of solo and dual type aircraft during their course of instruction. Whichever method or combination of methods are used, the objective will be to initially introduce you to the environment of flight whilst at the same time giving you experience in controlling the aircraft.

Because of these variations in microlight design and the differences in the training methods currently being used, this section of the manual can only be concerned with an appreciation of the factors involved in operating a microlight aeroplane and any coverage of the physical aspects of flying a microlight will, of necessity, be of a general nature only. In any event, although knowledge and understanding can be gained through manuals and books, your ability to fly a particular microlight can only be advanced by the briefings and demonstrations given by your instructor and through your own physical practice. No manual or book can be a substitute for the tuition and experience you gain from this source, and you must pay close attention to and abide by the instruction you receive, whether learning in dual or solo type aircraft. In this respect you are most strongly advised to choose one of the Flying Training Schools listed by the BMAA, in this way you will be taking steps to assure that you are receiving well organised and cost effective tuition.

Flying Training for a Licence with Operational Limitations

An applicant for a PPL(A) which includes an Aircraft Rating in Group D with Operational Limitations, shall produce evidence of having satisfactorily completed a course of training to a syllabus recognised by the Authority and pass a Flight Test. The syllabus of flying training must provide for a minimum of 15 hours of flight time in a microlight aeroplane including not less than 7 hours as PIC in the 9 months prior to the date of application.

Flying Training for Licence without Operational Limitations

An applicant for a PPL(A) which includes an Aircraft Rating in Group D without Operational Limitation shall produce evidence of having satisfactorily completed a course of training to a syllabus recognised by the Authority and a Flight Test. The syllabus of flying training must provide for a minimum of 25 hours of flight time supervised by a flying instructor in a microlight aeroplane. The total must include:

(a) not less than 10 hours as PIC in the 9 months prior to the date of application;
(b) not less than 5 hours training in navigation of which at least 3 hours must be solo and must include two solo 40 nm cross-country flights, during each of which the applicant landed at least at one other site not less than 15 nm from the take-off site at which the flight began. The two solo cross-country flights must be flown over different routes and to different sites.

FLYING TRAINING CONDITIONS

All flying training specified in the previous paragraphs must be carried out under the supervision of a flying instructor holding a valid AFI Rating or a FI Rating on the type of microlight on which the training is conducted. Solo flying may only be carried out when the flying instructor is present at the take-off site at which the flight commences.

Flight in any microlight aeroplane is acceptable irrespective of the method of flight control used and should follow either the dual training system for a two seat aeroplane or the solo training system for a single seat aeroplane.

THE GENERAL FLIGHT TEST

An applicant for a PPL(A) endorsed with an Aircraft Rating for Group D will be required to pass a General Flight Test (GFT) conducted by a CAA authorised PPL Group D 'X' Examiner in a Group D aeroplane.

Single Seat Aircraft GFT

Flying Tests conducted on single seat aircraft should include all the elements of the GFT conducted on two seat aeroplanes. The candidate will be required by the Examiner to carry out the various manoeuvres to a set sequence in an area in the Examiner's field of view. The test may be split into a series of short consecutive flights to enable the Examiner to re-brief the candidate on the next series of manoeuvres.

Flight Test Arrangements

Microlight flying training schools, the CAA and representative organisations will provide the addresses of PPL Group D Examiners.

Candidates should arrange the date and time of the test with the chosen Examiner who will enter the result of successful tests on the application Form FCL 102M. After completion the form should be sent to the BMAA.

The test will consist of a flight or series of flights of approximately one hour in total, during which the candidate will be assessed on all appropriate items detailed on this page and page 7–5.

GFT Pass Conditions

The whole of the Flight Test must be completed within a period of 28 days. A candidate who fails in any part of the Flight Test may be required to undertake further flying training before being accepted for re-test.

The written examinations will consist of multiple choice papers. In order to qualify, candidates must obtain not less than 70 per cent of the possible marks for each subject. A valid pass in the examination must be obtained in the 12 months preceding the date of application for the licence, except for the Aircraft (Type) ground examination where the time limit is 9 months.

FLYING SYLLABUS

This syllabus lists all the items which should be covered during training and which will be examined during the General Flight Test (GFT).

For single-seat aircraft of Group D the test will include all elements listed for the two-seat aircraft, with the candidate being required to carry out the various manoeuvres to a set sequence in an area within the Examiner's field of view. The test may be split into a series of flights to enable the Examiner to re-brief the candidate for the next series of manoeuvres.

The GFT will cover the following items and the candidate will be required to demonstrate satisfactory standards of knowledge and handling in each.

Preparation for Flight

Self briefing, weather suitability, aeroplane documentation, personal equipment check, weight and balance (calculate), weight and performance (calculate), fuel and oil state, aeroplane acceptability, ATC booking-out, and pre-flight inspection.

Starting, Taxying and Power Checks

Pre-start checks, post-start checks, taxying techniques, and power checks.

Take-off

Pre-take-off checks (vital actions), assessment of cross-wind component, during and post take-off checks, normal take-off, and cross-wind take-off.

Aerodrome Departure Procedures

Climbing

Straight and Level Flight

Descending with Power/Flap

Turning

Level, climbing, descending, high angles of bank.

Stalling/Incipient Spinning/Unusual Attitudes

Checks before stalling/spinning; flight at V_{s1} + 5 kts and at V_{s0} + 5 kts in straight and level, climbing, descending, and turning flight; recognition of incipient stall, recovery from incipient stall, recognition of incipient spin (dual only), recovery from incipient spin (dual only); straight and level, turning, climbing, descending and approach configuration flight; recovery from a developed stall from straight, turning and approach configuration flight; recovery from a spiral dive; side-slips (dual only).

Forced Landing without Power

Checks, procedure, judgment.

Navigation/Orientation

Recognition of features, assessment of position.

Circuit joining Procedures

Circuit Procedure

Approach and Landing

Pre-landing checks (vital actions), assessment of cross-wind component, powered approach, flap-less approach, glide approach, short field landing, bad weather circuit, cross-wind landing, missed approach procedure, checks after landing.

Simulated Emergencies

Engine fire in the air/on the ground, cabin fire in the air/on the ground, engine failure after take-off, other simulated emergencies.

Engines and Systems Handling

Airmanship/Awareness

Look-out, positioning (restricted airspace, hazards, weather), ATC liaison, aerodrome discipline.

Action after Flight

Engine shut down, parking and securing aeroplane, recording of flight details.

The training exercises which follow cover the dual training syllabus. Students who are learning on single seat aircraft will follow the general sequence of the solo training syllabus. In either case your learning programme will be arranged and supervised by your Training School.

Whether learning on solo or dual aircraft it will be most helpful to your instructor and of benefit to yourself if you read this section and review the various factors involved in each flight exercise prior to receiving your practical briefing/flying instruction for that stage of the syllabus.

AIRCRAFT FAMILIARISATION

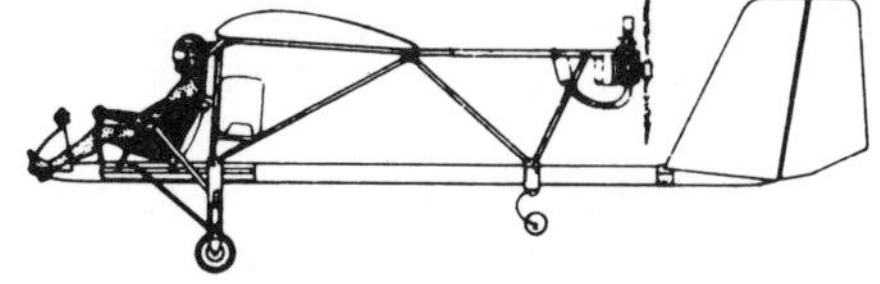

Objectives

To acquaint you with the aircraft type to be used in your training. In the main this exercise will cover an explanation of the controls, systems and equipment and in this respect it will be necessary to go into sufficient detail to ensure that you understand the basic purpose and method of operation of the relevant items.

Introduction

During the previous sections concerning Principles of Flight, Engines and Instruments many terms relating to an aircraft were covered, however before dealing with the more practical aspects of handling a microlight you should also be familiar with the following definitions:

COMPRESSION STRUT — A structural member which joins the leading and trailing edges of the wing.

CROSS BOOM — Normally fitted to flex wing aircraft and consists of a tubular member that is fitted spanwise across the wings to keep them rigid laterally.

ELEVON — A dual purpose control surface used for controlling the angle of attack and roll.

FLYING WIRES — The lower cables which connect the wing and fuselage structure. They are used to transmit lift loads to the fuselage.

KINGPOST — A vertical tube above the wing centre which anchors the landing wires and transfers negative loads to the fuselage.

LANDING GEAR — This includes the wheels, axles and supporting structure.

LANDING WIRES — These are upper cables which support negative loadings.

RIB — This item is used to provide the wing profile. Flex wing aircraft use stiffeners called battens.

RUDDERVATOR — This is a dual purpose surface used on 'V' tailed aircraft. It is a control surface which is designed to control pitch and yaw.

SPAR — The primary load carrying member of a wing.

SPOILER — A control surface which is normally located on the upper surface of a wing. It is designed to lie flush with the wing surface until used. When deflected it reduces lift and increases drag.

STICK — A control lever which is normally connected to the ailerons and elevators in 3 axis control aircraft. On aircraft fitted with 2 axis controls it is commonly designed to operate the elevators and rudder.

STRUT — A term used to describe tubes which are used to brace the wing to the fuselage. Struts transmit both flying and landing loads to the fuselage.

TAIL SKID – A component fitted to the aft portion of the fuselage and which keeps this end of the fuselage clear of the ground.

TAIL WHEEL – A wheel fitted at the aft portion of the fuselage which serves the same function as a tail skid.

In fulfilling the objectives of this exercise it should be appreciated that microlights have many of the basic characteristics of a conventional aeroplane e.g. a wing, fuselage structure, landing gear, engine mounting, engine and propeller etc. Normally the most unconventional characteristic lies in the types and methods of controlling the aircraft. For example, whereas conventional aeroplanes normally have a tail section upon which a horizontal and vertical stabilizer is fitted in conjunction with elevators and a rudder, the microlight is often designed with a rudder surface which is situated at the wing tips and/or a surface mounted in front of the main wing (canard) which is used to control the aircraft in pitch. Additionally many microlights are fitted with a flex wing and pitch and roll control is achieved by the pilot shifting his weight fore and aft and from side to side.

A further and distinct difference lies in the fact that many microlights are assembled prior to flight and dis-assembled afterwards. This means that a microlight pilot must know the method of assembly of his particular aircraft and this means understanding exactly how each part or component is fitted one to the other. The pilot must be capable of attaching the various tubes and cables, etc. safely and of making any necessary adjustments. Without this ability a microlight pilot will be inviting dangerous situations to occur instead of safely enjoying a pleasant and exhilarating pastime.

With this in mind it can be appreciated that if you intend to buy a microlight of your own it is absolutely essential that you learn the required rigging and de-rigging procedure applicable to the aircraft you will be flying. Therefore, although this aspect of microlight operation may appear to be a rather dull chore it is nevertheless one of the most fundamental lessons to be mastered. During this aircraft familiarization period you will be taken carefully over each step and given the necessary instruction to enable you to rig the aircraft safely.

Apart from this you will also learn the positions and purpose of the various controls including such items as the throttle, fuel taps, ignition switch and any engine or flight instruments which may be fitted to your training aircraft. You will also be taught how to strap yourself in properly and how to fit your protective headgear. Emergency procedures (as applicable) for the type of aircraft will be explained and where practical they will be practised on the ground.

The Aircraft Structure

In terms of structure microlights can generally be considered in the following forms:

1. Those which utilise a flex wing to which a triangular metal frame is suspended. This type is more commonly known as a 'Trike'.
2. Those in which the wing is assembled on rigid lines and fixed to a tubular metal framework. This framework is termed a fuselage and has a rear mounted conventional tailplane or a forward mounted control surface known as a canard.

3.A few microlights are designed with fuselage canopies of various designs all of which give the pilot some protection from the airflow. These types sometimes have covered fuselages similar to a conventional glider or aeroplane.

Amongst the various combinations of design features the complete airframe structure may be formed by any or all of the following units:

The Fuselage
Wing
Stabilizers
Flying Controls
Landing Gear.

These airframe components can be constructed from a wide variety of materials and are joined together by bolts, screws, rivets, welding and/or adhesives or other bonding materials.

The structural members have to be of sufficient strength to carry the loads and stresses which are a normal part of an aircraft's operation. For example, a single member of the aircraft structure may be subjected to a combination of stresses, i.e. end loads, side loads, tension or compression and torsion.

Although the strength and ability to flex are major requirements of most components, there are others such as fairings which do not carry loads but which are designed to provide smooth streamlined qualities in order to reduce the drag forces which occur as a result of movement through the air.

When designing an aircraft, every part must be considered together with the method of fitment in relation to the load to be imposed upon it, and the determining of these loads is an essential part of a subject called stress analysis. Although knowledge of this subject is not a requirement for the private pilot, it gives a pilot a greater appreciation of the importance that loads and stress play in the operation of the aircraft if he is aware of some of the basic considerations concerned with stress analysis.

The basic load is that which acts on the structure of the aeroplane in a condition of static equilibrium. This means the load caused by the weight of the aeroplane in unaccelerated straight and level flight.

The designer determines the maximum probable load which will be applied compatible with the type of operation for which the aircraft has been designed, and which might be applied during abnormal flight manoeuvres or occasioned by sudden gusts in the air.

The strength of any aircraft is limited by the need to keep structural weight to a minimum, and the various parts are designed to fail only at an ultimate load which is normally fixed at 1.5 times the maximum applied load. The ratio of the ultimate load to the maximum applied load (1.5) is known as the *Safety Factor.*

The load factor is expressed in multiples of gravitational pull or *g's,* and in normal straight and level flight will be 1. If a force is applied equal to 2*g's* the load factor will be 2. For example, an aircraft weighing 150Kg would weigh 300Kg if the load factor was increased to 2.

Apart from load factor, there are other stresses to which all aircraft are subjected, and before defining these in simple terms, it would also be helpful to realise that although the designer arranges for the individual aircraft components to meet all load and stress requirements compatible with normal flight and the operational purpose of the aeroplane, every pilot has the physical strength to exceed these limitations by brutal operation of the controls.

This means that a person of normal physical strength can apply forces to the aircraft controls which can cause a change in direction which will produce an acceleration in excess of 8*g*, and although the application of this force would cause a pilot to 'blackout' in a second or two, the airframe would already have been subjected to a load factor greater than 8.

Blackout can be explained by the following:

> *The forces of acceleration normally called* 'g' *can, upon reaching a certain level, cause the blood to be drained from a person's head. This action will cause the person to* 'black out' *and become unconscious. The average level for this to happen would be about* 5g,*although physical training and other methods can increase this level.*

Bearing in mind that some microlight aircraft are designed to withstand positive load factors of only 2g and most have only small negative load limits, it will be appreciated that a pilot could apply forces to the aircraft structure which are greater than those for which it was originally designed. Additionally, fatigue due to aircraft age and/or repeated stress loadings may cause a structure or component to fail at an earlier stage than that to which it was originally designed. These points must be born in mind by pilots when carrying out manoeuvres involving higher than normal loadings.

Having said this and bearing in mind that microlight pilots will commonly be assembling their own aircraft, it is clear that they should have a basic understanding of the types of stresses which may occur to an aircraft. For example, the application of a force to a unit area of material will induce within that material something called *stress,* such stress is always accompanied by a deformation within the material, called strain.

The five major stresses which act upon the parts of an aeroplane can be described as follows:

Tension

The stress that resists a force which tends to pull apart.

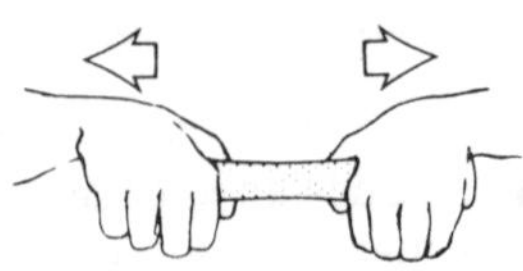

Fig. 7-1

An example of this would be the effect of the propeller pulling the aircraft forward, and the effect of air resistance which tries to hold it back. The result is a tension which tends to stretch the aircraft.

Compression
The stress that resists a crushing force, in other words, the stress that tends to shorten or squeeze the parts of an aircraft, e.g. the nose wheel strut whilst the aircraft is on the ground.

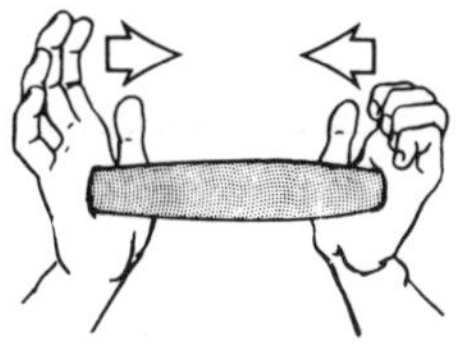

Fig. 7-2

Torsion
Torsion is a twisting stress and an example of this can be seen in the action of the propeller turning. An action which causes the fuselage to want to turn in the opposite direction.

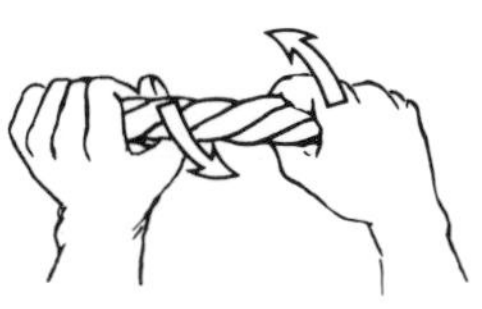

Fig. 7-3

Shear
Shear is the stress that resists the force tending to cause one layer of material to slide over an adjacent layer.

For example, if two strips of metal or wood were bonded together by a lap joint, then if the two strips were pulled, i.e., placed in tension the bonded joint would be in direct shear.

Alternatively, one could consider two components of an aircraft which are riveted together and which, when placed in tension, will develop a shearing stress in the rivets.

Bending

Bending is a combination of tension and compression stress as seen in Fig. 7-4.

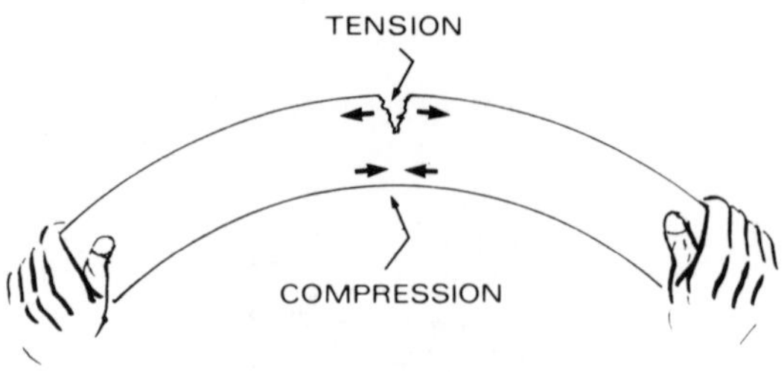

Fig. 7-4

Apart from the strains imposed by steady loads and stresses, there is also the factor of fatigue. Most parts of an aircraft are subject to strain brought about by steady loads and by vibration and flexing. The fatigue resistance of a material is that property which enables it to withstand cycles of steady and fluctuating stresses applied over a period of time.

Fatigue failure of the aircraft component is caused by stress and microscopic changes in the structure of the material. This is one reason why a careful pre-flight inspection is necessary prior to each flight in order that any deterioration or cracks in the visible components or surfaces can be attended to before flying.

The airframe section is the supporting structure for the wing and has to provide the seats for the pilot and, where applicable the passenger and any instruments. It also forms the base for the engine mounting attachments, fuel system etc.

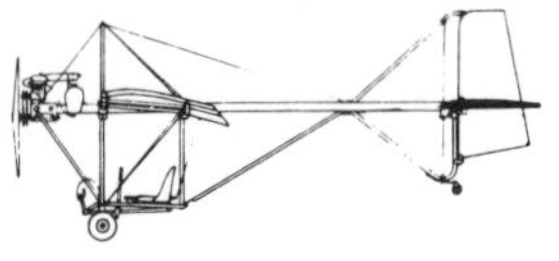

Fig 7-5

It may be constructed by the use of a single boom and bracing wires or multiple tubes and stay wires. Various methods are used for connecting booms, bracing or wires together and it is important that the correct materials are used and that the lock nuts or locking wire are properly fitted to ensure security against vibration. In this respect the mounting system used for the engine should include rubber shock absorbers to reduce vibration on the airframe to a minimum.

The position of the centre of gravity plays an important part in relation to an aircraft's stability during flights. In order to keep movement of the centre of gravity to a minimum the fuel tank(s) are normally placed over or near the centre of gravity so that as the fuel is used up the balance of the aircraft is not greatly affected. Clear plastic fuel containers are often used as these have the advantage of the pilot being able to see the fuel level during flight and their flexibility reduces the possibility of rupture in the event of a nose-in following a bad landing.

The fuel line connection point is normally positioned a short distance above the bottom of the tank in order to avoid drawing sediment or water into the fuel line. Moisture from water is always present in any fuel system but being heavier than petrol it sinks to the bottom of the tank or fuel system. A drain at the bottom of the tank may sometimes be incorporated so that the tank can, at intervals, be strained of any moisture or sediment which collects during normal operations.

The landing gear construction, like so many other aspects of microlight aircraft will vary between the different types of aircraft. Some are extremely basic and consist of wheels attached to the main airframe via members with little in the way of shock absorbtion, other mehods used spring coils or rubber bungees and or flexible attachment points. Particular attention should be paid to the condition of the shock absorbers and the security and condition of the landing gear assembly before flight.

PREPARATION FOR FLIGHT

Objectives

To teach you how to prepare yourself and the aircraft for flight. You will also be taught how to park the aircraft and check its condition after flight. Many of the items included in this lesson will have to be repeated several times before the objectives are achieved.

Introduction

The basis of all pilot competence and safe flight begins on the ground and in this respect the attitude and habits you develop in the early stage of your training will tend to fix the standards you achieve in all your flying. Therefore thoroughly learning the correct procedures which are used prior to every flight is a very important part of your training.

In the case of aircraft which have to be assembled before flight it is extremely important that the rigging and de-rigging is carried out in detailed accordance with the manufacturers instructions and the *Aircraft 'Owner's Manual'* will provide the necessary information for this operation.

In order to avoid damage to the aircraft and difficulty during assembly it will be advisable to have at least two persons available for this task. A sheltered site should, wherever possible, be chosen in order to avoid problems created by the wind when assembling the wing to the airframe.

During assembly all components should be carefully inspected for damage or stress prior to their being fitted together. Once the components are in position it is not always possible to see any damage, unusual wear or deterioration which may have occurred.

Following assembly of the aircraft a very careful pre-flight inspection must be made in a consistent sequence. The actual order in which you carry out this inspection will vary with the aircraft type and with the systems and equipment with which it is fitted. A fairly common and sensible procedure is to start at one point of the aircraft and continue around it until you return to the starting point.

In general terms you will be checking your aircraft for the following:

Nuts, Bolts, Turnbuckles

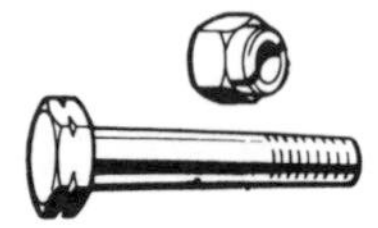

Check all bolts and nuts for wear. Bolts should be straight, no stripping of threads should be evident and they should be secure and safetied. Locknuts should not be removed and then re-used as the nylon insert wears out. A few threads of the bolt should appear past the locknut if it is to hold properly.

In order to adjust cable tension during the assembly, it is quite common to incorporate turnbuckles at the cable ends. Various types of turnbuckles are in common use, but essentially, they consist of a barrel with internal screw threads at either end. One end has a right hand thread and the other a left hand thread. When fitting the control cables and adjusting the tension the cable terminal is screwed into either end of the barrel an equal distance, and as a safety factor, not more than three threads should be exposed on either side of the barrel.

To ensure that vibration or wear does not loosen the cable terminals from the barrel ends, a locking wire method is used. Safety wiring is a method of wiring two or more units in such a manner that any tendency of one to loosen is counteracted by the tension of the wire.

The turnbuckles used in microlight aircraft are normally exposed so that they can be easily examined by a pilot and this is an important item to be included during the pilots pre-flight inspection of the aircraft.

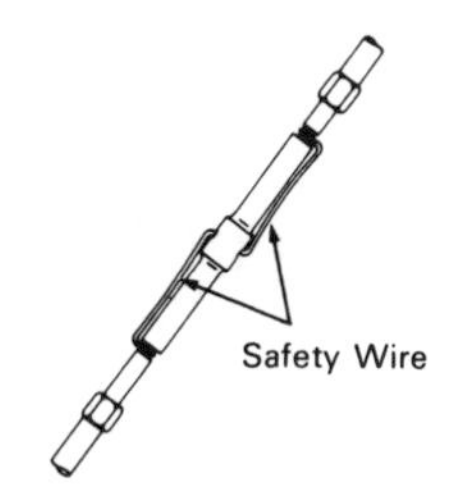

Cables

These should be tensioned properly and show no signs of fraying. Carefully run your hand down each cable and check to ensure there are no broken strands. Stainless steel cable is normally used for bracing and the approved method of connecting cables to bolts utilises a thimble which protects the cable from wear, a nicropress ferrule which swages the cable ends together, and a tang through which both the bolt and cable are joined together. These components should be inspected for security and to ensure that no unusual wear is present.

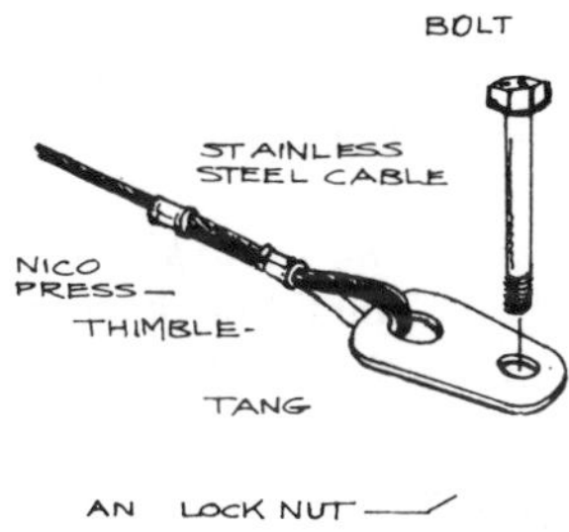

Rivets

These should be inspected for sheared heads and elongation of holes through which they pass, either of which indicates unusual stresses have been present.

Tubes and Struts

Carefully inspect all tubing and struts for dents or other damage, they should be straight and true and free from corrosion. Where bends are specifically incorporated these areas should be carefully checked to ensure that no deterioration or cracks are occurring.

Landing Gear

The tyres should be properly inflated and in good condition. The wheels should rotate freely and be safetied. The axles and supporting structure for the wheels should be inspected very carefully for any damage which may have occurred during previous landings.

Engine

The engine mounting should be checked for security and the engine attachment points should be inspected to ensure that all bolts and nuts are properly safetied. The sparking plug cables, throttle linkage and fuel line should be included in this inspection.

Propeller

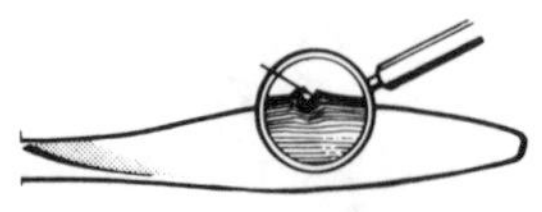

This should be checked for security and you should run your hand along each blade to ensure the surface is smooth and free from serious nicks and dents. Propellers are subject to extremely high twisting and rotational forces which can aggravate any cracks and result in disintegration of the blade.

Fuel Tank(s)
Should be checked for fuel quantity, and freedom from water and sediment. The fuel line should be firmly secured, and free from kinks. The fuel cap should be securely in place and the vent hole clear.

Ignition
A battery, if fitted, should be secure and in a charged condition. All electrical connections should be clean and tight, and any corrosion removed.

Instruments (as applicable)
These should be in working order, and securely fitted. The glass surfaces should be clean, and the dial markings must be legible.

Seating and Harness
Check the seat and harness attachment points to ensure that they are properly secured and showing no signs of wear.

Controls
Check all moveable components to ensure they operate freely, are secure and safetied. This will include such items as hinges, hinge pins, etc. Operate all controls to see that they work in the correct sense and are not restricted in any way.

Wing
Ensure that the wing surface shows no signs of damage and that it is clean, this latter applies particularly to the leading edges as any irregularity will be harmful to the production of lift.

Check that there is no fraying adjacent to those positions where bracing or control cables are close to, or come into contact with the wing surface.

At the end of your pre-flight inspection stand back from the aircraft and generally review it for overall appearance and trueness. Be careful to ensure that it is trimmed for your weight and that it is in a suitable area for the engine to be started.

Remember to check items of personal equipment such as overalls, helmet, gloves etc. If you intend to fly any distance from the take-off site you should ensure you are carrying a map of the area.

Engine Starting
Before starting the engine, ensure that the wheels are chocked to avoid the aircraft running forward immediately the engine starts. Advise any spectators to clear the area and stay well away from the aircraft.

Follow the starting instructions given in the engine manual, which usually contain the following general points:

- Set the throttle to the idle position
- Check the ignition switch is in the 'OFF' position.
- Prime the engine and turn it over a few times by hand.
- Call out in a loud voice 'Clear Prop' — then switch 'On' the ignition and pull the starter.

Once the engine starts and is running smoothly set it at idle RPM and allow it to warm up to the manufacturers recommended temperature. If the engine does not start, check to see whether it is flooded. This can be determined by the presence of a strong petrol odour and/or a wet sparking plug. If the engine has been flooded, follow the manufacturers instructions on this point before re-attempting to start.

It will be necessary to get into the habit of keeping your hand on the throttle whenever the engine is running, this will apply in the air as well as on the ground. Another very important point to remember is that the ignition switch should be kept in the 'OFF' position except when actually starting the engine. Handling the propeller with the ignition 'ON' is very dangerous and if the engine inadvertently starts serious injury could result.

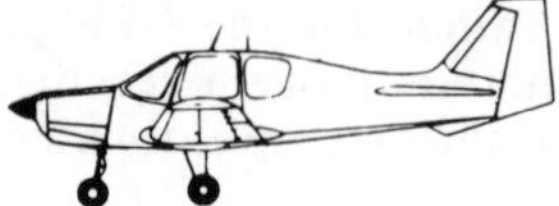

AIR EXPERIENCE

When learning on solo type aircraft this exercise is normally given in a conventional aircraft. Its purpose is to introduce and accustom you to the environment of flight, including the sensations of flying and the aspect of the ground as seen from the air.

Further flights can be undertaken in conventional aircraft to introduce you to the effects of the controls and other exercises depending upon the procedures used at your training school.

Whether air experience is given in conventional or dual microlight aircraft you will not normally be given much flying instruction during this exercise. The reason being that your initial flight is designed to enable you to become more at home in this new environment, and to experience the sensations associated with flying, before actually having to concentrate on actual learning. If you already have previous flight experience, then part of this flight may be used to introduce you to the 'Effects of Controls'.

The duration of the flight is variable and will be designed to suit individual students. After you have adjusted yourself to this new environment and associated sensations, you will be encouraged to participate by noting the readings of any instruments which are fitted and also identify ground features.

Later on in the flight you will most probably be given the opportunity to handle the aircraft controls and discover the light forces and small movements needed to alter the aircraft attitude.

EFFECTS OF CONTROLS

Objectives

This lesson is for the purpose of introducing you to the respective movements of the aircraft controls, their methods of operation and how their use affects the attitude of the aircraft during flight.

Introduction

The flight path of an aircraft through the air can be resolved into three planes of movement; the pitching plane about the lateral axis, the rolling plane about the longitudinal axis and the yawing plane about the vertical (normal) axis.

An aircraft is controlled in these planes of movement by means of the flying controls. In conventional (3 axis control) aircraft, the elevators control pitch, the ailerons control roll and the rudder controls yaw. The three planes of movement are fixed relative to the pilot and the aircraft, this means that if the aircraft is banked, the pitching plane of the aircraft is inclined to the vertical but the effect of the elevators will still produce the same movements of the aircraft's nose relative to the pilot, i.e. pitching. Further, whatever the attitude of the aircraft, the control movements will always produce the same pitching, rolling or yawing movements relative to the pilot and the aircraft.

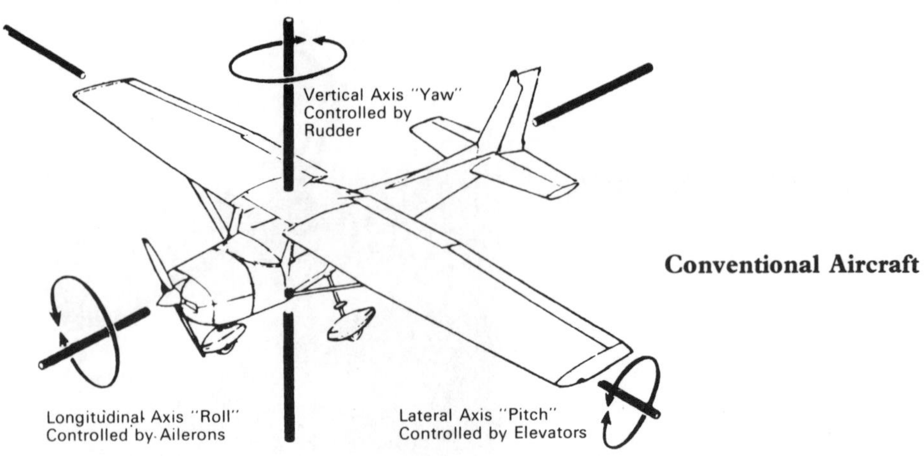

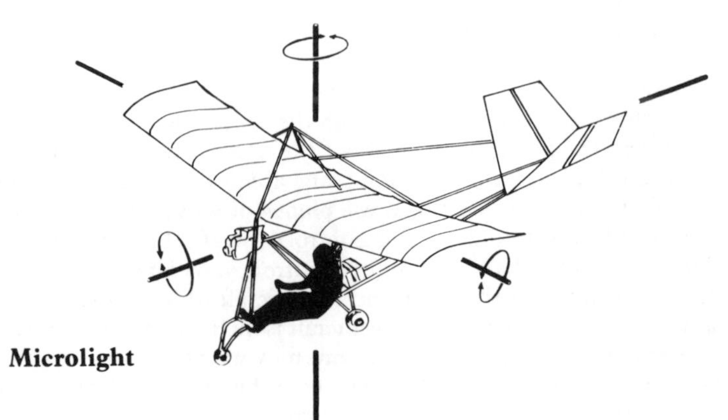

Fig. 7-6

Once these basic facts are understood you will be better able to appreciate the following paragraphs concerning the movement of the various controls and their effects upon the aircraft's attitude, whether it is flying straight and level, climbing, descending, or turning.

The illustrations below show the individual effects of the conventional primary controls, the elevators, ailerons and rudder.

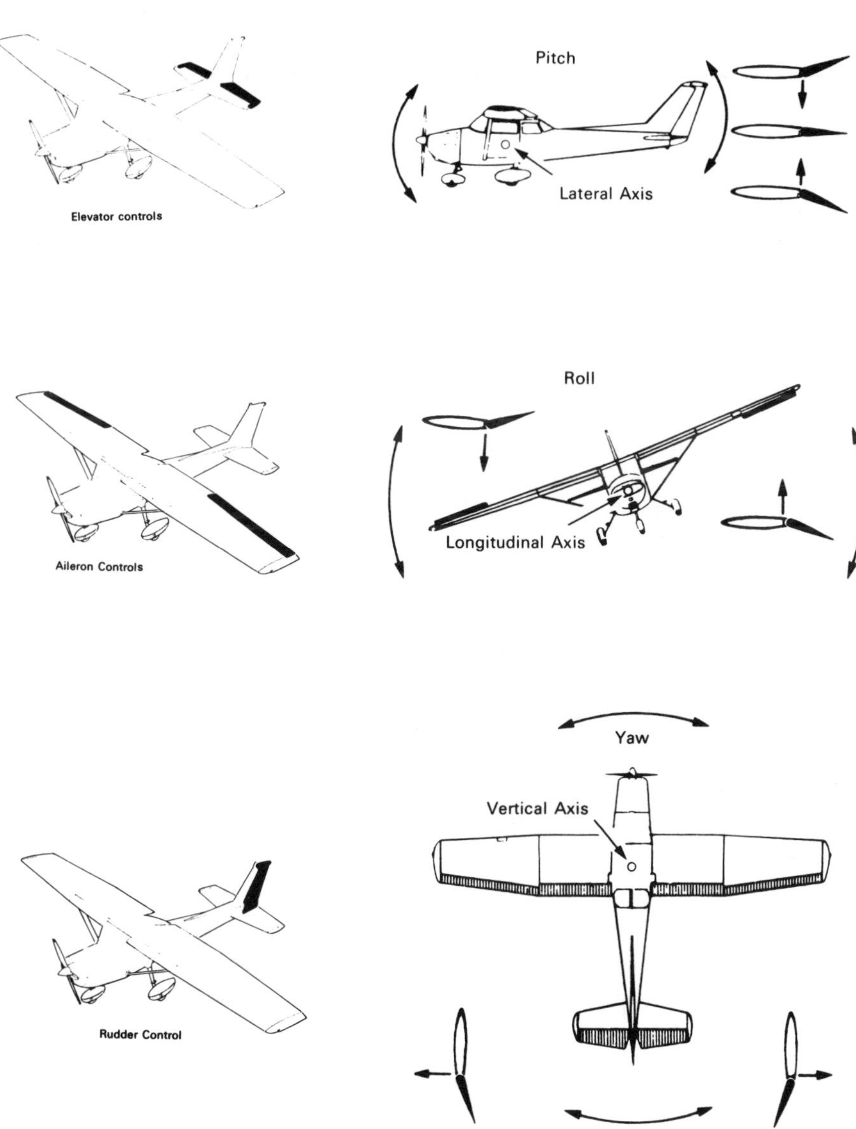

Fig. 7-7

Some microlight aircraft are now fitted with conventional control systems (known as '3 axis control'), in which case all the previous comments relating to the function of the controls in conventional aircraft apply. However a large number of microlights use a two control system, elevators and rudder(s), this is known as '2 axis' control. Other microlights are constructed on the principle of the hang glider wing, called 'flex wing' and rely solely upon 'weight shift' as the primary control, and are not therefore equipped with elevators, ailerons or rudders. Combinations of flex wing and some control surfaces may also be found, in that some weight shift aircraft are also equipped with rudder surfaces situated at the wing tips.

In the case of microlights which use elevators and rudder(s) only, the control in roll is achieved by the secondary or further effect of the rudder, which can be described as follows:

> When an aircraft is yawed about the normal axis there will occur a small differential in the speed of airflow over the left and right wings, this action will create more lift on one wing than the other. Added to this is the fact that inertia will cause the aircraft to continue for a short time along its original direction of flight. The effect of this upon dihedral or other methods used for lateral stability is to create a small increase in the angle of attack of the outer wing and the opposite on the inner wing. There will also be a minor masking of the airflow on the inner wing.
>
> Together these further effects are sufficiently pronounced to cause the aircraft to bank.

On a number of microlights the rudder controls are positioned at the ends of the main wing and are then variously referred to as, Tip Draggers, Tip Rudders, Ruddervons or Winglets depending upon their method of operation and the primary aerodynamic reason for placing them in this position.

Another method of control in roll is sometimes used on microlight aircraft and this consists of using wing spoilers. These are normally placed on the top of the wing along the outboard section as shown in the following illustration. The pilot will have the means to raise either spoiler independently, thus disrupting the airflow on that wing, decreasing the lift and increasing the drag. The net effect to cause the wing to lower and a bank will be induced. Sometimes they are also arranged so that they can be operated together and then can be used in the form of airbrakes permitting the aircraft to descend more steeply without an increase in airspeed.

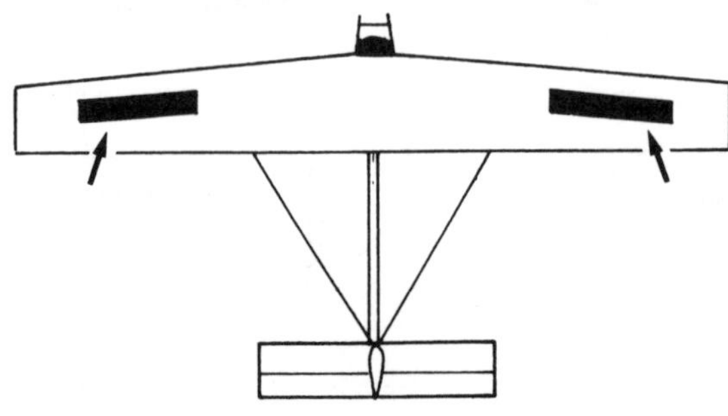

Fig. 7-8

When a microlight is designed in the canard configuration the same principles of pitch control will apply as with the more conventional tailplane. In the case of the canard however the elevators will have to be deflected upwards to reduce the lift on the forward wing section and so cause the nose to lower. The pilot will move the control stick or wheel in the same direction as in a conventional aircraft because the design of the canard control system ensures this.

One further variation in the arrangement of pitch and yaw controls is the design of the 'V' tail. The moveable control surfaces fitted to a 'V' tail stabilizer are known as Ruddervators since they perform a dual role (Fig. 7-9).

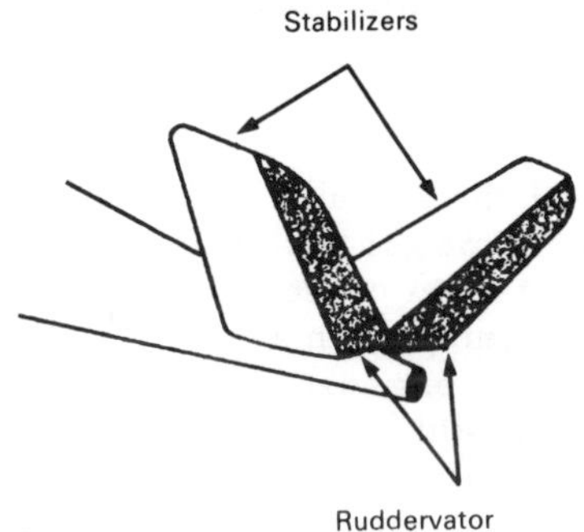

Fig. 7-9

The control surface system is so arranged that forward and backward movement on the control column causes both moveable surfaces to move up or down in unison thereby acting in the same way as elevators (Fig. 7-10). However, movement of the rudder pedals causes the moveable surfaces to move independently as shown in Fig. 7-11 to achieve the same effect as a rudder.

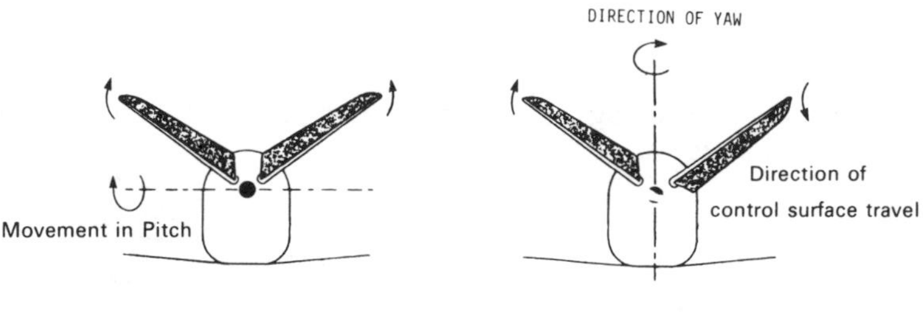

Fig. 7-10 **Fig. 7-11**

In those aircraft which use the flex wing principle the pilot uses a bar or stick attached to the wing as a means of controlling the aircraft in pitch and roll. The fuselage structure which contains the pilot, engine, landing gear, etc. is in effect slung under the wing and can pivot about the aircraft axes. Pitch control is effected by the pilot pulling on the bar, causing the fuselage structure (the Trike) to move forward relative to the wing. This effectively moves the weight forward and causes the aircraft to adopt a lower nose attitude. Pushing on the bar causes the aircraft to adopt a higher nose attitude.

Lateral control is effected by a lateral movement of the bar and a combination of lateral and longitudinal movement of the bar permits simultaneous movements in roll and pitch.

In relation to lateral control, the flexibility of the wing will, to a certain extent, change shape whenever lateral weight shift takes place or the tip draggers are operated. In effect the trailing edges of the wing on both sides of the trike will undergo a tightening or slackening when a bank is induced, this is known as 'billow shift'. In summary, the trailing edge of the rising wing tightens in the fore and aft direction bringing itself a little lower thereby increasing the angle of attack on that side. The opposite effect occurs to the trailing edge of the lowering wing. As a result a greater amount of lift is experienced on the upper wing (outside wing) and a lesser amount of lift is created on the lower wing (inside wing).

Effect of inertia

An aircraft, like all other masses, possesses inertia, it tries to continue on its original path even when the controls are operated to change that path. Thus, when the controls are moved there will be a lapse of time, even after the attitude has altered, before the flight path changes. This time lag will naturally vary with the size of the aircraft, and type of control method. Its importance will vary with the circumstances of flight, for example, when effecting a landing, an appreciation of inertia will be particularly important.

Effect of airspeed

The effectiveness of the flying controls depends on the speed of the airflow passing over the control surfaces.

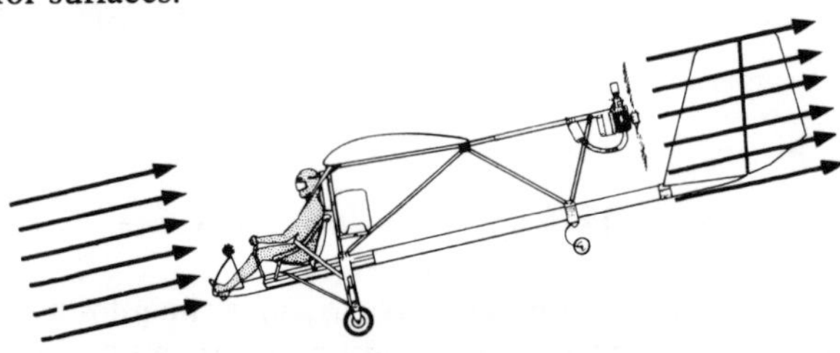

Fig. 7-12 High Airspeed — Strong Airflow More Effective Controls

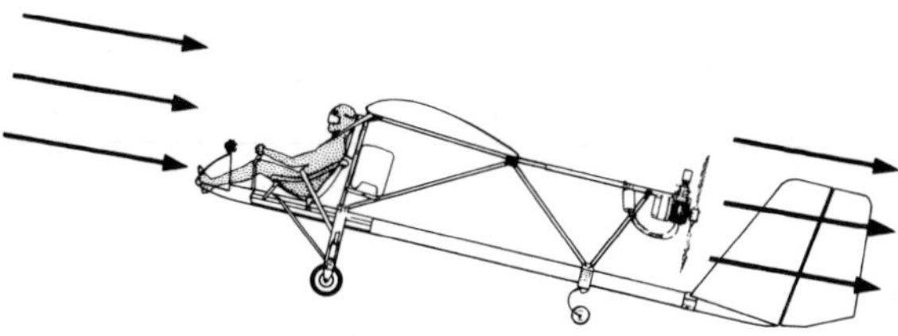

Fig. 7-13 Low Airspeed – Weaker Airflow Less Effective Controls

The greater the airspeed the more effective are the controls. At higher speeds, as well as becoming increasingly effective, the controls tend to become very firm and heavy, whilst at lower speeds they become light and sloppy. With the possible exception of the rudder they usually become ineffective below the landing speed.

From the practical point of view the most important lesson to be learned from the above comments is that airspeed is probably the most important consideration when controlling an aircraft. Without sufficient airspeed the pilot will not be able to control the aircraft in flight.

Effect of slipstream

Slipstream increases the effective airflow over the control surfaces it envelopes, usually the elevators and rudder. Throttling back will therefore reduce the effectiveness of these controls. The ailerons are outside the area of slipstream influence and will remain unaffected by changes in throttle setting. The effect of slipstream is most clearly observed when entering the climb or glide from level flight, and can be most noticeable on some microlight aircraft.

The spiral path of the slipstream as it passes the vertical stabilizer, creates an angle of attack, which in turn produces a horizontal 'lift' or sideways component which tends to yaw the tail as shown in Fig. 7-14. This angle of attack will vary with both RPM and airspeed. The lower the airspeed the tighter the 'coils' of slipstream will be, increasing the angle of attack relative to the vertical stabilizer. This, combined with a reduction in the directional stability of the aircraft at lower airspeeds will cause an increase in the yaw effect from the horizontal force.

At higher airspeeds the slipstream spiral becomes elongated and its angle of attack relative to the vertical stablizer becomes less, resulting in a smaller horizontal 'lift' or sideways force. This, together with the increased directional stability of the aircraft at higher airspeeds causes the horizontal force and its effect upon the aircraft to diminish, and yaw is less pronounced. It can therefore be seen that during normal flight operations the largest yaw effect will occur when the aircraft is climbing.

Fig. 7-14

In Fig. 7-14 the propeller rotation is clockwise as viewed from the cockpit. This causes a slipstream direction which produces a force to cause the nose of the aircraft to yaw.

Effects of power

On propeller driven aircraft, changes in engine power can also effect the directional trim. An increase of power will usually cause a yaw in the opposite direction to the rotation of the propeller. This is particularly noticeable in single engined aircraft due to the slipstream effect on the keel surface, and the changed angle of attack on the vertical stabilizer.

In the case of microlight aeroplanes any pitch changes resulting from engine power will depend upon the position of the thrust line relative to the mean drag line of the aircraft. For example if the thrust line is below the drag line a couple will exist between the thrust and drag forces which will cause the nose of the aircraft to tend to rise (ref. Fig. 7-15). If the drag line is higher than the thrust line the opposite will occur. In some aircraft the effects of power are offset or reduced by the design feature of inclining the thrust line at an angle to the horizontal and or lateral planes.

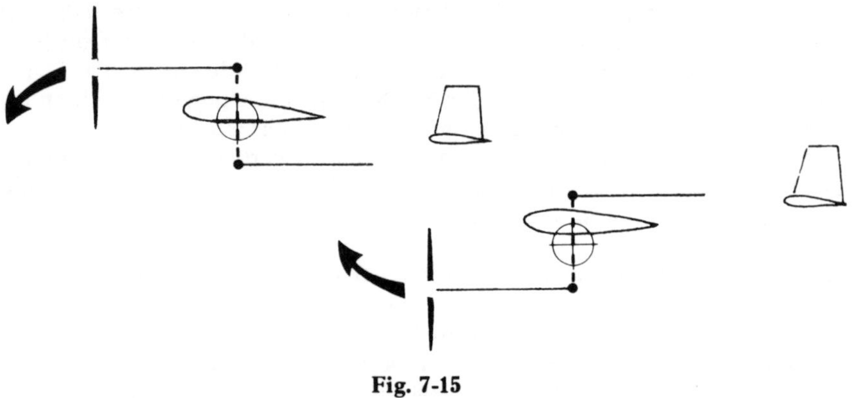

Fig. 7-15

Bear these considerations in mind whenever a power change is made during flight. You should appreciate that changes in power setting can cause changes in the aircraft's attitude in pitch, yaw and roll. The latter being due to the further effect of yaw.

Effects of Trimming Controls

Although very few microlights are equipped with trimming controls they are logically included at this point so that the microlight pilot has a basic idea of their purpose and how they work, should he ever have to use them.

Trimming controls are designed to relieve the pilot of sustained loads on the flying controls. The correct method of use is to select the required attitude by the use of the primary flying controls, and then to adjust the appropriate trimmer until no pressure is needed on the control column or rudder pedals. Changes in trimmer position are normally required after changes in power, speed, and flap setting, and also after a variation of the aircraft's disposable load.

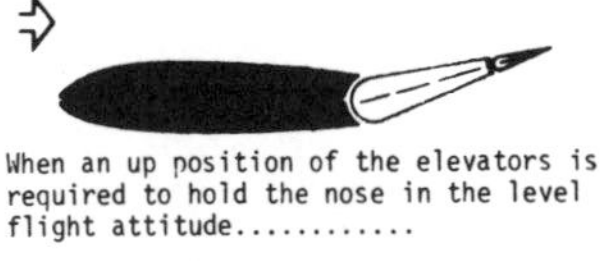

When an up position of the elevators is required to hold the nose in the level flight attitude...........

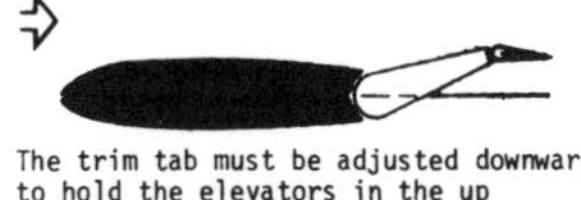

The trim tab must be adjusted downward to hold the elevators in the up position and so relieve the pressure on the control column.

Fig. 7-16

The above illustrations are shown in respect of the type of trimming control used on elevators or stabilators, however the basic principle of operation is the same when used in conjunction with ailerons or rudders.

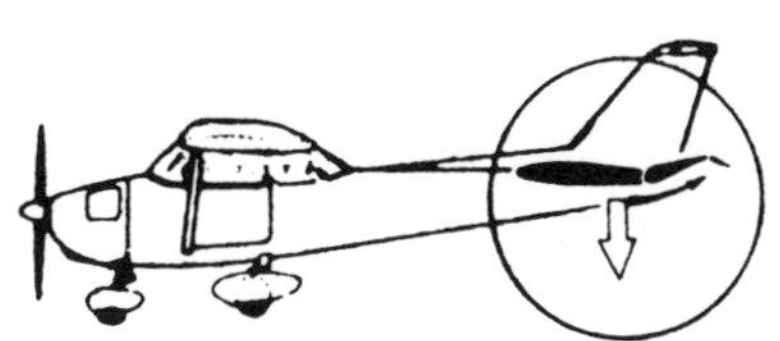

Trimming controls are a great help to the pilot, but as they are powerful and sensitive, they should be used carefully. Mishandling can lead to reduced aircraft performance and may also cause undue stress loads on the airframe. Trimming controls should not be used to relieve control loads of transient nature.

Effects of Flaps

As with trimming controls, there are few microlights which use flaps but an understanding of their purpose is included at this point.

Although many different forms of wing flaps are used on aircraft, they are all designed to vary the lift and/or drag. By increasing the lift, the flaps reduce the stalling speed and so enable the aircraft to fly safely at lower airspeeds. By increasing the drag, and acting as airbrakes, flaps make it necessary to glide at a steeper angle to maintain a given speed.

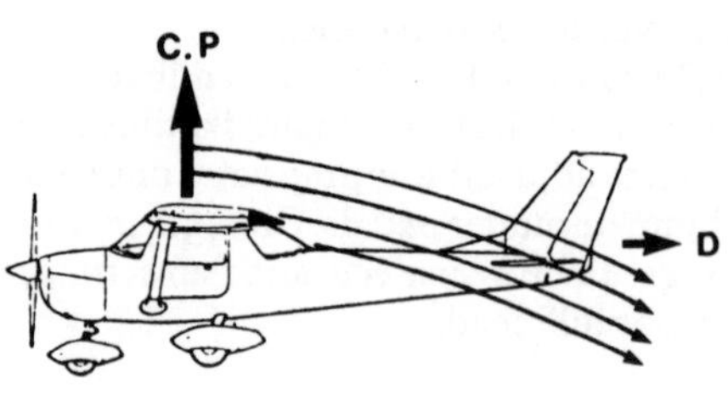

Fig. 7-17 shows the effect of the wing curvature and angle of incidence producing an angle of downwash over the tail surfaces. The Centre of Pressure (CP), and the Drag force (D) in the mean 'drag line' position are also shown.

Fig. 7-17

Fig. 7-18 shows the flaps in the lowered position. When flaps are lowered, they cause a change in the position of the Centre of Pressure, and alter the angle of downwash over the tailplane. The total drag is increased and the drag line lowered. These four major effects usually cause a pitching moment to take place. When the pilot resists this pitch change and holds the aircraft in its original attitude a lower airspeed will result.

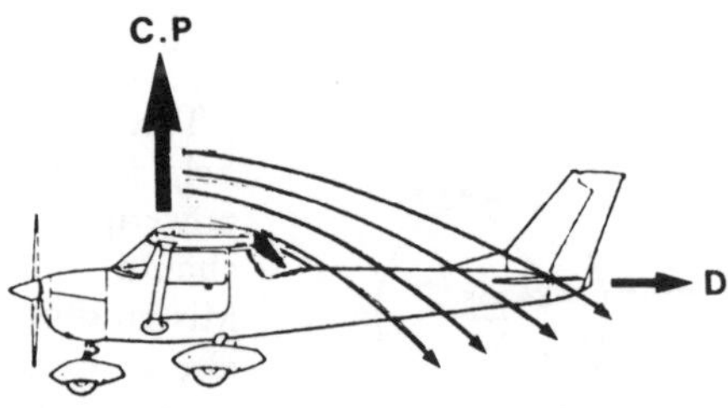

Fig. 7-18

On the majority of modern aircraft, the initial application of flap will increase the lift without causing much increase in the drag. However, a setting which varies with different aircraft will be reached, beyond which the lowering of further flap will start to make a substantial increase in the drag with little further increase in lift. This increase in drag will continue in proportion to the amount of flap lowered, but no appreciable increase in lift will occur after flap angles of about 60 degrees have been reached. The largest change of attitude usually takes place within the first 20 degrees or so of flap application, and may be nose down or nose up in direction, dependent upon the aircraft type.

Air Exercise

Dual Type Aircraft—Following a ground briefing on the control systems applicable to your training aircraft your instructor will demonstrate the movement of the controls (the actions and effects of weight shift in flex wing aircraft) and their effects upon the aircraft attitude in the air.

Following each specific air demonstration you will be given the opportunity to practise these control movements and learn the control forces involved and the rate and degree of aircraft response to the control movements.

Solo Type Aircraft—If you are training on a solo type microlight you will be given a thorough ground briefing on the control methods as applicable to your particular aircraft, and obtain experience of operating them during flight(s) in a conventional light aircraft, and/or through practice gained during towed flights, or short hops.

Performance Objectives
Upon completion of this exercise you should be able to identify and operate the various controls including the throttle and maintain a reasonably constant aircraft attitude.

TAXYING

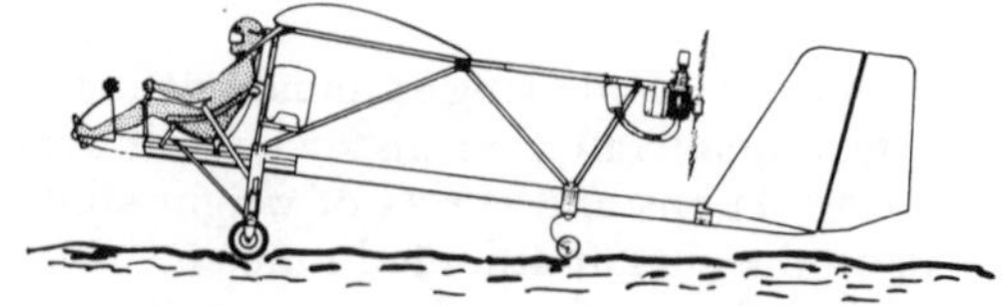

Objectives

During this stage of your training you will learn how to safely control the aircraft whilst manoeuvring on the ground, during which the following items will be covered:

Pre-Taxying Checks, Starting, Control of Speed and Stopping, Engine Handling, Control of Direction and Turning, Effects of Wind, Effects of Ground Surface, Procedures and Precautions to be Applied when Parking, and Marshalling Signals (as applicable).

Introduction

The actual order in which these items are covered will depend upon local circumstances, e.g. whether training in solo or dual type aircraft, and/or operating from grass or hard surfaces such as runways.

The first taxying exercise will nevertheless be concerned with getting the aircraft to move under its own power and controlling its speed and bringing it to a stop.

Pre-Taxying Checks

In areas where training is taking place, space is often limited and it is therefore important to ensure that it is all clear around the aircraft before the aircraft moves. The position of any obstructions and other aircraft should be noted and considerable care should be used when turning. Remember that on some microlights the tailplane is some distance behind the pilot's seat and a pilot who turns his aircraft tightly can easily foul the tailplane on obstructions or other aircraft. The use of power should be the minimum required to prevent the danger of the propeller slipstream damaging other aircraft, and also the inconvenience and danger to bystanders caused by blowing dirt and other material.

When ready to commence taxying open and close the throttle a few times to ensure that the engine is reacting properly and no obvious signs of unserviceability are apparent.

The first thing you will discover is that a microlight aircraft on the ground does not handle as well as a car. This is because it is a vehicle designed for use in the air and its manoevrability on the ground can often be difficult. With practice you will find yourself adapting to the ground handling characteristics of your training aircraft. Taxying techniques will vary slightly between different models of aircraft but the following basic points will generally apply.

More power is required to start the aircraft moving than to keep it moving because of the initial requirement to overcome inertia. You must be continually conscious of the wing span and be careful when manoeuvring in the vicinity of high hedges and trees. Taxying is conducted at relatively slow speeds and because little airflow is passing over the control surfaces the effect of rudder during turning will be small. If a steerable nose or tail wheel is fitted manouevrability will be improved. Some microlights have a steerable nosewheel where the pilot places his feet on the axle extension and when turning to the right will apply forward pressure on his left foot, and vice versa. Other types incorporate rudder pedals which are designed so that pressure on the right foot will turn the aircraft to the right.

Remember when stopping, to close the throttle first before braking with your feet or (when fitted) the aircraft brakes. Be particularly vigilant for the condition of the ground ahead and avoid crossing depressions in the ground at right angles, or the aircraft may tip onto the nose section. When taxying a trike aircraft it should be borne in mind that during a turn the trike section will turn first and a twisting moment will be applied to the wing through the trike/wing connecting assembly. Sudden and severe turning moments can place a large stress on this assembly.

If there is any wind, taxying downwind will cause the aircraft to travel faster and this should be prevented by using less power. When taxying into a wind the power will have to be increased. Taxying crosswind will tend to lift the wing in the direction from which the wind is coming and cause the opposite wing to lower. If the wind effect is strong enough the lower wing could touch the ground and be damaged, so one of your taxying lessons will be concerned with how to avoid this situation.

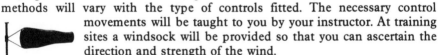

When taxying crosswind there will be a general tendency for the aircraft to line up with the wind and this is called 'weathercock tendency'. The stronger the wind the stronger will be this effect. The flying controls can be used to assist taxying and reduce weathercocking effect but the actual methods will vary with the type of controls fitted. The necessary control movements will be taught to you by your instructor. At training sites a windsock will be provided so that you can ascertain the direction and strength of the wind.

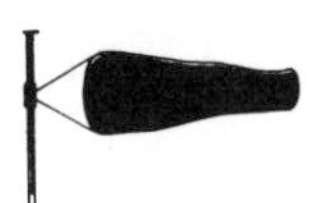

During training you will also learn the types of ground surface which can give you problems when taxying. In relation to parking a microlight it must be appreciated that they are most susceptible to strong winds and particularly to sudden gusts. Therefore it is extremely important to park the aircraft as closely as possible into wind and with chocks placed against the wheels. On those occasions when it will be left unattended, you should whenever possible improvise some form of tie down or anchor to ensure the safety of the aeroplane.

Practical Exercise

Dual Type Aircraft — When learning on a dual type aircraft the various demonstrations which relate to taxying will be introduced gradually from your first training flight onwards.

Solo Type Aircraft — Your knowledge related to the procedures and problems of taxying the aircraft will be obtained through careful briefings by your instructor and a series of practices in controlling the aircraft on the ground.

Performance Objectives
Upon completion of the whole exercise you should be capable of deciding when the wind conditions are not suitable for safe taxying. You must also be competent at controlling the aircraft on the ground in all normal conditions and situations and be aware of the requirements necessary to safeguard the aircraft after parking it.

STRAIGHT AND LEVEL FLIGHT

Objectives

During this lesson you will be given an understanding of how the aircraft is controlled so that a constant altitude, lateral level and direction is achieved. During the air exercise section you will also be consolidating the knowledge and ability gained from previous lessons.

Introduction

Before considering the use of the flying and engine controls to achieve this exercise it would be sensible to review how the forces of lift, weight, thrust and drag act on an aircraft when it is flying straight and level. In addition it would be useful to understand how the designer creates certain inherent characteristics in the aircraft so that the pilot's task is less demanding.

Straight and level flight involves keeping the aircraft laterally level with the altitude and direction constant. The aircraft will be in equilibrium when the lift equals the weight and the thrust equals the drag, this being recognised by the pilot when the airspeed and height remain constant. Accurate straight and level flight is essential for precise flight such as that required for reliable navigation and for obtaining the best performance from the aircraft.

Many variable factors are involved in this flight condition, attitude in pitch and roll, power setting, airspeed, altitude and direction all being important. An alteration to one normally affects the others. For example, an increase in power will produce an increase in airspeed or altitude or a combination of both; a change in attitude may vary height, airspeed and direction; an increase in airspeed will cause a reduction in altitude unless power is increased.

The Forces

In order to maintain a condition of horizontal level flight the lift produced must be equal to the weight of the aircraft (Fig. 7-19).

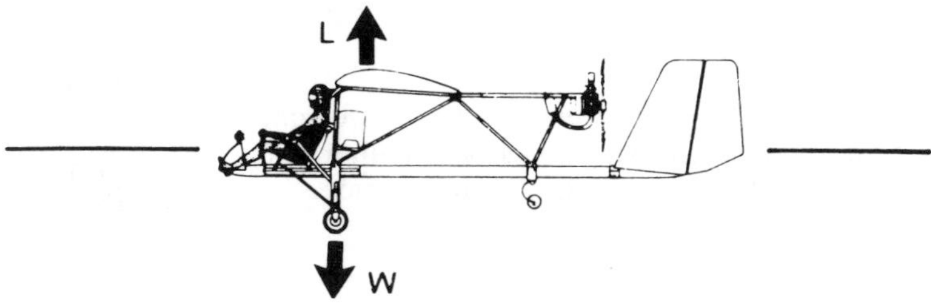

Fig. 7-19

In order to obtain the aircraft's forward movement through the air, thrust is achieved through the use of the engine and propeller. When the speed is constant the thrust will exactly equal the drag produced from all sources, including the aircraft's resistance to the airflow.

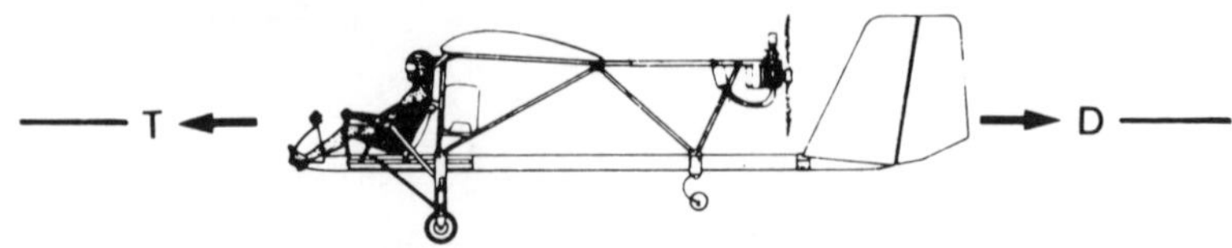

Fig. 7-20

When Lift = Weight and Thrust = Drag, a condition of equilibrium will result and only small control movements and adjustments will need to be made to maintain this condition.

A pilot does not need to have the detailed knowledge required of an aircraft designer but he should nevertheless have a basic understanding of the principles involved in stability and control. These principles will be of practical benefit to any pilot and will assist in his appreciation of those factors involved for example, in the stability about the three axes, control of the aircraft throughout its speed range, and the method of correctly loading passengers and baggage.

All these items are of primary importance to safe flight, and a lack of comprehension of these factors can completely negate the designer's efforts to provide the pilot with a safe and stable aircraft.

In flight the aircraft is controlled about three axes, the lateral (pitching axis), the longitudinal (rolling axis) and the vertical (yawing axis). The aircraft must also have adequate stability to maintain a uniform flight condition and recover from the disturbing influences of rough air. It is also necessary to provide sufficient stability to minimise the workload of the pilot and give proper response to the flying controls throughout the speed and loading range of the aircraft.

Stability in Pitch

Conventional aircraft use a horizontal tailplane to achieve stability about the lateral axis, i.e. stability in pitch. In the case of microlight there are several methods commonly used, these are:

Pendulous Stability — The weight of the pilot, engine etc., situated below the wing acts as a pendulum and helps to keep the wing in a horizontal attitude.

Fig. 7-21

Reflex — This is a built in aerodynamic characteristic of the wing which is based upon a similar principle to the action of a tailplane. For example, if the wing chord shape is arranged so that the angle of attack of the airflow meeting the wing is less at the rear section then a disproportionate increase of lift will occur along the chord of the wing when it is upset in pitch.

When an aircraft is disturbed by a gust, it will take up a different attitude, but due to inertia, it will remain temporarily on its original flight path. Assuming from the diagram below that point 'A' has an angle of incidence of 4° and point 'B' has an angle of incidence of 2° it will be seen that if a gust causes a 2° increase to the angle of attack the lift at point 'A' will momentarily be increased by 50% but at point 'B' it will increase by 100%. This will cause the rear section of the wing to rise and the wing will tend to assume its original attitude in pitch.

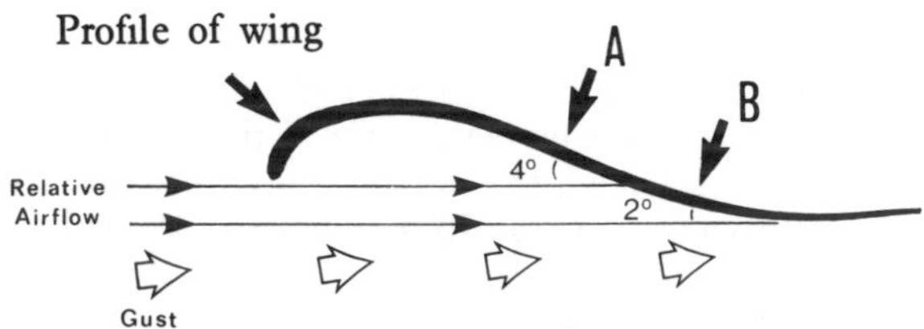

Fig. 7-22

The conventional tailplane works in a similar manner as can be seen by reference to Fig. 7-23.

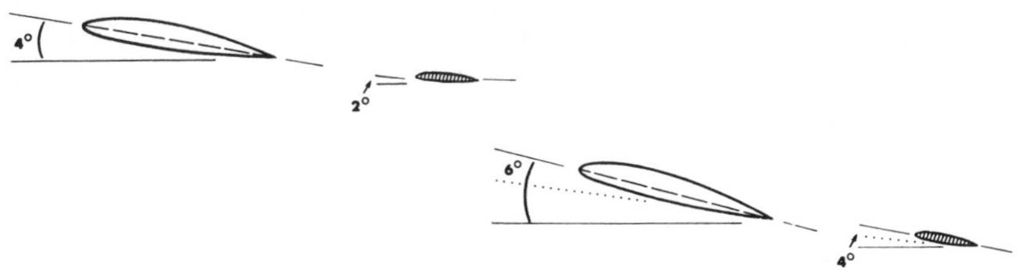

Fig. 7-23

Sweepback in conjunction with Washout — Some microlights have wings which are swept back from the wing root to tip. These are sometimes used to provide an element of stability in pitch. Normally they have a washout feature, which simply means that the angle of incidence is reduced towards the wing tip.

Fig. 7-24

Canard – Some microlights are designed with the horizontal lifting and control surface ahead of the main wing. When this type of configuration is used the forward wing is set at a higher angle of incidence than the main wing. The principle is exactly the same as with a rear mounted stabilizer, i.e. when upset by a gust the proportionate increase in the angle of attack of the main wing will be greater than that of the canard, therefore the increase of lift being greater on the main wing will cause the aircraft to lower its nose and return to the original attitude.

Relationship of Centre Of Gravity to Control In Pitch

All aircraft, including microlights are designed to be longitudinally stable over a very limited Centre of Gravity range. If the Centre of Gravity moves outside these limits, the performance of the aircraft and the pilot's control over it will be affected, in serious cases to the point where the aircraft's attitude could become uncontrollable.

The position of the centre of gravity relative to the stabilizing surface will obviously have to be taken into account when considering the effects of a forward or aft centre of gravity, and the following explanation relates to an aircraft with a conventional rear mounted tailplane. In this case if the aircraft is loaded so that the Centre of Gravity is at its forward limit, a relatively long lever arm between the Centre of Gravity and the tailplane will exist, and the aircraft will be most stable and if disturbed in flight it will quickly return to its original attitude. However, if the forward limit is exceeded, the aircraft will become tiring to manoeuvre in pitch due to its strong longitudinal stability. It can also become uncontrollably nose heavy, particularly at lower airspeeds when elevator control is less effective, as for example, during the landing phase. It is in this situation that full up elevator may not be capable of raising the nose to create a 'round out' prior to touchdown.

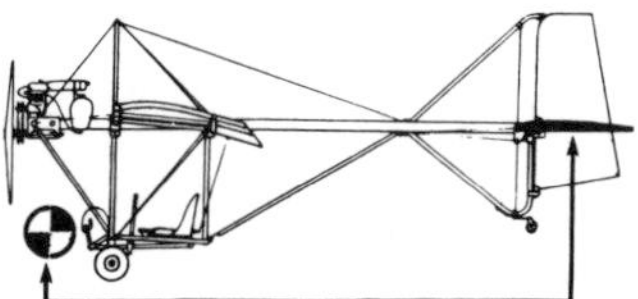
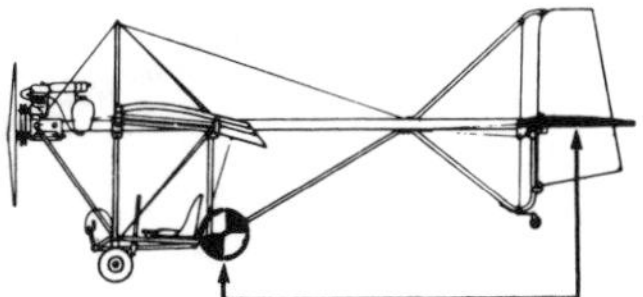

Fig. 7-25

When the Centre of Gravity is moved aft, the tail lever arm is decreased and the degree of longitudinal stability decreases, which means the aircraft will take longer to resume its original attitude when disturbed. If the Centre of Gravity position moves aft beyond a certain point, the aircraft will become uncontrollably tail heavy, the nose will rise and the aircraft will eventually stall. The permitted range of movement and forward and rear limits of the Centre of Gravity position are primarily based upon the effectiveness of weight shift, elevators or the stabilator to control the aircraft in pitch at the lowest possible flight speed.

It can be seen from these considerations that when operating an aircraft, the pilot must ensure the correct procedure for determining the weight and position of the Centre of Gravity is complied with.

Lateral and Directional Stability

As with longitudinal stability, the gusts and irregularities which occur in the atmosphere also affect the attitude of an aircraft both in the lateral and directional sense.

Here, an added complication arises, because any movement about the horizontal plane (rolling) also affects the aircraft in the vertical plane and produces a yawing action. Similarly, any movement about the vertical plane (yawing), will also cause a rolling action.

Therefore, lateral and directional stability are inter-related. However, for simplicity in the explanations which follow, the two types of stability are initially discussed separately following which, their inter-related effects are considered.

Lateral Stability

The lateral stability of an aircraft involves the rolling moments which result from sideslip. A sideslip tends to produce both a rolling and yawing motion, but if a favourable rolling moment can be built into the design, a sideslip will tend to return the aircraft to a laterally level attitude.

The design features which are normally employed in light aircraft design to achieve a favourable rolling moment are, a high wing in relationship to the Centre of Gravity, Geometric Dihedral or a combination of these features.

The high wing arrangement results in a Centre of Gravity below the wing where it therefore acts like a pendulum, the high wing offering a resistance to the airflow and thus becoming a type of pivot about which the Centre of Gravity acts. This effect upon lateral stability is by itself somewhat limited and tends to produce an oscillating motion.

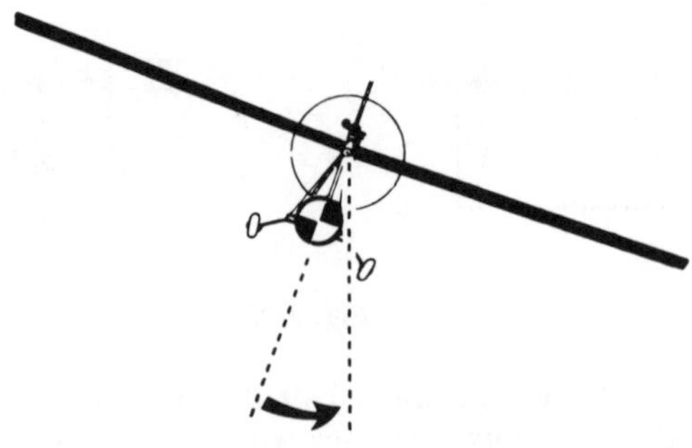

Fig. 7-26

Geometric dihedral however, offers a more positive action, and is accomplished in the following manner. The wings are arranged to produce an angle to the plane of symmetry as shown in Fig. 7-27.

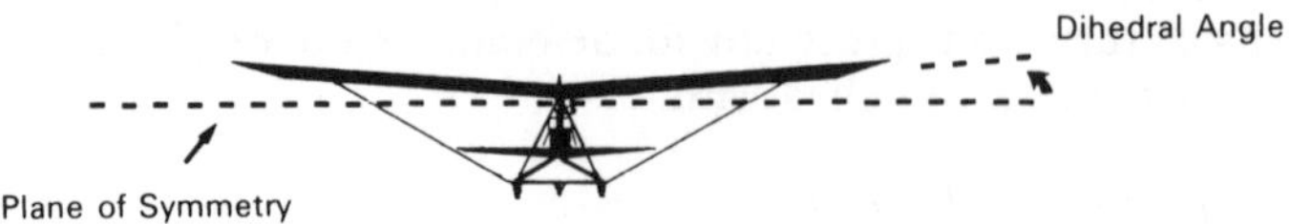

Fig. 7-27

Whenever a wing drops, the aircraft will sideslip in that direction due to the tilted lift line in relation to the weight.

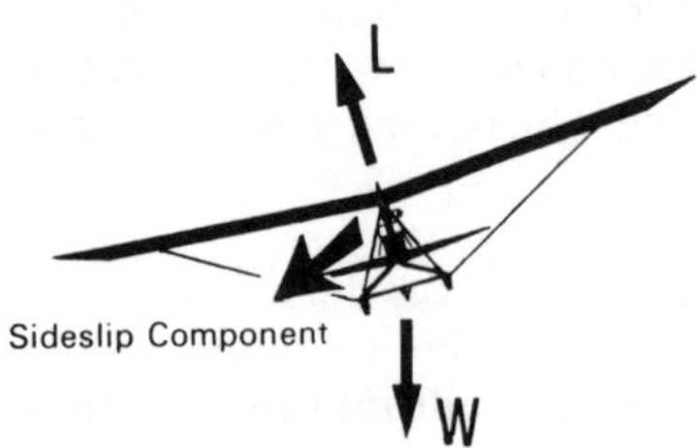

Fig. 7-28

Figure 7-28 illustrates this effect. A sideways component is produced and Lift being inclined, has a shorter vertical component and is no longer sufficient to balance the Weight. The result of this is to cause the aircraft to sideslip in the direction of the lower wing. The effect of sideslip is to change the direction of the relative airflow which now comes from ahead and slightly from one side (Ref. Fig. 7-29).

Fig. 7-29

This produces a greater angle of attack to the lower wing and a smaller angle of attack to the raised wing. The lower wing therefore obtains more lift than the higher wing and a tendency to restore the aircraft back to a laterally level position occurs. In this situation, a minor masking of the airflow occurs on the higher wing due to fuselage interference, but at the small sideslip angles incurred, the effect of such masking can be virtually ignored, unless of course, the aircraft is placed into a positive sideslip by the pilot.

It can be seen from the foregoing, that geometric dihedral has a beneficial effect upon lateral stability, but its actual restoring action is limited due to the fact that if the wing was returned to the laterally level position by the dihedral effect, inertia would cause the rising wing to continue beyond the laterally level position and the opposite wing would drop. This would produce a cycle known as oscillatory instability (commonly called *Dutch Roll*). This is a condition which would make the pilot's task more difficult in relation to the maintenance of lateral level. An aircraft with strong lateral stability would also be more difficult to manoeuvre in roll. The designer will therefore normally limit the dihedral angle to one which will give an aircraft a tendency to resist a rolling motion set up by disturbances of the air.

To sum up, it can be stated that the amount of effective dihedral will vary with the type and purpose of the aircraft. Normally the effective dihedral is kept low since a strong rolling tendency due to sideslip can lead to Dutch Roll, difficult rudder co-ordination in rolling manoeuvres, and excessive demands on lateral stability during crosswind take-offs and landings.

On some microlights which use basic hang glider wings a keel surface is fitted to aid stability in yaw. This 'keel pocket' also aids roll stability to a limited extent. Stability in roll is an inherent feature of well designed microlights, and this is especially so of 'Trikes' where the triangular structure which carries the pilot, engine, fuel etc., is suspended below a typical hang glider wing. In this arrangement the aircraft will be most stable when the pilot holds the control bar firmly because of the natural pendulous stability of this design.

Stability in Yaw

This is more commonly called directional stability which concerns the 'weathercock action' of the aircraft in flight, i.e. movement about the vertical axis. In common with the other types of stability covered previously there are several methods which are used to obtain sufficient directional stability and these will vary in relation to the configuration of the microlight type. For example the wing shape can be arranged to have sweepback and whilst this like other wing shapes will provide an equal amount of lift and drag when the aircraft is in straight flight, a different effect will occur if the aircraft yaws.

Referring to Fig. 7-30 it will be seen that if the aircraft yaws to the right the left wing will present a greater camber and depth of section to the airflow than the right wing. This will cause unequal drag between the two wings and result in a turning force which will tend to return the aircraft to its original path of flight.

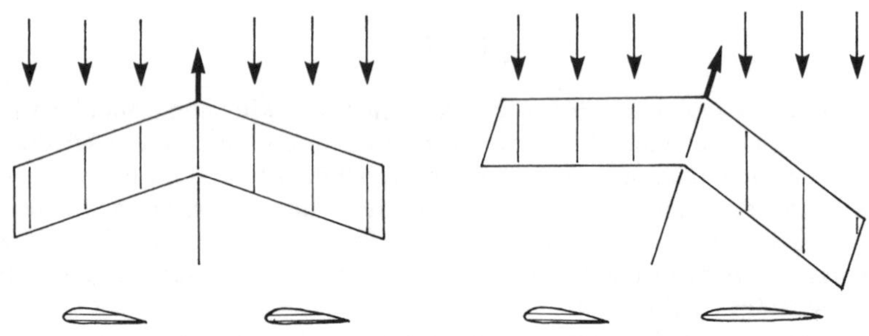

Fig 7-30

Another example of how directional stability can be achieved is in the use of a vertical stabilizer (fin) and when this is positioned at the tail end of the aircraft the fin will experience a change in its angle of attack to the airflow as shown in Fig. 7-31. If the aircraft is disturbed from its original heading the effect of inertia will allow it to continue for a short while along its original flight path, this will produce a relative airflow which results in a horizontal lift force setting up a restoring moment about the Centre of Gravity. This tends to return the aircraft to its original flight path. This corrective action will be increased by the effect of airflow direction upon the side surface of the fuselage behind the Centre of Gravity and the greater this area, the stronger the restoring effect.

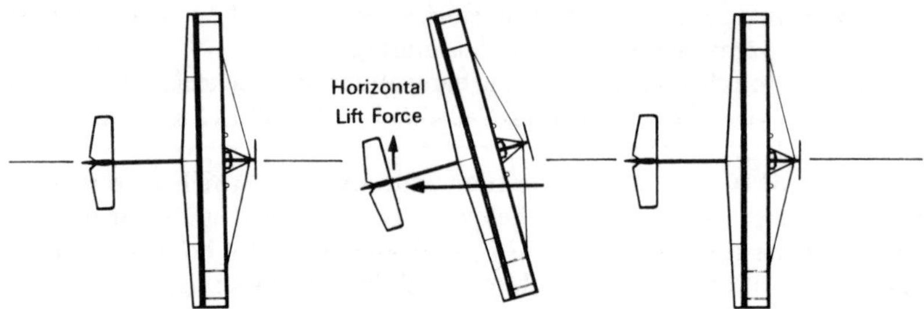

Fig. 7-31

Another method of providing directional stability is through the use of 'tip rudders' positioned above or below the wing tips, Fig. 7-32. They obtain their effect through the variation of horizontal lift and drag forces in a similar manner to that of a vertical fin. Yet another method is the use of keel pockets attached to the main wing which then act rather like a keel surface during flight (Fig. 7-33).

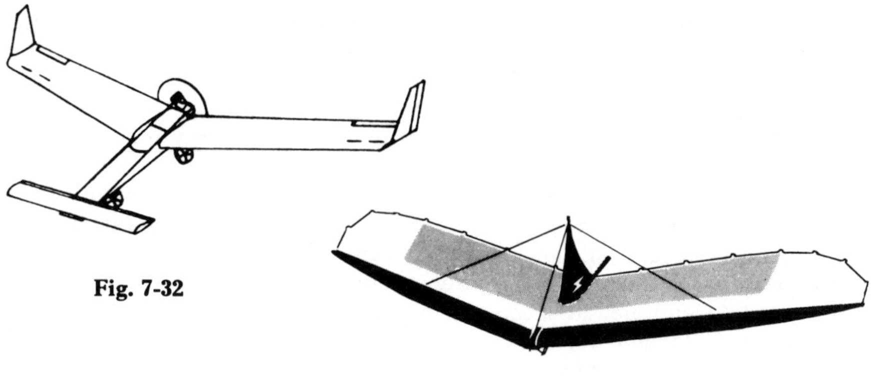

Fig. 7-32

Fig. 7-33

Inter-relationship of Lateral and Directional Stability

As stated at the beginning of this section on stability, there are many inter-related factors affecting the adequate provision of both lateral and directional stability. Due to the conflicting aerodynamic needs of these two stabilities in relation to sideslip and yaw, most aircraft are designed to have a lateral stability which will not overcome the properties of directional stability. This results in the aircraft having a weak spiral divergence, i.e. if a wing should drop, the aircraft will eventually go into a gentle spiral descent unless checked by the pilot. This action is known as spiral instability.

Aircraft Performance and Control

One aspect of an aircraft's performance is its capability to fly at different airspeeds in level flight, though in microlight aircraft this speed range is fairly limited. This range of airspeeds is achieved through a combination of aerodynamic and engine characteristics. The aerodynamic characteristics generally define the power requirement for specific conditions of flight, and the matching of the aerodynamic configuration with the power from the engine will be needed to obtain such performance requirements in terms of airspeed, aircraft range and endurance, and manoeuvres such as climbing, turning and descending.

In order to adopt a specific airspeed and hold a constant height it will be necessary to alter the power setting and the attitude at the same time. In addition to this the use of aileron and rudder (when fitted) will also be required to maintain the aircraft in balanced flight without slip or skid.

When adopting straight and level flight at a different airspeed it should be appreciated that if power is reduced and the aircraft attitude held constant the airspeed will reduce and the aircraft will descend or if power is increased and the attitude held constant the aircraft will climb. Therefore, in order to maintain altitude when changing power the elevators will have to be adjusted at the same time.

Air Exercise

Dual Type Aircraft — Once the aircraft has reached a suitable altitude your instructor will demonstrate how to attain and maintain straight and level flight at a specific power setting. Following which you will be required to practice this exercise on several headings. The use of ground features to assist you in the maintenance of a constant direction will be introduced.

Initially your instructor will maintain a careful watch for other aircraft. During this lesson you will also be introduced to such airmanship items as 'Lookout' and the development of orientation in relation to ground features. The modern concept of lookout is based upon the philosophy of 'See and avoid' and constant vigilance must be maintained at all times when airborne. However Lookout is not only concerned with other aircraft but also where your own aircraft is going in relation to clouds, towns, Controlled Airspace, etc. For example it is not conducive to safety to maintain a good lookout but allow your aircraft to fly so close to cloud that there is insufficient time to take avoiding action should another aircraft suddenly appear.

When you or your instructor report the position of aircraft to each other it is usual to report it by using the 'clock code'. This simply means that if an aircraft is seen directly ahead of your aircraft its position will be at 12 o'clock. Reference to the adjacent diagram shows an aircraft which is in the 3 o'clock position relative to the reporting pilot.

The vertical position of aircraft so sighted are reported by stating whether they are level, high or low. Level simply means that the observed aircraft is at the same altitude as the reporting aircraft.

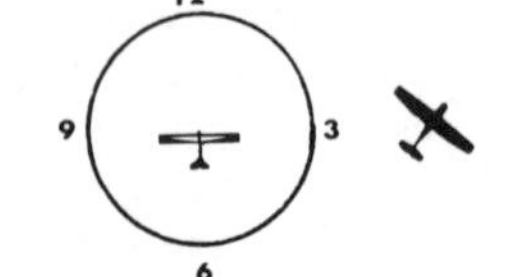

Solo Type Aircraft — The ability to maintain straight and level flight will only be developed through your instructor's briefing backed up by your own practice whilst airborne.

Performance Objectives

Upon completion of this exercise you should be capable of maintaining a reasonably constant altitude and direction together with the ability to keep a good lookout and be aware of your position in relation to your training aerodrome or site.

CLIMBING

Objectives

To teach you how to initiate a climb entry, maintain the climb and finally to return to level flight. A variation of climb entry will be to enter a climb from descending flight and this is practised in preparation for those occasions when it might become necessary to 'go round again' when the aircraft is in a descent on the approach to a landing.

Introduction

Normal climbing flight is achieved by the increase of propulsive energy over and above that which is needed to sustain the aircraft in level flight. Another method of gaining height is by raising the aircraft's nose, utilising airspeed to zoom to a higher altitude, this process in which the associated reduction in speed is converted into height, can only be a temporary one and is extremely limited on microlights due to the low cruising speeds of these aircraft.

Correct climbing flight will be a steady condition which is achieved by increasing power and adopting an aircraft attitude to give the proper climbing speed as recommended for the particular aircraft.

The Forces in the Climb

If the aircraft's path is altered from level to climbing flight the three forces of lift, thrust and drag will have a similar relationship to the flight path as they had in level flight.

However, since the weight will remain acting vertically downwards, there will be a component of the weight acting backwards relative to the aircraft's flight path thus augmenting the drag force.

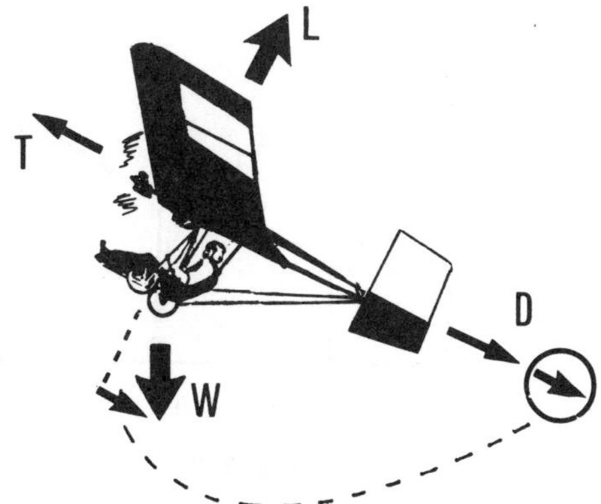

Fig. 7-34

This effect will cause the airspeed to decrease so that both lift and aerodynamic drag are reduced. However, the addition of the weight component along the line of remaining aerodynamic drag causes the total retarding effect to become greater, and in order to keep the forces in balance at a steady airspeed, the thrust must be increased.

When this additional thrust is added it will balance the aerodynamic drag plus the component of the weight, therefore, climbing flight is a steady state process during which additional thrust is used. If a constant airspeed is maintained, a steady gain in height is achieved, and the aircraft will be in equilibrium.

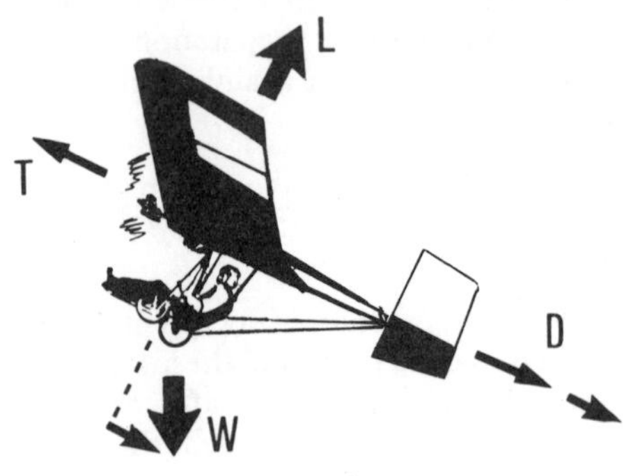

Fig. 7-35

The Relationship of Power an Attitude

In order to consider the relationship of power to the climbing attitude it will be necessary to briefly review the basic drag characteristics of an aeroplane. It should be remembered from the Principles of Flight Section that induced drag increases with increase in angle of attack, i.e. it will be greatest at the lowest speed of flight. However, on the other hand, parasite drag increases with increase of airspeed. This is illustrated in the following diagram where the drag curve shown is a combination of both types of drag.

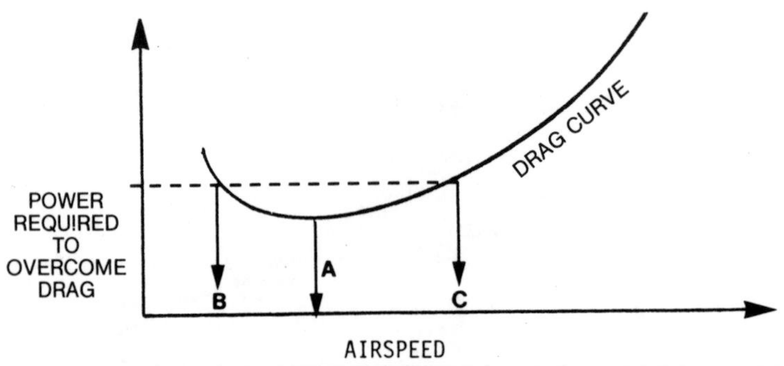

Fig. 7-36

The bottom of a curve A shows the particular aircraft endurance speeed which relates to the minimum power required to maintain the aircraft in level flight. On either side of this curve at B and C it can be seen that for the same power setting two different airspeeds can be achieved. The lower of these speeds will occur with the aircraft flying at a high angle of attack and the higher of these speeds will represent the correct attitude for level flight. Although this variation between aircraft attitudes is quite marked whilst in normal level flight it is far less apparent during climbing.

Therefore during a climb it is important not to get the nose attitude too high, or it will result in a lower airspeed, a reduced or nil rate of climb and a critical control condition which may then lead to the aircraft stalling. These factors illustrate the need to obtain and maintain the correct climbing speed.

Due to the low power of microlight engines there will be only a small amount of excess thrust available for the climb and if the engine should stop during level flight and particularly during the climb the airspeed will reduce very rapidly. Consequently it would be valuable to practise closing the throttle during the climb and lowering the aircraft's nose to maintain the speed. This way you will learn how quickly you must act to avoid a stall occurring should the engine stop when you are climbing.

Effect of Weight

A change in the aircraft weight affects both the angle and the rate of climb. An increase of weight will reduce the maximum rate of climb and (depending upon the shape of the power available and power required curves for a particular aircraft) the optimum rate of climb speed may be higher than when the aircraft is at a lesser weight. Reference to the Owner's Manual for the aircraft type will normally establish the correct climbing speed for the particular all-up weight of the aircraft.

Effect of Flaps on climbing

Although few microlights are fitted with flap systems the following information relating to the use of flaps may be of general interest.

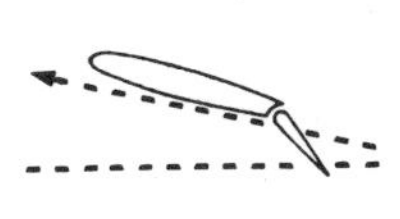

For a given speed the selection of optimum lift flap will give added lift with only a small increase of drag. Therefore it is possible to obtain the original amount of lift at a lower airspeed. At this lower airspeed the total aerodynamic drag may be less, and if this were the case in a particular aircraft the power required for level flight at this lower airspeed would also be less, resulting in more power being available for the climb. This would mean that there would be more thrust available to act against the aircraft weight, and as a result the aircraft would climb at a steeper angle. The rate of climb however is a function of both angle and airpseed and because of the lower airspeed with flaps down the rate of climb will usually be reduced.

Therefore at normal cruising heights there is no advantage in climbing with partial flap, but when flying near the ground, particularly after take-off, a steeper angle of climb may be of importance in clearing obstructions. Provided it is beneficial to use flaps in this situation (the Owner's Manual will indicate this) their use will normally be of value, provided a lower climbing speed is used. Following such a take-off and when a safe height and speed have been reached the flaps should be raised and a normal climb adopted.

When the flaps are lowered beyond the optimum setting for maximum lift, a considerable increase in drag occurs which needs more thrust to balance it. Therefore the amount of thrust available to act against weight becomes less and it is no longer possible to maintain the steep angle of climb. Thus it is wrong to climb with a flap setting greater than the optimum. At times when a climb must be started with this amount of flap down, as when 'going round again' following a mislanding, the flaps should be raised to the optimum setting as soon as a safe airspeed has been attained.

Effect of Temperature and Density

The power delivered from a piston engine will be dependent upon the weight of the fuel/air mixture taken into the cylinders during any particular operating condition.

The amount of air entering the engine will be determined by the size of the volume induced and the density of the air. The volume induced is related to the size of the carburettor system and the position of the throttle butterfly. The density which relates to the weight of charge is determined by the atmospheric pressure and temperature.

Since air density decreases with altitude, engine power will also decrease with altitude. The density of the fuel/air mixture will also vary with temperature and humidity in that the higher the temperature, and the greater the water content in the atmosphere, the lower will be the density.

This second statement is not always easily understood, as at first sight, it would appear that water being heavier than air would increase the density. A simple explanation of this apparent paradox can be related to engine power output, by considering the fact that when water vapour, which is less dense than air is held in a parcel of air of a given volume, there will be less room for the air particles. Since fuel flow rate is determined by the volume of air passing through the carburettor throat, this means that when water is present, the weight of the fuel/air mixture will be less, and therefore the engine will deliver less power.

Although the effect of an increase in humidity alone in relation to power output is quite small, in certain circumstances it could become significant.

e.g. taking off when heavily laden from a small airfield in conditions of little wind and high temperature.

The combined effects of temperature and air pressure upon air density are reflected in the effect of altitude upon the power needed, and the power available, at any aircraft configuration and airspeed.

Microlight aircraft are equipped with normally aspirated engines (non-supercharged) and therefore the maximum power available will vary directly with air density and will therefore commence to decrease from sea level upwards.

Air Exercise

Dual Type Aircraft

Entering and Maintaining the Normal Climb

Once the Airmanship considerations of Lookout, the direction of climb in relation to controlled airspace, the vicinity of cloud and the selection of a reference feature for maintenance of heading have been completed, the aircraft is placed in the climb by the following method:

Climb Entry

Power – Full power is selected whilst carefully keeping the wings level and the direction constant.

Attitude – The pitch attitude should be raised to the approximate climbing position and then held steady until the airspeed settles to a constant figure. If the airspeed is too high or too low the pitch attitude will have to be adjusted as necessary.

The correct climbing attitude with the wings level and the heading constant is maintained by the normal control actions as used during the maintenance of straight and level flight.

The aircraft is returned to straight and level flight by the following method:

Attitude – The attitude in pitch is decreased to the approximate position required for level flight at cruising power and held in this position.

Power – When the airspeed has increased to that required for level flight the cruising power can be selected. In the same way as for the climb entry the wings should be held level and the heading kept constant. If an altimeter is fitted, then at this stage cross reference can be made between the altimeter and the pitch attitude. If the altitude is not being maintained the attitude in pitch should be adjusted accordingly.

Airmanship

As with any other flight manoeuvre Lookout will be of primary importance both before and during the climb. A careful lookout must be made around the aircraft and particularly up ahead and to either side of the intended climbing path. The climb must not be commenced until it has been established that the climbing path is clear of other aircraft, cloud and controlled or other special airspace.

It is also during this flight and those which follow, that the rules of avoiding other aircraft can be applied when necessary, and in the case of converging or approaching head-on to other aircraft, a simple memory guide such as 'on the right in the right' will be found useful and will act as a quick reminder for taking decisions regarding the right of way rules for aircraft avoidance.

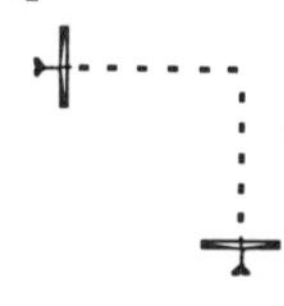

During the climb the engine is normally being operated at full power and it is a good practice to check the cylinder head temperature at more frequent intervals than when in normal cruising flight.

Once the aircraft has left the airfield traffic area the altimeter should normally be re-set to the Area QNH in order to obtain altitude information in relation to the terrain over which the aircraft is flying. Depending upon local circumstances and the type of terrain your instructor may decide to remain on the QFE setting. When operating outside Controlled Airspace and above 3,000ft amsl it is often advisable to set the altimeter datum to 1013 mb, however during practice of manoeuvres in the local area of the landing site it is usually more convenient to use the QFE or QNH as in these circumstances the aircraft will rarely be maintaining a constant heading for more than a few minutes at a time, and this will naturally restrict the application of the 'Quadrantal Rule'.

Solo Type Aircraft—When training on a single seat aircraft you will be faced with the climbing manouevre immediately you leave the ground following take-off. You will therefore need to know that once airborne you should lower the nose slightly to gain and maintain the correct climbing speed. This action is partially necessary due to the influence of 'ground effect'. To sum up the action of ground effect it can be stated that the drag on the aircraft is reduced whilst the aircraft is close to the surface, however as the aircraft rises more than a few feet above the ground the drag begins to increase to its free air value tending to reduce the airspeed. A slight lowering of the aircraft's nose once safely airborne will counteract this tendency to lose speed.

Normally you will have undertaken a number of tows or short hops before being faced with a proper climb and before you have to practice this exercise you will have had the necessary briefing from your instructor.

Performance Objectives

Upon completion of this training exercise you should be capable of entering and maintaining the climb followed by levelling off, whilst at the same time keeping the wings level and heading constant. You will also need to be able to apply the rules of airmanship and be aware of your position relative to the landing site.

DESCENDING

Objectives

The purpose of this exercise is to teach you the principles involved in changing from level flight to a descent. The contents of the practical exercise will include the two normal methods of descending an aircraft, i.e. gliding and descending with power.

You will also be taught to enter the climb from descending flight in preparation for those occasions when it might become necessary to 'go round again' during an approach to a landing.

Introduction

There are two practical ways of descending the aircraft, one is to close the throttle completely and glide, the other is to partially close the throttle and carry out a power assisted descent. In a glide descent the pilot flies the aircraft at the appropriate gliding speed and accepts whatever rate of descent this produces, but in the powered descent the pilot can select an airspeed and rate of descent compatible with his requirements.

The Forces in the Descent

By now it will be appreciated that once an aircraft becomes airborne and regardless of its flight path, there is but one force — weight (defined as the product of the aircraft's mass and acceleration of gravity) which always acts in the same direction i.e. straight down, and the geometry of the forces acting on the aircraft is dependent upon this factor.

Therefore, if the aircraft is placed in a nose down attitude i.e. as in a normal descent, the component of weight in the direction to the flight path will automatically augment the thrust. The aircraft will accelerate and lift and drag will change. In this case, to achieve a balanced condition with a constant airspeed, the thrust must be reduced.

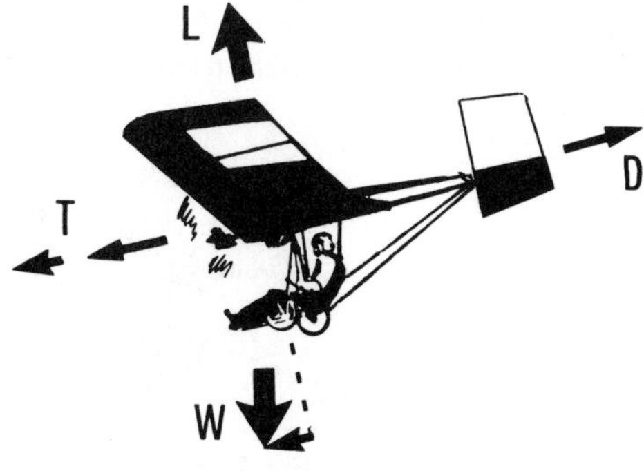

Fig. 7-37

Once the thrust is reduced to the correct value and the angle of the descent path established, the aircraft's speed and rate of descent will be constant and a condition of equilibrium will have been achieved.

If the aircraft is placed in a glide (a condition of no engine thrust) at constant airspeed, the aircraft's descent path will become steeper until the component of weight acting forwards along the flight path totally substitutes for the engine thrust.

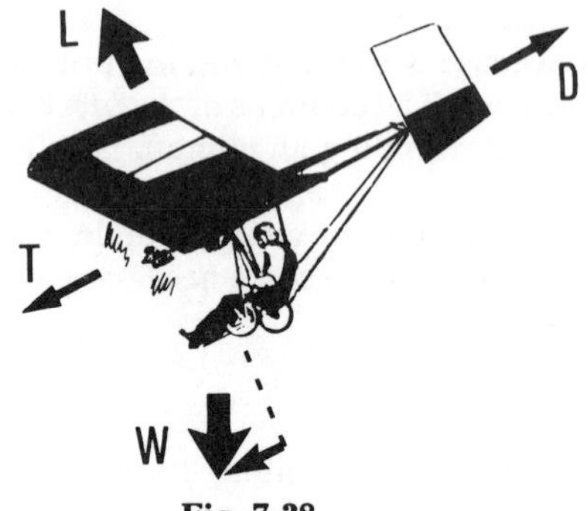

Fig. 7-38

The steeper the angle of glide, the greater will be the forward component of weight and therefore the greater the airspeed. The forces will still remain in balance, with lift balancing the component of weight perpendicular to the flight path, and the forward component of the weight parallel to the flight path acting as 'thrust', balancing the drag.

When the aircraft is flown at an angle of attack which gives the best lift/drag ratio it will glide the furthest distance. This angle of attack is related to airspeed and your Owner's Manual will normally give the best airspeed for the gliding situation.

Due to the shape of the drag curves of most microlight aircraft small deviations from the best lift/drag ratio speed will not cause a significant change in the glide angle. Flight at airspeeds greatly above or below the speed which coincides with the best lift/drag ratio will however result in a shorter distance travelled, therefore any attempt to stretch the glide by changing the speed will result in a shorter gliding distance. For example, any reduction of airspeed below that which gives the best lift/drag ratio will reduce the rate of descent but the reduction in descent rate will not be proportional to the reduction in airspeed and as a result the range of the glide will be reduced.

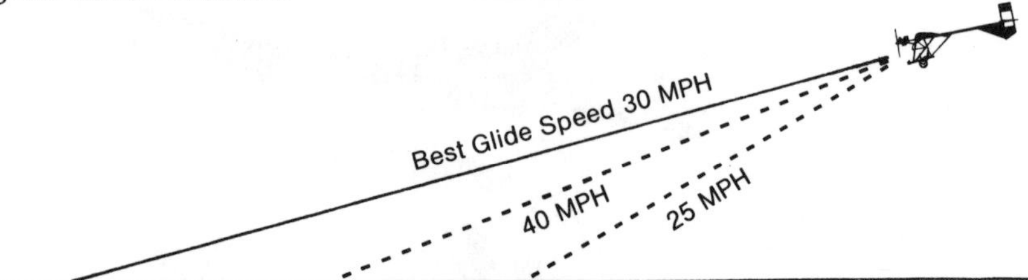

Fig. 7-39

Any increase of airspeed above the best range glide speed will also result in a reduction of distance travelled for height lost and the greater the increase in speed the lesser will be the distance travelled. A rough proportional indication of the effect of increasing or decreasing speed relative to the reduction in distance travelled is shown in Fig. 7-39.

Minimum Sink Speed
Although a lower airspeed will give less range in the glide it will also give a lower sink rate and although the practical use of a minimum rate of descent glide is limited, it could clearly be of value if it is required to extend airborne time while attempting to correct an engine malfunction. The minimum rate of descent glide will normally only be of value provided the reduction in distance travelled does not detract from the safety of planning for an arrival over a suitable area to carry out a forced landing. It could however be of some advantage when over the sea and out of range of land, or over mountainous areas where time airborne may be of more importance than distance.

Flight at the minimum sink speed will in the case of a light aircraft reduce the normal rate of descent by about 25%, the exact amount depending upon aerodynamic design features. Typical minimum descents speeds will be approximately 80% of the best gliding speeds for range.

Effect of Wind
Wind will have the same effect on gliding performance in relation to distance travelled as it does during normal cruising flight. That is to say, a headwind will reduce the gliding range and a tailwind will increase it (see Fig. 7-40).

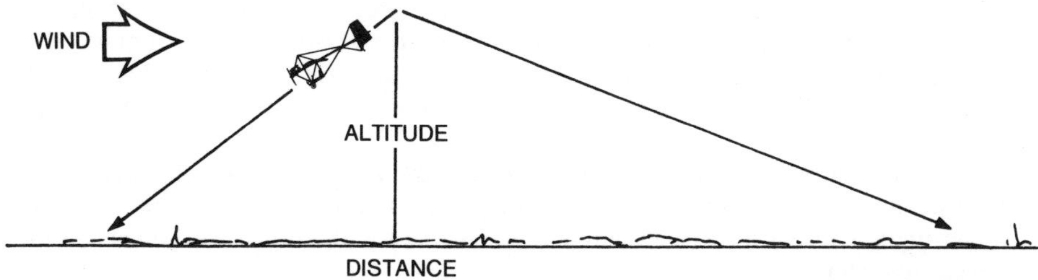

Fig. 7-40

In principle this means that it would be advantageous to decrease the gliding speed when a tailwind exists and increase the gliding speed when flying into a headwind. These actions should increase the proportion of ground distance covered to the altitude lost. However from a practical viewpoint there will be little advantage gained unless starting from a reasonably high altitude or operating in a very strong headwind or tailwind. Further, such changes in the gliding speed will not be very effective unless the wind strength is at least some 25% of the normal range glide speed.

Effect of Weight
Provided an aircraft is flown at the angle of attack which gives the best Lift/Drag ratio the actual weight will not effect its gliding range. The best gliding speed will however be affected in that the heavier the aircraft the greater must be its speed along the flight path.

To sum up therefore, the aircraft forces will remain in equilibrium and the effect of an increase in weight will be for the aircraft (in still air) to arrive at the ground sooner but the actual distance covered will be unchanged.

In practical terms a 10% increase in all-up weight will require a 5% increase in glide speed to maintain the angle of attack at the best Lift/Drag ratio. Gliding speeds quoted in aircraft manuals are normally based upon the aircraft's all-up weight. However with light single engined aircraft the variation in weight carried is fairly small, further to this, small deviations from the best Lift/Drag ratio will not significantly effect the glide performance and therefore in the practical sense a single value of glide speed can normally be specified and used.

Engine Considerations

During gliding the engine should be opened up at intervals for a variety of reasons as follows:

1. Although engines are designed to withstand extremes of heat or cold, it is poor operating practice to allow large variations of temperature to occur. Such temperature changes increase the onset of metal fatigue to both the moving and fixed parts.
2. Prolonged cooling of the engine results in the oil becoming very cold, a condition which reduces its capability to lubricate effectively.
3. When the throttle of a cold engine is suddenly opened a condition of imperfect vaporisation of the fuel/air mixture can easily occur which will result in uneven firing, power loss and sometimes a complete engine stoppage.
4. Although modern engines are not prone to oiling up plugs, all engines can suffer from plug fouling as a result of the carbon deposits produced from the burning of fuel. Whilst this is avoided during ground operations by maintaining the correct idling power it should be borne in mind that when an aircraft is gliding the cooling airflow over the engine is considerable and therefore cooler burning occurs leading to a higher possibility of plug fouling.

Certain engines are prone to carburettor icing and during the glide the usual symptoms of this condition, e.g. loss of power or rough running are not easily identified, even with engines which are equipped with some form of carburettor heating system.

The action of opening the throttle to the half way position for a few seconds at periodic intervals during the descent, will ensure that the engine and oil supply are kept reasonably warm and that imperfect vaporisation does not occur. Also the problems associated with failure to recognise or prevent carburettor icing and plug fouling will be avoided.

Attention should also be given to monitoring the cylinder head temperature gauge. Most aircraft manuals recommend optimum, minimum and maximum temperatures and indications to this effect are suitably marked on the cylinder head temperature gauge.

Effect of Flaps

When conventional flaps are fitted they can be used to increase the drag and steepen the descent path without any need to increase the airspeed. Normally they will also permit the pilot to approach for a landing at a steeper angle giving a better clearance over any obstacles on the approach) and reduce the float period during the hold off prior to landing. In addition, the use of flaps will enable a pilot to obtain a better forward visibility along the approach path in the case of a microlight which has a low mounted engine in front of the pilot. Conventional flaps also serve to reduce the stalling speed, but the same cannot be said of spoilers.

The Power Assisted Descent

The powered descent is basically used when a particular rate of descent at a selected airspeed is required. In this flight condition the airspeed is controlled by the elevators and the rate of descent by the throttle. The forces acting on the aircraft will be similar to those during the glide but the component of weight which acts forward along the flight path is supplemented by the amount of engine thrust selected. This additional thrust would result in the aircraft increasing its airspeed along the original flight path, but if the elevators are used to maintain the airspeed at the original figure the flight path will be shallower and the descent rate less.

In a powered descent at a constant airspeed the addition of power will require the nose to be raised slightly in order to maintain the speed and a reduction of power will require that the nose be lowered slightly to maintain the speed.

Air Exercise

Dual Type Aircraft

Entering and Maintaining the Glide

Once the Airmanship considerations of lookout have been completed, the aircraft is placed in the glide by the following method:

Glide Entry

Power — The throttle should be closed whilst keeping the wings level and the heading constant.

Attitude — When closing the throttle the pitch attitude should be lowered and held in the approximate gliding position.

Note: In microlights fitted with tailplane control surfaces the action of reducing power or closing the throttle completely, as in the glide, can reduce their effectiveness significantly.

The aircraft is returned to straight and level flight by the following method:

Power — Select cruising or higher power as required whilst keeping the wings level and the heading constant.

Attitude — As power is applied the pitch attitude should be adjusted to that required for level flight.

During a power assisted descent, power should be reduced and the pitch attitude adjusted to give the required airspeed. If the descent rate which follows these actions is insufficient, reduce the power slightly whilst lowering the pitch attitude to maintain the airspeed. Continued adjustments to power and attitude should be made until the aircraft is descending at the desired rate.

Airmanship

Prior to and during the descent the necessity for a good lookout retains its high degree of importance. Bear in mind that unlike climbing it is generally more difficult to spot aircraft lower down against the background of the earth's surface and greater care must therefore be exercised.

Lookout is not just a word to be remembered. It includes many things, for example, it is a positive action which must become instinctive and as such will require personal effort and practice to achieve, it also means the development of scanning techniques which will enable the pilot to direct his lookout into the right area at the right time.

All aircraft have inherent design features which restrict vision and these blind spots extend to infinity. Pilots must therefore adapt their lookout techniques to overcome this problem whenever possible.

Pilots must lookout in all directions within their field of view and periodically scan the entire viewing field. The most effective technique is for the pilot to systematically sweep his eyes over the entire visible region and increase the visual field by head and body movements and when this is insufficient the aircraft heading should be temporarily changed.

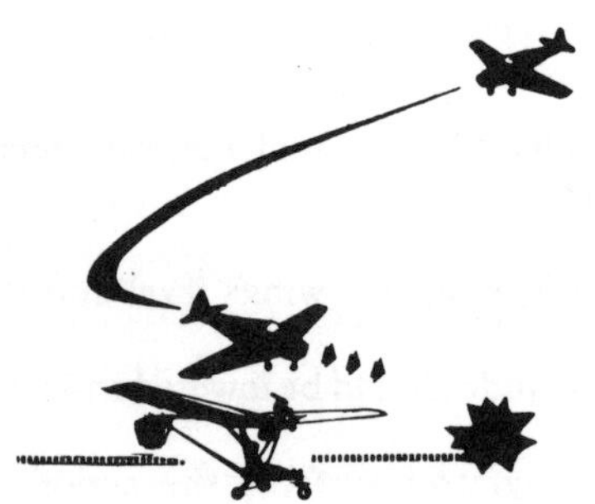

Descending is probably most commonly employed in the vicinity of an airfield and bearing in mind that statistics reveal that 80% or so of all mid air collisions occur within the traffic pattern area, the importance of lookout increases even more whenever the aircraft is operating adjacent to or within this area.

Solo Type Aircraft — The ability to descend safely will be a necessary part of your first solo circuit of the take off and landing site. You will be briefed in detail by your instructor and must ensure that you have understood the exact procedure and control actions required to control the aircraft throughout this flight manoeuvre.

Performance Objectives

Upon completion of this training exercise you should be capable of entering and maintaining both glide and power assisted descents and returning to level flight. During these changes of flight condition you must also be able to keep the wings level and maintain a constant heading. The development of a continuous lookout and awareness of the aircraft's position is an inherent part of these objectives.

BASIC TURNING

Objectives

The primary purpose of this exercise is to teach you how to carry out a controlled manoeuvre to effect a change in the aircraft heading. Initially you will be given an understanding of the principles and then taught how to achieve a turn whilst maintaining a constant height. Later you will be taught to turn the aircraft during climbing and descending flight.

Introduction

The co-ordination and timing of control movements to achieve and maintain the required attitude in pitch and bank whilst changing aircraft heading will require much practice. You will also find that turning will present a significant increase in your workload, and care will have to be taken to avoid deterioration in your standard of lookout.

By the time this exercise is introduced your instructor will be encouraging you to analyse your own mistakes and correct your own errors without waiting for directions from him.

The Forces in the Turn

During steady straight and level flight, the total lift produced equals the aircraft weight and a state of balance exists between the lift and weight forces. However, in order to produce a steady co-ordinated turn at constant altitude, a force must be present which acts towards the centre of the turn.

This force is produced by banking the aircraft and tilting the lift force. This effectively produces two components of lift at right angles to each other. One acting into the direction of turn and supplying a turning force, and the other acting upwards to support the aircraft weight.

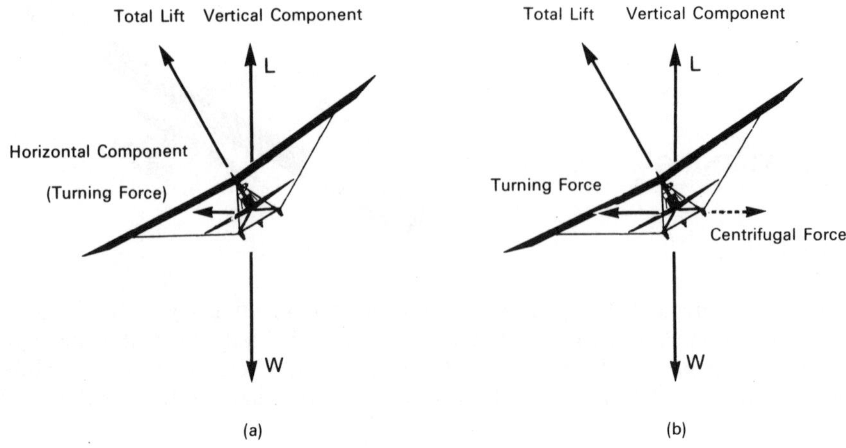

Fig. 7-41

Referring to Fig. 7-41 (a) shows the relationship of the forces on an aircraft during normal banked turning flight. It can be seen that the lift which acts at 90° to the wing is inclined at an angle to the vertical, and by resolving this into a parallelogram of forces, a horizontal component of the total lift produces the sideways, i.e. the centripetal, force which causes the aircraft to turn.

It is often convenient to refer to a centrifugal force rather than speak of the centripetal acceleration associated with curved motion. This is an apparent force, directed outward from the centre, and which the curved motion appears to exert in order to balance the forces producing the centripetal acceleration. Employing the concept of centrifugal force, the force diagram becomes as shown in Fig. 7-41 (b).

However, by banking the aircraft, and tilting the lift line, the amount of lift which was balancing the weight is decreased as shown in Fig. 7-42 (b). Therefore, either the angle of attack or airspeed will have to be increased to extend the lift line as shown in Fig. 7-42 (c).

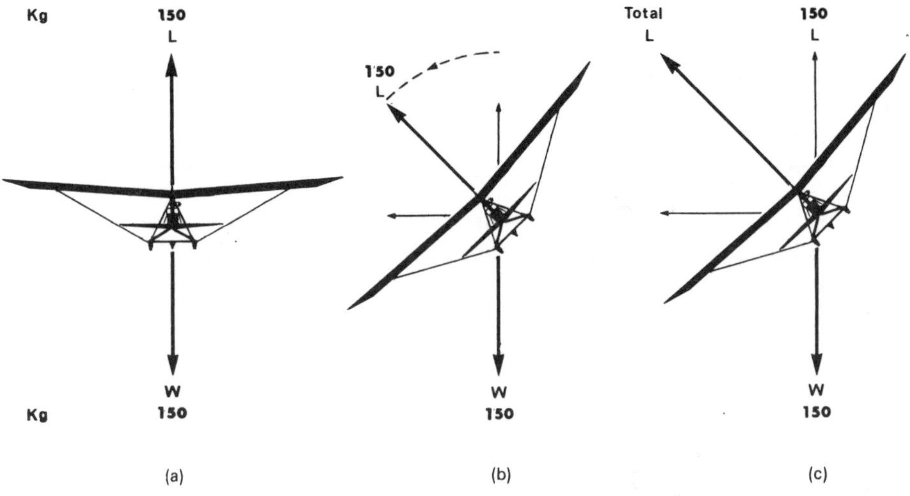

Fig. 7-42

In practice, the simplest method is to increase the angle of attack to achieve the required increase of lift so that constant altitude is maintained. Since increasing the angle of attack will also increase the induced drag, therefore, additional power will have to be used if the airspeed is to be maintained at the same figure, as for straight and level flight.

For shallow angles of bank, the small loss of airspeed from the slightly increased induced drag is acceptable and power need not be increased, but at steeper bank angles, the lift line is further inclined and significantly larger angles of attack are required with corresponding larger increases in drag. This must be overcome by a positive increase in power, otherwise, the airspeed will be substantially reduced leading to a significant loss of lift.

The following table illustrates how the effect of bank angle (when constant altitude is maintained) increases the induced drag.

Bank Angle Degrees	*Per Cent Increase in Induced Drag*
15	7.2
30	33.3
45	100.0
60	300.0

Use of Controls (3 Axis Control Aircraft)

Application of bank is achieved by using the ailerons to roll the aircraft to the desired bank angle. The rate at which the aircraft rolls is controlled by the amount of aileron deflection and the steepness of the bank is controlled by the length of time the ailerons are deflected. When the required angle of bank is reached the ailerons are returned to the neutral position and thereafter used to monitor the bank angle. On some microlights it may be advisable to increase the airspeed slightly before entering the turn.

It will be appreciated from the knowledge gained during the exercise 'Effect of Controls' that whenever an aircraft is banked there will initially be an adverse yaw, i.e. a yaw in the direction opposite to the applied bank. Yaw is prevented by the use of rudder and therefore whenever a turn is initiated the simultaneous use of aileron and rudder will be required to keep the aircraft in a condition of balanced flight. The rudder in this case will be used into the direction of the turn, that is, if a left turn is required the control column will be moved to the left and at the same time sufficient pressure must be applied to the left rudder pedal to maintain the aircraft in a balanced condition.

Once the aircraft is in a banking attitude there will be a tendency for it to slip sideways and also to drop the nose. This sideslipping tendency can be partially counteracted by applying back pressure to the control column which will increase the angle of attack and produce more lift. This action will in turn compensate for the effect of tilting the lift line as the aircraft is rolled into a banked attitude. The use of the elevators during the entry and throughout the turn will need to be sufficient to produce the increased angle of attack to provide the added lift which is needed for level flight to be maintained.

In conventional aircraft a balance indicator is fitted so that the pilot can determine whether the aircraft is slipping or skidding in the turn, however such instruments are rarely used in microlights and the pilot will have to assess the balance of the turn through the seat of the pants. When a well co-ordinated turn is being carried out the pilot will feel no sensation of slip or skid and with practice this simple recognition feature of the turn quality will be developed.

If the aircraft is felt to be slipping inwards during the turn the angle of bank should be decreased slightly if the aircraft is felt to be skidding outwards the angle of bank should be increased slightly. Rudder should also be used to correct either of these situations and when used it should be co-ordinated with the use of ailerons. For example slightly increasing pressure on the left rudder when the aircraft is slipping inwards to the left will assist to bring the aircraft back to the balanced condition, but as the further effect of rudder is to induce bank you will need to co-ordinate this action with the use of aileron to combat any increase in bank.

If the aircraft is skidding out to the right applying right rudder and increasing the bank angle with the ailerons will bring the aircraft back into a state of balance.

In the case of weight shift and 2 axis control aircraft the control of slipping or skidding as well as bank will be more limited. Raising the nose slightly to combat a slip and lowering it slightly to overcome a skid can nevertheless produce reasonably well executed turns. However it must be borne in mind that pitching up to combat a slip must be done with care as pitching the nose up too much can easily lead to a stall situation developing.

On the other hand lowering the nose too much to reduce a skid can lead to height being lost. Therefore whatever method of controlling bank is used it must be co-ordinated with the necessary pitching actions.

Use of Power

It has already been stated that in order to maintain a constant height during a turn it will be necessary to increase the total lift force by increasing the angle of attack. However an increased angle of attack will lead to an increase in the induced drag and if power is not increased to overcome this, a reduction in airspeed will occur. This would normally be an adverse situation as reduction in airspeed will lead to a reduction in lift which in turn will require a further increase in the angle of attack and this cycle of events will continue until there is insufficient airspeed for flight.

However at shallow angles of bank the amount of additional lift needed is small, therefore the increase in angle of attack and additional drag is also small. At moderate and steeper angles of bank the larger increase in lift required to maintain height produces a substantial increase of induced drag and an increase of power will be essential to prevent large airspeed loss and the cycle of events described above to occur.

In effect the increase of power required in a turn is similar to the increase of power required due to increased all-up weight in straight and level flight.

Air Exercise

Dual Type Aircraft

Entering and Maintaining a Shallow Turn

Following a careful lookout the aircraft should be rolled into a banked attitude by using the appropriate control action for the particular aircraft type. At the same time the pitch attitude should be raised slightly but care should be used to ensure the airspeed does not decrease too much. Once the required degree of bank is obtained the roll control action should be neutralized. This is achieved by centralizing the ailerons on 3 axis control aircraft or changing the pressure direction on the control bar on weight shift aircraft. If this is not done the angle of bank will continue to increase beyond the desired bank angle. Initially you may be taught to carry out these control actions in steps and one at a time but the ideal will eventually be for you to co-ordinate your various control actions in a smooth sequence.

Once in the turn small control actions will be required in order to maintain the correct bank angle. Returning to straight flight will consist of removing the bank whilst keeping the aircraft balanced (3 axis control aircraft) and adjusting the nose attitude so that the aircraft remains at a constant height.

The amount and sequence of control inputs can only be learned by practice on the particular aircraft being used for your training.

The control sequence for 2 axis control aircraft will vary dependent upon the combination of weight shift and rudder control used in the particular aircraft.

Once you have learned to perform level turns your instructor will introduce you to climbing and descending turns the basic control principles for these will be the same as for level turns but even more emphasis will be made on maintaining the correct airspeed.

Airmanship

Apart from being an exercise in the co-ordination of the three primary controls, turning will also require co-ordination in lookout allied to aircraft handling. Lookout is not merely a matter of maintaining a 'roving eye in the sky' it has to be controlled in such a manner that it becomes an efficient facet of pilot ability. It is unfortunately a basic fact that a pilot cannot achieve a 100% lookout due to the physical barriers which exist in relation to his head movements and the obstructions which present themselves in terms of cockpit and aircraft design, i.e. the pilot's seating position and his area of view relative to the position and size of items which are part of the aircraft structure.

The correct procedure prior to commencing a turn is to carefully look all round the aircraft, above, below and at the same level. This lookout sequence should however first start in the direction opposite to the direction of intended turn. This is to ensure that any aircraft which may shortly be passing directly behind the turning aircraft is not missed during the lookout phase immediately prior to the turn. For example,

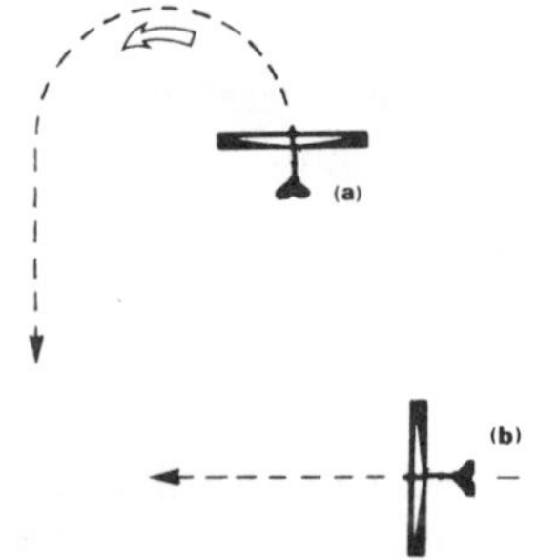

assuming the pilot of the aircraft at (a) intends to turn left then to look left and behind as a first action would not reveal the aircraft at (b) and by the time the pilot has looked out to the right and behind, the aircraft at (b) will have moved to the 6 o'clock position and may now be out of viewing range. In these circumstances the aircraft at (b) will not be seen until a hazardous situation is created.

Solo Type Aircraft — Turns will be a necessary part of your first solo flight and you will have to make these fairly shallow in order to avoid difficulties in controlling the aircraft at this very early stage of your practice. During these turns you must pay particular attention to your airspeed. Your instructor will brief you fully beforehand and you must ensure that you have understood all the points covered in this briefing.

Performance Objectives

By the time you have completed this stage of your training in a dual type aircraft you will be expected to be capable of carrying out the four basic flight manoeuvres of, straight and level flight, climbing, descending and turning. You should have reached the standard of controlling the aircraft safely throughout these exercises whilst at the same time maintaining a good lookout and demonstrating the ability to know your position in relation to the take-off and landing site used for your training.

When being trained in single seat aircraft you will normally have been introduced to the practice of making shallow turns through a limited number of degrees during the period spent in carrying out short hops prior to your first proper solo exercise.

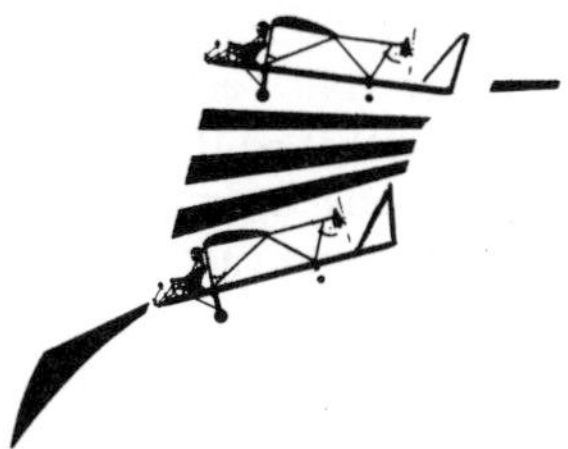

STALLING

Objectives

The purpose of this exercise is to develop your ability to recognise instinctively an impending stall situation, and by thorough training prevent you from ever entering an inadvertent stall. The exercise will normally start by giving you the opportunity to practise flying slowly for short periods whilst maintaining full control of the aircraft. Finally you will be taught how to recognise and recover from stalls at the incipient stage. These approaches to the stall should be practised in differing flight attitudes and power settings.

Introduction

Because a pilot must be able to operate his aircraft in complete safety over a wide range of circumstances and conditions it is difficult to decide on a relative order of importance for the flight exercises which he must master during training. However, because of the serious consequences of inadvertently stalling at low altitude i.e. during the approach to land, going round again or shortly after take-off, the ability to recognise the symptoms approaching a stall probably makes this exercise the most important one during your training.

An important feature in stall training is the development of the ability to estimate the margin of safety above the stalling speed by the diminishing response of the aircraft to movement of the flying controls. The student pilot must develop this awareness in order to fly safely at the lower speeds involved during take-off and landing.

The Forces and Aircraft Characteristics in Slow Flight

Slow flight can be defined as flight in the speed range close to but above the stalling speed. The amount of lift, and the control of an aircraft in flight depend upon the maintenance of a minimum airspeed. This speed will vary with the all-up weight and imposition of loads due to manoeuvre. The closer the actual speed to this minimum speed the greater the angle of attack and the less effective are the flying controls. The minimum speed below which it is impossible to maintain controlled flight is called the stalling speed.

Slow flight will normally be introduced from straight and level flight. The power is gradually reduced and the pitch attitude raised to maintain a constant height. The lateral level heading and balance must be maintained as the airspeed lowers to a figure just above the stalling speed. The actual speed used should be sufficient to permit manoeuvring flight but close enough to the stall speed for the sensation of reduced control effectiveness to be felt. In this situation the aircraft will be flying in an attitude where the induced drag will be large and in these circumstances any attempt to regain lost height by raising the attitude in pitch will result in a further increase of induced drag and without an increase in power the airspeed will lower still further. No height will be regained and continued raising of the attitude in pitch will only result in more height being lost and eventually the aircraft will stall. Therefore any attempt to regain height when operating at a very low speed demands an increase of power as the nose is raised.

Principles and Characteristics of the Stall

Lift obtained from a wing depends amongst other factors upon the smoothness of the airflow passing around it. As the angle of attack is increased the lift increases, until at a certain angle the smooth streamline flow breaks down and becomes turbulent resulting in a large loss of lift and increase in drag. During this 'stalled flight' condition height will be lost and the aircraft normally pitches nose down.

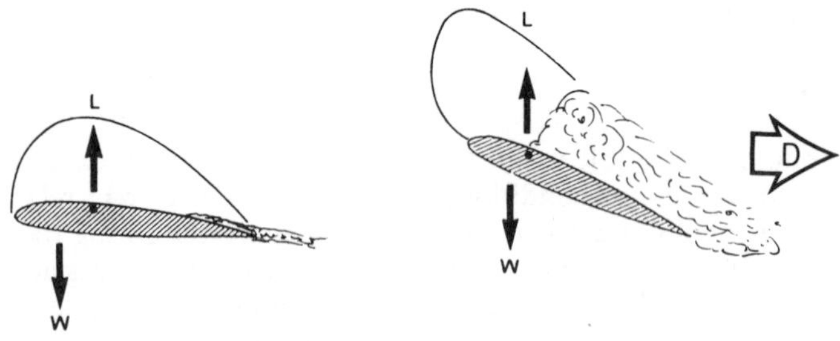

Fig. 7-43

Factors Affecting the Stalling Speed

The speed at which the stall occurs can vary, but as the angle of attack of the wings cannot be observed, speed is the only means of guidance as to when the stall will occur. The speed will vary with each particular aircraft type and its condition of flight, and provided this is understood there need be no confusion. The basic stalling speed of an aircraft means the speed at which the aircraft will stall from level flight with the throttle closed, the flaps up and the attitude in pitch being gently raised until the stall occurs.

For any particular aircraft the stalling speed will vary according to its all-up weight, the manoeuvre being performed (load factor effect) and the amount of power being used. These factors are summarized as follows:

The Weight — If extra weight is carried, greater lift will be needed to maintain the aircraft in level flight. Therefore, at all angles of attack including the stalling angle, more airspeed will be needed to provide the greater lift. In other words the stalling speed will be higher.

The Power — In those aircraft where the propeller is placed ahead of the wing in a position which causes slipstream to pass over the wing surface it will help to prevent the airflow becoming turbulent, as well as providing a small increase of lift from the wing surface immediately behind the propeller. The slipstream will also tend to reduce the angle of attack in this area.

The Load Factor (Refer to Advanced Turning) — In a turn the lift must be increased in order to maintain level flight, therefore the load factor and the stalling speed will be higher. Sudden accelerations in pitch will also increase the load factor and this is most noticeable when pulling out of a dive. During this manoeuvre the inertia of the aircraft prevents it from immediately following the new flight path suggested by the new attitude, and the angle of attack is thus momentarily increased. This type of manoeuvre can raise the stalling speed by a considerable amount.

The Symptoms of the Stall

The air exercise of stalling will commence by an introduction to the stall with the power off. This short period will be used to show you the change in aircraft attitude during the stall and to acquaint you with the physical sensations which will be felt during the practice of stalls. Following this, the symptoms of the stall should be demonstrated by slowly approaching the stall condition. These symptoms will be as follows:

A lowering of the airspeed, when the throttle is closed and the aircraft held in the approximately level attitude.

A reduced response from all control actions as the airspeed becomes lower. In some microlights, e.g. those fitted with tailplanes, a buffet may be felt through the controls.

The final symptom occurs at the stall itself in that full pitch up control may be applied, but the aircraft pitches down and height is lost, i.e. a complete reversal of what you have come to expect during your previous use of pitch controls.

The previous paragraph must not be interpreted as meaning that stalls will only occur when the aircraft is in a high pitch attitude. It must be understood that the attitude of an aircraft relative to the horizon bears no fixed relationship to the stalling angle of attack. An aircraft can in fact stall in any attitude relative to the horizon because it is the direction of relative airflow which determines the angle of attack for any condition of flight. For example, if the throttle is closed and the aircraft held in the level flight attitude it will commence to sink and the airflow will come up from below. This can produce a critical angle of attack even though the aircraft is in the level flight attitude.

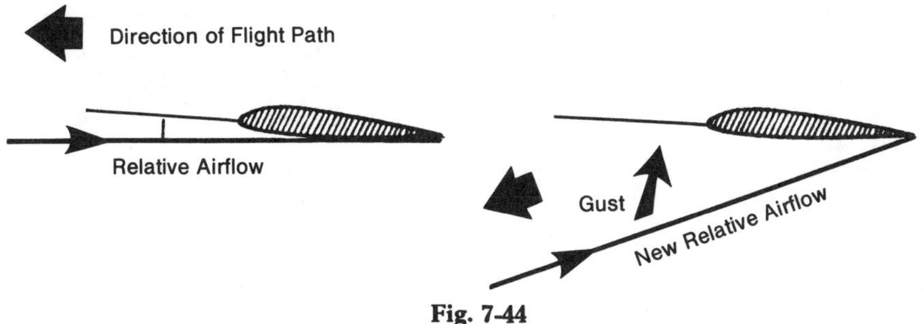

Fig. 7-44

Similarly the aircraft can be made to stall in a climb, descent or a turn, in fact at any time the wings are being presented at too large an angle to the relative airflow.

At the stall the aircraft's normal reaction is to pitch down and after a few seconds the airspeed will increase, the angle of attack will reduce and a smooth airflow over the wings will be regained. However, as will be seen from the next few paragraphs it is very important for a pilot to take positive action to hasten recovery. This is effected by the pilot carrying out the necessary control response to cause a pitch down movement and at the same time opening the throttle to gain full power.

This pitch down action will not only speed up the recovery process but it will also remove what may have been the most likely cause of the stall occurring, i.e. control inputs which have caused the aircraft to pitch up to a stalling angle of attack. In this connection it should be appreciated that if the approach to a stall is made relatively slowly it is quite common to arrive at a situation where the aircraft starts to 'mush' downwards with little change in pitch attitude, and in this situation a pilot will have to make a positive pitch down control action if recovery to normal flight is to be effected. Although a 'mush' may not technically be a stall, it is a very dangerous condition if it occurs when the aircraft is near the ground.

Some microlights, particularly those of the canard design are often described as 'stall resistant'. This really means that their design features are such that a mush is the most likely situation to occur should the pilot cause the aircraft to fly at high angles of attack. Whereas this is a good design feature it must also be understood by all pilots, that this safe design characteristic can be negated by sudden and large pitch up control action. Such actions creating a dynamic condition in which the aircraft is in effect zoomed past the point of mush and into a full stall condition.

Another characteristic of the stall is that one wing may stall before the other. This may be due to several reasons but in any event it is normally because one wing is producing less lift at the point of stall. For example with a glider which is turning at the moment of stall the outer wing will be travelling slightly faster than the inner wing, therefore the inner wing will tend to stall first. However in powered aircraft the main reason for asymmetric lift over the wings is due to the effect of yaw. A primary cause of yaw is the slipstream and torque effect of the propeller, therefore at low speeds when the effect of slipstream and torque effects from the propeller are greatest the tendency to drop a wing at the stall will be greatest.

Stall recovery is primarily a matter of pitching the aircraft downwards and thereby reducing the angle of attack. When this is done the tendency will be for the wing to stop dropping, following which normal control movement will bring the aircraft back to a wings level condition.

Although recovery from the stall is relatively simple, it must be appreciated that height will inevitably be lost. Therefore the stall is most dangerous when the aircraft is near the ground and when there is insufficient height available to recover before striking the ground. Accident statistics show that stalling at altitude rarely produces an accident, but stalling at low height can be lethal to the occupants of the aircraft.

It is for this reason that your stalling practice will be focussed towards recovery at the incipient stage.

Stall Recovery

The recovery from a stalled condition consists of pitching the nose downwards whilst at the same time smoothly applying full power and where possible controlling any yaw.

The expression 'Incipient Stall' relates to that flight condition just preceding the actual stall. Although a pilot can be trained to recover from a stall and lose a minimum of height in the process, such a recovery will be of no value if the height available at the time is insufficient for recovery to be completed before the aircraft hits the ground. Such a situation could occur during the final stages of an approach to landing, during a go round again, or immediately after the take-off.

Therefore the student's objective during the practice of stalling is to develop the instinctive ability to recognise the approach of a stall and return the aircraft to a safe flight condition before a stall actually occurs. This action will require the co-ordinated use of the flying controls and unless the aircraft is in a descent this recovery when successfully accomplished will involve no loss of height.

The normal method of practising this exercise will be to set the aircraft up in slow flight at a particular power setting. The speed should then be reduced to a stage where any further pitch up would cause a stall to develop. At this point recovery should be initiated by taking the necessary control action to cause the aircraft to pitch down whilst at the same time smoothly applying full power.

Air Exercise

Prior to being introduced to the practice of the stall and recovery it will be beneficial to practice controlling the aircraft at relatively low airspeeds.

Slow Flight

Once the correct power for level flight at the selected slow speed has been achieved turns of up to 30° of bank should be practised. However during the exercise of medium level turns it was seen that at a constant power and height a drop in airspeed occurred during a turn. Therefore to maintain a constant height and airspeed it will be necessary to increase the power during level turns in the slow flight condition.

Descents at slow speed should be practised with and without power. In the power on condition the desired rate of descent can be achieved at the selected airspeed by reducing the power and re-adjusting the pitch attitude to a lower position in the same manner as for a descent during normal flight.

The Stall and Recovery

Prior to stalling practice certain safety checks should be completed. Such checks may vary slightly between instructors but will essentially consist of the following points:

Height above the surface — Sufficient height must be available for you to be able to effect a recovery. If you are operating on the QNH you must bear in mind your altitude relative to the height of the terrain.

Location — This type of practice should be undertaken over open country and well clear of towns, aerodromes, microlight sites, etc.

Lookout — Remember that you will be losing height during your stalling practice and it is important to ensure there are no other aircraft in your immediate vicinity and particularly below you. A clearing turn will enable you to see any other aircraft which may be in your vicinity.

Other checks will relate mainly to the type of microlight in which you are conducting your practice.

When these checks have been completed satisfactorily the stalling practice can begin but lookout will remain a continuous factor throughout. You must not become so absorbed in your practice that you fail to maintain a good standard of lookout and orientation regarding your position over the ground.

The actual sequence and method used for stall training will depend upon your training organisation, the type of aircraft being used for training and whether it is a solo or dual type aircraft. The training notes issued by your instructor will therefore cover this aspect of the flight exercise.

SPINNING

Objectives

When spin training is carried out the objective is not to teach you how to spin but quite the opposite — 'How not to get into a situation where a spin could develop'. Therefore the primary purpose of this exercise is to teach you how to recognise the onset of a situation which may lead to an inadvertent spin. This training will enable you to instinctively take the necessary control actions to effect a recovery back to normal flight condition before a spin occurs, i.e. to recover at the incipient stage. (This is a dual only exercise.)

Introduction
Spin training is not included in the solo syllabus for reasons of safety, and because aircraft must normally be in a stalled or semi-stalled condition before a spin will occur, the emphasis on training in single seat aircraft will be placed on recovering from a stall at the incipient stage. In dual aircraft you will also receive training in recovering at the incipient stage of spin development. General training philosophy precludes the need to actually spin microlight aircraft because their spinning characteristics are often unknown. It is therefore considered as an unsafe exercise unless the aircraft concerned has been well proven in its ability to recover from a spin condition.

Characteristics of the Spin
A spin is a condition of stalled flight in which the aircraft describes a spiral descent. During a spin the aircraft will be simultaneously rolling, yawing and pitching until recovery is initiated by the pilot.

Causes of a Spin
If an aircraft is either inadvertently or deliberately brought to the stall a wing will often drop. There are several reasons which produce this condition but usually the primary reason is the development of yaw when the aircraft is close to or at the stalling angle of attack.

When an aircraft is brought up to or near a stalled condition, there will be an associated airspeed change leading to a constantly changing rate of response to the control pressures made by the pilot while at the same time the aircraft will be approaching a critical condition of lateral stability. From this it can be seen that the most difficult time to maintain a constant condition of balanced flight will be when the airspeed is continuously reducing and the control pressures which are required to maintain balance are constantly varying.

Fig. 7-45 shows a typical situation during which the aircraft is brought close to the stall and initially yaw is absent (the stalling angle is assumed to be 20°). At (a) the wings have reached an 18° angle of attack. At (b) a yaw to the left has occurred which will temporarily change the airflow speed about each wing and the slight differential of lift between the two wings causes the right wing to rise and the left wing to drop. This small rolling action leads to a change in the angle of attack affecting each wing. The lowering wing obtains a higher angle of attack while that of the rising wing decreases. The lowering wing now reaches the stalling angle and drops more quickly which will in turn lead to a higher angle of attack and a more stalled condition.

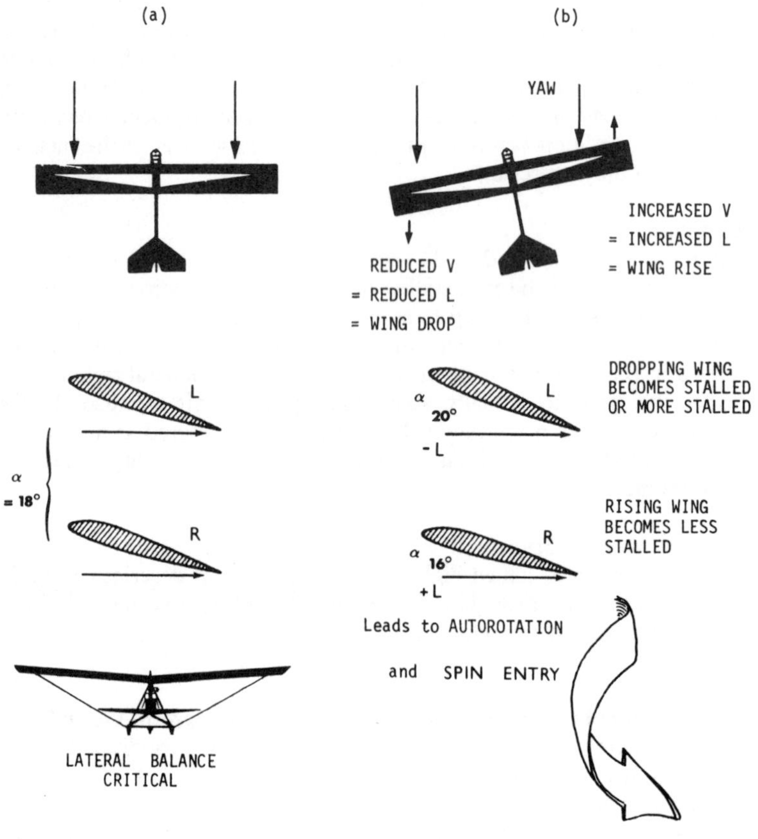

Fig. 7-45

The downgoing wing being more stalled will produce more drag causing the aircraft to yaw in the direction of the downgoing wing. Due to the upgoing wing being less stalled it will always have more lift than the downgoing wing and this action will be self perpetuating.

The circumstances which can cause a spin will be first, any condition of flight at or near the stall, and second, the development of yaw. The aircraft may assume some unusual attitude but unless yaw is present it will not spin. An aircraft will not spin directly from any state of normal cruising flight. In practice, it will be found that to spin, carelessness in the handling of the controls near the stall is necessary. It must be borne in mind that a single speed of entry is not significant, as a stall can occur at various speeds dependent upon configuration, weight, position of the c.g. and the load factor imposed.

A spin is a condition of flight in which the aircraft is experiencing rolling, yawing, pitching and sideslipping. It will be losing height rapidly and the airspeed will be low and descending along a vertical path about the spin axis, the helix of which is fairly small and can be less than the span of the wings. An important characteristic is that during a spin the predominant tendency is to continue the autorotation and the aircraft generally has a spinning motion which is primarily rolling, with moderate yaw and a degree of sideslip. If an aircraft has a large amount of directional stability it will be a favourable influence on the spin characteristics as it will minimise the displacement due to yaw and make it easier to effect a recovery.

Recovery From A Spin

Because of the different design features used in microlight aircraft it is not possible to define a universal recovery method and the Owner's Manual must be consulted to see whether any advice on spin recovery has been included. One method which has been established for aircraft with 3 axis controls (though it may not apply to all aircraft) is to carry out the following control actions:

Throttle closed
Ailerons (when fitted) held neutral
Full rudder applied — opposite to spin direction
  Pause — momentarily
  Ease the control column forward — continue this action until the spin stops
When the spin stops — immediately centralise the rudder and level the wings by the use of ailerons
When the wings are levelled — ease the aircraft out of the dive.

AIR EXERCISE (when applicable)

Dual type aircraft

Prior to practice at recoveries from any condition leading to a spin situation, the safety checks which have already been defined under Stalling should be carried out.

Recognition of the Incipient Stage

The incipient stage of the spin is that period after the entry and before the spin has progressed to the developed stage. From a training viewpoint the incipient stage is best described as that period before the wings first roll past the vertical, and as such it is similar to the situation of a positive wing drop at the stall.

Recovery action at the incipient stage — 3 axis control aircraft

Control column forward to unstall the wings
Rudder to prevent further yaw
Co-ordinated use of the elevators, ailerons and rudder is then made to return the aircraft to the level flight attitude.

The question of whether you will be introduced to this type of flight situation and the degree to which the incipient stage of a spin will be permitted to develop, will depend upon the aircraft being used and the procedures used by your training organisation and instructor.

TAKE OFF AND CLIMB

Objectives

Although the methods used to introduce students to the air exercise of taking off will be dependent upon whether a single or two seat training aircraft is being used, the objectives are the same. These include the need to provide you with a thorough understanding of the various factors concerned with getting the aircraft off the ground, and the development of your ability to get airborne safely and to fly the aircraft to the downwind position of the circuit.

Introduction

This phase of your training will consist of dual demonstrations and practice in the case of two seat aircraft, or short tows behind a land vehicle, or short hops of the aircraft under its own power with you learning how the aircraft responds to your control actions.

Apart from this there are many factors which have to be appreciated in relation to aircraft performance and control during the take-off and initial climb, and the following paragraphs will mainly be concerned with these aspects.

Microlight towing at Enstone Aerodrome

Factors Affecting the Length of Take-off Run and Initial Climb

Performance in this flight phase starts with a condition of accelerated motion and finishes with the aircraft being established in the climb at the correct airspeed and at a safe height. The criteria for the take-off will depend upon the length of take-off run available, the height of obstructions in the immediate climbing path, and the effect of ground surface, wind, weight, and atmospheric density.

During the take-off the aircraft will have to be accelerated from a standstill to the lift off speed. Therefore the immediate factors affecting this aspect of performance will be:

1. The lift off speed, which is normally derived from the stalling or minimum flying speed. In order to ensure a satisfactory degree of control immediately after the aircraft becomes airborne this speed is generally calculated as 1.15 times the stalling speed.

2. The acceleration experienced during the take-off run. The acceleration of an aircraft varies directly with the unbalance of the Thrust and Drag forces in relation to the retarding effect of the surface (rolling friction), and inversely as the mass of the aircraft.

3. The take-off length will be a function of both the acceleration and the aircraft speed.

The minimum take-off run and take-off distance will normally be of primary interest during the transition from the beginning of the take-off roll to the establishment of the normal climb. The take-off run is that distance the aircraft travels until it becomes airborne. The take-off distance is the distance taken for the aircraft to reach an arbitrary height of 50 feet.

Effect of Wind

Of the various factors which affect the performance of the aircraft during take-off the effect of wind is by far the most significant.

The effect of a headwind is that it enables the aircraft to reach the take-off speed at a lower ground speed, whilst the effect of a tailwind requires the aircraft to attain a greater ground speed to achieve the take-off speed. The direct relationship in practical terms of the effect of a head or tail wind can better be appreciated by reference to Fig. 7-46.

Taking an example, assume a lift off speed of 25 mph and a tailwind of 5 mph. 5 mph equals 20% of the lift off speed and using the graph shown at Fig. 7-46 it will be seen that in these conditions the take-off run will be nearly 45% greater than in conditions of zero wind. If a 5 mph headwind was prevailing the take-off run would be reduced by just over 35%. From a practical point of view it can be seen that a pilot who takes off downwind will be unpleasantly surprised to find out the increase in his take-off run. In this case and with only a light wind of 5 mph the difference in the take-off run between the headwind and tailwind situation comes to 80%.

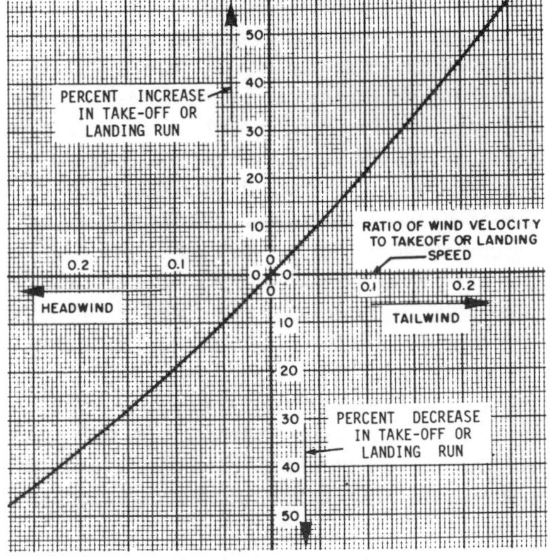

Tailwind 20% of the Lift-off Speed

Headwind 20% of the Lift-off Speed

Fig 7-46

The strength and direction of the wind also has a direct relation to the angle of climb in that a steeper angle is achieved into a headwind and a shallower angle of climb will occur if a tailwind condition exists. The angle of climb has a direct bearing upon the take-off distance (obstacle clearance) which can be achieved. A point which is not always appreciated is that when a zero wind exists at the surface a tailwind can often exist at a low altitude above the ground with a consequent deterioration in the climbing angle.

Due to certain inherent design characteristics and the low lift off speeds of microlight aircraft, directional control during the take-off run is limited. Therefore taking off across the wind is inadvisable except when the wind is very light. In any event crosswind take-offs are not advisable unless the aircraft has three axis controls. The reasons for this can be seen from the contents of the following paragraph.

Crosswind take-off

On microlight aircraft fitted with a tailplane, there will exist a side force on the keel surface during any crosswind take-off. As most of this keel surface is behind the centre of gravity there will be a strong weathercock action and the aircraft will tend to turn into the direction from which the wind is coming. This will have to be corrected by the use of rudder during the take-off roll.

Apart from the effect of wind upon the keel surface there will also be a strong tendency for the wing which is on the side from which the wind is coming to be lifted up throughout the take-off run. This effect will apply to any aircraft e.g. a flex wing without a tailplane as well as an aircraft with tail surfaces. This rising of one wing is normally counteracted by raising the aileron on that side and thereby reducing the lift produced from that wing. Depending upon the strength of the crosswind component a large amount of aileron movement may be required in the initial stages of the take-off. As the aircraft accelerates to higher speeds the ailerons become more effective and the amount of aileron movement can be reduced.

Due to the side force which exists during a crosswind take-off the aircraft will commence drifting sideways during and immediately after the lift off. To appreciate this tendency, it should be borne in mind that when the aircraft commences its take-off roll all the weight is being supported by the landing gear. As the speed increases this weight is gradually transferred to the wings and during this process the effect of the wind upon the side surface of the aircraft increases and if sufficiently strong can cause the aircraft to commence drifting sideways whilst still on the ground. This action could impose unacceptable stresses upon the landing gear and also give problems in the control of the aircraft.

It is particularly important on these occasions to use the correct lift off speed, this will give adequate insurance against the possibility of touching down again whilst drifting sideways. All aircraft have a limiting crosswind component and when this is exceeded during take-off the design tolerances relating to the landing gear sideways stress force will also be exceeded. This could lead to a weakening of the landing gear components and the danger of structural failure on that particular flight or on a subsequent one.

Once the aircraft is safely airborne it will be necessary to make a shallow turn towards the prevailing wind direction to counteract the drift experienced during the climb out. This will enable the aircraft to maintain a track over the ground which is coincident with the take-off heading.

A final point in relation to wind is that when gusty winds prevail it will be advisable to take-off at a slightly higher speed than normal to ensure adequate control of the aircraft when encountering such gusts immediately after lift off.

Effect of Weight

It will be remembered from the facts concerning stalling that an increase of weight increases the stalling speed, and as the lift off speed is related to the speed of stall (the lift off speed quoted in aircraft manuals is normally 1.1 to 1.2 times the stalling speed), and from this, it will be clear that any increase in weight will lead to a higher lift off speed.

To give an example, a 20% increase in weight will increase the lift off speed by 10%. But this is not the whole story, and any increase in aircraft weight will have a threefold effect upon the take-off performance.

1. An increased lift off speed
2. A greater mass to be accelerated
3. An increased retarding force.

Due to these 3 factors, the net result of increasing weight by just 10% will be to increase the take-off run of a light aircraft by at least 25% and also reduce the rate of climb. In the case of microlights it can be seen that the addition of a passenger could increase the weight by a large percentage and this in turn could result in a take-off run which is twice the length or even more of the take-off run when only the pilot is on board.

Pressure, Altitude, Temperature and Density

The effect of taking off from airfields significantly higher than sea level is to lengthen the take-off run and the take-off distance and reduce the rate of climb. This is due to the reduction of power available as altitude is increased and also, because of the reduced density a greater true airspeed will be needed to achieve the indicated lift off and climbing speed.

Whenever the temperature is higher than standard for a particular altitude, the density, and therefore the aircraft performance, will be reduced (the expression 'High Density Altitude' is often used to describe this situation).

Although the performance aspects of high density altitudes are normally absent when operating from relatively low altitude airfields in temperate climates, a pilot must have an appreciation of this effect so that he can make an allowance and operate safely when such conditions do exist.

Ground Surface and Gradient

Light aircraft commonly operate from grass surfaces, small airfields and landing strips, and sometimes also when the grass is longer than normal and/or the surface is wet, soft or covered with snow. Under these circumstances, the pilot should be particularly careful to consider the effects which the ground surface will have upon the performance of the aircraft.

The ground drag of an aircraft as it rolls along the surface is known as *Rolling Resistance* and because this rolling resistance can cause a substantial increase in the length of the take-off run when using surfaces which are soft or have long grass, it is an important consideration to be taken into account prior to take-off.

Another factor which must also be considered during take-off is the surface gradient, for whereas normal aerodromes are relatively flat, many landing strips have gradients which can significantly affect the length of the take-off run.

In this respect, a rule of thumb guide is that a 2° upslope will increase the take-off run by some 20%, and bearing in mind, the difficulty in estimating this angle with any degree of accuracy without some form of precision instrumentation, considerable care must be used when taking off in these circumstances. Particularly when other adverse performance conditions are present.

In this respect it is worthy of note that accident statistics relating to conventional aircraft have consistently revealed over many years that in the case of take-off accidents, it is not so much a single adverse performance condition which caused the accident, but rather a combination of the foregoing factors.

The Circuit Procedure

The circuit pattern is generally rectangular and left handed, but right hand circuits may be used when circumstances dictate, e.g. due to the position of high ground or local obstructions, or the need to avoid constantly overflying built up areas, etc. There may also be circumstances when an oval circuit is made, in which case the turn following the initial climb will be continuous until the aircraft is heading along the downwind leg.

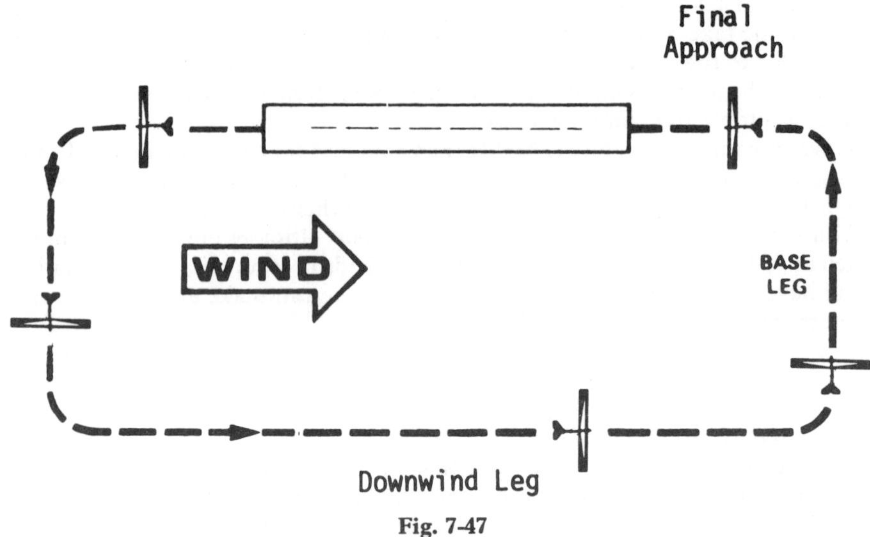

Fig. 7-47

When flying a rectangular circuit, the heading on the crosswind leg must be adjusted to take into account any drift which is experienced. A very careful lookout must be maintained throughout the circuit, and in this respect it will be very easy for a pilot to concentrate on his positioning in relation to the landing path to the extent that his attention is diverted away from other aircraft which may be re-joining or already in the circuit.

When the aircraft is a suitable distance out from the take-off path the aircraft should be turned onto the downwind leg. During this stage the heading should be adjusted as necessary to maintain a track over the ground which is parallel to the take-off and landing path. Dependent upon the aircraft used and the procedures in force at your place of training some Pre-Landing checks may be taught downwind in preparation for the approach and landing phase of the circuit.

Emergencies

When the aircraft is close to the ground the time factor to deal with emergency situations may be extremely small, and it is only alertness and training which will enable a pilot to handle this type of situation safely.

Abandoned Take-off

In the event that an engine misfires, runs roughly or does not develop the normal power during the take-off run the throttle should be closed and the take-off abandoned. The same thing will apply if you should lose directional control.

Engine Failure After Take-off

An engine failure immediately after take-off and when the aircraft is close to the ground is probably the most critical situation that could confront a pilot. The major problem will be the time available to adopt and carry out a safe course of action. The time factor is not entirely dependent upon height, for example if the area immediately ahead consists of open countryside with large fields the decision on where to land will be reasonably straightforward, but if woods, obstacles or built up areas are across the climb out path it will become more difficult to select a landing area quickly. **The most vital action will be to lower the aircraft nose and maintain a safe gliding speed.** Following this the exact method used to fit a particular situation will vary to a small extent but the best general advice is as follows:

Look either side of the nose to find the best landing area and head towards it, **turning no more than is necessary** to avoid obstructions. Maintain a safe gliding speed throughout as with speed available the aircraft can be manoeuvred to avoid single obstacles.

Keep in mind the wind direction and try to choose a landing path which is as nearly into wind as possible. The ground impact speed will be lessened if landing into a headwind.

One final point is that the throttle should be fully closed after the landing path has been selected. This is to ensure you do not become diverted from your original decision in the event that the engine temporarily comes back into operation. However, in the case of time being available to complete some form of cockpit check for engine failure, the throttle should not be fully closed until this procedure has been completed, or it will not be known whether the failure check and possible rectification has been successful.

Landing in an open field regardless of whether it is short grass, growing crops or ploughed ground, will not normally cause injury to aircraft occupants provided they are strapped in securely and the landing is made under control. Any decision to carry out checks to ascertain the reason for power failure will depend upon the time available and the type of aircraft you are flying. Advice on this point will be given to you by your instructor.

Air Exercise

The actual control actions used during take-off will vary with the type of aircraft being used, e.g. flex wing, 2 or 3 axis controls, nosewheel or tailwheel, etc. Therefore the following comments are mostly confined to aspects of procedure.

If you are being trained on solo type aircraft you will have already demonstrated your ability to control the aircraft and probably learned to carry out short deviations from heading and gentle turns during your tows or short hops.

Into Wind Take-off

The take-off is made into the direction of the prevailing wind for the following reasons:

It gives the shortest take-off run and the lowest ground speed at lift off.

There will be no tendency for the aircraft to drift sideways, and therefore will ensure better directional control and less strain on the landing gear.

It gives a steeper climb angle which together with the shorter take-off run will provide a better clearance from obstacles in the aircraft climb path, and a lower landing speed and shorter stopping distance should the engine malfunction during or immediately after take-off.

Pre-Take-off checks

1. Pre-Take-off Checks
   Prior to every take-off a system of checking certain essential items must be strictly adhered to.

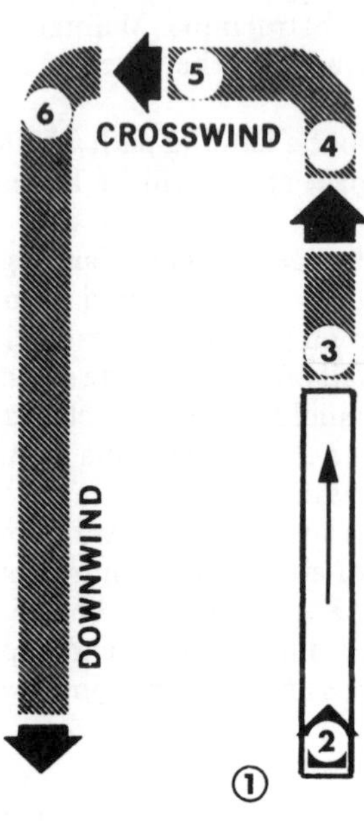

The exact checks and the order in which they are carried out will depend upon the particular aircraft and to a certain extent upon the training organisation where you are undergoing tuition. The basic purpose of these checks is to ensure a final review of the serviceability of the aircraft, engine and systems. The number of items included in this procedure will vary according to the aircraft type, its equipment and the operating environment.

The pre-take-off checks should be completed in a position from which the circuit area and final approach path of landing aircraft can be clearly scrutinised. This is a vital part of the airmanship considerations and will help to enforce the essential habit of checking the take-off and approach path to ensure that both are clear prior to taxying out to the take-off point.

2 When the checks have been completed and all found satisfactory the aircraft should be taxied into the centreline position of the take-off path or runway. If available a reference feature in the distance should be noted in order to assist in the maintenance of heading during the take-off roll. When a reference feature is not available you should look well ahead of the aircraft, and when runways are used their sidelines converging into the distance will be of considerable assistance.

3 Once safely airborne the aircraft should follow the same track line as used during the take-off. Any drift as a result of the wind should be corrected, and particularly attention must be paid to maintaining a safe speed.

4 Before commencing the turn onto the crosswind leg a careful lookout all around the aircraft should be made to ensure that it is clear to turn.

5 During the crosswind leg the effect of wind must be allowed for by pointing the aircraft slightly into the wind direction to counteract drift. Before the turn onto the downwind leg a careful lookout must again be made.

6 Once on the downwind heading you will need to monitor your position in relation to your distance out from the take-off path and adjust your heading as required.

During this leg you will be maintaining a careful lookout and completing your pre-landing checks as required.

Airmanship
The vital necessity for a vigilant lookout during the whole of the circuit pattern is highlighted by the fact that most airborne collisions occur in the vicinity of aerodromes and sites where take-off and landing operations are being conducted. It is in circumstances like these that pilot workloads and other distractions easily interfere with the maintenance of a good lookout.

Finally, apart from normal airmanship considerations the take-off will always need to be conducted taking into account the take-off run and distance available and the performance capability of the aircraft in relation to the conditions at the time.

APPROACH AND LANDING

Objectives

To teach the student a thorough understanding of the various factors concerned with developing the ability to maintain an accurate circuit pattern and to accomplish a safe approach and landing under varied conditions. The need to make positive decisions concerning the safe operation of the aircraft, e.g. when to initiate 'Go Round Again' procedure will be an integral part of the exercise.

Introduction

Statistics show that the largest number of aircraft accidents occur during the approach and landing phase despite the fact that this normally involves only a few minutes of each flight. Therefore it is clear that a thorough appreciation of the factors concerned will be vital to the implementation of the correct techniques, during which such existing conditions as wind, obstructions on the approach path, nature of ground surface, and the landing distance available must all be taken into account. It is therefore only from a review of these conditions that a pilot can decide upon the exact type of approach and landing to use.

In the initial stages of training the particular type of approach being used will depend largely upon laid down training practices rather than those related to specific weather, terrain and aircraft conditions. Nevertheless, such variables as wind and turbulence will form an integral part of the initial techniques employed. Eventually the student will be taught to assess each approach and landing situation and take into account not only the wind and weather conditions, but also those factors relating to landing distance, weight, effects of altitude and temperature, and the type and condition of the ground surface.

Experience has shown that provided a reasonable degree of continuity is achieved most people learn the physical skills needed to handle and control an aircraft without too many problems. On the other hand the thinking skills, those which are associated with putting knowledge to good use and making sensible decisions are not so easily gained. Pilot error is a predominating factor in aircraft incidents and accidents, and most of these errors are attributed to lack of thought, lack of preparedness, lack of planning, and incorrect decisions.

Landing an aircraft is not just a matter of placing the aircraft in the right position, pointing it in the right direction, adjusting the attitude and power, and holding it off before touchdown. Throughout the approach and landing phase of a flight certain specific observations should be passing through a pilot's mind. For example, what is the degree of wind gustiness?, is the wind direction fluctuating?, is the ground under the approach path lower than the landing site? It is only by being in a state of continuous awareness of the conditions existing at the time that you will be prepared to respond with the correct decision and actions.

But before you can make correct decisions you must know what to observe and when. This is why the factors relating to aircraft performance during the take-off and initial climb were detailed in the previous flight exercise. These same performance factors also have to be considered in relation to approaches and landings, however because of the knowledge you have already gained they can be covered more in the nature of a summary just to alert you that these factors are an essential part of your training in this exercise.

Effect of Wind

As in the case of the take-off, the effect of wind upon landing performance is very significant, and because an aircraft will land at a particular touch down speed regardless of wind strength, the main effect of wind is its ability to alter the ground speed during the landing therefore affecting the length of the landing run and distance.

The effect of wind upon aircraft deceleration during the landing run is identical to its effect upon the take-off run, which can be seen by reference to Fig. 7-46. A headwind which is 10% of the touch down speed will reduce the landing run by approximately 20% and a tailwind which is 10% of the touch down speed will increase the landing run by 20%.

The effect of a headwind upon the final approach path is to steepen the descent gradient for a given approach speed, and a tailwind will make the approach path more shallow. This is due to the effect on ground speed relative to the air speed. When crosswind conditions exist, there will be a correspondingly reduced headwind or tailwind component during the approach and landing roll. This effect is identical to the effect of a crosswind factor on the take-off.

Wind Gradient

When the wind strength is moderate to strong, the aircraft may encounter positive wind gradient effects as it nears the ground during the final stages of the approach to landing. Wind gradient (sometimes called 'Wind Shear') can have a significant effect upon an aircraft flight path and airspeed and is most likely to be met when the runway threshold is in the vicinity of buildings or trees, and also when the ground beneath the approach path is lower than the elevation of the runway.

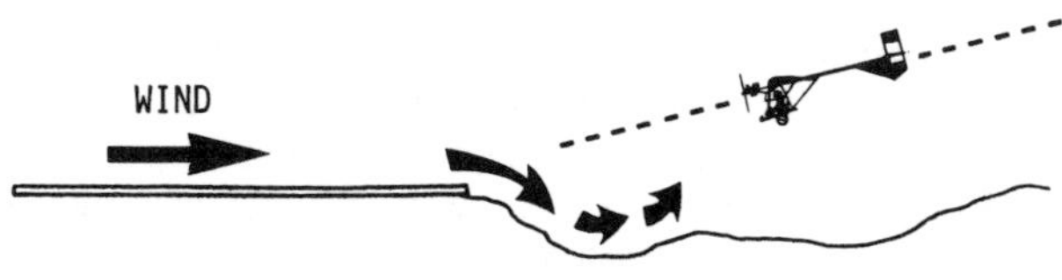

Fig. 7-48

Under these conditions horizontal or vertical wind shear and gusts creating up and down draughts will be prevalent and the pilot must maintain an added state of awareness and be ready to counteract any sudden loss of airspeed or sinking by prompt and correct use of power and elevators. When these conditions occur the immediate action should be to increase power and lower the nose to maintain or slightly increase the approach speed.

When meeting wind gusts or wind shear the changing direction of airflow can often cause a rapid alteration in the angle of attack of the wings, and sudden changes of airspeed. The problem associated with this occurrence at the lower speeds used for approaches lies in the possibility of the aircraft getting close to the stall at a time when little or no power is being used. The aircraft can suddenly sink in an attitude where it is in a high drag condition.

Effect of Weight

The effect of weight upon the stalling and aircraft performance has already been covered under the exercises of Stalling, and Take-Off. When related to the approach and landing this means that consideration must be given as to whether the approach speed should be increased if the all-up weight is increased, and by how much the landing run will be increased at the higher touch down speed associated with the higher stalling speed.

Normally Owner's Manuals will base their recommended approach speeds (if given) upon the permitted all-up weight of the aircraft, and therefore even if the aircraft is operating at its maximum all-up weight there will not normally be any need to increase the approach speed on this account. However the effect of weight upon the landing run is significant, in that added weight means a higher touch down speed, the actual figures being:

A 20% increase in weight will produce
a 10% increase in touch down speed.

To this must be added the greater energy to be dissipated during the landing roll. This energy increases with increased weights and touch down speeds and a 20% increase in weight will result in approximately a 20% increase in the length of the landing run.

Pressure Altitude, Temperature and Density

Increases in Pressure Altitude, Temperature and Density Altitude effect the landing run which will be increased due to the higher landing speed associated with a higher true airspeed.

In relation to the effects of density altitude a rule of thumb is to allow an additional 5% of the landing distance required, for each 1000 ft of landing site elevation.

The reduced engine power associated with altitude and density effect is normally not a critical factor during the approach to landing because of the reduced power settings needed. It must nevertheless be appreciated that altitude will have a very significant effect upon the aircraft's rate of climb should a go around be necessary, and in this situation it will be necessary to reduce drag to a minimum by raising flaps (if fitted and used) as quickly as possible after achieving a safe airspeed.

Ground Surface and Gradient

When a pilot is landing back on the site from where he took off he will know the type of surface conditions and be aware of any gradient or rough ground, long grass etc. However the greatest care must be taken when landing on a site from which he has not operated before or for a period of time. On these latter occasions a telephone call may be necessary in order to establish some information relative to the intended landing site and even then a careful inspection from the air should be carried out prior to attempting a landing.

The Base Leg and Final Approach

Apart from airmanship considerations it will aid your practice of the approach and landing if you always commence the base leg from the same height. Therefore the height should be monitored during the downwind leg and adjustments made as necessary to counteract any increase or decrease which may be brought about due to thermal activity or your own lack of attention. In the early stage of your circuit practice it will also be helpful if you commence your base leg from approximately the same position so you will need to pay attention to your distance out from the landing path as you proceed downwind.

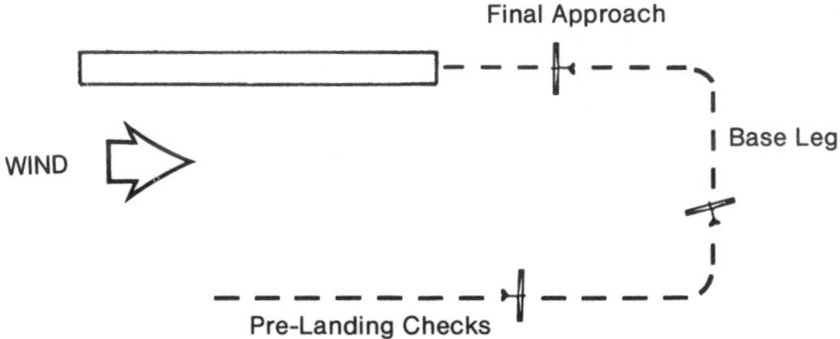

Fig. 7-49

The base leg is used to allow you to adjust the aircraft's position and height prior to commencing the final approach for a landing. During this leg the effect or drift will have to be counteracted by heading the aircraft slightly into the wind. When a powered approach is being carried out it is on this leg that the power is reduced and a descent commenced. When glide approaches are being practised the throttle will be closed and the descent rate will be greater. In either case extreme care should be used to maintain the correct airspeed.

The basic pre-requisite of a good approach is to maintain the aircraft at the right height, speed, attitude and position during its travel towards the runway or landing area. The use of power during an approach will assist considerably towards the accomplishment of this aim. Although the powered approach is the one most commonly used, there will be occasions when different types and variations of types of approach and landing will be employed.

Basically there are two types of approach and landing, the glide approach and the powered approach, the order in which they are taught will depend upon the procedure used at your training organisation.

The Powered Approach and Landing

This method is commonly used for the initial demonstration and practice of the approach to landing. It commences from a point approximately a quarter to one third along the base leg, where the power is reduced, and the attitude adjusted to maintain the correct airspeed.

The power initially selected will be determined by the direction and strength of the wind relative to the landing path and the position of the aircraft in relation to the intended touchdown area. It is from this stage onwards that considerable care must be given to keeping the airspeed correct. The importance of accurate speed control lies first with safety, and secondly, if the speed is allowed to vary continuously it becomes more difficult to judge the approach path in relation to the intended touch down area.

The rate of descent is controlled by the use of power and the airspeed maintained by the adjustment of the nose attitude in pitch. Assuming an into wind landing is being made, the turn onto the final approach should be commenced just prior to intersecting the final approach path, and the bank angle varied to bring the aircraft onto the centre line of the approach path. Care should be taken not to exceed the angle of bank recommended by your instructor.

In the event the aircraft overshoots the final approach path, the turn should not be steepened, but an adjustment to the aircraft heading can be made to bring the aircraft back onto the centre line after the final turn is almost completed. During this turn the airspeed must be monitored frequently.

Once established on the final approach path your instructor will point out the position and perspective of the landing area which will indicate the correct approach path is being achieved. One hand should be kept on the throttle throughout the approach and provided a reaction to errors in the approach angle is prompt, the amount of power variation and aircraft pitch adjustment will be relatively small. The actual height from which the final flare is commenced will only be learnt through practice but it can be said at this stage the aircraft will be flying parallel to and close to the ground, this is known as the hold off period. It is at this stage that the throttle is fully closed and pitch control is used to keep the aircraft just off the ground. Whether nose or tail wheel aircraft are being used the object will be to land in a tail down attitude.

Glide Approach and Landing

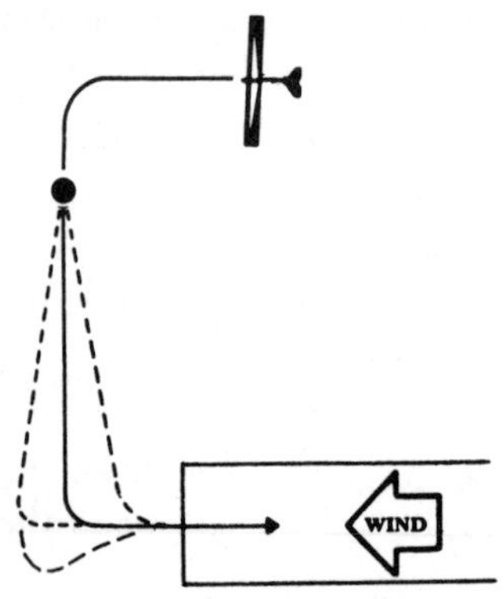

The primary function in teaching the glide approach is to develop the student's judgement for that stage of training when he will be practising forced landings without power.

When flaps are fitted to his aircraft a pilot can alter the steepness of his path of descent during the final approach into wind. However, without flaps the fundamental technique consists of manoeuvring the aircraft in relation to position and height from the landing area. For example, when the aircraft is in the base leg position a small alteration in heading either towards or away from the airfield will reduce or increase the distance the aircraft is away from the field when it turns onto the final approach. Therefore, in this way, undershooting or overshooting is primarily controlled when the aircraft is crosswind and before the turn onto final approach.

The procedure for the rectangular circuit commences on the base leg when the student will have to decide the point to close the throttle completely. The approximate position for this action will be when the touchdown area is approximately 45° to the aircraft track.

From this stage onwards the student will have to constantly monitor his position in relation to his height and distance from the point of touchdown. If it is felt that the aircraft is losing height too quickly the aircraft should be turned towards the landing area by an amount which is considered to be compatible with the aircraft height and distance from the aiming point. Conversely, if the aircraft appears to be too high it should be turned away just sufficiently to correct this situation. It should be noted that the roundout from a gliding approach will be greater due to the steeper descent which occurs when no power is being used.

Air Exercise

For the same reasons given in previous air exercises the following comments relate mostly to the general procedures used during the circuit approach and landing.

If you are training in solo type aircraft you will have already been introduced to and had practice at controlling the aircraft during the last stage of the approach and actual landing.

Normal Landing

Landings are normally made against the direction of the prevailing wind for the following reasons:

- It will give the lowest groundspeed and therefore the shortest landing run.
- It reduces any tendency for the aircraft to drift sideways due to wind effects, thus ensuring better directional control and less strain on the landing gear.
- It will provide a steeper approach path and therefore a better clearance from any obstacles below the approach path.
- Control of most microlight aircraft during landing is more difficult in crosswind conditions.

1. The Downwind Leg

The Pre-Landing Checks should be completed before turning onto the base leg. The exact checks and the order in which they are carried out will depend upon the particular aircraft and to a certain extent upon the procedures used by your training organisation.

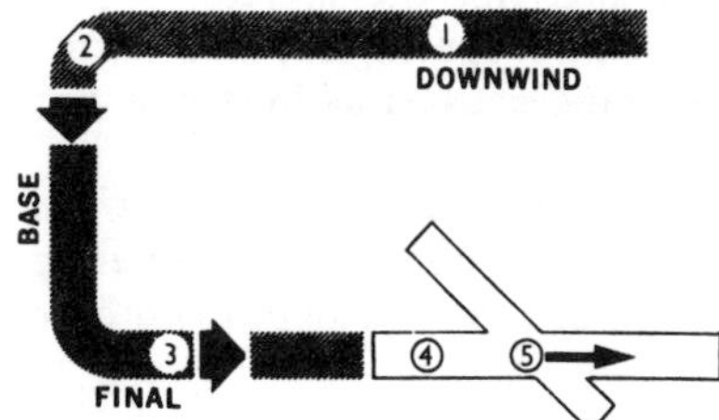

Care should be taken to maintain a track parallel to the intended landing path. It sometimes occurs that the wind direction and strength at circuit height is different to that which is experienced on the ground. When this is so, any effects of crosswind should be counteracted by altering the aircraft heading.

2. Your instructor will brief you on the best point to turn onto the base leg and before commencing this turn you will need to carry out a careful lookout all round the aircraft. It is a common tendency for student pilots to concentrate their lookout into the direction of the landing area and fail to give sufficient attention ahead and to the other side of the aircraft. During the base leg the descent must be initiated, however it is important not to get too low prior to the turn onto the final approach path.
3. On the final approach the aircraft's speed and height must be carefully controlled and at some stage a decision to land or 'go round again' must be made. The circumstances governing the need to go round again will vary, e.g. an unobstructed landing path is a paramount requirement for a safe landing and if another aircraft taxies into your landing path you will normally have to go round again rather than attempt a landing. Alternatively you may misjudge the approach and find yourself too high to allow for safe correction, in which case it will be wiser to abandon the approach and go round again.
4. The necessity for a 'Go Round Again' decision will exist right up to the touchdown and afterwards. For example if a badly executed landing takes place due to overcontrolling, or due to a difficult wind condition the aircraft may balloon into the air and in this situation it is usually preferable to apply full power and initiate 'go round again' action rather than trying to retrieve the situation by juggling with the throttle and flying controls.

   Providing the circumstances are normal and a proper 'roundout' has been achieved the landing should be accomplished safely, but this is not the moment to sit back and relax, because directional control of the aircraft becomes more difficult once on the ground.
5. At this stage you must remain alert to check any weathercock tendency produced from changing wind conditions. In the event that you have to land in a known crosswind it is vital that you are prepared to counteract the weathercock tendency remembering that the control surfaces become less effective as the aircraft slows down.

Airmanship and ATC Procedures

The proximity of other aircraft is close during the circuit, approach and landing, and pilot workload will be increased during this phase, therefore the airmanship considerations will be of the utmost importance. An extremely high standard of lookout and compliance with local procedures will be continuously necessary.

The following airmanship points should be observed throughout the take-off, circuit, approach and landing.

In many instances, the pilot's view of the surrounding airspace is restricted by the design of the aircraft and its flight attitude. Compensate for any blind spots by moving your head and where necessary by manoeuvring the aircraft.

Correct positioning and the maintenance of adequate spacing between aircraft is very important, and unless this is ensured dangerous situations can occur, particularly during the base leg and final approach.

When on base leg a very careful lookout must be maintained for aircraft which may be carrying out a long final approach. Blind spots between aircraft operating in this area are particularly hazardous. Lookout must therefore be made to both sides of the flight path and above and below it.

The final approach is the area where aircraft funnel into the landing path and during this period the workload on the pilot can easily reduce his standard of lookout. It is in this area that collision risk between aircraft is probably the highest, and this risk can only be reduced by constant vigilance.

A missed approach can be initiated at any time from the base leg onwards, and should always be carried out without hesitation when doubt exists as to the safe completion of the approach and landing. Getting too close to the aircraft ahead, or being inaccurately positioned on the approach path, or overhauling an aircraft too quickly for it to clear the landing path, are all examples necessitating missed approach procedures.

When using normal aerodromes, remember that some runways have 'no go' areas in the region of the actual threshold, this is to ensure that arriving aircraft do not approach too low over obstructions including roads and houses which are close to the airfield boundary. The type of runway marking used to signify the existence of these areas is shown in the adjacent diagram, and a landing aircraft must not touch down until it has passed over the line of V's or arrows.

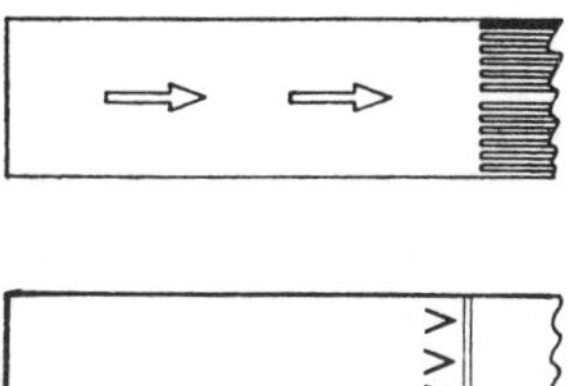

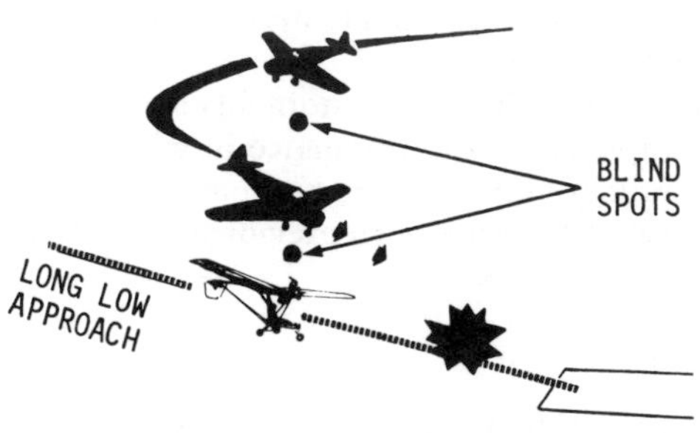

FIRST SOLO AND CONSOLIDATION

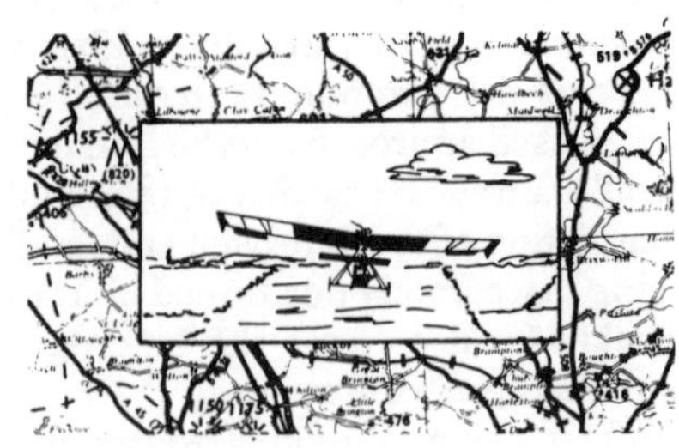

Objectives

The aim of the 'First Solo' flight is fairly obvious, but it can be defined as the successful achievement of the first major hurdle in flying training, and one which will allow the student to proceed to future flight exercises.

Introduction

This flight will be a significant occasion, and one which will stimulate your confidence. Although its accomplishment will often spur your rate of progress, do bear in mind that weather conditions can often interfere and delay the second solo flight. If this happens it is important not to become impatient about your progress or to be disappointed with your efforts.

Following your first solo flight you will normally spend several periods of flying to consolidate and improve your performance in take-offs, circuits, approaches, landings and the handling of missed approach and mislanding situations. Glide approach landings, if they have not been previously practised, may be introduced at this stage.

Airmanship
Your progress at implementing the various airmanship considerations, and the development of good airmanship will be a priority during this period of training. Good habits developed whilst practising solo circuits will have a considerable effect upon your ability to make sensible and safe decisions during future solo flying.

Local Flying
Following the consolidation period on the circuit you will be introduced to the procedures for leaving the circuit, developing orientation skills in the Local Flying Area, and rejoining the circuit for landing.

The method used for leaving the circuit area and departing for the local flying area will depend upon the procedures in use at your training organisation. There are various departure procedures which can be employed and the adjacent diagram shows the possible departure routes a student may be required to follow or which he may determine to use according to the prevailing circumstances. The path indicated by 3 illustrates the straight ahead climb out procedure and 4 and 5 are alternative methods. When climbing out straight ahead, due consideration must be given to the obscured area ahead and below the aircraft nose, and in these circumstances slight changes of heading to the left or right will be advisable.

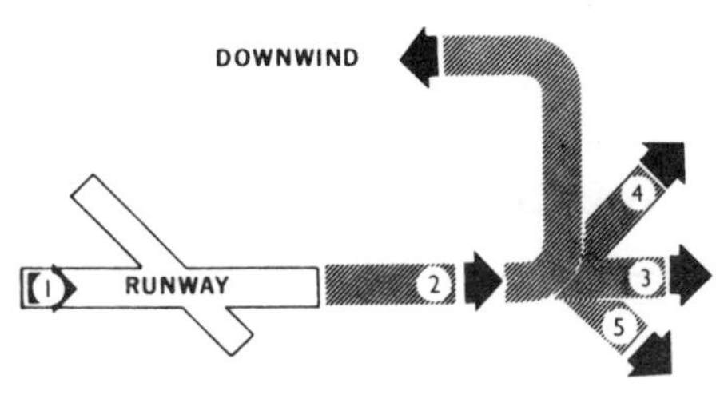

The departure track shown at 4 could be used in circumstances where rejoining aircraft are arriving on the crosswind leg for circuit entry, and the path shown at 5 would be a good method to use where the rejoining procedure is for aircraft to arrive directly on to the downwind leg.

All training airfields have a defined Local Area in which the student will carry out solo practice. When leaving the circuit the student will need to develop the ability to recognise landmarks, towns, etc., through local knowledge and map reading. The objective is to ensure that you can determine your position over the ground and develop a sense of orientation to ensure a return to the landing site.

In practice there are various methods used for joining the circuit pattern, and the use of any particular method will depend upon the weather in relation to visibility and cloudbase, or to the considerations involved during instruction demonstration and practice. The methods used at individual airfields will therefore vary, and the variations of the rejoining procedure must have been mastered before you are authorised for your first solo navigation flight.

Airmanship

A pilot must always keep in mind, wherever he may be, his responsibility for continuously maintaining a vigilant lookout, in relation to airfields, other air traffic or cloud. It must be noted that most 'near miss' situations between aircraft have usually occurred in conditions where the pilots involved should and could have seen the other aircraft.

A visual scan must take in all directions and should be made with the knowledge that the performance capabilities e.g. speed, rate of climb, etc., vary between aircraft, and that high closure rates are quite common. This limits the time available for detection for making correct decisions and taking evading action.

At least 50% of near miss incidents occur within or near the traffic pattern of airfields or landing sites, and these particularly involve aircraft which are climbing during departure, or descending towards the airfield and joining the circuit. During descending turns, there will always be blind areas and when descending into airfields and landing site environments hazardous situations can more easily occur.

ADVANCED TURNING

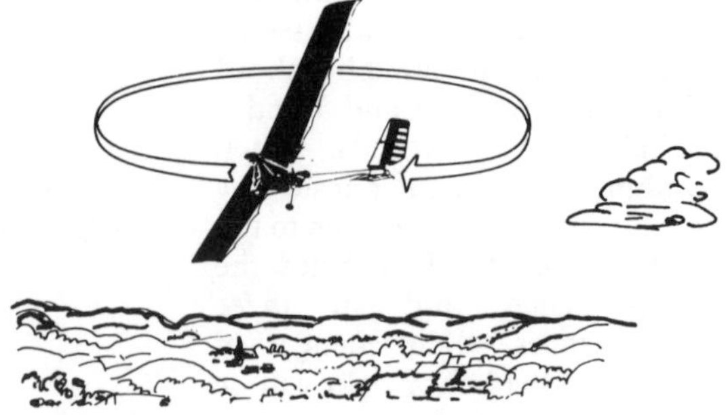

Objectives

Advanced turning is an exercise which is designed to improve your co-ordination and competency in handling the aircraft at steeper angles of bank. Additionally it will improve your confidence and also be of benefit should the need to take sudden evasive action arise.

Introduction

Although advanced turning is primarily taught to further develop the pilot's ability at co-ordination and aircraft handling, it must also be appreciated that incorrect handling of the aircraft during this practice can lead to overstressing the aircraft and/or stalling at higher airspeeds.

However it is not difficult to avoid either of these situations if the pilot has a thorough understanding of how incorrect control techniques can lead to circumstances which may place the aircraft and occupants at risk. During this exercise it is not the intention to teach private pilots to operate an aircraft to its limits, and the steepness of the turns and the airspeeds at which they are conducted must be carefully controlled with this knowledge in mind.

The Forces in Steep Turns

An aircraft in turning flight will have greater loads imposed upon it, thus increasing the structural stresses and also the stalling speed. In a steady co-ordinated turn during level flight, the vertical component of life must be equal to the weight of the aircraft in order that there will be no acceleration in a vertical direction. This introduces an important term in relation to manoeuvring flight, i.e. *Load Factor*. The load factor is the ratio between lift and weight.

The effect of load factor can be more easily explained by referring to Fig. 7-50. From this diagram it can be seen that the more the lift force is tilted the more total lift will be required to bring its vertical component (the component which balances the weight) to the original value. It will also be seen that a 60° angle of bank will necessitate a doubling of the total lift to achieve the original vertical lift force.

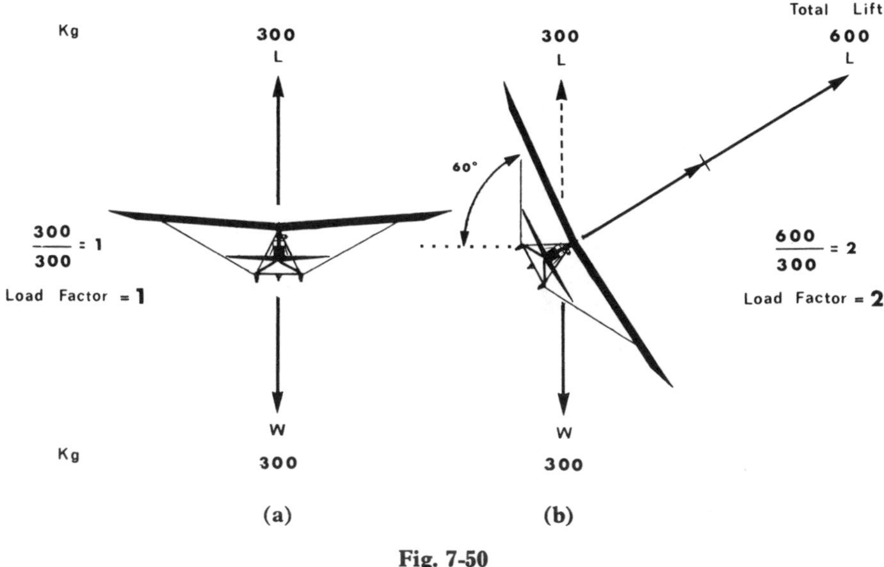

Fig. 7-50

Therefore, for a steady co-ordinated turn at a constant height, a specific value of load factor will be incurred, the value of which will depend upon the angle of bank, e.g. a bank angle of 60° will result in a load factor of 2.

Effect on Stalling Speed

Apart from the significance of the wing having to supply more lift than the weight to maintain the aircraft at a constant altitude, the resulting increase in load factor will cause an increase in the stalling speed.

During turning flight and manoeuvres, the effect on stall speed is similar to the effect of weight. A steady level turn requires the vertical component of lift to be equal to the weight of the aircraft and the horizontal component of lift to be equal to the centripetal force. Therefore, in a steady turn, the aircraft has to develop more lift than its weight.

During the turn at constant speed and altitude, the angle of attack will have to be increased to produce the extra lift required to support the aircraft. This causes an increase in the stalling speed which is related to the bank angle. Fig. 7-51 illustrates the percentage variation of stall speed with angle of bank.

Therefore, as the bank angle is increased, three factors of importance occur, the load factor, the stalling speed, and the drag, all increase. This increase in drag will cause the airspeed to decrease unless sufficient power is available to combat the added drag and keep the airspeed constant. It can therefore be seen that if insufficient power is available to overcome the additional drag, the flying speed will decrease and move toward the already increasing stalling speed as the angle of bank increases. A condition of stall will then occur at a substantially higher speed than would normally be expected.

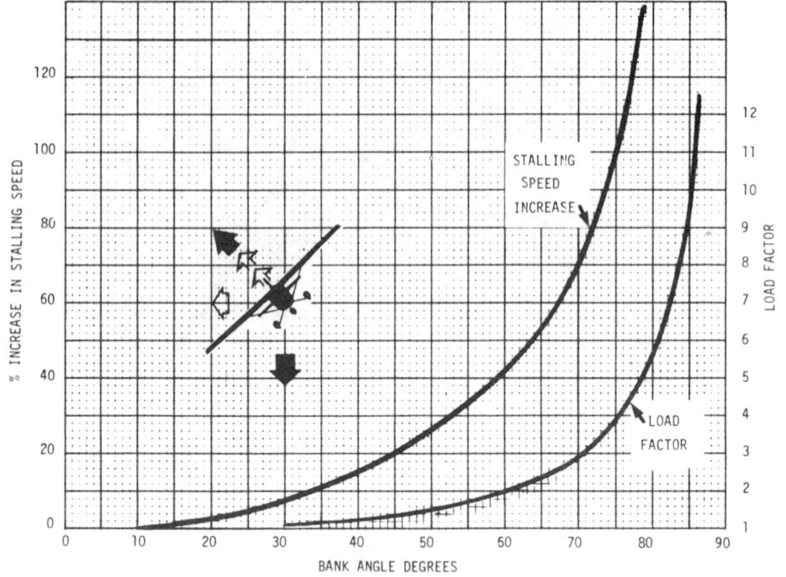

Fig. 7-51

It can also be seen from this illustration that whereas no significant change occurs to the stalling speed at moderate angles of bank up to 30°, the increase of load factor at greater angles than this has a startling effect upon stall speeds, i.e., at approximately 75° of bank the stalling speed is increased by 100%.

Structural Considerations

All aircraft are constructed to withstand any reasonable load factors which may be imposed upon them during flight, but the load factor limitation varies with different types of aircraft. The operation of any aircraft is subject to specific strength limitations, and overstressing can at best reduce the aircraft life and at worst can lead to catastrophic failure in flight.

The differences between the structural strength limitations of different aircraft types has a significant bearing when carrying out advanced turning or similar manoeuvres which impose high load factors on the airframe. Therefore, angles of bank must be limited in relation to the structural strength of a particular aircraft, and when the design load factor is not known it would be advisable to limit bank angles to below 45°.

Physiological Effects

During normal steep turn manoeuvres the body will experience positive 'g' loadings which will not usually be in excess of 2. This means that if a person weighs 75 kilos he will experience a body weight of 150 kilos at 2g. The effect of added 'g' force can be quickly adjusted to and will hardly be noticeable after several practice periods of Advanced Turning.

If the aircraft inadvertently gets into a low nose attitude during the turn and the pilot increases the load factor through the application of a large back pressure on the control column then a further effect of 'g' will become apparent. This is the effect of the blood draining down from the head towards the feet. At high accelerations, this draining of blood from the head can cause a 'greying out' and at higher accelerations a complete 'black out' of vision will eventually occur. The latter however, will normally be experienced only after the airframe has passed its limiting load factor, although the blackout threshold will also depend upon the pilot's degree of physical fitness.

Notwithstanding the comments made in the previous paragraph it should be appreciated that if a pilot causes a very sudden increase of 'g' to occur it will be possible to momentarily increase the 'g' loading to 8g or more before the effect of blood draining from the head and the consequent loss of oxygen to the brain causes a 'black out'. The airframe is less resilient than the human body and overstressing may easily occur.

During normal applications of 'g' the pilot will begin to see spots before his eyes at about 3g as the greying out process begins and this is a signal that back pressure must be released and the aircraft rolled into a laterally level attitude where it can be returned to normal level flight without excess 'g' force being exerted. Due to the different values of 'g' at which pilots grey out the foregoing must not be used as a means of assessing the load factor being applied.

Negative 'g' is more uncomfortable than positive 'g' but normally large negative 'g' forces are much more difficult to achieve either deliberately or inadvertently, but if they do occur the blood in the body will be forced up into the head and a 'redding out' condition will occur.

Air Exercise

The steep turn manoeuvre is an extension of the medium turn and can be executed in level, climbing or descending flight. However in relation to level and climbing flight the use of full power will be required to overcome the induced drag which is produced at the higher angles of attack which are needed to increase the total lift force.

Due to the significant reduction in airspeed at these higher angles of attack it will in almost all cases be necessary to increase the airspeed before increasing the bank angle beyond moderate amounts.

In relation to a descending steep turn it should be borne in mind that airspeed can be maintained and also increased by descending more steeply. This brings the structural considerations to the fore as it will be more easy to overstress the aircraft during this type of manoeuvre.

Stalling in the Turn

If insufficient power is available to overcome the additional drag the flying speed will move toward the already increasing stalling speed as the angle of bank increases. A stall will occur at a substantially higher speed than is the case when the aircraft is flown in level flight.

As stated and demonstrated during the stalling exercise an aircraft can be stalled from a level, descending or climbing turn. Stalls which occur from incorrect handling during a turn, particularly at steeper bank angles, are often associated with a positive wing drop particularly when the aircraft is flown with an aft c.g. As with the standard stall recovery the correct procedure to return the aircraft to a normal flight condition will be to move the control column forward and reduce the angle of attack.

Application of additional power will not have much effect if high power settings are already being used, as in the case of level and climbing steep turns. In the descending steep turn the nose will already be low and application of power will usually serve to accelerate the aircraft along the downward flight path, leading to additional height loss.

The Spiral Dive

If the nose is allowed to drop too far during the turn, this will be the result of not applying sufficient back pressure for the angle of bank being used, and the correction for this situation is to reduce the bank angle. However if recovery action is delayed or further back pressure is applied without also reducing the bank angle, a condition can occur where the turn tightens and the nose drops still further.

This condition is known as a 'Spiral Dive' and the use of back pressure alone will only serve to tighten and steepen the spiral as well as possibly overstressing the airframe. The correct recovery action is to close the throttle completely and positively roll the wings level, following this the aircraft can be eased out of the dive. When levelling the wings it must be appreciated that at the higher speeds associated with the spiral dive, the pilot will need to apply higher than normal control forces to the ailerons in order to roll the wings level.

Unusual Attitudes

Basically there are two types of unusual attitude taught during training, one where the aircraft nose is high and one where it is low. As these attitudes are being considered under Advanced Turning it can be assumed for the purpose of the following recovery procedures that a steep bank angle is present in either case.

Recovery Procedures

If the nose is high and the bank is steep:

- Level the wings and at the same time pitch the nose down and increase power smoothly (if additional power is available).
- Care must be used to control the aircraft gently as it may be in the region of the stall.

If the nose is low and the bank is steep:

The recovery from this condition is similar to the recovery from a spiral dive.

- Close the throttle.
- Roll the wings level and then recover from the dive in the normal way.

Airmanship

It is the pilot's responsibility to ensure that harnesses are tight and the surrounding airspace is clear of other air traffic before commencing practice steep turns. The height must be adequate enough to ensure sufficient time for recovery action to be taken should the aircraft inadvertently enter an unusual attitude, stall or spin.

The location must be one which is away from departure or arrival lanes near airfields and at a reasonable distance from any controlled airspace, aerodrome traffic zone, danger area or similar airspace.

Orientation will remain an important aspect of airmanship throughout this exercise and the student must monitor his geographic location between each manoeuvre to ensure that he is not drifted too far downwind, and does not depart too far from the area previously assessed as suitable for the practice.

A point worth noting is that during advanced turns the aircraft is flown at relatively high angles of attack, and in this condition it will produce moderate wake turbulence, thus if the aircraft loses some 20 to 40 feet of height during a 360° turn it will be flown through its own wake vortex, and this should be anticipated.

The strength of a wake vortex is related to the weight of the aircraft i.e. the greater the weight the greater the required angle of attack for any given airspeed. Once the effect of wake turbulence produced from a light aircraft has been experienced it will be easier to obtain a better physical appreciation of the considerably greater effect and added dangers of the wake turbulence produced by large General Aviation aircraft or airliners.

Owner's Manuals may state the airframe limitations which apply to a particular aircraft and caution must be exercised when practising advanced turning manoeuvres, to ensure these stress limitations are not exceeded. If a pilot thinks that overstressing has occurred at any time, his duty must be to report this to his instructor or to a ground engineer. Remember that in relation to overstressing an aircraft, a pilot not only has a responsibility for the safety of his aircraft and passengers, but also for those who may fly in the aircraft afterwards.

● LOOKOUT ASSUMES A GREATER DEGREE OF URGENCY DURING ADVANCED TURNING.

FLIGHT AT MINIMUM LEVEL

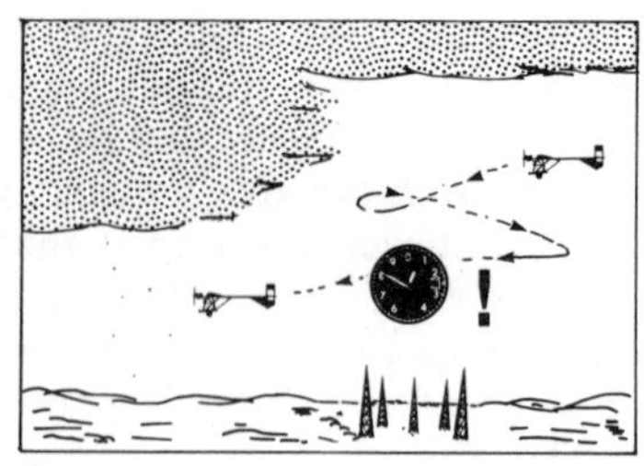

Objectives

The purpose of this exercise is to teach you how to operate the aircraft in safety when circumstances dictate the need for the aircraft to be flown at significantly lower heights than those normally used during the en-route stage of a flight. In the case of microlights these heights can be considered as being from 1000 ft to 500 ft above ground level.

Introduction

The primary reason for including this exercise in the syllabus is to cover the considerations of flying at lower than normal altitudes due to deterioration in the weather whilst you are in the circuit, the local area or conducting a navigation flight.

Without doubt one of the greatest problems the pilot has to face is the weather and its attendant hazards during flight. The ability to recognise the warning signs of weather deterioration and the knowledge needed to carry out the necessary procedures if caught out in these circumstances, is vital to the achievement of flight safety.

Low Level Familiarisation

During the operation of an aircraft at minimum level the pilot will need to understand certain environmental factors which he will not normally meet during flight at higher altitudes, for example the requirement to map read, interpret ground features and identify his position will become more difficult at lower levels. Further, due to the associated reasons necessitating operation at minimum level such as low cloud often in combination with poor visibility the exercise requires a higher standard of flying ability, self discipline and decision making qualities, all of which must be displayed during conditions which are more difficult than when flying normally at safer altitudes.

Preliminary Actions Prior to Descending

Immediately it becomes apparent that a flight cannot be conducted at a normal safe altitude and before descending to a lower level the following checks should be completed.

Fuel — The fuel contents should be noted, as running low or even out of fuel when the aircraft is near the ground will always be a more difficult emergency to handle when time is limited.

Engine — The cylinder head temperature should be checked to ensure that there is no indication of a developing engine malfunction, which might cause failure when the aircraft is at these lower levels.

Altimeter — Review the datum to which you have set the altimeter. During navigation flights this should be the QNH, thereby allowing you to determine your height above the terrain you are overflying.

Harness — Ensure this is tight and secure. There will always be the possibility of meeting turbulent conditions when low down, particularly if the wind strength has increased since take-off.

Position — Check the position of the aircraft immediately prior to the descent, and include a review of high ground, obstructions, danger and similar areas within or adjacent to the area. The changed wind velocity at the lower levels will also need to be anticipated.

The descent should be planned in relation to both time and position to ensure that it can be safely made without entering or becoming very close to cloud. The inadvertent entry to cloud in this type of operation would be particularly hazardous to a VFR pilot and if descending through gaps or broken layers of cloud, the pilot can easily experience spatial disorientation which would again lead to a hazardous situation.

Selection of Airspeed and Configuration

In small training aircraft the normal cruising speed will usually give an adequate margin for avoiding action in relation to high ground, obstructions or other aircraft.

Although range or endurance are not significantly affected by descents to lower levels in small training aircraft, an appreciation of the fuel remaining and that needed to return to the airfield must be conducted at short intervals. This will become of increasing importance if the pilot has to circumnavigate the weather.

Visual Impressions and Height Keeping at a Low Altitude

Once the aircraft has been levelled off at the selected height you will be able to more clearly appreciate the changed perspective of ground features and the difficulties experienced in maintaining the selected height by reference to the ground. Although one aim in this exercise is to develop your ability to judge height over the surface by visual reference, the altimeter should not be ignored as it will be of value as a secondary reference.

The lower the aircraft is flown the more oblique will be the view of the ground features which will lead to map reading becoming more difficult. One object of this exercise therefore will be to give you an opportunity to study this changed perspective, so that with practice you will be able to relate this changed impression of the ground features to your interpretation of the information shown on the map.

If snow has fallen the effect will be to mask certain ground features blending them with one another, affording greater difficulty in establishing the aircraft position.

In order to develop your ability to map read when flying at lower levels the aircraft will be flown at heights between 1000 ft and 500 ft during which you will get a first hand impression of landmarks viewed from an oblique angle. It will be important to keep in mind that symbols are not shown on air navigation charts for obstructions less than 300 ft above local ground level, and unmarked obstructions of all kinds may be present up to a height of 299 ft above ground level.

In view of this, you must make due allowance for unmarked obstructions up to this height in addition to the required terrain clearance, when determining minimum safe height, and although it is unlikely that there will be any need to fly at such very low heights, it must nevertheless be considered as a possibility when flying in areas where the ground has sharp vertical irregularities and the visibility is poor.

In relation to the weather conditions prevailing, it should be appreciated that poor visibility alone is no reason for flying at heights below 1500 ft. In these circumstances map reading can become very difficult and you will be much safer staying at a reasonable altitude. This will give you more time to concentrate on map reading and determining your position. Although at higher altitudes the slant visibility factor will reduce your visual range this effect is minimal at heights of 1500 ft to 2000 ft as shown in Fig. 7-52.

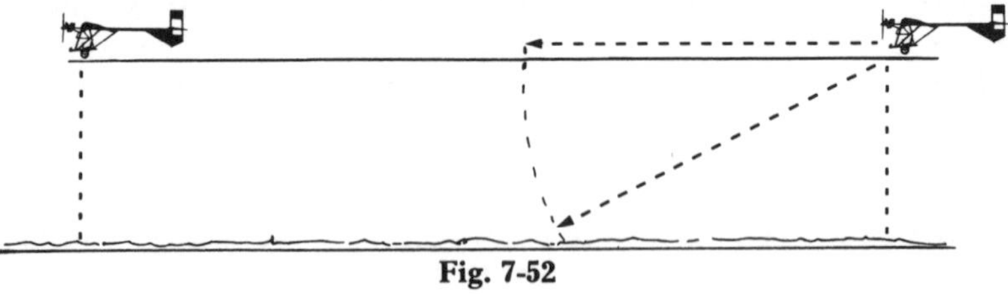

Fig. 7-52

Effects of Speed and Inertia During Turns

Whenever an aircraft turns, a degree of inertia will be present, this is highest at increased speed and less at reduced speeds. Whereas at altitude the effect of inertia is not particularly important it does become significant when operating near the surface. Whilst at low level you will be shown the visual effect during turns and made to appreciate the need for early decisions whenever obstacle clearance requires a change of direction.

Effects of Wind

This too is more noticeable during flight at low altitude, and its effect can produce erroneous impressions in the balance of the aircraft, for example when flying across the prevailing wind direction the amount of drift experienced can be clearly seen as shown in Fig. 7-53.

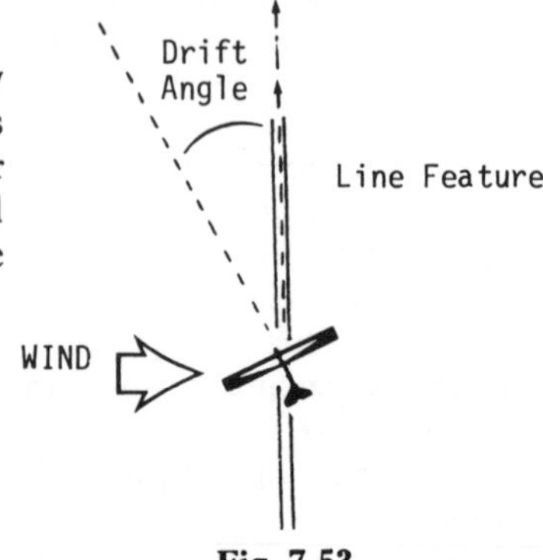

Fig. 7-53

If an aircraft being flown into wind is turned downwind the pilot will get the impression that the aircraft is slipping in towards the direction of turn. This is illustrated in Fig. 7-54.

When turning the aircraft to a downwind heading a distinct impression of 'slipping in' will occur.

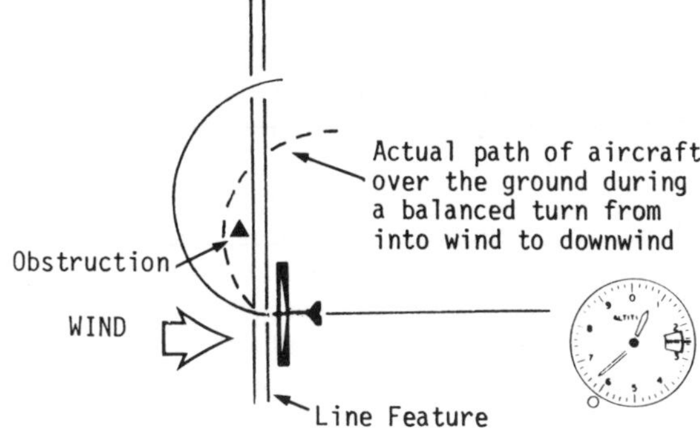

Fig. 7-54

Additionally, when flying downwind the impression of speed is greater and the pilot must guard against any instinctive tendency to reduce power in order to combat what is only a false impression of increased airspeed.

When turning upwind the opposite will be the case and the pilot will obtain the visual impression that the aircraft is in unbalanced flight and skidding towards the outside of the turn, Ref. Fig. 7-55.

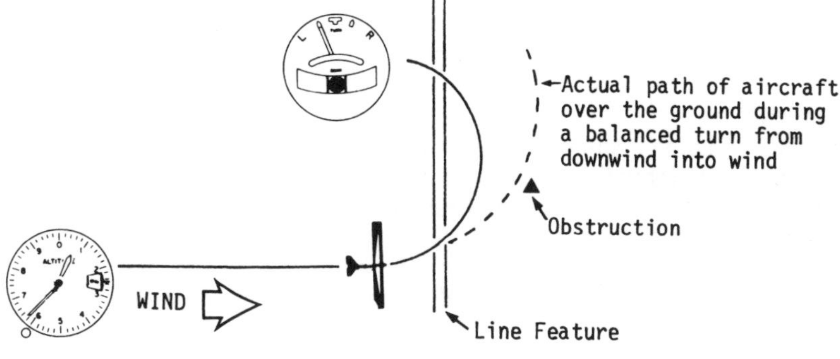

Fig. 7-55

Effect of Turbulence

When flying at relatively low altitudes over general terrain which is less flat and with more surface obstructions than an airfield, mechanical turbulence and wind shear effects are more marked, particularly in moderate to strong winds.

Turbulence and eddies will always exist in the vicinity of, and especially downwind of woods, forests, or hilly and undulating ground. Such turbulence can become a very real hazard to an aircraft in flight and the use of added power to avoid sudden height loss must be anticipated.

Air Exercise

Self discipline, methodical cockpit procedures and the development of an awareness of the problems will be essential for such a flight operation to be safely conducted.

When a low cloud base occurs with good visibility underneath, ground features can be seen well ahead and to either side of the aircraft flight path, however an awareness of the position of the aircraft in relation to high ground and obstructions will be necessary, and the importance of knowing the exact position prior to descending deserves special emphasis.

When conditions of both low cloud and poor visibility are experienced considerable care must be used to maintain a close check on the aircraft position, and an accurate appreciation of ground speed and intelligent use of the clock will be essential. It is just this type of weather condition which may call for a change in plan and an estimated heading and time required to an alternative landing site.

Some of the factors to be considered when arriving at a decision to continue or divert are listed below:

- The anticipated minimum base of the cloud in relation to the terrain to be overflown.
- The likelihood of the weather deteriorating still further.
- The visibility range to be expected when operating below the cloud, including the effect of precipitation.
- The degree of difficulty likely to be experienced in map reading and maintaining a reasonably accurate track in the existing weather conditions.
- The fuel state and daylight remaining in relation to the distance to the nearest suitable airfield or landing site.
- The weather conditions anticipated along the diversion route.
- The type of terrain to be overflown.

Airmanship

From the foregoing it can be seen that a continued state of awareness is essential for weather deterioration to be dealt with in a safe and sensible fashion. A lack of awareness coupled with unpreparedness can lead to hazardous circumstances in which a pilot who lacks decision making capability can be forced into a situation where he is unsure of his position or completely lost and flying into worsening weather, getting nearer the ground and becoming a potential hazard to himself and persons on the ground.

Lookout in relation to other aircraft is just as important at the lower levels as it is during operations at normal altitudes. It is sensible to assume that if a pilot is forced to fly low because of bad weather then other pilots may also be in the same situation.

KEEP IN MIND:

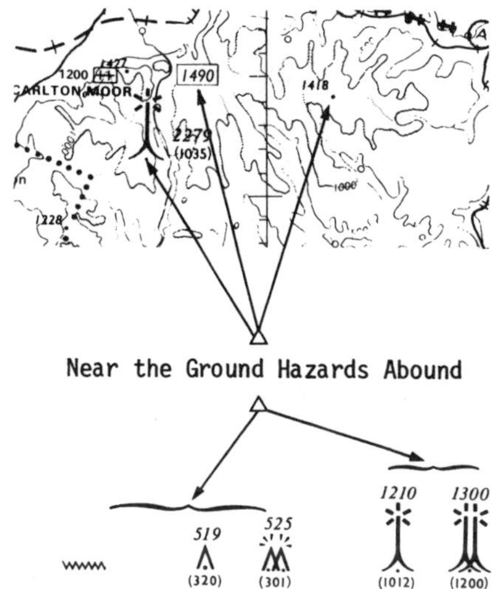

1200
CARLTON MOOR
1490
1418
2279
(1035)
1000
1228
Near the Ground Hazards Abound
519
(320)
525
(301)
1210
(1012)
1300
(1200)

Be Alert for Airspace Restrictions

FORCED LANDINGS WITHOUT POWER

Objectives

The purpose of this exercise is to teach you the procedure to adopt in the event of an engine failure occurring during flight at medium to high altitudes. The practising of this emergency procedure must be aimed at developing the required level of competence to handle this type of situation.

Introduction

Development of competence will only come from frequent practice during training and additional practice at intervals thereafter. When learning the procedures involved following an engine failure, it must be appreciated that in training for any emergency situation there are two fundamental aspects to consider.

1. The prevention of an emergency situation.
2. The action to be taken should an emergency situation occur.

Whereas this exercise is primarily concerned with the second of these aspects, you should appreciate that most engine failures occur because of fuel problems or lack of care in maintaining the engine. With this in mind it can be seen that if care is taken to ensure consistently good operating practices, the forced landing without power situation should rarely occur.

Forced Landing Procedures

The following procedures are mainly concerned with the execution of the forced landing without power, but there may be circumstances when partial power is available, and the decision to carry out a forced landing will then depend upon:

- The amount of power remaining and whether or not there are indications that a total power loss will follow.
- The distance to the nearest airfield.
- The type of terrain below the aircraft at the time and the nature of the surface en-route to the nearest airfield.
- Whether other factors, e.g. engine fire, are involved.

In such situations the pilot will have to weigh up all the factors before deciding to either continue to the nearest airfield using partial power, or

closing the throttle and initiating a forced landing without power, or

carrying out a forced landing using partial power.

Such a decision can only be made at the time, but a cautionary note can be introduced here, and that is if partial power is used to assist in the forced landing, the basic procedure once over the selected landing area should follow that used when no power is available.

This is to guard against the possibility of the engine stopping completely at some stage during the descent around the selected landing area. In other words if some power is available, use it when needed, but never rely upon it during the planning of the final descent route.

Choice of Landing Area

The surface of the landing area should preferably be grass or firm stubble. The presence of young crops indicates the surface will have been recently ploughed, and ripening crops will be long, leading in either case to the aircraft nosing over. The same will apply if the surface is particularly green, as this would indicate swampy ground with a very soft surface. Identification of suitable surface areas will only come from practice at recognition, and this will normally be carried out during earlier flights.

A marked ground slope will pose hazards and difficulties which increase with steepness. Down slopes should where possible be avoided as these will normally lead to a greatly increased landing run.

Field size and shape must be considered, and obviously if all other factors are equal the greater the size the better will be the chances of success, but shape will also be important, because a squarish field will offer alternative landing paths in the event that the aircraft is too low or too high at the end of the downwind or during the base leg. Fig 7-56 shows the benefits available from a square field and the restrictions of a long narrow field. The diagram at (a) shows the increased number of options a pilot will have if during the base leg or earlier he finds that he is too high or too low. It also affords a change in landing path if in the final stages he discovers that the original landing path is unsuitable. In the case of a narrow field these options will not be available.

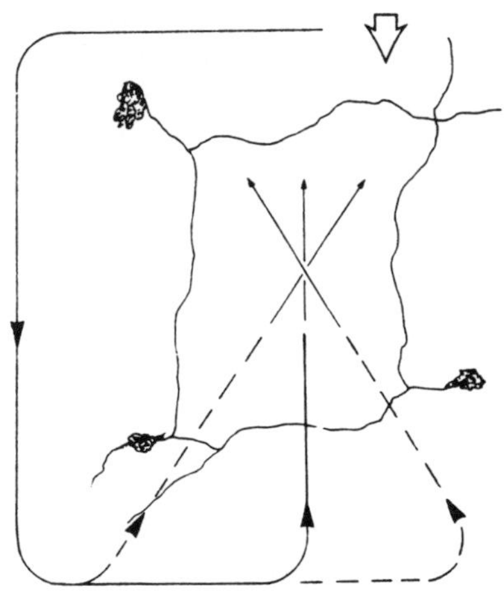

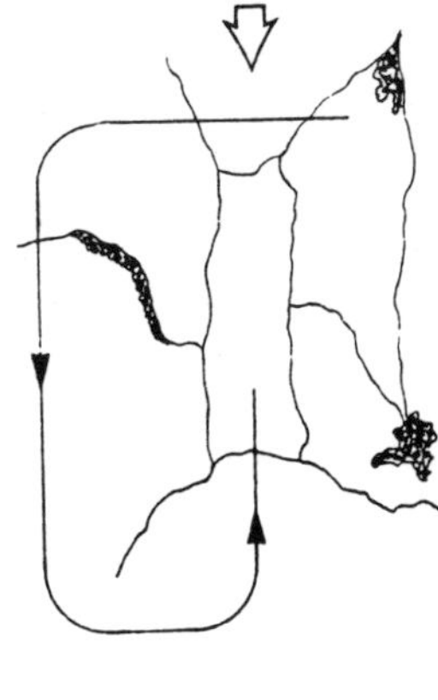

(a) **Fig. 7-56** **(b)**

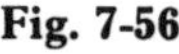

The overshoot, and particularly the undershoot area, must be free from obstructions as far as possible. Isolated trees can be negotiated if the aircraft is on the low side during the final stage of the approach, but copses or woods can form a hazard which cannot easily be dealt with when little manoeuvring height remains.

The selection of a landing area must be made as early as possible following the engine failure. This enables a wider choice to be made, with greater height. Nevertheless, when choosing a landing area from heights above 1500 ft a possibility will always exist that the initial choice will be unsuitable, due to the inability to discern from height such hazards as power cables suspended from small wooden poles, or ditches and stagnant streams with a greenish surface, any of which would cause considerable damage during the landing run (ref. Fig. 7-57).

Fig. 7-57

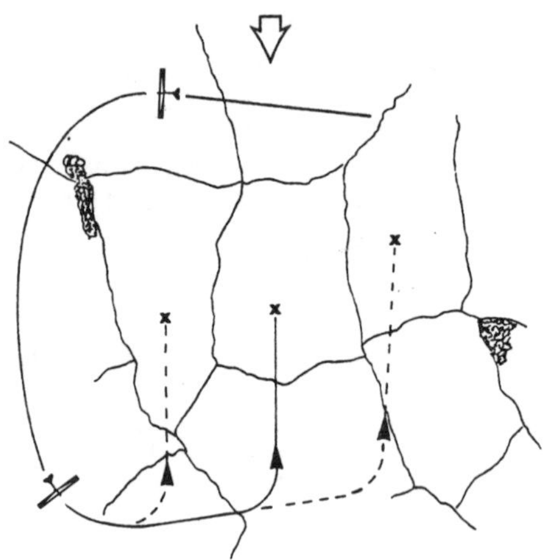

Fig 7.58

Provision for Change of Plan

Therefore when initially selecting an area to land it is advisable when possible to select a group of fields, choosing one of them which conforms to the requirements and is centrally situated. Having done this, a misjudgement or the discovery that the original choice is unsuitable, will enable a change of plan to be made without delay. Fig. 7-58 shows how an alternative choice of landing area can be implemented. The broken lines in the diagram show the alternative routes which can be followed.

Gliding Distance — Considerations

The choice of landing area must be made so that the aircraft can reach it at a height which allows the pilot to plan a descent pattern. A minimum of an angled base leg will be required to enable the pilot to re-adjust heading as necessary depending upon his height and the wind velocity, in order to reach the touch down area.

In the limited time available during this type of emergency, mathematical calculations and judgement of distances are not easily made. However when estimating the distance an aircraft can glide (assuming zero wind) one factor which remains constant is the descent angle. Therefore a radius about the aircraft will be the easiest method to use when judging gliding distance.

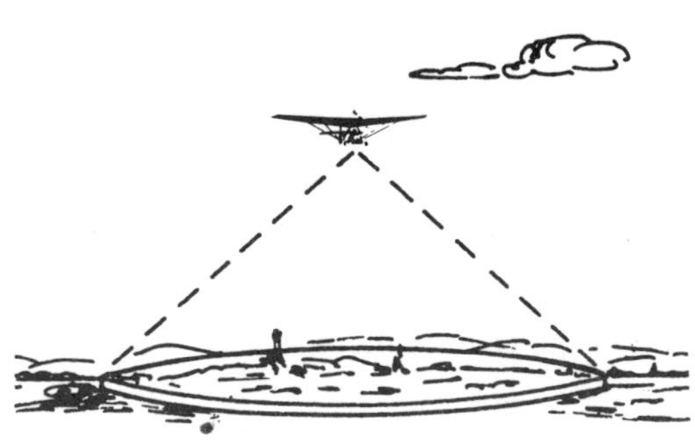

The Descent Plan

During the descent phase the route will be one that takes the aircraft towards and around the landing area. This will be achieved by establishing a descending circuit pattern during which a crosswind, downwind, base leg and final approach will be carried out. The distance out from the landing area will vary with the aircraft height at the time and its position in relation to the touch down area. Two possible variations of this circuit pattern are shown in Fig. 7-59.

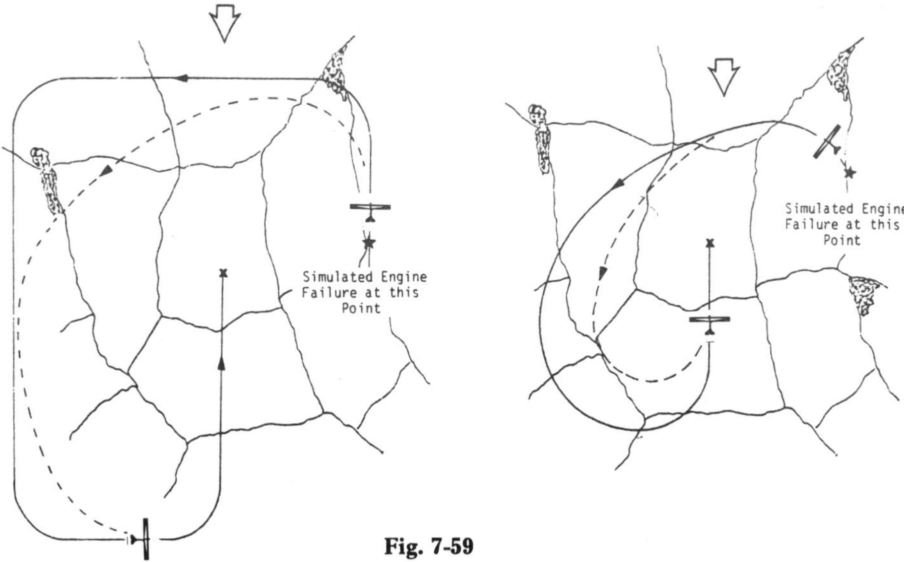

Fig. 7-59

The dotted lines show alternative routes which can be used if at any stage the aircraft is estimated to be too low in relation to its position in the pattern.

To what extent either path is followed will depend mainly upon the position and height of the aircraft relative to the chosen landing area at the time of the engine failure. Further to this, the strength and direction of the wind may require frequent amendment to the planned descent route.

In the case of engine failure occurring well below 1500 ft agl. the prior practice of forced landings from higher altitudes will stand you in good stead, as you will be able to appreciate where the aircraft should fit into this previously practised pattern compatible with the aircraft position and the height available.

You will have had frequent practice at flying rectangular patterns about an airfield, incorporating downwind and base legs, and the use of a similar pattern during a forced landing would be familiar to you. However being able to achieve this type of descent pattern will depend upon the aircraft position relative to the selected landing area, together with the wind velocity and height available at the time of the engine failure.

Air Exercise

The actual descent plan will have to be based upon the circumstances prevailing at the time. However during your initial practice of this exercise a simple descent plan should be used commencing from a reasonable altitude. Later on you should vary the aircraft's height and position relative to the selected landing area before simulating the emergency so that you obtain practice of handling forced landings in different situations.

The procedure to adopt will in general follow the principal steps outlined below:

- Adopt the glide, and search all around the aircraft for a suitable area within gliding distance. Turn towards this area and estimate the wind direction and strength.
- Select the best field within the chosen area bearing in mind the size, shape, surface, slope and surrounds.
- Choose the key position for the entry point of the descent pattern compatible with the height available. Assess the height of the ground in the immediate area and bear in mind that the altimeter will only give an approximate indication of height above ground regardless of what datum is being used.
- Choose a key area above the ground which is coincident with the end of the proposed downwind leg. The height of this key area should be consistent with the height you use for your normal circuits. Review any intermediate key areas at 500 ft intervals to aid judgement in arriving at the end of your downwind leg at the appropriate height.
- Complete the specified checks (for the particular aircraft type) in an attempt to rectify the engine failure.
- When carrying out checks and drills ensure that adequate surveillance of the selected landing area is maintained, together with the aircraft's progress towards the chosen key areas. Maintain or modify the descent route relative to the landing area as required.

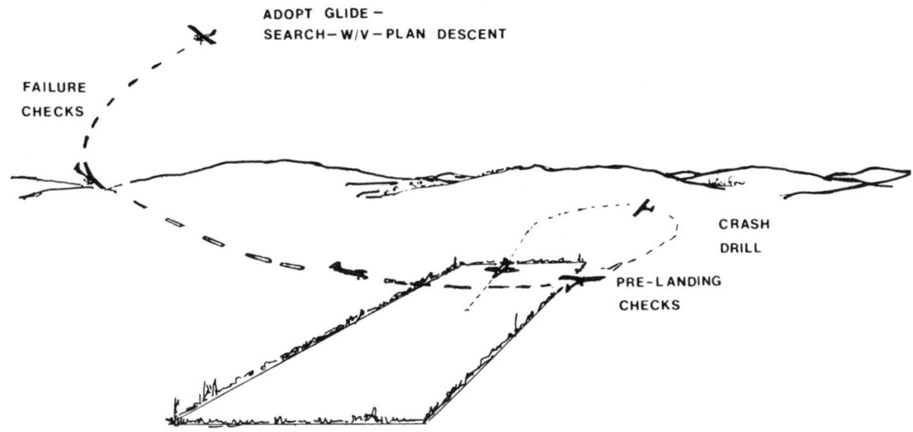

- The Downwind Leg. During that portion of the descent pattern which most closely approximates the downwind leg the normal pre-landing checks should be carried out, however during a real forced landing procedure these checks should be replaced by the 'Security Drills' which consist of turning OFF the ignition (and when possible the fuel), and ensuring the harnesses are very tight. During practice these latter drills should not be physically carried out but just said aloud.

  The end of the downwind leg terminates in your chosen key area. This area can be considered as a cube of airspace at which both the estimated height over the ground and the aircraft's position relative to the touch down point will need to be assessed, together with the wind strength and direction, when considering the exact point to turn onto the base leg.
- The Base Leg. The main value of the base leg lies in the fact that during this part of the descent the pilot can manoeuvre the aircraft into a position for the final approach, and at this stage the aiming point should be one third to half way into the field.

  The aircraft position can be varied in relation to the selected touch down point by diverging from the field if the aircraft is too high or converging if the aircraft appears to be too low. Alternatively if the aircraft is significantly low or high at this stage the landing line can be changed and the aircraft turned onto final approach earlier or later than originally planned. If a narrow field has had to be selected and an excess of height occurs on the base leg, then the aircraft's heading can be altered to diverge away from the field until the final turn. If this action is insufficient the aircraft can be flown past the approach centreline followed by a shallow 'S' turn to bring the aircraft back onto the approach path.

In the event that engine failure occurs low down the procedure will have to be modified depending upon the actual height above the ground, and the aircraft position relative to a suitable landing area. Some examples of alternative routes are shown in the adjacent diagram.

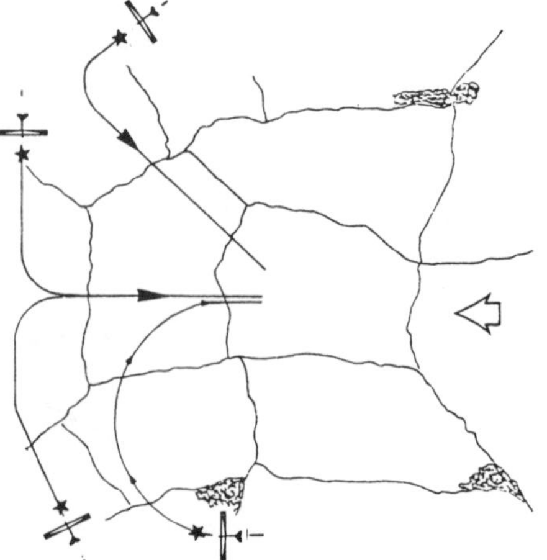

- The Final Approach. In most circumstances the final approach will be fairly short. This is due to the need to keep the base leg fairly close to the field when carrying out a glide approach in a microlight aircraft. Assuming the base leg has been handled properly and the position of the turn onto the final approach has been accurately judged the most important item at this stage will be the need to maintain a safe airspeed. If the aircraft is too high on this leg then there might be time to carry out one or two shallow 'S' turns to lose sufficient height before landing.
- Going Round Again. As soon as the outcome of the practice forced landing can be clearly seen, the aircraft should be climbed away. It is however important not to leave this until the aircraft is very low, and the minimum height to which the aircraft should be allowed to descend will be laid down by your training organisation.
- – – – – – – The Landing. In the case of an actual forced landing it may be that the length of the landing run available is rather short. In these circumstances there will be a strong tendency for you to place the aircraft onto the ground before the correct touchdown speed is reached. This may be a necessary action when available ground distance is becoming obviously short, but you must resist giving way to unwarranted anxiety in this respect, or the aircraft and occupants may be exposed to the hazard of nosing over. Bearing this point in mind it will nevertheless be advisable to place the aircraft firmly on the ground if an obvious over run is imminent, as this will utilise the deceleration effects of surface friction, to reduce the forward speed as much as possible.

  If brakes are fitted they could be used earlier than normal, but care should be used to apply them intermittently, increasing the pressure as the aircraft slows down, particularly if landing on a wet surface. In the event that the aircraft will clearly not stop before reaching the far hedge or any obstruction, a controlled ground loop should be initiated. This will obviate the sudden deceleration which occurs on collision with obstacles. This ground looping action will also hold good when the aircraft is running towards a ditch or similar ground feature at a moderately low speed.

Actions After Landing. In the case of a real forced landing, immediately the aircraft comes to rest, the safety harnesses should be released and the aircraft evacuated. When a passenger is on board you must give clear orders to this effect, and ensure that safety straps or harnesses are not unfastened until the aircraft has come to a complete stop.

When clear of the aircraft you should take stock of the situation, returning to the aircraft to ensure that everything is switched off.

Your next concern will be to protect the aircraft as far as possible, and in this connection it should be borne in mind that cattle are very inquisitive by nature and can easily damage an aircraft. Once the aircraft has been secured you should find the nearest telephone and inform your training organisation of the situation.

NOTE: If after landing, you find out the reason for the engine failure and can correct it, you must on no account attempt to take-off without consulting and obtaining permission to do so from your training organisation.

Airmanship

It will be important during the glide descent to open up to the half throttle position at intervals to ensure the engine is continuing to run correctly, to keep the plugs clear of excess carbon deposits, and to maintain a reasonably warm engine. The throttle should be left in the half open position for two or three seconds to be of value, and sudden and full power applications avoided as this will interfere with the smooth maintenance of the descent plan. In order to avoid upsets of judgement during the final stages of the approach the last opening of the throttle should be done during the base leg.

In relation to lookout it must be appreciated that other aircraft may also be involved in forced landing practice within the Local Flying Area, therefore the need to stay constantly aware of the position of other air traffic must be emphasised. This is necessary because of the danger of becoming over absorbed in the procedure to be followed.

This aspect of lookout is particularly important when specified fields are used for forced landing practice, especially in light winds when decisions as to the best final approach direction may vary between different pilots using the same forced landing area.

The minimum height down to which this exercise is practiced will depend upon the rules of the training organisation and the local environment. In any event the 500 ft rule must be observed, and it is very important that nuisance is not created to persons or livestock during the latter stages of the exercise.

During practice the selection of a suitable landing area must include an appraisal of the 'climb away' area. If this is covered with woods, buildings etc., then a totally unnecessary hazard will exist in the event of an actual engine failure occurring during the climb away phase. Therefore always ensure the climb out path is over relatively flat open countryside.

FORCED LANDING WITH POWER (PRECUATIONARY LANDING)

Objectives

The purpose of this exercise is to teach you the procedures to be followed should conditions occur which force you to land at a disused airfield or on an unprepared landing surface or an unknown airstrip.

Introduction

A forced landing when power is available can be considered as any unplanned landing which is forced upon the pilot due to circumstances encountered during flight. These circumstances normally relate to:

- Deteriorating Weather,
- Becoming Lost,
- A Low Fuel State,
- The Onset of Darkness.

When practising this exercise, the basic procedure used will apply to most landings made away from an active landing site, however variations will be dictated by the specific weather conditions at the time, e.g. cloud base, visibility, wind strength, and the type of terrain. One point to note is that the method of performing an approach and landing into a small field will also be applicable to the method used for landing at small airstrips. Therefore this part of the exercise will serve two purposes in your training.

Occasions Necessitating

The circumstances leading to a forced landing with power can be many and varied, but they usually arise from becoming lost, weather deterioration, running short of fuel or daylight. The difficulties encountered are normally of a compound nature, e.g. if the weather deteriorates, the likelihood of becoming lost is increased, and when navigation difficulties occur they can often result in unplanned additional airborne time leading to a shortage of fuel or the onset of darkness.

The important message emerging from these factors concerns the need to develop a state of awareness and the ability to take positive decisions before the situation changes from one of 'Urgency' to one of 'Emergency'.

In view of the foregoing it can be seen that when bad weather has led to the situation where a forced landing with power is necessary, many of the considerations are complementary to the lessons learned during Operation at Minimum Level.

The Procedure

A suitable field must be selected, and in assessing its suitability several factors must be taken into account. However the time available, e.g. fuel state, onset of darkness, and weather conditions will determine the scope of the search, and the choice may be restricted due to lack of time. The factors to bear in mind during the field selection are:

1. The length of the landing run available in relation to the wind direction and strength.
2. The nature of the ground surface and whether a pronounced slope is present.
3. The presence of obstructions in the vicinity of the undershoot and overshoot areas, keeping in mind that it may be necessary to go round again should the first approach to land be unsuccessful.

Having established that these criteria are satisfactory, standard circuit joining checks should be completed. Bear in mind that the altimeter will most probably be set to the QNH datum and if uncertain of your geographic position you will have to visually assess your height above the ground. Following these checks, the aircraft should be manoeuvred to a position which is into wind and slightly to one side of the selected landing path. The first inspection run should be done at 5/600 ft agl. and a safe cruising speed maintained.

Circuit and Approach Procedure
During the first inspection run the approach path must be assessed for suitability, and the position of any obstructions in relation to the descent path noted.

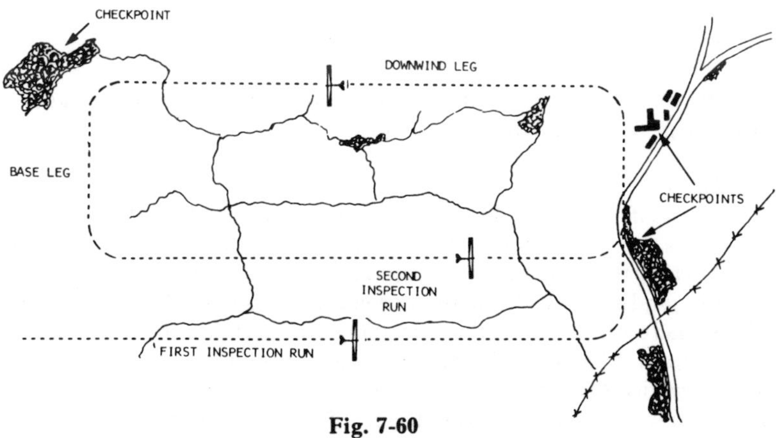

Fig. 7-60

By flying along one side of the intended landing path the surface will be more easily inspected for hidden ditches, light wire fences, rocks and other surface irregularities. The general appearance should be assessed in relation to whether it is relatively flat or sloping. If the inspection so far indicates the field is suitable the overshoot area should be checked for any obstructions, e.g. trees, power cables etc., which may be a hazard should the first approach have to be converted into a 'go round again'.

The aircraft can then be put into a circuit around the field and provided conditions permit, a second inspection run should be made, but this time an approach down to approximately 100 ft agl. should be flown, to coincide with the centre line of the selected landing path. This second inspection run will give you a final opportunity to re-assess all the points you were looking for during the first inspection and a more accurate assessment of the landing surface can be made.

Provided the results of this run establish the field to be satisfactory, the final circuit and approach can be commenced.

Actions After Landing
Wait until the aircraft has come to rest before releasing the seat harness. After this the normal shutting down and after flight checks should be carried out and the aircraft inspected for damage. Due to the possible hazards which may exist or be partially hidden by long grass, e.g. indentations, drainage strips etc., it is not advisable to taxy the aircraft after the landing is completed. In the event that the aircraft has to be moved to a safer position, e.g. shelter from the wind etc., a thorough inspection of the ground surface should be made on foot, and only after ensuring that the ground is suitable for taxying should the aircraft be restarted and moved to the required position.

The aircraft should be secured and protected as far as possible from damage by persons or animals and then you should contact your training organisation to inform them of the situation. Finally regardless of any improvement of the weather conditions, you should not attempt to take-off again unless you have received clearance from your instructor.

Air Exercise

The format of the air exercise has been covered on the preceding pages but the following aspects of airmanship will apply.

Airmanship
As in the case of Operation At Minimum Level the initial emphasis in relation to airmanship is the development of a sense of awareness to weather conditions, fuel state etc. so that the situation of a forced landing with power would never become more than a landing at an alternative airfield. This will only be achieved by correct decisions made early, rather than delaying the issue until the situation occurs where the aircraft has to be landed in whatever field can be found.

During practice the emphasis on airmanship will be in the need to choose a suitable field which not only meets the requirements of the exercise, but also one which will permit the practice to take place without infringing the 500 ft rule or causing annoyance to persons or livestock.

Due regard must be given to the maintenance of safety throughout the exercise, and adequate speed for the inspection runs and approaches must be maintained. This is particularly important when moderate or strong winds, gustiness and downdraughts are present.

During an actual situation:

Provided fuel state and weather conditions permit it will be essential to 'go round again' from the final approach to landing if the aircraft is not in the right position at the correct height and airspeed after the boundary of the field has been crossed.

SECTION EIGHT

PROGRESS TESTS

Progress Tests

This section contains a series of Progress Tests designed to enable you to test your level of knowledge in the subject materials included in this Manual.

You should bear in mind the following points when completing the tests:

They are designed to enable you to monitor your progress. Their objective is to provide a means whereby you can assess your knowledge and understanding at various stages in your learning task. If you can score good marks (75% or above) in these tests you will be able to sit the CAA written examination with a high degree of confidence.

The test items are not trick questions, each statement means exactly what it says. Therefore read each question, response or statement carefully and do not look for hidden meanings.

Be sure that you understand what the test item asks, and then review the alternate responses. Following this, decide which response is the correct one or work out the problem to obtain the correct answer.

Always select the response which gives the most complete and correct answer, the others will be responses which are totally wrong, partially wrong or those which you might select if you lack sufficient knowledge of the subject.

Upon completing each test, check your answers against those shown on page Q—29. Questions which give you difficulty or which you fail to answer correctly will give you an indication of those areas in which you lack understanding, and you should therefore review the appropriate parts of the subject before proceeding with your next stage of study

Quiz Answer Sheet

nter your Answer (a) (b) (c) or (d) in the appropriate box for the Quiz you are tackling.
Check your answers by referring to page Q—29

Quiz No. 1	
1	
2	
3	
4	
5	
6	
7	
8	
9	
10	

Quiz No. 2	
1	
2	
3	
4	
5	
6	
7	
8	
9	
10	
11	
12	
13	
14	
15	
16	
17	
18	
19	
20	

Quiz No. 3		
1		
2		
3		
4		
5		
6		
7 A		
B		
C		
D		
8 A		
B		
C		
D		
9 A		
B		
C		
D		
10 A		
B		
C		
D		

Quiz No. 4	
1	
2	
3	
4	
5	
6	
7	
8	
9	
10	

Quiz No. 5		
1		
2		
3		
4		
5		
6		
7		
8 A		
B		
C		
D		
E		
9		
10		

Quiz No. 6	
1	
2	
3	
4	
5	
6	
7	
8	
9	
10	

Quiz No. 7	
1	
2	
3	
4	
5	
6	
7	
8	
9	
10	

Quiz No. 8	
1	
2	
3	
4	
5	
6	
7	
8	
9	
10	

Quiz No. 9	
1	
2	
3	
4	
5	
6	
7	
8	
9	
10	

Quiz No. 10	
1	
2	
3	
4	
5	
6	
7	
8	
9	
10	

Quiz No. 1

Subject – Air Legislation

1. The statutory documents which cover the privileges of private pilots and the general flight procedures to be used by all pilots, are:
   (a) The Civil Air Publication 85.
   The Rules of the Air and Air Traffic Control Regulations.
   The (General) Air Navigation Regulations.
   (b) The Air Navigation Order.
   CAP 53.
   CAP 46.
   (c) The Air Navigation Order.
   The Air Navigation (General) Regulations.
   The Rules of the Air and Traffic Control Regulations.
   (d) None of the above responses are correct.

2. A pilot who suffers an injury or illness:
   (a) Must not fly as 'pilot in Command' for at least 6 days.
   (b) Must inform the CAA if the injury or illness prevents him from acting as a member of flight crew for a period of 7 days.
   (c) Must not fly as 'Pilot in Command' for at least 10 days.
   (d) Must inform the CAA if the injury or illness incapacitates him from acting as a member of flight crew for a period of at least 20 days.

3. The privileges of a Student or Private Pilot will lapse unless:
   (a) His medical certificate is renewed every 10 months.
   (b) The appropriate medical certificate is renewed every 13 months if the holder is less than 40 years of age.
   (c) The appropriate medical certificate is renewed annually if the holder is age 40 years or more.
   (d) All the above responses are incorrect.

4. In order to renew the Certificate of Experience included in a Private Pilot's Licence the holder of the licence will have to carry out the following:
   (a) 2 hours as 'Pilot in Command'.
   (b) Either 5 hours as 'Pilot in Command' or 2 hours as 'Pilot in Command' and 3 hours dual.
   (c) A minimum of 5 hours 'Pilot in Command', or alternatively 3 hours as 'Pilot in Command' plus sufficient dual flying with a qualified flying instructor to make the total up to 5 hours of flight time.
   (d) Only the 5 hours as 'Pilot in Command' can be accepted towards the flight time required for a renewal of the Certificate of Experience.

5. Which of the following are authorised to renew Certificates of Experience?
   (a) Any qualified flying instructor.
   (b) A Chief Flying Instructor.
   (c) A pilot who holds a Commercial Pilot's Licence.
   (d) Only authorised Private Pilot Group 'D' Licence Examiners.

6. The privileges accorded to the holder of a current Private Pilot's Licence include flights with passengers outside controlled airspace and above 3000' amsl in weather conditions which are not less than:
   (a) A flight visibility of 5 nm provided the aircraft remains clear of cloud and in sight of the surface.
   (b) A flight visibility of 1 nm provided the aircraft is not flown closer to cloud than 1000' vertically and 1 nm horizontally.
   (c) A flight visibility of 5 nm provided the aircraft is not flown closer to cloud than 1000' vertically and 1 nm horizontally.
   (d) A flight visibility of 3 nm provided the aircraft is not flown closer to cloud than 1000' horizontally.

7. For the purpose of private licensing there are 4 Groups of aeroplanes. These are:
   (a) Group 'A' — All single engined aeroplanes and small multi engined aeroplanes of which the maximum total weight authorised does not exceed 5700 kg.
   (b) Group 'B' — Certain types of aeroplanes having two engines (only) of which the maximum total weight authorised does not exceed 5700 kg.
   (c) Group 'D' — Aircraft which come within the definition of a Microlight.
   (d) Group 'C' — All single engined aeroplanes of which the maximum total weight authorised does not exceed 5700 kg.

8. The privileges of a Private Pilot's Licence will last for:
   (a) 13 months from the date of issue regardless of whether or not the medical certificate is renewed.
   (b) A statutory period of 13 months from the date of the pilot's initial flight test.
   (c) A period of 13 months including the remainder of the month in which the flight test was carried out.
   (d) A period of 13 months, but only provided the pilot carries out 5 hours flying as 'Pilot in Command' during the period.

9. Details which must be entered in your personal flying log book are:
   (a) Your name, address and particulars of your licence (if any).
   (b) Your name, address, and flight information in the form of;
   Date(s) of flights.
   Time of take-offs and landings.
   Flight duration and whether it was day flying, night flying or cross country flying.
   (c) The type of aircraft flown together with its registration marks.
   The capacity in which the licence holder acted during the flight.
   The details of any flight test undertaken, if such test was required for the issue or renewal of a Rating.
   (d) Although the items contained in responses (a) and (c) do not include all the information which must be logged, those items which are mentioned will be required for correct log book recording purposes.

10. Flying Instruction is defined in the Air Navigation Order as:
   (a) Any dual instruction given by a flying instructor as a part of a course of training to obtain a Pilot Licence or Rating.
   (b) Any time an instructor is on board the aircraft, whether the person handling the controls has a licence or not.
   (c) Including that time when an instructor is on board the aircraft and the pilot is undergoing a 'Check Ride' on an aircraft type which he has not flown before but is in the same 'Group' as that currently contained in his licence.
   (d) All the above responses are correct.

Quiz No. 2

Subject – Air Traffic Rules & Services

1. Control Zones are established around certain major aerodromes. The vertical dimentions of these zones extend from:
   (a) The surface to a common fixed level of 10,000' amsl.
   (b) A specified altitude to a specified altitude.
   (c) A specified altitude to a common fixed level of 10,000' amsl.
   (d) Ground level to a specified altitude.

2. Terminal Control Aress normally extend from:
   (a) Ground level to a specified upper limit.
   (b) A specified altitude to a specified upper limit.
   (c) A specified altitude to an upper limit which is coincident with the upper level of the attendent Control Zone.
   (d) Ground level to various upper limits dependent upon the size of the TMA.

3. A pilot operating in accordance with VFR and flying above 3000' amsl must have:
   (a) A flight visibility of 5 nm and remain clear of cloud by 1000' vertically and 1 nm horizontally.
   (b) A flight visibility of 3 nm and remain clear of cloud by 1000' vertically and 1 nm horizontally.
   (c) A flight visibility of 3 nm and remain clear of cloud.
   (d) A flight visibility of 1 nm and remain clear of cloud by 1000' vertically and 1 nm horizontally.

4. When operating under Instrument Flight Rules outside controlled airspace at between 3000' amsl and 24,000' amsl a pilot:
   (a) Is recommended to fly in accordance with the Quadrantal Rule.
   (b) Must fly in acordance with the Semi-Circular Rule.
   (c) Must fly in accordance with the Quadrantal Rule.
   (d) All the above responses are incorrect.

5. In order for a private pilot to operate within the privileges of his licence whilst carring passengers and flying in accordance with the Visual Flight Rules at or below 3000' amsl at an indicated airspeed of 140 knots or less, he must:
   (a) Remain clear of cloud, in sight of the surface and in a flight visibility of 3 nm.
   (b) Remain clear of cloud in a flight visibility of 1·5 nm.
   (c) Remain 1000' vertically and 1 nm horizontally clear of cloud and in a flight visibility of not less than 3 nm.
   (d) Remain 1000' vertically and 1 nm horizontally clear of cloud and in a flight visibility of not less than 1·5 nm.

6. When operating below Terminal Areas (excluding operations within an aerodrome circuit pattern) a pilot must use a particular altimeter setting to determine the base of the TMA. This setting is:
   (a) The area QNH of the associated ASR.
   (b) The QFE of the major airport below the TMA.
   (c) The QNH of any aerodrome situated below the particular TMA.
   (d) The 'Standard Pressure Setting'.

7. In the case of an aerodrome having a runway greater than 1850 metres in length, the horizontal and vertical dimensions of its associated Aerodrome Traffic Zone are:
   (a) 3 nm horizontally from the aerodrome boundary and 2000' vertically from the aerodrome surface.
   (b) 1·5 nm horizontally from the aerodrome boundary and 1500' vertically from the aerodrome surface.
   (c) A circle of 2 nm radius from the mid point of the longest runway and extending up to 2000' from the aerodrome surface.
   (d) 1·5 nm horizontally from the aerodrome boundary and 2000' vertically from the aerodrome surface.

8. The ground signal which indicates that the aircraft may land on a special grass area delineated by white corner markings is:
   (a) A white dumbell.
   (b) A red L.
   (c) A white cross.
   (d) A white disc displayed alongside the cross arm of the Landing T.

9. Which of the following responses is a correct cruising level for a pilot to operate at when flying in accordance with the Instrument Flight Rules above 3000' in uncontrolled airspace and on a magnetic track of 285 degrees.
   (a) Flight level 45.
   (b) Flight level 55.
   (c) Flight level 50.
   (d) Flight level 60.

10. In relation to aerodromes:
    (a) During the hours of operation of an aerodrome Air Traffic Unit a pilot must comply with the directions issued by Air Traffic Control unless he considers it unsafe to do so.
    (b) A pilot must obtain prior permission to land at a military aerodrome.
    (c) A pilot must obtain prior permission to use an aerodrome which is unlicensed.
    (d) All of the above responses are correct.

"At aerodromes, lamp signals may be used to direct aircraft within the Aerodrome Traffic Zone including the manoeuvring area."

11. The lamp signal 'Steady Green' directed at an aircraft in flight means:
    (a) Return to the aerodrome and land.
    (b) The aircraft is cleared to land.
    (c) Land at this aerodrome and proceed to the parking area.
    (d) The aircraft is cleared to return to the aerodrome but it should not land for the time being.

12. A red letter L displayed on a dumbell signifies that:
    (a) Light aircraft are permitted to take-off and land either on a runway or on the area designated by a white letter L.
    (b) The direction of take-off and landing do not necessarily coincide.
    (c) Landing on this area is dangerous.
    (d) Land in emergency only.

13. Which of the following signals indicates that a 'Right Hand' circuit is in force:
    (a) A red and yellow striped arrow placed along two adjacent sides of the signals area.
    (b) A red square panel with a diagonal strip.
    (c) A yellow cross on a red square panel.
    (d) A checkered flag or board.

"At aerodromes, marshalling signals may be used to assist pilots manoeuvring their aircraft on the surface."

14. The adjacent Marshalling Signal means:

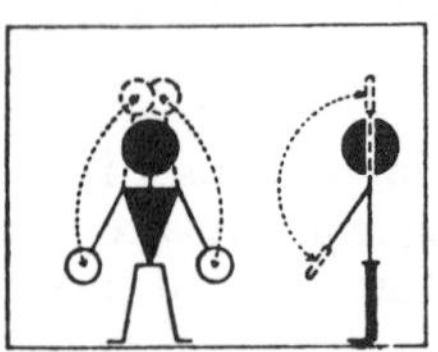

Arms repeatedly moved upward and backward, beckoning onward.

    (a) Slow down.
    (b) Start engine.
    (c) All clear, marshalling finished.
    (d) Move ahead.

15. Which of the following responses is correct:
    (a) An aeroplane shall not fly over any congested area of a city, town or settlement, below a height of 1500' above the highest fixed object within 2000 metres of the aircraft.
    (b) An aircraft shall not fly closer than 500' to any person, vessel, vehicle or structure.
    (c) An aircraft shall not fly without written consent, over or within 2000' of any assembly in the open air of more than 1000 persons who are assembled for the purpose of witnessing or participating in an organised event.
    (d) All the above responses are correct.

16. An aircraft which is flying in sight of the ground and following a road, railway, canal or coastline, or any line of landmarks:
   (a) Shall keep such line of landmarks on its right.
   (b) May keep such line of landmarks on either the left or the right of the aircraft.
   (c) Shall keep such line of landmarks on its left.
   (d) Shall keep such line of landmarks on its left only if the visibility is less than 2 nm.

17. In relation to 'Danger Areas' the term 'day' means:
   (a) That time between 30 minutes after sunrise to 30 minutes after sunset, sunrise and sunset being determined at the surface.
   (b) That period between 0800 and 1800 (Greenwich Mean Time).
   (c) That period between 0800 and 1800 (Local Mean Time).
   (d) The time between sunrise and sunset (Local Mean Time).

18. The adjacent signal is one of the International Ground/Air Visual Signals. It means:

   (a) Medical assistance is required.
   (b) Aircraft seriously damaged.
   (c) Unable to proceed.
   (d) Probably safe to land here.

19. The Code D406/15 in relation to a UK Danger Area means the Area, when active, extends from:
   (a) The surface up to 1500' amsl.
   (b) 1000' above the surface up to 5000' amsl.
   (c) The surface up to 15,000' amsl.
   (d) The lower limit is 1500' amsl and the upper limit will be notified by Notam.

20. Whilst flying over an aerodrome for the purpose of observing the Signals Area with a view to landing at the aerodrome, a pilot should whenever possible:
   (a) Remain below 500' above ground level.
   (b) Fly at least 2000' or more above aerodrome level.
   (c) Remain at 1000' above aerodrome level.
   (d) Fly below 1000' above aerodrome level.

Quiz No. 3.

Subject – Air Navigation.

1 Which of the following responses is correct in relation to a Rhumb Line?
   (a) Any line which crosses all meridians at a constant angle is known as a Rhumb Line.
   (b) A Rhumb Line is any straight line superimposed upon the Earth's surface.
   (c) A Rhumb Line will appear as a curved line on the surface of a sphere.
   (d) Both responses (a) and (c) are correct.

2. The most important property for an air navigation chart to possess is:
   (a) Correct presentation of area.
   (b) The portrayal of accurate angles in relation to those on the Earth's surface.
   (c) A constant scale.
   (d) The presentation of a Great Circle path as a straight line.

3. In relation to a 1:250,000 Series Chart, which of the following is correct?
   (a) Rhumb Lines (with the exception of the Meridians) will appear as curved lines concave towards the nearer Pole.
   (b) All Rhumb Lines will appear as curved lines convex towards the nearer Pole.
   (c) The scale increases continuously with change in lattitude.
   (d) None of the above responses are correct.

4. In relation to the Transverse Mercator Projection which of the following responses is correct?
   (a) The chart is not conformal.
   (b) Angles or bearings cannot be portrayed accurately.
   (c) Due to the large area covered on individual charts in this series the scale suffers distortion.
   (d) All the above responses are incorrect.

5. Magnetic Variation is caused by terrestial magnetism which:
   (a) Is of constant strength regardless of geographic location.
   (b) Varies in strength and depends on the aircraft's heading in relation to Magnetic North.
   (c) Is measured in degrees East or West of the Magnetic North.
   (d) Varies depending upon the geographic location in relation to the Magnetic Pole.

6. Compass Deviation occurs due to:
   (a) The proximity of the aircraft to areas of terrestial magnetism.
   (b) Local magnetic influences within an aircraft.
   (c) The influence of the local Isogonal.
   (d) All the above responses are incorrect.

7. Complete the following calculations:

	True Heading°	Variation	Magnetic Heading°
A	010	6E	
B	265	8W	
C	135	9W	
D	314	3E	

8. Using the information tabulated below, determine the Compass headings:

	Hdg°T	Var°	Hdg°M	Dev°	Hdg°C
A	352	9W		4E	
B	135	6E		7W	
C	261	5W		3W	
D	052	3E		2E	

9. Using the information tabulated below, determine the Variation and Deviation:

	Hdg°T	Var°	Hdg°M	Dev°	Hdg°C
A	077		084		081
B	299		293		291
C	146		141		143
D	301		295		299

10. Using the information tabulated below, determine the True headings.

	Hdg°T	Var°	Hdg°M	Dev°	Hdg°C
A		6W		2E	301
B		7W		3W	031
C		3E		2W	205
D		4W		2E	157

Quiz No. 4.

Subject – Air Navigation

1. In relation to the use of the 1:1000.000, 1:500.000 and 1:250.000 topographical chart series, which of the following responses is correct:
   (a) A disadvantage of the 1:1000.000 series is that because of their small scale, a large amount of cultural, geographic and aeronautical overprinted information appear very close together, and this often makes the chart difficult to interpret.
   (b) An advantage of the 1:500.000 chart series is that Danger and other similar areas including Controlled Airspace, are identified.
   (c) A disadvantage of the 1:250.000 chart series is that Controlled Airspace above 3000' amsl is not shown.
   (d) Responses (a) and (c) are correct.

2. In relation to contour lines on the 1:500.000 and 1:250.000 series topographical charts:
   (a) The deepest brown shades indicate the areas of highest ground.
   (b) On the 1:500.000 series ground contours below 500' amsl are not shown.
   (c) On the 1:250.000 series ground contours below 200' amsl are not shown.
   (d) All the above responses are correct.

3. Select the response below which correctly defines the following symbols:

   A . . .

   B . . . Ⓐ ↔ ↔ ↔ Ⓐ

   C . . .

   D . . .

   (a) A—Group Obstruction (Lighted).
   B—Cable Joining Obstructions.
   C—Group Obstruction below 200' (Lighted).
   D—Altimeter Setting Region.
   (b) A—Aeronautical Light.
   B—Altimeter Setting Region.
   C—Group Obstruction (Lighted).
   D—Cable Joining Obstructions.
   (c) A—Exceptionally High Obstruction (lighted) 1000' amsl or above.
   B—Altimeter Setting Region.

C—Group Obstruction (Lighted).
D—Cable Joining Obstructions.

(d) A—Exceptionally High Obstruction (lighted) 1000' amsl or above.
B—Cable Joining Obstructions.
C—High Obstruction (Unlighted).
D—Altimeter Setting Region.

4. In relation to 'map reading', which of the following statements is correct?

(a) The general shape of ground contours can always be used to obtain an approximate position check.

(b) In order to establish the position of an aircraft with reasonable accuracy it will be necessary to use a landmark or feature which is unique, or alternatively to use two features.

(c) A single ground feature should never be used regardless of its uniqueness.

(d) Disused airfields which are shown on an aeronautical map will be relatively easy to identify.

5. The purpose of selecting a 'Minimum Safety Altitude' during the flight planning stage is:

(a) To ensure the pilot studies his chart for information on en-route obstructions prior to flight.

(b) To note the highest obstruction and ground in the vicinity of the route, in the case of weather deterioration during the flight.

(c) To enable a pilot to make a positive and correct decision as to whether to continue, turn back or divert to an alternate aerodrome should the cloud base become too low.

(d) All the above responses contain correct statements.

6. Select the response below which correctly defines the following symbols:

A . . . ⌽

B . . . ○

C . . . ⊞

D . . . ◎

(a) A—Military Aerodrome.
B—Disused Aerodrome.
C—Heliport.
D—Civil Aerodrome.

(b) A—Military Aerodrome Available for Civil Use.
B—Aerodrome with No Facilities (or for Emergency Use Only).

C—Disused Aerodrome.
D—Civil Aerodrome.

(c) A—Disused Aerodrome.
B—Civil Aerodrome.
C—Free Fall Parachuting Area.
D—Military Aerodrome.

(d) A—Civil Aerodrome.
B—Aerodrome with no Facilities (or for Emergency Use Only).
C—Glider Launching Area.
D—Military Aerodrome.

7. The term 'Representative Fraction'
   (a) Means the ratio of unit length on the chart corresponds to the same number of similar units on the Earth's surface.
   (b) Will take the form of a statement in words, e.g. 10 cm = 1 km.
   (c) Is not applicable to topographical maps and charts.
   (d) Both responses (a) and (c) are correct.

8. If a chart length of $^3/_4$ inch = 3 nm of Earth distance, what is the representative fraction?
   (a) 1:291.840
   (b) 1:285.120
   (c) 1:246.000
   (d) 1:300.000

9. Using a chart with a scale of 1:250.000, what Earth distance would be represented by 7 inches on the chart? (1nm = 72960 in).
   (a) 21.76 nm
   (b) 23.98 nm
   (c) 28.98 nm
   (d) 22.39 nm

10. A chart has a scale of 1:250.000. Find the scale of the chart as a statement in words of inches to statute miles.
   (a) $1^1/_4$ inches to 1 st.m
   (b) $^3/_4$ inch to 1 st.m
   (c) $^1/_4$ inch to 1 st.m
   (d) $^1/_8$ inch to 1 st.m

Quiz No. 5

Subject – Air Navigation

1. An aircraft is flying into a headwind of 25 knots.
   (a) If the TAS is 65 knots the groundspeed will be 90 knots.
   (b) If the IAS is 100 knots the groundspeed will be 125 knots.
   (c) If the TAS is 45 knots the groundspeed will be 20 knots.
   (d) If the RAS is 98 knots and the IAS is 103 knots the TAS will be 123 knots.

2. Which of the following is correct?
   (a) A wind blowing from East to West is known as a Westerly wind.
   (b) The RAS (or CAS) will have to be established by first applying the 'density error'
   (c) The term 'DR' is used to describe the estimated position of an aircraft after a period of time.
   (d) A wind blowing from South to North at 25 knots would be reported as 360/25

3. 'Drift Angle' is the angle between the:
   (a) Aircraft heading and the prevailing wind.
   (b) Aircraft heading and the Track Made Good.
   (c) Aircraft track and the prevailing wind measured in degrees True.
   (d) Correction Angle and True North.

4. A pilot intends to maintain a track of 180°. If he were to fly a True Heading of 180° in a wind velocity of 090/20 kts the aircraft after one hour would be drifted:
   (a) 20 nm South of its intended track.
   (b) 20 nm North of its intended track.
   (c) 20 nm West of its intended track.
   (d) 20 nm East of its intended track.

5. The Triangle of Velocities is a method of determining the effect of the wind on an aircraft's passage through the air. In relation to this vector triangle which of the following responses is correct?
   (a) A knowledge of any two of the six variables concerned will enable a pilot to determine the other four.
   (b) It cannot be used to find out the wind velocity.
   (c) A knowledge of any four of the six variables concerned will enable a pilot to determine the other two.
   (d) None of the above responses are correct.

6. In relation to the adjacent diagram, select the responses which correctly defines 'X' and 'Y'.

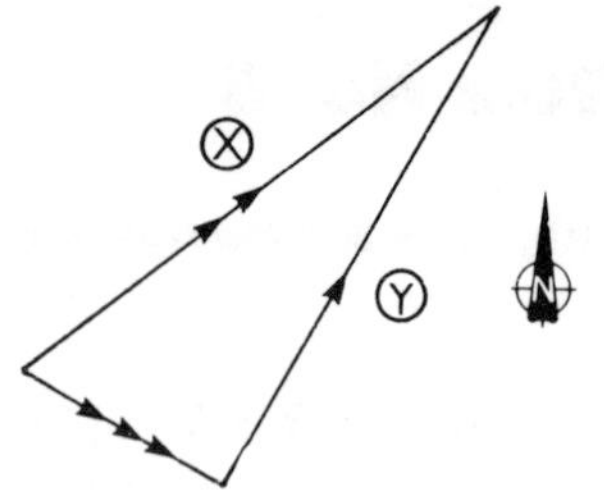

(a) X = TAS and Track.
    Y = Heading and Groundspeed.
(b) X = Groundspeed.
    Y = TAS.
(c) X = Track and Groundspeed.
    Y = Heading and TAS.
(d) X = TAS and Track.
    Y = Wind Velocity.

7. When measuring the direction of the required track on a 1:250.000 chart, between the point of departure and the point of destination, it will be necessary to:
(a) Measure the angle at the point of departure unless a North - South Track is planned.
(b) Measure the angle backwards from the point of destination unless a North - South track is planned.
(c) Measure the angle at the (approximate) halfway position along the track line unless an East - West track is planned.
(d) Measure the angle at the (approximate) halfway position along the track unless a North - South track is planned.

8. Given Track (T), TAS and W/V find: Hdg (T) and G/S (Kts)

	Track°(T)	TAS (Kts)	W/V
A	041	110	345/25
B	153	100	010/15
C	053	130	025/10
D	029	108	189/22
E	220	113	360/45

Hdg°(T)	G/S (Kts)

9. In relation to the adjacent diagram, select the correct response.
(a) The groundspeed is greater that the TAS
(b) The TAS is greater than the groundspeed
(c) The heading will be greater in number of degrees than will the track.
(d) Both responses (a) and (c) are correct.

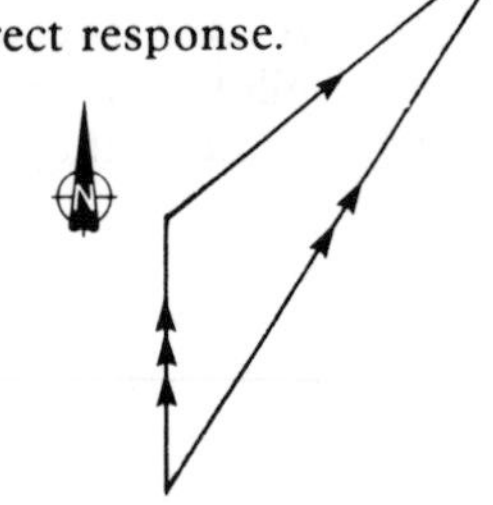

10. Using the following illustration, what are the relative bearings of A and B from the aircraft.

(a) A = 270
B = 360

(b) A = 090
B = 360

(c) A = 090
B = 180

(d) A = 270
B = 180

QUIZ No. 6

Subject - Air Navigation

1. Which of the following responses are correct?
   (a) The True Heading is coincident with the path of the aircraft over the ground.
   (b) The 'Track Made Good' is the actual path of the aircraft over the ground.
   (c) Track Error is the angular difference between the True Heading of the aircraft and Magnetic North.
   (d) None of the above responses are correct.

2. In relation to Danger Areas which of the following responses is correct?
   (a) A 'Notified' Danger Area is scheduled to be permanently active through any 24 hour period.
   (b) A 'Permanent' Danger Area is one which is active throughout every day of the year.
   (c) A 'Notified' Danger Area is one whose periods of activity will be promulgated in NOTAM'S.
   (d) None of the above responses are correct.

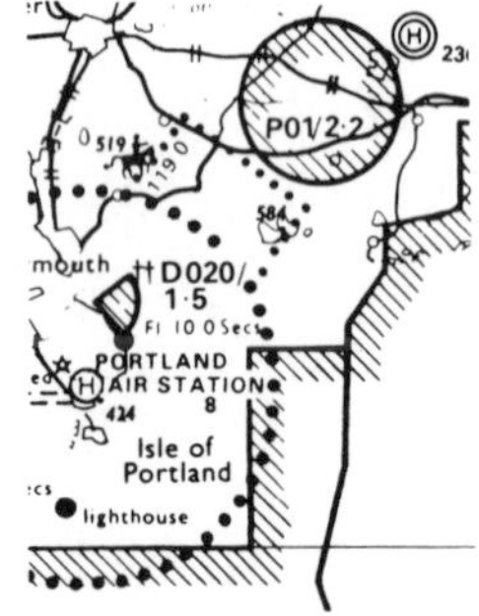

3. The adjacent Prohibited Area indicates that it is:
   (a) Permanently active from the surface to 2200' amsl.
   (b) Active on the first and second day of each week up to an altitude of 2000' amsl.
   (c) An area in which civil flying operations may not take place during the hours of 0100 to 2200.
   (d) Is permanently active up to a height of 2200' agl.

4. In relation to the position and height of the highest elevation on the 1:500.000 series topographical chart, which of the following is most correct?
   (a) This information is shown in the chart legend at the top of the 'vertical interval' column.
   (b) This information is only indicated by numerals against a black dot.
   (c) This information is indicated by numerals printed on a white background outlined by a black box adjacent to the particular spot height on the chart.
   (d) The responses (a) and (c) are collectively the most correct answer.

5. Which of the following responses is correct?
   (a) The base of a MATZ stub is 1500- amsl.
   (b) The horizontal radius of an Aerodrome Traffic Zone is 1 nm.
   (c) The vertical limit of an Aerodrome Traffic Zone is 2000 above the level of the aerodrome.
   (d) The base of a MATZ stub is 1000' amsl.

6. In relation to the selection of 'checkpoints':
   (a) Not less than four checkpoints must be found for every leg of the intended flight.
   (b) Discrimination must be used to avoid selecting a number which will give an unnecessary workload in identification.
   (c) It will be good navigational practice to select the maximum number available on each leg.
   (d) Select the first checkpoint so that it is not less than one quarter of the distance along the intended leg, otherwise it will be too close to the point of departure for a position check or fix to be of any value.

7. Select the response below which correctly defines the following symbols:

A . . . GND 2500'ALT

B . . . 3500'ALT FL245

C . . .

D . . .

   (a) A—Control Zone (CTR)
   B—Inner Boundary of a Control Area (TMA and CTA).
   C—Special Rules Zone.
   D—FIR Boundary.

   (b) A—Control Zone (CTR) Boundary.
   B—Outer Boundary of a Conrol Area (TMA and CTA).
   C—Military Zone or Radar Advisory Zone.
   D—FIR Boundary.

   (c) A—FIR Boundary.
   B—Inner Boundary of a Control Area (TMA and CTA).
   C—Low Level Corridor or Special Route.
   D—Military Zone.

   (d) A—Advisory Route (ADR) Centre-line.
   B—Outer Boundary or a Special Rules Area.
   C—Special Rules Zone.
   D—FIR Boundary.

8. At the half way point an aircraft has drifted to the right of track and the closing angle at this point is 10°. The correction angle to the aircraft's heading will be:
   (a) 20° to the right.
   (b) 10° to the left.
   (c) 20° to the left.
   (d) 10° to the right.

9. A heading error of 1 degree will result in the aircraft being 'off track' by:
   (a) 2° in 60 nm.
   (b) 1° in 30 nm.
   (c) 1 nm in 60 nm.
   (d) 1 nm in 30 nm.

10. Using the 1:60 rule the track error can be calculated by the following formula:

(a) $$\frac{30}{\text{Distance Flown}} \text{ x Distance Off Track}$$

(b) $$\frac{60}{\text{Distance Flown}} \text{ x Distance Off Track}$$

(c) $$\frac{\text{Distance Flown}}{60} \text{ x Distance Off Track}$$

(d) $$\frac{\text{Distance off Track}}{60} = \text{Track Error}$$

QUIZ No. 7.

Subject - Aviation Meteorology

1. If the air temperature or the air pressure decreases during flight, and the altimeter datum is not changed, the altimeter:
   (a) Will under read.
   (b) When both temperature and pressure decrease the effect of the lower air pressure will cancel out any altimeter error produced by the lower temperature.
   (c) The altimeter will over read.
   (d) None of the above responses are correct.

2. In relation to Density Altitude and its effects, which of the following responses are correct:
   (a) Whenever the International Standard Atmosphere conditions are present, the Pressure Altitude and the Density Altitude will be the same.
   (b) If the air density is less than normal, the lift produced by the aircraft wings will be less.
   (c) If the air density is less than normal an aero engine will produce less power.
   (d) All the above responses are correct.

3. In relation to Adiabatic temperature change:
   (a) When rising air expands, it leads to compression and adiabatic warming.
   (b) When warm air rises, it heats the surrounding atmosphere and adiabatic warming will occur.
   (c) When warm air rises to higher levels, it will expand and adiabatic cooling will occur.
   (d) An "Inversion" is created when the temperature lapse rate is constant.

4. When a significant quantity of water vapour is present in the atmosphere:
   (a) The power output from an aero engine is reduced but the lift from the aircraft wings is increased.
   (b) The power output from an aero engine will be reduced.
   (c) There will be no appreciable effect on the aircraft performance.
   (d) The density of the air will be increased and the aircraft performance improved.

5. If during flight, the pilot maintains a constant altimeter reading, he will be :
   (a) Maintaining a constant vertical distance above the surface, provided he uses the QNH as his altimeter datum.
   (b) Maintaining a constant height above the ground, provided he uses the aerodrome QFE as his altimeter datum.
   (c) Following a line of constant pressure, regardless of which datum he has selected.
   (d) Maintaining a constant vertical distance above mean sea level.

6. Buys Ballot's law can be summarised as follows:

(a) In the northern hemisphere a person standing with his back to the wind will have an area of high pressure to his right, and an area of low pressure to his left.
(b) In the northern hemisphere a person facing into wind will have the area of higher pressure on his right.
(c) In either hemisphere a person facing the wind will have the area of lower pressure on his left.
(d) When experiencing port drift in the northern hemisphere the area of low pressure will be ahead of the aircraft.

7. In relation to "mountain waves", when crossing a mountain range a pilot would be advised to:

(a) Fly at least 2000' above the highest ground in the vicinity of the route, and cross the range at an angle of 45 degrees.
(b) Fly at least 500' above the highest ground within 5 nm either side of track, and cross the range at an angle of 45 degrees.
(c) Fly at least 2000' above the highest ground in the vicinity of the route and cross the range at an angle of 90 degrees.
(d) Fly at least 500' above the highest ground in the vicinity of the route and cross the range at an angle of 90 degrees.

8. Wind Shear may be associated with the following conditions:

(a) Thunderstorms or squall line activity.
(b) Moderate to strong local winds.
(c) Light or zero wind conditions at the surface in conjunction with an inversion of temperature.
(d) All the above responses are correct.

9. Wind Shear can occur near the surface or at altitude. When a marked wind shear is present near the surface, the most hazardous situation will occur:

(a) Immediately after take-off.
(b) During the final stages of the approach.
(c) During the roundout prior to landing.
(d) All the above responses are correct.

10. In relation to the following illustration, choose the correct response to fit the anticipated conditions at, A, B, and C.

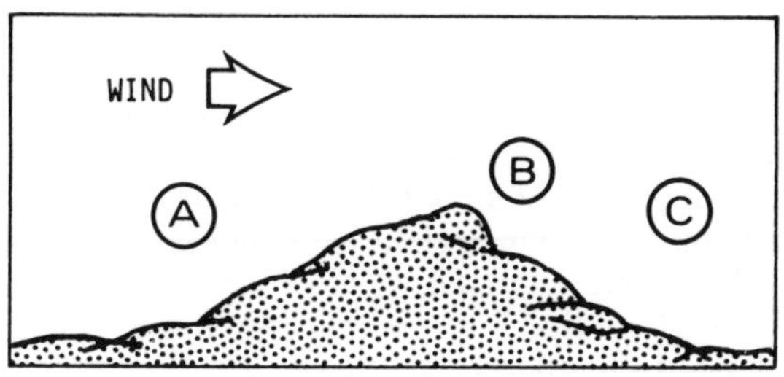

(a) A Downdraught area.
B Updraught area.
C Downdraught area.

(b) A Updraught area.
B Relatively smooth flying conditions.
C Updraught area.

(c) A Updraught area.
B Downdraught area.
C Area of possible updraughts and downdraughts.

(d) A Downdraught area.
B Updraught and downdraught area.
C Downdraught Area.

QUIZ No. 8

Subject - Aviation Meteorology

1. In relation to the water content in the atmosphere:
   (a) Relative Humidity is the term used to express the temperature at which a particular mass of air will become saturated.
   (b) Dew Point Temperature is the temperature at which a particular mass of air will become saturated.
   (c) Relative Humidity is the amount of water vapour per unit volume contained in the particular mass of air.
   (d) All the above responses are incorrect.

2. Which of the following responses gives the most complete answer in relation to the various casual actions which may produce cloud?
   (a) Widespread ascent of an air mass.
   Local convection currents.
   Widespread irregular mixing of air.
   Local orographic disturbances.
   (b) Widespread ascent of an air mass.
   Widespread irregular mixing of air.
   Stable conditions.
   (c) Air Masses from different source regions coming together.
   Frontal activity.
   Unstable conditions.
   (d) Local convection currents.
   Irregular surface heating.
   Stable conditions.
   Surface cooling.

3. The type of precipitation and its intensity varies with cloud type. Which of the following responses is most correct?
   (a) Continuous rain or snow - Thick altostratus and nimbostratus.
   (b) Rain or snow-showers - Altocumulus, large cumulus and cumulonimbus.
   (c) Hard or soft hail - Cumulonimbus.
   (d) All the above responses are correct.

4. The effect of ice forming on the surfaces of an aircraft will result in:
   (a) A reduction of lift and drag, an increase of weight and a possible reduction in thrust.
   (b) A reduction in thrust, an increase in weight and a reduction in lift and drag.
   (c) An impairment of the lift characteristics together with a decrease in drag and increase in weight.
   (d) An increase in drag and weight, a reduction in lift and a possible reduction in thrust.

5. Under which of the following conditions is carburettor icing most likely to occur?

   (a) Outside air temperature above 0°C, clear of cloud, and with a high humidity.
   (b) Outside air temperature of -10°C clear of cloud, and a low degree of humidity.
   (c) When the aircraft is flying through cloud with an outside air temperature of - 20°C and a low atmospheric humidity.
   (d) When the aircraft is flying through hail regardless of the air temperature.

6. Radiation fog is most likely to occur when the:

   (a) Sky is clear.
   Relative humidity is low.
   Wind is light.
   (b) Wind is light to moderate.
   Relative humidity is low.
   Sky is clear.
   (c) The air is moist and moving over a relatively warm surface.
   Light winds are present.
   (d) Relative humidity is high.
   Sky is clear.
   Wind is light.

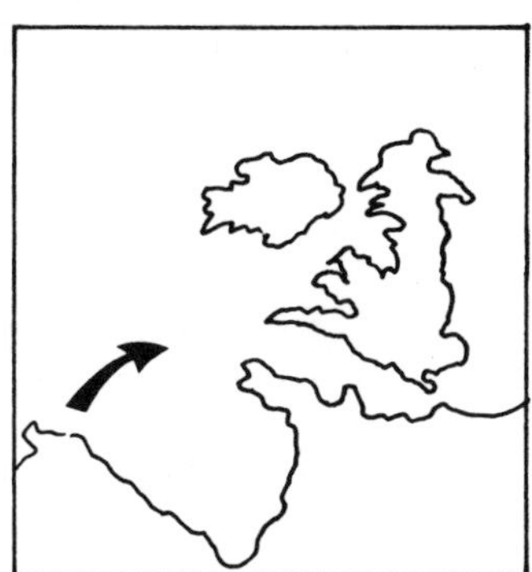

7. Referring to the adjacent illustration the air mass shown by the arrow is a:

   (a) Tropical Maritime.
   (b) Polar Continental.
   (c) Polar Maritime.
   (d) Tropical Continental.

8. During flight in conditions of haze or mist a pilot will have:

   (a) A better range of visibility by looking down-sun.
   (b) A better range of visibility by looking up-sun.
   (c) The same range of visibility regardless in which direction he looks relative to the sun.
   (d) The best chance of recognising surface features if he looks to one side and ahead of the aircraft.

9. Some typical cloud forms associated with a cold front are:
   (a) Stratus.
       Stratocumulus.
       Nimbostratus.
   (b) Stratocumulus.
       Cirrostratus.
   (c) Altostratus.
       Nimbostratus.
       Cirrostratus.
   (d) Cumulus.
       Cumulonimbus.

10. Warm frontal weather is associated with:
   (a) Lowering cloud base.
       Increasing visibility.
       A general drying out of the atmosphere.
   (b) Lowering cloud base.
       Reducing visibility.
       Precipitation.
   (c) Instability type clouds.
       Good visibility.
       Strong winds.
   (d) The possibility of line squalls.
       Sudden lowering of the cloud base.
       The wind backing and becoming stronger.

QUIZ No. 9

Subject - Principles of Flight

1. A symmetrical aerofoil section which is moved through the air at a zero angle of attack:
   (a) Will cause the air passing over the top of the aerofoil to travel faster than the air passing below it.
   (b) Will produce a low pressure above the wing and a high pressure below the wing.
   (c) Will cause an acceleration to the airflow passing round it and the speed of the airflow above and below the wing will be the same.
   (d) Will produce a high pressure above the wing and a low pressure below the wing.

2. An asymmetric shaped aerofoil as shown in the adjacent diagram will upon being passed through the air at sufficient speed create:

   (a) An upward lift force, but only provided the angle of attack is more than zero.
   (b) A negative lift force when placed at an angle of attack of zero degrees.
   (c) An upward lift force at a zero degree angle of attack.
   (d) Will produce an equal reaction both upward and downward when at a zero degree angle of attack.

3. Which of the following statements is correct?
   (a) The Total Reaction of a wing acts at 90° to the relative airflow.
   (b) The camber of a wing is the imaginary line between the leading and trailing edges.
   (c) The angle of attack is the angle between the chord line and the relative airflow.
   (d) All the above responses are incorrect.

4. If the angle of attack of an aerofoil in a given airflow is increased, the:
   (a) Lift and drag will decrease.
   (b) Lift will increase and the drag will decrease.
   (c) Drag will increase and the lift will decrease
   (d) Lift and drag will increase

5. Which of the following statements is correct?
   (a) As the angle of attack is decreased the Centre of Pressure will move rearward.
   (b) As the angle of attack is increased there will be a change in the pitching moment of the wing.
   (c) As the angle of attack is decreased the Centre of Pressure will move forward.
   (d) None of the above statements are correct.

6. Induced drag is caused by the:
   (a) High pressure area over the wing moving outwards to the tips.
   (b) Air below the wing moving outwards towards the tips.
   (c) Turbulence produced by the joining of the wing root to the aircraft fuselage
   (d) Frictional effect of the air passing over the wing surface

7. During flight the wing will produce "Profile Drag" and "Induced Drag". In relation to induced drag, which of the following is true?
   (a) It increases with increase of airspeed.
   (b) It remains constant regardless of variation in airspeed.
   (c) If the speed decreases and level flight is maintained, the induced drag will increase.
   (d) Induced drag is least at high angles of attack.

8. The term Lift/Drag Ratio:
   (a) Can be used to illustrate the aerodynamic efficiency of the wing.
   (b) Can be defined as the ratio of the amount of lift to drag produced from an aerofoil.
   (c) Is obtained by comparing the amount of lift and drag produced from an aerofoil at different angles of attack.
   (d) All the above responses are correct.

9. A wing of high Aspect Ratio will:
   (a) Be less efficient than one with a low aspect ratio.
   (b) Produce a larger drag force at any angle of attack than that of a low aspect ratio wing.
   (c) Be more efficient than one with a low aspect ratio.
   (d) Have a long chord and a short span.

10 Which of the followng statements is correct?
   (a) The curvature of the aerofoil from its leading edge to its trailing edge is known as "Camber".
   (b) Thicker wing sections will in general produce more lift for a given airspeed and angle of attack.
   (c) The wing is normally attached to the fuselage at a particular angle known as the "Angle of Incidence".
   (d) All the above responses are correct.

QUIZ No. 10

Subject – Engines and Instruments

1. In relation to two stroke engines which of the following responses is correct?
   (a) The valves are operated by push rods.
   (b) The valves are operated by a camshaft.
   (c) There are no valves except in rare engines of special design.
   (d) None of the above answers are correct.

2. In relation to two stroke engines which of the following responses is correct?
   (a) The exhaust system can be easily modified for better performance.
   (b) There is no conventional exhaust system.
   (c) Each exhaust system is designed for a particular engine, and it is unwise to modify it without obtaining expert advice.
   (d) None of the above answers are correct.

3. With regard to two stroke engine lubrication which response is correct?
   (a) The engine oil is stored in the part of the engine known as the sump.
   (b) The engine oil is carried in a separate oil tank.
   (c) The oil must be changed at every 50 hour interval.
   (d) All the above answers are incorrect.

4. In relation to a two stroke engine which is the correct answer?
   (a) The fuel is fed to the carburettors sometimes by gravity, but more often by mechanical pump.
   (b) The fuel is always fed to the carburettor by gravity.
   (c) Fuel is always fed to the carburettor by an engine driven pump.
   (d) All the above answers are wrong.

5. With regard to two stroke engine fuel - which is the most correct response?
   (a) A fuel/oil ratio of 20:1
   (b) A fuel/oil ratio of 100:1
   (c) A fuel/oil ratio of 50:50
   (d) A fuel/oil ratio of 40:1

6. With regard to the carburettor which is the correct response?
   (a) Engine performance is easily improved by changing the jets.
   (b) No adjustments must be made to the carburettor under any circumstances.
   (c) Only the adjustments authorised in the engine handbook should be made to the carburettor.
   (d) Performance is improved by varying the needle size.

7. With regard to fuel, which is the correct response?
   (a) Any petrol may be used for two stroke engines.
   (b) Only the fuel recommended in the engine handbook should be used.
   (c) Only 4 star fuel should be used.
   (d) 2 star fuel is normal for all two stroke engines.

8. In relation to the altimeter, which of the following responses is correct?
   (a) The aneroid capsule is sealed and affected by changes of air pressure fed through a static tube into the instrument case.
   (b) If the datum scale is correctly set to read the current QFE, the altimeter will indicate the aircraft's height above the particular aerodrome.
   (c) Part of the pilot's serviceability checks will be to ensure that the instrument glass is secure and unbroken.
   (d) All the above responses are correct.

9. Regarding engine oil which response is correct?
   (a) Any grade of good quality engine oil is suitable.
   (b) Only 10W/50 engine oil is suitable.
   (c) Only Detergent type oil should be used.
   (d) Normally a good quality straight 30 SAE non-detergent oil should be used.

10. In relation to carrying magnetic (ferrous) materials on board an aircraft:
    (a) They should be stowed as far away from the magnetic compass as possible.
    (b) They will have no effect upon the magnetic compass.
    (c) Unless they are stowed well away from the magnetic compass, they will cause a change in variation.
    (d) They will have no effect upon the value of deviation.

Answers to Progress Tests

Quiz No. 1	
1	**c**
2	**d**
3	**d**
4	**c**
5	**d**
6	**c**
7	**c**
8	**b**
9	**d**
10	**a**

Quiz No. 2	
1	**d**
2	**b**
3	**a**
4	**c**
5	**a**
6	**c**
7	**c**
8	**b**
9	**a**
10	**d**
11	**b**
12	**a**
13	**a**
14	**d**
15	**b**
16	**c**
17	**c**
18	**a**
19	**c**
20	**b**

Quiz No. 3		
1	**d**	
2	**b**	
3	**a**	
4	**d**	
5	**d**	
6	**b**	
7 A	**004**	
B	**273**	
C	**144**	
D	**311**	
8 A	**357**	
B	**136**	
C	**269**	
D	**047**	
9 A	**7W**	**3E**
B	**6E**	**2E**
C	**5E**	**2W**
d	**6E**	**4W**
10 A	**297**	
B	**021**	
C	**206**	
D	**155**	

Quiz No. 4	
1	**d**
2	**d**
3	**c**
4	**b**
5	**d**
6	**d**
7	**a**
8	**a**
9	**b**
10	**c**

Quiz No. 5		
1	**c**	
2	**c**	
3	**b**	
4	**c**	
5	**c**	
6	**c**	
7	**d**	
8 A	**030**	**9**[illegible]
B	**148**	**11**[illegible]
C	**051**	**12**[illegible]
D	**033**	**12**[illegible]
E	**235**	**14**[illegible]
9	**d**	
10	**c**	

Quiz No. 6	
1	**c**
2	**c**
3	**a**
4	**d**
5	**c**
6	**b**
7	**b**
8	**c**
9	**c**
10	**b**

Quiz No. 7	
1	**c**
2	**d**
3	**c**
4	**b**
5	**c**
6	**a**
7	**c**
8	**d**
9	**d**
10	**c**

Quiz No. 8	
1	**b**
2	**a**
3	**d**
4	**d**
5	**a**
6	**d**
7	**a**
8	**a**
9	**d**
10	**b**

Quiz No. 9	
1	**c**
2	**c**
3	**c**
4	**d**
5	**b**
6	**b**
7	**c**
8	**d**
9	**c**
10	**d**

Quiz No. 10	
1	**c**
2	**c**
3	**d**
4	**a**
5	**d**
6	**c**
7	**b**
8	**d**
9	**d**
10	**a**

Notes

Notes

Notes

Notes

Notes

Notes

Notes